INDIAN SUN

INDIAN SUN

THE LIFE AND MUSIC OF
RAVI SHANKAR

OLIVER CRASKE

hachette
BOOKS

New York

Hachette Books
Hachette Book Group
1290 Avenue of the Americas
New York, NY 10104
hachettebookgroup.com
twitter.com/hachettebooks
Instagram.com/hachettebooks

Originally published in 2020 by Faber & Faber in the UK
First U.S. Edition: April 2020

Hachette Books is a division of Hachette Book Group, Inc.
The Hachette Books name and logo are trademarks of Hachette Book Group, Inc.

The publisher is not responsible for websites (or their content) that are not owned by the publisher.

The Hachette Speakers Bureau provides a wide range of authors for speaking events. To find out more, go to www.hachettespeakersbureau.com or call (866) 376-6591.

Print book interior design by name.

Library of Congress Cataloging-in-Publication Data has been applied for.

ISBNs: 9780306874888 (hardcover); 9780306874871 (ebook)

Printed in the United States of America

LSC-C

10 9 8 7 6 5 4 3 2 1

CONTENTS

CONTENTS

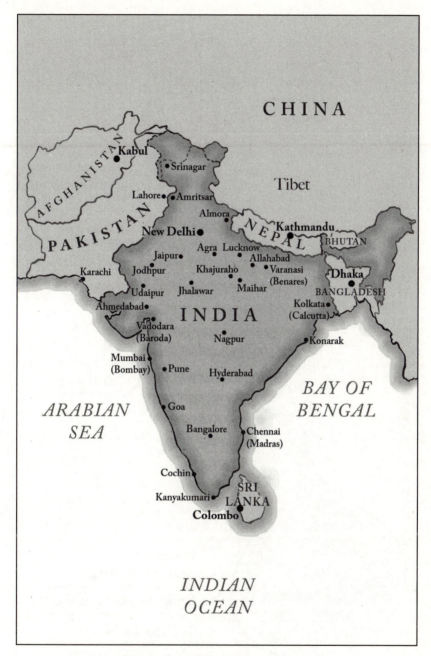

The Indian Subcontinent, 2020

The boundaries on this map are representational only. They do not purport
to be accurate and do not imply endorsement by either author or publisher.

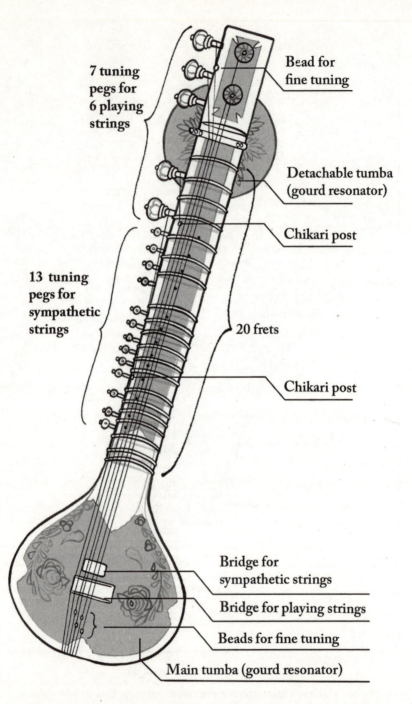

7 tuning pegs for 6 playing strings

Bead for fine tuning

Detachable tumba (gourd resonator)

Chikari post

13 tuning pegs for sympathetic strings

20 frets

Chikari post

Bridge for sympathetic strings

Bridge for playing strings

Beads for fine tuning

Main tumba (gourd resonator)

The Sitar (Ravi Shankar Model)

THE OCTAVE IN INDIAN CLASSICAL MUSIC

In everyday usage, the Indian octave resembles the Western equivalent in being divided into seven principal notes (*swaras*) or twelve semitones. The seven notes are most commonly known by their abbreviations—*sa, re, ga, ma, pa, dha* and *ni*—from which they derive their collective name, the *sargam*.

The Indian *sargam* is movable in that these names do not stand for absolute pitch values. They are comparable to the terms *do, re, me, fa, so, la* and *ti* in Western terminology (where a "movable *do*" solfege system is followed).

In Indian musicology the octave is sometimes further subdivided into twenty-two *shrutis* or microtones, which are said to be the smallest changes in pitch that a human ear can detect.

Ravi Shankar's principal sitar was usually tuned so that his *sa* (the tonic or first note) was C sharp. When he played with Western orchestras he used a sitar tuned to D.

NOTE	NAME	ABBREVIATION	NOTATION	EQUIVALENT IN KEY OF C
1st	*Sadya*	*sa*	S	C
flattened 2nd	*komal Rishabh*	*komal re* (or *ri*)	R̲	C sharp/D flat
2nd	*Rishabh*	*re* (or *ri*)	R	D
flattened 3rd	*komal Gandhar*	*komal ga*	G̲	E flat
3rd	*Gandhar*	*ga*	G	E
4th	*Madhyam*	*ma*	M	F
sharp 4th	*teevra Madhyam*	*teevra ma*	M̆	F sharp
5th	*Pancham*	*pa*	P	G
flattened 6th	*komal Dhaivat*	*komal dha*	D̲	A flat
6th	*Dhaivat*	*dha*	D	A
flattened 7th	*komal Nishad*	*komal ni*	N̲	B flat
7th	*Nishad*	*ni*	N	B

RAGAS CREATED BY RAVI SHANKAR

Nat Bhairav

Ahir Lalit

Rasiya

Yaman Manjh

Gunji Kanhara

Janasanmodini

Tilak Shyam

Bairagi

Mohan Kauns

Manamanjari

Mishra Gara

Pancham Se Gara

Purvi Kalyan

Kameshwari

Gangeshwari

Rangeshwari

Parameshwari

Palas Kafi

Jogeshwari

Charu Kauns

Kaushik Todi

Bairagi Todi

Bhawani Bhairav

Sanjh Kalyan

Shailangi

Suranjani

Rajya Kalyan

Banjara

Piloo Banjara

Suvarna

Doga Kalyan

TALAS COMMONLY USED
BY RAVI SHANKAR

Dadra tal	6 beats, divided 3–3
Ardha jaital	6½ beats, divided 3–2–1½
Rupaktal	7 beats, divided 3–2–2
Keherwa tal	8 beats, divided 4–4
Mattatal	9 beats, divided 4–2–3
Jhaptal	10 beats, divided 2–3–2–3
Sadhe Das	10½ beats, divided 4–4–1–1½
Chartal ki sawari	11 beats, divided 4–4–3
Sadhe Gyarah	11½ beats, divided 4–4–2–1½
Ektal	12 beats, divided 4–4–2–2
Jaital	13 beats, divided 2–2–2–2–2–1–2
Dhamar	14 beats, divided 5–2–3–4
Ada chautal	14 beats, divided 2–4–4–4
Chanchar	14 beats, divided 3–4–3–4
Pancham sawari	15 beats, divided 3–4–4–4
Teental	16 beats, divided 4–4–4–4
Shikhar tal	17 beats, divided 4–4–4–2–1–2

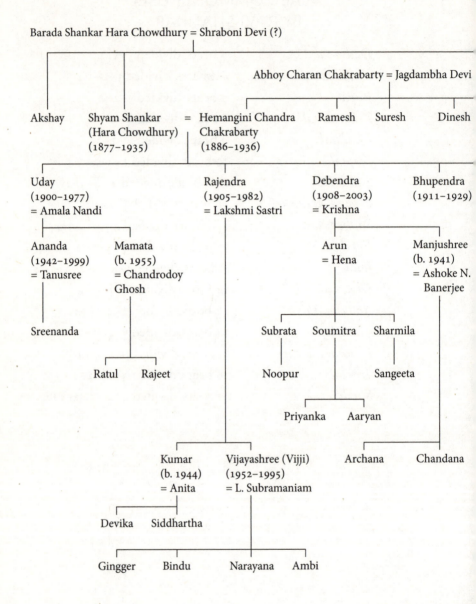

SHANKAR FAMILY TREE

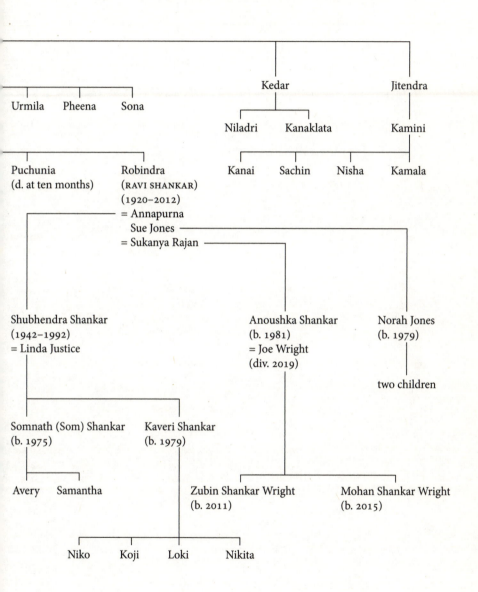

Urmila   Pheena   Sona

Kedar   Jitendra

Niladri   Kanaklata   Kamini

Puchunia   Robindra   Kanai   Sachin   Nisha   Kamala
(d. at ten months)   (RAVI SHANKAR)
                      (1920–2012)
                      = Annapurna
                        Sue Jones
                      = Sukanya Rajan

Shubhendra Shankar   Anoushka Shankar   Norah Jones
(1942–1992)   (b. 1981)   (b. 1979)
= Linda Justice   = Joe Wright
                            (div. 2019)

                                                 two children

Somnath (Som) Shankar   Kaveri Shankar
(b. 1975)   (b. 1979)

Avery   Samantha   Zubin Shankar Wright   Mohan Shankar Wright
                         (b. 2011)   (b. 2015)

        Niko   Koji   Loki   Nikita

INTRODUCTION

AN UNENDING QUEST

Why are you writing about me now? You should wait
until I'm gone, otherwise how can you possibly write
a fair and unbiased story?

RAVI SHANKAR[1]

In an old Indian parable, a group of blind men who have never before encountered an elephant inspect one using their hands. Each
touches a different part of the animal: the man who feels the trunk
believes the object is a huge snake; the one who grabs the tail thinks
it is a rope; the one who touches a leg thinks it is a tree. In 1966, at
the height of what he called "the sitar explosion," Ravi Shankar related
this story to a London press conference. It was, he explained, the same
with Indian classical music: in whichever country it was played, the
locals saw resemblances to their own music. Americans said it was like
jazz; Japanese compared it to their folk music. "But the similarities are
very superficial," he said. "Beyond that, there is something very deep
that is yet to be appreciated by Westerners."[2]

Ravi Shankar made it his life's mission to spread understanding and
love of Indian classical music. When he took it up himself in the 1920s
and 1930s, it was an elite art form that was struggling to survive on the
waning patronage of maharajas and rich landowners. First he played a
leading role in its revival in India as a national classical art form; then,
from the mid-1950s onward, he took it abroad to the world's foremost
concert halls, festival stages and airwaves. He had a rare gift for making new audiences thrill to a previously alien music. It was as if the
incense sticks that smoldered during his concerts were slow-burning
fuses setting off chain reactions across the worlds of rock, pop, jazz,
folk and Western classical music.

By the end of 1967, it was clear that he was having a global effect. He was *Billboard*'s Artist of the Year, the *guru* to a Beatle, and—alongside his legendary tabla accompanist Alla Rakha—the show-stealing sensation of the Monterey Pop Festival. He was in the middle of a six-month run at the top of the classical album charts, and had just performed a duet with Yehudi Menuhin in the United Nations General Assembly, East meeting West in a symbolic encounter. Hollywood had commissioned him to write a film score, and a feature documentary was being made about him. John Coltrane had named his son Ravi, the Doors were attending his music school, and Marc Bolan had been inspired to remodel himself. Demand was so high that a dozen Ravi Shankar albums were released that year alone in America. "Due to the influence of Shankar, the music of the East is no longer strange to the occidental ears," proclaimed *Billboard*.[3]

If the mid-1960s passion for all things Indian was only temporary, Ravi Shankar's impact outlasted the craze. Over time he became a one-man representative of not only a system of music, but an entire culture. As an icon of India, he ranks not far below Gandhi or the Taj Mahal. At one stage there were three Indian restaurants named after him on Manhattan's Fifth Avenue alone (none with his endorsement).[4]

He also lived one of the twentieth century's most extraordinary lives. He had an uncanny habit of being an eyewitness to historic events all around the world. He was born in India when the nation was struggling to evict the British, toured Weimar Germany as a child star just as Hitler was rising to power, danced at Carnegie Hall and partied at the Cotton Club, met Clark Gable and Joan Crawford in Hollywood, sang for Gandhi and was blessed by India's great poet Rabindranath Tagore—all this before he was eighteen. Only then did he switch his focus from dance to music. He came to national recognition at the time of India's independence, toured the Soviet Union at the height of the Cold War, was invited to America in 1956 thanks to the CIA, and moved to California just in time for the Summer of Love. He shone a spotlight on Bangladesh's liberation struggle, played inside the Kremlin in the midst of *glasnost*, and served as a member of India's parliament.

Ravi obviously liked the parable of the blind men and the elephant. In 1974 he deployed it as a metaphor again, this time in a book on India, when he wanted to portray the extraordinary diversity of the country—from the Himalayan glaciers to the tropical backwaters of Kerala, from the turbaned desert nomads of Rajasthan to the tribal hill peoples of the northeast.[5] But the metaphor is equally apt for describing public conceptions of Ravi Shankar himself: the sitar maestro, the musical missionary, the counterculture hero, the orchestral pioneer, the traditionalist, the innovator, the soundtrack composer of the *Apu Trilogy,* the "Godfather of World Music," as George Harrison labeled him, or the "part-*sadhu*, part-playboy," as *India Today* once called him.[6] He was so multi-faceted and long-lived that everyone knows a different part of him, and most have struggled to understand the whole person.

This book, the first biography of Ravi Shankar (apart from his own), takes on that challenge. I first met and worked with him in 1994, when he was seventy-four. Over the eighteen years he had yet to live, I came to know him well and we met on many different occasions. At first I was his editor, but he subtly encouraged me into the role of future biographer, happy to update me regularly on the latest developments in his life. It was easy to like him; he had a rare ability to connect with people of all backgrounds, and I was awestruck by his prodigious musicality. Yet he understood the need for his life story to be told objectively. When Richard Attenborough went to see India's prime minister Jawaharlal Nehru about making a film on Gandhi—the film that, with a soundtrack by Ravi, would triumph at the Oscars two decades later—Nehru's advice was that it would be wrong to deify the Mahatma: "He was too great a man for that."[7] Ravi Shankar deserves the same approach.

Many music-lovers find Indian music to be impenetrable on first encounter. A hundred years ago, it was little known outside its homeland. On the rare occasions that foreigners encountered it, they would typically describe it as mystifying, monotonous and unending: "a maze of noises," as the narrator puts it in E. M. Forster's 1924 novel *A Passage to India*.[8] Ravi Shankar would change all that.

He knew from his youthful experiences, touring the world as a dancer in his brother Uday Shankar's troupe, that even sympathetic audiences would need to be eased into the rituals and practices of Indian music. In his early days as an overseas pioneer, he liked to preface his concerts with a short spoken preamble. Seated on a carpet on a raised dais, with *agarbathi* incense burning, and illuminated by gold-hued stage lights, he would first introduce the instruments— typically just three of them. There was the tabla, the two-piece, tuned drum played by an accompanist; the tanpura, a simple lute whose open strings are plucked to produce a drone, usually played by a junior musician or disciple; and then there was the sitar, the instrument with which Ravi is synonymous. One early American review described the sitar half jokingly as "that Indian plectrum instrument which Western museum directors love to exhibit because it is one of the most complex-looking machines ever invented by the mind of man."[9] The sitar is a long-necked lute with curved, movable frets, twenty tuning pegs and, in Ravi's model, nineteen strings. It is certainly striking in appearance, often beautifully carved and decorated, and when it is played with skill it seems impossible that one instrument could produce so many different sounds simultaneously, ranging from a thunderous *meend* on the bass strings to the buzzing brightness of an upper-octave melody, or the glinting arpeggios of the sympathetic strings.

Next, Ravi would briefly familiarize his audience with two key musical concepts, *raga* and *tala*. The *raga* is the most important element in Indian classical music, and it has no equivalent in Western music. A *raga* is a precise melody form; it sets the framework for any performance, which must be composed or improvised within the rules of that *raga*. Hundreds of *ragas* are in regular use, and Ravi used to say that he had about 250 of them at his fingertips. Each *raga* has its own character. Most are associated with a mood (such as joyful, sad, romantic, erotic or devotional) and a time of day, and some with seasons. Ravi would liken *ragas* to people, or even deities. "You cannot treat a *raga* as if it was your servant," he once wrote. "You cannot sit on its chest and order it to go your way. You should delve deep into its mysteries, dedicate yourself totally to its spirit and allow it to seek expression through you as a medium."[10]

A *raga* is identified by its characteristic melodic phrases, its emphases on certain notes, its subtle embellishments and microtones, and by the sequences of notes that are permitted in ascending and (since they often differ) in descending phrases. *Ragas* might thus be imagined as strange staircases, on which one has to climb the steps in one pattern and descend them in a different pattern, perhaps pausing in contemplation on a particular stair, or zigzagging back up before continuing down.

One aspect that gives *ragas* such emotional power, and makes them so distinctive to foreign ears, is that the scales they employ are not limited to the two scales, major and minor, that dominate Western music. Ravi used to say (following south Indian teaching, despite himself growing up in the rival north Indian system) that there are no fewer than seventy-two different parent scales into which all *ragas* can be categorized.[11] Indian music thus explores a much greater variety of scales than does Western music, allowing for a wide range of moods.

Western music often obtains its mood shifts by the use of key changes or harmony, but neither of these features is available to an Indian classical musician, who usually plays solo, with only one melody line at any one time, observing the same tonic or root note throughout a performance—typically C sharp when Ravi was playing sitar. This note is further underlined by the constant background drone of the tanpura. The drone acts as a kind of mental anchor, tethering the musician and listener to a fixed pitch, a familiar home to return to after every daring foray into melodic invention. Long ago, this use of a single melody line against a background drone was common in the West too, in the drone organum form of Christian plainchant in the first millennium. Whereas Indian music retained the monophonic melody line, Western music evolved into harmony and counterpoint and largely forgot about drones for centuries (although they lived on in folk instruments such as the bagpipes), until they were reintroduced in the modern encounter with Indian music led by Ravi Shankar.

Thus, the thrill for the listener is to be found not in harmony, chords or key changes but in the melodic creativity that a performer demonstrates—a thrill intensified by the overwhelming emphasis on improvisation. Indian music is performed without scores, foregrounding instantaneous invention within the constraints of the chosen *raga*. Not surprisingly, jazz musicians were prominent among Ravi's earliest overseas fans. One effect of this emphasis on improvisation, allied to the oral tradition that still defines how the music is passed on, has been a continuous growth and evolution in styles over the centuries. In the words of another sitar player, "In Western music, land is cleared, a new building is raised, music is created. In Indian music, it is always a blend, an improvement."[12]

The second key concept Ravi would introduce to his new audience was the rhythmic cycle, or *tala*, the fundamental element of time and rhythm. A performance of a *raga* often begins unaccompanied, in the slow, exploratory, free-tempo movement known as *alap*. Once rhythmic accompaniment is added, however, it is always structured in the form of a *tala*. Each *tala* is defined by a fixed number of beats per cycle, and the divisions of beats within that cycle, as well as characteristic rhythmic syllables and the stresses on certain beats. The chosen rhythmic cycle is repeated again and again, with subtle variations and periodic shifts in tempo, until the end of the piece, which always concludes on the first beat of a cycle (known as the *sum*). The most common cycle is the sixteen-beat *teental*, which is divided equally into four groups of four beats, and approximates to Western 4/4 time. But the number of beats in a *tala* can range from three to

108, and the system of rhythm is based on a very high level of mathematical complexity, especially in south India. In my own experience, the virtuosity, precision and invention that Indian percussionists and soloists display in their handling of rhythm tend to astound novice audiences. These interactions between percussionists and soloists, which can range from soulful to playful or exhilarating, are at the heart of Indian classical music. Indeed, its central dynamic is located in the tension between the melody of *raga* and the rhythm of *tala*.

Ultimately, the formal intricacies of the music and the technical virtuosity of its performers can take you only so far in appreciating a particular *raga*. You also have to surrender yourself to its soul. So Ravi might complete his brief introduction by encouraging the audience to listen with their hearts, rather than their heads, and then the recital would commence, typically in the solemn *alap* style. He considered this to be the highest form of the music, capable of evoking a profound sense of serenity. When John Coltrane came to Ravi for lessons, it was this feeling of peace that he was seeking. Ravi was very conscious of Indian music's power to put a listener into a relaxed or meditative state, to calm the racing, chattering mind, as he reflected in old age:

> Our music has become more appreciated around the world, but
> what makes it special is not the exotic part, the virtuosity. This
> element of speed and playing for the gallery is found in other
> music also. Every music has speed . . . But the very serene part
> of our music—you can call it spiritual, devotional, soothing,
> peaceful, whatever you call it—this is the most unique thing in
> our music.[13]

In assessing Ravi Shankar's impact, it is crucial to retain the Indian perspective. One result of his success as a global pioneer, which dominates his reputation, is that his impact in his homeland is often forgotten. The name Ravi means the sun, and in 1997 the *Times of India* acclaimed him as "The Sun who Rose in the West," but the newspaper had a short memory.[14] Before he began touring abroad as a sitar player, his standing was already unrivaled in India. He was prolific, fiercely creative and a superb communicator. As the country shrugged off its colonial shackles, he told Indians to be proud of their cultural riches. Through his record releases, concerts, film scores and theatrical productions, and especially through radio, which had blossomed late in India, he led the way in creating, for the first time, a mass market inside India for the nation's classical music.

In the generation of great musicians that emerged after India's independence, he was first among equals. He was the only classical musician to have a film star's profile. Vishwa Mohan Bhatt, who became the fourth Indian to win a Grammy Award (Ravi was the first), remembers how, when he was growing up in Jaipur, "We would play a game where I would say, 'I am Ravi Shankar'; another fellow would say, 'I am Alla Rakha,' and then we would pretend to go on stage and have people clap."[15]

Yet in India Ravi seemed to be deified and vilified in almost equal measure. He was accused of straying from musical purity and marital fidelity. Long before any rock stars had even picked up a sitar, he had been condemned for allegedly Westernizing his music, so when he became an idol to the hippies his detractors went into overdrive. Meanwhile, gossip circulated in India about his stormy first marriage to his *guru*'s daughter and his many later love affairs. Although he could be thin-skinned about any criticism, the attacks on his morality did not bother him as much as those on his art. He was hypersensitive to the charge that he was polluting Indian music, because on his foreign travels he was in fact obsessed with asserting its dignity and integrity. In his own words, "What everyone thinks is that Ravi Shankar has got a lot of roses but they do not know that he was showered with an equal number of thorns."[16]

It is perhaps a consequence of these attacks that, while his fame remains unrivaled among Indian classical musicians, he is sometimes underestimated as an artist. There are listeners who, on hearing music that is so seductive and impeccable, that is presented so engagingly, and that had such a colossal mainstream appeal, conclude that there must have been something insubstantial about the musician. Surely he must have sold out?

We often think of the serious artist as one who is difficult or contrary, who struggles in anonymity. Ravi Shankar does not fit this description: he was a charismatic extrovert who earned and loved the limelight, a polished performer who brought a new professionalism to Indian music. There was something irresistible about him, as millions of fans (and dozens of lovers) would attest. A perception grew, especially in India, that, compared with some contemporaries—especially his brilliant fellow sitar player and frequent antagonist, Vilayat Khan—he was more lightweight, too showbiz.

Others, especially abroad, consider him to be one of the twentieth century's most significant musicians—probably India's most important cultural figure of the era, and certainly its most enduring. After all, he charted the map for thousands of global musicians who traveled the world in his wake. Yehudi Menuhin, Ravi's first great champion in the West, declared that he was indebted to him "for some of the most inspiring moments I have ever lived in music."[17] Zubin Mehta has called him the Jascha Heifetz of India.[18] Philip Glass, who considers him to be one of his two principal teachers, said of him in 2006, "It is easy to fall into the habit of thinking of the great masters of music as beings who existed in some distant time—a hoary past celebrating its bi- or tercentennials. Yet one of those masters is here among us now."[19]

This book seeks to interrogate such divergent judgments by tracing, for the first time, a full record of Ravi Shankar's life and achievements, and by putting them in context. To this end I have spent the past six years reimmersing myself in his life, carrying out more than 130 new interviews and researching in archives on three continents, the most important such resource being his own voluminous, extraordinary and previously untapped collections, which are maintained by his second wife, Sukanya. I have also explored in his footsteps, beating a trail from his birthplace in Varanasi and his mother's village in Nasrathpur, via his *guru*'s house in small-town Maihar, where he spent six pivotal years, to the homes, hotels, studios and concert halls he frequented everywhere from Malabar Hill to Manhattan, Dartington to Delhi. Well though I had known him, it was a shock to discover just how much he accomplished and just how widely he ranged. I came to realize that capturing Ravi Shankar's entire life and music in one book is, to borrow David Sheppard's verdict on Brian Eno, like folding down a skyscraper into a suitcase.[20] Or, as Tanmoy Bose, a regular tabla accompanist for his last thirteen years, once put it, "like trying to measure the ocean."[21]

It became apparent to me that this sophisticated showman in fact worked incredibly hard to make what he did look so effortless. Amit Chaudhuri, the writer and musician, who composed the libretto for Ravi's final work, his opera *Sukanya*, judges that he was "incomparably skilled, and his facility often made what he played seem easy."[22] It was a style of playing that Ravi cultivated in his disciples; he would admonish them if they let the hard work show.[23] I also realized that his life often resembled the music: swan-like serenity on the surface, but furious paddling underneath, with all kinds of turbulence rippling around him.

Along the way, I came to understand better his attitude to music. At the sixteenth-century court of Emperor Akbar in Agra, there was a musician called Mian Tansen, of whom it was said that he had yogic control of sound. He could make it rain by singing *Raga Megh Malhar*; he could light oil lamps by singing *Raga Deepak*. He became the most hallowed name in the entire history of north Indian music. Yet he embodied the spirit of *vinaya*, or humility, in his approach to learning music. "My knowledge is like a drop in a vast ocean of promise," he told Akbar.[24]

For Ravi Shankar, too, the learning never ended. He strove ceaselessly to improve, to discover new riches of musical experience. In sifting through drawer after drawer of his tour itineraries, programs, memoranda, cuttings and correspondence, I realized just how driven he must have been to maintain such a hectic schedule for so many decades: all those *ragas*, *talas*, *bandishes* and *bhajans*, film scores, albums, musicals and songs. Concertos and a symphony, too; even that opera, which he was still composing in hospital when he was ninety-two. And in between, the perpetual motion of touring. Once, when asked why he made music, he joked, "There's an insect gnawing in my head."[25] There was some truth hidden in his jest. He had no choice; it was as if there was always something else impelling him on his unlikely and often lonely mission.

"I feel God mostly in the musical notes," he once said.[26] For a man who so often exuded joy and frivolity, there was something very serious at his heart. Music, he discovered, could evoke serenity, bliss or melancholy; it could heal; it could even transcend life and death. He often talked of the "beautiful sadness" that he felt in the search for musical and spiritual perfection. He lived a life of passion and pain, and of enormous artistic and material success, but above all of constant quest—musical, emotional and spiritual. "For me there is always that sadness in a *raga*," he once said, "that wanting to reach something that I know beforehand I never will, and each note is like crying out, searching."[27]

So this book sets out to explore a series of questions: how did Ravi Shankar first become a national star in India, and then achieve global acclaim for Indian music? Why was he such a successful evangelist for it, and why did he also provoke so much criticism? And the puzzle that lies at the heart of the man and the artist, and of this biography: what was it that drove him on his unending quest?

I
STAR FORMATION
1920–1944

The prodigy, aged about thirteen, dressed up for a press shot in London

1

BENARES

In the holy city of Benares sound is everywhere.
RAVI SHANKAR[1]

Sitting in his southern Californian home, where he usually spent about half the year, Ravi Shankar surveyed the lush greenery and tropical flowers in the garden and the azure Pacific skies above. He was eighty-eight. His pen was poised, for he had been invited to write about his favorite place on Earth. He loved this suburban idyll, but at heart he had mostly been an urban creature. He often reminisced about Paris, New York and London. Kolkata, Mumbai, Delhi and Los Angeles had played important roles in his life too. Yet one place stood out. "Varanasi seems to be etched in my heart," he wrote.[2]

The north Indian city of Varanasi, or Benares as Ravi usually called it, has been a place of pilgrimage and learning for many centuries. It is said to be one of the world's oldest surviving cities. Hindus still arrive from all over India because they believe that dying here and having their ashes scattered in the sacred River Ganges enables them to attain *moksha*—freedom from the cycle of rebirth and suffering. The city's abiding magic somehow resists the encroachment of commercialization and the pressure of population growth. Benares is believed to be the eternal abode of Shiva and the holiest of all *tirthas*, those special crossing points on Earth where the barriers are thinnest between this world and the other. It was here, just before dawn on April 7, 1920, that Ravi Shankar was born.

"The city is a feeling in your bones; it is beyond comprehension," he said.[3] The *ghats*, the tiers of stone steps that descend into the west bank of the Ganges, with temples and palaces towering above, were the place Ravi loved most as a child. All human life was there: ritual bathing, wrestlers in training, *sadhus* worshipping amid wandering cows, boatmen sheltering under bamboo parasols, cricket games and theatrical plays, even childbirth and death. He could pass hours there, relishing the sound of the shehnais, the oboe-like reed instruments that resonated at auspicious hours from the palaces. They began at dawn, as the city was greeted by the sun rising across the Ganges. But his favorite time was sunset. Such was the ecstasy he felt then that he sometimes had to be taken home at night against his will. This was India as it might have been two millennia ago. The adult Ravi wrote of how the view from the *ghats* at dusk still filled him with "a very deep spiritual peace that makes me forget all the material world."[4]

Benares was a profoundly formative influence, but there were other forces shaping the boy. He was born at a pivotal time in India, on the cusp between the ancient and the modern worlds. Power was draining away from the princes and the landed aristocracy; there was an educated middle class growing in size and confidence, and the British Raj was entering its final phase. It was a time of political ferment. It was only a year since the Jalianwala Bagh massacre, when troops under British command fired on an unarmed crowd in Amritsar, and during Ravi's first summer Mohandas Karamchand Gandhi began his two-year Non-Cooperation Movement of peaceful resistance to British rule. The British were building a new imperial capital of startling hubris at New Delhi, while at the same time trying to suppress the surging nationalist movement. As a child it was normal for Ravi to see the British beating up and arresting Indians, and he was aware of the attacks carried out by freedom-fighters. When he read *Ananda Math*, a book banned for its nationalist sentiments, he felt he had to hide it in case he was caught and sent to prison.

But there was little in Ravi's first decade to suggest that he would become a world-changing musician. He was a lively, curious boy, his horizons limited to the city and the surrounding area. His family increasingly struggled for money and he had only two years of schooling in Benares. He sang well and occasionally played musical instruments but did not study music formally.

Ravi Shankar's given name was Robindra. He was the last of seven sons, five of whom survived infancy. During his youth most people called him Robu, or occasionally Robin, or Robi—Bengali for the sun. To this day most Bengalis call him Robi Shankar. He did not change his name to Ravi until he was about twenty. His eldest brother, Uday, born in 1900, left for Europe when Robu was only four months old and did not return for over nine years. The second son was stillborn. Then came Rajendra, born in 1905, and Debendra, in 1908, who were both at school in Benares at the time of Robu's birth. Rajendra, or Raju, had inherited an intellectual streak from their father, and young Robu was fond of his gentle nature. Debendra, or Debu, was sterner and Robu was less close to him. Bhupendra, born in 1911, was the tallest of the brothers at five foot eight, and the most artistic: he enjoyed drawing, writing poetry and songs, and singing along to the harmonium. He was Robu's favorite brother, but there was an age gap of nine years between them. After Bhupendra there had been one more boy, Puchunia, who died at only ten months. They had no sisters.

Robu's mother, Hemangini Chandra Chakrabarty, was from a family of *zamindars* (landowners) who had fallen on hard times, while his father, Shyam Shankar, also from a landowning family, rose to become foreign minister in the state of Jhalawar. His parents were both Bengali Brahmins, belonging to the priestly caste. It was an arranged marriage, and their horoscopes were favorably aligned, but they were very different from each other. She had an inner strength but was soft-spoken, poorly educated, knew no English and had the Bengali handwriting of a child. He was intellectual and cultivated, a high achiever with a questing spirit, and had a beautiful calligraphic hand. Born in 1886, she had been only eleven at their wedding, and fourteen when she had Uday. Shyam was nine years older than his wife.

By the time of Robu's birth, almost twenty years after Uday's, his parents were effectively living separate lives. In Jhalawar, where the family had spent the previous four years, and long stretches of the previous two decades, Shyam had begun living apart from his wife. After a nine-year relationship with an Englishwoman called Miss Morrell, whose family had cut her off for being the mistress of a "black-devil," he had married her in 1917 or 1918.[5] They had a Hindu ceremony, and she took the name Vrinda Shankar. Shyam had not divorced Hemangini and this second marriage did not prevent him getting her pregnant with their youngest son. Having two wives was not unlawful for a Hindu at the time, but it was rare and generally disapproved of.

Shyam traveled frequently on matters of state and in 1920, after a brief period in Calcutta, he left for Europe with His Highness Bhawani Singh, the Maharaj Rana of Jhalawar. Shortly before the birth of Robu, Hemangini settled in Benares with her sons and Shyam appointed a friend, a Mr. Biswas, as their guardian. At first they stayed in Biswas's house on Tilebhandeshwar Galli, a lane that weaves its way through the Bengali neighborhood in the middle of the city, about four hundred yards from the river. It was here that Robu was born, in a home haunted at night by both fireflies and a ghost. Robu never saw the ghost himself, but apparently it manifested itself as different people. On one occasion Hemangini saw one of her brothers in the bathroom, but on returning to the bedroom found he had been fast asleep there all along.[6]

In Jhalawar, the family had enjoyed the privileges and prosperity of court life, and in Robu's early years they remained comfortably off. Apart from returning to Jhalawar for five months in 1921, Shyam remained in Europe with his second wife until late 1924, and then decided to leave state service. There was a free spirit within him in conflict with his establishment instincts. "I have always fought for freedom and gave mortal offense to His Highness when I tried to break away from the bondage of slavery," he explained. "I could not stick to it any longer."[7] The Maharaj Rana reacted by seizing land that Shyam had earlier been granted and denying him fair compensation. He was, however, awarded a pension of 200 rupees per month, which in theory should have been enough for Hemangini to raise the family in Benares. In reality, after various courtiers had taken their percentages, she received only 60 rupees, which was clearly insufficient. Shyam never sent her anything extra, even as he went on to establish an international portfolio career as a barrister, lecturer, consultant and composer.

Hemangini and Robu were especially close. His fondest childhood memory was lying on the flat roof of their three-story home with his head in his mother's lap as she sang and told him stories of happier days, of her childhood in her village of Nasrathpur, or the palace life at Jhalawar, where his older brothers had been treated like princes and even had a pet tiger cub. "All those stories sounded like a fairy tale," he later mused.[8] Life had become a struggle for Hemangini. She cooked well, and Robu developed a lifelong taste for traditional Bengali dishes such as *shukto*, but she often went without so that the boys could eat. Later the family moved to a house further along the same street, renting from a landlord called Dukhi Teli. Their hardship was thrown into relief by a wealthy family living in a mansion opposite. This was where Robu saw riches for the first time: there was marble everywhere, mouthwatering sweets and fruits to eat, plenty of land, a tennis court and a motor car.

In her Jhalawar days Hemangini had often received gifts from the maharani, and of necessity she now resorted to pawning them. In the evening she would remove a bangle or sari from her trunk, drape a shawl over her head, grab Robu's hand and scurry through the shadows to Dukhi Teli, who would pay her for each item. Robu's brothers were unaware she was doing this. It was unthinkable for a woman of her status to take a job, but she earned some money by making blouses at home on a sewing machine. She showed no bitterness, but Robu felt her sadness and solitude as though they were his own wounds.

The family's only pet was a mynah bird called Gangaram, which was kept in a cage next to the outdoor water tank. One sultry afternoon, when Robu was four or five, he thought he would give the bird a refreshing bath, but the cage slipped from his grasp and plummeted to the bottom of the tank. By the time he managed to retrieve it the bird was dead. He was horrified, although the fear of being caught was greater than his grief. At his shouts, his mother came running. "Who has killed Gangaram?" he howled, pretending that someone else had done it, but she realized what had happened.[9]

Indian classical music is an oral tradition, passed on direct from *guru* (teacher) to student, and to this day many of its protagonists follow in a family lineage and begin training at an early age. Robu might not have been a hereditary musician but the family was, as he once said, "rather more musical than most."[10] In Jhalawar his mother had attended musical events at court, and in her melodious voice she sang him many semi-classical or folk songs that she had learned there. His father, he later discovered, had a deep love of music. As a young man studying in Benares, Shyam had been trained to sing in the old classical *dhrupad* style, and he learned Sanskrit hymns from the Vedic scriptures. He had a rich voice and had learned how to project it in the days before amplification. When he was staying in Britain during the First World War he had arranged wartime entertainments for Indian soldiers, and even composed the first Indian ballet to appear in London's West End, *Hindu Mystic Ballet*, which was staged at the Playhouse Theatre in 1915.

Rajendra was the most musically inclined of Robu's older brothers. He played in the ensemble at a cultural club, Sangeet Samiti, and there were some instruments he had acquired or borrowed in the home, including a flute, a harmonium and, up on a shelf, a dilruba and an esraj, both fretted, four-stringed instruments played with a bow. Robu was particularly drawn to a small sitar that stood in the corner of the room. Initially he was forbidden to touch it. When he was about five or six, he would try it out in secret. He loved the buzzing sound, the sympathetic strings resonating in response when he plucked the main melody strings. Later he would surprise the family by playing some of the compositions that Rajendra had been practicing. There was rather more encouragement for his singing. Rajendra's friend Annada Charan Bhattacharya, nicknamed Bechu, taught him some songs by the living titan of Bengali culture, Rabindranath Tagore, which are known collectively as *Rabindra Sangeet*. Robu also picked up songs from gramophone records. He often sang in front of guests at home and, later, at school, where he first experienced nerves about performing in public.

Benares is famous for its Banarasi-style silk, and a Muslim family of weavers lived nearby. Robu sometimes saw their daughters on their rooftop, and he was transfixed by one of them, who would have been about seventeen: "She used to smile at me and I was in love with her! She was so beautiful. I had a weakness for women from that very time."[11] When he was six, there was an incident with a young aunt in Nasrathpur that lit a spark of erotic curiosity in him.[12] "Falling in love was one of those natural things I was born with," he said.[13] "My body was small but in my heart I already felt mature. I looked very sweet when I was young. Women used to fondle and kiss me. They thought I was a boy, but they didn't know the passion aroused."[14]

Robu would have been about eight when he first met his father. Shyam arrived at the house one morning to pick him up. Wearing his best Savile Row suit and with his fair complexion, he looked like a British sahib, thought the awestruck Robu. Shyam took his son to the Hotel de Paris in the Cantonment, the British quarter, where he was staying. He had two female companions: Madame Henny, a Dutch woman, who was his latest girlfriend, and Miss Jones, a cousin of Vrinda, who had died a couple of years earlier. The four of them sat down to a breakfast of fried eggs but the experience was humiliating for Robu, who was used to eating with his hands and had no concept of European table manners. He was bombarded with instructions on how to use the cutlery and the serviette, and he was on the verge of tears when he spilt egg yolk on his clothes. "I don't know how I got through that breakfast!" he said.[15]

Shyam stayed in Benares for only about a week. One day he bought Robu a balloon and took him down to the *ghats*, where he bumped into Biswas and began a long conversation. Robu was bored and kept playing with the balloon until it burst with a loud report. Shyam said nothing, but when Biswas eventually left he grabbed Robu by his shoulders and shook him. Robu was not sure what he was being punished for, but he remembered how upset he was. "I had never felt any love from him; he had never taken me in his arms or touched me with affection," he recalled. "I cried, although I tried not to. I really didn't have much feeling for him then."[16]

Shyam did something on that visit that seems out of character. Debendra had completed two years at college, but his father said to him, "What is the use of studying? You should try something adventurous."[17] He bought him a Chevrolet van and Debendra began running a private bus service. It was a surprising gesture from someone who valued education so highly.

Shyam was born in 1877 in Kalia, in the district of Jessore, in what was then the eastern part of undivided Bengal. Governed by his intellect, he was not interested in being a *zamindar* like his father, Barada Shankar Hara Chowdhury. From an early age he had unusual self-belief and determination. At South Suburban School in Calcutta, he used to study so hard that he slept for only four hours a night. He read classic authors in English and Bengali.[18] He was a product of a modern Bengali society that prized education and the professions, that was molded by British rule but also drew strength from the nineteenth-century Bengal Renaissance and demanded the right to participate in a universal culture.

He entered Calcutta University aged just fifteen, transferring to Benares shortly afterward. At twenty-one he began his career in the governments of Indian princely states by becoming private secretary to the chief of Piploda, in what is now Madhya Pradesh. There was a British restriction on Bengalis working in state service in the region, so the chief instructed him to drop "Hara Chowdhury" from his name, because it identified him as Bengali. He abridged his surname to Shankar. The transformation to "a pucca Rajput in habits" was complete when he donned a turban and learned to ride, shoot and play polo.[19]

Subsequently he worked as a teacher at the high school in Udaipur, where Uday was born (and named after his birthplace), and as headmaster of the Darbar high school in Jhalawar state, where his singing made him a favorite of the Maharaj Rana. As he became more influential at court in Jhalawar, he progressed from being the Maharaj Rana's librarian, investment adviser, judge and private secretary to eventually becoming his foreign minister. He spent the years from 1912 to 1916 with his employer in London, where he took a master's degree in law and qualified as a barrister at the Middle Temple. He lectured widely on Indian affairs, and in 1914 published his first book, *Buddha and His Sayings*. Six more books contracted by the publisher, Francis Griffiths, were canceled when type was melted down to make bullets for the war effort. It was at this point that Shyam threw himself into staging entertainments for Indian soldiers. After four years back in India, he resumed his theatrical projects on his return to London in 1920, culminating in 1924 in a one-act ballet, *The Great Moghul's Chamber of Dreams*, staged by an Italian company at the Royal Opera House, Covent Garden. Choreography was by the Russian émigré Ileana Leonidoff, while the music, according to *The Times*, was "based on native melodies collected by Pandit Shyam Shankar, and orchestrated by Western musicians."[20] In the same year he published a second book, a volume of folkloric yarns entitled *Wit and Wisdom of India*.

There were two sides to Shyam. There was the worldly, clubbable politician and lawyer who networked formidably among Indian princes and British knights of the realm. He traveled frequently and juggled multiple commitments. Like many in his position, he accepted British imperial power. He disapproved of Indian agitation against the 1905 Partition of Bengal, attended the 1911 Delhi Durbar, and received a medal for his war efforts. He identified with the establishment. Then there was the lone spiritual seeker. In his twenties he spent time as a renunciate, practicing yoga in the caves of Mount Abu or on the sea beaches of Bombay. He wrote an unpublished book, *The Religion of Universal Brotherhood*, and gave lectures on subjects such as "Mystic Power and Love."[21] This dual personality, immersed in the world yet detached from it, was inherited by his youngest son, who recognized it as "the feeling of having everything but having nothing."[22]

These characteristics made Shyam an unusually remote father and husband, even for the time. He acknowledged this himself. In a remarkable document addressed to his children, which appears to form part of his last testament, he sought to explain and justify himself: "I was not made for a homely home-life as a domesticated animal. I was fortunate in a wife who did not care much for constant company." This description of Hemangini sounds conveniently self-deluding. "My children I wanted to be self-reliant in the same way as I trained myself without a father's care and protection. I sought to combine a Sannyasi's non-attached life with a family life." Then, in a line that reveals his sense of a higher calling, he added, "Anyhow the world is my real family—I have never been narrow in my views or in my ambition to do some good to the world and to my mother-country, which outweighed all the other conditions in my life."[23]

Then there was his marriage to Vrinda. "Only a brute," he explained,

could refuse to give the use of his name to a lady who adhered to him with constant love and devotion for nine years and was praying to God to have the honor of a wedlock to die leaving a respected memory among her own people... She was the first English lady who was married and cremated according to

Orthodox Hindu rites and who married a Hindu knowing that he had a wife and children and did her best to love and help them. She never tried to hurt their interests. My children ought to be proud of her, as I am.[24]

The village of Nasrathpur lies on the road north of the market town of Ghazipur, about eighty miles east of Benares. The bucolic calm that would have reigned here ninety years ago is hard to imagine now, when Maruti vans, auto-rickshaws, Hero Honda motorbikes and hand-painted Tata trucks, each decorated with the redundant request "Horn Please," bellow and clatter along the road north to Mhow.

It was here that Robu's mother Hemangini spent most of her childhood, in a two-story house. Today there are some serviceable rooms and a small indoor shrine, but it is somewhat dilapidated. A large, dry depression behind the building, covered in foliage, is all that remains of what was once a deep pond teeming with fish. Abhoy Charan Chakrabarty, Hemangini's father, was the local *zamindar*. The estate had been amassed by her rich and profligate grandfather, who also built a mansion at Ghazipur. All the fields that stretch back from the road as far as the eye can see once belonged to him. Here, in the Hindi-speaking United Provinces (today in Uttar Pradesh), the Bengali Chakrabartys were well known and locals nicknamed this spot on the road "Bangla."

Fifty yards south on the same side of the road is a neatly white-washed bungalow where Robu's cousin Habul lived until his death in 2016 at the age of eighty-seven. This is where the family used to stay during the fiercest heat of summer. A wildly excited Robu and his mother would arrive from Benares on the slow steam train run by the Bengal and Nagpur Railway. In Nasrathpur there might be as many as two dozen cousins and younger uncles and aunts for Robu to play with. In a field behind the house an old lychee tree and a mango tree still stand, all that remains of a large orchard where the children used to scramble up the branches and gorge themselves on the fruit. Robu's favorites were custard apples, jackfruits and—above all—mangoes. The canopy of scarlet-flowered gulmohar, laburnum and frangipani trees provided some shade, but the summer heat, at its most intense from April to June, could exceed 110°F (43°C). After their exertions the children were doused with buckets of cold water drawn from a well that still reaches deep into the earth behind the rear wall of the house. For lunch everyone would sit down to a feast prepared by Robu's great-aunt. Then the youngsters took siestas indoors, soothed by some ingenious early air-conditioning: blocks of vetiver straw filled the windows and were sprayed with water to cool any breeze blowing into the house. There was also a servant who pulled on a rope to operate the *pankha* (ceiling fan).

The arrival in July of the *varsha*, or monsoon, was a time of great excitement:

> Everything was scorched. The parched earth cracked with expectation. Then, one day, a slight breeze stirred the topmost leaves in the trees. It grew stronger. Ominous clouds that had been gathering speed over the Bay of Bengal hovered above us. A smell of rain hung in the air. Lightning forked over the orchards, and then, suddenly, huge, heavy drops of rain turned into sheets of water. The *varsha* had arrived. Special *ragas* were played, and people danced with joy in the rain. It was a time of regeneration, and the rice crop was planted.[25]

Back in Benares, the end of the rainy season saw preparations begin for the biggest festival of the year, the Ramlila. This is the local version of Dussehra, celebrating the life of Rama and his defeat of the demon Ravana. But for Bengali Hindus, including the Shankars, the focus of this season was worship of the goddess Durga. For five days running, Robu and his brothers woke at 4 a.m. to join other devotees in the two-mile walk to the Durga temple.

The little streams of people soon formed a great procession, carrying scented flowers of *bel*, *chameli* and *juhi* and burning incense. Some of the groups chanted Sanskrit hymns or sang devotional songs as they walked. There were people from all over India, singing in many different languages, and I could feel all around me the vibrations of intense religious love and devotion.[26]

The climax was to have a *darshan* (glimpse) of the Durga icon at the temple. Musical plays, in which Rajendra was involved through his cultural club, were performed throughout the festival.

Winter brought relief from the heat. In the cool dawns, the mist hovering over the Ganges gave the *ghats* an even more intense air of otherworldliness. In contrast March brought Holi, the color festival, marking the start of spring and the blossoming of new loves, when Hindus playfully spray each other with vividly pigmented paints. It has a strong association with the romance of the gods Radha and Krishna, who would become a fixation for Robu.

When Ravi remembered his childhood in later life, the most striking theme—perhaps surprisingly—was loneliness. The problem, he said, was a lack of children of his own age to play with. The age gap with his brothers was too great: "Even if they had their friends round they were in another room, laughing away at their jokes, and I couldn't participate with them."[27] For some years he was tutored at home, and this too must have increased his sense of isolation. Although he lived in the middle of a city and spent much of his time roaming outside on the *ghats*, he did not make friends. This changed only at the age of seven, when he entered Bengalitola High School, which was situated nearby, behind a high wall at the end of Tilebhandeshwar Galli. There he befriended Bulu, from the rich family who lived opposite, another boy called Ratan, and two others whose names later eluded him.

From about the age of five Robu began to read children's books and fairy tales in Bengali. He had a lively imagination and liked to act out fantasy stories in front of the mirror. When he was lucky his brothers took him along with them to the cinema, which made him feverishly excited. It was the age of silent films. Two early Calcuttan productions he enjoyed were *Kapal Kundala* (1927) and *Durgesh Nandini* (1929), both directed by Priyanath Ganguly and based on stories by Bankim Chandra Chatterjee, a leading light of the Bengal Renaissance and the author of *Ananda Math*. Some Hollywood films were available in Benares too, and he remembered seeing Elmo Lincoln, the first Tarzan, and Douglas Fairbanks Senior.

Later he came to love reading stories from the great Indian epics, the *Mahabharata* and *Ramayana*. Here he found "all the beauty of the mortal and the grandeur of the divine."[28] In the Hindu tradition gods are often presented as characters with familiar human emotions: they fall in love, they make mistakes, they experience anger and jealousy, they are heroic. Pictures of deities adorned the walls of the Shankars' home as if they were film stars. The family worshipped the goddess Kali in particular. Using white chalk on slate, Robu enjoyed drawing the four-handed Narayana, Krishna playing his flute, Rama holding his bow and arrow, with Hanuman at his feet, and Saraswati, goddess of learning and music, seated on a swan and playing the veena.

From as early as he could remember, he had a leaning toward the spiritual. The Tilebhandeshwar temple, dedicated to Shiva, was just along the road, and Robu loved to wake before sunrise and listen to the priests chanting as they processed toward it. He liked to explore temples, either alone or with his mother. He had a memorable encounter with Ma Anandamayi, a Bengali woman who was believed by her legions of devotees to embody the divine. She made her first visit to Benares in 1927, soon after she had adopted the pattern of incessant travel that marked her life thereafter. It was probably on that occasion that Robu was told by a schoolfriend that the gods Shiva and Parvati had come to earth in human form, and the two boys played truant in order to visit the house where they were staying. There they found Ma Anandamayi and her husband, Bholanath, surrounded by devotees singing devotional *bhajans*. She radiated such love that Robu believed she really was Parvati. He later described this encounter as one of the miracles of his life.

Robu was a very sensitive boy. He responded emotionally to the rhythms of the days and the seasons, and he reveled in the city's spiritual intensity. If he later remembered his earliest years as times of loneliness and deprivation, he also recalled them with yearning, the sadness mingled with memories of devotional joy. As an adult, the most sublime music made him feel as if he was teetering between ecstasy and melancholy, and this feeling seems to have originated in his formative years, in the city that still beguiled him at life's end.

But he was about to learn that life brought dangers too. One day another classmate invited him to come and see his family's new house being built, promising "something fantastic" there that would make him feel nice. The boy told Robu to touch a bare copper wire, and he was electrocuted. He felt furious, humiliated, foolish: "It was so cruel of him, and so stupid of me."[29] It might have been more serious than he let on at the time. Ravi's second wife, Sukanya, believes that a life-long scar on his temple was caused by him landing on his head as he was thrown back.

An even more sinister menace lurked. At the age of seven, a nightmare began that violated his innocence and abruptly curtailed his childhood. He was raped by a man whom he later described as "an uncle," a hitherto loved and trusted figure. The assault was repeated on other occasions in the years that followed. Terrified, on several occasions Robu tried to hide from the abuser or ran away. What must have compounded his trauma and bewilderment was that there was no one he felt able to confide in, not even his mother. It became his great secret. Indeed, it was not until he was in his seventies that he revealed what had happened, and then to only one person, Sukanya.

For some time he used to wet his bed (he was still doing so aged ten), and it could be that this was a sign of his emotional distress at the abuse. Otherwise, the impact on him has to be inferred from his later patterns of behavior. Effectively a fatherless boy already, he must have lost trust in other adult male figures, and his strong attachment to women, which began in childhood and continued for his whole life, was probably a compensating search for refuge and security. His daughter Anoushka says that in later life he showed a remarkable empathy with women, and an unusual sensitivity to any instances of violence toward them—for example, in films he watched. He had deeply emotional memories of his mother, even though (or perhaps precisely because) he had been unable to share his pain with her.

It also seems likely that there was more to his sense of childhood loneliness than a lack of siblings of a similar age. As an adult, he described this sense of isolation as if it were an existential condition inherited at birth. But in all probability the abuse was the original trigger for that feeling of being alone in the world.

There was more trauma to follow in 1929, when Robu was nearly nine years old. Bhupendra had recently joined Debendra in running the bus service and was driving the route between Ghazipur and Mhow, where there was an outbreak of plague. He fell ill and died three days later at Nasrathpur. Robu was in Benares at the time, and the Chevrolet van brought Bhupendra's body back on the day of Holi. It was the first time Robu had seen a dead body close up, and Bhupendra was his favorite brother. He could not bear to go with the cremation party to the burning *ghats*. Sixty years passed before he felt able to celebrate Holi again. "Boy, I was crying, and I remember my mother crying, when they brought his body," he recalled in 2006. "He was so handsome, just eighteen, can you imagine?"[30]

Ultimately the impact of Ravi's childhood traumas can best be traced in his music, and specifically in what he described as his favorite narrative arc, which shows up in several of his later works. This theme always had three parts, which on their first appearance he named Dream, Nightmare and Dawn. The first part represents a prelapsarian dream, a utopia of times gone by. There follows a nightmare phase, in which innocence is ended and exploitation, violence and conflict bring despair, before, in the final part, the nightmare is overcome and there is the optimism of a new dawn. This was surely his way of processing the violation he had suffered and comprehending it in a framework that meant he could come to terms with it.

On February 3, 1930, a couple of months before his tenth birthday, life changed again for Robu when Uday arrived in Benares. It was his first visit to India in almost a decade. To Robu, he resembled a returning hero, charismatic and sophisticated. Robu called him Dada (eldest brother), but at almost twenty years his senior, Uday was also a surrogate father figure.

Back in 1920 Uday had been summoned to London by Shyam, initially to help out with his variety shows. Uday, then nineteen, was a promising painter who had just completed two years at Sir J. J. School of Art in Bombay. He was also fascinated by dance. He had no dance training, but he had an excellent eye and imagination, and the ability to mimic and improvise. He had begun to dance after watching the movements of a village shoemaker in Nasrathpur, Mata Din. He had then seen court displays in Jhalawar, including the swordplay of Rajput warriors, and folk and tribal dances. At first his father put him to work in his British shows as a musician, magician and scene painter. He also enrolled him on a fine-art degree course at the Royal College of Art, through his acquaintance with its principal, Sir William Rothenstein, a noted Indophile and friend of Tagore. Rothenstein was, according to Uday, "the first to open my eyes to the greatness and beauty of India and her arts," and encouraged him to undertake research at the British Museum.[31] He was enthralled by the representations of dance in Indian sculpture and paintings.

Uday metamorphosed from fine-art student to pioneering dancer, first appearing on stage in his father's productions. In 1922 he danced for King George V at a garden party in Regent's Park, and he subsequently came to the attention of the Russian prima ballerina Anna Pavlova, who had recently visited India. She was so impressed that she invited him to choreograph two dances on Indian themes, and persuaded him, against Rothenstein's wishes, to give up painting in favor of dance. "He is endowed with one of the most perfect bodies I have ever seen in a man in any country. God never gives rhythmic bodies to painters and sculptors," she told Shyam. "He is a born dancer. He must dance."[32] It was a turning point for Uday. The two pieces he choreographed, *Hindu Wedding* and *Krishna and Radha,* the latter a duet for Pavlova and himself, became part of her *Oriental Impressions* program, which opened at Covent Garden in September 1923 and then toured America for nine months. Ultimately Pavlova encouraged him to pursue Indian dance rather than Western ballet, believing that it was his destiny to present it to the world, as Tagore had done with Indian poetry.

After dancing at the British Empire Exhibition in 1924, the great imperial festival for which the original Wembley Stadium was built, Uday spent the next five years in Paris, developing a repertoire of solo and duet pieces that sought to represent an ideal of Indian dance. It was his own composite style, in no way Westernized. After a while he settled on a regular French partner who was very convincing as an Indian dancer: Simone Barbier, better known by the name he gave her, Simkie. But he always felt hamstrung by dancing to music played by European musicians or to gramophone records, as opposed to Indian musicians playing Indian instruments.

Hence his return to his homeland in 1930. His plan was principally to assemble and train a band of musicians and dancers, but also to journey for several months around India, studying its dance, music, sculpture and iconography, to amass musical instruments and costume materials, and to secure sponsors for a return to Paris with a professional troupe. Accompanying him was a wealthy patron, Alice Boner, who was paying for this grand tour. She was a forty-year-old Swiss painter and sculptor who had been mesmerized when she first saw Uday dance in Zurich in 1926. She was already fascinated by India, and to her he represented an ideal of Indian beauty and creativity. In Zurich he posed for her camera and sketchbook, and after she had moved to

Paris in 1928 she had begun to support him, not only financially, but as "costume designer, director, impresario and adviser."[33] He prompted her to break out of her comfortable bourgeois life. He was her project.

When Uday and Alice arrived in Benares, the whole Shankar family took them to visit the historic Buddhist site of Sarnath, a few miles outside Benares. There Alice took some wonderful photographs, including some of Robu with Uday and their mother. The newsreel company Pathé had supplied Uday with a cine camera, and there is a short clip of Alice taking an elephant ride with Robu, who beams as if this is an unprecedented treat.[34] "Little Robu has wonderful eyes, serious and alert, passionately expressive," she wrote in her diary.[35]

Uday spent a week in Benares explaining his dream to his family, and they also visited Nasrathpur. There they watched Mata Din dance, and Robu was stunned to see Uday respectfully touch the feet of this low-caste villager. Then Uday and Alice set off around India, armed with letters of introduction from Shyam to various princes who they hoped would back their venture. First stop was Baroda, where they went to petition the Gaekwad, the progressive and fabulously wealthy ruler, who was a renowned patron of the arts. Yet Uday's plea was fruitless. It was the same all over India: despite Uday's credentials, every maharaja or nawab declined to sponsor him, probably because of the dubious reputation that dance had acquired over recent decades. Most of what we now think of as Indian classical dance originated with highly trained female dancers who performed at courts or in temples, such as the *devadasi* temple dancers of south India. The *devadasis* were often accomplished scholars and wealthy patrons, but the British, imposing their Victorian morality, conflated what they called *nautch* dancers with prostitutes, and led an "anti-*nautch*" campaign to stigmatize and even outlaw them, with support from some Indians. The British had the added incentive that the *devadasis*, as guardians of the temples, often owned land that could be confiscated.

Uday's tour of south India coincided with another tumultuous phase in India's journey toward independence. On March 11, Gandhi began his march to Dandi in defiance of the British monopoly on salt production, unleashing mass civil disobedience, which provoked a vicious crackdown. The independence struggle was starting to leave its mark on the arts too. Dance revivalists were inspired by the nationalist cause to stand up for their imperiled traditions. The *devadasi* style of *sadir attam*, which Uday saw in the Madras area, was soon to gain a mainstream profile under the new name of Bharatanatyam. In the Malabar region there was a similar push to revitalize the dance-drama style of Kathakali. Traditionally featuring only male dancers wearing elaborate costumes and makeup, it is staged outdoors at night and tells the stories of the religious epics through music, choreography and a codified language of facial and hand gesture. Uday was electrified by Kathakali, which became the biggest new influence on his style. Further north, he witnessed Chhau dance in Bihar and Orissa province, and Manipuri in the northeastern state of Manipur, as well as various folk and tribal dances, including Bhil and Santhal. He also visited the caves of Ellora, Ajanta, Badami and Bagh, and the figurative sculptures at Konarak and Mahaballipuram, to see the dance poses depicted in ancient art.

Each dance style Uday saw was at the time restricted to one part of the country. What he did was to integrate elements of them into his unified style, which he presented as an authentic sampling of India's historic arts in an attempt to revive and popularize them. It was in effect the first all-India dance form, making him, in the words of critic Joan Erdman, "India's first dance patriot."[36]

In Calcutta in July Uday met Timir Baran Bhattacharya, who played the sarod, a popular fretless lute with a metallic neck. He had recently studied for four years with Allauddin Khan, a revered courtly musician from Maihar, two hundred miles southwest of Benares. Inspired by his *guru*, Timir Baran had formed a small ensemble of Indian instrumentalists, which he used to accompany Uday in recitals that August at the New Empire Theatre. Now that he was dancing to music created by an Indian ensemble, Uday was transformed, and the packed house was enthralled. Reviewers marveled at the poetry, suppleness and control of his movements and hand gestures, and it was said that his body seemed to manifest the moods of the gods. Much was made of his association with Pavlova. "When he came here, he was still an unknown figure," Alice wrote to her aunt from Calcutta, "and after a few performances he became the idol of the whole city."[37]

Given the failure to attract financial support from Indian princes, a new plan was needed. To minimize costs, Uday decided that the core of his new venture should be his own family: his brothers Rajendra and Debendra; his father's younger brother Kedar Chowdhury; Kedar's daughter, Kanaklata; and Brijo Bihari Banerjee, known as Matul, who was a cousin of Hemangini. Timir Baran agreed to join as music director, and the only other recruit from outside the family was Rajendra's friend Bechu. Initially, at least, the primary role of most troupe members was as musicians. It took some months to persuade everyone to take part. This meant Rajendra abandoning his master's degree and Debendra his bachelor's, but Uday deployed all his charisma to talk them round. He also asked his mother to come and supervise the household, and so Robu had to be included too. Alice agreed to become Uday's principal patron, an arrangement formalized a year later in the establishment of a French company owned fifty–fifty by Uday and Alice. For a ten-year period Uday undertook to provide his services to the Compagnie Uday Shankar Danses et Musique Hindoues, and on that basis Alice funded and underwrote its activities.

Trunks were shipped to Paris full of costumes, textiles, ornaments and an astonishing collection of 150 musical instruments—classical, folk and tribal—from all over India. Then, shortly after Durga Puja, the band of travelers left Benares by train. The first stop, Bombay, was itself extraordinarily exciting for Robu: a modern colonial city, with wide streets, immense buildings, trams, people in Western dress. Here they paused to visit the rock-cut cave temples at Elephanta, and Robu was thrilled by the "talkies," having up to now encountered only silent movies. In mid-October an Italian liner embarked from the docks, destined for Brindisi. It was the same ship that had brought Uday and Alice out to India in January. Now they were returning as a party of eleven. The SS *Ganges* was carrying Robu to a new life.

2

DANCING COMES FIRST

I haven't seen anything for ages which has thrilled me more.
BENJAMIN BRITTEN[1]

Paris was the second city to have a profound influence on Ravi, and the bond was lifelong. "I have a strong feeling that I belong here," he told a French television documentary in 1986. "The smell, the taste and something in the atmosphere still excites me."[2] It was in Paris, then the world's cultural capital, that he first experienced Western life, and he relished instant immersion in the city's arts scene, which gave him access to the leading musicians, dancers and writers of the age. At the same time his awareness blossomed of India's own cultural riches, which the troupe was showcasing to the West, and his love for his homeland grew stronger. This dual perspective, looking to the East and the West, shaped him for life.

The troupe arrived in Paris on October 31, 1930, the final leg completed by train from Venice. "How fast you can get around the world," Alice Boner wrote to her aunt on arrival. "Fourteen days ago in the radiant, glowing, tremulating heat of Bombay and today in wet, cold, gray, gloomy Paris!"[3] Ten-year-old Robu did not share her sense of deflation. The boat journey alone had been a procession of wonders, as he tore around the decks and marveled at the hot and cold taps in his cabin. Although it had been a stormy passage and everyone was seasick, the Suez Canal had offered the respite of calm water and Port Said had seemed like a charmed land. As for Venice, "I could never have even dreamed up a city so beautiful," he said.[4]

The entire troupe moved into a rented house that Alice had found for them just south of the Bois de Boulogne at 121 rue de Paris. It was a four-story building with a downstairs hall large enough for dance rehearsals. Robu shared a bedroom with his mother. The trunks had already arrived from India and once they were unpacked he had free rein to wander among their contents, trying on the antique-style costumes or experimenting with dozens of stringed, percussion or wind instruments—all of them Indian, as Uday was fanatical about not using Western instruments.

There were two new troupe members to meet: Uday's dance partner and lover Simkie, who had her own apartment in the city, and Vishnudas Shirali, an Indian singer and multi-instrumentalist from London who had met Uday just before his departure to India and had agreed to join when he returned. So the troupe had two first-class musicians, Shirali and Timir Baran, and two professional dancers, Uday and Simkie. The rest were very much amateurs.

Rehearsals began straight away—there had been none in India— and Robu was in awe of what Uday achieved over the next four months: "Dada transformed us, by some magic I should think, into dancers and musicians."[5] As part of the dance training, led by Uday and Simkie, they were taught a system of daily exercises, which Uday said was designed to tune up every part of the body and instill gracefulness of thought as well as of movement.

Robu also credited Uday with helping to devise a style of music for creative dance that was, like the dance itself, "entirely new but basically Indian."[6] Uday sang his preferred melodies to Timir Baran, and they discussed tempos and moods, before Timir Baran shaped them into compositions and honed them in tandem with the dancers. Rare folk and classical percussion instruments, such as finger cymbals and tribal drums, were used to produce unusual accents. The parts for each musician were taught orally and, as is the norm with Indian classical music, played from memory in performance. Robu listened to the ensemble practicing, and he liked to imitate the tunes on the sitar or esraj. The musicians encouraged his obvious talent and involved him in rehearsals. No one had time to teach him correct technique, so he devised his own fingerings and hand positions. Like a sponge, he was soaking up all these new sounds and experiences.

Meanwhile, Alice, who had an apartment nearby, was negotiating with theater managements and cultivating the local arts scene. The first recital was booked for March 3, 1931 at the Théâtre des Champs-Élysées. Before his Indian trip Uday had been exciting interest in Parisian artistic circles, and now a stream of visitors came to watch the exotic new arrivals as they rehearsed. A photographer captured them in the hall and the garden, with little Robu wielding a sitar comically too big for him.

Of the nine dances in the first show, eight were solos or duets performed by Uday and Simkie that had survived from their old programs, although Uday's choreography was probably modified in response to the new music and influences. The only completely new item was *Tandava Nrittya*, in which Shiva slays the elephant demon Gajasur. This also featured Kanaklata and Debendra, and showed most clearly the influence of Kathakali, with Uday's free-form interpretation of its hand-gesture language and the heavy costume and make-up worn by Debendra as Gajasur. In between the dances six musical interludes, performed mostly by Timir Baran and Shirali, presented a concise selection of Indian classical music and covered the costume changes. Robu, whose photograph and name ("Robindra") were printed in the program, appeared briefly in the item *Kalia Daman* as a snake on top of whose head Krishna dances, and he played in the ensemble accompanying the dance items.

The debut was a triumph. Hundreds of people were turned away and the reviews were sensational.[7] The European fascination with the East was no new thing, but Uday's dancing was so luminous and the dances apparently so piercingly authentic, with their lavish costumes and "bizarre" instruments (as a Pathé newsreel described them), that audiences were transported into an ethereal realm.[8] One critic even commented, "It is by listening to a work like *Tandava Nrittya* that we understand what is barbarous about Western civilization."[9]

The troupe then took to the road, initially in France and Switzerland. During these first tours Robu remained with his mother in Paris. Each morning he would don his school blazer, plus-fours and beret, strap on his satchel and walk the two miles to school. L'École St. Joseph, near Michel-Ange–Molitor Métro station, was a Catholic school, and his time there was not altogether happy. Initially unable to speak French, he was placed in classes with children a year or two younger than him, and felt his fellow students were uncultured brutes and bullies. Fortunately he was a fast runner. He took to hitting his tormentors pre-emptively and running away before they could react. After a while the bullying stopped. He gained little from the school academically, but acquiring French was invaluable. When Rajendra and Debendra were at home they gave him extra tuition in English and mathematics. He turned out to be a natural autodidact.

In September the troupe took up an engagement at the Exposition coloniale, Paris's answer to London's Empire Exhibition. Over a period of six weeks they gave sixteen performances of just fifteen minutes each. It was not satisfying artistically but it was high profile, and the money was good. The underlying purpose of the exhibition was French imperial propaganda, but it did bring artistic treasures from around the world to new audiences. Robu was mesmerized by the Balinese gamelan orchestra.

Another musician who responded to the gamelan was the violin prodigy Yehudi Menuhin, who was taken to the exhibition by his teacher, the composer George Enescu. The gamelan opened his ears to the wider possibilities of music. At fifteen, Yehudi was already world famous. Enescu, who was interested in Indian music, was a friend of Uday and a frequent visitor to the Shankars' house. The following year he took the troupe members to watch Yehudi in rehearsal with his sister Hephzibah at the Salle Pleyel. It was the first time that Robu's path crossed with Yehudi's, and he was overwhelmed by the sound produced by this preternaturally gifted violinist, who, at the insistence of his parents, was still wearing short trousers to prolong the wunderkind image for as long as possible.

While in Paris Robu received a rich introduction to Western classical music. He went to concerts given by Arturo Toscanini, Feodor Chaliapin and Ignacy Jan Paderewski, by the great cellist Pablo Casals, and by the two reigning gods of the violin, Fritz Kreisler and his younger rival Jascha Heifetz. The guitarist Andrés Segovia lived nearby, and Robu used to sit on his lap when he came to visit. On the gramophone at home he listened to works from the Western classical repertoire as well as Spanish flamenco and French accordion music. He also saw the Spanish dancers La Argentina, La Teresina and Vicente Escudero. Later, when he began touring, he encountered folk and classical music from a wider range of countries. Other celebrities he met included Gertrude Stein, Henry Miller and Cole Porter. He lapped it all up and loved the attention he received. "I was a spoiled creature then," he recalled. "Everyone made a fuss of me because I was so small and had such big dark eyes."[10]

Musicians who came to the house were often intrigued by Indian music. However, Robu noticed how time and again they announced that, while it was suitable enough as accompaniment for dancers, on its own it was repetitious and monotonous, no more than an ethnic curiosity. "Even when they were being 'decent' and 'kind' to our music I felt furious," he later reflected. "And at the same time sorry for them. Indian music was so rich and varied and deep. These people hadn't penetrated even the outer skin."[11]

His father was another occasional visitor. He was now living in Geneva, but he took pride in the troupe's activities and came to see them on three or four occasions in Paris. In 1931, drawing on his years negotiating Jhalawar's foreign affairs, he completed a doctorate at the University of Geneva entitled *The Nature and Evolution of the Political Relations between the Indian States and the British Imperial Government*.[12] He also did some work of a legal nature for the League of Nations, while continuing to travel around Europe giving lectures.

On one occasion he invited Hemangini, Robu and Kanaklata to visit him in Geneva. Robu was again overawed by his father, who stayed in a huge apartment that Madame Henny funded with her investment dividends (until they dried up during the Depression). Miss Jones lived there too, in a domestic set-up that Robu never deciphered. They stayed for two weeks, the longest time he ever spent with his father. Although he still felt hostility toward him—fueled by Hemangini, who could not help but show her bitterness—Robu was getting to know him a little. Hearing his father sing Vedic chants in a Geneva chapel revealed a previously hidden side of him. Uday, having spent years with him in London, helped Robu to understand him better and appreciate his achievements.

Uday was Robu's first hero: "His radiant personality, dynamism and creative reservoir altogether dazzled me in my early years."[13] Uday nurtured his young brother's appreciation of Indian culture, and inculcated a whole philosophy of performance. In north India there was a thin tradition of public concerts, since court musicians tended to perform only for their patrons in private. During his years of apprenticeship in London and Paris, Uday had learned how to create a spectacle, how theatricality could be employed to elevate the art. The show needed to be varied and well paced in order to appeal to a European audience with its limited attention span. Each item lasted between three and eight minutes, apart from longer dance-dramas such as *Tandava Nrittya*, which was used as a finale. According to Uday's daughter Mamata Shankar, "My father always told us to keep the audience hungry. Don't overfeed them."[14] He also imposed a rigorous professionalism on the troupe. Everyone had to be punctual, disciplined, immaculate and fully rehearsed.

There was a transcendent quality to Uday's own dancing. Like Kathakali dancers, for whom meditation and yoga are integral parts of their training, he seemed to draw on a kind of psychic power when he was on stage. If he was playing Shiva it seemed to audiences, especially in India, that he really *was* Shiva incarnate. After one concert in Salzburg he re-emerged onto the stage to acknowledge the ovation and simply said, "Thank you." From the front row a woman let out a startled exclamation: "He speaks!"[15]

Over the next year demand for the troupe grew and they toured France, Spain, Belgium, the Netherlands, Luxembourg, Czechoslovakia, Hungary, Italy (a rare flop), all over Scandinavia (huge successes), Latvia and Lithuania. But it was in Germany where they met with their strongest response. They made their debut there in September 1931, when a brief bus trip to Hamburg was Robu's first excursion outside France. By the time they returned in November for a month-long tour without him, a Shankar frenzy was building. The German fascination with India dated back to the nineteenth-century Romantic movement, to Schlegel and Schopenhauer, and Uday struck a chord. The country was in economic and political crisis, and there was widespread deprivation, but even in small towns the halls were sold out. At the National Theatre in Mannheim they received a twenty-minute ovation.[16] Audiences saluted them with hands clasped in the Indian-style *namaskar*.[17] "I am really in love with the German people. They have a real understanding and affection for art and science," Rajendra wrote to Alice.[18] As the most responsible Shankar brother, he handled money, liaised with promoters and kept their patron updated on progress.

When the troupe returned to Germany in January it had gained an extra dancer. Amala Nandi was a twelve-year-old Bengali girl who had been visiting the Exposition coloniale with her father. Hemangini welcomed her like a daughter, and Robu gained a partner in mischief. "In Robu I had found a brother," she says. "The whole day we were together, either stealing something from the kitchen or playing in the garden."[19] When her father had to travel to America, he left her in Paris in the care of Hemangini at the troupe's new house, 17 rue de Belvédère. Amala took up dancing, and when Uday suggested she join them on the German tour Hemangini went along to accompany her. Robu stayed behind in Paris with Alice.

Although the troupe continued to play to full halls, this winter tour was exhausting, with hazardous night-time drives on foggy country roads, and financially the margins were slim. The political mood was tense. The Nazi Party was the second largest in the Reichstag and Adolf Hitler was standing for election as president. The troupe began to feel vulnerable, but the biggest risk was not hostility because they were Indians but because they came from France. In Stendal some of the audience demanded their money back when they discovered the performers had arrived in a French vehicle. Thereafter they tried to cover up all the French markings on the bus, and pretended that Simkie was Indian.[20]

"The whole atmosphere is fraught with an evil odor of suspense on account of the presidential election," Rajendra wrote in March. "If Hitler comes into power, our condition in Germany will not long remain enviable. From what I see, he has a very big party."[21] A remarkable photograph shows Vishnudas Shirali reading bill posters in Berlin. Alongside an Uday Shankar flyer are two posters for the Eiserne Front, an anti-fascist paramilitary organization backing Paul von Hindenburg, Hitler's rival in the election.[22] Hindenburg won on that occasion, but in the two parliamentary elections during 1932 the Nazis emerged as the largest party. These coincided with Robu finishing his schooling for good, aged twelve, and beginning to tour regularly, initially with his mother alongside him. Showing his developing knack for being present as history was in the making, he was in Germany during both parliamentary campaigns. "There were posters everywhere, the swastika, the fanatic fervor of the Nazis," he recalled.[23] That year he also toured Belgium, Austria, Switzerland, Czechoslovakia and Poland. It was an extraordinary education.

In later years Ravi often described how the endless new thrills made him feel feverish with excitement. Sometimes these fevers were medical rather than metaphorical. He had always been a sickly child, and at some stage he had perforated his left eardrum. It did not heal properly and affected his hearing for the rest of his life. This might have been

in June 1931, when he was treated in Paris for an unspecified ear problem.[24] Then in January 1932 he came down with whooping cough. His
mother was away in Germany and Alice Boner took him to Hyères
on the south coast for the milder, cleaner air. The many photographs
she took are witness to her affection for him. She served as a kind of
additional mother to the troupe's younger members. Kanaklata once
moved in with her for a while after having a "nervous crisis."[25] Evidently
the troupe's house, dominated by extrovert adults, was not the calm
environment she needed at the time.

Robu still loved reading, and enjoyed popular Bengali authors
whose books his brothers left lying around, including Dwijendralal
Roy, Bankim Chandra Chatterjee and his favorite, Sarat Chandra
Chatterjee, author of *Devdas*, a writer whose works gave him a vivid
picture of Bengali people and traditions. He devoured Uday's collection of picture books on Indian cave and temple art. When he was
about thirteen he graduated to reading the essays, poetry, plays and
stories of Tagore. At that age he appreciated the beauty of the writing,
if not its full meaning, and was moved to tears by some of the poems
based on the Buddhist Jataka tales. Although he also read books in
English and French—everything from children's comic books to
Émile Zola and Victor Hugo—his heart increasingly yearned for
India and Bengal, a burgeoning passion encouraged by Uday's advocacy. "I really fell in love with India and its past," he explained.[26]

He was making great advances as a performer, taking on more prominent dance roles in the show, including a masked devil in the *Demon
Dance*. But he was growing up too fast in a world that was too adult
for him, and at times it was positively dangerous. His brothers were all
now in their twenties or thirties. They lived European lifestyles: they
had girlfriends; some of them drank alcohol. Sometimes they would
take him with them to nightclubs in Paris. If there was a nude sequence
during the cabaret, they would hustle him home, but Robu's inquisitive eyes missed nothing. However, this loss of innocence was far from
the worst that happened to him in Paris. Sadly, hideously, he suffered

further episodes of sexual assault there involving at least one new abuser. Again he felt unable to confide in anyone at the time. The true damage caused by the cumulative impact of these repeated assaults, starting in Benares and continuing in Paris, can only be guessed at.

The effect must have been intensified when his mother decided to return to Benares in October 1932. Over the previous two years she had stayed mostly in Paris, caring for Robu and cooking for the troupe when they were in town. She was never at ease in Europe, and as he had become an integral part of the troupe she decided that he no longer needed her. Presumably she knew nothing of what he was secretly enduring. He was still only twelve, and some part of him must have felt abandoned by his beloved mother.

Decades later, when he was driving Ravi Shankar into London, George Harrison put some music on his car stereo. "Who's that?" Ravi asked, and Harrison replied, "Oh, it's Cab Calloway, you won't know him." Deadpan, Ravi said, "Oh yes, I saw him at the Cotton Club around 1933."[27]

If the reception in Germany was overwhelming, it was surpassed by what America had in store. The impresario Sol Hurok, who had presented Pavlova during Uday's time with her, had attended the troupe's Paris debut and soon signed them up for three seasons. In December 1932 they steamed into New York harbor. As the Statue of Liberty loomed out of the dawn mist, followed by the newly completed Empire State Building and Chrysler Building, it was a moment of unequaled excitement for Robu. Hurok gave them star treatment. Dressed as Rajput princes in turbans and sherwanis, they posed on deck for the press photographers. They stayed at the luxurious Hotel St. Moritz, opposite Central Park, and he booked them to appear at the New Yorker Theater in his International Dance Festival, which also featured Vicente Escudero and Germany's queen of modern dance, Mary Wigman. There was a huge publicity campaign and Uday was greeted everywhere like a matinee idol. "Shankar" was soon the world's third-best-known Indian, after Gandhi and Tagore. Review coverage centered on Uday, although *Time*, which described him gushingly as "a perfectly proportioned male with a sensitive, feminine face," also picked out "twelve-year-old Brother Robindra, masked as a foolish little king of the monkeys."[28]

Hurok believed the predominantly female audiences were drawn by Uday's sex appeal. The shows foregrounded him as the sole male form of the divine, the object of worship surrounded by adoring female dancers, with all the sensual and mystical resonances that the Orient held for a Western audience: half *Kama Sutra*, half Krishna. Indeed, Uday cultivated the idea of himself as a Krishna figure. In the story of the Raslila—the subject of one of the troupe's dances—a group of *gopis* (milkmaids) is drawn to the flute-playing Krishna, all of them in love with him. A god in mortal form, he dances with each of them simultaneously, and each believes that she is the entire focus of his attention. It is perhaps the most loved of many devotional Hindu tales that parallel human love with the spiritual love that each soul has for Krishna, or God. Uday, who adored women, seemed to take the mortal element of the story literally, observed Robu, who was watching and learning. "Wherever he went, women flocked to him," he said. "His sexual prowess was God's gift to him. He enjoyed life to its fullest extent."[29]

The tour took in the northeast and the Midwest, and Chicago made a big impression, not least for the temperature of minus 17°F (minus 27°C), the city's coldest for 34 years. But Robu was most intoxicated by New York, from its skyscraper hotels with central heating and en-suite bathrooms (then unknown in Europe) to the dazzle of Broadway. He spent as much time as possible in the movie theaters, especially the Paramount. On days off he sometimes watched three films, his favorites being the Ernst Lubitsch comedies starring Maurice Chevalier, and he fell in love with Joan Crawford and Myrna Loy. He adored the vaudeville acts, too: he saw the Marx Brothers, W. C. Fields, Will Rogers, Eddie Cantor and Ed Wynn. His brothers took him out to Prohibition-era nightspots, and they saw Duke Ellington, Louis Armstrong, Count Basie and Cab Calloway playing live, and the Rockets dancing at Radio City Music Hall. On New Year's Eve they mingled with the crowds in Times Square.

London's critics also received the troupe enthusiastically on their first British appearance in April 1933, when they played for a week at the Arts Theatre before transferring for a fortnight to the Ambassadors Theatre. These were two of the West End's more intimate venues. "Chance meetings with Oriental song and dance often give the impression that they are bare and monotonous to the Occidental," noted a review in *The Times*, before countering that viewpoint by asserting, "These beautifully mounted dances are exquisitely rich and have powers of expression fully equal to those of any European people."[30] But the warmth was not fully reciprocated. London's grandest sights were undeniably impressive, and Robu loved the underground railway, but overall he found the city depressing, with its grimy houses in identical terraces shrouded in pea-souper smogs. After Paris and Amsterdam— not to mention the luxury of America—his London hotel seemed like a barracks. The city had some curry houses but there was also overt racism—children would run after Indians in the street shouting, "Blackie!"—and he felt unsafe at times.[31]

The imperial mindset seemed to impede Britain's appreciation of Indian arts, which, especially outside London, lagged behind the reception the troupe met with in France or Germany. But there were notable exceptions. Watching in rapture at the Ambassadors was the nineteen-year-old Benjamin Britten, then a precocious student at the Royal College of Music. Asian music would be an important influence on his later compositions, and this was his first experience of Indian music or dance. "I haven't seen anything for ages which has thrilled me more," he recorded in his diary. "Marvelously intellectual & perfectly wrought dancing. Finest I have yet seen. Music, full of variety, rhythmically & tonally." He also singled out the dancing of "Simkie & Robindra."[32]

Another spectator was Margaret Barr, head of dance at Dartington Hall, a sprawling estate in Devon dedicated to rural regeneration, progressive education and the arts. It had been founded by Leonard and Dorothy Elmhirst, inspired by Tagore's similar institution at Shantiniketan in Bengal. Barr invited Uday to visit Dartington, where he danced an informal solo in the medieval hall—under the stars, as the roof had yet to be restored.[33] Dorothy Elmhirst listened entranced as Uday expounded his dream of establishing his own cultural center in India, inspired by Dartington and Shantiniketan. She proved to be a vital connection. She was, after all, one of America's wealthiest women. Uday also met her eighteen-year-old daughter Beatrice Straight, and they were very attracted to each other.

In May the troupe left Paris for their first tour of India. A tearful Alice Boner waved them off at the station, and the normally undemonstrative Shyam admitted to her that he too was sad to see his sons go. "Uday is still as simple as a child. Raju and Debu have grown much wiser and broader in their views and Robu is a marvel for his age," he wrote, adding that he was proud they had not lost "the better side of Indian characteristics."[34]

Uday's homecoming was a triumph. As his train progressed cross-country from Bombay, at every stop there was a crowd to greet him—thanks to his impresario Haren Ghosh publicizing the arrival times. At Patna the mob forced its way into the carriages and garlanded everybody. On arrival at Calcutta conch shells were blown, there were giant welcome placards and a Rolls-Royce was waiting to spirit them away.[35] The mayor of Calcutta held a reception in the town hall. Meanwhile, Robu spent a week in Benares catching up with his mother. When the concerts began at the New Empire, Calcutta, there was such a fervor that a crowd of people who had been unable to get tickets smashed windows at Ghosh's shop.[36]

It was two and a half years since Robu had been home, and several events during this visit combined to increase the passion for Indian arts that had been developing in him abroad. The most important was a meeting with Rabindranath Tagore. From reading Tagore's books, Robu already considered him a legendary figure, and in later years he often described this as one of the most inspiring moments of his life. Tagore had become globally famous as a poet after winning the 1913 Nobel Prize for Literature, and was revered as an artistic polymath within India, especially among Bengalis. Uday took the whole troupe to Shantiniketan, the rural estate a hundred miles north of Calcutta where Tagore had established a university in the ashram style, with classes held under the trees. Tagore, now seventy-two, had invited them after watching one of the Calcutta shows. With his long white beard, flowing mane of hair and piercing eyes, he had the aura of a great sage or monarch, and as Robu approached he was sitting regally on a high-backed chair. When Robu knelt down to touch his feet, he felt the poet's hand on his head and heard his blessing: "Be great like your father and your brother." Electricity seemed to course through him. That evening one of Tagore's musical plays, *Chitrangada*, was performed on the open-air stage, but Robu barely noticed it. The great man sat watching it from a chair at the side of the stage, and Robu could not take his eyes off him.[37]

He was also spellbound by the countryside of his ancestral land, Bengal, which he first saw on this visit to Shantiniketan and then during another trip for a special reception in Kalia, Shyam's home town. "I remember Bengal's early morning light dancing in the water-logged paddy field, green with young rice, and the yellowy-green light in the banana leaves," he later wrote.[38] This was the Golden Bengal that Tagore had immortalized in his song "Amar Shonar Bangla," today the national anthem of Bangladesh.

The tour—forty-two dates in all—took the troupe all over the sub-continent in the scorching heat of summer, from Rangoon in the east (Burma was still part of British India) to Delhi and Lahore in the north and Madras in the south. Uday's shows were a revelation to his compatriots. As the *Times of India* pronounced, "He has brought coals to a Newcastle badly in need of refueling, an India that has almost forgotten that it possesses one of the most ancient artistic cultures in the world."[39] Equally, India was a revelation to young Robu. He had traveled to America and all over Europe, yet until now he had seen almost nothing of his own country.

At this stage Robu saw himself primarily as a dancer. There is an eerily beautiful double-exposure photograph of him taken during the months after his first arrival in Paris. In it, he is both seated, playing a sitar, and standing in a dance pose. Uncannily, Uday, the photographer, seems to have anticipated the twin routes open to his youngest brother. For a long time it seemed clear which would prevail. Uday certainly assumed dance was where his future lay, and their father wrote, with boundless encouragement, "For Robin dancing comes first, music second, correct knowledge of languages third. He must work very, very hard to master the art of dancing and become the world's best dancer some day."[40]

Now, however, music started to rival dance. He was already an admirer of the sitar-playing of Vishnudas Shirali, but when he heard Timir Baran's nephew Amiya Kanti Bhattacharya playing the sitar in Calcutta on this trip, he was amazed by his technical virtuosity. He began to take the instrument more seriously and resolved to become a student of the boy's *guru*, the renowned Enayat Khan, when he next returned to Calcutta.

Another pivotal encounter occurred in Madras, where Robu had a privileged introduction to south India's music and dance cultures. There are parallel systems of classical music in India. Until that point, all of Robu's exposure had been to the Hindustani music of the north, but the south has its own Carnatic music. The two traditions have a common root and are based on the same fundamental principles. In the West music can usually be defined by three elements: melody, rhythm and harmony. Both the Hindustani and Carnatic systems foreground melody and rhythm while avoiding harmony—something that can make Indian music sound alien to Western ears. Musical works are most commonly solos, often with percussion accompaniment. Within the carefully defined rules of the chosen *raga* and *tala*, each artist performs compositions from memory or improvises. The key measures of a performer's achievement are proficiency and imagination in improvisation, rather than the interpretation of a written composition, as in most Western classical music. Notes are born in mid-air, rather than remaining on the printed page.

From the thirteenth century onward the Hindustani system came under the influence of Persian musical culture, while the Carnatic system remained untouched by it as, even at its height, the Mughal empire failed to control much of south India. The two systems then evolved separately over the centuries, resulting in clear differences in musical practice. The Persian influence encouraged the development of a courtly, secular music culture in the north, with musicians performing for private elites. In the south music and dance remained centered on Hindu temples, so Carnatic music was still predominantly devotional, with more lyrical content; there was a stronger tradition of public concerts, and performers were notably more professional (and punctual). Instrumentation was different too. By the early twentieth century the most popular stringed instrument in the north was the sitar (originally *seh-tar*, from the Persian for "three strings"), while the veena had that honor in the south. As for percussion, the two-piece tuned tabla drum led the way in the north, while the south preferred the double-headed mridangam drum. Vocal music was popular everywhere.

The musical content differed as well. While many *ragas* were shared by the two systems, they often had different names or slightly different rules, and there were also some *ragas* present in one system but unknown in the other. Improvisation comprised a higher proportion of the music in the north (perhaps 80 percent of the duration) than it did in the south (where it took up about half), and pieces tended to be briefer in the south. Both systems boasted astonishing technical proficiency in the use of complex rhythmic cycles, but the south had a more advanced, mathematical, "calculative" approach to rhythm. Carnatic concerts even had solo spots (*thanis*) for the percussionist, something unheard of in the Hindustani system.

In 1933 there was still very little crossover between the two systems. Robu's first encounter with the southern form came when the troupe attended one of the regular Friday evening soirées run by Veena Dhanam, the grand old lady of Carnatic music, at her small house in the George Town district of Madras. On August 25 Robu climbed a steep staircase to the music room. Many local dignitaries were present, because attendance bestowed a social cachet as a music connoisseur. At 5 p.m. sharp the doors were shut. The audience listened in complete silence as the hostess began to play the veena, and within two minutes Robu had tears in his eyes.[41] In later years Carnatic music became a burning passion for him, and this was the first spark.

Madras provided a further revelation the very next day, with the second ever public performance by the dancer Balasaraswati, the fifteen-year-old granddaughter of Veena Dhanam. Balasaraswati was determined to defy convention and revive her hereditary tradition of *devadasi* temple dance. The term Bharatanatyam had recently been coined, and the emergence of this supremely talented exponent gave impetus to the fledgling campaign to rehabilitate and promote what was then a regional style—a campaign ultimately so successful that today Bharatanatyam is danced by the daughters (and some sons) of middle-class Indian families all over the world. An electrified Uday endorsed her publicly and then, after she had come to see the troupe perform at the Museum Theatre, hosted a dinner at Hotel Connemara to try to persuade her to join them. Although she wanted to accept the invitation, her family was opposed. As for Robu, he fell wildly in love with her.

In late September, the troupe sailed from Bombay to New York, changing ships in Italy. Once again they were a hit in America. This time Hurok had arranged a longer tour, four months in all, covering the whole country. Robu loved their train journeys: "I used to lie on

the top bunk, reading comics and reveling in the sound of the churn-
ing wheels, the steam whistle blowing and the smiling black porters
singing out "All aboard!" as though they were performing negro spiri-
tuals."[42] This time they traveled to the West Coast, and Robu's excitement peaked when Hurok arranged for them to visit the Hollywood
film studios. There he saw his favorites in the flesh: Joan Crawford,
Myrna Loy, Greta Garbo, Clark Gable, Ramón Novarro and John
Barrymore.

The troupe was invited to a tea party hosted by Marie Dressler, star
of *Tugboat Annie* and *Dinner at Eight*. With so many actors there,
Robu was in heaven, but then he noticed Dressler trying to persuade
his brothers of something and them adamantly saying no. It turned
out she was so taken by their youngest brother that she was asking
to adopt him. Robu was furious at his brothers' refusal. What bliss it
would be to live in Hollywood! Dressler would not let it go, and continued to correspond with his brothers even after the troupe's return
to India. They would not budge.

Robu excitedly recounted his Hollywood adventures in a letter to
his father, who was now living in New York. Shyam replied encourag-
ingly, "The best use you can make of it is to be resolved to work hard
so that you may become a Star or a Sun ('Robi') someday. Nobody can
become great without working hard."[43] Twice during this trip Robu
stayed in New York with his father, who had been invited earlier in
the year to Chicago, and was now lecturing at the Roerich Museum
and Columbia University. Their relationship was improving. Shyam's
role as a teacher of Hindu philosophy had transformed him into a
wise elder to his eager disciples, and Robu felt he was a changed man.

There was an ignominious end to the American tour. Uday was
causing problems with his drinking and his autocratic nature. In
Cleveland a minor dispute backstage between him and other members of the troupe escalated into a brawl in which Uday damaged two
fingers so badly that several shows either had to be canceled or went
ahead without him. Ticket sales plummeted. Hurok claimed he was

left with a loss of almost $15,000 at the end of the tour, and he with-
held $8,000 of their earnings.[44] Although their contract had another
year to run, Hurok refused to bring them back the following season,
and they sued for the withheld fees. Suddenly, the future did not look
so secure.

After seasons in Paris and London, the troupe returned to India
in July 1934, leaving Uday and Simkie in Europe to try to resolve the
dispute with Hurok. It became clear that there was no prospect of
an American tour the following winter, and they ended up staying in
India for the next thirteen months.

3

THE CALL OF MUSIC

It was a big pull between two personalities.
RAVI SHANKAR[1]

Abroad, much was made of the authenticity of the dances that Uday's troupe presented. But at home, after the initial exhilaration created by his 1933 Indian tour, there were some attacks on his alleged lack of authenticity. The south Indian critic G. K. Seshagiri condemned Uday's dance style for departing from established canons, describing it as "a typical example of present-day decadence in one of our arts."[2] At this time there was no such thing as Indian classical dance, only a series of regional styles, such as the Bharatanatyam practiced only around Madras. However, there was a new impetus from dance revivalists toward codifying some of those styles and enshrining them as classical forms. Battle lines were being drawn up between those who wanted to define and preserve traditions unchanged and those who preferred innovation and evolution. Uday was in the latter camp—he had chosen to create his own hybrid form that drew from many sources and thus represented all India. Ironically, it was he who had done so much to persuade people nationally and internationally that Indian dance was a rich art form. His response to Seshagiri was effectively to ask in what way his work was not authentic. All art forms change over time, he asserted. "Does he expect that we should go back to two hundred years or five hundred years ago and blindly imitate what our forefathers were doing at that particular period?" He demanded the right to "adopt the best from the past and mold it to the requirements of our present-day life. That way real progress lies."[3]

The year spent in India was a good time to take stock. The plan was to research Kathakali in more depth, devise new dances, tour the country, and make plans. In practice, it marked a turning point for everyone in the troupe. For nearly four years they had been based in France and had concentrated their efforts on Europe and America, generally with spectacular success. However, it was expensive to keep a dozen salaried performers on the road and maintain a house in Paris. The debacle in the States revealed the underlying weakness of the company's situation. It had minimal reserves, and had relied on Alice Boner intermittently injecting new funds. The situation in Europe had deteriorated too. The country with the biggest audience for the troupe, Germany, had been off-limits since the Nazi seizure of power in 1933. So the Paris house was relinquished, and everyone returned to India for retreat and renewal.

While Uday was still in Europe, Robu took the opportunity to study the sitar. In Calcutta Rajendra bought him a new instrument and rented an apartment for them both, where Robu practiced hard in preparation for becoming a disciple of Enayat Khan. Arrangements were made for his *ganda* ceremony, in which the hands of *guru* and disciple are symbolically tied together. But within a week of his arrival he developed a high fever, and the night before the planned ceremony he was diagnosed with a severe case of typhoid. He was admitted to Howrah General Hospital, on an expensive private ward in the European block, where a worried Rajendra initially remained with him round the clock.[4] Robu made a full recovery, but he was in hospital for six weeks. After such an ill-starred beginning, there was no question of becoming Enayat Khan's disciple. It was not meant to be.

In October a house with a large hall was rented for the troupe across town at 35 Elgin Road, and Uday arrived to take charge of rehearsals for an entirely new program. Over the next three months the house was a hive of creativity. It was as if the rue de Paris had moved to Calcutta, as Alice recounted:

The tailors are working in a room in the back of the building, on the veranda someone is carving a Shiva headdress, and in the main room there is a pile of instruments and new masks. On the tennis court in the yard a marquee has been erected from where the drums are banging from morning to evening (much to the pleasure of the whole neighborhood) and in a metal shack the hard-working Chinese produce fabulous new boxes for us.[5]

Once restored to health, Robu sensed a new awakening in his body and mind.[6] He suddenly felt like an adult and, aged fourteen, had his first love affair in Calcutta—with none other than Simkie. For two years he was in love with her, and he lost his virginity.[7] He also threw himself into the dance training at Elgin Road. Both he and Uday received lessons from the Kathakali master Shankaran Namboodiri, who had traveled specially from Malabar, while Robu also had lessons in the north Indian style of Kathak from Sohan Lal of the Jaipur *gharana* (tradition). He still considered dance his forte, although Alice saw things differently. "He helps most with the music," she told her father. "He is fabulously gifted."[8]

Uday's recruitment of the versatile Gokul Nag in late 1934 encouraged Robu's growing interest in the sitar. Nag, a lean young man with a toothbrush mustache, played the instrument in a style different from anything Robu had heard before. It was also the first time he had seen a chromatic sitar, one with a fret for every semitone, like a guitar; on most sitars there is no fret for the flattened second or flattened sixth notes.[9] Robu absorbed much by listening, although he did not formally study with Nag, as some have claimed.[10]

Indian music festivals are traditionally called conferences. In December the first All-Bengal Music Conference gave Robu the chance to attend performances given by some of India's greatest musicians and dancers in the neoclassical grandeur of Calcutta University's Senate Hall. Among the sitar players, he was most taken with Mushtaq Ali Khan and Enayat Khan. The vocalist he was most impressed by was Faiyaz Khan, who dressed like a turbaned maharaja, with medals pinned to the breast of his tunic, and sang in a succession of vocal styles in his resonant bass baritone: *alap, dhrupad, dhamar, khyal* and, to conclude, the lighter *thumri* and *ghazal*.[11] Representing dance were the Kathak exponent Achchan Maharaj and the two south Indians invited by Uday: Balasaraswati, whom he was still hoping (in vain) would join the troupe, and Shankaran Namboodiri. Balasaraswati gave the first performance of Bharatanatyam seen in Calcutta, and it caused a big stir. To add to the occasion, Rabindranath Tagore was observing from one corner of the stage.

However, the person who made the biggest impression on Robu was Timir Baran's *guru*, Allauddin Khan. On the first day he presented the Maihar Band, an ensemble he had formed from local orphaned boys to entertain guests at the royal palace in Maihar, where he was the court musician. Between them, they played sitar, sarod, tabla, violin, cello, clarinet, harmonium, a homemade sitar–banjo hybrid, and a xylophone-like invention of Allauddin Khan's called the naltarang, made by cutting down twenty-four old gun barrels belonging to the maharaja's guard. Allauddin Khan led them from the violin. The band played classical and semi-classical pieces in unison or with simple harmony. Robu was used to playing in Uday's Indian ensemble, but orchestral playing was rare in India, and to combine Indian and Western instruments was a real novelty. Allauddin Khan had a legendary temper and if he heard a mistake he would hit the culprit with his bow—even, to the amusement of the audience, during the performance. Fortunately Robu had been briefed in advance by Timir Baran to discount the freak-show element as his *guru* had a tender side, too, and was a musical genius.

The following day Allauddin Khan played a recital on the sarod, which was his main instrument among the many he had mastered. He was a nervous performer and there was more strange behavior, including withering glances directed toward his son Ali Akbar Khan, who was assisting on sarod in the subordinate role often allotted to a disciple accompanying his *guru*, providing answering phrases as required. Ali Akbar was still musically immature, and patently terrified of making a mistake. Despite all this, Robu was deeply moved by

Allauddin Khan's music making, which had a degree of feeling that he had never heard before.

The festival takes on an even more significant cast in retrospect because four young people were present who thirty years later were spearheading India's cultural mission to the world: the performers Balasaraswati, then aged sixteen, and Ali Akbar, who was only twelve, and, in the audience, not only Robu, aged fourteen, but the thirteen-year-old Satyajit Ray, the future film director.[12] Robu and Satyajit Ray did not meet on this occasion but both were thrilled by Bala's dancing, and Robu developed a close friendship with her during the weeks she spent in Calcutta.

In the early years the troupe's personnel had been very settled. Only Bechu had left, a year earlier, but now there were more departures. Timir Baran left to take a job in film music in Calcutta, but his absence was eased by the arrival of Gokul Nag, while Shirali took on his role of music director. More serious was the rising tension among the brothers. By this point Rajendra's contribution as a performer was minimal and his role was increasingly administrative; he had even suggested he take over as troupe manager. Financial pressures remained and in June 1935, at the end of a three-month tour during which the troupe had struggled somewhat in Ceylon and the south, there was a confrontation in which Uday complained that Rajendra was being paid to do nothing. Rajendra chose to leave, explaining to Alice, "I do not really like the attitude prevalent there, and could not bring myself to please and flatter him on that account."[13] He was followed by Debendra, and within a couple of months by Kanaklata and her father Kedar. Of the original troupe, only Uday, Simkie, Shirali, Matul and Robu remained. As new lead dancers Uday enlisted Madhavan Nair, a Kathakali exponent, and Zohra Mumtaz (later better known as the actress Zohra Segal), an aristocratic young woman who had trained in modern dance under Mary Wigman in Dresden. The other new musicians were Timir Baran's brother Sisir Sovan, flutist Nagen Dey and sarod player Dulal Sen, who became a good friend of Robu.

The first concert with this new lineup took place at the New Empire, Calcutta, in August 1935. Then followed a tour of Southeast Asia, taking in Rangoon, Moulmein and Mandalay in Burma, and Kuala Lumpur, Penang and Singapore in British Malaya. The plan was to continue to China and Japan and then, subject to reaching an agreement in time with an American promoter, to cross the Pacific to California. But at Singapore a telegram informed Uday and Robu of the sudden death, on October 17, of their father. Mystery surrounded what happened, but once the high commissioner in London had pieced together the story, it was clear that he had been murdered.

Shyam had recently given up lecturing in America, having been offered two prestigious jobs in India: as chief minister to the Gaekwad of Baroda and a senior government role in Delhi. En route he took on a legal case being heard by the Privy Council in London, a bitter and long-running dispute between two Bengali *zamindar* brothers. In the middle of the case, he was hit over the head one morning outside his hotel, where he was found by a policeman. Although he was still conscious when he was taken to hospital in Paddington, he had lost the ability to speak English and died without being able to say what had happened.[14] The culprit was never identified, but the family was advised that Shyam had probably been killed because he was performing so well in court. Oddly enough, two days after his death Uday received a letter from him intimating that he had not much longer to live.[15] The troupe cut short the Asian tour and returned to Benares so that Uday and Robu could mourn with their mother and brothers.

Counting up all the occasional days in different countries, Robu had spent no more than about a month with his father in total. He barely knew him, and yet he grew up to resemble him to a surprising degree. There was the dualistic personality, both highly professional and at the same time unworldly. There was the ferocious drive for self-improvement, the restless need for constant motion, the ability to function on little sleep, and—of course—the sensitivity to music.

Most likely Robu's brothers, especially Uday, acted as conduits, passing on some of their father's characteristics to their youngest sibling. Shyam himself was not much concerned with nurture, although in his rare letters to his sons he did aim to pass on the value of hard work and a higher calling. Sadly, the one trait that Shyam definitely passed on by direct example to Robu was that of being an absent father.

A new tour itinerary was devised, which would take the troupe westward through the Middle East and into Europe. Gokul Nag decided not to join them, which left Uday short of one high-quality musician, so he invited Allauddin Khan instead. This was to prove a fateful decision for Robu. Allauddin Khan was granted extended leave by the Maharaja of Maihar, Brijnath Singh, and in December he arrived in Bombay for rehearsals, bringing his son Ali Akbar with him. There the troupe played a well-received farewell week at the Excelsior Theatre. The *Evening News of India* had praise for all the dancers, noting the "delightful ability" of Madhavan, Robindra and Zohra.[16] Ali Akbar, however, did not want to travel, because he knew that on tour he would be unable to escape his irascible father. So he approached Matul, pretending to be distressed by a bad dream about his mother and saying he did not want to leave her alone in Maihar. When Allauddin Khan heard the story, he agreed to send his son back to Maihar.

Alice Boner, after spending the previous year in India, also opted to stay on rather than join the tour. She remained a partner in the dance company but felt she had neglected her own creativity long enough. She probably felt let down by Uday after the debacle in America, and there are later letters from him in which he tries to reassure her that he has given up drinking. Her decision was also driven by her burgeoning fascination with the iconography of Indian sculpture, which she wanted to study. She took a house at Assi Ghat in Benares, which was to be her main home for the next forty-three years.

Uday was always on the lookout for patrons. In Dartington the previous year he had persuaded Dorothy Elmhirst to advance him $2,500 and he hoped she would back his proposed Indian cultural center. In the run-up to departure Dorothy's daughter Beatrice Straight arrived in Bombay to spend time with Uday over Christmas. He took her to see the ancient rock-cut Buddhist caves at Ajanta and the Buddhist, Hindu and Jain caves at Ellora, and arranged for the musicians to play inside them for her. It was a magical experience, she recalled, and she fell "madly in love" with him.[17] He was also petitioning leading Indian figures to endorse his center. Tagore was supportive; Gandhi less so. Robu was among the small group who visited Gandhi at his residence in Bombay. On the rooftop they sang him his favorite *bhajan*, *Raghupati Raghav Rajaram*, also known as the *Ram Dhun*. But Gandhi explained that music and dance were not a priority for him: "We really need more than anything for people to eat food and wear clothes. The art can follow later."[18]

Hemangini came to Bombay to see them off in January 1936. She had a premonition that she might not see Robu again, and as they stood on the pier she took his hands and placed them in Allauddin Khan's. "He is still so young and recently lost his father," she said to the veteran musician. "As I am not coming with you and do not know whether I will see him again, please look after him as your son." She asked him to spare Robu if he made a mistake at music. Allauddin Khan became emotional. "Ma, you are *ratnagarbha*!" he said, meaning the mother of a jewel—Uday. "Until now I had only one son, Ali Akbar, but from today I have two."[19] All three were in tears. As the SS *Britannia* eased away, Robu watched his sobbing mother on the dockside as she receded into the distance.

Allauddin Khan was as good as his word, showing Robu love and affection and, after they began music lessons on the boat, refraining from losing his temper with him. Up to this point, Robu was largely self-taught on the sitar and thought he played quite well, but now he was made to relearn his fingering technique. Lessons also covered vocal music, which is at the root of all Indian classical music—

everything that can be played can be sung. In turn, Robu acted as his new teacher's guide, interpreter and companion. At first he addressed him as "Ustad," the term for a respected Muslim musician (the equivalent of "Pandit" for a Hindu), but in time he switched to "Baba," or father, which was widely used by those who knew Allauddin Khan well. In Robu's case he really was a substitute father.

They stopped in Aden, Cairo, Alexandria, Tel Aviv, Jerusalem and Haifa. It was the era of the British Mandate in Palestine and on the day they reached Tel Aviv the British were marking the accession of King Edward VIII. From there they sailed to Greece and toured through Yugoslavia, Bulgaria, Romania, Hungary, Czechoslovakia, Austria, Italy and Switzerland, playing concerts all the way. They reached Paris in April. At first Baba Allauddin Khan appeared in only one solo musical item, accompanied on tabla by Sisir Sovan, but, frustrated at being underemployed, he insisted on playing in the ensemble accompanying the dance items as well. Robu was struck by this example of the master musician's humility, a quality conventionally prized in Indian music. Like Tansen, Baba believed that music was a vast ocean and he had imbibed merely drops of it.

In most respects Baba was strict and ascetic. He never drank alcohol, he prayed five times a day, and he adhered to the old belief that indulging in sex reduced a musician's powers. The culture in the troupe was very different. Following Uday's example, Robu was used to living as he pleased. He chased girls and dressed in fine suits. With a hint of the dilettante, he spread his energies across painting, writing and reading as well as dance and music, and within music across the sarod, flute, esraj and tabla as well as the sitar. He visited some of Paris's more explicit nightspots, including the salon at Le Sphinx, the upmarket brothel frequented by the artistic set, including Alberto Giacometti, Jean-Paul Sartre and Henry Miller. Being in Paris with Baba presented him with the starkest of culture clashes: "I was brought up in that very strange bohemian atmosphere and meeting him was my first jolt."[20]

One day Baba asked Matul whether it was true there were places where women danced in the nude. "Oh yes," said Matul. "I have seen them. Dulal and Robu can take you there." So Baba was taken to a cabaret, which made for an uncomfortable evening for Robu:

> There we were, sat at a table, and the girls serving us were wearing next to nothing, just a little apron for their modesty. Baba was sitting like a statue, very nervous, and I was feeling so self-conscious—I was sitting like a good boy, not looking either side! Then the show started—and now not even an apron!

Baba's only remark was, "Their bodies are like candle wax, so white." Embarrassment peaked when one woman sat on his lap. He whispered in Bengali, "Tell her to move away!" Robu told her, "He's a priest, celibate—please move."[21]

In contrast Robu also took Baba to see Notre-Dame Cathedral. As the organ played one Sunday morning, Baba fell into a trance. There were tears in his eyes as he said, "Here is God."[22] Although he was a devout Muslim, he had grown up in a Hindu village in Bengal and was unusually receptive to different faiths. For him, music was the ultimate divinity. As Robu got to know Baba, he grew to love this aspect of him.

A long summer followed at Dartington Hall. This five-month residency was the first time Robu had stayed for an extended period in a rural environment, and it changed his negative feelings about the British too. Amid the beautiful grounds, the troupe was allocated a studio in which to develop new material, and they gave a few shows in the Barn Theatre. Alice Boner joined them in July. It was there that Robu met Zohra's sister Uzra Mumtaz, who joined as a new dancer, and he formed an instant bond with her even though she was three years older than him. There, too, he choreographed his first solo dance, *Chitra Sena*, with much Kathak-inspired movement. Dartington fostered a fertile creative atmosphere. Also present were the modern dance pioneers Kurt Jooss and Sigurd Leeder, who had been given safe haven from Nazi Germany by the Elmhirsts, and the Russian actor Michael Chekhov, who was preparing to open his drama studio, where he would specialize in the method acting of his teacher Konstantin Stanislavski.

The greatest exhilaration, though, was in learning from Baba. He represented pure creativity: every day he wrote five or ten new compositions and taught them. Through disciplined practice Robu made speedy progress and felt that he was going much more deeply into music. He began to understand its spiritual dimension. Baba perceived that he had a remarkable musical gift, but berated him for squandering it on a frivolous life. He had a saying: "*Ek sadhe sab sadhe, sab sadhe sab jaye.*" ("Do one thing well and you can achieve everything. Do everything and you achieve nothing.") Before returning to India in October, he told Robu that if he wanted to study properly he would have to give up dance and come to Maihar in a spirit of renunciation. Learning music was a lifetime's work. Robu was stunned: "He was the first person frank enough to tell me that I had talent but that I was wasting it. Everyone else was full of praise, but he killed my ego and made me humble."[23]

Back in India Hemangini had retreated to her village of Nasrathpur. Her father gave her ten acres of land, across the road from her own home, and she dedicated herself to building a house there for her children. Debendra and his wife Krishna moved in after their marriage and lived there for the next six decades. Today the house still stands, tired and sunbeaten despite the relieving shade of a huge peepul tree, with cows tethered in the forecourt. Bricks in the retaining wall bear the marks "AG 1935" or "DB 1936," indicating the years they were fired.

Hemangini was so determined to finish the house before Debendra's wedding that she worked outdoors through the 1936 monsoon season and caught a chest infection. Days after the ceremony, she died of pneumonia. Her body was taken to Benares for cremation. On November 24, the day she died, Uday, Shirali and Matul all spent a sleepless night in Amsterdam, where they were playing ten shows in a week. "I imagine it was a telepathy," Shirali wrote to Alice Boner, who had returned to India with Baba.[24] A telegram informing Uday of his mother's death reached him on arrival in Paris. It was not until the next day that he summoned Robu to his hotel room to break the news. The whole troupe was sitting around looking glum as he walked in. He picked up the telegram, read it and sat still without saying a word to anyone or shedding a tear.[25]

He might have looked composed but he was devastated. He had felt so close to his mother. "We are very sad as you can imagine to hear about mother's departure," he wrote to Alice. "It will be terrible for us when we go to India, specially for Matul, Dada and me, because we shall miss her in every corner. At the present moment I can't believe even that she is gone. I feel always that she is living still!" He added that he was worried that his new sister-in-law might be blamed for bringing bad luck: "You know how our Indian people are superstitious."[26]

As for Uday, he admitted that it broke his heart. "Just when I was on the way to do something worthwhile and wonderful dream to realize [sic], she should leave us and go away. It pains me so much to think that I could not do anything for mother or father."[27] According to Zohra Segal, "He tried to cry but couldn't, so he drank and drank. If he had cried he might have released his pain in tears; trying to drown it in drink didn't work."[28]

After Christmas in Paris, the troupe embarked on its third American tour, a resolution finally having been reached with Sol Hurok. With his mother's death following hard on the unequivocal parting message from Baba, Robu suddenly found himself in turmoil. From the SS *Lafayette* he wrote to Alice, "We shall arrive in New York this evening, but I don't feel excited about it at all—I wonder why! Truly I feel very homesick and want to return to India as soon as possible. Nothing interests me in these countr[ies] any more."[29] Over the following year, he was torn between dance and music, between the glamourous world of showbusiness and an austere journey toward an uncertain future, and between two strong personalities, Uday and Baba. His first reaction to Baba's departure was to put aside the sitar in favor of the sarod, Baba's instrument, and at the same time he threw himself with even greater determination into dancing. Yet he kept gravitating back toward the sitar. Uday, meanwhile, had come to appreciate his brother's dual talent. "Robu is going to be a great musician and dancer—his solo is a great success," he told Alice.[30] Yet Robu was not comfortable discussing his dilemma with Uday. Tellingly, he felt that, with both his parents dead, he had no one to turn to for advice.[31] Even surrounded by friends and with much in life to enjoy, he felt alone.

This tour of North America was shorter, less than two months in all, taking in major cities in the northeast, including ten nights at the Majestic Theater on Broadway, plus Chicago and four dates in Canada. Despite their three-year absence, they once more met with packed houses and effusive reviews. But Uday's focus was increasingly on his proposed cultural center, which, he announced to prospective American backers, would be in Benares. He could see that Europe was heading for catastrophe.

In New York, before they caught the boat home, the troupe made a historic recording, the first album of Indian classical music to be released in the West. The ten tracks were spread across five 78 rpm shellac discs, one cut per side, each about four minutes long. There were five dance items and five musical interludes selected from the stage shows. Apart from a solo by Shirali on the twelve tuned drums of the tabla taranga, all are ensemble pieces, played with great proficiency by Shirali, Sisir Sovan, Dulal Sen, Nagen Dey, Matul and Robu (credited as "Rabindra," playing the sitar and esraj). There are two vocal numbers: *Danse Ramachandra*, which features two devotional songs based on the Carnatic *ragas Simhendra Madhyamam* and *Hamsadhwani* (evidence that the troupe incorporated south Indian music), and a *bhajan* sung engagingly by Shirali. The album was issued in April 1938 by RCA Victor. It is invaluable as the only substantial audio record of the troupe's sound in the 1930s, which was a formative influence on the later ensemble compositions created by its youngest member.

There was a European tour in the spring of 1937, taking in Belgium, the Netherlands, Denmark, Poland, Switzerland, Italy, Hungary and France, sandwiched between seasons in London at the Savoy Theatre and the Gaiety Theatre. At the latter, the Viceroy of India, Lord Linlithgow, came backstage.[32] Indeed, Uday's star power was undiminished. In America the troupe met Walt Disney, Basil Rathbone and Mickey Rooney. It also continued to fascinate some of the world's fledgling composers. Leonard Bernstein and Alan Hovhaness were both inspired by seeing concerts in Boston, while Benjamin Britten and Imogen Holst attended in London, Britten for the second time. Now aged twenty-three, on this occasion he wrote in his diary that the music was "highly subtle, developed and consequently marvelously beautiful. The dancing is the same—and technique of everyone beyond conception...I have the intuition that I was taking part in a very significant festival."[33]

The autumn was then spent in London, where Beatrice Straight rented a house for them for three months at 9 The Mount, Hampstead, with a studio space across the road. Here Uday led more rehearsals. After a week of shows at Dartington, they sailed from Southampton for what they already knew would be their final tour of America. This was another coast-to-coast adventure, three and a half months in all. During the four visits there since 1932 they had appeared in forty-four states. The highlight this time was their first two performances at Carnegie Hall, where Robu danced his *Chitra Sena* solo as well as playing the sitar. The second of these shows closed the tour on March 12, 1938. On that very day, the German army crossed the border into Austria and annexed the country in the *Anschluss*. The catastrophe was approaching. The troupe returned to Europe, but prospects there were too bleak. Simkie stayed on in Paris, while Uday and Zohra sailed off to explore Java and Bali, and the rest returned to India.

Over the last year Robu had still been reveling in a life of pleasure. He had many girlfriends, the most constant being Uzra Mumtaz. He had also developed a taste for beer and wine. Although he always said that drinking never became a problem for him, as it had for Uday, he sensed in himself a vulnerability to alcohol. The atmosphere around Uday was often one of excess, and with uncommon maturity Robu recognized that he needed to get away from it. Fortunately music was calling. Meanwhile, his admiration for Uday was undimmed. "My appreciation for the world's color, romance and music was inspired totally by my brother," he said. "He was like my God. It is true he had his human failings, too, but that does not detract from the fact that he was indeed extraordinary… He was for us a superman."[34]

Seven and a half years with Uday had given Robu a confidence in performing and mixing with stars, an appreciation of the Western world and its music, and an understanding of how Indian performing arts could be successfully presented abroad. It was a training that no rival Indian musician had experienced. Even more significantly, he had met his future *guru*. On the other hand, the years on tour had drilled into him the habit of restless motion and had done nothing to cure his fundamental loneliness—issues that would haunt him in his adult life.

4

THE PATH OF MOST RESISTANCE

For us, *guru* is sometimes greater even than God. He is the
teacher from whom all knowledge is passed on.
RAVI SHANKAR[1]

As if gathering himself before a long journey, Robu stayed in Nasrathpur for a couple of months on his return to India. There, in his
mother's village, he tried to come to terms with her death, which had
seemed unreal from afar. There was further sadness when his grandfather, Abhoy Charan, died during his stay, following a fall.[2] At least
Rajendra—always a supportive presence—was there. This visit also
gave Robu the opportunity to undertake his *Upanayana* (sacred
thread) ceremony, the rite of passage that admits a Brahmin boy into
adulthood. Usually it happens by the age of twelve, but he had never
been around long enough. Some family members even feared that he
had been eating so much foreign food that he might no longer be a
Brahmin. In preparation, he shaved off his shoulder-length hair and
learned the Gayatri Mantra so that he could recite it during the rituals.
At the ceremony, which took place in May in his mother's house, he
was initiated alongside his young uncle Dinesh Chandra Chakrabarty
and a cousin.[3] Afterward he felt cleansed. He observed the custom
of living like a monk for a few weeks, following an ascetic diet and
abstaining from worldly concerns.

The family worried when Robu went down with a fever, reviving
memories of when he had typhoid, and there was a fear that he was
now too accustomed to cooler climes to tolerate the summer heat in
what Zohra called "the disease inferno of Benares."[4] But this time the
illness was not serious, and he readied himself for his next destination,
Maihar. He had been secretly writing to Baba Allauddin Khan during

the previous year, and the offer remained open to study with Baba in the traditional *gurukul* style, in which a disciple lives with his *guru* and practices music full-time, as part of the family. Uday, who was still away in Bali, was expecting Robu to continue in the troupe once a location had been found for the cultural center, but he agreed to him studying with Baba in the meantime. Robu had not told him what kind of commitment Baba was demanding.

It required a certainty of mind remarkable in an eighteen-year-old for Robu to choose what one critic has called "the path of most resistance," spurning the comforts of his flourishing career in dance in order to learn classical music the hard way.[5] Ahead of him, as it transpired, lay six and a half years of fanatical dedication in Maihar. As he traveled there with Rajendra, a journey of about eight hours from Benares by train, he was still in turmoil, doubting his own powers of self-discipline, knowing how spoilt he was, how sensitive to criticism: "I felt as though I were committing suicide and knew that I would be reborn, but had no way of knowing how the new life would be."[6]

Baba was shocked to see him. No longer a luxuriantly maned dandy in a tailored British suit, Robu arrived with a few weeks' growth of hair on his head and wearing a coarse, white, hand-spun *kurta* (tunic) and *pajama* trousers of the same material. He carried his few belongings in a cheap tin trunk. "What have you done to yourself?" Baba asked, but Robu's transformation pleased him, for he had evidently understood the need for renunciation.[7]

Baba's imposing house, arranged around a colonnaded central courtyard, had been built for him a few years earlier by the Maharaja of Maihar. Robu installed himself in a small dwelling next door at a rent of five rupees per month. Facilities were spartan. There was a simple bed made of hard coconut coir bound to a wooden frame. Rajendra stayed for the first week to settle Robu in and engage a maidservant to prepare his food. After his brother had left, Robu was alone. From time to time another student moved in—at least thirty of them over the next couple of years—but each one ran away within ten days because of Baba's temper. Otherwise Robu's only company in his house was mosquitoes, flies, cockroaches, scorpions, lizards and even snakes. At night he could hear frogs and crickets outside, and was scared by the howling of wolves and jackals. The house was on the edge of what was then a small, remote town. There were no cinemas, no entertainments. It was the biggest contrast possible with the fine hotels and frantic social life he had been used to abroad.

Baba had a gentle and generous side to him, and he could be very sentimental; later, he would weep when watching the film *Fantasia*. Robu loved this aspect of him, but he knew that when Baba was teaching he was very strict indeed. He was startled, though, to discover just what a tyrannical disciplinarian Baba became on his home turf. Everyone was scared of him, including his wife Madan Manjari (also known as Madina Begum), his son Ali Akbar, now sixteen, and his daughter Annapurna, who was twelve, and particularly the other students. Robu realized that Baba had no patience with mediocrity: "To him music is a sacred and completely religious thing. How, therefore, could he allow any impurities or defects to remain?"[8] Baba was unpredictable and sometimes violent. He assaulted all his students— even, on one occasion, his own patron, the Maharaja of Maihar, when he made a mistake during a lesson. One tabla student ended up in hospital for several months after being struck by Baba with a tuning hammer.[9] Robu was the only student to escape this treatment. Baba never laid a finger on him, true to his promise to Robu's mother.

Only once did Baba even lose his temper with him. Robu was struggling to play a fast exercise, and Baba rebuked him, saying, "Go and buy some bangles to wear on your wrists. You are like a weak little girl!"[10] Robu was unused to being chastised, and reacted angrily. He packed his bag and stormed off to the station to wait for a train home. It was Ali Akbar who persuaded him to return to the house at least to say goodbye. There he found an emotional Baba cutting out a photograph of him and putting it in a frame. "I just told you to wear bangles, and it has hurt you so much that you are going to leave?" said

Baba. "You remember at the pier in Bombay how your mother put your hand in mine and asked me to look after you as my own son? This is how you want to break it?"[11] Tearfully, Robu changed his mind.

Baba's harshness was rooted in his childhood struggles to become a musician. His family were Bengali Muslim peasant farmers in Tripura, bordering East Bengal. His father and older brother were amateur musicians but they refused to let him devote his life to such a disreputable profession, so at the age of eight he ran away to join a traveling group of musicians, claiming to be an orphan. Over several years they taught him both folk and classical styles, and he then spent long periods struggling to support himself in Dhaka, Calcutta and Rampur. As well as learning vocal music, he mastered the violin, clarinet, cornet, trumpet, shehnai and various drums—tabla, pakhawaj and dhol—even before he took up his principal instrument, the sarod. He was fanatical in his drive to learn, and forced himself to abstain from sex so that his energies were focused solely on music. Sometimes when he practiced, he would tie his hair to the ceiling with a long cord, to force himself to stay awake.

It was his first sarod *guru*, Ahmad Ali Khan, who instilled in him a higher appreciation of classical music. But Ahmad Ali also drank and frequented courtesans and dancing girls. One night Baba was sent to retrieve his *guru* from a bordello. "I have come to take him home," he announced, but the woman who answered the door found him attractive and tried to persuade him to stay the night too. At first he misunderstood, in his naivety, but when he realized what she meant he fell at her feet. "My Ustad is like my father," he said. "He comes to you, so you are like my mother." That cooled her off quickly, and he was able to carry his drunken *guru* home.[12]

For generations north Indian classical music had been structured according to the *gharana* system. A *gharana* is an artistic tradition or house, founded around a figurehead, location or instrument, with its own distinctive approach passed on by direct oral transmission, often within a single family. The same term applies to everything from dance to wrestling. Historically, separate *gharanas* had emerged because classical music had been shut away in palaces, and communications were slow, so there were few chances for musicians to listen to each other. There had always been some evolution in the system over time, as *gharanas* arose, faded away or developed in new directions, but the pace of change accelerated in the late nineteenth century as the decline of princely power and the coming of the railways brought Hindustani musicians out into public view and into contact with each other.

Baba's principal *gharana* was Senia Beenkar. He had studied it with his last and greatest *guru*, Wazir Khan of Rampur, whom he met after Ahmad Ali had stopped teaching him. Senia Beenkar dated back to Mian Tansen (hence the name Senia), who had perfected the classical *dhrupad* singing style, in which a *raga* was slowly unfolded through an unaccompanied, free-tempo opening section known as *alap*, and then progressed into a *jor* section with a measured pulse. It had a deep spiritual quality and was highly formalized. *Raga* purity was prized, and each musical piece was designed to express one of the nine standard emotions or *rasas* originally detailed in a two-thousand-year-old Sanskrit text, the *Natya Shastra*.

Dhrupad was principally a vocal style, with rhythm accompaniment provided by the barrel-shaped pakhawaj drum. However, the Beenkar strand of Tansen's tradition, which descended through his daughter's line, interpreted *dhrupad* through the stringed instrument that its members played, the been, a north Indian version of the veena. Wazir Khan was a direct descendant of Tansen. Baba became a master of this style, playing it mainly on the sarod, and he was rigorous about policing musical purity within it. But he was also, as Robu noted, a remarkable "impurist," because of all the different styles he had absorbed in his earlier days.[13] During his year in Europe, he had revealed to Robu just how much affection he had for Bengali folk music. In Maihar he kept this side more hidden, but Robu was tremendously attracted to Baba's vast knowledge and his combination of musical purity and eclecticism.

From the start of Robu's training, his life was supposed to consist of nothing but music. He woke around 4 a.m., after about four or five hours' sleep, washed, drank a cup of tea, and worked on scale exercises on the sitar until six. Following a bath, morning worship and breakfast of two boiled eggs and a piece of bread, he returned to the sitar until seven, when he crossed nervously to Baba's house for a lesson lasting anywhere between thirty minutes and three hours. Baba was not a sitar player—it was one of the few instruments he did not play—so he taught by singing phrases or playing them on his sarod. His touch and sensitivity were such that Robu often shed tears listening to him. Baba knew enough about the sitar to instruct his pupil on left-hand fingerings and right-hand strokes, but Robu had to work out his own methods for many effects. After the morning lesson, the rest of the day consisted of more *riyaaz* (practice), apart from lunch and a siesta of about an hour, and there might be another late-afternoon session with Baba. Robu practiced for at least eight hours every day, and twelve to fourteen was not uncommon. Occasionally, for the sake of his ego, as he put it, he reached sixteen hours.[14]

It was unusual for someone as old as Robu to be starting formal training, but he had the zeal of a convert. Mentally, he was already quite an advanced musician, given his wide-ranging experience, but physically his technique needed to catch up, and there were many hard months of unrelenting exercises. "In the beginning it was more perspiration than inspiration," he said.[15] There was an element of mental torture as he struggled to concentrate and adjusted to the mindset required of a *shishya* (disciple) of Baba, who demanded humility and the surrender of the ego. Such was the way with the *guru–shishya parampara*, the old tradition of learning. The *guru* provided free tuition and as far as possible removed material burdens so that the *shishya* could focus on music. In return, the *shishya* imbibed uncritically the gift of music, and served the *guru* in whatever way he required—"doing the needful," in the Indian expression.

At first, Baba mostly taught him on his own. Ali Akbar was two years younger than Robu, but a couple of years ahead in his musical training. He had been through a brutal regime: Baba had even tied him to a tree and beaten him when his progress was unsatisfactory. Although Baba had arranged for Ali Akbar to marry at the age of fifteen, he still expected him to remain celibate—married to music. Twice Ali Akbar ran away. Ultimately the harsh discipline brought out his talent and made him into a master of the sarod, although one wonders about the emotional cost.

Robu could not believe Ali Akbar's musical transformation from the tentative boy he had seen in Calcutta. The two became close friends. Ali Akbar was calm on the surface, the opposite of his father. He was, as his daughter Lajwanti Gupta put it, "a country bumpkin, total simpleton," and Robu assumed the role of experienced older brother, instructing him in the ways of the world, even in how to make love.[16] They spent hours talking together as they went on local walks— to the temple, along the river or on Robu's favorite excursion, the long walk up the conical Trikuta Hill, topped by the temple of Ma Sharda, an incarnation of the mother goddess. Baba, with his eclectic spirituality, worshipped Ma Sharda. He considered her his protectress and the fount of his music. Every year on the day of Saraswati Puja, he climbed the steep hill to make an offering at her shrine.

After a while Robu started learning alongside Ali Akbar in lessons that formed the basis of their later celebrated duets. Sometimes Annapurna joined them. When Robu arrived in Maihar she was playing the sitar, but she progressed to the surbahar, a bass version of the sitar that is heavier, longer, broader in the neck and usually tuned five tones lower. In time Robu also took up the surbahar. A lucky fly on the wall could have watched the three greatest successors to Allauddin Khan's art learning music together at his feet—the ancient oral tradition at its best.

Robu's musical inheritance was particularly rich. Previously, India had been in what he called "the age of specialization."[17] Some musicians

spent all their lives playing only *alap* and *jor* styles. Others concentrated on aspects of later styles, especially *khyal*, which became popular
in the nineteenth century as courtly entertainment, emphasizing vir-
tuosic improvisation on *bandishes* (short vocal or instrumental compositions bound by a rhythmic cycle). Ali Akbar Khan once said that
dhrupad is like plain dal, but *khyal* is like dal with added onion and
garlic. *Khyal's* emergence saw the sidelining of the been in favor of
instruments such as the sarod, sarangi and especially the sitar, which
had evolved from the veena in an earlier era. As Robu liked to say,
"The sitar isn't very old—just seven hundred or eight hundred years."[18]
But the modern sitar design did not begin to take shape until the
nineteenth century.

As communications between musicians improved over time, different schools took the best elements from each other. What marked
out Baba was just how many traditions he amalgamated. "He himself
was like an ocean," said Robu. "He had all the different styles, all the
different forms. In him I found everything! Therefore—I know it
sounds high-handed, but the fact remains—I was the first to have
all these things in one...I tried to combine this technique in my
sitar."[19] Under Baba's guidance, Robu developed a new performance
structure, elaborating one *raga* in a succession of styles. He began
with slow, *dhrupad*-style *alap* and *jor* sections, which he adapted
for sitar and always felt were the most powerful and distinctive elements for him (and for Ali Akbar on the sarod). Then he progressed
to *khyal*-style improvisations on *gats* (fixed instrumental compositions) in both slower and faster tempos, accompanied by the tabla.
In the final *jhala* section, when the melody strings were plucked in
rapid alternation with the open *chikari* (drone) strings, he accelerated into awe-inspiring displays of virtuosity. At the end of a concert
he usually added a lighter, semi-classical *thumri* piece or a folk-like
dhun passage, drawing on Baba's folk influences, and here he often
included flashes of many different *ragas* in a style known as *raga
mala* (meaning a garland of *ragas*). In subsequent years this format

became so well known around the world that most have assumed it has an ancient origin, but the structure was devised in Maihar, with Robu developing it on the sitar and Ali Akbar on the sarod. "I was the first one in sitar to combine all these elements on one canvas," Robu said. "Then little by little it was taken and accepted, and many other people started doing it."[20]

He developed at a phenomenal rate, and Baba was impressed. Quite soon Robu began to join him on stage, either plucking the tanpura or assisting on the sitar. After less than eighteen months of training— remarkably soon—he was permitted to play a duet with Ali Akbar, at the Allahabad Music Conference in December 1939. There was much appreciation from three great vocalists sitting in the front row, Faiyaz Khan, Mushtaq Hussain and Omkarnath Thakur.

The following year he was invited, at Baba's recommendation, to perform on All India Radio in Lucknow, beginning a long relation-ship with the national broadcaster. Every other month he traveled to Lucknow to record two programs on consecutive days. He took this opportunity to rename himself Ravi Shankar, initially just for radio audiences, and then as a permanent and significant change. The Hindi name Ravi (short for Ravindra) had the same meaning as the Bengali Robi (Robindra)—"the sun"—but it presented him as a universal Indian figure rather than as a Bengali. The name change made sense in an era when Indians were asserting their national iden-tity more strongly as independence edged closer, and it revealed his ambition. There was a strange echo of his father's shedding of "Hara Chowdhury" from the family name nearly forty years earlier in order to obscure his own Bengali identity.

From now on he was India's Sun, Ravi Shankar.

After rejecting first Benares and then Bombay as the site for his cul-tural center, because they were too hot in summer, Uday alighted on Almora, two hundred and fifty miles northwest of Delhi. This was one of the more remote hill stations in the Kumaon Himalaya, a good place for working without interruptions. The Elmhirsts' friends Boshi and Gertrude Emerson Sen, who lived there, recommended an abandoned eight-acre tea estate with heavenly views of the snow-crested peaks around Nanda Devi.[21] Everything fell into place: a further ninety-four acres of forest land at the nearby Simtola ridge were offered by the United Provinces government for future expansion, and there were donations by the Gaekwad of Baroda and the industrialist J. K. Birla, although the Elmhirsts were the principal benefactors with a gift of £20,000. However, Uday's plans brought about the end of his friendship with Alice Boner, which had been so vital for his troupe. Alice agreed to dissolve their dance company, thus writing off most of her investment, but she was upset by Uday's failure to consult her.

In its brief existence the Uday Shankar India Culture Centre at Almora became a fabled institution. It combined the traditional ashram style of school (a remote establishment in a rural location) with the workshop atmosphere Uday had encountered among modern-dance pioneers in the West. Dartington was the principal model. Work began in 1939, when a large studio cum performance hall was constructed, a series of buildings on the Ranidhara ridge was rented for accommodation, and preparations were made for a nationwide tour in the winter of 1939–40. This saw many members of the old dance troupe reunited, including Simkie, Zohra, Uzra, Shirali and even Rajendra and Debendra, as well as Amala Nandi, who was now twenty and secretly became engaged to Uday during the tour. Baba revived his role as the guest soloist, and as before insisted on also playing in the ensemble accompanying the dancers, even when it involved him simply striking a huge Balinese gong. Uday asked Baba to allow Ravi to dance in the troupe, and to Ravi's amazement Baba agreed, so for two winter seasons he joined the tour as both dancer and musician—a respite from the ascetic intensity of Maihar. During Uday's modern ballet *Labour and Machinery*, Ravi had the surreal experience of dancing a two-and-a-half-minute Kathak item to Baba playing the Bangla dhol drum.[22] He also rekindled his affair with Uzra, with a passion fueled by the abstinence of his life at Maihar.

For the classes at Almora, which commenced in March 1940, Uday engaged four teachers, each a master in his field: Balasaraswati's *guru* Kandappan Pillai for Bharatanatyam, Shankaran Namboodiri for Kathakali, Amobi Singh for Manipuri dance and Allauddin Khan for music. Both Ali Akbar and Ravi assisted with the music classes, while Ravi also joined in with the dance program and continued learning the sitar. He loved the center. There was no institution like it in India, not even Shantiniketan. The student body was small, starting with about ten and growing to sixty, but many alumni went on to national acclaim, including the film director Guru Dutt, the dancers and choreographers Shanti Bardhan, Narendra Sharma, Sachin Shankar (Ravi's cousin) and Ghanshyam, and the arts mogul Sundari Shridharani. Kumudini Lakhia, today the doyenne of Kathak, visited as a child and was inspired by the ambience: "Everybody wanted to dance. I think even the cooks and the servants danced in Almora. It was in the air."[23]

Most important for Ravi's future was a pair of Tamil sisters who arrived as young dance students: Kamala Sastri, who was to become one of the great loves of Ravi's later life, and her older sister Lakshmi, who would marry Rajendra. Their father, who edited Gandhi's journal *Harijan*, had been so impressed by seeing the troupe perform in Madras that he moved the family to Almora to enable fourteen-year-old Lakshmi to study there. Soon Kamala joined the classes too. Both were so talented that they were quickly included in the troupe. They were in a creative heaven. "The four years I spent there was the most fantastic time in my life," said Lakshmi.[24] As for the eleven-year-old Kamala, everything was exciting for her, but she particularly noticed that Ravi was full of life, zest and humor.[25] "Even then he would compose little songs and make us all sing," she recalled.[26]

For a while Almora thrived as an artistic sanctuary at a time of upheaval. Much of the world had descended into the darkest horrors of the Second World War, and India was not immune: in 1942 the Japanese occupied Burma, invaded parts of northeastern India and bombed Calcutta. This was also the time of the Quit India movement, with Gandhi calling for mass protests to demand immediate independence as the price of India's support in the war. The British reacted with widespread repression and most of the leaders of the freedom movement were imprisoned. The cause of national liberation found expression in Uday's first full-length ballet, *The Rhythm of Life*, which was created at Almora, but mostly the center's activities sought to rise above the turmoil—as Gertrude Emerson Sen put it, "like a beacon-light on its Himalayan hilltop."[27]

That Baba never beat Ravi was evidence of the unique position that Ravi occupied in his heart. An even bigger sign was that Baba agreed to him marrying his daughter, Annapurna.

It was Ravi's sister-in-law Krishna, Debendra's wife, who first suggested the union, during a visit to Maihar in 1939. It had never occurred to Ravi that he might marry his *guru*'s daughter. Annapurna was still only thirteen and was in the habit of doing *pranam* whenever she greeted him—touching his feet in a respectful manner, as one traditionally does with an elder. Krishna pursued the idea and suggested it to Baba, who reacted with humility, asking how a Muslim might even dream of marrying a high-caste Brahmin. But the idea appealed to Baba for two reasons: his fatherly love for Ravi, and his yearning for Annapurna to marry someone who would allow her to continue with her music. He was haunted by the experience of one of his three older daughters, Jahanara: he had taught her music, but she had married into a devout Muslim family that had forbidden her from singing, and she died young, a broken woman. At first Baba had refrained from teaching Annapurna, fearing a similar outcome for her, but her talent was too strong to ignore, so instead he wanted her to marry a husband who loved music.

The following year, the matchmaking continued at Almora, with Ravi's uncle Matul encouraging the idea. Ravi gradually warmed to the plan, reasoning that through an arranged marriage he would benefit from formally joining a musical *gharana*, rather like wedding the boss's daughter. Yet he remained conflicted, not least because he was continuing his affair with Uzra throughout that summer in Almora and on the winter tour that followed. When Uzra eventually found out about his wedding plans, she was so upset that she left the troupe at the end of the tour.

The marriage took place in Almora on the evening of May 15, 1941. Ravi was twenty-one, and Annapurna had just turned fifteen. It was almost unheard of at the time for a Muslim to convert to Hinduism on marriage; any change was usually in the other direction. But earlier that day, in another indication of Baba's religious broad-mindedness, Annapurna had converted to the monotheistic Hindu reform sect Arya Samaj. Annapurna, as it happens, is a Hindu name, that of the goddess of food. She had been given it at birth by the Maharaja of Maihar, alongside her Muslim name of Roshanara. Baba had always called her Annapurna.

The marriage triggered a wave of other weddings in the romantic setting of Almora: Rajendra and Lakshmi Sastri, Uday and Amala, Simkie and the dancer Prabhat Ganguly, and Zohra and one of the students, Kameshwar Segal. After spending two months together at Almora, Ravi and Annapurna returned to Maihar, where Baba insisted, against Ravi's wishes, that they move into a pair of rooms in the main house, directly above Baba's bedroom. Early married life was full of passion and almost immediately Annapurna became pregnant. As love blossomed between the pair, Ravi decided to confess his past affairs, including his relationship with Uzra. This honesty was spectacularly ill-judged. Annapurna had led a sheltered life and was always reading romantic novels. It made her feel very insecure.

Ravi's progress on the sitar was astounding. When Alice Boner heard him playing in March 1941, she was "amazed to hear what a remarkable musician he has already become." She noted that he had now left the center at Almora, to devote himself entirely to music in Maihar. "I think it is the right thing he did from every point of view," she observed.[28]

Uday did not agree. He seemed unable to accept that Ravi had chosen music over dance. Ravi's relationship with him had been deteriorating for a couple of years. Uday consented to the marriage, and there is a story that he took Baba up to the shrine of Ma Sharda in Maihar to seal the agreement.[29] Yet the following winter there occurred what Ravi called the "final clash," when he went to join the troupe on tour.[30] Uday disapproved of Ravi's appearances on the radio and at music conferences, perhaps because, as Debendra said, he felt threatened by any of his brothers having his own public profile.[31] But the main flashpoint arose, according to Ravi, when he criticized the way some things were done at the center: "That made him mad like anything." Uday then asked Ravi why he should continue supporting him if his loyalty was to music rather than to the center.

"Dada," replied Ravi, "if money is the only connection between you and me—stop it. I don't want any help from you!"[32]

Uday did terminate the monthly allowance of forty or fifty rupees he had been giving Ravi. When Baba went to Almora and tried to persuade Uday to excuse Ravi for his hotheaded response, he refused and said he wanted to teach him a lesson. That was the last straw for Ravi, and he severed his links with Uday.

This left him in financial difficulty. He refused to accept money from Baba, and his earnings from recitals were still meager and irregular. Rajendra and Matul sent some money when they could, and in desperation Ravi sold some gold jewelry. Matters came to a head after Annapurna gave birth to their son on March 30, 1942. The birth took place at home and they named the child Shubhendra, Shubho for short. Ravi, who was present, felt proud and delighted, although he did not feel ready for fatherhood. All went well at first, but after eight weeks Shubho developed an intestinal obstruction and a severe chest cold. "[For] 25 days we had to fight with death every second," Ravi wrote at the time.[33] Shubho pulled through, but he had developed the habit of being unable to sleep at night. The strain on his parents was great. Sleepless nights alternated with days still structured around an intense regime of music training and the need to retain Baba's fickle favor, even while caring for a delicate child. Ravi was left with a debt of 250 rupees to the doctors, and he asked Alice Boner whether she knew any benefactors who might sponsor him. He was haunted by the fear that he would fail to achieve his potential. "I have great dreams and ideas...but they'll be all shattered being cheaply in search of money," he wrote to her.[34]

Under the pressure, Ravi's and Annapurna's marriage began to buckle. She became preoccupied with his past sex life, and accused him of being unfaithful when he was away giving recitals. He was handsome and charismatic, and as he made a name for himself there were often women giving him "green signals," as he put it, but he resisted temptation. "Even when I went hundreds or thousands of miles away, I tried to be like Baba, as if I were anti-sex and anti-women, always thinking how I must be pure," he said.[35] But Annapurna did not believe him.

One key to understanding the relationship is something that is rarely mentioned in the gossip about them that persists even today: despite it being an arranged marriage, love did flourish between them in the early years. If it had not, it is unlikely feelings would later have become so embittered. In truth they were two very different people, a worldly sophisticate and a very sheltered young woman. They were ill-matched and ill-equipped for their challenges as partners and parents. Neither had grown up within a healthy family dynamic. Ravi's father had been absent and cold. Annapurna's ruled his household with fear, and she grew up with a severe lack of self-worth, needing his approval and dreading his rages. Their mothers were both submissive women. Neither Ravi nor Annapurna knew anything about the compromises and negotiations required for a successful marriage. Added to this were the pressures of a relationship where one partner was a traveling musician and the strain of still living in Baba's household. A pattern was established: suspicion, resentment and living increasingly separate lives. Musically, the Maihar years were an astonishing blessing for Ravi, but emotionally they were grueling: "It was one of the most terrible ordeals that one can imagine."[36]

Ravi's traveling was at least bearing fruit professionally. He first made an impact in Bombay in August 1942, when he and Ali Akbar performed at the School of Indian Music, founded by the singer and musicologist B. R. Deodhar.[37] Soon after, he played a radio session in Bombay in which he was accompanied for the first time on the tabla by Alla Rakha, who was then an All India Radio staff artist and later became his greatest accompanist. Like Ravi, Alla Rakha combined classical training with a mosaic of influences; in his case these included both pakhawaj and tabla rhythm styles. "The radio broadcast went off well and I felt that musically too our chemistry matched, and I was sure that we would be playing again at more important concerts," said Ravi.[38]

He found patrons in the family of the industrialist Lala Shri Ram, who had built up the Delhi Cloth Mills empire in the early twentieth century. Shri Ram and his younger brother Shankar Lal lived on Curzon Road in the capital in a pair of adjoining mansions. During a family holiday in Almora in 1942, Shri Ram's daughter-in-law Sheila Bharat-Ram had visited Uday's center and had begun learning the sitar with Baba. Her son, the vocalist Vinay Bharat-Ram, remembers the visit clearly because after seeing Simkie dance he declared that he wanted to marry her. "Rather early, don't you think?" he was asked. He was only five.[39]

After that, whenever Baba visited Delhi he stayed with Shri Ram and continued Sheila's lessons. He was as exacting as ever. Once when he had reduced her to tears he snapped, "I knew you people can't handle this art. It's not for rich people." But then he saw that her finger was bleeding—a common hazard for sitar players—and he immediately became considerate, apologizing and fetching her warm salt water.[40] Soon Ravi took over training her, and she began to support him with an allowance, which, according to Debendra, was a very useful 150 rupees a month by January 1943.[41] Ravi and Annapurna spent almost six months with the Shri Rams that year, while she was being treated in the city for a digestive problem. Baba might stay for a month and then return to Maihar, but Ravi continued his sitar training regardless.

Shri Ram was a great benefactor of education, science and the arts. He was in fact almost tone deaf, but nevertheless enthusiastically supported music and dance. Once Uday Shankar's entire troupe stayed in the larger mansion while they were performing in the city. Shri Ram also hosted concerts at the house by Baba, Ali Akbar, Ravi and others.

The best investment Ravi ever made was surely the 500 rupees he paid in March 1944 for what he called his "immortal" Kanai Lal sitar.[42] This embodied changes he had made to sitar design and set the template for what is known as the "Ravi Shankar model," one of the two main sitar designs popular today. In his first four years in Maihar he had been playing three different sitars made by Baba's younger brother, Ayet Ali Khan, and one by Yusuf Ali Khan of Lucknow, all of which had been commissioned for him. Since Baba was not a sitar player, Ravi took the initiative himself, working with craftsmen to develop his own distinctive sound, and his rapid turnover of instruments shows how quickly his ideas were evolving. By 1942, when he placed the order with Kanai Lal, a renowned luthier who worked from an unmarked shopfront in north Calcutta, he had settled on the design features he wanted.

In a sitar, the sound produced by plucking the strings with a wire pick (*mizrab*) resonates throughout the hollow neck and the soundbox (*tumba*). The neck is usually made from teak or toon wood, while the *tumba*, as on many other Indian stringed instruments (and on the

West African kora), is made from a seasoned gourd or calabash—a large dried vegetable. The Ravi Shankar model also has a second, detachable gourd resonator at the top of the neck. Only a handful of farmers grow instrumental gourds, and the best-known place of cultivation is around the village of Pandharpur in southern Maharashtra. The "sitar-makers," as the farmers are known, turn the gourds regularly on the ground to encourage them to grow in a rounded shape, and after harvest they are dried out before the best are shipped off to instrument workshops.

Aside from the selection and the crafting of the wooden materials, it is the arrangement of the strings that makes a sitar's sound distinctive. Western classical music, since the rise of the keyboard, has tended to experience each note in a scale as an island unto itself, and playing a melody as jumping between these islands. In Indian music, however, notes are not islands; they are played in a rounded, often ornamented style, and the expressive core of the music is in the microtonal journey between notes. Sitars are designed so that the main playing strings can be bent sideways over the curved frets by up to about five tones—an effect known as *meend*, which allows the musician to produce microtones. (Blues guitarists also bend strings, but sitarists do it much more, and with extreme precision.) Ravi's new sitar had six playing strings, four of them for playing the melody and two for *chikari* (drone) notes. In an idea borrowed from the surbahar, two of the melody strings played thunderous bass tones: the *kharajpancham*, tuned to the fifth note (usually F sharp) two octaves below the tonic in the middle octave; and the lowest string, the *kharaj*, tuned to the tonic below that (C sharp). The bending of notes in this bass register became the most distinctive element of his new sound, used most prominently in his powerful, meditative *dhrupad–alap* passages.

The other element that produces the sitar's characteristic sound is its second track of strings, the *taraf* or sympathetic strings, which run underneath the curved frets and resonate in response to the playing of the main strings. Sympathetic strings became a feature of sitars only in the early twentieth century. Ravi's design had thirteen of them. The way that all nineteen strings resonate against the two *jawari* bridges gives the sitar its characteristic buzzing sound, what one British critic has called its "porcupine timbre."[43] Kanai Lal was a master at crafting the *jawaris*, and this also helped to establish Ravi's sound.

Ravi's new sitar was embellished with beautiful wood carvings in leaf designs on the gourds and tuning pegs, and varnished with a rich shellac lacquer, while the neck and *tumba* were bordered with white celluloid inlays decorated with intricate floral designs. It was a masterpiece of artistic as well as musical craftsmanship, and it set a standard that others copied. It served as Ravi's principal performance instrument for the next seventeen years. "It was like a whole new era," he said.[44]

When Ravi visited Calcutta to collect the sitar, he arrived at the tail end of perhaps the most shameful chapter of the entire British Raj: the devastating Bengal famine of 1943–4, which killed about 3 million people in his ancestral province. When the writer and film director K. A. Abbas, with whom Ravi would soon work on a film on the subject, had visited Calcutta in late 1943 he had described it as "the city of horrors." Starving people had streamed in from the country-side and were everywhere on the streets, begging for *phaan*, the water thrown away after rice has been boiled. Middle-class Calcuttans were unaffected. In an obscene juxtaposition refugees lay dying in front of luxury hotels, restaurants and sweet shops. "Often the glass partition was all that separated the hungry destitutes from the rich display of food," Abbas wrote.[45] Ravi did not witness the most horrific scenes himself because by March 1944 those who had managed to survive had mostly returned to their villages following a bumper new har-vest, and deaths by starvation were tailing off. However, the weakened population continued to die in large numbers from malaria, cholera and smallpox. Ravi was deeply affected by the stories he heard. Abbas felt that "Bengal, with all its rich heritage of political dynamism, and cultural flowering of art and literature, was dying, too."[46]

The causes of the famine were complex but it was essentially man-made rather than a natural disaster. India's Nobel Prize-winning economist Amartya Sen, who observed the famine's effects firsthand as a child in Shantiniketan, has shown that food production in Bengal was actually higher in 1943 than it was in 1941, when there was no famine. He labeled it a "boom famine." After the fall of Burma, Allied soldiers and money had poured into Calcutta, and priority was given to the military when it came to resources. The surge in demand pushed up the price of rice far beyond what millions of the rural poor could afford, and the market was allowed to let rip, resulting in famine. The disaster was exacerbated by the Raj's scorched-earth policy of confiscating boats and surplus rice stocks in Bengal in anticipation of a Japanese invasion and restricting the movement of food supplies within India. The British reaction, once evidence emerged of the developing catastrophe, was characterized by apathy, confusion and callousness. The government never even formally declared a state of famine, and the all-powerful viceroy, Linlithgow, did not visit the area. As the independence leader Jawaharlal Nehru declared from Ahmadnagar Fort, where he was imprisoned following the repression of the Quit India movement, the Bengal famine was "the final judgment on British rule in India."[47]

In February 1944, as if no longer able to rise above this apocalypse of war, famine and pestilence, the Almora center closed. Uday blamed the wartime conditions, which were certainly difficult, but he bore a heavy responsibility himself. For all his creative brilliance and inspirational teaching, he was a poor administrator, and discontent had been increasing among staff and students. Debendra described the atmosphere, somewhat melodramatically, as like living under a dictatorship.[48] Meanwhile, Uday became fixated on suspending the work of the center in order to concentrate on what eventually became his feature film *Kalpana*. The denouement was unedifying. At the end of the troupe's last winter tour he gave his students an ultimatum: to join him for *Kalpana* or to leave. They left. It was the end for the center. Uday returned to Almora for two days to pack up his personal possessions and then headed south. Later that day five new students arrived, having traveled all the way from Ceylon. Gertrude Emerson Sen and her husband Boshi were left to deal with the chaos Uday had left behind. They loved what he had created in Almora, but Gertrude felt "very sad that he needlessly spoiled his own bright dream and let down those who financed him."[49]

Ravi's time in Maihar was also drawing to an end, although for very different reasons. In June he became ill with rheumatic fever. With a temperature of 106°F at one stage, he was so delirious that when Baba came to see him Ravi shouted at him using his father-in-law's own intemperate language. Rheumatic fever was a serious illness, particularly before the availability of antibiotics, and his doctor informed him that there was a risk that he had sustained permanent damage to his heart valves. Recovery entailed bedrest over many weeks. As his strength returned, Ravi concluded that he needed to make a fresh start. After six and a half years, he was ready to move on from Maihar. Reluctantly, Baba gave his permission.

II
THE SUN RISING
1944–1956

Playing his Kanai Lal sitar during the late 1940s or early 1950s

5

MUMBAI MADE ME

*In our fight for freedom we are also finding our feet
and getting back our lost soul.*
RAVI SHANKAR[1]

"Though I was born in Benares, I feel my birthplace is Mumbai," Ravi once said. It was there, in the four and a half years after his arrival in October 1944—a period of extreme turbulence both for Ravi and for India—that he began to make a name for himself as a sitar player and composer. "As such," he said, "Mumbai made me."[2] He might have added that the city almost destroyed him, too.

Ravi's move to Mumbai, or Bombay as it was then known, made a lot of sense. It was clear that he had to leave small-town Maihar if he was going to forge a career as a musician. Earlier that year Ali Akbar Khan had moved to Jodhpur as court musician to Maharaja Umaid Singh, and if Ravi could not secure a position with a patron of similar artistic tastes—and they were becoming rarer, given the waning influence of the princely states—then he needed to be in a big city. Owing largely to its textile factories and film studios, Bombay had become both the commercial and cultural capital of India.[3] It was attracting artists from across the country, including many of those leaving Almora. The city offered prospects for musicians in the form of the record industry, the Bombay branch of All India Radio, the nascent Indian People's Theatre Association, and especially the Hindi film industry, which Ravi initially viewed as his likeliest source of work.

However, the immediate prompt for Ravi to move to Bombay was that Rajendra, concerned about the standard of medical care in Maihar, wanted him to continue his treatment for rheumatic fever there. Ravi, Annapurna and two-year-old Shubho moved into a house in the northern suburb of Malad, immediately next door to Rajendra, who had recently taken a job as a screenwriter at Bombay Talkies. Rajendra's wife Lakshmi, whose sights were set on a dance career, had just given birth to their son Kumar. Also staying with them were Lakshmi's sister Kamala and their mother, who were both helping to look after Kumar and could assist in Ravi's care during his convalescence. Kamala, who turned sixteen that November, caught Ravi's eye. "I was absolutely dazzled," he said. "By this time she had become a beautiful young lady, and I was very attracted to her."[4]

Ravi's strength returned in Bombay. He found his first job, serving briefly as an apprentice in the music department at HMV India, and looked around for recital opportunities. He soon realized how hard it was to earn a reputation and a living as a performer. There were only a few major music conferences in northern India at that time, and he had to rely mostly on giving recitals for local music circles in Bombay and in cities further afield, such as Pune, Kolhapur, Nashik, Aurangabad and Baroda. Music circles were a long-standing institution in India, membership organizations that usually arranged recitals in which a single artist performed for an entire evening. Venues were simple halls, with audiences of between 150 and 400 seated on the floor (known as *baithak*-style). The fees were lower than for music conferences, but the opportunities came around more often, and Ravi loved playing for these intimate, knowledgeable crowds. If he came up with a particularly beautiful piece of improvisation, he could see and hear the audience's appreciation. Without any time restriction, he sometimes played for seven or eight hours. His record was ten hours, with only one interval.[5] On another occasion when he had played through the night, he was confused because a section of the audience encouraged him to keep going, even though they were not engaging with the music as connoisseurs would. Afterward he realized that they had missed the last train home and were waiting for the service to resume at 4:30 a.m.[6]

He also gave private performances. At the home of a maharaja or a tycoon he could command a better fee, but audiences were typically less knowledgeable. Baba had imbued him with a spirit of reverence for classical music, and he could not bear to play in front of crowds who lounged around drinking, smoking, eating or chatting. So began a small but significant act of rebellion. No matter how grand the gathering, he would put down his sitar, explain the sanctity of the music and ask everyone to pay attention during his performance. He began insisting that organizers provided a low platform for him, reasoning that it was the music that he wanted to be symbolically elevated, rather than the performer. That most people accepted his strictures was a tribute to his powers of persuasion as well as his musicianship.

Sometimes he played at the homes of friends. A favorite venue was 41 Pali Hill, home of the director Chetan Anand and his actress wife Uma Anand, who were trying to break into theater and film. For a while it was also home to the Mumtaz sisters, Zohra and Uzra, and their husbands. Uzra was now married to the actor Hameed Butt, and becoming recognized for her stage acting. She was the leading actress for Prithvi Theatres, the dynamic company founded by Prithviraj Kapoor, patriarch of one of Hindi cinema's foremost families. Both Ravi and Ali Akbar played at Pali Hill. The house, then on the city's northern outskirts, was a hub for an ambitious group of young actors, writers, directors and musicians who went on to national fame, including Guru Dutt, the actor Balraj Sahni and Chetan's younger brothers Dev Anand, later one of India's greatest romantic leads, and the writer–director Vijay Anand. According to Dev Anand, "The place used to be full of restless minds, sharp and high on talent, bubbling to pour forth and create new vistas."[7]

Just as Ravi started to settle into life in Bombay there was a big disruption. He and Kamala fell in love with each other. In Malad they were effectively living in an extended family unit, with the door often open between the two houses, so the pair met on a daily basis.

From initial flirtation they progressed to hushed confidences and the exchange of love notes. "Annapurna was doubting me with everyone anyway," he recalled, "so it was nothing new for her to doubt me with Kamala—only this time it was true."[8] Before the relationship could become physical Annapurna found out, and so too did Rajendra and Lakshmi. They were all extremely upset. Annapurna returned to Maihar for a few months, taking Shubho with her, and Rajendra searched for a husband for Kamala. His friend Amiya Chakravarty, a Bengali director who had already made three films in Bombay, was fond of Kamala, and a marriage was swiftly arranged.

With fortuitous timing Ravi received an invitation to join the Indian People's Theater Association (IPTA) in Bombay. This was a progressive, anti-imperialist collective founded two years earlier, which used theater to oppose not only the British but also exploitative Indian landlords and capitalists. The Bengal famine was a particularly potent subject. Like many socialist movements of the time, the IPTA embraced traditional and folk-art forms as the true expression of the people. Among its members were Prithviraj Kapoor, K. A. Abbas, the film composers Sachin Dev Burman and Salil Chowdhury, and most of Chetan Anand's household. There were branches in several other Indian cities, with a particularly militant one in Calcutta involving Shombhu Mitra and Utpal Dutt, who were in the vanguard of the next generation in Bengali theater.

In Bombay the IPTA had set up a special unit for dancers and musicians, the Central Cultural Squad, which was funded by the Communist Party. Shanti Bardhan joined as its chief choreographer, and was assisted by fellow Almora alumni Sachin Shankar, Narendra Sharma, Prabhat Ganguly and Ravi's brother Debendra. Ravi was offered the role of music director. Confused and upset about the situation with Annapurna and Kamala, he grasped this opportunity and moved into the squad's headquarters at Khushru Lodge. He made it clear that he was not a communist, but like almost all Indian artists at the time he had leftist leanings. He shared the enthusiasm for native

Indian arts over European forms, and identified with the collaborative, egalitarian ethos and the anti-imperial message. He publicly lamented that India was "a country under foreign yoke and education, where musicians starve," but his instincts were optimistic rather than angry. "With the people awakening to their cultural heritage, to the wealth of their musical riches, folk, secular, devotional and classical, a new era is dawning," he wrote.[9] Music could herald a bright future.

Khushru Lodge was a mansion in the suburb of Andheri East. It had a spacious garden with coconut palms, mango trees and a huge hundred-year-old banyan. This was both workplace and residence, and was run as a cross between a commune and a militia. Everyone woke at five, took breakfast together at 6:30 a.m. and began working at seven. Ravi liked the disciplined environment, and in turn he made a very positive impression on the movement. There were, he recalled, more "green signals" from women staying at the house, but he was in a celibate mood. At the end of the working day, he often practiced sitar until late at night. "Even today I can visualize him doing that on moonlit nights on the roof of the veranda," said the writer Rekha Jain, who was studying dance there. "The notes from his sitar seemed to touch our very heart-strings."[10]

For the next few months Ravi immersed himself in work and practice and thrived on it. He had artistic freedom, he had a corps of musicians and dancers to teach and train, and there were exciting projects. For the first time he was composing for the stage. Before he joined, two IPTA dance productions, *Bhookha Hai Bengal* and *Spirit of India*, had toured with some success, and another production was planned: *India Immortal*. This was billed as "a patriotic ballet" and presented a history of India told through dance. Ravi felt inspired and found that music flowed out of him very quickly. He loved working with his friend Shanti Bardhan, whose roots were in the dance of his native Tripura. He was similar to Uday in his approach to choreography, combining inventive modern dance with Indian classical and folk styles. In late 1945 and early 1946 *India Immortal* went on a tour of north India, taking in Calcutta, Patna, Delhi, Kanpur, Lucknow, Lahore and Bombay.

Soon afterward, Ravi was asked to make his debut as a film composer. Two commissions came along at almost the same time through the IPTA. Both were films that championed the downtrodden in society; they pioneered social realism in Indian cinema and were influenced by the work of Sergei Eisenstein and Vsevolod Pudovkin in Russia. *Dharti Ke Lal* ("Children of the Earth"), the directorial debut of K. A. Abbas, dramatized the horrors of the Bengal famine. It was developed from the Bengali IPTA play *Nabanna*, which had toured widely in aid of famine relief. The film gave the first major screen roles to Balraj Sahni, Shombhu Mitra, Tripti Bhaduri and Zohra Segal. This was the only film that the IPTA actually produced, but the collective did give support to the other film that Ravi worked on, Chetan Anand's debut, *Neecha Nagar* ("The City Below"). Based on Maxim Gorky's *Lower Depths*, this is the story of a rich landowner who knowingly diverts the sewage from his hilltop mansion to pollute a village in the valley below. The villagers fall sick, and it is the death of Rupa, played by another screen legend in her debut role, Kamini Kaushal, that inspires the villagers to militant protest. It also starred three other members of the director's household, Uma Anand, Hameed Butt and (once again) Zohra Segal.

Ravi's music was crucial for the emotional impact of both films. He saw his choral effects in the title sequence of *Dharti Ke Lal* as "endeavoring to capture the wail of humanity uprooted from its home and on the march in search of food and shelter."[11] For *Neecha Nagar* he wrote rousing songs—based on classical *ragas*—for the villagers who rise up in protest. But it was in the incidental music where his contribution was most significant. In the fifteen years since India had first made films with sound, most of the industry's musical focus had been on the songs, with less thought given to what happened in between them. "I have always felt that the purpose of background music is not merely to fill the silent gaps in a film," Ravi wrote in 1958, "but to enhance the mood of the picture and endow it with a poignancy which words and actions cannot convey."[12] He believed that songs and incidental music should play equally important roles. At a time when Western orchestral arrangements were the norm for Indian films, he also went against received wisdom in believing that Indian classical music could render the full range of required emotion, and could do so using small ensembles of Indian instruments. Ravi was particularly happy with the music in *Neecha Nagar*, and found it rewarding to work with Chetan Anand, who was a good violinist and had a sensitive ear.

Both films were made against the odds, the inexperienced casts and crews having to contend with low budgets and rationing. They had to apply for special wartime licenses, only three of which were granted to independent filmmakers (the third went to Uday's dance epic *Kalpana*). Ultimately the films were too demanding for a general audience, and both flopped at the domestic box office, although they were critically acclaimed and proved to be influential. At Cannes in 1946 *Neecha Nagar* actually won the Grand Prix, the top prize at the time, although uniquely in that first year of the film festival it shared the honor with ten other films, among them *Brief Encounter* and *Rome, Open City*. As for *Dharti Ke Lal*, after receiving Stalin's personal approval, in 1949 it became the first Indian film to be dubbed into Russian, opening up a huge market for Indian cinema in the Soviet Union.

However, Ravi's soundtracks sank without trace. Then, as now, film songs were India's popular music, and a film could succeed or fail depending on the appeal of its songs. A few years later, and Ravi's songs might have achieved some broadcast coverage, but radio was still in its infancy in India. "The films had such scattered and short runs that the songs had no chance of becoming popular. Promotion by radio did not exist then," Ravi said.[13] That said, his songs would by their nature have probably struggled to make an impact outside the cinema. The film music fashion of the moment was the dholak beat, introduced by the 1944 hit *Rattan*, which sold gramophone records

in the thousands and established Naushad as one of Bombay's leading music directors. Ravi came to accept that he had been "innovative
ahead of the times...My compositions were wedded to the theme
so closely, welded in fact, that they hadn't a chance with the public
unsupported by the film."[14]

The most lasting product of Ravi's time in Andheri was not his
stage or film work; it was the tune he wrote for "Sare Jahan Se Accha,"
which today is a ubiquitous Indian national song. Only the national
anthem, Tagore's "Jana Gana Mana," is better known. The first line
translates as "Our India is the best place in the world." It started out as
a patriotic lyric written in 1904 by the Urdu poet Mohammed Iqbal,
whose authorship is ironic given his subsequent support for a separate
Pakistan, but it served as an anthem for the nationalist movement.
When Ravi joined the IPTA the group was singing it as the opening
of *Spirit of India*, but it was set to a slow, mournful melody. At some
point during 1945 Ravi wrote a new, brighter tune to suit the uplifting lyric and taught it to the Cultural Squad. Through their performances, the new version was widely taken up. Today Ravi's arrangement of the song is heard everywhere, from the smallest school
gathering to the "Beating of the Retreat" parade that closes Delhi's
Republic Day celebrations on January 29 each year. India lacked a music copyright system, and for decades it infuriated him that few people
were aware he had written the tune, which was often attributed to
Iqbal or assumed to be "traditional." After a minor campaign he ran in
later years—he even licensed a ringtone—Ravi's composing credit has
become widely accepted.

Ravi's honeymoon phase at IPTA lasted about eight months, before
an "Orwellian straitjacket" started suffocating him.[15] The Communist
Party felt *India Immortal* had lacked a sufficiently trenchant political message, and thereafter issued directives instructing the Cultural
Squad about the topical issues its art should address. A progressive
purpose was one thing, but Ravi was not prepared to make agitprop
to order. Nor were several of his colleagues. Shanti Bardhan left first,

followed in the summer of 1946 by Ravi, his music assistant Abani Das Gupta, Sachin Shankar and Narendra Sharma. The Cultural Squad did not survive their departure for long.

Ravi retreated to Borivli in the far northern suburbs. Here he and Annapurna were reunited, and they began living again with Rajendra and Lakshmi, this time in Madgaonkar Bungalow, a large house opposite the station.

Alongside his IPTA duties, Ravi had continued to give live performances. For most who heard him, his brilliance was obvious, yet he had to toil ceaselessly to build up a following, and he described these years as "a bitter time for me in many ways."[16] The story is still told in Calcutta of him calling at the house of Hiru Ganguly, a well-known tabla player. When the servant asked who he was, Ravi replied, "Please tell Hiru-Babu that Uday Shankar's brother has come."[17] His own name meant nothing; he was Uday's brother or Baba's disciple. That began to change after his first major concert in Calcutta in late 1945.

By the mid-1940s Ravi and Ali Akbar Khan were also becoming known for playing as a duet, or *jugalbandi*. This was novel, because Indian classical music is overwhelmingly a solo form. *Jugalbandis* were unusual between vocalists, very rare for instrumentalists, and unheard of between two different instruments. Ravi and Ali Akbar defied convention. Ravi had to sacrifice a little brightness in his sitar by tuning it down from C sharp to C, so that they were playing in the same key. But psychologically no two musicians were ever more in tune: they had spent so much time together in Maihar, learning from Baba and practicing, that they had an almost telepathic understanding, and their melody lines dovetailed beautifully. At first they performed together mainly in Lucknow, when Ali Akbar was music director at the city's All India Radio studios, and in nearby Kanpur and Allahabad. As their popularity rose, they played all over north India. "There was so much love between us, and for the next dozen years it was fantastic," recalled Ravi.[18]

Another distinctive element in Ravi's music was his mastery of
rhythm. This had been evident ever since his second year in Maihar,
when he had begun practicing for two to three hours a day with a
blind tabla player from the Maihar Band. The convention at the time
was for an unadventurous approach to *talas* (rhythmic cycles). Sitar-
and sarod players clung to the 16 beats of *teental*, the most popular
of all *talas*. Encouraged by Baba, who among his many talents was a
superb drummer, Ravi and Ali Akbar were responsible for popularizing many other rhythmic cycles in instrumental repertoire, including
rupaktal (7 beats), *jhaptal* (10) and *ada chautal* (14). Ravi personally
set a further vogue for rarer odd-numbered *talas* such as *chartal ki
sawari* (11 beats) and *pancham sawari* (15), and half-beat *talas* such
as *ardha jaital* (6½ beats). Whatever *tala* he was playing, he loved to
improvise sitar phrases that were filled with rhythmic patterns. He
was unsurpassed as a spontaneous composer of the *tihai*—the device
with which pieces usually finish—a musical phrase that is repeated
three times and must finish on the first beat of the cycle. Rhythm
could bring out the most playful side of him. As the vocalist Ajoy
Chakrabarty said recently, "Raviji was the first to play all these games
with the *tala*."[19]

During his childhood exposure to the Carnatic system Ravi had
been thrilled by the quickfire exchanges between its percussionists.
These might feature the mridangam drum, ghatam (clay pot), kanjira
(a type of tunable tambourine) or morsing (a Jew's harp). The percussionists traded improvisations of phenomenal complexity, starting
with, for example, each playing a 16-beat solo passage, then each playing an 8-beat solo, then a 4-beat solo, progressively halving the length
until everyone joined in for a frenzied unison climax. Baba employed
something similar in his tuition: he would sing a long passage and
ask Ravi to play it back on the sitar, and follow up with shorter and
shorter ones. Ravi became famous for these exchanges in his concerts,
the *sawal–jawab* (question–answer) phrases bouncing between his
sitar and his accompanist's tabla, and he and Ali Akbar made them

a feature of their *jugalbandis* too, with the sitar and sarod swapping phrases at blistering speed. They generated tremendous excitement.

That said, for Ravi performance was never just about virtuosity. In the concert format he was developing, everything was in proportion, the pyrotechnics of the climax counterbalanced by the long build from the meditative *alap* opening. Ultimately all of this was in the service of creating depth of feeling. Music is nothing without emotion, and Ravi was outspoken in criticizing those musicians who had wondrous technical gifts but sucked the life out of the music. "If our music is so great that it has brought rain, caused fire, moved animals and melted hearts, why should it prove so dry, boring and lifeless today?" he asked in a 1947 interview. "It is for the musicians and lovers of music to realize this, to put an end to repetitious and prolonged vocal and instrumental acrobatics and to feel the necessity of transcending grammar and technique in order to bring out the beauty and soul of the music."[20]

Ravi's career was blossoming simultaneously in several different directions. According to tradition, learning from one's *guru* never ends, and Ravi continued to spend two to three months each year studying with Baba, either in Maihar, or in Bombay if Baba were visiting, or at Shri Ram's house in Delhi. But now Ravi became a *guru* himself, too—a milestone in his development. If his life's professional activities are envisaged as a triangle, the three corners would be performing, composing and teaching. He believed wholeheartedly in the system by which Baba had taught him, the *guru–shishya parampara*, and the intense bond it created between the two musicians, and he took on disciples on the same basis. His first was Rebati Ranjan Debnath, a schoolteacher who had studied with Baba in Maihar. After Ravi and Annapurna left for Bombay, Baba asked Debnath to follow them so that he could continue studying the sitar with Ravi while teaching Shubho Bengali and English.[21] Soon Ravi took on a number of other students, including two of his most devoted, Harihar Rao, at the end of 1945, and Amiya Dasgupta. As with all his disciples, he never charged them. In return they assisted him in all areas of his life. Harihar, who was highly organized, helped to arrange his concerts in and around Bombay and was always being asked to book tickets, run errands or meet Ravi at the station or airport.

In Pune in 1945 Ravi heard B. R. Deodhar singing a composition that had elements of two well-known *ragas*, *Nat* and *Bhairav*, and included both the natural and flattened second notes in its scale. In a moment of inspiration, Ravi thought of a way to improve it by using only the natural second, and he elaborated it further by defining ascending and descending patterns and distinctive phrases and emphases. He had created his first original *raga*, and he called it *Nat Bhairav*. The real test of a new *raga* is whether it becomes part of the repertoire. After he started playing *Nat Bhairav* in concerts and on the radio, other musicians picked it up and performed it regularly without knowing that he had created it. Later some claimed it had already existed, but although the scale used was common to other *ragas*, what Ravi had created was a new *raga* in that scale (a *raga* being a form far more detailed and specific than a scale). "It pains me when young musicians claim it as an old north Indian *raga*. For this version of *Nat Bhairav* did not exist before I played it in 1945," he asserted five decades later, still smarting.[22] This was the first of at least thirty-two new *ragas* that he composed, and it was far from the only time that his role in creating one was unacknowledged. To some extent this is an occupational hazard in an oral music tradition, but the same happened when he created *Bairagi* in 1949, even though he published that *raga* (and a *bandish* composition in it) in *Sangeet*, a specialist classical music magazine. These two *ragas* have become universally accepted as standards.

Another career development was Ravi's debut as a solo recording artist for HMV India, part of EMI's global empire. The format of the day was still the 78 rpm disc of up to four minutes per side, and his first release paired his concise renderings of *Raga Hemant* on one side with *Raga Marwa* on the reverse. On these he was accompanied by

Jnan Prakash Ghosh, a favorite tabla player from a wealthy family of harmonium-makers in Calcutta. It was issued in late 1946 or early 1947 through HMV in Calcutta, and began an association with the record company that lasted for most of Ravi's life.

As Ravi became better known, press photographs started to appear in programs and newspapers. No longer a gaunt teenager, he now had the looks of a matinee idol: the same mesmerizing large eyes were set into a face that had filled out to become stronger and more confident. On a visit to Gemini Studios in Madras, where Uday was spending four years on *Kalpana*, he was spotted by S. S. Vasan, the owner of the studios. Vasan was casting his own film in the same studios, and he offered Ravi a leading role in it. It is said that Ravi declined after checking with Baba, who judged that acting would be a distraction from music. The film was *Chandralekha*.[23] With its own spectacular dance sequences (probably influenced by *Kalpana*), it was at the time India's most expensive film, and it became the first Tamil production to have nationwide success.

After the end of the Second World War, and the change of government in London, it became clear that the British were at last going to leave India. Even while battling to shape the terms of independence, leaders of the freedom movement were looking to the future. One example was the Asian Relations Conference held in March 1947. Representatives of twenty-eight nations emerging from colonialism gathered at the Purana Qila, the sixteenth-century fort in Delhi. The driving force was Nehru, who astutely saw India's coming freedom as part of a long-term resurgence of Asia's role in world history. "One of the notable consequences of the European domination of Asia," he said during his inaugural speech, "has been the isolation of the countries of Asia from one another."[24] He sought to strengthen pan-Asian ties independent of the retreating European powers or the rising Cold War rivals, an attitude that soon gave birth to the non-aligned movement.

For the conference's cultural program, Kamaladevi Chatto-padhyay, president of the fledgling Indian National Theatre (INT), decided on a dance production for its accessibility to an international audience, and contacted the group of artists responsible for *India Immortal*. The plan, once described by Ravi as "the most bizarre thing I ever did," was to stage a ballet based on Nehru's bestselling nationalist history, *The Discovery of India*, published just a year earlier.[25] Shanti Bardhan was given responsibility for the choreography, Ravi for the music, and Rajendra for the script.

Work began in mid-January at Madgaonkar Bungalow. This was now home not only to the extended Shankar family, including Matul, but also to much of the thirty-five-strong troupe, including the ex-IPTA colleagues involved: Bardhan, Sachin Shankar, Naren-dra Sharma, Abani Das Gupta and Prabhat Ganguly. Lakshmi took a lead role as a dancer, while Annapurna played the sitar and sang in the chorus. Feeling that they were contributing to a national cause, all the artists took only nominal fees; Ravi was on just 50 rupees per month. Beginning in the house's inner quadrangle, and continuing in the garden once a *pandal* (marquee) had been erected, rehearsals proceeded at a furious pace, with just seven weeks to prepare a 2½-hour show. *The Discovery of India* was treated as a historical panorama from Vedic times to the present day. Along the way, using music and dance appropriate for each era, it ranged from the Golden Period (the age of Kalidas, around the fifth century) and the Dark Period (the fourteenth and fifteenth centuries, after the death of the great Sufi poet–musician Amir Khusru), through to the Mughal empire and the British Raj. There is no record of Ravi's music, but he did say that he used only Indian instruments.

The premiere followed the formal opening of the conference on March 9. Most of the leaders of the independence movement were there, including Gandhi, Nehru, Rajagopalachari, Vallabhbhai Patel and Sarvepalli Radhakrishnan. The show was enthusiastically received, and at the end Nehru went up on stage to announce that the ballet was "much better than my book."[26] After further performances in Delhi, the production moved to Bombay's Excelsior Theatre, where it ran for at least seven nights.[27] After that, the INT terminated its commitment, but the troupe wanted to tour the production nationally, and five of its principal members formed a theatrical company for the purpose, including Ravi, his brothers Rajendra and Debendra, and Shanti Bardhan. They called it India Renaissance Artists.

The Discovery of India was the first time that Ravi's solo work was acknowledged at the level of national government. Given his various activities and his growing fame, it would seem that all was going well. Yet one day during the monsoon season of 1948 he wrote two suicide notes: one addressed to his brother Rajendra, the other for the local police in Bombay. He planned to throw himself under a train at Borivli, and even selected the day of his death.

For Ravi the two years from March 1947 were a time of extreme emotional turmoil. "Many great national events occurred and simultaneously most of my major struggles began," he said.[28] By the time of the Asian Relations Conference the country was in crisis. That week, dozens died in sectarian riots in Calcutta, Bombay and Amritsar—the bitter harvest of Britain's long-term policy of divide and rule. Simultaneously Lord Mountbatten was being sworn into office as the last viceroy. Mountbatten's controversial contribution was to accelerate the timetable for independence, bringing it forward by over nine months, to midnight on August 15, 1947, and to agree to the partition of the subcontinent, creating a Muslim-majority Pakistan—consisting of entirely separate western and eastern territories—and a Hindu-majority India lying between them. Both states were envisaged as secular in nature.

Ravi spent the day of independence with family and friends at home in Borivli, where thirty or forty people gathered around a radio to listen to Nehru's "Tryst with Destiny" speech and others by Radhakrishnan and Mountbatten. "It was such a feeling to realize that we were free, totally free," said Ravi.[29] Yet the longed-for moment was soured by the suffering that accompanied it. Like many of his generation, Ravi did not talk much about these events.

The 1940s were, in a way, Ravi's personal "Dark Period." There is far-less documentation of his activities than there is for the 1930s or the 1950s, and when he later talked about these troubled times he seemed to skim over some aspects, perhaps unconsciously. He did write, in 1997, that "I was deeply hurt by the partition of our country and its consequences—the ruthless communal killings of multitudes and the tribulations of the millions of refugees, uprooted from their homes and forced to cross the new borders."[30] But he never recorded what he actually witnessed, even though from late 1945 until August 1947 there were riots in Bombay, and much of the city's large Muslim population fled to Pakistan. As a performer, he traveled to Calcutta, Delhi and other affected cities too.

There were appalling scenes in Punjab on both sides of the border, and by the autumn the two new nations were at war over the princely state of Jammu and Kashmir. There was much torment in the east too. Calcutta had been the scene of slaughter in August 1946, when over four thousand were killed in one day, triggering a wave of rioting across north India, and at independence Ravi's native Bengal was split between India and Pakistan. Before the 1940s Calcutta had been renowned for its pristine elegance, but no city could have emerged unscathed from the successive influxes of refugees caused by the Bengal famine and by partition. By the 1950s Calcutta had unfairly become a byword for poverty.

During the summer and autumn of 1947 India Renaissance Artists engaged about thirty-five people and worked on a revised production of *The Discovery of India*, updated to cover the events around independence. It was all but complete when, on January 30, 1948, Gandhi was assassinated by a fanatic Hindu nationalist. Ravi was profoundly affected. A few days later, with the nation in shock, he made an afternoon radio program for All India Radio Bombay. He was asked to play a suitably somber unaccompanied *alap*. As he tuned his sitar and prepared himself mentally, an idea came to him. He took the third, seventh and sixth notes of the scale, *ga*, *ni* and *dha* in Indian terminology, which approximated to Gandhi's name. He flattened both the seventh and sixth, and with occasional use of the second note (*re*) he devised a haunting melodic theme based around the *ga-ni-dha* motif. He elaborated it more and more, and before long he had once again created a new *raga*. It bore a family relationship to the pentatonic *raga Malkauns*, so he told the continuity announcer to introduce the new creation as *Mohankauns*, an allusion to Gandhi's given name, Mohandas. Judging by his only recording of it, in 1980, this premiere would have gripped his radio audience.

The new production of *The Discovery of India* was updated again to include Gandhi's death, and then ran for two weeks in Calcutta, with a further two in Bombay. After that, the new company collapsed owing to a rift among the owners. The three Shankar brothers found themselves being sued by their two colleagues, accused of misappropriating funds. Ravi and his brothers were arrested and taken to a police station, and the story reached the newspapers. A shopkeeper friend posted bail. Ravi was adamant that the charges were false, and he was devastated that two close friends had suddenly become enemies. So began a legal battle that lasted for about two years. The company was disbanded, and *The Discovery of India* shelved. It was hard for Ravi to accept, and he never forgave Shanti Bardhan. "It was a beautiful new ballet that we did and it was unnecessarily destroyed. And I, too, was almost finished," he said.[31]

Ravi and his brothers felt responsible for the thirty-five newly unemployed people who had given up jobs to join them at Madgaonkar Bungalow. Until the others could find work, the only source of income was what Ravi could earn from his infrequent sitar recitals. As he took on the burden of earning enough money to feed his household, he descended into a desperate struggle. Within six months he had reached breaking point and drew up his suicide plan. "I had no strength left, no will, no hope, and I felt that I was failing completely as an artist and as a person."[32]

By chance Ravi received an invitation to play a private recital at the Taj Mahal Hotel on the very evening he had planned to take his life. The patron was the young Maharaja of Jodhpur, Hanwant Singh, who had succeeded to his throne the year before and was a close friend and supporter of Ali Akbar. Ravi made the decision to postpone his suicide for twenty-four hours as the substantial fee would help those he was leaving behind. On the morning of the recital, he took out his sitar for the first time in several days. He was acutely distressed. He wept with despair and self-pity as he tried to practice. Then, as if in a fable, a passing holy man knocked on the door and asked to use his bathroom. His name was Tat Baba. Ravi had heard of him, and knew that he was a saintly *yogi*. He dressed humbly and Ravi was struck by the radiant aura around him.

Over tea, Ravi found himself agreeing to play the sitar for Tat Baba that evening, at first forgetting his recital engagement. When he remembered, he sent his apologies to Hanwant Singh, sensing this new commitment was more important than the most extravagant fee. As he played for Tat Baba that evening, Ravi had tears in his eyes again, but now he was inspired, and Tat Baba went into a trance. Afterward, he told Ravi that his struggles would continue but he would overcome them if he were blessed with strength by a spiritual *guru*. "The money you missed tonight will come back to you many times over. Don't do anything foolish."[33] In that moment, Ravi abandoned thoughts of suicide and became a devotee of Tat Baba.

Ever since childhood, whenever he was drawn to religious matters he had felt in need of a spiritual *guru*. "Sometimes I feel blindfolded, completely susceptible to spiritual atmosphere and prepared to believe whatever I am told, like a simple village person," he reflected in old age. "I know I am someone who likes and often needs to depend on someone or something."[34] He had found what he needed at that moment. As he recited Tat Baba's *mantra* in his mind over the following months, his problems receded and his career picked up. "Most important, I felt a new, special strength within me, a surge of power."[35]

What is most perplexing about these events is not so much the episode of his salvation, for Ravi's heart was open to the world of the spirit, but what had caused him to sink into such profound despair. Even if his early progress was uneven, he was making a startling impact on many people, and this was his first major professional setback. The man I knew in his advanced age was a life-affirming personality with an infectiously joyous laugh. His younger self seemed to have a similar sense of fun, and understood the need for dedication. How did he as a twenty-eight-year-old come so close to suicide?

In 2014 I put this question to Kamala Chakravarty. She did not see a contradiction. "Usually only people who are like this, full of the zest of life, wanting to live, wanting to enjoy everything, commit suicide," she said.[36] It is true that a sense of betrayal, of public humiliation and—perhaps most wounding—of failure would have been a toxic cocktail for a man as sensitive as Ravi. His tempestuous marriage was probably also a factor, but this seems inadequate as an explanation. More pertinent is the sense of profound loneliness that dogged Ravi, a sign of the damage that was hidden beneath the surface from his childhood traumas.

It also seems relevant that Ravi's personal crisis occurred in the wake of a vast national trauma, events that would cause many people to question their faith in human fellowship and, for the spiritually inclined, like him, in the benevolence of God. This would explain why Tat Baba's visit was so decisive: Ravi sensed that the universe was not silent, that watching over him was a greater power that had responded to his crisis. From this encounter, he gained a sense of certainty, of a destiny revealed—and that destiny was music.

As Tat Baba had forecast, the turnaround in Ravi's fortunes took its time. The court case still hung over him, and he was under the same financial pressure. During five weeks in Calcutta at the beginning of 1949 he was able to secure only one radio broadcast and two private recitals. "You can well imagine the mental agony I'm going through! The whole burden of Bombay (Borivli) expenses is expected to be bourne [*sic*] by me. I really don't know what is going to happen," he wrote to Harihar Rao on February 3, the day before the case was due to be heard in Bombay.[37] Yet in his letter he revealed his own answer. He had been offered the post of director of music at the External Services division of All India Radio's national headquarters in Delhi. The salary was a generous 1,000 rupees per month. He accepted, although he committed initially for only three months, wanting to ensure that the role suited him. He began work on February 21.

6

ALL INDIA STAR

I lived through an age of musical renaissance and
grew in the shadow of giants.

RAVI SHANKAR[1]

A revolution had arrived in the lives of north Indian classical musicians. The previous system, whereby the best and brightest had worked for maharajas or rich *zamindars*, had been ebbing away since the late nineteenth century. Independence tolled its death knell, as the power of the 565 princely states was swiftly dismantled. The new Indian state now assumed the role of the nation's principal patron of music. A new type of career became possible, with India's musicians earning their livelihoods from public concerts, recordings and radio broadcasts. For the first time some of them became famous throughout the country.

Nehru, the first prime minister of independent India, had no great feeling for the arts, but he believed the state had a responsibility to support them, and that they might help to bind together India's extraordinary diversity into a national culture. He led a government that was interventionist by instinct, embracing the socialist concept of five-year plans. Now he sought to redress the decades of neglect suffered by musicians and dancers during the colonial era, when they had been demoted to a lowly status in the class and caste hierarchy. A government program was instituted to revive and support their work.

This took several forms. In the early 1950s the government founded three national academies: one for literature, one for fine art and one for the performing arts, the Sangeet Natak Akademi, which became a significant patron of musicians through its program of grants, awards and research programs. Recognition as a fellow of the Sangeet Natak Akademi became a key indicator of career achievement. Another source of state patronage was the Indian Council of Cultural Relations (ICCR), which was established in 1950 to handle cultural diplomacy. It was comparable to the British Council or the United States Information Service. Through its network of foreign missions and Indian regional bureaux, it organized cultural exchanges and awarded travel grants to artists. Then there was Films Division, founded in 1948, India's state production studio, which created documentaries and news reports. From the early 1950s until 1978 all cinemas had to screen newsreels made by Films Division before a main feature. The soundtracks for these newsreels provided regular work for musicians. But the most important organization supporting classical music was Ravi's new employer—All India Radio.

In India, radio had been pioneered in the 1920s by private radio clubs providing local coverage. The state had assumed control by 1930, and under the first controller of broadcasting, Lionel Fielden, who held the post from 1935 to 1940, the stations at Bombay, Calcutta, Madras and Delhi were unified as a monopoly broadcaster, All India Radio (AIR). Its purpose-built Broadcasting House, on Parliament Street in central New Delhi, was opened in 1943, and gradually more regional studios, transmitters and languages were added. However, the audience grew slowly, and Fielden blamed the viceroy, Linlithgow, for underfunding the service.[2]

In 1947 there were only 90,000 license holders in the whole country (compared with about 11 million in the UK), and just 3,000 radio sets were manufactured that year. It was independence that gave radio a massive boost. In 1951 60,000 sets were manufactured.[3] By then AIR was broadcasting from a network of 25 stations, in all of India's major regional languages, and could be received by 21 percent of the population.[4] Ravi arrived in his new job just as the audience was exploding for the first time, and he was one of the first to appreciate the radical potential of music. As early as 1947 he had declared, "Now is the time for great musicians to let millions have a chance to hear and appreciate our music rather than remain aloof in impotent indifference."[5] It was his seven years at AIR that made Ravi into a national star.

AIR's External Services division had recently been separated from the Home Services division. Modeled on the BBC Overseas Service (the forerunner of today's World Service), External Services transmitted in eleven languages to Europe, the Middle East, Africa, South East Asia and the Far East. For a twenty-eight-year-old outsider to be chosen as its director of music was a sign of the regard in which Ravi was held, for all his recent crisis of confidence. The man who had spotted him was Narayana Menon, who was a south Indian veena player, a literary scholar and a rising power in broadcasting. He was nine years older than Ravi and would become his friend and mentor.

After being awarded a PhD from Edinburgh University for a thesis on W. B. Yeats, Menon had joined the Indian section of the BBC Overseas Service in London, where George Orwell was among those who commissioned his wartime radio talks. Ravi, listening from Maihar, had been impressed by a show he presented called *Music of the East and West*, and they had met around 1946. When Menon left the BBC in 1947, he recommended that he be replaced by Ravi, who was keen to accept the offer. "Narayana was the first to notice and appreciate the creative side of mine," he recalled. However, according to Ravi, Annapurna refused to contemplate the move to London.[6] Menon returned to India and, after serving briefly as director of broadcasting in Baroda, joined AIR, where this time he was successful in appointing Ravi.

Ravi's role involved working with the administrative staff to plan all the External Services broadcasts that required music, as well as serving as composer–conductor of its proposed new instrumental ensemble. The creative possibilities in particular appealed to him. As well as arranging solo, duet or ensemble recitals for broadcast, he was given the opportunity to create tone poems or provide incidental music for radio plays. For the first three years, the programs Ravi worked on were not usually heard within India, but he became well known for his solo recitals, which were broadcast domestically.

His sitar recitals had an impact all over the nation. To take one example, Rama Rao was a recent college graduate in Bangalore. His family included no serious musicians and did not own a radio, but when Rao went to a neighbor's house to listen to a broadcast by the new sitar player who was causing such a stir, it was to change his life. It inspired him to take up the sitar himself. When Ravi played a concert in Bangalore soon after, Rao asked to study with him. Two years later, in 1951, he made the three-and-a-half-day train journey from Bangalore to Delhi and began several years of intensive study there as Ravi's disciple.[7] Such was the power of radio. A similar story was recounted by Balwant Rai Verma, another sitar disciple of Ravi's who began to study with him in the 1950s. He, too, first encountered Ravi's music on AIR.[8]

Ravi's greatest satisfaction at AIR came from experimenting with his ensemble. One approach he developed was to drill his musicians in playing a classical *raga* in such a way that it sounded as if they were improvising, even though they were playing his score and he was conducting them. They maintained classical purity within a single *raga*, and there was no harmony or counterpoint, but they did not simply play in unison; Ravi arranged the parts so that his melodies were passed from one part of the ensemble to another, taking advantage of the tonal color and range of all the instruments. "The effect was breathtaking and new," he said.[9]

As well as classical works, Ravi also composed pieces in light classical and folk idioms. The light pieces were often in the *thumri* style, a semi-classical vocal form historically related to Kathak dance. Typically, the songs tell of a lover's longing for Krishna and have a romantic, erotic or devotional quality. Ravi had already embraced playing *thumri* in instrumental form on the sitar. One innovation when he applied it to the ensemble was to introduce "a very free kind of counterpoint, where one group of instruments played against another, executing different phrases with any number of rhythms"— comparable, he said, to the melodic exchanges in his *jugalbandi* concerts.[10] His most popular pieces were those based on folk songs and dances. He aimed to revive the soul and spirit of such forms as *Kajri*, from the Benares area, which he had learned from his mother, or *Vidai*, a marriage farewell song from the region of Awadh.[11] He also created many pieces based on fairy tales, historical episodes, the lives of Buddha or Tansen, or poems by Tagore. With these he kept to the appropriate spirit, period or region, but allowed himself the freedom to bring in other styles and to vary the instrumentation.

In his ensemble work, Ravi was confronted by several obstacles. Most Indian classical musicians saw themselves as soloists, since ensembles rarely featured in their musical culture. Some people held that orchestration was antithetical to the genre, the essence of which was the single linear melody line. Indian instruments themselves also presented technical problems when used en masse. Some, such as the sitar, are inherently quiet. Most are designed for solo use and their sound production is not uniform, with the buzzing sympathetic strings all too likely to clash. "Our Indian instruments are more or less like Indian people," Ravi once observed. "We are very individual, and seldom agree with each other."[12] At AIR he tried to minimize some of these technical difficulties, bringing the instrument-maker Bishandas Sharma onto the staff in 1950 to maintain and adjust the ensemble's instruments.

There were orchestral precedents at AIR. Lionel Fielden had aimed to maintain Indian orchestras of between eight and fifteen players at all stations "for accompaniments, rehearsals and for performance."[13] The most intriguing of them was in Delhi, where the British composer John Foulds, who was fascinated by Indian music, had run an experimental Indo-European orchestra, consisting entirely of Indian instruments, that broadcast his compositions for a few months before his untimely death in 1939. He even wrote a large-scale *Symphony of East and West* for Western and Indian instruments, now sadly lost.[14] The historian David Lelyveld has described Foulds's ensemble as the model for Ravi's, while the musicologist Nalini Ghuman contends that "Shankar effectively inherited the post-Foulds ensemble."[15]

However, a decade had passed since Foulds's short-lived venture, and any continuity in personnel was of limited benefit to Ravi, as he revealed in a letter written shortly after starting the job: "I have got rotten hands to work with," he told Harihar Rao.[16] Much training and recruitment was required to raise the standard. The similarities between Foulds's and Ravi's working methods were superficial. Both used scores, but Ravi used Indian notation, as opposed to Foulds's Western notation. Both explored folk melodies, but Ravi's were drawn from two decades of his own rich experience. And although Ravi's instrumental palette was similar to Foulds's—sitar, sarod, sarangi, veena, vichitra veena, bansuri flute, tabla, dholak and jaltarang (tuned bowls of water)—these were familiar north Indian instruments that he had first heard brought together years before. His models were Timir Baran, Vishnudas Shirali and Baba, rather than Foulds.

Foulds and Ravi did share a fascination with the fundamental question of how to orchestrate an Indian classical *raga* without sacrificing its essence. Foulds, despite being a novice at Indian music, was on the right track. He declared he wanted to harmonize *ragas* "purely by the true inherent Ragaic harmonies."[17] Another British composer, Imogen Holst, during a winter spent studying Indian music at Shantiniketan in 1950–51, despaired when she discovered Indians writing "modern," harmonized Indian music by adding inappropriate Western chords. "I'm still hoping to find someone who is thinking in terms of Indian counterpoint to suit Indian tunes—apparently Tagore suggested it during the last two years of his life," she wrote to Leonard Elmhirst at Dartington, where she was a teacher.[18] This was exactly the territory that Ravi was starting to explore with his semi-classical ensemble works, and it was to captivate him for the rest of his life.

In B. V. Keskar, Nehru's minister for information and broadcasting, classical musicians had a passionate advocate. Keskar wanted Indians to free themselves from the habits of the British and appreciate their own high art. Believing that Indian film songs were a vulgar,

Westernized form, he banned them from the airwaves for a few years. Indian classical music filled the vacuum, and most stations played several hours of it every day. When the English tenor Peter Pears visited Agra in December 1955 he noted that "Indian music on the wireless starts at 7 a.m. and goes on to 9 p.m. with few breaks."[19] Keskar's ban sparked a boom in popularity for Radio Ceylon, which shrewdly began broadcasting Hindi film music into India, and in 1957 he staged a tactical retreat by launching a separate AIR station for film music, Vividh Bharati. However, he had achieved his ambition. "I don't think people have recognized his role in reviving Indian classical music," says Lalit Mansingh, who was Director General of the ICCR from 1985 to 1989.[20]

Keskar accelerated the initiative, begun in the late 1930s, of putting musicians (as well as poets and dramatists) on AIR's staff, and giving them production as well as performing responsibilities. By the late 1950s there were 10,000 musicians on the payroll. By 1983 AIR employed over 27,000 Hindustani and 30,000 Carnatic musicians.[21] Having the security of a government salary made a career in music viable. "Almost every great musician that you can think of started off as a staff artist at All India Radio," says Mansingh. Among them were Ali Akbar Khan, Alla Rakha, the shehnai virtuoso Bismillah Khan and the flutist Hariprasad Chaurasia.[22] From 1955 onward the nation's broadcaster also began organizing annual festivals of live classical music, known as Radio Sangeet Sanmelan, held in up to fifteen different cities around the time of the annual Diwali festival. These performances were recorded and filled the airwaves for a month.

On arriving in Delhi in 1949, Ravi stayed initially with the Shri Rams at 22 Curzon Road. Once he was settled, Annapurna and Shubho joined him. Subsequently he was provided with government accommodation as a perk: first an apartment in Mandi House, then another on Ferozeshah Road, and finally a large bungalow at 34 Ashoka Road, each home grander than the last. All these addresses were in the heart of New Delhi, the British imperial district that had been completed just two decades earlier. There was much to be said for life in this modern city. Ravi could cycle to work on the wide, tree-lined streets. "Delhi was clean, green and unpolluted," he recalled.[23]

He also felt ready to take on further formal disciples, including the sitarists Jamaluddin Bhattacharya and Uma Shankar Mishra, the flutist Vijay Raghav Rao, the violinist Satyadev Pawar, and Gopal Krishan, who played a Hindustani form of the veena, the vichitra veena, in Ravi's AIR ensemble. Harihar Rao remained in Bombay for the time being, where he continued to be a linchpin for Ravi, but he eventually followed him to Delhi, as did Amiya Dasgupta. These two were among the first disciples whom Ravi invited to live in his home and learn in the *gurukul* style. Others studied with Ravi on a less formal basis. Ali Akbar's son Aashish Khan visited from Maihar when he was about thirteen and stayed on at Mandi House to study.[24] Birju Maharaj, who became the greatest exponent of the Lucknow *gharana* of Kathak, was also about thirteen or fourteen when he moved to Delhi to teach at Sangeet Bharati, a new institute, and he was a regular at Ferozeshah Road, where he listened to Ravi practicing with and rigorously training Chatur Lal, a promising young tabla player on AIR's staff. Sometimes Ravi would ask Chatur Lal to pass the tabla to Birju and he would accompany him. Birju always felt that he could see the dancer in Ravi, in his rhythmic intricacy, in the elegance with which his fingers moved over the strings. "His playing was dancing," he says.[25]

One disappointment for Ravi was that the capital lacked the music circles of Bombay. Almost the only institution presenting concerts was Gandharva Mahavidyalaya, a music school founded a decade earlier. In fact the classical music scene had been marginalized ever since the British had sacked the old city and sent the last Mughal emperor into exile in 1858. According to Ravi, "There used to be a saying that Delhi's musicians were paupers in their own land and could earn their living only by traveling and performing outside the city, in Calcutta or Lucknow."[26] So he took the initiative. He began playing Saturday evening sitar recitals for connoisseurs at the adjoining mansion on Curzon Road, hosted by two of Shri Ram's daughters-in-law, Sumitra Charat Ram and Sheila Bharat-Ram. He named it the Jhankar Music Circle. The first recitals took place outdoors on the lawn, as there was hardly a car to be heard in Delhi in those days. Gradually they built up an audience, and later switched to a large salon indoors or other, bigger venues.

According to Sheila Bharat-Ram's second son, Arun, "Raviji was already by that time, compared to other musicians, much more educated and worldly and had more organizational skills. So, along with my mother, my aunt and a few more patrons, he actually started inviting many musicians to come."[27] The performers included both AIR staff artists and visiting musicians. Among them were some of the most revered names of the older generation, such as the sarod player Hafeez Ali Khan, the vocalists Bade Ghulam Ali Khan, Faiyaz Khan and Kesarbai Kerkar, and the tabla players Ahmedjan Thirakwa and Kanthe Maharaj. Once or twice Annapurna played a surbahar duet with Ravi.

In those days visitors to Delhi might easily have traveled for a couple of days by train, so these musicians often stayed on at the Curzon Road house for up to a fortnight. "It became a kind of open house for a vast variety of people," says Arun's older brother, Vinay Bharat-Ram, who was a teenager at the time. "At the center of this, as far as music and art is concerned, was Ravi Shankar. He also became a promoter of the arts in Delhi."[28] Jhankar went from strength to strength, and with Sumitra Charat Ram at the helm it evolved into Bharatiya Kala Kendra, a major Delhi institute of the performing arts that continues to thrive today, and also spawned the annual Shankarlal Festival.

Vinay recalls the impact of an early Jhankar recital, when Ravi and Ali Akbar played one of the *jugalbandis* for which they were becoming increasingly famous:

I was watching the expression of the middle-class and upper-middle-class families who had come, who had never actually heard this kind of music. When the *jhala* began they said, "This must be what it was like in the courts of Tansen." That music could be like this was unbelievable to them. It was such a vast difference between what people had heard and what they witnessed here.[29]

It was an era of musical renaissance. Prospering in this remade world, Ravi was a part of a generation of Indian classical greats who came to national prominence around the time of independence and dominated for decades to come. Among these musicians was Ravi's brother-in-law Ali Akbar Khan, a new master of the sarod. There was also the brilliant sitar player Vilayat Khan, eight years younger than Ravi, the son of the late Enayat Khan. Given that fate had prevented Ravi from becoming Vilayat's father's disciple, perhaps it was destiny that these two should become great rivals, the two leading sitarists of their day, each with his own camp of followers. Even their instruments were in competition; the "Vilayat Khan model" was the only sitar design to rival Ravi's in popularity. It differed in lacking the second gourd resonator and the bass strings that were such a feature of Ravi's sound, and it covered a three-octave range rather than Ravi's four octaves. Vilayat used it to develop his own distinctive style. Where Ravi drew so profoundly on the older *dhrupad* style, Vilayat's emphasis was on the poetic imagination of *khyal*, and he was also known for singing as he played sitar. Over the following years, Ravi, Vilayat and Ali Akbar became established as the country's most famous instrumental triumvirate. They were, Ravi liked to joke, India's Three Musketeers.

Another star in this new firmament was Bismillah Khan, who came from a family of hereditary court musicians in Bihar, but grew up in Benares and single-handedly brought the shehnai, hitherto a ceremonial instrument, to the concert stage. One of the showpiece events on the eve of independence was a recital he gave at Delhi's Red

Fort, which became an annual tradition. Then there were the new percussionists, including the outstanding trio of tabla players Alla Rakha, Kishan Maharaj and Samta Prasad. Meanwhile, rising up from the south was the Carnatic vocalist M. S. Subbulakshmi. After both playing the lead role and singing the songs in the blockbuster film *Meera*, she became revered nationwide as a musical deity, described by Sunil Khilnani as "a new-age bhakti saint."[30]

At the start of the 1950s, all these musicians were in their twenties or early thirties. They came to prominence on the cusp between the old and the new systems, benefiting from both the rigorous focus of the ancient tradition and the mass-media exposure and state support of the modern world. It was not unlike the change in status of European composers during the nineteenth century, when they became public figures and national icons. Indian music, a system previously based on *gharanas*, on families and traditions, now embraced the modern concept of the star performer. No matter where you lived in India, you could hear the nation's leading personalities playing on the radio. With this new meritocracy, the profession gained a more elevated status. The honorific "Pandit," originally accorded to Brahmin scholars and priests, was extended to respected Hindu musicians of any caste. Muslim musicians were similarly prefixed with "Ustad," another term previously used only for learned teachers. Musicians had broken out of the lower levels of society.

Among these new idols, Ravi gradually emerged as first among equals, a position that made him a target for others, most famously Vilayat Khan. In fact their rivalry was mostly one-sided. While Ravi was media-friendly, charming and collegiate, Vilayat was a natural rebel who fell out with All India Radio and could not resist showing his resentment of Ravi's greater popularity. There was private warmth between them, and early on they were close enough for Vilayat to stay with Ravi in Delhi for ten days in 1950.[31] But his behavior was different in public. "He was such a wonderful musician," said Ravi, "but whenever he played, the first thing he would do would be to make digs at me!"[32]

The most infamous episode occurred at a Jhankar concert at the Red Fort in 1952. In a unique lineup, Ravi, Vilayat and Ali Akbar all performed together, with Kishan Maharaj on tabla. Ravi was skeptical beforehand, not least because he was running a 102°F fever, but Vilayat told him, "*Dada, prem se bajayenge.*" ("We will play with love.")[33] Baba was present and they agreed to play his creation, *Raga Manj Khamaj.* As it transpired, the concert was characterized not by love but by competitive rivalry, cheered on by partisan elements in the audience. According to Vilayat's brother Imrat Khan, the crucial moment came when Vilayat played a particular *taan*—a rapid phrase, a kind of complicated riff—that was the trademark of his *gharana.* "It takes many, many hours of practice for months to get it," said Imrat. "Raviji tried and couldn't do it. Ali Akbar tried and couldn't do it either. Then my brother played it again and added more to it, and at that point pandemonium broke. People started roaring that Vilayat Khan had outshone Raviji."[34]

Although he was offended by Vilayat's competitive ambush, Ravi at first played down what had happened. But when the newspapers printed reports from Vilayat's followers that Ravi could not keep up with their hero, he became riled and, in front of Ali Akbar, Kishan Maharaj and the vocalist Amir Khan, challenged Vilayat to a rematch. "Dada, let's not get into this," replied Vilayat. "People indulge in idle talk and unless you hear me say something in person, don't go by hearsay."[35] Ravi was not prepared to let it go, and responded that they should play once again "*prem se*" (with love). He told Harihar Rao that he would not be "melted" by Vilayat's "crockodile [*sic*] tears and apologies."[36] Meanwhile, he became convinced that Vilayat was sending spies to find out what he was playing in his concerts. He was still pursuing the rematch as late as March 1954, when they both played solo at the Bharatiya Kala Kendra festival at the Red Fort, but Vilayat never did accept the challenge. It was probably a good thing; as Kishan Maharaj said, "If these two eyes of India play together again, one will shut forever."[37]

There was often friction between the top musicians. A third consummate sitar player to emerge during the 1950s was Nikhil Banerjee. Eleven years younger than Ravi, Nikhil became a fellow disciple of Baba in Maihar in 1947, but Baba deliberately shaped his sound to be distinct from Ravi's. Ravi rated him very highly and taught him a couple of *ragas*. In 1949 or 1950 Ravi was performing on the rooftop at Gandharva Mahavidyalaya in Delhi when he debuted a new *raga* that he had written, called *Manamanjari*. He noticed Nikhil in the audience. Ravi did not play *Manamanjari* much thereafter—it was not one of his favorite *ragas*—but years later he was "not only appalled but deeply hurt" to discover that Nikhil had released a recording of it and claimed it as his own creation.[38]

There was a story, probably originating from Nikhil himself, that Ravi had felt so threatened by the new prodigy that he had asked Baba to stop teaching him in 1952, which was when Nikhil switched to studying with Ali Akbar. While Ravi certainly enjoyed his superior status, this does not ring true for either Ravi or Baba. Where music was concerned Baba knew his own mind, and it seems inconceivable that he would have been influenced in this way. But this jungle tended to generate tension between its biggest beasts.

In 1952 Ravi became director of music at AIR's Home Services division, a move that meant all of his creations could now be heard within India. Here he made two lasting innovations. The first was the *National Programme of Music*, a weekly show consisting solely of one classical musician performing live, like a music-circle recital condensed into 90 minutes. Although AIR broadcast all over the country, programming was controlled regionally, with each station opting whether to relay shows from Delhi on shortwave frequencies. The *National Programme* was specifically aimed at the whole of India, and was quickly picked up by most stations. It launched on Sunday July 20, 1952 with a performance by Ravi himself, playing the monsoon *raga Mian Ki Malhar* on surbahar. It made a huge impression.

One writer, later vividly recalling that first evening, described Ravi's fingers toying with the strings, "coaxing sounds out of them by deflecting, caressing and teasing them, till the instrument itself became an extension of the magic spell that he evoked, opening up vistas of sonic possibilities that were to set a new trend."[39]

Ravi gave the next show to Baba, and then the following week to Bismillah Khan. A pattern was established. Settling into a regular slot on Saturday evenings at 9:30 p.m., the *National Programme* became the gold standard of Indian classical music broadcasting, the single most important factor in developing a national consciousness of the form and making stars of its leading exponents. It gave Ravi, as its gatekeeper, enormous influence in shaping and reflecting the nation's taste, and allowed him to indulge his questing spirit, seeking out the best of what India had to offer in all its variety—including both Hindustani and Carnatic musicians.

His other innovation at Home Services was to organize an expanded ensemble known as Vadya Vrinda, or the National Orchestra. Not only did it have a larger complement of musicians than the earlier ensemble, it had a wider choice of instruments, including, for the first time, some Western ones—the violin family and the clarinet. Until now Ravi had followed Uday's example in rigid ideological adherence to the use of Indian instruments alone, but he had come to appreciate that the violin family, in particular, was well suited to rendering the subtleties of Indian music. He was not the first to realize this. The violin had been adopted into Carnatic music a couple of centuries before as both an accompanying and a solo instrument. In the north its appearance was less common, but Baba played it, as did another of his leading disciples, V. G. Jog. What Ravi realized was that these stringed instruments could be used en masse without producing clashing overtones. He particularly loved how the cellos and double-basses extended the orchestra's lower range.

Like the *National Programme*, Vadya Vrinda encapsulated Ravi's embrace of Carnatic music. The orchestra included musicians from

both Carnatic and Hindustani traditions, while the assistant conductor was a south Indian, T. K. Jayaram Iyer. The ensemble regularly played Carnatic *ragas* and compositions. This meant it attracted a
truly national audience.

Meanwhile, Ravi had become the first Hindustani instrumentalist
to appear regularly in Madras's annual music season. He had made his
solo debut there in December 1949, beginning a tradition that was
to last many years of him performing at the Madras Music Academy
every New Year's Eve. At the academy he got to know M. S. Subbulakshmi, who was sitting in the front row during his debut, and he was
enraptured when he first heard her sing. He often visited her palatial
home, Kalki Gardens, where they lunched sitting cross-legged on the
floor, eating from a plantain leaf. He gave at least one private recital
there.

It was during this period that, inspired by the southern example of
percussion exchanges, he developed what became known as the *Tala
Vadya Kacheri* concert format, which showcased multiple percussionists trading improvisations. In his own sitar recitals he also raised the
profile of tabla players, who traditionally had a subordinate role on
stage, sitting behind the soloist to one side. Ravi was the first to bring
them forward, partly so that they could face each other, and partly to
show off their fabulous skills. He introduced a solo spot for the tabla-
player—initially Chatur Lal—at his concerts.

He began to bring Carnatic *ragas* into his sitar repertoire, playing
them in Hindustani versions with his own embellishments, and he
succeeded in popularizing them in the north for the first time. These
included *Charu Keshi*, *Kirwani*, *Vachaspati* and *Simhendra Madhyamam*. Ravi's later disciple Gaurav Mazumdar tells the story of meeting
a south Indian passenger on a train who wanted to thank him because
"Your *guru* took *Charu Keshi* from us and gave it back better."[40] Ravi
had an admiration for the wider culture of the south, which produced
so many scientists and mathematicians. "South Indians are so brainy,"
he was fond of saying. "Is there something in what they eat?"[41]

*

Until Harihar Rao moved to Delhi, probably around the end of 1954, Ravi wrote regularly to him in Bombay, and these letters give insights into his state of mind. Most commonly he wrote asking Harihar to arrange concerts for him there. There was a surprisingly strong financial imperative behind them; during 1953–4, especially, he was complaining of being short of funds. But this was about more than money; in fact he often took unpaid leave from AIR in order to play these concerts. He was driven by a compulsive need to play live. Part workaholic, part missionary, he pushed himself physically, covering vast distances criss-crossing India on planes and trains, sacrificing sleep for music. He thought nothing of playing on a Sunday evening in Bombay, taking the night plane back to Delhi and returning to AIR on Monday morning.

This lifestyle placed a strain on his already tense family life, and he experienced a new crisis in 1954, this time apparently arising from marital problems. Three times early in the year he wrote to tell Harihar of his despair, while explaining that he was unable to put the details in writing. In March, for example, when Harihar was hoping to stay with him, he begged him, "Please don't come if you at all care for any peace or happiness (?) in my life and household…It is impossible really for me to explain in [a] letter."[42] The following week he added, "Lord alone knows—as I can't write to you—the details [of] how helpless I am." But this time, he reassured Harihar, he was not going to descend into a suicidal state. "I am not dying now and know that you will be living long too! And time will tell as well as heal everything."[43]

Ravi's letters also reveal how emotionally dependent on Tat Baba he was in these years. Tat Baba was a spiritual bedrock, whose support could mitigate Ravi's lowest moods and fuel his most blissful flights of creativity. Ravi encouraged others to meet him, including Annapurna, who was skeptical, and Ali Akbar. He even arranged for Tat Baba to visit Baba in Maihar in October 1952. To Harihar he wrote,

You are really lucky, he has taken a liking to you. You take my word... that you'll benefit in every sense of the word if you have *shraddha* [concentration] on him and get his blessings!! Don't care if your friends tease you for becoming a religious or spiritual fool and all that![44]

Indeed, Tat Baba became well known among musicians. In the 1950s and early 1960s the devotees performing at or attending his soirées in Bombay included Ravi, V. G. Jog, vocalists Bhimsen Joshi and Hirabai Barodekar, santoor pioneer Shivkumar Sharma, and a Muslim contingent too: Ali Akbar, Alla Rakha, Bismillah Khan, Amir Khan and Bade Ghulam Ali Khan.[45]

Established as the rising star among Indian musicians, Ravi began lifting his gaze beyond India's borders. Uniquely among his contemporaries, he had gained international touring experience in his youth, so he knew what was possible. Those years had also implanted a kind of missionary impulse. He had never forgotten the disparaging remarks toward Indian music made by Western musicians in the 1930s, and events now conspired to persuade him that he could be its champion, carrying it to new worlds.

Living in the capital, close to ministries and the diplomatic community, presented opportunities to Ravi. When foreign dignitaries visited Delhi, their Indian counterparts usually showcased music at state functions, and Ravi was sometimes asked to give such recitals. In 1953, for example, he played at Nehru's official residence, Teen Murti Bhavan, at a reception for the visiting prime minister of Pakistan, Mohammed Ali Bogra, and dined with both heads of government.[46]

One evening he was invited to play at the home of the Belgian consul, Louis de San, who was a good friend. The small audience consisted mostly of fellow diplomats, and Ravi prefaced his recital by giving a spoken introduction to Indian music, including a demonstration of each *raga* and *tala* before playing it. This went down extremely well.

Musical prowess aside, he was an engaging public speaker and proficient in English and French. Some of those present told him it was the first time they had been able to enjoy Indian music. They decided to form an Indian music appreciation group and invited Ravi back. Louis de San also planted an idea in his mind: "Ravi, why don't you go out and make our people in the West understand Indian music? You're the first person we've seen who can do it."[47]

An even more consequential encounter was with Yehudi Menuhin in February 1952. Twenty years after Ravi had seen the short-trousered sensation at the Salle Pleyel, Yehudi was now the world's most famous classical musician. He had come to India for the first time, fulfilling a long-held desire, in order to give five concerts in aid of Nehru's National Relief Fund. The tour was organized by Mehli Mehta, a Parsi from Bombay who had studied violin at the Juilliard School in New York and founded the Bombay Symphony Orchestra. It was during the orchestral rehearsals that Mehta's fifteen-year-old son Zubin had his first taste of conducting.

As honored guests of India, Yehudi and his wife Diana stayed at Rashtrapati Bhavan, formerly the viceroy's palace and now the residence of the Indian president. Yehudi was bewitched by India from the first. He had recently discovered yoga, and it was on this trip that he met his yoga teacher, B. K. S. Iyengar, an encounter that had lifelong benefits for his health and his music-making. At a reception in Delhi guests watched on as Yehudi demonstrated his best *shishasana* (headstand) in full evening dress, minus his shoes and socks. Unfazed, Nehru removed his Gandhi cap and responded in kind.

One morning at Narayana Menon's house, Ravi and Chatur Lal played privately for Yehudi. "That was a music-making that I could have only dreamt of," said Yehudi.[48] The corseted emotion of his upbringing had given way to a search for pure spontaneity, which, for all his mastery of Western music, he sensed that he needed to find elsewhere. He had located it first in the Romanian gypsy fiddlers he had heard as a child. Now he found it again in Indian classical music, and this time the sense of abandon was founded on an exacting training, one far more disciplined, he believed, than was practiced in the West. On the one hand there was the microtonal control of pitch and the mind-boggling mastery of rhythm; on the other, all this virtuosity was in the service of improvisation. He felt humble, a mere interpreter acknowledging the higher power of instantaneous creation. The recital was to him like a sacred ritual, and forever after he drew inspiration from "that moment when the tapers are lit, and Ravi and his colleagues begin working, making their offering, going as close as one can to the earth and then, using this tremendous training, producing this which is in the heavens."[49] Ravi had never seen a Western classical musician respond so emotionally to Indian music. Instinctively they bonded on a personal level too, and a warm friendship was formed.

Yehudi wanted the world to know about his two epiphanies. He brought Iyengar to Switzerland, triggering the international breakthrough of Iyengar Yoga. Similarly he encouraged Ravi to look abroad. They stayed in touch and when Yehudi returned to India in 1954 he received another dose of Ravi's music. "Yehudi my friend came to my place one evening for nearly three hours," Ravi reported to Harihar on that occasion. "Sat, chatted and heard me—was in raptures."[50]

Ravi's sights were now set on taking Indian music overseas. This was the era of India's non-alignment between East and West, and when his first opportunity for a foreign tour came through the ICCR, the destination was the Soviet Union. In late 1953, the Soviets sent a party of thirty-six musicians and dancers to India on a two-month tour. India responded in kind the following year with the first of its own cultural delegations. In the USSR this was the time of the post-Stalin thaw, and India was fashionable. A Hindi film was dominating the Soviet box office: *Awara* by Raj Kapoor, the son of Prithviraj. It had a script by K. A. Abbas and a dream sequence choreographed by none other than Simkie, and it is one of India's most successful films of all time. That year, an estimated 64 million people bought tickets to see it in the USSR.[51]

Over six weeks, from late August to early October 1954, the Indian delegation performed all over the USSR, in Moscow, Leningrad, Kiev, Sochi, Yerevan, Tbilisi and Tashkent. They met with political leaders including Nikolai Bulganin, composers such as Dmitri Shostakovich and Aram Khachaturian, and the ballerinas Galina Ulanova and Maya Plisetskaya. They were paraded around all the essential sights: the Hermitage Museum, the pioneers' schools, the Moscow metro and the Red Square mausoleum, which at the time contained Stalin's body as well as Lenin's. They were also filmed for a Russian documentary, *Masters of Indian Arts*, which, despite its obvious intended use as propaganda, is a wonderful historical record. "I have never had a busier time than the last one & half month[s]," Ravi wrote from Moscow. "I am wonderstruck at what wonders I have seen—specially in the art world here!"[52] He was transported by watching the Bolshoi Ballet performing *Swan Lake* and *The Fountain of Bakhchisarai*, and by Ulanova dancing *Giselle*.[53] But he also knew that along with the VIP treatment came KGB surveillance, and he was troubled by the lack of freedom and the stifling of creativity.

With forty artists involved, the concerts resembled variety shows, and Ravi's solo slot was a mere 15–20 minutes, although he also led a small choir in singing his arrangement of "Sare Jahan Se Accha." It was an unforgettable experience to play at venues such as the Bolshoi Theatre or Tchaikovsky Hall. The delegation included many leading artists, mostly of Ravi's generation, including the dancers Tara Chowdhury, Indrani Rahman and Guru Gopinath, the singers Asa Singh Mastana and Meera Banerjee, and the tabla players Kishan Maharaj and Jnan Prakash Ghosh. But Ravi was its unofficial star, as is clear from a wonderful photograph of the whole party strolling among the pavilions of the All-Union Agricultural Exhibition in north Moscow. The entire group seems to be composed around him; there is no doubting who is the center of attention. From Moscow he sent a report of the tour to Indira Gandhi, who was then personal assistant to her father, Nehru. He was even approached with an offer to play Alexander Pushkin in a Russian film, for, as he was repeatedly told, he bore an uncanny resemblance to the national poet. There was certainly a likeness, especially when Ravi was wearing his trademark long black Nehru jacket and had that determined, slightly impatient look about him that suggested coiled energy.

The tour was completed by ten days each in Poland and Czechoslovakia, after which Ravi added on two weeks in London for Jnan Prakash Ghosh and himself. The London interlude is puzzling because it was his long-planned return to the West after sixteen years away, yet for the rest of his life he never publicly referred to it. His itinerary has come to light only from correspondence. From Moscow he wrote to Harihar Rao confirming that he would arrive on October 30 and could be contacted care of an Ashok Ghosh at 8 Barter Street in Bloomsbury.[54] On the 8th Narayana Menon wrote to two BBC contacts in London, Peter Crossley-Holland, controller of music for radio's Third Programme, and Philip Bate, who produced music programs for television. He told them that Ravi was one of the two or three best sitar players in India and recommended they record him for broadcast while he was in London.[55] After a flurry of memos within the BBC, the Third Programme authorized a recording and its "Indian Programme Organiser," John Linton, wrote to Ravi on the 26th via the Indian High Commission in London, apparently as instructed. Linton suggested Ravi create a signature tune for the BBC, but surmised that it might be better recorded in India, where an Indian orchestra would be available.[56] There the trail goes cold. There is no reply in the BBC files, and no sessions were recorded that year.

He definitely arrived in London, for he later told Sukanya that he had stayed at the Hyde Park Hotel in the year that she was born, 1954. This means he chose to omit the visit from the résumé that he later formulated, according to which he did not set foot in the West between the final tour with Uday in 1938 and his triumphant return in 1956. The most likely explanation for this missing fortnight is that, having arranged no concerts in advance, and being offered only a radio commission for a recording back in India, he found that there was no demand for him to perform during his short stay, so there was nothing to report. Once he was back home, it was better to concentrate on his accomplishments in the USSR. So he erased the whole visit from his biography.

7

THE WORLD OF APU

I hear music in the waves, the breeze, the rain and
even in the rustle of the leaves.
RAVI SHANKAR[1]

By late 1954, aged thirty-four, Ravi was the most prominent star of
the independence generation of classical musicians. He had achieved
recognition through his work in a variety of media: radio broadcasts,
record releases, prolific touring and some songwriting and composition for theatrical shows. There was one area crucial to his career
that he had yet to develop fully: film music. This was about to change.

In some ways he was ideally suited to working in film. His imagination was endlessly fertile: an unceasing flow of melodies and rhythmic compositions poured out of him on demand. He was blessed with
the ability to conceive an entire arrangement in his head. He worked
best to deadlines. And from childhood he had been an avid film fan.
He also brought to the field the innovative mindset of an outsider.
Although he would create some of India's best-known soundtracks,
he always kept his footing in classical music, never being swept away
by the mighty currents of the commercial film world.

From the very first films he worked on, *Neecha Nagar* and *Dharti Ke
Lal*, Ravi's soundtracks were distinctive for the emphasis he placed on
three elements: the use of Indian instruments, Indian classical forms,
and incidental music as opposed to song. In the eight years following
that initial foray, Ravi had not gone out of his way to pursue cinema
work. The box-office failure of both those films, he admitted, "acted
as a great mental setback" for his new concept of film music, and he
lost heart.[2] During this time he played on the soundtrack for Uday's
Kalpana (credited as "Ravindra Shankar"), but that was under the

music direction of Vishnudas Shirali. Similarly, when he played sitar and surbahar for Chetan Anand's *Aandhiyan* (1952), Ali Akbar was the principal composer. The turning point came after Ravi returned from London in November 1954, when he received a letter from Satyajit Ray inviting him to provide the music to his debut feature, *Pather Panchali*, the first installment in what became the legendary *Apu Trilogy*. Four times in the next six years films scored by Ravi won the President's Gold Medal for India's best feature film at what is now known as the National Film Awards.

Although they had both been present at the All-Bengal Music Conference in 1934, it was not until late 1944 that Ravi first met Ray, at Malad in Bombay, where Ravi was living. Ray had relatives there, one of whom was a female singer known to the Shankar family.[3] It is possible Ray had gone there to meet Rajendra, who was working for Bombay Talkies, but it was the introduction to Ravi, whose music Ray had heard on All India Radio, that turned out to be more important. They stayed in touch. Ray was not yet working in film; he was art director for a British advertising agency in north Calcutta, D. J. Keymer. He was a striking figure—six foot four, with a booming voice and intellectual gravitas—and he came from a distinguished artistic family; his father was the much-loved children's writer Sukumar Ray, Bengal's equivalent of Lewis Carroll or Edward Lear. Musically, his tastes were predominantly Western classical, but he was familiar with Indian music (especially *Rabindra Sangeet*) from his childhood, when he had met Allauddin Khan. After attending Ravi's breakthrough concert in Calcutta in late 1945 he became a regular in the audience whenever Ravi played in the city over the next few years. Ravi usually stayed at the Great Eastern Hotel, which was near Keymer's office, and they got to know each other over coffee or lunch.

Ray was a fan and critic of American and European cinema, and several years passed before he decided to make his own films. He felt that most Indian directors had failed to grasp the potential that the medium offered for creating a distinctively Indian film aesthetic.

However, in 1948 he was so enthralled by one Indian film—*Kalpana*—that he watched it at least ten times. "I never knew Indian music and dancing could have such an impact on me," he wrote at the time.[4] Having earlier made woodcut illustrations for a children's edition of *Pather Panchali*, the 1929 novel by Bibhutibhushan Banerjee about a boy growing up in a Bengali village, he now focused on the idea of filming the book. He received encouragement from Jean Renoir, when the French director was in Calcutta filming *The River*. His eureka moment came during a six-month posting in London in 1950, when he saw Vittorio De Sica's *Bicycle Thieves*. "It just gored me," he said.[5] It showed him that a masterpiece could be made on a low budget, working on location with non-professional actors.

At the same time, Ray was developing another idea: a short film on Ravi. His 32-page storyboard from 1951, entitled *A Sitar Recital by Ravishankar*, still exists.[6] In watercolor-and-ink sketches, with penciled annotations, frame by frame he tracks Ravi playing a *raga*, from slow *alap* through to a climax in a fast *gat*. The focus is on the sitar player, with some poetic shots of nature or shimmering water and details from a Rajput miniature of *Ragini Todi*, as well as a tabla-player's hands. The *raga* Ravi plays is usually agreed to be *Todi*, because of the *raga mala* miniature, although Sankarlal Bhattacharjee has argued that it is *Desh*.[7] The purpose of this tantalizing unmade film has long been a subject of debate, but there is an overlooked 1956 interview in which Ravi explained it quite succinctly: "Satyajit wanted to make short films on the classical Indian *ragas* with my cooperation. It was a beautiful idea but somehow it could not materialize." He added, "Once he sent me an album of remarkable sketches drawn by him showing me in various moods and expressions while performing. I was struck by his imagination and artistic skill."[8] The project had evidently died a death by then, but its echoes can perhaps be detected in the *Apu Trilogy*: Andrew Robinson has compared the structure of the trilogy to that of a *raga*, developing all the way from exploratory simplicity and wonder through to emotional catharsis.[9]

As a first-time filmmaker, with little budget or experience and no shooting script, Ray faced enormous difficulties making *Pather Panchali*. In October 1952 he began filming at the weekend in a village outside Calcutta, but had to stop when the money ran out. It was more than a year before he secured the government funding that enabled him to pick the project up again. He then enjoyed a gift from providence. The Museum of Modern Art was organizing a short festival to introduce New Yorkers to *The Living Arts of India*, in tandem with a pioneering exhibition it was mounting on Indian textiles and ornamental arts. When the museum's head of exhibitions, Monroe Wheeler, was in Calcutta in February 1954, he viewed stills from Ray's rushes and was so impressed that he said he would screen it in New York if it was finished in time for the festival in April 1955—the only film to have this honor. It was a visionary act of curating.

Orchestral music, with or without songs, was still the norm in film—in India as in Hollywood—but Ray was attracted to new approaches, such as the use of the zither in *The Third Man*.[10] He had watched *Neecha Nagar* and *Dharti Ke Lal*, and he admired Ravi's music for *The Discovery of India*, which he had probably seen during its Calcutta run in 1948. "I thought instead that it would be a good idea to work with someone like him, who would be able to introduce a fresh approach—quite unlike conventional Bengali film composers at that time," said Ray.[11]

Ravi accepted the commission immediately, before seeing any footage, and they agreed a fee of 2,500 rupees, although Ray could pay nothing up front (and Ravi later said that he ended up accepting a token one rupee).[12] Ravi's diary was packed but he scheduled a two-day visit to Calcutta in early 1955 for the recording. When he arrived, Ray came to meet him at Jnan Prakash Ghosh's house at 25 Dixon Lane, where he was staying. There are several discrepancies in the accounts of what followed. Ray later claimed Ravi had not read Banerjee's novel, whereas Ravi was adamant that he had done so in the early 1940s.[13] Ravi also remembered his brothers reading the original serialization in *Bharatbarsha* magazine, published when he was eight.[14] Ray said that Ravi first sang him his main theme music when they met at Dixon Lane. Ravi, though, said the theme came to him spontaneously when he was watching the rushes at Bhavani cinema later that day. What is undisputed is the impact of that screening. "It was not until I saw the rushes of the film that I became aware of the intense human drama he had created on celluloid," Ravi said.[15]

As a composer, one of Ravi's advantages was that he could play the sitar part himself; his performances on *Pather Panchali* are exquisite. The other musicians were sourced locally. "To ensure the required simplicity and to prevent the background music from being obtrusive, I employed the minimum possible number of instruments," he explained a year later. "There were only four instrumentalists to play the music individually and collectively. I myself played the sitar. Then there was a pakhawaj player, a flutist and a dilruba player, who also at times played on the tar shehnai."[16] The tar shehnai, which was to play a key role in the hands of Daksinarayan Tagore, is an esraj with an added gramophone horn, which amplifies its sound and lends this bowed instrument the timbre of a reed instrument, hence the name tar shehnai ("stringed shehnai"). The flutist was Aloke Dey, who also assisted Ravi by transcribing his compositions into Indian notation where needed. The pakhawaj player has not been identified.

Ravi's session was squeezed into the only day available before he had to be back at All India Radio in Delhi. So he composed, arranged and recorded the soundtrack in a single night session, variously estimated at between four and eleven hours (the latter is more likely). After composing each passage spontaneously, he instructed Aloke Dey and the ensemble, ran through a couple of rehearsals, and then recorded immediately, usually taking the role of conductor himself. With time so short, he recorded music of well beyond the required length for each scene, and an additional half-dozen three-minute sitar pieces in various *ragas* and tempos, to provide flexibility for Ray when he came to edit the film.[17]

Ravi's folklike main theme is one of the most memorable melodies in cinema history. When it is first heard on the flute at the end of the title sequence it sets up a wistful, lyrical mood to complement the intimate, rural sensibility of the film. It reappears throughout, the tune sometimes carried on the sitar or sarod rather than the flute, the feeling sometimes more playful, sometimes more melancholy. The way Ravi reworked this theme to match the changing moods of the scenes is remarkable—"most certainly the work of a master," as Shubha Mudgal has observed.[18]

Among the other fine musical passages in *Pather Panchali* is the scene of insects skating over the pond as the land comes alive before the monsoon. This section was inspired by Ravi's soundtrack recording. One of his extra pieces was this sitar improvisation in the rainy-season *raga Desh*. Ray loved it and, remembering some unused pond footage he had shot, he matched up the two and inserted the scene during the final edit. In another scene a furious Sarbajaya, having discovered that her daughter Durga has been stealing, drags her by the hair and throws her out of the home. It is shot so that the violence is almost all implied rather than seen, but what gives the scene its force is the frantic rolling swell on the pakhawaj.

Most moving of all is the harrowing scene in which Sarbajaya reveals to her husband that Durga has died. For a whole minute we hear only the high wail of the tar shehnai in *Raga Patdeep*. The result is searingly powerful, far more so than it would be to hear the characters' howling grief. The music is Ravi's, but Ray claimed that the idea was his, and that he conceived it while viewing the rushes. This may be the case, but it is worth comparing a scene from *Neecha Nagar* in 1946. When the mourners are gathered around the body of Rupa and the white shroud is peeled back to reveal her face, the sound is reduced to a similar musical lament on the sarangi and sarod. Consciously or not, Ray probably picked up the idea from Ravi anyway.

Uncannily, narrative elements in the trilogy parallel Ravi's own life. The protagonist Apu, a large-eyed, ever-curious, Bengali Brahmin boy, could almost be the young Ravi himself as he explores the lanes of Benares in the 1920s, suffers the tragically early deaths of an older sibling and both his parents, and then struggles to relate to his own son. Such resonances seem to have pushed Ravi to rare heights of creativity. When he was asked where his music came from, his response was that the film had touched his heart.[19] For all the technical and mathematical mastery in his music-making, in its expression it is highly emotional; the rest is the substructure that allows him to rise up and fly free. His method of composing for film means that we hear his spontaneous response to what is on screen (mediated sometimes by Ray's editing). It is as if we are taking his pulse. Given that the death of Durga would have reminded Ravi of Bhupendra's premature demise, the tar shehnai's lament surely also expresses Ravi's own primal grief at an unbearable loss.

Pather Panchali had its world premiere in New York in May 1955. Reactions were positive and it gained some influential supporters, although the film had yet to be subtitled and there were only two screenings. Its Indian release was more significant. It was the first truly modern Indian film, and a generation of Bengalis remember the buzz it created—among them my own father-in-law, who watched it on the day of its release in Calcutta. Abroad its profile was boosted by the 1956 Cannes Film Festival, where it received a prize for "best human document." When at last it received extended international releases, in London in December 1957 and in New York in September 1958 (where it ran for thirty-six weeks at the Fifth Avenue Playhouse), it became hugely important for both Ray and Ravi. This was the first Indian art film to resonate worldwide. At home Ravi was already an established star, while Ray was an unknown, but they arrived on the international scene simultaneously, heralding a new wave of fascination with India. When Martin Scorsese watched the *Apu Trilogy* in a New York theater a couple of years later, it was "one of the great cinematic experiences of my life," he recalled. "Ray's use of music impressed me so much that I sought out and eventually found soundtracks to his films, such as Ravi Shankar's music to *Pather Panchali*."[20]

The sequel, *Aparajito*, continues the tale of Apu from the age of ten, when he and his parents arrive in Benares in 1920 (the very year Ravi was born there). In March 1956, when filming began, Ravi told Ray that he had already worked out his ideas for the music, which was based around another lyrical main theme that he worked into different arrangements. The soundtrack session was arranged for August 17–18. The instrumentation was much the same as on *Pather Panchali*, and the session proved to be just as hectic, with Ravi, as Ray later remembered, "humming, strumming, improvising and instructing at a feverish pace, and the indefatigable flutist-cum-assistant Aloke Dey transcribing the composer's ideas into Indian notation and dealing out the foolscap sheets to the tense handful who had to keep plucking and blowing and thumping with scarcely a breathing space."[21]

One factor in the success of Ravi's scores to Ray's films was the way that the pair interacted. "Many directors are very fussy about the music, but they don't really know what they want," Ravi later reflected. "When you press them they are vague. I always ask for this freedom: either the director must tell me exactly what he wants—exactly what mood—or he must leave it to me."[22] Ray was so artistically confident and clear that Ravi could never be in any doubt.

Ravi's film music was now much sought after in Bengal, and he accepted a commission from Tapan Sinha, considered to be one of the four leading Bengali directors of the Parallel Cinema movement, along with Ray, Ritwik Ghatak and Mrinal Sen. *Kabuliwala* was based on a short story by Tagore about the friendship between an Afghan peddler of nuts and fruits and a young girl in Calcutta who reminds him of his daughter back home. Fortuitously, Ravi was flying to Kabul immediately after the *Aparajito* session to play a series of recitals during the Jashn festival marking Afghan independence day. The king, Mohammed Zahir Shah, was a great patron of Indian classical music, and Ravi found a real fervor for music among the audiences. They almost tore their shirts with emotion, as he put it.[23] During this trip he sourced some Afghan folk tunes that he then used

for the opening sequence of *Kabuliwala*, and on his return he recorded the soundtrack in another marathon overnight session. Sinha com-
plimented him for his commitment to authenticity and for his ability
"to feel the right mood of the film and decorate it with his music." He
added, "I have never seen such devotion to music in any other person. He could compose throughout the night, yet in the morning he
came out of the studio looking as fresh as ever."[24] Though not quite in
Apu's league, *Kabuliwala* triumphed at the National Film Awards and
Ravi's music won a Silver Bear at the Berlin Film Festival.

Apart from the Afghan elements, Ravi employed a familiar palette
of Indian instruments, principally sitar, flute, sarangi, sarod, shehnai
and tabla. He firmly believed they were capable of fulfilling the necessary cinematic requirements:

> It is true our instruments, by nature of their construction and the
> methods of playing, do not lend themselves to comprehensive
> orchestration as effectively as their Western counterparts do. But
> they can serve the purpose equally effectively if they are used in
> small numbers and individually as I did in *Pather Panchali*. If one
> draws properly from the fund of the classical and folk music and
> improvises skillfully to suit the needs of a film, there is no reason
> why every shade of mood and sentiment cannot be expressed.[25]

It would be wrong to see this preference as a sign of conservatism.
Film work actually encouraged Ravi's experimental side. His next
film for Ray was *The Philosopher's Stone* (1958), a comedy about an
everyman Bengali clerk who becomes rich after finding a stone with
alchemical powers. Following Ray's wishes, Ravi created a soundtrack
of "weird and musically fantastic sound effects," as he put it: shimmering percussion, ominously hovering strings, or drones produced
by playing harmonics on a tanpura. There are none of the trilogy's
memorable tunes. Ravi declared shortly afterward that it was his best
score yet, but this was his instant reaction rather than a lasting verdict,
reflecting his excitement at being given license to use instruments in

unusual ways to enhance cinematic effects.[26] He took a similar approach in Utpal Dutt's *Megh* (1961), a murder mystery with a psychological twist in which he used discordant sounds to illustrate the mindset of an unhinged crime writer who believes himself responsible for a murder he has not committed.

By the time Ray came to make the sublime final installment in his trilogy, *The World of Apu* (1959), he was in need of a success. *Aparajito*, *The Philosopher's Stone* and *The Music Room* (for which he had engaged Vilayat Khan, Ravi being abroad at the time) had all disappointed at the box office. One problem with *Aparajito*, Ray felt, was that it had some oppressively silent passages because Ravi had not left him with enough music on his flying visit. This resulted in some tension between the two of them.

It was not just that Ravi's hectic schedules meant he could not give Ray enough time. He positively thrived on working to tight deadlines. He felt he created his best work at the last moment, whether it was for radio broadcasts, cinema or live shows. The method worked for him because it was like improvising in a recital: once the tap was opened under the force of necessity, all his creativity could flow. "It has been the story of my life," he admitted in 2005.[27]

The World of Apu is masterfully constructed and intensely moving. It launched the long careers of its two lead actors, Soumitra Chatterjee and Sharmila Tagore, and boasts another inspired score. As the story of the trilogy progresses from childhood through youth to adulthood, and from village to city, so too the music becomes more sophisticated, folklike refrains giving way to serious classical *ragas*, here with the instrumentation augmented by sarod and strings. At the film's resolution, Ray brings back the tar-shehnai theme that has haunted the whole series, the instrument's sporadic appearance until now always ominous and reminiscent of Durga's death. But this time, when Apu at last opens his heart to his son, the theme signifies Apu's redemption.

There was no problem with the recording this time, as Ravi managed to schedule three sessions, and the film gave Ray the big hit he needed.

It was the last time they would work together. Ray turned to Ali Akbar Khan for his next film, *Devi*, but found him even more frustrating; Ali Akbar, for his part, felt that Ray was not a connoisseur of Indian classical music. Thereafter Ray stopped working with classical musicians, boldly deciding instead to create his own soundtracks. "The reason why I do not work with professional composers any more," he explained in 1961, "is that I get too many ideas of my own, and composers, understandably enough, resent being guided too much."[28] In particular, he did not want to be restricted to Indian classical music; he preferred a hybrid form drawing also on folk and popular songs as well as Western classical.

Although Ravi understood that his hit-and-run approach did not suit Ray, he probably still felt a sense of rejection, and over the years there were occasional public hints of underlying friction between these two giants of Bengali culture, even as they remained on friendly terms. They certainly respected each other's work. *Pather Panchali* was Ravi's favorite among Ray's films, although he acknowledged that some of his later works were technically better. "He was undoubtedly the greatest director I worked with—meticulous, disciplined and an expert in every aspect of film making," he said.[29]

By 1957 Ravi was acclaiming "the dawning of a new age" in Bengali film.[30] Calcutta certainly excited him. With a population of 4 million, it was still India's biggest city, and it was the one most shaped by its colonial history, having been capital of the British Raj until 1911. The city of the Bengal Renaissance had emerged as a modern hybrid of Bengali and European culture. Its proud elite had long considered itself to be in intellectual and cultural dialogue with its Western counterparts. It was also India's greatest center of instrumental music. "This was a wonderful period in Calcutta," said Ravi. "It had such vibrancy, such appreciation for musicians, and there were so many artistic activities going on. In this respect, it used to be far in advance of other Indian cities. The earnings of the leading Hindustani musicians were at their maximum in Calcutta."[31]

Bengalis prized Ravi as one of their own but also noticed how different he seemed. As a *prabasi* Bengali (one living outside the motherland) he blew in on a breeze of modern professional glamour. He was the first classical musician in Calcutta to have a "secretary" to manage his affairs—his maternal cousin Jogu Chatterjee. At a time when very few people owned or hired vehicles, and most musicians relied on taxis, Ravi used to rent an expensive air-conditioned car and hire a driver whenever he came to the city. But he was not yet rich; this was about projecting an image. He also had professional portrait photographs taken and ensured that they were printed on glossy paper in souvenir concert programs.[32] Where some musicians deliberately turned up late in order to create a stir, Ravi was a promoter's dream, arriving punctually, soundchecking thoroughly, controlling his presentation on stage. He resisted encores, leaving the audience wanting more. He even kept note of what he performed live so that he avoided repeating the same *ragas* in each city.

As Ravi's fame spread, first within India and then across the world, his appeal stretched far beyond connoisseurs of music. "For the average Bengali," says Partha Bose, a Calcuttan sitar player and another member of what has become known as the Maihar *gharana*, "he represents the global Bengali and makes all Bengalis very proud, even if they don't all listen to classical music. Here is someone who gives us a cultural identity in the world. Satyajit Ray and Ravi Shankar, these two—Bengalis consider them their prize possessions."[33]

In two Bengali films that Ravi made in 1958, Salil Sen's *Nagini Kanyar Kahini* and Tapan Sinha's follow-up, *Kalamati*, Ravi returned to writing songs—for the first time since *Neecha Nagar*—as well as background music. This pattern continued with *Anuradha*, a Hindi film made in Bombay. This was a loose adaptation of *Madame Bovary*, starring Leela Naidu, a first-time actress whom Ravi himself had recommended to director Hrishikesh Mukherjee. In Hindi-speaking India this film's music is perhaps even better known than the score of the *Apu Trilogy*. Ravi provided six songs, one of them sung by Manna

Dey and the other five by Lata Mangeshkar, whose voice, spanning an astonishing range with tonal precision and melodic versatility, has come to epitomize the Bollywood sound. In the studio Ravi was meticulous in his instructions to her. "He would sing the songs himself to make me understand what exactly he expected out of me," she recalled. "Very few people know that he was a good singer, too."[34]

All six songs had words by Shailendra, Ravi's favorite lyricist. What also distinguishes them is that Ravi rooted them all in classical music. The title song, *Sanwarey Sanwarey*, is written in *Raga Sindhu Bhairavi* and features classical elements such as the opening use of the sarangi, the *teental* rhythm and the *sawal–jawab* structure, with Lata's voice being answered by the strings. Strip away the lush orchestration and it is essentially a *thumri* composition.[35] Ravi's deep relish for complex rhythm is also evident in the effervescent love song *Jaane Kaise Sapnon Mein*, based on his own *Raga Tilak Shyam*. Two of the songs were rewrites from his recent Bengali films with new Hindi lyrics, including his favorite, *Kaise Din Beete Kaise Beeti* (in *Manj Khamaj*), and *Haye Re Woh Din*, in which the classical substructure is clear in the use of *Janasanmodini*, another of his own *ragas*, and the *rupaktal* rhythmic cycle.

When *Anuradha* was released in September 1960 it was a substantial hit. Tagged "the big show that draws big crowds," it ran for 14 weeks in Bombay. On its release, Ravi had mixed feelings about it, but in Calcutta he arranged a private screening and was pleased to report that "everybody liked it—even I liked it better."[36] Its extended run in theaters was particularly impressive given it was competing with the phenomenon of *Mughal-e-Azam*, released a month earlier, which (adjusted for inflation) is still thought to be the highest-grossing movie ever in the Indian domestic market. *Anuradha* also beat *Mughal-e-Azam* to the best feature film of the year at the National Film Awards, the fourth of Ravi's such triumphs after *Pather Panchali*, *Kabuliwala* and *The World of Apu*. In cinema his stock was soaring. *Cine Advance* declared, "The modern composer whose music, in its complete alliance with classical tunes, can be described as suitable for any film, is that celebrated international figure Ravi Shankar."[37]

There were several reports that Ravi was being considered as the lead actor in a Bombay film about a sitar player—"if negotiations between him and producer Vasant Joglekar reach a successful conclusion."[38] Playing opposite him, the speculation went, would be either Meena Kumari or Lata Mangeshkar. If Ravi and Lata teamed up as a screen couple, reckoned one breathless account, it might be "the biggest ever scoop in the annals of our screen history."[39] Ravi confirmed in June 1960 that he was contemplating the film, but the flurry of activity in the gossip columns has the ring of a producer testing the market. A year later there was talk that Ravi was planning to produce his own film about a sitar player, based on his own life. His brother Rajendra would write the script, either Utpal Dutt or Ashit Sen would be engaged as director, and the stars would include Supriya Choudhury and the south Indian dancer L. Vijayalakshmi.[40] Neither project seems to have been pursued. What does emerge from this fog of rumor is the fact that Ravi was star material.

If there was any danger of Ravi being sucked too deep into the Bombay film world, he was cured of the temptation by his experience with Trilok Jetly's *Go-daan*. For this he again wrote songs based on classical music, albeit with folklike elements from rural Uttar Pradesh, where Premchand's famous story was set. They were performed by a forty-piece orchestra, including local folk instruments, and a stellar lineup of playback singers—this time not only Lata Mangeshkar and Manna Dey, but also Asha Bhosle, Geeta Dutt, Mohammed Rafi and Mukesh. Production dragged on and Ravi lost faith in the director, who did not seem to know what he wanted. Ravi's involvement was first announced in 1959, but, after initial recordings in 1961, he did not finally finish the music until August 1963. The music is excellent, with highlights including *Janam Liyo Lalna*, sung by Asha Bhosle, the equally talented sister of Lata Mangeshkar. Released at the end of 1963, the film sank almost without trace.

Through the early 1960s Ravi continued to work regularly on films in Calcutta. There was Ashit Sen's *Swayambara*, which features the gorgeous *Prithibité Jara Konodino*, sung by Hemant Kumar. There were two more films by Utpal Dutt, *Ghoom Bhangar Gaan* and *Phagun Ashbe Phire*; on the latter Ravi was credited as a producer as well. He also provided the music for a handful of documentaries in Bombay, notably Serbjeet Singh's docudrama *The Avalanche*, which was shot at 16,000 feet in the Himalayan mountains at Kullu, with narration by India's iconic broadcaster Melville de Mellow. It won best feature film in English at the National Film Awards in 1964.

But Ravi was coming to the end of his prolific decade in Indian cinema. The results had often been outstanding, but at the time he felt ambivalent about the process. Sometimes, for no apparent fault of the music, a film was a failure. At other times films for which he had recorded the music were never finished because of financial problems. More than once a director added new scenes after the final soundtrack session and redeployed Ravi's background music in ways Ravi was unhappy with, but critics blamed him for the results. Increasingly the Indian film industry frustrated him, and with so many opportunities elsewhere—including more attractive offers from foreign filmmakers—he did not need to rely on it. In later years he could be withering about mainstream Indian films, lamenting the trend for "shallow, hybrid, unreal monstrosities," especially in Hindi cinema.[41]

In 1965 he announced that in future he would not work on any more films unless they were "something special."[42] After Purnendu Patri's *Swapno Niye* in 1966, he never recorded another soundtrack in Calcutta. A threshold was crossed: by then he had been music director on seventeen films in India and three overseas. After *Swapno Niye* he made just two more Indian films (and one of those was recorded in Paris) and ten overseas.

8

GOING SOLO

I have been thrashed and hammered with one failure
after another, and it has been a lot of working and toiling
and I have advanced at the pace of a turtle toward
the great ideal—which is yet so so far!

RAVI SHANKAR[1]

The telegrams forwarded by Narayana Menon brought exciting news: "We are most anxious invite Ravi Shankar plus drummer and one or two other musicians of his choice to formal launching April 19 when Indian ambassador Chester Bowles and I will introduce them."[2] It was 1955 and Yehudi Menuhin was inviting Ravi to New York to appear in the same festival that was staging *Pather Panchali*'s world premiere. There Ravi could perform not only at the Museum of Modern Art, but also on *Omnibus*, CBS's network TV arts show hosted by Alistair Cooke. It was all arranged. No Indian musician had received such an invitation before. "Ideal opportunities. Urge immediate action," cabled Yehudi.[3]

Ravi was desperate to accept. AIR granted him the necessary leave, but there was also a financial issue. The Museum of Modern Art had offered to pay subsistence expenses in New York, while the Ford Foundation, which underwrote *Omnibus*, was contributing $500 "pocket money" each to Ravi and the dancer Shanta Rao, who was also invited, but they would cover only return flights between London and New York. So Narayana Menon, now the deputy director of AIR, immediately wrote to Indira Gandhi, asking the government to pay for six artists to fly from Delhi to London with Air India.

And yet, despite these barriers being cleared, Ravi turned down the invitation. On March 18 he wrote to his station director to explain that, apparently with appalling timing, he had been prevented from going by serious illness:

> As you are aware, I was recently operated upon for appendicitis which has left me very weak. In view of the rare opportunity this offer provided, I, however, consulted my physician in the hope that if he allows I could undertake the journey. But my physician has very strongly advised me against any such exertion under my present conditions. I, therefore, regret very much my inability to avail of this opportunity now.[4]

This was a lie. Ravi was not ill. Rather, his resolve had faltered due to the growing crisis at home.

"Two persons sometimes don't match. It is very simple and happens all the time."[5] This verdict, perhaps the wisest take on Ravi's marriage to Annapurna, was delivered years later by her second husband, Rooshikumar Pandya. Ravi was the nation's only classical musician to become as famous as a film star, and the marriage has fascinated India for decades. As Partha Bose says, "People have not bothered about the personal lives of other comparable musicians, but in the case of Ravi Shankar each person could write a kind of a biography. They do what we musicians call *upaj*—coloring the melody with improvisations."

As Ravi said himself, with inimitable phrasing, "A marriage is a thing that no one can say; when it doesn't work, it doesn't work."[6] His own marriage had not been working for years. As a professional musician, gregarious and workaholic by nature, he was often away from Annapurna, and after the relationship's early peak of intense passion, they had become more distant and fractious with each other over time. He was still channeling Baba's puritanical streak, and he used to dread getting close to female singers, but Annapurna continued to suspect him of having affairs. In the rare public comments she later made (either personally or through disciples), she blamed the deterioration of the marriage on two things: musical tensions and other women.

Annapurna was by all accounts a superb musician, and an influential teacher revered by her brilliant disciples. Ravi maintained that she was the best performer of all on surbahar.[7] In contrast to his enormous body of work, there is sadly very little available by which to assess her as a musician. There are no official recordings of her music, and on the internet only three *ragas* by her: two solos and one live duet with Ravi, all muddy in sound quality. She plays the *alap* divinely, and some fast *jhala* passages, but none of the recordings feature tabla accompaniment, so there is no opportunity to assess her rhythmic skills and mastery of *tala*. Her musical reclusiveness was her choice. There are many ways to serve the goddess of music: Ravi was a public evangelist, while Annapurna chose to teach and play privately. The consequential shroud of mystery around her has not harmed her standing. That she left so few traces has encouraged the sense that she was a hidden genius—or perhaps a suppressed one.

In her entire life Annapurna played public recitals only on about ten occasions, most of them *jugalbandis* with Ravi. They first performed together in Bombay, about three times for music circles in 1947–8, and continued sporadically in Delhi, including at least once for Jhankar. He said he encouraged her to play live, but she did not want to perform solo, so he agreed to join her in surbahar duets. "She was very nervous by nature to play," he said. "She was admired very much, which was very good, and we had wonderful duets. But she didn't really want to perform. It was something to do also with Baba— he was not very happy with her playing."[8] Baba always said music was sacred, and not something to be sold, and she accepted this literally. "I did not enjoy performing," she said in 2010. "For me music has always been my offering to God."[9]

Rumors have circulated for years that Ravi became jealous of the acclaim Annapurna received when they performed their duets. She revived the allegation in an interview after his death. "Panditji was not happy, as I received more appreciation than he did from both the audience and the critics whenever we performed together in the

1950s. And that had a negative impact on our marriage," she said.[10] In some versions of the rumors, Ravi is said to have made her swear an oath never to play live again. She refuted that charge herself, but she added, "Though he never categorically stopped me from performing in public, he made it clear in several ways that he wasn't happy with the fact that I was drawing more applause. I was an introvert, more of a family person. I was keener to save the marriage than to earn name and fame."[11] The tragic precedent of her older sister Jahanara conditioned her to see music as a potential cause of marital conflict, and ultimately she did give up performing live, although not yet.

Reconstructing what happened at their few concerts is difficult, not least because reviews, with one exception, do not seem to have survived. Certainly, Ravi rejected strongly the notion that he felt threatened by her prowess, or that he wanted her to give up playing. If she later renounced live performance because she thought it would save their marriage, it was nothing to do with him, he asserted. It was her decision alone, perhaps encouraged by her father. Moreover, it made no difference to the marriage. By the time she ceased performing it was almost certainly too late to save it anyway. Long after their eventual divorce Ravi was still publicly urging her to play live: "It is of her own will that she has stopped. This is very sad because she is a fantastic musician."[12] According to him, what brought about the crisis in his marriage had nothing to do with music at all.

He was adamant, too, that it was not provoked by *him* having an affair. Feeling torn by his duty of loyalty to his *guru*, he never publicly elaborated what really happened, although he did discuss it privately.[13] Eventually he went on the record in 2005, during an interview that has never before been published:

> For all those years I controlled myself. I had a few light flirtations—
> that I admit—but I really controlled myself. And then I found
> out after a few years that she had an affair with one of my students.
> That was something which was so shocking to me. After I had

seen what happened with my student, and a few other incidents, I
let myself go. Whenever I had a chance, here and there, an affair.
Casual, nothing serious, but I didn't care any more.[14]

He did not say when he discovered Annapurna's affair, but it was
probably in early 1954, when he went through the crisis that he could
not discuss in writing with Harihar Rao. Divorce seemed to be out
of the question: this was his *guru*'s daughter, after all. But the way he
reacted instead, by embarking on his own extramarital relationships,
served only to intensify the dysfunction in their marriage.

By March 1955 they had been married for nearly fourteen years. The
relationship was now in a deep crisis, and Annapurna would not countenance Ravi spending at least two months in New York. "I was having
such restrictions from the home front," he later wrote, "and with these
tensions I decided not to go. However, I could not tell this to anyone;
it would be such a stupid reason to have to give, that family pressure
was the reason." Hence the story he put out—that he was ill.[15] Ironically one of their rare duets took place at the Constitution Club in Delhi
on March 30, exactly when he should have been flying to New York.

Ravi wrote to Yehudi Menuhin suggesting that his best replacement
was Ali Akbar on sarod. Yehudi, still a newcomer to Indian classical
music, cabled back, "Who is Ali Akbar Khan, and what is sarod?"[16]

Unlike Ravi, Ali Akbar was reluctant to go to America. He did not
have Ravi's gifts as a proselytizer. It had been hard enough to establish an audience for his recitals in Bombay, where the sarod had not
previously been a popular instrument, and he feared that foreigners
would be unmoved by it. "My friends pushed me more or less through
customs and onto the plane," he admitted.[17]

He need not have worried. He arrived in New York on April 1, along
with Chatur Lal. Together they made a strong impression accompanying Shanta Rao's dance on *Omnibus*, gave two compelling recitals at
the museum and recorded an album for Angel Records, *Music of India:*

Morning and Evening Ragas. This was the first long-playing record of Indian classical music issued anywhere in the world. Yehudi, once he had heard Ali Akbar play, acclaimed him as "an absolute genius...the greatest musician in the world," and introduced the pair before their appearances on television, stage and vinyl, and in a *New York Times* article.[18] They stayed on for six weeks in New York and Washington, and on their way home they stopped in London, Paris and Brussels to give further recitals and talks. Not everything went smoothly—Paris was an "unhappy experience" because of unresponsive audiences—but overall the *Times of India* hailed the tour as an "astonishing success."[19]

Ravi's music was not completely absent from New York because of the *Pather Panchali* screenings. Nevertheless, he felt intense frustration at missing out on a tour that should have been his breakthrough in the West. As news filtered back, he was happy at the plaudits for Ali Akbar and Indian classical music, but it would have been hard for him not to imagine Yehudi extolling him, rather than his brother-in-law, as the greatest musician in the world.

On Ali Akbar's return in June, he, Ravi and Chatur Lal began making plans for another tour of America, this time as a trio.[20] Something had changed with regard to Annapurna. Perhaps she had given her assent this time because her brother was also going, or perhaps it no longer mattered to Ravi whether she approved or not. By late August Ravi had secured or saved up the funds necessary for their international travel, and Yehudi was showing interest in the plan, so Ravi asked him for his "frank and personal advice" as to the feasibility of arranging "a series of regular concerts of either duets or solos in concert halls or other suitable places in big cities like New York, Boston, Chicago, Philadelphia, etc.," along with American television and radio broadcasts and lecture-demonstrations. After his disappointment in London, he did not want to leave things to chance. He envisaged leaving India by the end of December 1955.[21]

Separately he made a breakthrough in the pursuit of European dates. Through his friend Jamshed Narielwala, a trusted lieutenant of the Tata family, he made contact with an agent in London. John Coast, the European representative of Columbia Artists Management, had managed Shanta Rao on her UK visit in June and knew of Ravi by reputation. Narielwala wrote to Coast on August 30 inquiring about the possibility of a month-long tour of Britain and Europe by the trio. Ravi was presented as its leader.[22]

Coast was an Englishman with an astonishing history. During the "phoney war" of 1939–40 he had been on MI5's watch list as a fascist sympathizer and virulent anti-Semite, and was on the fringes of a Nazi spy ring. But the war cured him of his far-right politics. After enlisting in the Coldstream Guards, he was captured by Japanese forces at the fall of Singapore and became a prisoner on the notorious Burma railway, an experience he recounted after the war in a bestselling book, *Railroad of Death*. He then joined the Indonesian fight for independence from the Dutch, married a Javanese woman, settled for a while in Bali, and began his career as an impresario by taking a troupe of Balinese dancers and musicians on tour to the West in 1952–3. It seems unlikely that any of the artists he represented would have been aware of his fascist phase, which has only recently been revealed.[23] His later—Jewish—partner Laura Rosenberg says the war brought about a "180-degree change" in his beliefs.[24] Subsequently David Attenborough, inspired by Coast's book *Dancing Out of Bali*, would collaborate with him on television films about Balinese culture, and his respect for Coast persists to this day.[25]

Coast, who was in the process of setting up his own agency, sent a proposal for a tour of Britain, based around one television and three radio programs, two or three concerts in London and one in Oxford. He was cautious about prospects across the Channel, where there was little interest from the commercial sector. Paris would be almost impossible, he advised. He envisaged total earnings of between £250 and £750, less his commission.[26] Initially Ravi would not commit to Coast until Yehudi had confirmed a U.S. tour, which was his priority. Yet at the end of November, without anything firm from

America, he accepted Coast's terms.[27] He knew that he was "taking a big risk with this adventure."[28] He seems in fact to have been Coast's first client as an independent agent—and the first of a distinguished list. Coast would go on to represent Mario Lanza, Luciano Pavarotti and José Carreras, and was the first person to present Bob Dylan in London.[29]

The target departure date had already slipped—Ravi was now thinking of reaching England in late March or April—and would shift again. But in the meantime there were other encounters with Western artists in India that encouraged him in his plans. In December he met Benjamin Britten in Delhi. At forty-two, Britten was now the leading British composer of his era. This was his first opportunity to explore Indian music since being thrown into raptures by watching Uday's troupe two decades earlier. It was his first visit to Asia, and it proved seminal for him: the music of India, Indonesia and Japan, all of which he visited on this trip, would influence his later compositions.[30]

Britten was traveling with Peter Pears, his partner in life and music, and they gave recitals in Bombay, Delhi and Calcutta. On December 21 the pair lunched in Delhi with Nehru and Indira Gandhi. The next day they were given an introduction to Indian music by Ravi at Broadcasting House. It was common for visitors to AIR to watch the staff artists at work, and by then Ravi was the star attraction, a situation that sometimes made him feel "like a freak."[31] First Britten and Pears heard Vadya Vrinda, but the orchestra left Britten lukewarm.[32] Ravi then gave a brief tutorial on Indian music and a private sitar recital, accompanied by tabla and two tanpuras. The visitors were bowled over. Pears wrote in his diary that Ravi was "the real thing" and "a wonderful virtuoso," and praised the musicians' "unbelievable skill & invention."[33] Britten was effusive too: "We have heard lovely & exciting music. I was pleasantly surprised that with only a little instruction, we were able to get so much from it."[34]

A day later, they wrote a joint letter home:

Yesterday we had our first real taste of Indian music, & it was tremendously fascinating. We had the luck to hear one of the best living performers (composer too), & he played in a small room to us alone...Like everything they do it seemed much more relaxed & spontaneous than what we do, & the reactions of the other musicians sitting around was really orgiastic. Wonderful sounds, intellectually complicated & controlled. By jove, the clever Indian is a brilliant creature—one feels like a bit of Yorkshire Pudd. in comparison.[35]

For Ravi, one encounter now followed another. In Calcutta he was briefly introduced to Alfred Hitchcock, who was on his own Asian tour, promoting his film *The Trouble with Harry*. In April 1956, on a concert visit to Karachi, Ravi and Chatur Lal met the jazz trumpeter Dizzy Gillespie and his band, who were on a tour organized by the U.S. State Department. Gillespie's musical director was the twenty-three-year-old Quincy Jones, who befriended Ravi and was inspired to study Indian classical music.[36]

Ravi also met the French photographer Marc Riboud, who was based in Calcutta while he roamed the country in an old Land Rover. They became lifelong friends.[37] This was early in Riboud's career, but some of his most memorable images come from the year he spent in India, including an evocative portrait of Ravi pensively tuning his sitar, dressed in a saintly white *kurta–pajama* and waistcoat. Ravi had earlier got to know Marc's older brother Jean, a leftist industrialist and fervent Indophile. The Riboud family was rich and well connected. Jean was married to a Bengali, Krishna Roy, a great-niece of Rabindranath Tagore. Ali Akbar had stayed with Jean and Krishna in their Paris home the previous summer.

Meanwhile, Ravi had come to the attention of the London *Times* for the first time as a solo musician. At the end of 1955 its correspondent attended his New Year's Eve recital at the Madras Music Academy. The resulting review concentrated on the performance of Ravi's

AIR orchestra, admiring in particular the "astonishing left-hand versatility" of the violinists, but it also featured the briefest coverage of a separate recital: "A duet on two surbahars, an instrument of the vina type now in danger of dying out, was given by Ravi Shankar and his talented wife Annapurna."[38]

The writer Sakuntala Narasimhan, who was also present, recalled:

> The music they made together! It unzipped my soul and poured honey to overflowing. Husband and wife challenged each other to greater heights of speed and showmanship. He played and she returned it, note for note, in a particularly racy passage. He threw up his hands in a gesture of mock defeat, smiling broadly, and the gathering broke out in delirious applause.[39]

This would have been the last time the couple performed live together.

In the early hours of January 17, 1956 there was what Ravi described as a "serious breakdown" in the marriage.[40] Through some of his students he had come to hear that Annapurna was becoming close to one of his friends, Biman Ghosh of HMV India. How he chose to address this was an indication that the feud had become petty and self-destructive. "By that time I wanted to really catch her," he said in 2005.[41] So, with the help of his friend Ashwini Kumar, he devised an elaborate plan. Kumar, as well as organizing one of India's biggest classical music festivals, Harballabh in the city of Jalandhar, was director general of the Border Police Force. He proudly boasted of being wounded seventeen times in shoot-outs with bandits, and Ravi loved listening to his stories.[42]

Ravi was leaving for a concert in Patna and he suspected Ghosh would visit Annapurna in his absence. He left Amiya Dasgupta in charge. At about one o'clock in the morning Ghosh was spotted by some servants entering by the back door and going to Annapurna's room. The plan was set in motion by Dasgupta. Kumar's police officers burst in with torches and found Ghosh in the bedroom. According to Ravi, "They were on the bed, not doing anything really." But the circumstantial evidence was damning.[43] The following day Dasgupta sent a telegram to Harihar Rao, who was in his family's home town of Mangalore: "Biman caught red-handed. Come imdtly."[44]

Annapurna, who must have been horrified by the involvement of the police in a marital dispute, later dismissed it as a "cooked-up scandal" devised by her husband to turn people against her.[45] Whatever had actually happened, Ghosh's role resembles that of a pawn in the endgame between a feuding couple, unwittingly bringing matters to a head. It is a mark of Ravi's double standards in this episode that his bond with Ghosh seems to have been little affected; they remained friends for decades.

The destructive behavior then spiraled further out of control. First Ravi traveled to Maihar and informed Baba of what had just happened:

I was so mad at that time really. I did the wrong thing, maybe— I just told him, "This is it, you do the judgment. This is what has happened. I don't pretend to be a saint." I wanted him to tell me what to do. He was so angry, he said, "Just go and kill her, I don't want to see her face any more!"[46]

In turn, Annapurna went to see her father along with her sister-in-law Zubeida, the first wife of Ali Akbar (who had by now taken a second wife, Rajdulari). "That's when they also made a plan," said Ravi.

Ali Akbar used to stay once or twice a year. I used to buy for him small bottles of brandy, whisky…I drank very little. But she had collected all these empty bottles, and they took all these bottles and everything to Baba—Zubeida and her—and told him how bad I have been all these years, I have been womanizing and drinking—holding the bottles. And then—he was like a child— now I was the devil, of course.[47]

Annapurna moved out of the family home at Ashoka Road and went to Calcutta to stay with her brother, who, fresh from his American triumph, was opening a music school there. On April 14, as part of an all-night program to inaugurate the school, she gave a solo performance at the Ranji Stadium (today better known as Eden Gardens, India's largest cricket ground). This was probably the last concert she ever gave. She started teaching music at the new Ali Akbar College of Music. Shubho, aged fourteen, remained in Delhi, where he was attending the Modern School, but he moved in with his uncle Debendra and aunt Krishna, since his father was away so frequently, and he subsequently boarded in the school's hostel for pupils. At this point Ravi believed the marriage was probably over. Alone now in Delhi, he tried to be philosophical. "What happens has to happen—I have ceased to worry," he wrote to Harihar Rao.[48]

The events of January 1956 were not the cause of the marriage breakup; rather, they marked the sad implosion of a relationship that was already collapsing. Yet their rancorous nature probably prevented any chance of a true reconciliation later on. The split had an immediate and traumatic effect on the whole family, in different ways. It further encouraged Annapurna's inclination toward solitude. Shubho was torn between his riven parents, but living with neither of them.

As for Ravi, he was left disillusioned with the whole concept of marriage. "That was the horrible period in my life, and it shook me up so much. I didn't care any more, as far as women or sex was concerned. I really went wild for a few years," he said.[49] Separated from Annapurna, and no longer observing self-imposed restraint, he pursued instead what he called a "butterfly lifestyle," which would characterize his private life for the next three decades. At first it was as if he was eighteen again: multiple relationships, all passion, no commitment.[50]

Relations with Baba had been badly damaged. "He became mad with rage, cursing me," recalled Ravi.[51] At length he tried to clear the air with a long discussion. "It was so pathetic, he and myself both cried so much," Ravi wrote on March 8. At this meeting Baba gave permission for Ravi to play a duet with Ali Akbar for the Jhankar Music Circle in Delhi, a positive sign. But Ravi was conscious that his *guru*'s mind could be changed once more when he next spoke to Annapurna. "He'll again be influenced if he goes to Cal[cutta]," he wrote. As he later reflected, "Baba was always believing the latest bulletin."[52]

Ravi now turned with renewed impetus to his travel plans. Ali Akbar had withdrawn from the touring party; he had a new school to run, and relations with Ravi had been strained by the marital split. Chatur Lal, though, remained committed to the tour. In April Ravi confirmed to John Coast that they would arrive in London in October, and then he took the plunge and gave his notice to AIR. In his resignation letter he explained that he had film soundtracks, concerts and an overseas trip in the offing, and he knew it would be hard to obtain sufficient leave, so he had decided to relinquish his staff position. However, he reassured his employer, "I will always be too happy to serve the AIR through casual contracts for solo programs, composing and conducting orchestras, or for producing such other musical productions, as I intend making Delhi as my headquarters."[53] He marked his leaving day, July 15, by giving a sitar recital for the nation, his last broadcast on AIR for more than a year.[54] His replacement as composer–conductor of Vadya Vrinda was the flutist Pannalal Ghosh, a fellow disciple of Baba.

Resigning was a risky career move. He was giving up a prestigious and secure government job, and the Ashoka Road residence that came with it, for a foreign tour, the outcome of which could not be predicted. But there was a missionary in him and the idea of taking Indian music to the West was irresistible. Moreover, he had the sense that there would be diminishing returns from remaining at AIR. His natural restlessness resurfaced. The seven years he worked there were the longest that he ever held any job.

Ravi understood about news management. When his resignation was revealed in the *Times of India*, it was tagged onto an announcement of his upcoming tour, which at this stage comprised concerts in

England, France, Germany, the Netherlands and Italy. The USA was still not confirmed.[55] In August Coast wrote to EMI in London suggesting they record an LP by Ravi when he arrived, to follow up on Ali Akbar's release on Angel Records, which was part of EMI's global empire.[56] Meanwhile, Yehudi Menuhin supplied a stirring endorsement to use in publicity, declaring, "I am indebted to him for some of the most inspiring moments I have ever lived in music."[57]

On hearing the news that Ravi was leaving AIR, Satyajit Ray encouraged him to relocate from Delhi to Calcutta.[58] But in the time left before departure Ravi had other priorities. He recorded the soundtracks to *Aparajito* and *Kabuliwala* and made the trip to Afghanistan. During September, he played concerts in Calcutta, Bangalore, Hyderabad and Bombay. *Pather Panchali* won its National Film Award and *Aparajito* was released.

At a press conference in Bombay, Ravi was at last able to confirm that—after six weeks in England—he would be going on to America. He had been invited to New York for the first meeting of the planning board for the East–West Music Encounter, an international festival cum conference that would take place later in Tokyo. This was the brainchild of Nicolas Nabokov, Secretary General of the Paris-based Congress for Cultural Freedom. Nabokov, cousin of the novelist Vladimir, was enthusiastic about Indian classical music and had probably first met Ravi during his visit to India in late 1954. Others on the board included the American composers William Schuman and Virgil Thomson; the invitation was a mark of Ravi's growing international standing. After America he would return to Europe for a tour of the continent. He would be away for between three and a half and six months.[59]

After a farewell appearance in Delhi on October 4 in front of many friends and some family, Ravi set off the next day for Bombay, where he caught a flight to Paris.[60] It had been a traumatic year, but a defining one too. Three developments in the previous twelve months would shape much of the rest of his life. After the acrimonious split with his wife, he felt his marriage was over and had embraced a foot-loose approach to relationships with women. He had resigned his job at AIR, opting to survive on his own freelance earnings. And he had decided to take Indian music to new worlds. He was going solo.

III
WANDERING STAR
1956–1965

New York, 1957, on his first solo tour—his first time back in America since 1938

9

LIKE DRIVING THROUGH A MIST

The finger dexterity of the two men is so uniformly miraculous
that it was necessary to watch them closely to assure oneself
that several other instrumentalists were not playing also.
NEW YORK HERALD TRIBUNE[1]

Late on Saturday, October 6, 1956, Ravi descended the aircraft steps
at London Airport after an interminable journey from Bombay. In his
hand, wrapped in a double-layer bag of quilted silk and waterproof
fabric, was his Kanai Lal sitar. It was too delicate and important to
trust to the hold. When traveling by plane or train he liked to book
an extra seat for the instrument under the name of "Mr. Sitar."

Normally the most resilient of travelers, Ravi arrived in a bad
mood. The propeller-driven Lockheed Constellation had made stop-
overs in Cairo, Athens, Rome and Geneva, before reaching Paris after
twenty-six hours, where he had to change planes for London. There
had been delays in Paris, and poor service throughout the flight. He
vowed never to travel TWA again. And he held no great affection for
his destination—his memories of pre-war London were of a grimy,
foggy, cold and depressing city in which Indians did not feel safe.

But this time the British capital lifted his spirits. He admired the
cosmopolitan restaurants and the modernist architecture that had
sprung up post-war. He noted the much improved air quality; it had
reached its nadir with the deadly Great Smog of four years earlier, but
the Clean Air Act had come into force that summer. "London is good
and peaceful!" he wrote home. "Really I give the first prize to this city
for all the good points which a big city should have—and with a special
ref to the wonderful system and discipline here!"[2] Thereafter, he often
said that—weather apart—London was his favorite city in the world.

Traveling with him was Chatur Lal. His young protégé would never quite attain the highest grade of tabla players (tragically, he died young), but he was a real asset in popularizing Indian music abroad. His natural exuberance was so infectious that, according to one critic, he looked "as though he might roll into a ball and bounce up to the ceiling any moment." The same writer noted Ravi's "elegant, refined beauty"; he and Chatur Lal made a handsome, effervescent duo.[3] The prim, dependable Nodu Mullick, a brilliant craftsman who joined the tour to provide the tanpura drone and maintain Ravi's sitar, followed four weeks later, once he had received his visa. In the meantime the tanpura was played in concerts by Prodyot Sen, a London-based Bengali who became a close friend.

At Ravi's debut recital, on October 12 at Friends House, the Quaker center on Euston Road, he was introduced by Yehudi Menuhin. But it was the audience at the second concert, five days later at the same venue, that gave the first inkling of the impact Ravi was making. Among those present was Krishna Menon, Nehru's sharp-elbowed global spokesman, who was at that moment busy trying to defuse the Suez crisis. He had recently founded the India Arts Society, which was promoting this first pair of concerts. Several more of Britain's classical music elite turned out, including Ravi's new friends Benjamin Britten and Peter Pears. It was Pears who introduced him from the stage this time. Also attending were Imogen Holst, who was now an artistic director at Britten's Aldeburgh Festival; Sir Steuart Wilson, a former music administrator at the BBC and the Royal Opera House; and George Lascelles, the 7th Earl of Harewood, along with his first wife, the pianist Marion Stein.

Of these, Lord Harewood was to prove the most important for Ravi's early solo career in Britain. He was a first cousin of the Queen, and from a young age had demonstrated an ear for music uncommon in the British royal family. "It's very odd about George and music," the Duke of Windsor once remarked of him. "His parents were quite normal." As a prisoner of war in Colditz, he had passed his time studying

Grove's Dictionary of Music, reaching as far as the letter T.[4] In 1956 he was working as a senior administrator at the Royal Opera House, while also serving as president of the Aldeburgh Festival. He and Marion were close to Britten, who had invited them that evening at Friends House for their first taste of Indian music, which soon became "little short of a passion," as Harewood put it.

> I had never thought much about India before, but Ben had recently been there and what interested Ben tended to interest me. I found an immediate fascination in the new sounds and rhythms and shapes—the shapes far harder to get hold of than the colors or the rhythmic patterns—and soon started to fall under their spell.[5]

Ravi made friends with the Harewoods and became a regular visitor to their London home in Orme Square, where he gave private recitals. So, after his first pair of concerts in the UK, he already had the support of three of the most significant figures in British classical music: Yehudi Menuhin, Benjamin Britten and Lord Harewood.

There were other London recitals at the Imperial Institute, Conway Hall and Holborn Hall, and Ravi played for the student Majlis Society in Oxford, and at the Union Debating Chamber in Cambridge. He also rekindled happy memories at Dartington Hall. These were small venues, each with a capacity of a few hundred, but even so full houses were a rarity. Some of these concerts were promoted by the Asian Music Circle, a small, impecunious organization that helped introduce Indian performing arts to the UK. Its key figure was Ayana Deva Angadi, who ran it from his north London home. He was a charismatic amateur with a talent for persuasion who had managed to rope in Yehudi as president and, for a short while, Britten as vice-president. Encouraged by Yehudi, he and his wife Patricia would also help to popularize yoga: B. K. S. Iyengar became their house guest and gave his first classes in England to a handful of musicians in their living room and garden, the teenaged Jacqueline du Pré among them. Patricia, who was an amateur artist, painted a portrait of Ravi.

Ravi was impressed by John Coast's gentlemanly efficiency, but earnings were often low, and the half-empty halls reminded Ravi of his times of struggle in India a decade before. Coast described the venues as "scruffy little clubs and obscure halls."[6] The British still had little awareness of Indian music, especially outside London. "It took a long time for me to break through in the regions of Britain, much longer than in any other country," Ravi recalled.[7] Angadi, for his part, was good at attracting attention but poor at managing it, according to his son Shankara. Some reports suggest that half the audiences were from the local Indian diaspora, although Shankara Angadi's memory is that the community was largely uninterested: "It was always one of our family jokes: the only Indians who went to Asian Music Circle concerts tended to be trying to impress their white girlfriends."[8]

The city that disappointed Ravi most was Paris, where he spent the first week of November staying with Jean and Krishna Riboud in the Latin Quarter. He played twice at the Musée Guimet, the museum of Asian art, but the money was poor again, and the audience, of which he had high hopes, exhibited "a hard coldness, except on the part of a very few."[9]

Back in London, he was becoming a regular at the BBC's various studios—Maida Vale, Bush House, Oxford Street and Lime Grove. There were three sessions on BBC Radio's Third Programme and three more on its overseas services, and he was commissioned to record a signature tune for its Bengali station (presumably the theme that had been mooted two years earlier). He also made his first appearance on British television on the BBC's *Music for You*, presented by the conductor Eric Anderson. This was broadcast at 9:15 p.m. on a Wednesday night, significant exposure in an era when there were only two channels to choose from. For all this broadcast work, he was paid nearly £290 (worth over £7,000 in 2019), minus his agent's 10 percent and an unknown share for Chatur Lal, making the BBC probably his biggest single source of income on this UK tour.[10]

In letters home, his stress was on the upbeat: "All my progs have been successful till now by God's grace," he wrote on October 23. A fortnight later he was even more positive: "Future seems to look bright."[11] The tour was certainly giving a boost to his reputation back in India, where the BBC radio broadcasts could be heard. The verdict of the *Times of India*'s London correspondent, Stella Alexander, was that "Ravi Shankar is a brilliant performer and the sitar is a ravishing instrument." Comparing his concert to Ali Akbar's sarod recital the previous year, she wrote that the sarod was "an instrument which sounds austere and even harsh to Western ears. But the sitar presents no such difficulties with its liquid, running notes and enchanting harmonies."[12]

One of the reasons Ravi was gaining followers was his understanding of how he should tailor his recitals to appeal to this new audience. His youthful experiences on stage had impressed on him the importance of showmanship and stagecraft. As he later said, "I realize the reason for success is not just art, but it is presentation—the look, the atmosphere you create, and the vibration you create—that is equally responsible for making a successful artist."[13] In Britain, just as he had done in India, he aimed to establish a reverent atmosphere. Attention was paid to lighting, the musicians' entrances and exits, their clothes, the carpet they sat on, the backdrop, the burning of incense. In larger venues (although not in private homes) he required that the musicians perform on a raised platform. He insisted on there being no eating, drinking or smoking while he was playing.

In these initial tours abroad, he found it was much easier to foster concert decorum in his audiences than it had been in India, given the stronger tradition of formal concerts in the West. What these Europeans did need, however, was to be familiarized with Indian music and its customs. Confusion could arise, for instance, if Ravi shook his head while Chatur Lal was playing, or vice versa. Audiences often took this for a mark of reproach, when it in fact signified delight. Chatur Lal's occasional use of a small hammer to strike the drumskin mid-recital was sometimes misconstrued, too; this is how a tabla player adjusts the tuning, but one early reviewer even praised the syncopations created by his skillful use of the hammer. Soon, Ravi decided to avoid such misunderstandings by giving a short talk before each concert, explaining some fundamentals of Indian music and its performance rituals, demonstrating the instruments and introducing each chosen *raga* and *tala*. He was always conscious of the need to keep his remarks clear and concise. He asked his audience to relax, and to listen to him with their hearts rather than their heads.[14]

In India Ravi's recitals sometimes lasted for over five hours, but he knew that this would not work in Europe, so he aimed for the duration of a conventional Western classical concert, between two and two and a half hours. This set the pattern for most of his international career. In condensing his program he drew on sixteen years' experience of playing radio broadcasts in India, which typically lasted for under an hour. He also found that new audiences met with less of a cultural barrier when it came to appreciating the exhilarating drumming than they did with the sound of the sitar, so—as he had been doing in India—he gave the tabla a greater prominence than had traditionally been the case. There came a moment in most concerts when he put his sitar down and simply demonstrated the rhythmic cycle on his fingers while Chatur Lal played a solo.

On November 7 Ravi arrived at London's Abbey Road Studios, almost six years before the Beatles famously set foot in the building. He was there to record his first album, John Coast's approach to EMI having borne fruit. This was only the second time that Indian classical music had been recorded specifically for the LP format anywhere in the world, and the album title, *Music of India: Three Classical Ragas*, deliberately echoed that of Ali Akbar's earlier album.[15] The new format had space for about 25 minutes per side, compared with 4 minutes on 78 rpm discs, but Ravi's knack for condensing a program was still invaluable. The track selection is effectively an abbreviated version of one of his recitals. Side 1 is taken up with the evening *raga Jog*, which is elaborated at length through *alap*, *jor* and *jhala* phases, concluding with a *gat* improvisation in a *teental* rhythmic cycle (16 beats), which develops with a gathering sense of excitement through slow, medium and fast tempos. Side 2 contains two more *ragas*. First is the morning *raga Ahir Bhairav*, but this time, after a short *alap*, Ravi jumps straight into a *gat* in *rupaktal* (7 beats). This is followed by *Simhendra Madhyamam*, a Carnatic *raga* that Ravi performs in a *gat* alone, this time in *jhaptal* (10 beats). There is a carefully judged variety throughout, of *ragas*, moods, arrangements, rhythmic cycles and tempos—and, as so often throughout his career, a Carnatic *raga* is included.

Present at this session was a young EMI management trainee from India, whose Keralan parents were friends of Ravi in Delhi. His name was Bhaskar Menon. He went on to become one of the global music industry's great moguls, and by some serendipity this was his first day working at Abbey Road.[16]

Ravi wrote his own liner notes, introducing Indian music's history, its Carnatic and Hindustani incarnations, the instruments, *ragas* and *talas*. His reference point was Western classical music:

> For the better and finer enjoyment of Indian music, Western audiences should forget about harmony and counterpoint or the mixed tone colors which may be considered the prime essentials of a symphonic or similar work, and relax rather in the rich melody and rhythm, and with the exquisitely subtle inflections through which the *atmosphere* of a *raga* is built up.[17]

On November 18 Ravi's trio left for New York. This trip had been confirmed so late that Ravi and Chatur Lal had to apply for their U.S. visas in London rather than in Delhi, and when the papers arrived they initially covered "talks and business" only, because the reason for the visit was to attend the meeting with Nicolas Nabokov. Ravi wanted to play recitals too, so the visas had to be upgraded.[18] But at last he was returning to America. He had no idea who was ultimately behind this invitation. It was the CIA.

Ravi arrived at a pivotal moment for American society. The early signs of the momentous changes to come were in the air. The year 1956 saw Elvis Presley breaking through; as Ravi disembarked, "Love Me Tender" was number 1 in the Billboard Top 100, and the film of the same name headed the U.S. box office. That November the Supreme Court made its landmark ruling against racial segregation on the busses of Montgomery, Alabama, while in literature Allen Ginsberg's *Howl* was published. Meanwhile, the center of the Western art world had shifted from Paris to New York, thanks to the revolutionary paintings of Jackson Pollock, Mark Rothko and Willem de Kooning. Interest in foreign cultures had increased after 1945, following the return of vast numbers of GIs who had served overseas. Television and jet travel were also shrinking the world. Minds were being prized open, despite the efforts of many to snap them shut.

Nevertheless, most Americans had little or no knowledge of Indian arts. Ali Akbar's tour the year before was the only precedent for an Indian musician of the first rank performing as a soloist in the States. Records of Indian music were scarce too. The French musicologist Alain Daniélou's *Anthology of Indian Classical Music*, a triple-album UNESCO compilation, which included two tracks by Ravi, had been released in 1955, and there was also Ali Akbar's album. Otherwise the only records available were 78 rpm discs such as Columbia Records' catalog of "ethnic music" releases with distinctive green labels, or the Ethnic Folkways Library series, which compiled similarly brief recordings (with the artists often uncredited) from AIR. Ravi's London album *Three Classical Ragas* did not appear in America until May 1957. The new arrival was faced with an uphill task.

It was also a time of nerve-racking international tension. While Ravi had been in London, Soviet tanks had crushed the uprising in

Budapest, even as Britain, France and Israel were invading Egypt over control of the Suez Canal. President Eisenhower, who that same week was concluding his reelection campaign (he won by a landslide), managed to de-escalate the situation in Egypt, but this was one of the Cold War's most dangerous moments. It was on the very day Ravi left London for New York that Soviet leader Nikita Khrushchev notoriously declared to a roomful of Western diplomats in Moscow, "We will bury you!"

This was the backdrop to the meeting with Nicolas Nabokov. Nabokov was a minor composer whose real talent lay in cultivating elites. Igor Stravinsky nicknamed him "the culture generalissimo."[19] The East–West Music Encounter was one of many conferences that Nabokov organized during the 1950s and early 1960s through the Congress for Cultural Freedom, but there was more to them than musicology. The Congress was secretly and lavishly funded by the CIA. With offices in 35 countries, including a bureau in India, it was at the heart of what is now known as the Cultural Cold War. Because of its rivalry with the Soviet Union, America sought to counter communism's appeal to artists and intellectuals around the world by showcasing the creative benefits of liberal democracy. Its main focus was Western Europe, but its attention was turning to the new post-colonial nations. The CIA was a major player in this cultural battleground. There were other, more overt efforts to court India, including the State Department tours that brought Dizzy Gillespie, Martha Graham and Benny Goodman to Asia in 1955–6. Private organizations also played a part: the Ford Foundation had sponsored the Museum of Modern Art's Indian textiles exhibition, which was still touring nationwide.[20]

When the Congress's CIA funding was later exposed, there was widespread alarm because some artists found themselves wrongly suspected of being spies. Nabokov himself claimed ignorance of the source of the funds. Many critics have not believed him.[21] Others were pleasantly surprised: Yehudi Menuhin told Nabokov that his opinion of the CIA had gone up when he discovered it had been associating with "people like us."[22] Ravi surely had no idea then of the CIA's involvement, and there is no record of him commenting on it later. But the fact remains that it was a CIA-bankrolled project that brought him to America.

When Ravi reached New York he discovered that the meeting with Nabokov had been delayed because of the events in Hungary and Egypt. His focus turned to performing instead. He had no agent in America, but he arranged a number of concerts with some help from Ann and James Laughlin, a prominent couple on the Upper East Side arts scene. Ann Laughlin was a governor of the Museum of Modern Art and a trustee of the newly formed Asia Society. She had assisted with Ali Akbar's visit a year earlier, and it was she who had arranged Ravi's performance visa.[23]

Her husband's contribution was to provide Ravi with a grant through his company, Intercultural Publications.[24] James Laughlin was the founder of the literary publishing house New Directions. With Ford Foundation funding, he had set up Intercultural as a side project in order to publish *Perspectives USA*, a journal of American arts and letters that was another front in the Cultural Cold War. But Laughlin, like Nabokov, was genuinely fascinated by India. On his first trip there he met Alain Daniélou in Varanasi and would have become aware of Ravi. In 1953 Intercultural produced *Perspective of India*, the first of a series of supplements for *Atlantic Monthly* that gave Americans a flavor of high culture abroad.[25] Intercultural also funded an art exhibition in India. Sponsoring an Indian musician was a natural progression. There is no record of how much Laughlin gave Ravi, but he had a "president's discretionary fund" of about $5,000 per annum for small grants to needy artists.[26]

In New York Ravi stayed with friends, including the cinematographer Gopal Sanyal at 233 West 16th Street in Chelsea and Karuna Maitra on Riverside Drive. On his last visit in 1938 he had been captivated by the city, so he was thrilled to be back, although this time he was struck also by the dirt and the disarray. Surprising as it might sound today, he sensed its similarity to Calcutta, in that both were characterized by a chaotic, inventive energy.

His first performance was a private recital given to thank the Laughlins for their support. This was held on November 29 at the Manhattan apartment of Ann's parents, Stanley B. and Helen Lansdowne Resor.[27] James Laughlin had written to invite Tennessee Williams and his partner Frank Merlo: "This is really the way to hear them best, when they sit right on the floor in the middle of a small group, and you get right into the 'jam.'" He described Ravi and Chatur Lal's music as "a sort of mixture of quite intellectual chamber music and a jazz jam session. They start off rather formally on a *raga* and then it gets hotter and hotter and the rhythms are terrific. I think you would like it."[28]

A photograph shows the musicians gathered with their hosts at the Resors' apartment. The Laughlins occupy the center of the frame: Ann the picture of gracious ease, the lofty James leaning on her chairback with uxorious pride. Beyond them is the slight figure of Nodu Mullick, elegant in his Nehru coat and as usual retreating into the background. Chatur Lal sits on a settee in the foreground, for once not grinning at the camera. Ravi sits next to him, but all his attention is on an attractive, self-assured twenty-seven-year-old American woman at the far right. He grins at her conspiratorially; she leans back in her seat, ankles twisted together, returning his smile. She is Marilyn Silverstone. She was making her name as a photographer and was soon to become one of the first women elected to the elite Magnum agency. Here in New York, she took some fine portraits of Ravi, images with a serenity and grandeur to match his most soulful *alap*. Ravi soon started to use these photographs as his publicity stills, and one of them adorned the cover of his official retrospective box set forty years later. If these photographs are testimony to her rare talent, they also reflect her intimacy with her subject. She and Ravi began an affair.

A week later Ravi appeared at the Kaufmann Auditorium, part of the Young Men's Hebrew Association complex on the Upper East Side known today as the 92nd Street Y. Three years previously it was here that Dylan Thomas had staged the earliest performances of *Under Milk Wood*. Now, on December 6, it presented the U.S. public debut of Ravi Shankar. Santha Rama Rau, a friend of the Laughlins and author of the bestselling memoir *Home to India*, was there to introduce him. In the audience was Anaïs Nin, who described the recital in her famous diary: "Such a beautiful, subtle, complex, incredible performance, all of it improvised...An exhilarating challenge between drum and sitar as if trying to trip each other up but never able to do so, and they enjoy it as jazz musicians enjoy their own feats." Ravi, she noted, "smelled so strongly of sandalwood that we all went away impregnated with his perfume."[29]

Some early American press coverage grappled with the task of comprehending Indian music. On the day of his debut, the *New York Times* billed Ravi as a "sitar (Hindu guitar) player."[30] The following morning's review misnamed him "Rani Shankar." The reviewer struggled to appreciate the opening *alap*, due to "the seeming sameness of the music, a sort of mournful repetitiousness without apparent rhyme or reason," but was eventually won over by the thrilling interaction between sitar and tabla, as the crowd burst into cheers.[31] According to Ravi, "the show was a splendid triumph," and two days later the *New York Times*'s Sunday magazine underscored this by hailing a "master musician...Indians call him the 'Sitar wizard.'"[32] From the start, major publications covered Ravi's concerts. The reviews often expressed mystification at the alien nature of the music, but they raved about the musicians' virtuosity and skill, which cut through the fog of incomprehension.

The New York jazz world gave its early seal of approval to Ravi when he was guest of honor at an extraordinary party held at the Greenwich Village residence of the jazz historian Marshall Stearns. This took place just eleven days after Ravi's debut in the city, which gives a sense of the buzz he was creating. Dizzy Gillespie, who knew Ravi from Karachi, brought half his band and performed "A Night in Tunisia," with Willie "the Lion" Smith on piano. A fledgling Toshiko Akiyoshi played the piano too. In turn, seated on the floor beneath a wall of twelve thousand jazz records, Ravi and Chatur Lal gave a recital for this appreciative audience of musicians, hipsters and finely dressed socialites. Dizzy Gillespie, Count Basie and Roy Eldridge sat cross-legged on the carpet in the front row. Quincy Jones was in the second row. Further back in the packed room were Shelly Manne and the critic Nat Hentoff. The music-making continued into the night, until neighbors called the police, but when Stearns told the officers who was playing they listened for a while, collected some autographs and left. *Life* magazine ran a photo feature on the gathering, its verdict glowing: "The most popular stringed instrument in India is the sitar...and the best sitar player in India is Ravi Shankar."[33]

In January the delayed meeting for the East–West Music Encounter was at last fixed for late April in New York. With the likelihood of more performances to come, Ravi decided to stay on for the meeting and postpone his return to India. An extension had to be sought for Chatur Lal's leave of absence from AIR. Ultimately three and a half months away became ten and a half months.[34] Concerts in Washington, Philadelphia and Boston were added to his itinerary, and extra performances in New York. One of them, in the annex of the Museum of Modern Art, was attended not only by Narayana Menon, who happened to be in the city, but by India's great novelist R. K. Narayan, who had been touring coast to coast on a Rockefeller fellowship; it was on this trip that he wrote *The Guide*. This was Narayan's first meeting with Ravi. One challenge Ravi faced was the reserve of Western audiences—the downside of their concert decorum—and he encouraged the pair to leave their chairs and sit on the carpet, Indian style. Others followed suit. He also urged the audience to express appreciation during the recital because Indian performers were used to getting an instant response. "He misses it in this country where the convention is for listeners to sit still, maintaining a sort of grim silence throughout," wrote Narayan.[35]

In New York, as in London, word of mouth was bringing Ravi's music to the attention of leading musicians and record company executives. George Avakian was director of popular music at Columbia Records and one of the shrewdest men in the business. During the war he had developed reconnaissance skills in an infantry intelligence unit operating in the Philippines; after it, he had applied the same skills to spotting opportunities in the music industry. He was one of the pioneers of the 12-inch LP, introduced by Columbia in 1948. As a jazz producer, he was responsible for signing Miles Davis, Louis Armstrong and Dave Brubeck, but his antennae were tuned to international possibilities as well. Recently he had shifted 8 million copies of *I Love Paris*, an album of lush French instrumentals by Michel Legrand.[36] Indian music was more of a leap but his first exposure to it had come when he was a young man. He had been taken by his mother to see the Uday Shankar troupe in New York in 1937 or 1938, and had been so impressed that he had bought their album. Subsequently the only Indian music he had heard was on Columbia's 78 rpm "ethnic music" discs.

Avakian and his wife, the violinist Anahid Ajemian, had just moved into an apartment on Central Park West, and when their telephone was installed the first call he received was from the composer Alan Hovhaness. A friend and fellow Armenian American, Hovhaness had been fascinated by Indian music ever since his own encounter with Uday's troupe in 1937. He had studied the sitar and the veena with amateur Indian musicians in Massachusetts, and his compositions, very much in the ascendant in the mid-1950s, bore the influences of Armenian, Indian and other Asian music. "A magnificent musician, Ravi Shankar, has come from India," he told Avakian down the line. "He'll be concertising next week, but you should meet him before that." As Avakian had to wait in for the removal van, there was no time like the present. Twenty minutes later the two arrived on his doorstep, the lanky Hovhaness towering over Ravi.

"Welcome, Mr. Shankar," said Avakian. "I'm afraid we can't ask you to sit down; all we have so far is that telephone and the chair it's on."

Ravi promptly dropped, lotus-style, to the floor of the foyer. "Not easy for Westerners, but very easy for us Indians."[37]

Ravi formed an immediate bond with Avakian, whom he described as "a happy face with an honest smile."[38] So Avakian was present on February 1 when Ravi played at the biggest venue of this first tour, New York Town Hall, presented by jazz promoter Kenneth Lee Karpe. Although not a commercial success, this performance had historic repercussions. One source says the hall was only about a third full, but among the audience were five people who would play key roles in furthering Ravi's career.[39] Avakian was one of them. He found the concert so enchanting and dazzling that he asked Ravi to record for Columbia.[40]

Also at the show was Richard Bock, who became the most important record producer of Ravi's career. Bock had founded Pacific Jazz in 1952 in order to release the first LP by the Gerry Mulligan Quartet. This had defined a new West Coast jazz sound, with its piano-less rhythm section and the young Chet Baker on trumpet. (Bock's mentoring role in Baker's own solo career and turbulent life is dramatized in the 2015 movie *Born to Be Blue*.) For Bock, like so many in the new jazz scene, the war had been formative. He returned from his Navy service with a fascination for foreign music and a taste for hashish, both acquired while floating around in the South Pacific. He was certainly a jazz obsessive, but above all, according to his son Ron, "He was always in search of that magic moment of improvisation."[41]

Bock had flown in from Los Angeles to discuss Avakian joining Pacific Jazz, and it was Avakian who invited him to Town Hall. Bock had never heard Indian music before, and about forty minutes into the concert he nodded off to sleep—not through boredom, but because Ravi's music created a deep sense of peace within him. "Even though Indian music has its moments of great excitement," he said, "the most powerful aspect is its ability to put the listener in a relaxed mood and a calm state of mind, which carries the listener into an area of serenity."[42]

Bock had struck at once on a characteristic of Indian music that has been key to its success, and one that was not highlighted in most early press reviews. Ravi himself was very conscious of it:

> Our music has become more appreciated around the world, but what makes it special is not the exotic part, the virtuosity. This element of speed and playing for the gallery is found in other music also. Every music has speed…But the very serene part of our music—you can call it spiritual, devotional, soothing, peaceful, whatever you call it—this is the most unique thing in our music.[43]

Bock was introduced to Ravi after the concert and they arranged to meet again when the sitarist came out to Los Angeles in April.

A third member of the audience was Conrad Rooks, who later commissioned Ravi to write a film score. Rooks, young and rich, was the son of the Avon Corporation's CEO. He already had chronic issues with substance abuse, which had been triggered by a series of childhood operations during which he had been given painkilling narcotics. By the age of fourteen he was guzzling the school communion wine. By twenty-two, when he met Ravi, he had been kicked out of three schools and the Marines and was a drinking partner of Jack Kerouac. "I remember my first image of Shankar was this tiny little man scurrying down 57th Street in a long Nehru jacket carrying an enormous sitar instrument," said Rooks. He ran after Ravi and told him he had attended his concert. "I sat down with him in the bar of the Great Northern and said how fantastic I felt his music was and what it did to me, and we struck up a friendship."[44]

The fourth person was Penny Estabrook, an American then pursuing a PhD in Indian music at Columbia University. She did not meet Ravi until three years later, but after she moved to India she became for several years his student, musical assistant, touring companion and lover, and she remained a dear lifelong friend. "I thought he was a genius from the start," she recalls. "And till the end. I still think that." Early on, although it could be hard to get people through the doors for Ravi's concerts, once they were there it was rare for them to be disappointed. Estabrook observes, "It's just that you had to be *introduced* to understand it or to like it."[45]

The last of the Town Hall five, the musicologist Rosette Renshaw, was definitely not disappointed. She turned up at Ravi's hotel and tearfully declared her love for his score to *Pather Panchali*.[46] She invited him to Montreal, where on Valentine's Day he gave a sixty-minute lecture-demonstration on CBC's *Concert Hour*, which she introduced. This was his first full-length television show, for which he was paid Can$1,100. "That man Shankar is incredible," she wrote afterward, marveling that he had worked so successfully without a script, defying the TV rulebook by improvising both his music and his commentary. "I don't make the mistake of thinking that Shankar is a typical Easterner," she continued. "What saved his neck as well as mine is his miraculous sense of timing; he…has it to a degree that few musicians, East or West, can match."[47]

Ravi's momentum remained patchy during the chilly New York winter, and typically he went through some low periods, with plenty of time to brood alone. The high-profile coverage and influential supporters did not yet translate into large fees and full houses. "The concerts here are going well but unfortunately the financial gaines [*sic*] are not as I expected. Comparatively and considering how much less prosperous it is, England was much better!" he wrote to Harihar Rao.[48]

On March 28 and April 2 Ravi was booked in for two recording sessions with Avakian. The venue was Columbia Records' 30th Street studio, where many classic jazz records were recorded. He had to perform sitting on a coarse hessian carpet and, affected by the environment, was slightly disappointed with the results. His April diary was tight, as he was spending the middle of the month in California, followed by five days in meetings with Nicolas Nabokov, but two further sessions were shoehorned in on April 29 and May 1, just before Ravi departed for Europe. This time more attention was paid to the ambience. He invited friends to the studio, and played seated on a Persian carpet, which the producer had borrowed from his father. Avakian Brothers, the family firm, was a wholesale oriental-rug business. This began a tradition whereby for many years Avakian Brothers lent Ravi an exquisite Persian or Indian carpet to cover the podium when he appeared in New York.[49]

Ravi felt suitably inspired in the second pair of sessions. The result was his first U.S. album, *The Sounds of India*, released on Columbia. For decades now, this has for many people been their first encounter with a Ravi Shankar recording, a product of its instructive character as well as its peerless performances. As Yehudi Menuhin had done on Ali Akbar's album two years earlier, Ravi opens by giving a short spoken introduction to Indian music, four minutes long, demonstrating on the sitar. When prompted, Chatur Lal demonstrates the tabla, and Nodu Mullick the tanpura. Ravi similarly prefaces three of the four *ragas* he performs by playing the ascending and descending scales and the rhythmic cycle. The liner notes, which included Western notation of the scales, were written by Alan Hovhaness, under close guidance from Ravi, who asked that he refer to the notes on his recent EMI album and his concert programs, and avoid Western musicology. "I do not want Alan to read a lot of technical and backdated views of foreigners," he told Avakian, and he amended Hovhaness's text before the album's release.[50]

The two earlier sessions were stored away in Columbia's vaults and did not see the light of day for another decade. Meanwhile, Richard Bock told Avakian he was keen to add Ravi to his roster. Avakian had no objection, knowing that Columbia foresaw only a connoisseur market for two "catalog items of exotic music"; indeed, he was delighted that his new friend had found another label.[51]

Following the first two Columbia sessions, Ravi headed over to the West Coast for a short tour, still with no agent. He fell in love once again with California's natural beauty and climate, and was particularly drawn to the diversity and vivacity of Los Angeles. "Coming on my own and performing for such a different kind of audience, I saw things from a new perspective," he said. "I noticed quite a change in the country itself—so much more affluence and self-assurance, and the attitude of the young people seemed to have changed so much since the war."[52]

First Ravi played two concerts in San Francisco, including one at the San Francisco Museum of Art, and then at least five shows in Los Angeles during a week-long stay. One concert with special resonance was held on April 17 at the Self-Realisation Fellowship's Hollywood Temple on Sunset Boulevard. Here he played in the basement hall, built just five years earlier while the SRF's founding *guru*, Paramahansa Yogananda, was still alive. Ravi had met Yogananda in the 1930s and had later been inspired by his book *Autobiography of a Yogi*, a classic about spiritual searching. Both the *Los Angeles Times* and the *San Francisco Chronicle* acclaimed Ravi in reviews, while back in India an image appeared in the newspapers of a radiantly beaming foursome: Ravi, Chatur Lal, Nodu Mullick and Gene Kelly. Ravi had been invited to MGM Studios by its house composer, David Raksin. There he watched Kelly dancing on the set of George Cukor's *Les Girls* and was shrewd enough to be photographed with him afterward. Kelly knew of Ravi, and over lunch in the studio restaurant quizzed him about Indian music.

Richard Bock threw a welcome party at his West Hollywood home to introduce Ravi to the Los Angeles music scene, and then arranged a recording session in the Forum Theater on West Pico Boulevard. This was a disused cinema that Bock hired regularly; he had taped albums there by Chet Baker, Art Pepper and Hoagy Carmichael. This session produced Ravi's second U.S. album, *India's Master Musician*. Its five tracks again replicate in condensed form the range covered by one of his live concerts. This time he included a classical evening *raga*, a light-classical *raga*, a folk-like *dhun*, a *thumri*-style *Mishra*

Piloo played with references to other *ragas*, and a Carnatic *raga* that he had adapted and incorporated into his Hindustani repertoire. This Carnatic *raga*, *Charu Keshi*, was one of Ravi's favorites among all his recordings because of its "spiritual crispness and playful quality."[53]

It was during this year that Bock renamed his label World Pacific and gradually diversified away from jazz and toward Indian and other global music traditions. Most of his staff thought the audience for Indian music records would always be minuscule, but Bock followed his instincts. Reflecting later on all his releases by Ravi, he said, "The first one, I think, is a gem. It still holds up and it was a marvelous performance." His initial impressions of Ravi were of not only an extraordinary musician, but also a generous and gentle person, well traveled, cosmopolitan and somewhat aristocratic. "He was a very universal man. He was sort of a symbol to me of Indian culture," he said.[54] George Avakian, who wrote the liner notes for *India's Master Musician*, described Ravi as "probably the most gifted and imaginative master of improvisation that the musical world has ever encountered"—high praise indeed, coming from the producer of Miles Davis.

Ravi had two classic albums ready for release, but there was a snag. He had an exclusive worldwide recording contract with EMI, through its subsidiary HMV India. Avakian felt that Ravi's attitude toward these commitments was somewhat cavalier.[55] The news of EMI's objection arrived after Avakian had signed Ravi to Columbia and paid him an advance, and probably after Ravi had left the country. So Columbia embarked on negotiations with EMI in London, with the local assistance of John Coast. For a while the release of *The Sounds of India* was in jeopardy, but an agreement was reached by July. "I myself had given up the hope of Columbia! Was thinking how to return the advance! I am glad of the settlement," Ravi wrote to Avakian.[56] The album was released on December 30. But the issues proved more protracted for the World Pacific album, which did not appear until September 1958.

*

Who were Ravi's early adopters in North America? Anaïs Nin was surely embroidering her account when she wrote of his debut concert that "the entire YMHA was filled with Hindus."[57] According to Conrad Rooks, the sparse audience at Town Hall consisted mostly of "staunch beatniks" plus some people drawn to "Orientalia."[58] *Billboard*'s review of *Three Classical Ragas* judged that it would appeal to a "highly sophisticated or ethnic-minded audience."[59] In fact four groups can be identified, with some overlap between them. Indian immigrants comprised one group, but they were still few in number, restricted by annual national quotas in the hundreds that prevented substantial South Asian migration to the USA until the 1965 Immigration and Nationality Act. There were the "ethnic-minded" elements in liberal arts circles or the classical music world. Two other groups are worthy of particular attention: music students and professors, particularly the ethnomusicologists, and jazz aficionados, including the beatniks.

The formal study of musical cultures around the world had its origins in the early twentieth century, but in the 1950s ethnomusicology, as it was becoming known, was still only a fledgling discipline. Mantle Hood, one of its founders, established the Institute of Ethnomusicology at the University of California, Los Angeles (UCLA) in 1956. He promoted the then novel idea that in order to understand the music of another culture students should learn how to play in that system as well as in their own.[60] UCLA had assembled an impressive collection of instruments, but it could not yet boast expertise in Indian music. So the master's degree students in Hood's first intake were particularly fortunate to have Ravi visit: not only did he perform at UCLA's Schoenberg Hall, enabling them to hear a full-length *raga* by an Indian master, he also gave a lecture on Indian music. Among those students was Robert Garfias, later a distinguished professor in the field. Garfias and some fellow scholars got to know Ravi, Chatur Lal and Mullick and took them to dinner. "We were very naive twenty-somethings, but we recognized these guys were really *great* musicians," says Garfias. "Ravi would sit on the beach and play for a party. He was just trying to get anyone interested in Indian music. He'd go anywhere and play."[61]

Ravi disliked the term "ethnomusicology," which he felt relegated Indian classical music to an inferior "ethnic" category, and argued that it should be given the same weight as Western classical music. Otherwise he was delighted at the interest shown by the academics. He came to know most of the major names in the emerging field, including Hood, Garfias, Rosette Renshaw and Bob Brown, and pointed Brown in the direction of south Indian music, which became his specialism. Gradually knowledge of Indian music was growing in Western universities, especially in America, which became a source of support that continues today. On this tour Ravi played at the universities of Princeton, MIT, Philadelphia and Southern California, as well as UCLA, and when he next returned to America it was for a coast-to-coast tour focused on college venues.

Above all, though, there was the jazz audience. Several of his foremost champions, including Avakian and Bock, were jazz experts. Having been hailed by the New York jazz crowd, a similar thing happened to Ravi in Los Angeles: at Bock's welcome party Ravi was introduced to Laurindo Almeida, Bud Shank, Jimmy Giuffre, Shelly Manne and Emil Richards. During the trip he also met Dave Brubeck, Gerry Mulligan and Chet Baker. Ravi thought that jazz musicians and fans made up "the major part" of his early followers in the USA.[62] What attracted them to Indian music was often the emphasis on improvisation common to both systems, as well as a shared appreciation for rhythmic complexity and the soloist's virtuosity.

But Ravi was keen to detach Indian classical music from jazz. In his spoken introduction to *The Sounds of India* he denied that it was "akin to jazz."[63] Jazz is typically characterized by the use of harmony and chord progressions as the framework on which the soloist improvises. This is very different from Indian classical music, which does not employ chords or harmony; instead the intricate rules of the chosen *raga* and *tala* provide the framework. Ravi repeatedly voiced his objections to the comparison, and *Life* magazine, reporting on the party at Marshall Stearns's apartment, got the message:

> The jazz experts were deeply impressed by Shankar's *ragas*, because just as U.S. jazz has improvisational flights, his Eastern music improvises on traditional themes and rhythms. But though the *ragas* are far more complicated and refined than even the best Western jazz, Shankar said happily, "I love jazz. Its wild rhythm is so much like our Indian folk music."[64]

This comparison of jazz to India's folk music, rather than its classical music, was one that he repeated in other interviews.

Sometimes it was these very differences in Indian classical music that most strongly attracted jazz musicians. For Dave Brubeck, it was the novelty of its complex rhythms, reinforced by his experiences on an official tour of South Asia and the Middle East in early 1958, that inspired his greatest works. Back home, instead of playing in the usual 4/4 time—what he called "march-style jazz"—he recorded tracks in less common time signatures, including "Take Five" in 5/4 and "Blue Rondo à la Turk" in 9/8. The resulting LP *Time Out* became the first jazz album to sell a million copies. Avakian even devised a plan for Ravi to tour the U.S. jointly with Brubeck in 1959, but it never transpired, probably because of Ravi's determination to preserve Indian music's integrity. As Avakian acknowledged, "He seems to want to keep away from jazz as much as possible."[65]

For Quincy Jones, encountering Ravi for the second time, it was not only the rhythms of Indian music that thrilled him, but its use of microtones in its melodies. "It was stuff I'd never heard before," he recalled in 2016. "The tabla and sitar are such great examples of the incredible use of polyrhythms and quarter-tone." He also identified with its melancholic sensibility, what Ravi liked to call the "beautiful sadness" in a *raga*. "I always felt that Indian and Arabic music were similar to the blues," says Jones. "It's an expression of a life of endured pain.

It opened my eyes and allowed me to get deep into other cultures. It opens your mind and soul."[66]

Other jazz musicians were drawn to the sense of peace that suffuses a *raga*, particularly in the opening *alap* section. John Coltrane, hitherto a self-destructive heroin addict but undergoing a life-changing detox and spiritual epiphany at the very time Ravi was in New York, was soon wondering how to attain that serenity. He was inspired to pursue it through studying Indian music, and in time sought out Ravi.

A further area where jazz was influenced by Indian music in this period was in experimenting with different modes or scales. Modal jazz minimized the use of chords and mostly maintained an unchanging key, emphasizing instead melodic creativity, sometimes against a drone background. In these respects it echoed Indian music. The modal approach was not entirely new in jazz, but it was about to be explored like never before. Brubeck recorded the modal "Calcutta Blues" in 1958. Miles Davis recorded his first modal piece the same year, and in 1959 came his modal masterpiece *Kind of Blue*—probably the best-known jazz album of all time. Davis drew his modal inspiration from African rather than Indian music, but Coltrane, who was playing tenor saxophone on it, took modal jazz even further over the next few years under a heavy Indian influence.

Ravi was lukewarm about some of jazz's incarnations, such as free jazz. He loved the earlier styles of Duke Ellington, Count Basie, Louis Armstrong and Cab Calloway that he had encountered in America in the 1930s. "The old jazz of that time is still so deeply ingrained in me, because I found so much innocence, life and soul in it," he recollected in 1997. "Their music was not as intellectual as the atonal, modern and avant-garde varieties you hear today, but it appeals to me more."[67] Robert Garfias remembers Ravi voicing his reservations about a gig by the Jimmy Giuffre Trio that he and some fellow Indians had attended in Los Angeles in 1957. What apparently disappointed Ravi was how the jazz musicians "weren't able to really let go, or get more deeply into it." He and his compatriots were "curious and amused by the jazz but far from deeply impressed," says Garfias.[68] But despite Ravi's reservations, his mutual love affair with the U.S. jazz world continued: over the next few years jazz fans remained his core audience there.

As word spread, Ravi's music came to the attention of film directors in North America. One was Norman McLaren, a Scot based at the National Film Board of Canada. He specialized in experimental short films, and had won an Academy Award for *Neighbours* (1952). This employed a novel method called pixilation, in which stop-motion or variable-speed shooting enables live actors to interact with animated objects. It is the technique later made familiar by the films of Jan Švankmajer or the video for Peter Gabriel's "Sledgehammer." In early 1957 McLaren had just finished editing another film using similar methods, *A Chairy Tale*, which was a short fable about a man who wants to sit down and a chair that won't let him. It is only after the protagonist, played by co-director Claude Jutra, has allowed the chair to sit on him that it reciprocates, after which, the film concludes, "They sat happily ever after." *A Chairy Tale* is, as Ravi put it, "a beautiful metaphor for relationships," and he felt McLaren was "a sheer genius."[69] The chair takes on a personality of its own, by turns disdainful, coy or ecstatic. The film was complete except for one element: it had no soundtrack. McLaren had initially conceived it as a silent film, before accepting that the market demanded sound.

McLaren had reached this point when, on February 14, he saw Ravi playing the sitar on television, in the episode of CBC's *Concert Hour* introduced by Rosette Renshaw. "It struck me immediately as being the solution to the problem," he said. He arranged a meeting with Ravi through Renshaw. McLaren had visited India four years earlier and had become intrigued by the structure of Indian music: "You get one germ in the *raga*, and that germ is developed and developed and developed…It's just a constant build."[70] This chimed with the accumulative structure he had used for some of his earlier films. However, for *A Chairy Tale* he did not want a linear performance of a classical *raga*. He told Ravi, "I want a kind of halfway house between Hindu music and Western music. Can you do a *raga*...in such a way that it's international music?"[71] Ravi accepted the challenge. The meticulous McLaren went so far as to give his composer a timeline of the film on squared-off graph paper, each square representing one second, using colors and shapes to show the mood required for each scene. He spent an afternoon screening the film about a dozen times for Ravi and Chatur Lal.

They returned to Montreal about three weeks later for the recording session. There were practice run-throughs for fine-tuning (and, probably, some instant composition), and then, according to McLaren, "When the music was felt to be right, we did not stop the projector, but continued running, and made several takes immediately; for Shankar it was important that they be recorded while at the peak of their warming-up rehearsals."[72] They also recorded some special effects on the sitar and tabla that could be edited into the final mix as required.

The finished soundtrack features only Ravi's music; there is no dialogue or any other sound. Ravi's solution to the challenge was to create flashes of melody and bursts of percussion, rather than to develop a single *raga*. These suited the episodic nature of the film, and often served as comic commentary on the action. His music is very different from the sparseness of his *Aparajito* soundtrack recorded a few months earlier, but it is delightfully apt, and *A Chairy Tale* had huge success on the festival circuit. McLaren was so happy that he toyed with the idea of making a documentary on Indian music with Ravi.

Another filmmaker drawn to Ravi's music was the young James Ivory. They met in Los Angeles in April, when Ivory was an unknown director working on his second short, *The Sword and the Flute* (1959), a documentary on Indian miniature paintings. Ivory had bought Ali Akbar's *Music of India* on its release and listened to it until his ear became accustomed to it. However, no records by Ravi were available yet in America, and the trigger for Ivory to use Ravi's music in his film did not come until he saw *Pather Panchali* eight months after their meeting, when it was shown at the first San Francisco Film Festival in December 1957. Ivory recalls that Ravi then sent him a copy of *India's Master Musician* after it was released in 1958.[73] In return for a share of any profits (there would be none), Ravi allowed him to use two pieces from the record: a vigorous tabla–sitar exchange in *Mishra Piloo* and an excerpt from *Charu Keshi*.

The Sword and the Flute explores miniatures from the Mughal (Muslim) and the Rajput (Hindu) schools that were produced under the emperors Akbar and Jahangir in the sixteenth and seventeenth centuries. The narrator is the actor Saeed Jaffrey, who knew Ravi from AIR in Delhi and was building a career in America. Sadly Ravi never saw this absorbing twenty-four-minute short, although Ivory did tell him about it when they later met at the Films Division center in Bombay. Yet *The Sword and the Flute* was significant: not only did it initiate Ivory's fascination with India, but it was at a screening of it in New York in 1961 that Jaffrey introduced him to Ismail Merchant, leading to one of the great partnerships in cinema history. Over the next decade Merchant Ivory established its identity with English-language features made in India, including *The Householder* and *Shakespeare Wallah*, with Indian classical soundtracks by Ali Akbar and Vilayat Khan. James Ivory never used Ravi's music again, but their paths would cross in the future.

After the breakdown of his marriage, Ravi found being on tour far from home liberating. He had become used to a peripatetic life in India, and now he enjoyed the freedom to roam—in both senses of the word—on the other side of the globe. It's unclear whether he expected the separation to be permanent but he rationalized that it was Annapurna who had walked out on him. He now behaved like a single man, with many casual relationships over the years to come.

Partly this was down to opportunity. To many women in America, Europe and elsewhere he was handsome, charismatic, bursting with talent and exotic. He seemed to them to hold the secrets of a wiser culture. He reveled in the attention. Richard Bock found him to be "very much of a sensualist...a fun-loving person. Very loving, and very loyal."[74]

There was more to it than just being a player. He had a sensualist's ardor for beauty, in women as in music. He thrived on company, and always loved to have a roomful of friends, but after everyone had gone home he was prone to extreme emotional lows, especially after the high of a concert. At those moments, when others might turn to alcohol or drugs, he longed for company, for love and tenderness.

During this long stay in America he undoubtedly had more than one affair, but of these the relationship with Marilyn Silverstone went the deepest. She spent time with him during the colder months in New York, and brought a passionate glow to his last few days there. She was among the crowd of friends present when he recorded in Columbia Studios, and photographed the occasion—as she did two days later, on May 3, when she, along with George Avakian and Anahid Ajemian, came to see him off as he boarded the SS *United States*, the Blue Riband passenger liner, bound for London. Later she reminisced to him about

> that day on the sunny New York dock, as we really waved goodbye—
> or au revoir—so close inside in the sharing of our castle, having
> given each other so much—so happy and warm and poignant in
> parting...and no promises or commitments or grimnesses—only
> love and comradeship and the loveliness of what we had had
> together and would always in some way, somewhere have...[75]

Previously stifled by the high-society expectations of her family, she credited Ravi with transforming her, as well as sparking a lifelong fascination with India. The day he left, she wrote to him,

> You've really become such a big part in my life and you've changed
> me...You are really like a Sun—so warming and radiating & so

lovely inside & out... You know you've little by little made me come outside and become more really myself... I never want to go back & hide anything again... We've both been through a valley this winter—and now it's spring and we're out and it's so lovely & free.[76]

Both of them were in complicated personal situations—Ravi separated from his wife, Marilyn having second thoughts about an absent and hesitant lover—and they chose a carefree parting, determined to avoid possessiveness. However, they kept in regular correspondence over the summer; he wrote her two letters from the boat alone. For the next three months he was touring Europe: Britain, the Netherlands, France, Belgium, Norway, Denmark and Sweden, and about twenty concerts in West Germany. Missing him, she arranged to come over. Ostensibly this was partly for work—she had an assignment to cover Ho Chi Minh's visit to Warsaw—and partly to tour around Europe with her parents. Her father was a Hollywood executive, and on the Côte d'Azur she stayed with Joan Fontaine. Despite Ravi's initial intentions, in Marilyn's absence he ached for her and wondered whether she might be the lover to end all others. His letters made her uneasy and there was an intense but anguished reunion in Paris, he complaining that she was keeping "2 feet in 2 boats," she wanting to move more slowly but mortified at hurting him. She was convinced that the relationship would "reach full flower and madness in India" and was hoping for a commission to shoot a big story there in 1958.[77]

In the meantime they tried in vain to keep their affair secret from her conservative parents. He started to sign off his letters to her as "Robert Sherman," and she replied as "Archie Lee," "Ellis" or "BD." "I got into big trouble with her," he remembered. "Her father was the president of Twentieth Century Fox, and he put a private investigator after it. They used to smuggle [intercept] all my letters which I wrote to her. Then he approached her and scolded her."[78]

*

During Ravi's European tour a pattern was becoming established: a relentless stream of concerts, radio broadcasts and effusive notices. The London *Times*, which had not covered his British concerts the previous autumn, now reviewed two concerts at London's Wigmore Hall, calling him a "virtuoso performer" and hailing his "dazzling demonstrations" of Indian music.[79] Yet the British were not as enthusiastic as the Americans or the Germans. In West Germany there was a particularly powerful response, with echoes of how Uday's troupe was received there in the 1930s. It was while Ravi was in Germany that he won the Silver Bear for *Kabuliwala* at the Berlin Film Festival.

Ravi also took his music to the International Summer School of Modern Music in Darmstadt, the cauldron of twelve-tone serialism and other avant-garde music. The juxtaposition was exquisite: at 8 p.m. on July 18 the audience in the Orangerie could hear works by Arnold Schoenberg, Pierre Boulez, Edgard Varèse and Humphrey Searle; at 10 p.m. Ravi took the stage. According to Ravi,

> about four hundred musicians, composers, and musicologists of international repute listened till late in the midnight to the unending variations of melody and rhythm on our instruments. A sublime feeling of ecstasy and pleasure seemed to hang on the faces of the audience in the tense atmosphere of the Theatrical Hall.[80]

Unfortunately the sentiment was not reciprocated. Ever curious, he listened to other concerts at the festival and found he had a visceral reaction against *musique concrète*: it gave him a headache and made him feel nauseous. But he took encouragement from the possibility that Indian music might make an impact in this setting. Intriguingly, some of the avant-garde musicians enthused about its "modern" characteristics. "I felt that Western musicians were somewhat tied up with the limitations of staff notation," said Ravi. "Now they are trying to find a way out of the mist of troubles enveloping them and some of them had evinced interest in Indian music."[81]

At the end of the tour, a week was set aside in early August to record another film score, this time in London for Arne Sucksdorff, an Oscar-winning Swedish director. But when that recording was postponed until November, Sucksdorff invited Ravi instead for eight days' holiday at his home in Remningstorp, near Skövde in central Sweden. Here is perhaps the most telling detail of Ravi's entire trip: despite feeling as though he was staying in "a dreamland," in a forty-room lakeside mansion on a private estate, at the end of a draining ten-month tour, he spent this break practicing the sitar for seven or eight hours each day.[82] There could be no resting on laurels if he hoped ever to attain true mastery of the instrument. As he had told *Time* magazine, "It is like driving through a mist. The more you drive, the more you realize the road is still there."[83]

On August 16 he flew back from London to Bombay. He reflected later that his epic tour had been "successful in many ways but not financially"—and yet his hard work would eventually pay off in that respect too.[84] He had planted seeds abroad: small but committed live audiences motivated to spread the word; many influential friends; four LPs recorded, three of which were out by September of the following year; and his first two soundtracks for overseas films, with a third in his diary. Already his Indian film scores were winning garlands abroad. After the triumphs of *Pather Panchali* at Cannes and *Kabuliwala* in Berlin, there were further wins at Venice in September 1957, where *Aparajito* earned the Golden Lion, while *A Chairy Tale* was named the best avant-garde or experimental film. The following year *A Chairy Tale* received a BAFTA Special Award and a Canadian Film Award, and was nominated for an Academy Award for best live-action short.

In time these seeds sown in the West would germinate and bear fruit. But that would take another decade, and immense efforts by Ravi on future visits. The more immediate impact of the tour could be seen at home in India.

10

A HERO'S WELCOME

I am mobbed in the street by admirers, almost like a Film Star.
RAVI SHANKAR[1]

Privately, Ravi admitted to being nervous about how he would be received on his return home in August 1957. The Indian arts scene could be intensely factional. The tall-poppy syndrome was rife: if anyone grew above the rest of the crop, he was at risk of being cut down by critics and rivals. Marilyn Silverstone had tried to boost Ravi's self-confidence in a letter he received in Sweden a week before his flight back to Bombay: "Don't be afraid of the crocodiles...Stand on your accomplishments, which are great, and on your own self & what you know & believe...don't doubt yourself or let others make you do so even temporarily."[2]

Ravi's preparations for his return had been thorough. He was determined to hit the ground running. The previous month he had written from Germany to three of his friends, asking them to arrange press conferences in Bombay, Delhi and Calcutta, as well as half a dozen recitals within a fortnight of his arrival. In order to present the glory of his overseas successes as India's rather than his alone, he asked for the recitals to be fundraising events for the prime minister's National Relief Fund. He also instructed Harihar Rao to find him a new home in Delhi as he no longer had the government house on Ashoka Road.

While Ravi had been abroad, his reputation had been enhanced by regular reports of his progress in the Indian press. When R. K. Narayan had arrived back in June after his own long foreign tour, he brought news of how Indian music had acquired a patina of glamour in the West thanks to Ravi: "I was tremendously impressed with the response his recitals evoked," Narayan was quoted as saying. "Eminent musicians and composers in London and New York were simply captivated by the music... They wanted to know all about Indian music and all about musical instruments."[3]

Ravi plunged into a round of concerts, interviews and "felicitations" in his honor. His first recital, on August 22, took place under the dome of the Cowasji Jehangir Hall, Bombay. Today the building houses the National Gallery of Modern Art, but it was then a premier concert venue. One reviewer praised Ravi's "triumphant tour," commenting on the arrangements—"for the first time, the concert began on the scheduled hour"—and describing the performance of the rainy season *raga Mian Ki Malhar* as a "superb display of the sitarist's art." However, the journalist was disappointed with the *Charu Keshi* and *Dhun*: "Both left me with the impression that, perhaps, the foreign tour had been far too arduous for the artiste."[4] This was surely the earliest example of what was to become a persistent critical theme in India: that Ravi's music had been ruined by foreign touring. But for now this was the exception. A day later, there was unqualified praise in the same newspaper: "No greater ambassador of goodwill has gone out of this country in recent times than the famed virtuoso of the sitar, Pandit Ravi Shankar. Nor has a single artiste going abroad earned for himself and his country that much of respect."[5]

On August 29 he performed at a private musical soirée at the home of music director Shankar (no relation), the senior half of Shankar–Jaikishan, probably the leading Bombay film composers of the 1950s and 1960s. Their filmography already boasted the Raj Kapoor classics *Awara* and *Shri 420*, and they had just won their first Filmfare Award, for *Chori Chori*. The evening began with the classical vocalist Amir Khan—one of Ravi's favorite artists—accompanied by the sarangi-player Ram Narayan (Chatur Lal's brother) and the percussionist Mohammed Ahmed. Then Ravi played, accompanied by Chatur Lal. The guests, sitting on the floor close to the performers, comprised "a galaxy of filmdom's top-notchers," all at the peak of their careers: as well as Shankar, Jaikishan and fellow music director Roshan, and the actor-director Raj Kapoor, there were playback singers Lata Mangesh-kar and Mukesh and actors Dilip Kumar, Prem Nath and Motilal.[6] Dilip Kumar and Raj Kapoor arrived late but listened at the door until a break in the performance to avoid disturbing the musicians and the audience. The concert lasted six hours. By the time Ravi had finished, at 4:45 a.m., and the five-minute ovation had died down, it was too late for sleep. He had to catch the 8 a.m. plane to Delhi. On arrival he was photographed exiting the plane, clad in kurta, dhoti and dark glasses, clutching his sitar in its soft bag, and was cheered by a group of waiting fans.[7] He had a dinner engagement with Nehru that evening.

In Bombay Ravi had stayed for a week with his friend B. I. Joshi-pura at his Sonawala Buildings apartment in Tardeo. Harihar Rao had apparently been unable to find a suitable apartment for Ravi to rent in Delhi, and between frequent trips away he lodged temporarily with his brother Debendra at 51 Lake Square, where Shubho was living, and where Amiya Dasgupta and Harihar sometimes stayed.

In press interviews, he was at pains to assert that the integrity of his music had survived his travels unscathed. "I do not think Western notions, particularly with regard to harmony, should or will influence my playing technique," he said.[8] He pointed out that one way the Indian live music scene could learn from the West was to become more professional: "The thing that impressed me most in foreign countries was the discipline of music lovers and the beautiful arrangements that exist for such gatherings. I want Indians to learn concert manners." He contrasted this with recitals in India, where "music performances often turn out to be social gatherings. The clatter of the cups mingles with the gossip and the artist is forgotten. You must give full attention to art to derive pleasure out of it."[9] He was also keen to restate his belief in the universality of art, which had been strengthened by his touring experience: "Artistes know only one language and that language is understood by peoples the world over. Art is the quickest medium to reach the hearts of the people."[10]

"I got a hero's welcome on my return to India," he wrote to George Avakian.

The success and demand for my recitals seems to be unbelievable. I have accepted two contracts for film music direction and refused at least twenty! I am mobbed in the street by admirers, almost like a Film Star. I am glad I have a seasoned head on my shoulders— so there is no fear of its swelling and bursting. Just like you, my friend, the keynote in my life seems to be "speed," with tremendous activity and no relaxation.[11]

Marilyn Silverstone, responding to one of Ravi's letters, wrote, "I'm so glad you're having such a terrific success. It is really wonderful & shows that if you have guts to take a chance, in the end it works & everyone comes round, slightly envious that they didn't think of it in the first place."[12]

He was in Calcutta in mid-September, for "three weeks of hectic film work and concerts."[13] As usual he stayed at his friend Lala Sridhar's house on Ballygunge Park Road. In his recitals at the New Empire and the Lighthouse, he deployed for the first time the condensed, intelligently paced concert format that he had honed abroad. This made a huge impression, but a local critic attacked him fiercely.[14] Six years later the press was still describing the New Empire concert as historic for the "inimitable style" with which it was presented.[15] While in Calcutta Ravi also recorded the two film scores he had mentioned to Avakian: Satyajit Ray's *The Philosopher's Stone* and Tapan Sinha's *Kalamati*. Ray sat in on both sessions.

It was probably on this visit to Calcutta that Ravi saw the Little Theatre Group's Bengali production of Gorky's play *Lower Depths*. Ravi's friend Utpal Dutt, the driving force behind the company, was by now a prolific actor-director on stage and screen and occasionally found himself in trouble with the law for his radical-left activism. He had made his name touring Shakespeare around India with Geoffrey Kendal (father of actors Jennifer and Felicity), and would be in the cast when Merchant Ivory later dramatized the troupe on screen in *Shakespeare Wallah*. His Bengali theater and film work was often politically committed and not always commercially successful. Nemai Ghosh, who was acting in *Lower Depths*, recalls that there were only twelve people in the audience that evening, including Ravi, Uday and Amala Shankar, and that Ravi was so moved that he offered to provide music for Dutt's next production.[16]

Back in Delhi for two weeks, Ravi prepared a mixed choral group for Delhi University's entry in the prestigious all-India Inter-University Youth Festival, which was opened by Rajendra Prasad, the President of India, on November 1. Ravi also assisted with choreography and music for a student ballet, and gave his services at a concert to raise 20,000 rupees for Triveni Kala Sangam, today one of Delhi's finest cultural institutions but then still fundraising to finance construction of the center on land allocated by Nehru.[17]

At a reception in December hosted by Triveni's director, Sundari Shridharani, Ravi played for the American contralto Marian Anderson and presented her with a tanpura as a gift. She was in India on a State Department-sponsored tour; the USA was still courting India through music.[18] As one of her country's greatest classical singers, Anderson was a barrier-breaking inspiration to black Americans, an ideal figure to counter Asian attitudes to America's perceived racism. While in Delhi, she was given the honor of singing in Mahatma Gandhi Park beneath the statue of the "father of the nation," leading America's legendary broadcaster Ed Murrow to observe, "If you wish to influence the Indians, rather than a thousand missionaries send one saint. The United States sent Miss Anderson."[19]

On October 28 Ravi caught a flight from Bombay to London for the postponed recording session for Arne Sucksdorff's *The Flute and the Arrow* (*En Djungelsaga*). This docudrama depicts the Muria tribe of Madhya Pradesh, best known for its mixed, communal *ghotul* huts in which adolescents live and practice free love with the compulsory changing of partners—one of a number of rituals that reinforce the tribal culture of sharing. The story focuses on a young man who is ostracized for marrying outside the tribe, and his efforts to regain favor by hunting a leopard. Luxuriously filmed on location in wide-screen Technicolor, it is an earnest and glossy piece of anthropology that tends to exoticise its subject matter. Musically, it is notable as a further example of the spare soundtrack treatment Ravi had employed on Ray's *Pather Panchali* and *Aparajito*. Unusually he had traveled without a tabla player, instead taking instruments with him and relying on uncredited Indian musicians resident in London to play the flute, sarangi and drums that feature sporadically along with his own sitar. In an article four months later, he said he had "experienced the greatest thrill" making this soundtrack because he had relied on "simplicity and the direct approach."[20] It is unlikely that he had seen the finished film at that stage. Only four scenes have background music (there are no songs), which suggests that Sucksdorff declined to use a fair proportion of what Ravi recorded. Ravi stayed in London for only a week and gave no performances, but there was an opportunity to meet up with George and Marion Harewood. Lord Harewood was the incoming artistic director of the Leeds Festival, and he invited Ravi back the following October to perform at it. On his return journey to India Ravi stopped off in Rome to give a recital and appear on television.

By this time Ravi was already planning to return to the UK in the autumn of 1958. John Coast had persuaded him to be more ambitious: rather than play several smaller London venues, as he had done in 1956–7, he should hire the Royal Festival Hall and announce it as his sole London appearance. The hall was booked for a deposit of £75. With Leeds now scheduled for a week later, Coast could work on adding other British and European dates. Ravi hoped the tour would extend across the Atlantic. He missed America, as he had realized when Gopal Sanyal visited Delhi in October 1957: "We were talking about all the common friends and all the trifles that we have left behind in the States which left me with such a heavy heart and a feeling of homesickness," he wrote to George Avakian.[21] However, he was still without an American agent or promoter who could put together a new tour. He seems to have sounded out Sol Hurok—who had brought Uday back to the USA for two post-war tours—but without success. Perhaps Avakian and Richard Bock could help? He tried an appeal to the former: "It is up to you, Dick and a few other good friends who could join the heads together and plan a way out for my next, short but well-planned tour."[22] Six months later, he was still pinning his hopes on Avakian arranging something for mid-January 1959, asking if he could set up "one proper big-scale recital at Town Hall New York? Then we could concentrate on universities and few cities such as Philadelphia, Boston, Washington, Cleveland, Canada—and California. I'm trying for Mexico & South America—and return via Islands—& Japan! Let's see."[23] It was at this point that Avakian investigated the possibility of Ravi touring with Dave Brubeck, but nothing was to come of that idea.

For the first half of 1958 Ravi focused on two major projects. In January, while maintaining a typically hectic schedule (Madras—Hyderabad–Nagpur–Calcutta–Bombay–Delhi), he was preparing for what he later described as his first magnum opus. *Melody and Rhythm* marked a return to stage productions for the first time since he had had his fingers burned by *The Discovery of India* a decade earlier, and was the first of half a dozen similar shows over the next six years. It comprised a survey of Hindustani music history through multiple items, all composed or arranged by Ravi. There were no dance elements, which was unusual for an Indian stage show. But with Indian music still being seen very much as the realm of soloists, the most ground-breaking and controversial feature was the use of a chorus and orchestra, some sixty musicians in all, conducted by Ravi.

For the staging Ravi was influenced by the Western classical tradition. Whereas Indian singers traditionally sit cross-legged to perform, most of the choir stood in tiered rows, apart from a single seated line at the front holding long-necked bass tanpuras. This style of presentation has become more common in India today, courtesy of ensembles such as Delhi's Gandharva Choir, but in 1958 it was a new departure.

The music itself was untouched by Western influences. The show grew out of Ravi's fascination with the evolution of Indian music forms. "I want to present different facets of Indian music from the most traditional to the most modern, folk, thematic and abstract," he explained to Harihar Rao, who served as the production manager.[24] For example, a piece in *Raga Bhimpalasi* sung in *dhrupad*, probably the most ancient form of Indian classical music still extant today, was followed by a suite beginning in *khyal*, to illustrate the historic progression of styles.

Ravi preferred to use only Indian instruments—sarod, sitar, bansuri flute, sarangi, tabla and tanpura—although he did add the violin, justifying its presence on the grounds that it had long since been embraced by Indian musicians. Drawing on his orchestral experiments at All India Radio, he knew that the violin's uniform timbre worked well in unison and counterbalanced the more idiosyncratic sounds of the other instruments. His own recent work with the Delhi University students, who formed the choir, might have served as a dry run for the choral elements.[25]

Melody and Rhythm, co-produced with Triveni Kala Sangam, was presented on five consecutive nights in March at the Arts and Crafts Hall in central New Delhi, one block from the parliament building. Ravi was touched when Baba attended the opening night and gave his blessing. Another night, Nehru, personally invited by Ravi, came to the performance.[26] During the rehearsal period, Ravi had been heartened to hear that Nehru had praised him in parliament for his efforts as a cultural ambassador for Indian music. Nehru "was like a superstar at that time," said Ravi, so it was quite a coup to have him in the audience. There was an extraordinary moment during the *Lori* (lullaby) sung by Lakshmi Shankar. Nehru, who sometimes worked eighteen-hour days, had a reputation for falling asleep in theaters and, exhausted after a long parliamentary session, he nodded off. As he was sitting in the central box this was obvious to everyone. So when the lullaby drew to a close the audience refrained from applauding to avoid waking up their prime minister. After the finale, Nehru embraced and congratulated Ravi.[27] The production was "a thundering success," reflected Ravi a couple of weeks later, "and has been acclaimed as 'something new,' 'for the first time,' a 'landmark' etc.—very gratifying really—and worth the death of a hard work I went thru!"[28]

The second project was his first tour of Japan. He had been waiting for this moment since 1935, when the death of his father had curtailed the dance troupe's Asian tour before it reached Japan. Acclaim in the West made Ravi, like Rabindranath Tagore before him, all the more curious to explore the Far East, and by the beginning of 1958 he was describing visiting Japan as "an obsession I must get through with."[29] On April 1 he arrived in Tokyo, leading an official cultural delegation on a four-week trip visiting twelve Japanese cities: Tokyo, Nagoya, Tokushima, Hiroshima, Fukuoka, Kobe, Osaka, Nara, Kyoto, Hakodate, Sapporo and Asahikawa. On the way home the group spent a further two weeks in Bangkok and Hong Kong. Ravi's debut at Yomiuri Hall in Tokyo was attended by Princes Takamatsu and Mikasa, the two younger brothers of the Japanese emperor, as well as numerous diplomats. "Very great success everywhere," Ravi reported from Tokyo.[30] He was "dazzled" by the country's economic vigor and technological sophistication barely a dozen years after the war. Here was an Asian nation outpacing the West while retaining its distinctive and ancient culture. He felt that the coexistence of bamboo interiors, kimonos and cherry blossom on the one hand with state-of-the-art cameras and cars on the other could offer a role model for an independent India navigating its own way between tradition and modernity.[31]

The ten-person party consisted of two classical dancers—Damayanti Joshi (Kathak) and Kamala Lakshman (Bharatanatyam)—and their accompanists, plus Ravi, Harihar Rao on tanpura, and Ravi's tabla player, Alla Rakha—a significant choice. Chatur Lal had flourished in the West when the spotlight had been focused on him, but once back in India he had become deflated. Within a couple of months of their return, Ravi was commenting, "It is sad to see Chaturlal as he has lost confidence in himself being one among so many. But I try to keep him in good humor and cheers, though it is not so easy as there are so many good drummers all over the country who want and expect me to give them chances too!"[32] There was no reason why he had to take the same accompanist each time he went abroad. So for Japan he asked Alla Rakha, by now the doyen of the Punjab *gharana* of tabla players. "I always liked him as a drummer," Ravi later said. What marked out Alla Rakha was "a certain showmanship, and the happiness that he sort of exudes."[33] Foreign audiences picked up on this sense of fun and the palpable electricity that flowed between these two masters when in flight. A historic international partnership had begun.

Meanwhile, over in New York, George Avakian had resigned from Columbia Records in March, after eighteen years, in order to join forces with Richard Bock. The plan was that, as a new vice president of World Pacific, Avakian would be in charge of the company's East Coast operations, while Bock would continue to run the West Coast. Ravi's two American producers would combine their expertise, especially in jazz, pop and spoken-word, and run a dynamic independent label to rival the majors. Avakian invested in the company and set up a New York office within Carnegie Hall.

The contractual impasse continued over *India's Master Musician*, and it was Avakian who now tried to resolve it. The issue remained that Ravi had recorded it while under exclusive contract to EMI. From Tokyo, in response to a letter from Avakian, Ravi proposed a subterfuge to get around this: when he returned to Delhi at the end of May he could ask either the United States Information Service (USIS) or the American Women's Club to arrange a concert for him, Chatur Lal and Nodu Mullick. They would play exactly the same *ragas* as they had for their Los Angeles recording, to the same timings, record the concert and send the tapes to Avakian. Ravi would have the show photographed and perhaps covered by *American Reporter*, USIS's Indian newspaper, "to make the whole thing look above board."[34] As a result, World Pacific could release the original album, claiming that it had been recorded in India in 1958 rather than in America in 1957, and presumably avoid any contractual issues. Ravi asked Avakian to send him the exact track timings, and it appears that Avakian agreed to the deception, according to a letter he wrote to Bock on April 24. But there is no evidence that it went any further. The liner notes for the album, which Avakian wrote over the following weekend, omit any reference to the date or place of recording.[35]

By late May, however, the dream team of Avakian and Bock was falling apart. In the midst of a market downturn, Bock decided that World Pacific needed to make severe cutbacks and ordered a temporary freeze on recording new artists. Avakian, already frustrated over several matters, including the delay to his own contract, lost faith in the way the company was being run and wanted out. On July 16, perhaps after hearing of the split, Ravi cabled Avakian from Delhi that he wanted the album release to be halted.[36] But presumably he changed his mind because a month later Bock confirmed that it would be issued in September "as we recorded it at the Forum Theater."[37] A resolution had been reached with EMI: he signed a new three-year contract that allowed him to record for both companies in the years ahead.[38] Avakian, who remained friendly with Ravi, severed his connection with World Pacific and shortly afterward co-founded a new major label, Warner Brothers Records.

By June 1958, ten months had passed since Ravi's return from the West. He was still separated from Annapurna and pursuing his "butterfly lifestyle." He had recently moved into 16 Hailey Road, an attractive bungalow in New Delhi near to the Modern School, which Shubho attended, and the new cultural quarter around Mandi House Circle. Principal among his girlfriends was Kamala Sastri—or, as she now was, Kamala Chakravarty. After her marriage, years had passed without any contact. It was in September 1956, just before his overseas tour, that they had begun their affair. In March 1957, while Ravi had been in America,

Kamala's husband Amiya had died at the age of just forty-four. Ravi had resumed his relationship with her on his return to India and she became the constant presence in his love life, essential but not exclusive.

Although he no longer believed in monogamous relationships, he was still married. It was Annapurna who had walked out on him, but divorce was rare in Indian society, and not straightforward. Moreover, the marriage had bound together his domestic and musical lives, and the rancorous split had turned his *guru* against him. Adverse publicity or a legal case would make things even worse.

Marilyn Silverstone, with whom he must have discussed his painful dilemma (and who had an interest in the outcome), had expressed the hope that "the other matters will also work out the way you want & not a compromise to suit other purposes. You have worked too hard and come too far to fall back." In April, when he was in Tokyo, she had written to him again, asking pointedly, "How are *you otherwise*? What if any decision reached?"[39]

A series of letters from Annapurna during 1958 reveal her emotional dependence on Ravi, despite two and a half years' separation. She uses a respectful tone, addressing him as "Sri Charan Kamaleshu," and signs off "Pranam, Annapurna," or "Your Anni."[40] She misses him; she can't wait to hear from him again. Only his presence or his letters can lift her mood. And her mood is very low at times.

It is clear that her attitude had changed and she wanted a reunion. Her motivation was less clear. Over the marriage there always loomed the figure of Baba. On June 4 Annapurna asked Ravi to "let me know as soon as you can what's happening," so that she knew what to say to her father.[41] By the time of her next letter, on August 9, Ravi had been to visit her. "Since you left I am missing you and feeling sad," she wrote. "How quickly the time went when you were here, but now the time just doesn't want to go."[42]

Two weeks later Baba wrote a letter to Ravi that must have upset him deeply. The tenor was distant, angry, even sarcastic, completely unlike Annapurna's letters. He referred to an incident when Ravi had told him off and said he would not forget it; he didn't want anything from him. There was a suggestion of emotional blackmail: "I am free now, you don't have to think about me...My life is finished, just a few days left. Keep a family life and be happy, that's all I can wish for." But he did at least add, "God has made you big, but I give you the blessing that you become even more so."[43]

On September 24 Ravi was in Bombay, preparing for two concerts. That day Annapurna wrote him a farewell message as he was about to leave for his three-month European tour: "Whenever I hear about your praises it is impossible to write how happy I feel. Every day you will rise and make new things. This is what people expect from you." She added, "Please write to me. I'm counting the days until you come back and don't know when the counting will end."[44]

Ravi's relations with Annapurna's brother, strained by the separation, appear to have eased by this point. They had resumed playing their *jugalbandi* sets to great acclaim, a notable example being Ravi's send-off concert at the Cowasji Jehangir Hall on the 27th. "Not only is each an acknowledged master in his own field," raved one reviewer, "but [he] has a near-perfect understanding of the style and thought of the other." Such intuition did not extend to the recital's organizers, who employed "a distraction on the stage" to cut short a sublime ninety-minute *alap* in *Puriya Kalyan*, apparently because they thought it had gone on too long—an extreme example of the kind of unprofessional Indian staging that Ravi so lamented.[45] More appreciative was Lata Mangeshkar, who congratulated the pair backstage.[46]

The next day Ravi left for London. The letters from Annapurna foreshadowed a major development: she was about to come back to him.

11

A COMPROMISE TO SUIT OTHER PURPOSES

My whole life is but from the very beginning this kind
of a suspense drama, thrill-miracle—full of climax and anti-climax.
RAVI SHANKAR[1]

Ravi's appearance at the Royal Festival Hall, London, on Saturday
October 4, 1958 was his biggest overseas concert so far, and marked
Indian music achieving a new status in Britain. During the summer
Ayana Angadi had followed up Ravi's 1956–7 tours by organizing
a UK visit for Vilayat Khan and the tabla player Nikhil Ghosh. As
well as appearing at the Aldeburgh Festival and Dartington, they had
played in the 250-capacity Recital Room within the Festival Hall
building (the space now occupied by the National Poetry Library).[2]
But Ravi was the first Indian musician to headline the main hall,
which had a capacity of nearly three thousand.

Ravi was not a regular diarist, so it is fortunate that he kept journal entries for the first seventeen days of this trip, as they reveal the
drama behind this landmark concert. Even before he left Bombay he
had been struck down with a fever, and had played a recital there "intoxicated with a profusion of medicines—ears ringing, head swirling."[3]
Then, as he was leaving from Santa Cruz airport, well-wishers presented him with flowers, a generous gesture that went seriously wrong. All
his life he was prone to allergies, and during the flight to London he
came out in an angry rash, initially on his fingers, where he had handled the garland, but eventually his whole body was itching. He tried
rinsing his hands in Dettol, but this only caused his fingers to blister.

In the five days between his arrival and the concert, he chron-
icled with growing desperation the medical interventions he tried,
his inability to practice and his dread of not being able to give the

performance. What made it even more galling was that interest in him was mounting. When at short notice he was invited onto BBC TV's *Tonight*, a prime-time magazine program broadcast live to 7 million viewers, he was unable to play the sitar properly; he could only strum it to demonstrate its timbre, with the *mizrab* pick worn lightly on his swollen forefinger. Afterward a doctor lanced the blisters and bandaged his fingers. Ravi's diary entry that night closed like a soap-opera cliff-hanger: "What will happen at the Festival Hall?!? Will it? Won't it? Dear Lord—only you can tell!!"[4]

On the morning of the show, with his bandages removed, he tearfully prayed to Durga, surrendering his fate to the goddess. The concert began shortly after 3 p.m. and there was a packed house, with around three hundred people turned away. Defying the odds, Ravi and Alla Rakha delivered what Tapan Sinha, who was in the audience, described as "an unforgettable experience."[5] Ravi himself was convinced that his inspiration was divine in origin. "Where did that music come from?" he asked his diary.

> I do not know, do not comprehend—except for the Lord's mercy! Filled with melody and emotion, ready for everything. (The hands felt light as a flower, doing what I wanted, taking risks at will.) Have not played like this for ages!! Alla Rakha played extremely well too…My whole life is but from the very beginning this kind of a suspense drama, thrill-miracle—full of climax and anticlimax. I bow to you, Lord! You have given me so much, so much. All the pain, sorrow, misery—joy, delight and happiness coming together…O Lord, please do not take away from me my ability to feel enlightened like this.[6]

"The audience were wonderful, casual, chattering, a true Asian audience for the most part," recalled John Coast. "Ravi was very happy and rewarded us with a little tin of his special sandalwood powder."[7] But Ravi's diary also reveals the crash after the high:

Everybody was excited and genuinely overjoyed at my success. I sat and chatted with them for a while, played games. After everybody left, we went back to Allahabad [hotel restaurant], and I lay down straight away. Very tired, melancholy, helpless—felt lonely like a child. If only somebody was there to lovingly massage my forehead.[8]

First thing on Monday, Ravi and Alla Rakha were at Abbey Road to record a new EMI album, *Ragas and Talas*. The most revelatory track on it is the morning *raga Jogiya*, which expresses the sadness of parting and is associated with the pre-dawn hours. Listening now to the *alap* movement, in the light cast by Ravi's weekend diary entry, one can sense the afterglow of his desolation and loneliness in the early hours of Sunday, when he desperately needed human love to substitute for the spiritual euphoria of his performance, and perhaps for the addictive high of wild acclamation. It is a supremely sensitive passage. As so often, his most beautiful playing balanced on a razor's edge between melancholy and bliss.

That day he learned from Angadi that Vilayat Khan had been disparaging about him during his summer tour. "Feel more hurt than angry—the very person who gives the impression of such cordiality—calls me 'Dada' [elder brother]—but all this talk behind my back... Nowadays he seems to have turned even nastier," he wrote.

Most amusing is the fact that he suddenly seems to have become all traditional and conservative—and hell bent to point out to all that I am incorporating Western music in mine. What do you do with such childishness—if there is so much anger and bitterness, why does he not come to me and spit it all out—so easily resolved. It is as if I have everybody, music director, audience, crowd—at home or abroad—in my grasp, involved in a massive conspiracy against him—that's how he feels, it seems. He plays so well, is in such demand—so much respect—what's lacking, what more does he want? Why this complex?[9]

After a concert at Manchester University Union, Ravi arrived in Leeds. The city's music festival was essentially a choral affair, seasoned with chamber concerts and opera, but for this centenary celebration Lord Harewood, directing it for the first time, had diversified into jazz (including appearances by Duke Ellington, Johnny Dankworth and Humphrey Lyttelton), blues (Muddy Waters) and two Indian music recitals by Ravi in Leeds City Art Gallery. At the Queens Hotel, where the artists were staying, and on a visit to Harewood House Ravi socialized with Ellington, Yehudi Menuhin, Benjamin Britten and Peter Pears, pianist Annie Fischer and conductor Rafael Kubelík. The festival was also notable for the presence of Harewood's first cousin, the Queen, although Ravi was not introduced to her on this occasion. Among the audience for Ravi's first recital were Harewood himself; his mother, the Princess Royal; and his cousin, Prince Ludwig of Hesse and the Rhine. An ecstatic Yehudi was in the front row. Ravi himself attended a number of concerts: by Ellington's orchestra; by Britten, Pears and Norma Procter at Temple Newsam; and by Yehudi. At Yehudi's recital, Ravi was struck by an Enescu piece that followed a Beethoven sonata: "What a difference from Beethoven's grave and deeply thoughtful soul!! Wild—the unbridled passion of the gypsies, sorrow, tears—everything is there."[10]

A week later George and Marion Harewood were leaving for their first trip to India, on a lecture tour. Their original plan had been to explore the country with Britten, Pears and Ravi—a tantalizing band of travelers—but the other three had all canceled, Britten and Pears owing to work commitments and Ravi because Coast had booked him on a European tour. This made for an awkward moment for Ravi at the festival banquet:

> I sat at a table with Marion and Prince Hesse. Countess Marion was looking extremely beautiful. The one-piece dress with open shoulder on one side suited her admirably. She was a little cross with me... Last year I had given them my word that I would

show them around in India—can't do that anymore, so had to endure a few words from her.[11]

Despite the countess's reaction, the Harewoods hardly lacked for connections where they were going: they stayed in Delhi with the president of India at Rashtrapati Bhavan.[12] Nevertheless, from half-way across the world Ravi went to great lengths to arrange an evening of live music for them at his Delhi home, giving Harihar Rao instructions about the musicians he wanted, as well as the flowers and sweets. He even specified the exclusive guest list of nine, which included, interestingly, Annapurna.[13] He had acted in a similarly thoughtful fashion when James and Ann Laughlin had traveled to India in January 1957, writing then to Harihar from New York, telling him to assist them.[14] This kind of meticulous hospitality to friends was a mark of his generosity, but it was also an excellent way of cultivating relationships with influential people. For the flutist Hariprasad Chaurasia, this was one of Ravi's unique skills: "He knew whom to meet and whom to make friends with and whom to play with. To have such a convincing power, nobody else has that—how to make yourself known to that kind of crowd."[15]

After concerts in Birmingham and Oxford, Ravi embarked on a six-week tour of Europe, starting with a major event to celebrate United Nations Day (October 24), which took peace as its theme. Three venues in the USA, France and Switzerland staged coordinated performances: each was televised in its own country, with an international radio broadcast of the integrated concert. The event began at the UN General Assembly in New York, where Pablo Casals was making his first appearance in America since the Spanish Civil War; then it transferred to the Salle Pleyel in Paris for a Soviet–American duet by violinists David Oistrakh and Yehudi Menuhin, playing Bach's Double Concerto, followed by Ravi with Alla Rakha; and finally moved to the Victoria Concert Hall in Geneva for a performance of Beethoven's Ninth Symphony. The prestige of the event was such that for a few years it was what Ravi was best known for in the West. At a party in Paris, Ravi met Henri Cartier-Bresson and Nicolas Nabokov, and discussed a shared love of Chaplin's films with Jean Renoir. Ten days later he played another gala show in Paris, appearing for just ten minutes (for a fee of £84), to mark the opening of UNESCO's new headquarters. Ravi was already being perceived as an artistic representative not only of India but of the entire non-Western world—the preferred ambassador for what later was to become known as world music.

The tour continued to West Germany, the Netherlands and Italy. Ravi had not succeeded in securing an American leg, and by mid-December he was back in India, where Annapurna had moved into his Hailey Road home, presumably during his absence in Europe. It is hard to reconstruct exactly how he felt about this development at the time. In later years he presented it as unwelcome, and it is unclear whether he even knew in advance that she was coming back to him. The first indication is the return address on her letter of October 29, sent to Ravi in Paris. For months she had been sending him letters seeking reconciliation, and there is some evidence that he initially thought they could reach a modus vivendi. "After a long time I've got the most beautiful letter from you," she wrote to him in Bombay in February 1959.[16]

Sixteen-year-old Shubho, who had spent so much time apart from both his parents, had hoped for a reunion. A letter he wrote shortly afterward to his father, who was away in Bombay, paints a picture of a cozy home at Hailey Road, complete with family dog, Rana: "I am happy and enjoying myself among friends. Mother too is happy and well. Our sweet little nest is as sweet as before. Rana the old little thing too acts still as a young one."

There was an expectation that Shubho would be a musician, but he had started his music studies relatively late and was at the same time equally attracted to the visual arts. Private lessons had been arranged with a fine art teacher. Ravi felt conflicted between encouraging his son to follow in his footsteps and allowing him to find his own path.

In the same letter Shubho expresses his wish to prioritize the sitar, despite not having his father's all-consuming drive for classical music:

> I will take music seriously whether I have to struggle a lot and forget everything about film music, Rock'n'roll etc. I feel that he who have no ambition in his life and has not struggled in order to fulfill his ambition is just like a dead man. (Do you agree.) So my main ambition at present is to be a sitarist no. 1. Do help me in having an opportunity to fulfill my only wish. I am rather taking an oath my dear father that I will never change my mind and do watch me slowly slowly I will change my own self entirely.[17]

It is telling how he seeks validation; the impression is that this is an attempt to please his father.

Even after Annapurna's return, her letters to Ravi show that her self-esteem was still disturbingly low. "I just hate myself so much I cannot explain to you. My soul is dead. I can't even recognize myself. I like it only whenever you are here," she wrote just after moving into Hailey Road, a message that seems to have upset him.[18] This did not bode well for the future of their marriage. Whatever Ravi had at first hoped, in retrospect he believed that the attempt at a new start had been doomed: "Though Annapurna and I tried hard, something had snapped between us."[19] Trust had given way to suspicion. Ravi was told that the Indian legal system would have made divorce much more straightforward after a three-year separation. They had spent about three months less than that apart, and Ravi came to suspect that the only reason Annapurna had come back was to prevent him seeking a divorce: "She said she was very sorry. 'Let's start all over again.' I said OK. There was nothing else I could do. But then our relationship was really broken. It was just staying together."[20]

Why did he feel there was nothing else he could do? There were two reasons he was not prepared to push for a contested divorce. Certainly, he was sensitive to his public reputation. But probably more important was the sense that divorcing Annapurna would be tantamount to divorcing his *guru*, a step he could not bring himself to take. A *guru* was supposed to be for life.

The marriage became largely a facade. This was surely the "compromise to suit other purposes" against which Marilyn Silverstone had warned Ravi. It was an unhappy situation that was to persist for the next eight years. Annapurna's last solo concert performance had been in Calcutta during their separation, so if she did give up performing live in an effort to save the marriage, as she later claimed, it must have been during this period. Her gesture, whatever her motivation, had no effect on the breakdown of the marriage.

It appears that Annapurna did offer, at least initially, to reach an accommodation with Ravi. "As you suggested, I really do not want any lies between us," she had written to him in the letter of October 29. "I want to see your true face, even if it is very hard for me to accept, but it will be my only consolation if you are not lying to me and you will not lie to me. If the tie between us is not of truth then it will break again." But what Ravi wanted now was an open relationship. He had become convinced that marriage—and his extended embrace of self-denial—did not suit him. Like a love addict long denied his fix, he swung to the other extreme.

Before 1959 the only love letters in his archives are from Marilyn Silverstone during 1957–8, but from 1959 onward others start to appear. The jewel in the collection is the twenty-year, two-way correspondence with Kamala. This had become a serious relationship. They would meet in Bombay, where she lived in the Khar district with Lakshmi and Rajendra, or occasionally in Calcutta, where Ravi rented a one-bedroom flat in Presidency Court, an apartment block on Ballygunge's Gariahat Road. Given his hectic touring, not to mention Annapurna's return, he and Kamala were usually apart. So they wrote to each other, sometimes daily, and he sent telegrams or, very occasionally, used the telephone. His letters were usually two sides long and his handwriting betrays a sense of urgency. Frequent topics were his upcoming schedule or his bouts of ill health (especially stomach problems, which plagued him throughout his life), but above all they were saturated with love and longing: "You are very much with me here…I kiss you ardently," he wrote; or "I think of you so often, my love…I want you so desperately and urgently."[21] At the end of October there was a night in Calcutta that Kamala still cherished seven years later, when she told him, "Nothing can be compared with the Diwali…I spent with you in Cal in 1959. It is still imprinted in my memory."[22] Of another night, he wrote, "Really it seemed like a beautifully perfect awareness of supreme bliss! Darling, I love you so!"[23] Often he used his letters to express erotic desire for her, switching from English to Bengali for the more explicit lines, which he playfully liked to punctuate with a modified exclamation mark in the shape of a phallus.

There is the sense of a very passionate relationship, a fire that was being carefully tended (and sometimes vigorously stoked) over a long distance. The practicalities were complicated and stealth was required. Ravi often sent his letters to her office in Churchgate, or through Joshipura. If he planned to telephone, he might write in advance telling Kamala to be downstairs at a particular time. When he hoped to stay with her in Khar, he might ask her to confirm that "the weather is good," perhaps indicating that Lakshmi and Rajendra would be away.[24] Communications were unreliable too. Although the postal service was fast—there were night-mail trains between the big cities—letters went missing now and then, causing anxiety about who might read them. He sometimes had to wait a whole morning to get a phone line from Calcutta to Bombay.[25]

There is no doubt that their frequent separations intensified Ravi's passion for Kamala. She tolerated him having other lovers (he had many), and he was free to tell her about them. As far as he was concerned, this was a matter of being honest with each other, rejecting hypocrisy in matters of love and desire. There is no evidence that Kamala herself took any other lovers; she was playing Radha to his Krishna. Ravi seems to have been open with each woman that she did not have an exclusive claim on him.

At some point in 1959 Marilyn Silverstone finally arrived in India, where, as she had earlier told Ravi, she hoped their relationship would "reach full flower and madness." Ravi's somewhat vague account years later was that "she came for me actually, and we had a plan. But something happened—in the meantime I was not available there."[26] He might have meant that Annapurna's return prevented him from making any kind of commitment, although perhaps an equal obstacle was his affair with Kamala, which had not been so important when he had last seen Marilyn eighteen months earlier. Marilyn's letters imply that it would have been all or nothing for her, but Ravi's feelings for her had waned. There was no resumption of their affair, although they did meet and, as he told Kamala, he did write a "sentimental" letter to her.[27] As it happens, she was soon introduced to Frank Moraes, editor-in-chief of the *Indian Express* and biographer of Nehru, and fell in love with him. What she had intended to be a four-month visit ended up being fourteen years of living with Moraes in New Delhi, during which she built a considerable reputation as a photographer.

But Ravi's impact on Marilyn lasted until the end of her life. Following Moraes's death in 1974 she embraced Buddhism and spent the last two decades of her life as a nun in Nepal. After she died of cancer in 1999, it was found that among the few religious objects and family photographs she had kept in her small cell at the Shechen Monastery in Kathmandu there was a print of Ravi playing his sitar. It was inscribed, "To Marilyn, with love Ravi Shankar, May 2nd, 1957"—the last full day they had spent together in New York.[28]

After he returned to India in December 1958, Ravi did not leave the country for seventeen months, but made regular concert tours within its borders. Reviews in this period were divided between effusive praise ("brilliant by any standard") and complaints that he lacked "the usual sparkle" or "the flashes of brilliance and imagination associated with Panditji's play." Some writers promoted the idea that foreign travel had affected his style. The *Times of India*'s uncredited music critic (probably

Mohan Nadkarni, who held that position for half a century), wrote, "It is obvious that the creative genius of Ravi Shankar is searching for new directions in expression and in this he has been influenced by his recent experiments in orchestration and Western music." However, all reviewers, regardless of their verdict, recognized his status. Shortly after Ravi turned forty, he was described as one of "the big three of the music world," along with the vocalists Bade Ghulam Ali Khan and Omkarnath Thakur, both of whom were a generation older.[29]

One remarkable project in 1959 was *Angar* ("Coal"), a new play performed by the Little Theatre Group in Calcutta. It was based on the true story of a coalmine accident in which trapped coalminers were gradually submerged by rising water. Lighting designer Tapas Sen created a memorable effect with pinpoints of light shining through holes in tin cans. "The whole effect of disaster and panic was very powerfully rendered," said Ravi. "To be able to produce such plays on the small old stage of the Minerva Theatre in Calcutta was mind-boggling."[30] Ravi honored his promise to Utpal Dutt and supplied the music, recording it with a small ensemble at National Sound Studio in north Calcutta. In contrast to the commercial failure of *Lower Depths*, *Angar* was a phenomenon, the public drawn by the gripping realist story and Ravi's music. It ran for 300 nights in the city, of which 297 were sold out, before touring to Bombay in 1961.[31]

Commissions from Bengali filmmakers meant that Calcutta was assuming a greater importance in Ravi's life. He had many friends there and his apartment was well located. Gariahat Road carried nothing like the thundering, choking volume of traffic that it does today. He installed his cousin Jogu Chatterjee in a nearby flat, and he occasionally called in on the painter Jamini Roy, the grand old man of Indian art, whose studio was almost opposite Presidency Court.[32] Meanwhile, in Bombay Ravi had accepted the commissions for *Go-daan* and *Anuradha*. He was spending increasing amounts of time in these two cities because they were where most of the work was— but perhaps it also suited him to stay away from his Delhi home.

Without the All India Radio job, and with most of his work else-where, Ravi finally came to the conclusion that it made no sense to stay in Delhi. He had done as much as anyone to nurture the city's musical life, but there was still a lack of cultural opportunity. One option was basing himself in Calcutta, but he had a lifelong ambivalence toward the city, and he decided that maintaining the flat there was sufficient commitment. Instead he chose to return to Bombay, attracted by the artistic prospects there, as well as Kamala's presence. In spring 1960 he bought a spacious second-floor flat with a sea view in an apartment block auspiciously named Pavlova, in the upmarket area of Malabar Hill. He decided to decorate the flat in Indo-Japanese style, with bamboo featuring heavily. While he was waiting for his new furniture to arrive he hired some second-hand pieces and insisted on disinfecting them all.[33] He prized cleanliness and could be very fastidious.

Shubho, who was coming to the end of his time at the Modern School, remained in Delhi with his mother for about eight months before they joined Ravi at Pavlova. Another addition to the household was a dachshund named Munna, whom Annapurna taught to sing.[34] In Bombay Shubho entered the Sir J. J. School of Art, a venerable institution of Victorian origin, to study fine art. One of the school's earliest members of staff had been Lockwood Kipling, whose son Rudyard was born on the campus. Previous students included Uday Shankar and Francis Newton Souza. Shubho also continued learning the sitar, but Annapurna now took over teaching him, as Ravi was not around consistently enough to perform that role.

Before Annapurna and Shubho moved in, an early house guest at Pavlova was the young Shivkumar Sharma. Ravi had first met him in his native Jammu in 1956, when, aged eighteen, he had accompanied Ravi on tabla at the radio station and given him a private demonstration of his proficiency on the santoor. This type of hammered dulcimer was commonly used for folk music in Jammu and Kashmir, but Sharma adapted the instrument and then for years waged an

ultimately triumphant campaign to gain acceptance for it as appropriate for classical music. Ravi was one of Sharma's keenest early supporters, and used him in a number of his own ensemble compositions.
The first of these was probably *Angar*. In 1960 Sharma moved from
Jammu to Bombay to seek his musical fortune, and Ravi brought
him in to play on the *Go-daan* soundtrack; his santoor features on
the instrumental title music and on *Janam Liyo Lalna*. Sharma's early
months in the city were financially precarious. He recalls how during
a rehearsal at Pavlova he asked Ravi if he could leave early, because he
had discovered that his flatmate had been pocketing his rent money
rather than paying it to their landlord. "Maybe I will have to move
out of my house," he told Ravi. "I'll have to organize a hotel room and
shift over there."

"Nothing doing," was the reply. "You are not going to a hotel. Bring
your bags over here."

So Sharma moved in. Ravi was about to head out of town, but told
his cook to ensure that his guest ate well. "This I can never forget,"
says Sharma. "I stayed there about a month or so until I rented my
own flat. This large-heartedness, this love—this shows the tender side
of his heart."[35]

When Ravi traveled abroad in the 1950s and early 1960s, his airport
departures and arrivals were covered by the Indian press as newswor-
thy in themselves. He was often pictured emerging from a pile of garlands, no doubt keeping his hands well away from the flowers. The
global music circuit was tiny in comparison with its scale today, and
Indian musicians had little access to it. Travel costs and foreign exchange controls were prohibitive, and the international demand for
Indian arts was still at an embryonic stage. The one body that could
overcome these difficulties was the Indian government, which, under
Nehru, used culture to punch above its diplomatic weight. It provided
support either through subsidizing travel expenses, as it had offered to
do following Ravi's invitation to New York in 1955, or by organizing

official cultural delegations, including his visits to the Soviet Union and Japan. At their best, such official trips bestow prestige, improve international relations through cultural exchange and provide artists with access to people and places unreachable through commercial ventures. Unforeseen benefits often result. However, there can be disadvantages.

Between mid-May and the beginning of October 1960, Ravi undertook four foreign trips in fairly rapid succession, all in response to official invitations. First he spent four weeks in Czechoslovakia, Austria and Switzerland, taking with him the tabla player Shashi Bellare, nephew and disciple of Taranath Rao (Harihar's half-brother). Ravi's main performance was a two-and-a-half-hour set at Prague's showpiece Rudolfinum Theatre, one of five concerts he gave during the Prague Spring festival of classical music, to which the Indian government had sent him as participant and observer. He delighted the locals by weaving the strains of Czech folk songs into his final *thumri* number, and there were many reviews in the Czechoslovak press. At the city's Hotel Esplanade he mixed with the Western classical titans Sir John Barbirolli, Isaac Stern and Mstislav Rostropovich, but he was just as stirred by an encounter with six Romany musicians in the Slovak spa town of Bardejov. This prompted in him the same feelings as the Enescu piece had in Leeds: "I was immensely moved by their music, which has tremendous passion and pain, and many of their melodies strangely echo the strains of some of our *raags* [ragas] like *Bhairavi* and *Nat Kirvani*." Ravi was intrigued by their claim that their gypsy ancestors were migrants from India—then a little-known theory, but recently borne out by genome sequencing. His fascination with the musical links between European gypsies and Indians was the seed of a collaboration with Yehudi Menuhin four decades later. Equally thrilling on the trip were the films he watched: *La Dolce Vita* and *Hiroshima mon amour*, which he saw in Zurich (where he played at the Museum Rietberg), and Jiří Trnka's color puppetry masterpiece *A Midsummer Night's Dream*. "Never since *Fantasia* have

I seen a creation like this one," he said of the Shakespeare realization, and appealed to the Indian film industry or government to create animated versions of the *Ramayana* or *Mahabharata*.[36]

The second trip, to Iraq, illustrated the potential drawbacks when culture is subservient to diplomacy. Ravi led a select group of Indian artists, including Alla Rakha and the young Kathak stars Kumudini Lakhia and Birju Maharaj. The omens were hardly propitious, since the three concerts in Baghdad were staged to celebrate the second anniversary of the revolution of July 14, 1958, when the Iraqi king had been murdered in a military coup. Every evening Prime Minister Qasim, who had led the coup, arrived late at the venue, at which point the audience was obliged to stand and sing the national anthem. Somehow, even though Ravi varied the running order each night, the interruption always occurred in the middle of his recital, forcing him to pause until the anthem was finished. He saw the funny side, but he must have seethed inside at the disrespect for music. A short tour by train followed; Ravi shared a compartment with Maharaj, who took the top bunk, while Ravi, as the senior artist, had the bottom one.[37]

The third invitation, in August, to give a concert tour of Ceylon (later Sri Lanka), came from the Ceylon government. Highlights included a sightseeing trip to the Buddhist ruins at Polonnaruwa and a photocall with the prime minister, Sirimavo Bandaranaike, who just two weeks earlier had become the world's first female head of government.[38] "This is an enchanted land," Ravi wrote home. "It's beautiful—so green and soothing to eyes! I have been given a heroes [*sic*] welcome—and ovation. My photo with the new (lady) P.M. was on the front page."[39] Ravi caught up with his friend Lionel Edirisinghe, principal of the government music college in Colombo, but a meeting that proved more formative was with Penny Estabrook, the American musicologist who had seen Ravi play at New York Town Hall in 1957. She had since completed a doctorate in Indian music at Columbia and taken elementary tabla and sitar lessons. Her trip to Ceylon was a graduation present from her father, and she met Ravi briefly at his final concert in Colombo. The next morning her 5 a.m. alarm call was accidentally switched with the 4 a.m. call for Ravi, who was staying at the same hotel. The result was that they encountered each other in the hotel lobby—she killing time, he rushing like a whirlwind, late for his flight. Perhaps because of the odd way fate had brought them together at that instant, something clicked between them. "Please look me up if you ever come to India," he told her.[40]

The fourth trip was to Kathmandu, where Ravi led a cultural delegation and met with King Mahendra and Queen Ratna of Nepal. Soon afterward, he was much taken by a recent bestselling novel set in Nepal, *The Mountain Is Young* by Han Suyin. Perhaps the subject resonated with him; it is about a woman on a journey of self-discovery, falling in love after a long and stifling marriage.[41]

Although he was barely installed in his Bombay flat (and still awaiting his Japanese furniture), Ravi was soon spending more time away—if not for concerts, then for writing commissions. By now his reputation as a composer for both cinema and theater was firmly established. His next major theatrical project was a new Indian ballet by Uday. Ravi had put aside his mixed feelings about his brother and had for a while been telling Uday that they should collaborate on a project. At last Uday agreed, and so Ravi spent much of November and December 1960 in Calcutta. *Samanya Kshati* was the result; it was the first time they had worked together since *Kalpana* and their only collaboration as true equals. It was staged in 1961 to mark the centenary of the birth of Tagore, who had written the story of an arrogant queen who destroys some of her villagers' houses to use for firewood. The subject had been suggested by Amala Shankar, who danced the lead role. Ravi poured his heart into the project, and loved the result: "It was one of my works where I felt most inspired."[42] There is a remarkable photograph taken after the premiere of Ravi being congratulated by India's Vice-President Radhakrishnan and Prime Minister Nehru. It was a moment that Ravi remembered well: Uday, who was standing beside him still wearing the king's regalia, was saying, "Before he was Uday Shankar's brother, but now I am Ravi Shankar's brother."[43] Lord Harewood, who visited Calcutta during the dress rehearsals, was thrilled by the production and hoped it could be staged in Britain. That did not prove possible, but Uday made it the centerpiece of his show during his 1962 U.S. tour, when Ravi's score was described by the *New York Times* as "the lifeline of the work, which is filled with exotic vocal and instrumental color, and which seems to give all the dances and dramatic incidents their rightful shape and duration."[44]

At the same time Ravi was composing the music for a pair of dance pieces choreographed by his cousin Sachin Shankar. *Utsav* and *Jay-Parajay* were produced by the Indian National Theatre and performed in March 1961 at Tejpal Auditorium in Bombay, before touring around the country. Ravi also recorded an orchestral suite for All India Radio's Tagore centenary celebrations in May.

There were more signs that Ravi's standing among the elite was rising. In Calcutta, during a garden banquet at the Raj Bhavan, the governor of West Bengal presented him to Queen Elizabeth, who was on a state visit. When his name was announced she asked animatedly, "Weren't you at the Leeds Festival?"[45] Back in Bombay he celebrated his forty-first birthday at Pavlova by playing for a select gathering, including Guru Dutt, Waheeda Rehman, Alla Rakha and the cast of *Angar*, who were in town for its short run at Rang Bhavan's open-air theater.[46]

The drawback to being in such demand was that—even by his own standards—he was pushing himself too hard, as his letters to Kamala make clear. "Going still through the usual mad rush work & without sleep," he told her in January as he was completing *Samanya Kshati*. On February 17, while working on the film *Sandhya Raag*, he wrote, "I have been working average of 14 hours a day since the 13th ... I wish I could sleep at a stretch for at least 20 hours."[47]

After *Samanya Kshati*, Uday and Ravi decided to work together on *Life of Buddha*. This was a shadow-play theater piece that Uday had first created in New Delhi five years before, at the time of the Buddha Jayanti festival, which marked the 2,500th anniversary of the

Buddha's attainment of nirvana. Now Ravi wrote music for a new production. As the sweltering Calcuttan summer wore on, he continued at a hectic pace on this and the *Sandhya Raag* score. "I've been working like a madman, though the work (Buddha's music) is almost complete—and seems to be good," he wrote in August.[48] However, for reasons that remain unclear, *Life of Buddha* was never staged with Ravi's music. He and Uday were never to work together again.

Despite the outward appearance of Ravi's restored marital harmony, relations with his father-in-law remained uneasy. Publicly there was no hint of a rift and, when Ravi had told *Link* magazine in September 1958 that the standard of instrumental music in India was higher than ever before, he said that this was "in large measure" because of "the great Allauddin Khan."[49] Yet, as Ravi later wrote, "Even after Annapurna came back to me near the end of 1958 he was still furious with me. It was only after some years that he seemed to calm down, although things were not quite like they had been before."[50]

In Ravi's letters the first sign of the improvement comes in September 1960, when a visit to Maihar made him feel wistful: "Here I am at the place where I was born (though not physically) and have become whatever I am today!" he wrote to Kamala. "I feel strangely at peace and devoid of all worries. Though am a little sad—to see Baba so old and weak and lonely—same about Ma. Poor things! I owe him and them so much."[51]

Matters were complicated by Baba's frailty. According to Ravi, he was now "slightly senile." His age had become another part of his legend. Officially he was ninety-seven, although Ravi was skeptical and one scholar has plausibly proposed he was really seventy-eight.[52] When he was taken ill that November, Ravi canceled concerts and dashed to Maihar, fearing the worst: "Hope it's not too late."[53] There was another scare the following July when Ravi reported that Baba had undergone "a very serious prostate operation. He is out of danger now, but very weak, dejected and ill-tempered."[54]

Ravi told Kamala that he had attempted a showdown with Anna-purna on this July 1961 visit: "I had longest and frankest talks this time, and firmly have stated many facts, hitherto untold! It has been decided not to take any drastic step at this crucial period. But it has been mutually agreed upon that things can not go on like this—and some definite decision has to be taken—sooner the better!"[55]

Returning to Maihar a month later, Ravi found that the "poor old man is in bad condition. Poor A[nnapurna] is going through real hell—suffering seeing Baba's condition." But he concluded that he was again being bad-mouthed to Baba by Ali Akbar's first wife. "Jobeda [Zubeida] is up to her usual dirty tricks," he wrote.[56]

Four days later, when Ravi was leaving for Kabul as part of another government delegation, he once more had the feeling that Baba was nearing the end of his life: "Saw Baba in a terrible state before leaving. Hope the catastrophe doesn't happen before time! I'm truly so worried." But there was another feeling too: "You know something? There was such thick fog of misunderstanding meaning—distrust, anger from his side—etc. (thanks to Jobeda's calculated propaganda all these years)—and a lot of *abhimaan* [hurt] from my side too! But during the last few weeks (specially last few days) somehow all those seem to have vanished. We both feel how deep rooted love and bond-age we have. In spite of so many small pettiness and being of a very angry and doubting nature the man is truly such a great great artist. I only pray for his last moments to be peaceful."[57]

Ravi was writing on August 20, 1961. A month later, he departed on a four-month tour of America. As he left, he must have felt that the end was drawing near for his *guru*, and it seems he felt his facade of a marriage was winding down in parallel, given his view that "things can not go on like this." Both had a lot more life left in them than he realized.

12

COAST TO COAST

The greatest ambition of mine from childhood is to compose
& create the ideal Indian orchestra.
RAVI SHANKAR[1]

Ravi often pointed out in later years that his huge success in the West
was no overnight phenomenon. His first solo tours were in 1956–7
and he built on that initial groundwork during the early 1960s.
Crucial was the new Performing Arts Program set up by the Asia
Society in New York in the autumn of 1961. Ravi was one of three
acts invited to tour America in the first season, and the exhausting 40-date schedule sent him all over the country. This perfectly
timed opportunity, satisfying a growing American interest in South
Asian arts, enabled Ravi to cultivate a nationwide college following.
During the scheme's initial four-year incarnation he was its favorite
and most profitable artist, and the only one to be invited back for a
second tour.

Ravi left India in late September 1961, along with Kanai Dutta, a
leading tabla player from Calcutta who had trained with Jnan Prakash
Ghosh. The third member of the trio was once again Nodu Mullick,
who had recently presented Ravi with a new sitar. The instrument was
a masterpiece, completely handcrafted by Mullick himself, with the
neck fashioned from a single piece of toon wood. Mullick had copied
Kanai Lal's ornamentation, now established as the Ravi Shankar style,
but the sound created by his *jawari* (bridge) was even more distinctive. "My bass strings were like thunder," said Ravi.[2] Mullick had made
two sitars at the same time, the other for Amiya Dasgupta. After a
while Ravi decided he preferred the sound of his disciple's and they
swapped instruments. This was to become his principal performance

sitar for the next three decades, replacing the 1944 Kanai Lal model, and he dubbed it his "Stradivarius."

The musicians broke their journey to the USA in London to record three tracks at Abbey Road for Ravi's new album. First, appropriately, was *Hamsadhwani*, a pentatonic Carnatic *raga* restricted to the notes of a major ninth chord. As its bright sound is considered auspicious, it often opens concerts in south India. Next was *Kafi*, the spring *raga* with associations to Holi and the romance between Krishna and Radha, which had also appeared on Ravi's first World Pacific album. As before, he recorded it as a *thumri*-style folkish *dhun*, but this time improvised in a 16- rather than 7-beat cycle, and infused it with what he described as an "erotic spirit."[3] Last came *Ramkali*, a morning *raga* with a devotional mood; Ravi's recording builds through all the phases, from a slow *alap* to a rapid climax, in another 16-beat *gat*. EMI issued the album in December under the generic title *Music of India*. In the USA World Pacific gave it the cumbersome title *India's Master Musician/Recorded in London*, before settling years later on the simpler *In London*.

While in London Ravi met his new agent, Basil Douglas, who had been recommended by Lord Harewood. A one-time flatmate of Peter Pears, Douglas had managed the English Opera Group for seven years, before becoming one of Benjamin Britten's "corpses," the label sometimes given to those whose services and friendship the composer had dispensed with. Douglas had established himself as a classical music agent, bringing with him the invaluable Maureen Garnham, who became a partner in the new business and was devoted to this perceptive and energetic impresario. In time his roster also included Julian Bream, Charles Mackerras and Jean-Pierre Rampal.

It is not certain why Ravi had decided to part company with John Coast. According to Douglas, the decision was mutual, and Ravi reassured him that Coast was a good friend and would be helpful if he wanted any information or materials. Most likely Ravi was swayed by Douglas's greater cachet in the classical world. Ravi also told him that he had been disappointed with the fees Coast agreed with the BBC, claiming that he had accepted them only in order to get publicity: "This time I would like to have the highest [rates] available, and the programs also arranged for a good time and peak hours."[4]

Ravi was in London only briefly, but there was something about the city that seemed to make him prone to accident or injury. An incident on September 27 left his right hand "horribly burnt" from thumb to wrist. "What an experience! Went through hell!" he told Kamala once he was able to write again, three weeks later, still wearing a bandage.[5] He had managed to play through the pain.

The Asia Society had been established by John D. Rockefeller III in 1956, with a remit to strengthen ties between the USA and Asia through arts and education. In 1961, after a survey of U.S. universities, it set up a Performing Arts Program "to give American audiences across the country a first-hand experience with the music, dance and theater arts of Asian countries."[6] The program had an impressive advisory committee, most of whom already knew Ravi, including Ann Laughlin, Yehudi Menuhin and Marian Anderson, as well as dance pioneers Martha Graham and Ted Shawn.[7] Overseeing the scheme was Beate Gordon, a remarkable woman who had spent her childhood in Japan and had helped to draft the country's post-war constitution at the age of just twenty-two. More recently she had been managing the cultural exchange programs for the Japan Society in New York (another Rockefeller vehicle), where one of her young students was Yoko Ono.[8] To run the scheme the Asia Society engaged Isadora Bennett, a sixty-one-year-old publicist specializing in modern dance. She was "a born-in-a-dressing-room theatrical figure," industrious, forthright and very experienced.[9] She took Ravi under her wing, and he was soon writing to her as "Isy dear."[10]

There were two other acts booked for the 1961–2 season. Indrani Rahman with her company of six dancers and musicians toured in parallel with Ravi, and the twelve Ceylon National Dancers followed in the spring of 1962. Indrani's performances never coincided with Ravi's, although they did some pre-tour press together in New York, where they were photographed on his hotel roof. Ten years Ravi's junior, Indrani had a similarly cosmopolitan background. Her mother was Ragini Devi (née Esther Sherman), one of the first Americans to study dance in India, and the young Indrani was drawn to the stage during her childhood, which was divided between India and the USA. She was an early popularizer of Odissi dance in India, and also included Bharatanatyam, Kuchipudi and Kathakali in her repertoire. The highlight of her Asia Society tour was performing for President John F. Kennedy at the Indian Embassy in Washington during Nehru's state visit. Indrani was a famous beauty, the first ever Miss India—an accolade she spent her life trying to live down. According to her daughter, she had a succession of lovers, and it was rumored that after seeing her dance Kennedy tried to engineer a date with her—something she never confirmed or denied.[11] She certainly had an affair with Ravi.

Given the political dimension that the performing arts often had in Asia, it was essential to the Asia Society that the acts were successful. "Anything else could be a boomerang," said Bennett. The scheme, which was a nonprofit, underwrote the tours so that the artists were protected from financial loss and were guaranteed to return home with some money. "Our arrangement with the companies we bring is the most generous and protective one which has ever been worked out in the concert field," Bennett claimed.[12] The State Department provided a grant of about $43,000 to cover international travel expenses. Each venue was charged a fixed fee per appearance: $750 for Ravi, $850 for Indrani and $1,000 for the Ceylon National Dancers. Any profit from the U.S. performances was split equally between artist and program, with the Asia Society's share capped at 20 percent of gross income, but no limit to the artist's take. Ravi's gross income from this tour was $13,314, which was worth a small fortune in India—although he did have to meet the fees of his two fellow musicians and other tour expenses out of this sum. He made much more than the other two acts because the running costs for the trio were far less than for the larger troupes.[13]

Ravi's first tour date was October 1 at Worcester Art Museum, Massachusetts, followed by New York Town Hall the next day. He loved being back in New York. He liked to remind the press that, far from being fresh off the boat, he was in fact on his sixth tour of the USA, and the city felt like home. One reporter playfully tested his fluency in the local patois. Did he know what street was south of 34th Street? "Toity-Toid Street, yes?" Ravi responded, smiling, then added, "You still say Beat It, and Scram?"[14]

In 1961 New York's vibrant new music scene was based in Greenwich Village, where folk clubs had sprung up at venues such as Café Wha? and the Gaslight. Bob Dylan was in the middle of a two-week residency at Gerde's Folk City at the time of Ravi's Town Hall concert. Just four days earlier he had signed to Columbia, after being spotted playing the harmonica on the album sessions for an established folk singer and friend of his, Carolyn Hester.

Hester was in the audience at Ravi's concert. "We were all swept off our feet that evening by the music, and the sitar itself, and *mesmerized* by Ravi," she recalled in 2010.

> There was a certain aroma that swept the hall, like burnt beans. A neighbor sitting there said to me, "That's Acapulco Gold—marijuana." So I guess people were enhancing their enjoyment, but our row didn't need anything to enhance our state. We were in a veritable trance. I have to say Ravi took New York that night.[15]

The show was a commemoration of Gandhi's birthday, and part of the proceeds went to the India Students Association. Isadora Bennett priced balcony tickets at $1.50 so that students could afford them. "A day before the performance it looked like not one would be coming," she recalled. "Then the entire balcony sold out on the night of the performance. I was told that Indians, like the Spanish audience, wait until the last minute."[16] This time the Town Hall performance was an unmitigated triumph. The *Village Voice* said the electricity between the performers was "shooting blue flame...It was nothing less than mesmerizing, hair-raising, giddy, elegantly controlled, aesthetically pure pandemonium...In comparison, barrelhouse, bop and rock'n'roll are positively funereal."[17]

Variety hailed "a performance...that was so lively, so amusing and so dynamic that a tradepaper reviewer must ask, why only college campus dates?"[18] The answer was that the Asia Society's program was conceived as an educational service. Isadora Bennett was careful to preempt any accusation that the generously underwritten scheme operated in unfair competition with commercial agents. Consequently the venues were generally universities and colleges, alongside the occasional museum or other cultural institution. Major commercial halls were avoided. New York Town Hall was an exception because it was affiliated to New York University.

Ravi was in New York for only one night, but he planned to return to the city after the tour ended. His hedge-hopping schedule was grueling. Travel was by a mixture of train, plane and car, all coordinated in meticulous detail by Isadora Bennett. The first three weeks were spent mostly in the northeast, including recitals at Cornell, Colgate, Vassar, Yale, Wesleyan and Johns Hopkins universities, followed by a week in the Midwest. Occasionally Ravi also gave lecture-demonstrations. By November 7, in a letter written from Chicago, he was grumbling to Kamala about the "terribly hectic tour; 5 to 6 recitals a week & traveling constantly. It's so tiring—and my arms and whole body ache so much—as there are very few porters to carry luggages at Airports, Stations, etc. The little that there are—gosh they are so expensive!" He had also been worrying about a financial problem in Calcutta, but was now able to send $500 to Rajendra to repay part of an outstanding loan.[19] He would have been buoyed by the press reaction. Harvard's student paper called him "the Richter of the Raga," an allusion to the Russian pianist Sviatoslav Richter.[20]

Ravi reached Seattle on November 10 and spent a week working his way down the West Coast to Los Angeles. In his three days in the city he recorded two new albums for World Pacific. Dick Bock now had his own studios at 8715 West Third Street and for the first album, *Improvisations and Theme from Pather Panchali*, he assembled a group of four fine jazz musicians: Bud Shank on flute, Dennis Budimir on guitar, Gary Peacock on upright bass and Louis Hayes on drums. Harihar Rao, who had just taken up a Fulbright scholarship at UCLA, came too, bringing a dholak folk drum.

The album showcases Ravi in multiple guises, as if he slips into a new garment for each track. First was Ravi as film composer. By this time the entire *Apu Trilogy* had been released in America, and all three films had been acclaimed as classics, contributing no little to his growing reputation. On tour he had been playing his *Pather Panchali* theme as an occasional encore, and it was an obvious move to record a new version of it. Here the theme is stated first in *alap* style by Ravi on sitar and then by Bud Shank, who was playing the Western flute rather than the bamboo flute used on the soundtrack. Then Ravi improvises in three distinct sections, accompanied by Dutta on tabla and Mullick on manjira (small hand-cymbals): first in the 7-beat *rupaktal* cycle, then in *dadra* of 6 beats, and lastly *keherwa* of 8 beats. After each improvisation, Shank restates the theme on flute, before Ravi's unaccompanied sitar gently closes the piece after just seven minutes. The cloth is perfectly cut, with nothing wasted.

On the second track, *Fire Night*, the tailoring is looser. This was the first time an Indian classical musician had written music recorded by Western jazz musicians—the forerunner of many such collaborations. Ravi did not play, but he arranged and conducted the track, which owes its title to a major brush fire that had burned down hundreds of nearby homes a week earlier. This experimental piece opens with Dutta playing the damaru, an hourglass drum associated with Shiva as god of destruction. The flute then introduces the folklike main melody in the *raga Dhani*, the pentatonic scale of which has a kinship with the blues. A series of solos follow on drum kit, flute, tabla, guitar, drum kit (Hayes playing with mallets this time), bass and, again, flute. The feel is less precise than the previous track, the rhythmic pulse varying between sections. Hayes, who was twenty-four and had already recorded with John Coltrane, was impressed by the Indian musicians but recalls that there was no time to learn about Indian music. "I didn't try to figure a time signature that they were playing in, because that wouldn't have made any sense to me back then," he says. "I just played what I felt would accompany it and make it work."[21] Interestingly, the press release given to the Indian media described this as "a beautiful new fusion of Indian light and Western jazz music," an early use of the F-word in connection with music.[22]

Side 1 closes, characteristically, with Ravi in south Indian attire, playing the Carnatic *raga Kirwani* in north Indian style, and finishing in a *sawal–jawab* exchange between sitar and tabla. But the true masterpiece of *Improvisations* is on side 2: the evening *raga Rageshri*. Ravi's superlative classical performance in three parts—*alap*, *jor* and a short *gat* in *rupaktal*—remains one of his daughter Anoushka's favorites among all his recordings. "East Meets West on this strange but fascinating disk," ran the *New York Times* review, "and East wins."[23]

The other album from World Pacific was a recording of Ravi's November 19 performance at UCLA, where he had been upgraded to Royce Hall. Two twenty-minute cuts were issued: the romantic afternoon *raga Madhuvanti* and a playful nocturnal *Mishra Mand* in the form of a folk-like *dhun*, with which he had ended the concert. In contrast with the *Rageshri* recorded in the studio, both tracks feature only brief (*aochar*) *alaps*, majoring instead on the sitar–tabla teamwork in the extended *gats*. The *dhun*, especially, radiates joy and frolic. "None of our jazz boys can hold a stick of incense to this particular combo," admitted the *Los Angeles Times* review of the concert.[24] Continuing the trend for World Pacific album titles that seem to be extended improvisations in themselves, the LP was issued as *India's Most Distinguished Musician in Concert*. Later releases preferred the simpler *In Concert*.

Revitalized by his time in Los Angeles, Ravi flew the next day to Oklahoma, continuing on to Dallas and Iowa City, before retracing his steps to the northeast for nine more venues in the final fortnight. By the time he reached Dallas he was feeling more positive, as he wrote to Kamala:

> All the financial torture plus the terrible accident of burnt hand put me in horrible state of dazed numbness for nearly 2 months— but now I seem to be coming out of it and gathering up courage & strength enough to fight everything against me & overcome. Just be with me...always, will you my love? No matter what happens?...I love you, want you—passionately.[25]

After the final concert of the tour in Washington, DC, a reception was given in Ravi's honor by Ambassador B. K. Nehru at the Indian Embassy. The day before, India's armed forces had entered Goa. The territory, on India's west coast, was at the time a colony of Portugal, a situation that Prime Minister Nehru had described as a pimple on the fair face of India. Ever since Indian independence, the Portuguese regime of António de Oliveira Salazar had refused demands to withdraw. Goa was captured within thirty-six hours and annexed as a union territory of India. The American government objected to this use of force (there were about fifty deaths) and the media whipped up a moral storm at the supposed hypocrisy of Nehru and Krishna Menon, who for years had lectured the West on non-violence. The numerous Capitol Hill officials invited to Ravi's reception were instructed to boycott it in protest. Ravi, who liked to keep out of politics, found himself giving a somewhat surreal recital in the dining room to a scattering of guests, including the Russian ambassador, who was loudly praising the "war of liberation," and Jackie Kennedy's mother, Janet Auchinloss, who had apparently not received the directive.[26]

Ravi spent three weeks in New York over the New Year, relaxing, catching up with films and plays, and spending time with a new girlfriend, Hallie Scott, who had been at his Town Hall performance.

He also took the opportunity to explore more of the city's jazz scene. He met up again with Conrad Rooks, who had returned from three years in Asia with a worsening drug habit and a passion for India and cinema—Raj Kapoor had given him a tour of his film studios in Bombay. Rooks invited Ravi to play at his apartment on Perry Street in Greenwich Village, and later claimed that he had introduced him to John Coltrane and the Modern Jazz Quartet.[27] There has long been confusion about the chronology of Ravi's encounters with Coltrane. Ravi himself was unsure of the dates, but he remembered it was Dick Bock, not Rooks, who first brought them together; that he gave Coltrane some private lessons in Indian music at his New York hotel; and that he once went to see him perform live. It now seems certain that all these events took place during this three-week period.

For Coltrane these encounters were momentous. After *Kind of Blue*, his pursuit of modal improvisation had led, in late 1960, to his brilliant interpretation of "My Favorite Things"—from the new Broadway musical *The Sound of Music*—which seems to bear traces of Indian music and encouraged other jazz players to move in that direction. Coltrane said that the Indian influence was "at that time more or less subconscious," although the bright nasal tone he produced on soprano saxophone is reminiscent of the sound of the shehnai.[28] By early 1961 Coltrane was immersing himself in Indian music, as well as in music from other cultures. This exploration bore fruit in his album *Africa/Brass*, released in September, another modal set that foregrounds melody and rhythm.

In November, the Indian influence in Coltrane's music became explicit when he recorded a track entitled "India" live over four nights at the Village Vanguard in New York. This piece is rooted in a drone on twin double-basses, and on three of the nights there was even a tanpura in the ensemble. Above them soared Coltrane's melody, which was based on a Vedic chant he had heard on a Folkways LP, but his shrieking, hallucinatory improvisation on soprano sax is otherworldly. His convoluted melodies on just one or two chords stirred up violent reactions for and against; a scathing review in *Down Beat* described the new style as "anti-jazz" and "gobbledegook."[29]

In Paris later that month Coltrane discussed Ravi with a French journalist. "I collect the records he's made," he said, "and his music moves me. I'm certain that if I recorded with him I'd increase my possibilities tenfold, because I'm familiar with what he does and I understand and appreciate his work." He was brandishing a letter from Dick Bock confirming a meeting with Ravi when he returned to New York.[30]

Ravi knew from experience that while black jazz musicians were admired in America, the law enshrined racial discrimination and they were denied the full respect they deserved. Many lived hard lives and struggled with drug problems. Knowing what Coltrane had contended with made Ravi appreciate him all the more when they met: "He had sophistication, dignity and at the same time such humility."[31] After kicking heroin four years earlier, Coltrane had become a dedicated musical and spiritual explorer, embracing vegetarianism and reading spiritual texts, including those by Yogananda and by the nineteenth-century saint Ramakrishna Paramahansa. It seems that Ravi recognized something of himself in the saxophonist. Coltrane had sought to re-route his addictive tendencies toward music and was now renowned for his intensive practice regime.

They talked first over dinner, during which Coltrane ordered a vegetable cutlet, while Ravi ate chicken, apologetically explaining that meat boosted his strength on tour. They liked each other, and the following day they met again at Ravi's hotel. Coltrane talked only a little about his own music and had not brought his saxophone, preferring to ask Ravi questions about Indian music. The American was profoundly moved, and Ravi's exquisite demonstrations on sitar brought him to tears.[32] Coltrane, said Ravi, was "amazed by our different system of improvisation within the framework and discipline of fixed melody forms, by the complexity of our *talas*, and more than anything by how we can create such peace, tranquility and spirituality in our music."[33]

Coltrane invited his new mentor to come to one of his concerts. During the first half of January he was playing the Jazz Gallery at 80 St. Mark's Place, an East Village address that already had a fabled history: Leon Trotsky had stayed upstairs in early 1917, and W. H. Auden still lived across the street at No. 77. Coltrane played sets every day, and twice on Sundays, with Monday off. On one of these days Ravi came to the Jazz Gallery and spoke to Coltrane again and to his pianist, McCoy Tyner. The three discussed recording an album together.[34]

"The music was fantastic," said Ravi.

> I was much impressed, but one thing distressed me. There was turbulence in the music that gave me a negative feeling at times, but I could not quite put my finger on the trouble...Here was a creative person who had become a vegetarian, who was studying yoga, and reading the *Bhagavad-Gita*, yet in whose music I still heard much turmoil. I could not understand it.[35]

The time spent with Ravi confirmed Coltrane in his new musical direction. "I feel I'm just beginning again," he told *Down Beat* in April 1962, the month when he formed what has become known as the "classic" John Coltrane Quartet, along with Tyner, Elvin Jones and Jimmy Garrison.[36] The following year he said:

> I like Ravi Shankar very much. When I hear his music, I want to copy it—not note for note of course, but in his spirit. What brings me closest to Ravi is the modal aspect of his art. Currently, at the particular stage I find myself in, I seem to be going through a modal phase...There's a lot of modal music that is played every day throughout the world. It is particularly evident in Africa, but if you look at Spain or Scotland, India or China, you'll discover this again in each case...It's this universal aspect of music that interests me and attracts me; that's what I'm aiming for.[37]

*

It wasn't just jazz. Like a wandering star coursing through the galaxy, Ravi was exerting a gravitational pull on the music of many different spheres, among them the newest incarnation of Western classical music—minimalism. Terry Riley, one of its founding fathers, was in the audience for Ravi's concert on November 12, 1961 at Berkeley, where he had recently been a student. This was Riley's first encounter with any non-Western music. Forty years later he recalled how inspired he had been that night by the interaction between Ravi and Kanai Dutta:

> What impressed me was the joy in their performance. They were looking at each other, smiling, and feeling joy in what they were doing. I came away from that concert thinking to myself, "Boy, that's a very satisfying way to make music." To create such joy, not only for the musicians, but also for the audience.[38]

At this period the dominant movement in the classical world was serialism, which had been developed in the early twentieth century by Arnold Schoenberg and his disciples of the Second Viennese School, including Alban Berg and Anton Webern. This was the music of European high modernism—intellectual and radical in spirit, its structures dictated by the twelve-note series, and often dissonant to the ear. The rise of Nazism displaced its center of gravity to America, where its leading lights found work in exile on university campuses and Hollywood soundtracks. Its sense of fragmentation and tension mirrored the ruined landscapes and ravaged psyches of the post-war world. By the 1950s it had created its own avant-garde establishment, with a new generation of European patriarchs in Pierre Boulez, Karlheinz Stockhausen and Luciano Berio. Serialism dominated the conservatories but, as the composer George Rochberg said, it was like "an orthodox cultural church, with its hierarchy, gospels, beliefs and anathemas."[39] Over time what had once been liberating and challenging began to some to seem rigid and alienating. Ravi was not the only one who got a headache at Darmstadt.

During the 1960s young composers on both coasts of America began to look for a new approach. The most notable were the Californians La Monte Young and Terry Riley, who had met at the University of California at Berkeley, and the New York-based Philip Glass and Steve Reich, who had studied together at the Juilliard School of Music. They eventually became known as minimalists, although, like the impressionist painters of the nineteenth century, they resisted the label. This loose grouping was united by a belief that, although they had trained within the twelve-tone system and liked some of its music (Reich had studied with Berio), its moment was over. It was too uptight for a new era of adventure and optimism. Riley labeled it neurotic music. Glass called it creepy. Reich dismissed it as "the dark-brown *Angst*" of central Europe, no longer relevant to 1960s America with its tail fins and burgers, bebop and Chuck Berry.[40]

Non-Western music was important in the development of each of these composers. Young, Riley and Glass were all drawn to Indian music, while it was African drumming that inspired Reich. All four were also strongly influenced by jazz, and especially by John Coltrane. Glass spent many nights at the Village Vanguard listening to him. Reich saw him play at least fifty times and was particularly influenced by his modal improvisations on *Africa/Brass*.[41] For Riley, hearing him at the Jazz Workshop in San Francisco was "a very powerful transformative experience" of a devotional nature.[42] Young noticed how Coltrane "would take a fixed constellation of tones and do these very interesting mathematical permutations on them...He had refined the process because of his exposure to Indian classical music and other Eastern traditions of modalism."[43]

Each of the four followed his own path but shared impulses with the others. They all wanted to make more open-ended, democratic music, to take it out of concert halls and into the worlds of theater, dance and art. Like Indian musicians, they all reunited the roles of composer and performer. There were also overlaps in their fascination with repetition, drones, sustained tones, trance and transcendentalism, or the new technology of tape-recorders and electronics. Many of their early works, in particular, feature a cyclical approach to rhythm and melody, characterized by small shifts in repeated patterns that could produce surprisingly intense emotions.

La Monte Young had his lightbulb moment when, as a Webern-loving music student at UCLA in 1956–7, he heard Ali Akbar Khan's album *Music of India* on the radio. He played his copy of the disc so much that his mother wrote "Opium Music" on the sleeve. He became obsessed by the drone of its tanpura. Drones had been a feature of early Western music before slipping out of use almost a millennium ago, although they persisted in folk music.[44] From childhood Young had been fascinated by extended, unchanging tones. Subsequently he experimented with sustained notes and long silences in pieces, including his 1958 *Trio for Strings*, which evolves at a glacial speed. He also advocated just intonation, the tuning system based on the natural harmonic series, as opposed to equal temperament, which is standard in the West. Catalyzed by equal parts mescaline, Indian music and John Cage-style conceptual compositions, he began staging long-form improvisations that he termed the Theatre of Eternal Music.

Before Terry Riley heard Ravi play in 1961, the only music he had previously encountered with the same sense of relish and ritual was jazz. In 1962 he was to have a similar response when he heard Arabic music in Spain and Morocco. On his return to California he became involved with the San Francisco Tape Music Center, a pioneering house of electronic sound, where he experimented with tape-loops. In February 1964 he heard Young's Theatre of Eternal Music in New York and compared it with "the sun coming up over the Ganges."[45]

These experiences drove Riley to produce his most influential work, *In C*, which was premiered in November 1964. This radically simple ensemble piece consists of 53 short melodic modules, using notes mostly from the scale of C major—an abomination to a serialist. In a democratic spirit, it specifies neither its length nor its timing nor the number of musicians. Each player moves on to the next module whenever he or she chooses, and those who arrive first at the final module wait for the others to catch up. Every performance is thus unique. Pulsing throughout the work is a pair of high Cs on a keyboard (played in the premiere by Steve Reich), underpinning it rather as a tanpura does in Indian music. The effect is of shifting, looping waves of complex rhythms and shimmeringly bright harmonies over a chiming drone, mesmerizing and meditative. This was the public birth of minimalism, and with its modal form, droning effects and boundless cyclical repetition, *In C* bore the genetic imprint of Indian music.

Of the four, Reich was the odd one out in not being particularly drawn to Indian music. Young and Riley both went on to explore Hindustani vocal music in depth through studying with Pran Nath after 1970. Philip Glass's Indian epiphany was yet to come but would have the most profound impact of all.

Ravi stopped over for two days in London on the way back to India, but failed to meet up with Basil Douglas as he did not have his new address. Douglas had just moved to 8 St. George's Terrace, the home and office overlooking Primrose Hill from which he was to operate for the rest of his career. The missed meeting and the fact that Ravi had been in touch with his former German agent caused what Ravi described as "a slight misunderstanding" between the two, but the relationship soon recovered and in February they began to plan Ravi's 1963 European tour.[46] He had been booked that summer for the Edinburgh Festival, where Lord Harewood was now the artistic director. He was also being lined up by Mantle Hood for a visiting position at UCLA.[47]

"Pandit Ravi Shankar has done it again," wrote one reporter after Ravi's homecoming press conference in Bombay on January 24.[48] There he related the successes of his tour: the forty-one recitals, the three offers he was considering for American film scores, the growing appreciation for Indian music abroad, and the unnamed U.S. musicians to whom he had given lessons. He was unquestionably the world's best-known Indian musician. But the *Sunday Standard* noted that "some of our orthodox *ustads*" had again accused him of dumbing down Indian music. As in 1957, he was determined to confront this charge. "To popularize any music does not necessarily mean cheapening it," he said.[49] It was a matter of presentation, not content.

In India he typically opened with a long *alap*, of perhaps an hour or more, before moving on to the *jor*, *jhala* and *gat* of the same *raga*. He explained that if he began a concert in this way with a Western audience unfamiliar with Indian music, they might just walk out. He was also conscious that, unlike in India, any latecomers had to wait outside the hall until the end of the first piece. So in America he reversed the sequence. He took his cue from the Carnatic tradition of opening with a lighter piece in fast tempo. "This method of music presentation is nothing new; the south Indians have always understood the value of it," he later explained.[50]

We can take as an example his concert at Chatham College, Pittsburgh, on November 28, 1961. We know exactly what he played because he annotated a copy of the program.[51] He and Kanai Dutta opened with two *gats*, probably prefaced by the briefest of *alaps*: the first was in *Yaman Kalyan*, played in *ektal* (12 beats), the second in *Kirwani*, in slow, medium and fast *teental* (16 beats). After the interval, Dutta played a tabla solo in the 10-beat cycle *jhaptal*. Only then, with the audience initiated, did Ravi play unaccompanied sitar, rendering *Malkauns* through full *alap*, *jor* and *jhala* sections. Kanai Dutta joined in again for the final number, *Pancham Se Gara*, one of Ravi's own *ragas*, played in the lighter *thumri* style in two different rhythmic cycles, *dadra* and a fast *teental*.

Ravi used this five-act sequence throughout the tour: two *gats* before the interval, then a tabla solo, a sitar solo (*alap*, *jor* and *jhala*) and a final *gat* in a lighter style to end with—plus the *Pather Panchali* theme as an encore if required. No doubt the Pittsburgh audience was treated to a rapid-fire *sawal–jawab* exchange between sitar and tabla toward the end of one of the *ragas*—either the *Kirwani*, to create a talking point for the interval, or the *Pancham Se Gara*, to send them home buzzing. He knew how to put a concert together.

Uma Vasudev, in a major article on Ravi's music, had recently defended his right to innovate in this way: "He plays with forms, experiments with techniques, gives a flash and brilliance to his music which is very contemporaneous, very pertinent, very daring…He never tampers with the melodies themselves, the *ragas* of the Indian system upon which its whole melodic structure is built." She mocked those traditionalists whose reaction was to exclaim, "'What? Only an *alap* in one *raga*? Only a *gat* portion for the other?'…They shook their heads sadly, 'Western influence! He is losing his Indian-ness.' Or, 'He's becoming a showman, he does not wish to test his audience too far.'"[52]

At the press conference Ravi also announced his forthcoming new music institute in Bombay, part academy and part production house for the creation of orchestral, theatrical or cinematic works. His ideas had been percolating for several years. Shortly before leaving for America the previous September he had set out his vision in a nine-page handwritten document, "My Dream."[53] He was hoping to build his institute on a verdant plot of two to three acres, away from the downtown hubbub, in one of the more pleasant suburbs, such as the Bandra hills, Khar, Santa Cruz or Vile Parle—a *rus in urbe* idyll. If it all came to fruition, which would require at least five years and some major funding, it would eventually include a school, a sound studio, a concert hall of 750 to 1,100 seats, a studio theater of up to 500 seats, a library of music tapes, and guest rooms for students who did not live in Bombay. The name he initially proposed was Sangeetalaya, but eventually he decided on Kinnara, after the half-human–half-bird celestial musicians of Hindu mythology.

His motivation is revealing:

> The greatest ambition of mine from childhood is to compose
> & create the ideal Indian orchestra—which would be based on
> different styles…such as pure Dhrupad, Dhamar, Khyal, Thumri,
> light, folk & thematic styles! I have had experience enough to say

that "It can be done"—and I CAN DO IT!!! Because of my earlier
love & glamour for stage (as well as experience) and because they
are closely connected with "Orchestration" I want to do new ballets—
and operas & also compose for interesting, novel & artistic films.

He explained that, although he had worked in these fields for other
institutions and individuals over the previous seventeen years, he had
been unhappy because of his "lack of independence & so many other
factors." Although he stated that he wanted to encourage young talents, the school itself seems to have been secondary, conceived in part
as a means of supplying the orchestral projects with trained musicians.

The combination of creative factory and school, the ashram-style
setting in a green space, performance spaces on site, the student accommodation—all these elements point to the principal model and
inspiration for Kinnara being Uday's India Culture Centre. Ravi was
around the same age as Uday had been when he founded his school.
Almora was still exercising its pull on Ravi.

"I am forty-one now, & expect to run about a few more years only
giving concerts," he wrote, "but I intend to settle down whole-time
basis steering the handle of this big venture." But how serious was he
about seeing an end to his perpetual touring? In February 1962 Isadora Bennett promised him that either the Asia Society would invite
him back for a further tour in the autumn of 1964, or else she would
try to arrange "a reputable and leading management" for him in the
USA. He sketched out for her his proposed tour schedule for 1963
and 1964: Australia, Fiji, Indonesia, the Philippines, Japan, Hong
Kong, Thailand, Burma, Edinburgh, Europe, Australia (for a second
time), South America and "West Indies etc.," before the American tour.
Only three months in those two years were blocked out for India.[54]
This does not sound like a man winding down his touring in order to
spend his time running a school. Perhaps the success of the American
tour had modified his thinking, and he was trying to make the most
of the opportunities while he had the energy.

In April 1962 Baba was taken seriously ill with typhoid, and once more Ravi dashed to his bedside in Maihar.[55] Annapurna stayed with her father during his slow recovery, but his fever kept flaring up and she was dissatisfied with the treatment given by the local doctors. She wanted to move him to either Bombay or Calcutta, where the best care was available, and appealed to Ali Akbar and Ravi to arrange it. "He will never get better, he will always have different kinds of complications," she wrote to Ravi on May 1. "This is nearly the end of his life now. He should be where he is comfortable and happy."[56] However, he remained where he was. Whenever Annapurna bought him medicine he made himself ill worrying about the cost, so it is possible that he resisted the expense of a move.

Ravi pressed on with plans to open Kinnara, and canceled a provisional booking at the Royal Festival Hall in October in order to focus his attention on it.[57] Without an investor willing to purchase land for the school, Ravi agreed to open it in July in temporary rented quarters at Breach Candy School on Bhulabhai Desai Road. This was a pleasant seafront location not far from his Malabar Hill apartment, but it was a long way south of the suburbs Ravi had envisaged. Breach Candy has been an upmarket area ever since the city's cotton boom in the nineteenth century. On Bhulabhai Desai Road was the childhood home of Salman Rushdie, whose grandfather had been one of Bombay's textile magnates. In Rushdie's novel *Midnight's Children* the author's fictional alter ego Saleem Sinai grows up on this street, too.

"Till very recently I was unsure about me & Kinnara," Ravi wrote to Kamala. "But now I feel positive about the whole thing. This responsibility is the only thing which would hold me and sober me up. The effing around (aimlessly) days are over!"[58] Given his frantic diary commitments during the previous couple of years, it is surprising, and revealing, that Ravi felt he had been wasting time. His ambitious goals for Kinnara seem to have aggravated his constant tendency to doubt himself. However, after spending the first half of June in Delhi and Calcutta concentrating on his plans, he returned to Bombay with renewed confidence.[59] He was given a boost by the news that he was to receive the Sangeet Natak Akademi Award from Indian president Radhakrishnan on August 20.

Kinnara's formal opening took place at 6 p.m. on July 17, chosen because it was Guru Purnima, the day when students pay homage to their *gurus*. *Puja* offerings were made first to Ganesh and then to a portrait of Allauddin Khan. Tat Baba was present too. The school initially offered classes in sitar, flute, tabla, pakhawaj and vocal music for pupils aged from eight to fourteen and also for advanced students. *Screen* reported that it was overwhelmed with applications.[60] Sitar was taught by Ravi's disciples: Shamim Ahmed, Kartick Kumar, Shambhu Das and Amiya Dasgupta. Vocal classes were taken by Tulsi Das Sharma, tabla by Taranath Rao and Ravi Bellare (the twin brother of Shashi), and flute by G. S. Sachdev. Kamala was joint honorary secretary and the chief administrator. Ravi took the title of director.

Another member of the staff was Penny Estabrook, who had returned to India to study the sitar on a Ford Foundation grant. Despite Ravi's open invitation, she did not look him up on arrival because, as she put it, "You don't go to Menuhin if you are just starting the violin."[61] Instead she enrolled at Bharatiya Kala Kendra. Ravi heard she was in Delhi, and when they met again they rediscovered the instant connection they had felt in Colombo and became lovers. Ravi also started teaching her the sitar, and she moved to Bombay to help him run Kinnara. Once again Ravi was open with Kamala about this new relationship, and the two women became lifelong friends. They were both key figures at Kinnara. Penny helped with the administration and in time began teaching classes in the piano and Western ballet. She also took on an archival role, compiling the scrapbooks of Ravi's activities that provide such an invaluable record today.

Ravi began a Kinnara Music Circle, with regular recitals for its members. At the inaugural concert on July 28 he and Ali Akbar Khan played a *jugalbandi* with Chatur Lal. Ravi had the crowd laughing when he told them that Kinnara's woodcut logo of a bird-man playing the sarod was inspired partly by a sculpture at Ajanta and partly—he was jesting now—by his brother-in-law.[62] Ravi was keen to train audiences as well as his students. In a program essay entitled "Good Listening" he appealed for all to be seated on time at Kinnara concerts, "relaxed and receptive." It was announced beforehand that the doors would be closed at precisely 8:30 p.m. and reopened only between numbers.[63]

The musicians who appeared in the Music Circle's first year were the cream of that generation, including V. G. Jog, Shivkumar Sharma, Samta Prasad, vocalists Kumar Gandharva, Hirabai Barodekar, Lakshmi Shankar and the Dagar brothers, and even Vilayat Khan, who played at the Birla Theatre on June 23, 1963, with Ravi in attendance. Their relationship remained complicated, rivalry alternating with appreciation, and on this occasion Ravi was giving a platform to Vilayat. A photograph of them grinning and hugging each other appeared in the press.[64] Kinnara also arranged a "felicitation" event in September 1962 at the Tejpal Auditorium to honor Uday and his troupe (including Lakshmi as music director) before he departed on his first American tour for a decade.[65]

After a couple of months at Breach Candy School, Kinnara moved down the street to new rented premises on the first floor of the Bhulabhai Memorial Institute. The institute took its name from the late lawyer and Congress freedom-fighter Bhulabhai Desai, who had set it up in a complex adjoining his home. It was run by Desai's one-time aide, Soli Batliwala, a passionate supporter of the arts described by Ravi as "one of the most unusual and remarkable people I have ever come across."[66] He had divided the old house into studio spaces offered at peppercorn rent to dozens of fine artists, including two painters who were to become modern greats, M. F. Husain and Vasudeo Gaitonde. This was also where artist-collector Bal Chhabda founded Gallery '59, one of the city's earliest private galleries. Ebrahim Alkazi ran the School of Dramatic Art and staged plays on the terrace.

Dancers, musicians and actors—among them Waheeda Rehman, Hema Malini, Sonal Mansingh and Sachin Shankar—rehearsed in the house or on its spacious lawn. Shyam Benegal recalls attending a workshop there led by Martha Graham.[67] For a few years the institute was Bombay's most dynamic creative hothouse. According to Gaitonde, "It was the center of cultural activity and it was very exciting to be there. One was not enclosed. Everything that you saw affected you—theater, music, dance. It was full of color."[68]

"I never dreamt there was so much to do in running a school," Ravi wrote to Isadora Bennett.[69] On top of Kinnara's regular classes, functions and recitals, and organizing the move, his energies were taken up by a new production of *Melody and Rhythm*, staged at Bombay's Birla Theatre on four nights in mid-November. This was based on the 1958 Delhi show, with even more performers. Among the orchestra of fifty-one and choir of forty-two were rising names such as Shivkumar Sharma, Shankar Ghosh and Shobha Gurtu, as well as Shubho and most of Kinnara's teaching staff. Ravi was composer, arranger and conductor. Penny Estabrook conducted the choir, while Vijay Raghav Rao, now music director at Films Division, was assistant conductor of the orchestra. Gaitonde acted as art consultant.

The show was once again a panorama of Indian music, with a mixture of old and new items. Among the latter was a sitar concerto. Unlike Ravi's later experiments under this title, involving a full symphony orchestra, this piece was a very liberal adaptation of the chamber concerto form of Western music, in which a soloist is accompanied by a small ensemble. The sitar soloist—Ravi—played against seven other sitars and two tablas. There was also a *Tala Vadya Kacheri*–style rhythm-ensemble piece in which seven drummers—on two tablas, a tabla tarang, nal, pakhawaj, mridangam and dholak—played the 7-beat cycle *rupaktal*. At first individual players took turns to improvise at length, before gradually the pace quickened and the duration of each solo slot reduced, until all the drummers converged in a climax. This item proved wildly popular.

During the rehearsal period, Ravi paid a visit to Bhopal on October 7 to perform in the Madhya Pradesh government's celebrations for his *guru's* hundredth birthday. Ritwik Ghatak was working on his Films Division tribute to Allauddin Khan, which described him as "the grand old man of Indian music" who had "built up the greatest musical family of modern India."[70] The documentary included footage of him seated on the *charpoy* in his Maihar courtyard, with Ravi and Ali Akbar sitting at his feet once again. Time with Baba always returned Ravi to the deepest roots of his music. "Baba Ustad Allauddin Khan belongs to a school that seems so far removed from our modern industrialized era," he wrote in a centenary newspaper tribute. "His music knows no age."[71]

Meanwhile, ominous shadows were being cast across the country from the Himalayas. Much of the world spent late October fearful of nuclear armageddon during the Cuban Missile Crisis. But for India war was already a reality, as China had crossed the high mountain frontier on October 20. During the 1950s the catchphrase "Hindi-Chini-bhai-bhai" had been coined to describe the fraternal relations between socialist India and communist China, and Indian performers including Uday and Indrani had been dispatched to Beijing on cultural delegations. But Nehru had badly misjudged the rising tensions over border disputes and Indian support for the Tibetan cause. The Chinese army caught India by surprise and inflicted heavy casualties as it advanced sixty miles into the northeastern state known today as Arunachal Pradesh. A national emergency was declared, and the opening night of *Melody and Rhythm* was given in aid of the war effort, raising some 8,000 rupees.[72] On November 22 China withdrew unilaterally, apparently satisfied with its punitive incursion.

Ravi felt the new show was "a much improved production" and "a grand success," and he envisaged it being staged every year.[73] It certainly provoked discussion, and a typical review deemed it "a show no progressive music lover can afford to miss." But when it came to the detail the critics could diverge wildly. The sitar concerto, for example, was either "a rare specimen of technique and creative imagination" or else dismissed as giving "the impression of a sitar training class in a music school."[74] More generally, there was the question of whether Indian music was suited to orchestration. Earlier in the year Yehudi Menuhin, still Indian music's greatest friend abroad, had lamented in the British press that "a particularly untimely and embarrassing effort has been made to harness Indian musicians into 'orchestras' requiring 'conductors.' This does violence to the very nature of Indian classical music." In Indian music, Yehudi said, "each individual is on an almost solitary search for an aesthetic and spiritual state of balanced perfection," and he felt this ideal was threatened by orchestral regimentation and the wider effects of mass culture.[75] His target was Bombay film music rather than Ravi's orchestral compositions, with which he would have scarcely been familiar, but the comments were picked up in India, adding fuel to an already smoldering controversy. After all, as Ravi had recently confided, creating the perfect Indian orchestra was his greatest ambition.

Ravi addressed the subject at length in the concert program and in an interview in *Screen*. He stressed that while *Melody and Rhythm* was an experiment and "an entertainment," it was created "with authenticity, keeping the beauties of Indian music in mind."[76] Having explored the orchestration of Indian instruments for twenty-five years, he said, there was no one more aware of the technical problems. Orchestration, he well knew, allowed little space for improvisation, and orchestral harmony compromised one of the pillars of Indian classical music, the integrity of a melodic line. But he argued that group forms of music, from film scores to police bands, were already in existence in India. The goal was to orchestrate while remaining faithful to the essence or character of each *raga*—its *bhava*. He was convinced this was possible without undermining traditional solo forms. Orchestras would provide more opportunity and increase participation. "Has the ballet killed the pure Bharatanatyam or the Kathak?" he asked. "On the contrary, the ballet has given a new impetus to our classical dances by roping in wider audiences to appreciate them and patronize them...why shouldn't traditional music and modern innovations like the orchestra coexist and flourish?"[77]

Ballet was on his mind. Barely had the last show finished than he was in Mehboob Studios creating music for a new staging of Tagore's 1938 dance-drama *Chandalika*. This was a passion project for Vyjayantimala, reigning queen of Hindi and Tamil cinema, who was also accomplished in Bharatanatyam—"a mesmeric dancer blessed with a gorgeous figure," as Ravi noted.[78] She choreographed the production and starred as the Dalit heroine who is inspired by Buddha's disciple Ananda to see the injustice of her caste-based oppression. Rather than use Tagore's original songs, she commissioned Ravi to record a new, song-less soundtrack, considering him perfect for the job because of his expertise in both Carnatic and Hindustani music, as well as his familiarity, as a Bengali, with Tagore. They worked closely together coordinating the music and dance, through rehearsals at Bhulabhai Memorial Institute and five recording sessions, in time for the opening at Bombay's Birla Theatre on December 22. *Chandalika* was a major theatrical production, with a dozen dancers, lighting by Tapas Sen and set design by M. R. Achrekar, art director to Raj Kapoor and Guru Dutt. President Radhakrishnan attended the premiere, while Nehru brought the king and queen of Belgium to see the show. "The most praiseworthy aspect of the dance-drama was Raviji's unsurpassable music," Vyjayantimala wrote in her autobiography.[79] It used an ensemble of Indian instruments supplemented by Western strings and clarinet, and was described in one review as "out of this world, so enchanting is it in its appeal to the senses, so moving in its message to the emotions."[80]

Annapurna and Ravi were living increasingly separate lives. During 1962 Annapurna had been away in Maihar for extended periods, and it speaks volumes that it was Kamala whom Ravi asked to be so involved in running Kinnara, rather than his wife. He was also encouraging

Kamala to get closer to his son. "Please help me in keeping the fire burning in Shubho, to work work & achieve something great and become someone great with his own entity!" he wrote to her in summer 1962. "Poor thing, he is weak in mind, let us help him & give him strength." And again, in January 1963, from Allahabad, "Please inject his mind that he should *A.* get up early. *B.* Practice sitar. *C.* Work on painting—work, work & WORK—and prepare himself and get ready for going abroad in August with me."[81]

The prospect of a trip to Edinburgh did not have the desired effect on Shubho. Over the New Year it was Penny who accompanied Ravi on his customary trip to Madras to play at the Music Academy, and while they were away tensions at home boiled over. Shubho, who had become resentful of his father's girlfriends, confronted Kamala and told her he had written to Annapurna in Maihar, telling his mother all about both her and Penny. He could not understand why his mother seemed not to react, but then she knew about Kamala already. Shubho assumed that she would put her foot down when she returned to Bombay and the girlfriends would be shown the door. Around this time Ali Akbar's daughter Lajwanti, who was ten at the time, remembers accompanying her mother Rajdulari to the station to meet Annapurna off the train. As soon as Annapurna saw Rajdulari she burst into tears. Lajwanti did not know what had happened, but she has always felt that this marked "the fag end" of the on-off relationship between Ravi and Annapurna. The extended families were intimately enmeshed, she explained:

> That was a very strange time, because you felt all this closeness, and we were going for recording sessions, and there were lunches and dinners and all those kinds of things happening, and on the other hand there is my aunt weeping uncontrollably and inconsolably on my mother's shoulder. It was a crazy confounded family, bound by love but sort of fraying away at the edges.[82]

The first half of 1963 saw Ravi juggling his commitments to Kinnara with the usual busy tour schedule in India. After Madras, there was Allahabad, Katni, Jabalpur and Calcutta. Amritsar, Madras, Vijaya-wada, Bangalore and Nagpur followed, and Calcutta again, as well as regular concerts for various Bombay music circles and societies. In March he was invited to Delhi for the opening by Radhakrishnan of Triveni Kala Sangam's building, designed by Joseph Stein, and played the inaugural concert in the garden theater. His restlessness resurfaced whenever he was in one place for much more than a week. His letter to Isadora Bennett in February, confirming his second Asia Society tour for the autumn of 1964, reveals his yearning for foreign parts when he asks if it is snowing on the other side of the world: "It makes me think nostalgically of my slipping and sliding days on the lovely streets of New York."[83]

Kinnara marked its first birthday in July with a flourish, but apart from gala occasions Ravi tended to leave the day-to-day administration to Amiya Dasgupta, Penny and Kamala. By January Penny was becoming concerned that the atmosphere was too relaxed, and that Kinnara would not reach its potential unless Ravi drilled it into the staff that more was expected of them. The deeper problem for him, and one that he was reluctant to admit to himself, was that, passionate though he was about music education, he did not want to spend his days dealing with personnel issues or teaching beginners. It was not a good use of his time. What motivated him was producing ambitious shows such as *Melody and Rhythm*, giving recitals or teaching brilliant students. In retrospect Penny feels that "Panditji shouldn't [have] ever set up a school, because he got bored with it so soon." Yet Kinnara was largely dependent on him. Sometimes students asked Kamala, "Where is Panditji?" and she would explain that he was away on tour. "When will he be back?" She came to realize that whenever she told them the truth about his absence they skipped classes.[84]

He had one new major commission during this period, a forty-minute orchestral and vocal piece for All India Radio based on

Tagore's 1930 poem "The Child." He was challenged by this complex job and its tight deadline, which required two visits to Delhi in June. He went into his most productive mode by working "like a madman" as the deadline approached, and the other musicians struggled to match his energy levels. At the end of June the finished work was played for the radio station's management and warmly received. "I have worked so hard all these days—without lunch rest or proper sleep," he wrote the next day on the plane back to Bombay. "Though I'm not satisfied completely (when am I over any of my creations?) it was the best I could do. A marathon work—within such a short time!"[85]

As his departure for Europe drew near, he also had to finish the music for *Go-daan*, shooting for which was finally completed in August. His last recording session, with Lata Mangeshkar, began at 4 p.m. on August 25 and went on till 7 a.m. the following morning.[86] Typically Ravi had taken it right down to the wire, but it was complete, and the film would be released in December. Later the same day he left for London on Air India's sole Boeing 707 jet. M. S. Subbulakshmi was on the same flight. Shubho was not.

13

PROPAGANDIST-IN-CHIEF

Indian classical music fell down from the air like a healing balm,
like soft rain on my head, that original Edinburgh morning:
purple haze of jacaranda trees in Princes Street Gardens, drongos
and bee-eaters on the telephone wires, and the sounds of crickets,
mynahs and cattle bells oozing from the cracks between
the granite cobbles of the Grassmarket.

RORY MCEWEN[1]

The 1963 Edinburgh International Festival, with Lord Harewood as artistic director, was built around an "Indian invasion," and proved to be a landmark in the growing popularity of Indian music in Britain.[2] Harewood booked Ravi, Ali Akbar Khan, Alla Rakha, M. S. Subbulakshmi and Balasaraswati, whose Bharatanatyam had mesmerized him at the East–West Encounter in Tokyo in 1961, her first appearance outside South Asia. Bismillah Khan was billed in the program too, but in the event did not come. All the Indian concerts were introduced from the stage by Narayana Menon, while Yehudi Menuhin was a ubiquitous and supportive presence. Meanwhile, there was an exhibition at the Royal Scottish Museum on *Music and Dance in Indian Art*, and every afternoon a film from the *Apu Trilogy* was screened.[3]

Ravi played three recitals in Edinburgh: a free event at St. Cuthbert's Church, where he and Ali Akbar shared the bill with Yehudi and the harpsichordist George Malcolm, each playing separate parts of the concert; and two at Freemasons' Hall, both recorded by the BBC Third Programme for broadcast the following spring. The critical notices were among the most effusive of Ravi's career. After his solo performance of morning *ragas* on August 30, the *Daily Telegraph* acclaimed his "breath-taking agility," while *The Times* was startled by "the utterly spontaneous and prodigiously brilliant improvisational feats of both sitar and tabla," and felt it "impossible to imagine how the charge of monotony ever came to be leveled at Indian music."[4]

On the duet between Ravi and Ali Akbar on September 2, which met with a foot-stamping ovation in the hall, *The Times* went even further: "Having listened to these thrilling musicians one continues for some time to feel that musicianship is given to mankind for this, and not for plowing yet again through long finite compositions by dead composers. Interpretation, however polished and penetrating, is not so vital an artistic function, after all, as musical creation."[5] Edinburgh elicited a renewed rapport between Ravi and Ali Akbar. "It was something like a few years ago," Ravi wrote immediately after the concert, "the reason being that we have had a chance (staying together) after long time to have close touch and had a heart to heart talk! I gave him hell & told off many things. He seems to be so much better & his sweet self. But God alone knows for how long."[6]

Rory McEwen, the folk singer cum TV presenter cum botanical artist, wrote evocatively of Ravi and Ali Akbar "threading their way delicately through the suffocating Edinburgh atmosphere, gradually pulling free of the shut faces, the gluey gentility, the cold gray strings of rain, spreading their net of shimmering mathematical certainties, till the whole gray city was altered, enmeshed, made to vibrate and glow in iridescent peacock colors."[7] For a folk musician McEwen's background was unusual: second son of a Scottish baronet, Eton, Cambridge University and the Queen's Own Cameron Highlanders. His country seat even had its own railway station. But he was influential in British music: he hosted *Hullabaloo*, a short-lived British television program that featured musicians playing live in the studio, a format continued today by his son-in-law, Jools Holland. In 1958 Rory and his brother Alex had appeared on the same episode of the magazine program *Tonight* as Ravi, which is presumably when they met, but it was not until Edinburgh in 1963 that he had his transfiguring encounter with Ravi's music. There Rory and Ravi became firm friends.

Ravi also made a guest appearance at the start of the *Tala Vadya Kacheri* percussion concert on September 4, which featured Alla Rakha and five stellar Carnatic musicians: Balasaraswati's brothers T. Viswanatham (flute) and T. Ranganathan (mridangam), two more mridangists, Palghat Raghu and T. K. Murti, and Alangudi Rama-chandran on the ghatam clay pot. The critic William Mann wrote,

> What I shall never forget is the comic turn in which Ravi Shankar explained the tabla while Alla Rakha gave examples: "This sound is called *Ktar*," said Shankar. "Clunk," responded Rakha's drum. "And this is *Ktol*." "Clunk," answered the drum. "*Tarakatatariko*" — "Tarakatatariklunk," came the reply, pat and *prestissimo*. On television it would go like a house on fire.[8]

The "Indian invasion" became a triumphant conquest, "the great converting revelation of the festival," according to Mann.[9] It was a breakthrough for dance as well as music: Balasaraswati had been booked for six nights in a small lecture hall at the museum, but she was such a sensation that two more shows were added, and all eight sold out. Narayana Menon judged her the star of the festival.[10]

In the evenings there was socializing at a town house rented by Harewood, where a jam session took place featuring Julian Bream (lute), Larry Adler (harmonica) and Ali Akbar (sarod)—or Ali Snack-bar, as Adler nicknamed him. They improvised late into the night on "Greensleeves," with Ravi, Yehudi and the Princess Royal listening.[11] At another party, thrown by Rory and Alex McEwen, the guest of honor was Princess Margaret. Carolyn Hester, who was present, re-membered the Indians mixing with the Portuguese *fado* singer Amália Rodrigues and the Manhattan Brothers from South Africa, but her favorite moment was asking Ravi how he managed to transport his sitar around the globe. Did airlines make him check it in as baggage?

"Oh no, the sitar travels the world between my knees," he told her.[12]

The enthusiasm for Indian music shown by Carolyn Hester and Rory McEwen was an indication of another emerging audience for

Ravi, the transatlantic folk-music scene, which regarded him as the herald of a vibrant, ancient culture. Ravi came to see this phenomenon as a precursor of the hippie movement. Even at Edinburgh Menon had noticed "long-haired young men in blouses and short-haired young women in trousers squatting in nooks and corners of the recital halls listening to Indian music with eyes shut as if in a trance."[13] A different harbinger of the near future could be seen piled high in the local record stores: "She Loves You" had been released three days before Ravi arrived, with half a million advance orders. Beatlemania had arrived in Britain.

Ravi spent much of September in London. He played at five or six private soirées but gave no public concerts, except for one at Claydon House in Buckinghamshire. There were two more recitals for BBC Radio, which was now paying him a much improved fee of £105 per session. Penny Estabrook arrived to accompany him on a six-week European tour, which began at Charlottenburg Palace in West Berlin. There *Die Welt* confirmed that he was "without question" the best-known Indian musician internationally, and judged that for technical brilliance Ravi and Alla Rakha could be compared only to Jascha Heifetz, David Oistrakh, Vladimir Horowitz and Shura Cherkassky, reigning gods among classical soloists.[14]

After concerts in Zurich, Berne and Basel, Ravi returned to London for his second appearance at the Royal Festival Hall, on October 13. It was a Sunday afternoon and there was a full house of over three thousand, divided roughly equally between Indians and Europeans. He was using the same five-act concert format as he had in America two years earlier, with no sustained *alap* passage until after the interval and, as he explained to the audience, it was condensed to cater for Western concertgoers' expectations. Colin Mason in the *Guardian* suggested that next time he might try playing one *raga* for two hours to see how Western audiences would react.[15] That evening, a mile away, the Beatles were sealing their national fame on *Sunday Night at the London Palladium*, Britain's top-rated TV show.

Not that they registered yet in Ravi's world. On Monday morning Ravi flew back to Berlin for another concert, this time at the Kongresshalle, a stone's throw from the two-year-old Berlin Wall, in the same venue where a defiant Kennedy had three months earlier declared, "West Berlin ist mein Land." Next was Brussels for two shows, Paris for four in three days, and Madrid, where he also attended a bullfight and was sickened by the experience. "These Toreadors are fine but couldn't bear it till the end. It's so cowardly & pathetic the way they kill the bull little by little," he wrote in a postcard home, adding, "Loved the Flamenco music & Dance."[16] During a further week in Paris his show at the Musée Guimet was eulogized in *Le Monde* as the equivalent of listening to Chopin improvising.[17] The tour was rounded off in Munich and Frankfurt.

Back in India Ravi plunged into another round of concerts, twenty-five of them in the run-up to the New Year. He was even less impressed by Indian audiences and spoke out about how poorly they compared to their Western counterparts. At one concert he was distracted by a VIP in the front row laughing and talking loudly, and at another by women knitting. He struggled to play his best through these interruptions. He was notably severe on Delhi's music scene, arguing that its interest in classical music was superficial, motivated mainly by status consciousness.[18] Nowadays we might be tempted to see his reverence for the perfect concert manners of American and European audiences as a manifestation of "the cultural cringe," the phenomenon whereby post-colonial societies have tended to undervalue their own cultures in comparison with the supposedly superior West. Ravi would have rejected this interpretation. He had a mission, after all, to reveal the greatness of Indian music to the whole world, and that included to India itself. It was a matter of establishing concert etiquette in a society where public recitals were relatively new.

It would not be surprising if Ravi's head had been turned a little in the West. It was reported that after Edinburgh Julian Bream had added three of Ravi's compositions to his repertoire. André Previn, who had made his name as a jazz pianist and composer of Hollywood film scores, told *Down Beat* that "The Ravi Shankar records absolutely put me away. I think they're so marvelous."[19] The experimental filmmaker Don Levy included short excerpts of music by Ravi (and other Indian musicians) in his extraordinary collage film *Time Is*, a meditation on the nature of time. That autumn Ravi's music was also selected by two castaways on BBC Radio's *Desert Island Discs*: Leonard Cheshire, founder of the charitable homes for the disabled, and Ron Grainer, composer of the original *Doctor Who* theme. Grainer chose *Dhun-Kafi* from *In London* as his favorite track of all. And in its Christmas quiz the London *Times* asked its readers to name the instrument played by eight musicians, among whom were (e) Ringo Starr and (h) Ravi Shankar. The Beatles were not the only artists who had a British breakthrough in 1963.[20]

Yehudi Menuhin's relationship with Ravi had clearly not been affected by the disagreement about orchestration. Indeed, after hearing Ravi perform at a private concert in London in September, Yehudi had written to thank him in effusive terms for "a memorable evening— one of the most entrancing and inspiring Diana [his wife] and I have ever known."[21] At this point Yehudi began to explore the possibility of performing Indian music himself. He had for some time resisted the idea of a violin–sitar duet, first suggested by Ravi, but he now felt ready and he spotted an opportunity. Ian Hunter, who was Yehudi's British agent and one of the great festival directors of the era, was planning a Commonwealth Arts Festival in Britain for 1965. Yehudi's first move was to ask Benjamin Britten to compose an "East–West" piece for it. "Is it theoretically and aesthetically possible," he wrote to his friend in December, "to conceive of a work of music which would unite an inspired Indian artist, as Ravi Shankar or Ali Akbar Khan, with a pedestrian Western artist, as yours truly? Is it conceivable to compose a piece allowing rhythmic and melodic freedoms within a set pattern to the one, and dotting the i's and crossing the t's for the other?" He explained that it was because such hybrids had been "done so often so badly, as witness the incidental music to most of the Indian films," that he was asking Britten.[22]

"I'm afraid my reaction to your East–West idea is rather negative," replied Britten.

> I'm not saying it *can't* be done, but like you, I am immensely put off by what I've already heard of the mixture. And, I can't forget what Ravi S. himself did on Radio India in Delhi, which I didn't frankly enjoy. What the two arts are aiming at seem to me quite different... But thank you for thinking of me in the connection— I must admit the idea of working with personalities like Ravi, & Ali Akbar & you, my dear Yehudi, was tempting![23]

Ravi had his own reservations. Asked in Edinburgh about fusing jazz and Indian music, he said, "There is a danger of this East–West-*bhai-bhai* stuff being overdone. Experimentally it is all right, but an attempt to put this seriously on the musical map would entail a loss to the great traditions of Indian music, and also to jazz."[24] But with Britten a dead end, Yehudi must have discussed his idea with Ravi when they met in Delhi at East–West '64, Nicolas Nabokov's latest music conference. Afterward Ravi sent Yehudi a tape of a composition in the south Indian *raga Nat Bhairavi* (not to be confused with Ravi's own *Nat Bhairav*) along with its Western notation (transcribed by Penny Estabrook), and explained that this was "just an experiment— a little fun—with a hope that we can do more sometime!"[25]

The Delhi conference, which opened on February 7, 1964, was hosted by the ICCR at its Azad Bhavan headquarters and presided over by Indira Gandhi. The thirty-one delegates comprised the elite of the world's musicologists and an A-list of Indian classical musicians, including Ravi, Ali Akbar, Vilayat Khan, Imrat Khan, Bismillah Khan, Amir Khan, M. S. Subbulakshmi, Balasaraswati and Palghat Mani Iyer, all of whom gave recitals to leaven the six-day diet of papers. Ravi and Ali Akbar played a *jugalbandi*. The medley of characters taking part made for some odd moments. "There was a lot of disdain between the performers and the musicologists," recalls one of the latter, Robert Garfias. "I found it amazing that Indian theorists would get up and demonstrate these *ragas* in front of these guys. I would hesitate to do that."[26] A letter from Ravi confirms the impression:

> The whole East–West Encounter went off quite well. Though lot of our old foggies [*sic*] wasted a lot of style in saying what "Bharata" said, what "Matanya" said—our friends from south (in purest Tamil–English) what Ramamatya, Venkatamakhi & Tyagaraj said... You should have seen the faces of Foreign delegates![27]

Meanwhile, Nabokov, ever the cold warrior, scented Bolshevism in the Indian air: "It smells all like the good old Kerensky-time, just a wee bit before the take-over."[28]

Ravi's own paper expanded on the themes he had been addressing in public.[29] The audience for Indian classical music, he argued, had greatly expanded in recent times at home and abroad, so musicians must be educators, sensitive to the different nature of their audiences. "The ideal situation for performing," he wrote, "is an intimate atmosphere, a well-initiated audience and no time restrictions but in the world of today that is not always possible." Critics of his supposedly "Westernized" approach were forgetting that not long before there had been a similar concern for presentation at the *mehfils* and *mujrahs* of the royal courts. They were also, with their attacks on him for playing shorter *ragas*, confusing quality with quantity, for *ragas*, he asserted, have no fixed length. "Haven't the great old Masters always admonished their students that they should be able to give the essence of the *raag* within the first moments of presentation?" He expressed his continuing faith in the *guru–shishya* tradition of learning, even though social changes were eroding it, and he asserted the right of musicians to pursue creative experimentation, rebutting five specific criticisms he faced: for *sawal–jawab* exchanges between sitar and tabla, *jugalbandi* duets, the introduction of new *ragas*, the development of a notation system and, of course, orchestration.

Almost every film used an orchestra, he said, and that was not going to change, but the problem was too little consideration being given to refining the instruments and techniques used: "Some of our song writers are truly masters but when their works are orchestrated, much of their beauty is often lost." This subject in particular polarized opinion. In the ensuing discussion, Nabokov declared that orchestras went against the very nature of Indian music, while Professor Pichu Sambamoorthy of Madras University replied that the tradition was two thousand years old. Ravi conceded that while orchestration did of course restrict musicians, "When we think of orchestra we don't think of improvisation, but composition."[30] Even so, he posited in his paper that there might be scope for improvisatory passages within orchestral compositions, "in much the same way as the cadenza is found in the concerto."

That month, February, Ravi was due to record the music for India's first son-et-lumière presentation, to be mounted at the Red Fort in Delhi, telling the history of India, from the high Mughal era to independence. Ian Hunter, who had been appointed to run it, had visited Ravi in Bombay in December, along with Somnath Chib, director general of Indian tourism, and Ravi began work, intrigued by the challenge.[31] However, Hunter's commission was canceled by the ministry, and it is not clear whether Ravi had recorded anything by that time. Chetan Anand took over as director and opted for Ali Akbar Khan as music director instead. The finished son et lumière became one of Delhi's major tourist attractions, and daily showings continue today in a revised version.

As in the previous year, Ravi was based in India for most of 1964, his grand plans for global tours not having materialized—at least, not yet. At Kinnara he focused first on six public lecture-demonstrations on "Design and Style in Music," which he gave on Thursday evenings, beginning on March 12. This "monumental series" (as he referred to it) may have been influenced by the debates at Azad Bhavan as he covered the history and development of both Indian and Western music;

the melodic forms discussed, for instance, included *dhrupad*, *dhamar*, veena, chants, canons and madrigals.[32] Penny Estabrook assisted him with the Western elements. Out of this series grew *Music Memory*, a short educational book written by Ravi and Penny in the form of an extended quiz on Indian and Western music.

A film crew visited in May to shoot Ravi as part of a trilogy of short films about Indian arts, made for PBS television under the banner "Esso World Theatre." *Ravi Shankar Plays a Raga* is a fifteen-minute film reminiscent of Satyajit Ray's unmade documentary in that it presents his live performance of a *raga* (with Alla Rakha) and intercuts it with poetic images—in this case, the sensual sculptures of Khajuraho, courtly scenes from Ajanta frescoes, tableaux of modern village life, and girls dancing in Bharatanatyam and Kathak styles. There is a rather bland narrative, voiced again by Saeed Jaffrey. The director was Robin Hardy, later famous for *The Wicker Man*, and he also shot the other documentary in the trilogy, about the Little Ballet Troupe's distinctive production of *Ramayana*, in which the dancers moved like puppets, originally devised by Shanti Bardhan. The third film was Satyajit Ray's *Two*, a piercing wordless fable about privilege and conflict. The trilogy was broadcast in the U.S. in September. "Good timing, isn't it?" Ravi wrote to Isadora Bennett on May 25, as they refined plans for his autumn tour.[33]

That day, he was busy with the first choral rehearsal for *Nava Rasa Ranga*, Kinnara's biggest event of the year. Despite Ravi's intentions, there had been no *Melody and Rhythm* show in 1963, as he was abroad in the autumn. In 1964 he developed a new musical extravaganza, once again presenting his own compositions in ancient and modern forms, but this time with dance and variety-show elements too. The more familiar pieces included a chorus sampling the evolution of vocal styles down the ages, through *alap*, *numtum* (*jor*), *dhamar*, *khyal*, *tarana*, *tappa* and *thumri*, and separate vocal pieces in *kirtan* and *Rabindra Sangeet* styles. There was an instrumental group playing *Raga Jog*, conducted by Vijay Raghav Rao; another "sitar concerto," in *Raga Desh*; and a percussion ensemble, Tal Tarang. *Screen* ran a photograph of the youngest of the drummers, a tabla wunderkind absorbed in his craft. It was the eleven-year-old son of Alla Rakha, billed as Zakir Qureshi—soon to be known as Zakir Hussain.[34]

The concept of the show was to present a colorful entertainment (*ranga*) expressing all the nine *rasas*, the principal moods of Indian arts. The word *nava* has the dual sense of "new" as well as "nine," and there were many innovations. One highlight was a puppet operetta. *Madhu Gulguli* was a comedy about a princess who falls in love with a poor woodcutter and has to overcome her pride in order to win his favor. Ravi wrote the music and the story (with poetry by lyricist Nilkanth Tiwari), and recorded the high-pitched dialogue for all three characters at double speed on a Ferrograph tape recorder, even singing the princess's *thumri* song himself.[35] For the puppetry he called on Bombay's leading exponent, Madhavlal Master, who later created the clown marionette in Raj Kapoor's classic movie *Mera Naam Joker*. The grand finale featured choral, instrumental, dance and audio effects, and dancers appearing to fly through the air against a black backdrop. For all the novelty, the show also marked the end of an era by opening with an instrumental tribute in *Raga Hem Kalyan* to Jawaharlal Nehru, who had died in office in May.

Nava Rasa Ranga opened on July 16, marking Kinnara's second birthday, and was mounted for four nights at the new Bhulabhai Desai Auditorium at Nariman Point in Bombay, before moving to Ravindra Natya Mandir, a concert hall across town in Worli, for three more shows. Ravi felt the production was "mind-boggling" in its range and ambition, but the box-office takings were disappointing.[36]

Kinnara Music Circle continued to showcase top performers, including a major show by Balasaraswati, shoehorned into the middle of *Nava Rasa Ranga*'s run. Meanwhile, Ravi created the scores for three documentaries, including *The Avalanche*. The two-day "music take" for Ravi's soundtrack in September featured thirty-four musicians, including Lakshmi Shankar, Hariprasad Chaurasia, Jnan Prakash Ghosh, Kartick Kumar, Shubho and Kamala. He then spent four "beautiful" days with Kamala at the Oberoi Grand in Calcutta before leaving for Europe on September 28.[37]

Ravi's traveling companions were again Alla Rakha, Nodu Mullick and Penny Estabrook. Penny, who had no driving license, had learned late on that she was needed as chauffeur in America, and had spent the previous ten days taking lessons in a Hillman Minx on the steep streets of Bombay. With a deadline brinkmanship she might have acquired from Ravi, she took her driving test on the day of departure, scraping through only because the examiner's boss, who was married to a friend of hers, changed her fail to a pass.

The trip began with three nights in Paris, where Ravi recorded a session for ORTF radio and gave recitals at the Musée Guimet and the Salle Gaveau, and three nights in London. The Royal Festival Hall was closed for improvements, so instead Ravi was booked to appear at the Wigmore Hall. With its 500-seat capacity, this was now too small to cater for his audiences. He played two sets in one day, with tickets sold out five days in advance. He also recorded at the BBC for the Third Programme before the group left for the North American tour, which opened in Toronto.

By now the Asia Society Performing Arts Program was in peril. In the first year it had broken even, helped by the healthy margin on Ravi's tour and by the State Department's one-off travel grant. In the following two years, six more groups had toured, including the Bharatiya Kala Kendra from Delhi, which had featured two blossoming talents in its ranks, twenty-year-old Kathak dancer Uma Sharma and seventeen-year-old sarod prodigy Amjad Ali Khan, the son of Hafeez Ali Khan, on his first U.S. trip. The scheme was fulfilling its artistic aims, but in both years it made losses of around $50,000. It was granted a stay of execution when the JDR 3rd Fund, a new Rockefeller-backed funding body for Asian arts, stumped up $27,300 to sponsor Ravi's tour, judging him worth the investment. After that the Performing Arts Program went into a five-year hibernation.[38]

In many respects Ravi's second Asia Society tour echoed his first. He played 43 cities in 72 days, and every concert was sold out. By mid-October he was writing to Kamala from Boston, "It has been great success, success & SUCCESS everywhere up til now, touch wood!"[39] As before, the first month concentrated on the East Coast, followed by a fortnight in the Midwest, before they arrived on the West Coast in mid-November. There was the same focus on colleges, even though Ravi had appealed to Bennett—in vain—to play at the New York World's Fair and a handful of major commercial venues. New York Town Hall was another rampant hit, this time inspiring the *Herald Tribune* to rank Ravi and Alla Rakha "among the greatest musicians of any sort of music in the world today."[40] Robert Shelton, who had written a famous early review of Bob Dylan three years before, wrote a big piece in the *New York Times* reporting a surge in interest in Indian music and describing Ravi as its "Propagandist-in-Chief."[41]

Ravi was now extending the length of some concerts to nearly five hours.[42] Audiences had more experience of Indian music and were becoming more diverse. *Time* magazine described his University of Philadelphia appearance as "more a musical seance than a concert."[43] He played two shows at Antioch College in Ohio, which had a reputation for progressive politics and recreational drugs. Penny remembered:

It was winter, and the hippies in those days didn't wash very often. The theater was awfully smelly, and he wouldn't like that. So we took his *agarbathi* incense sticks and put them all around the stage. Then he gave a lecture on drugs before he started. He said, "You should be able to get your 'up' without having anything extra." There was pin-drop silence.[44]

As ever, Ravi wore elegant Indian clothes on stage, but he tended to wear a sports jacket and tie when he was traveling. His ease of switching between dress styles mirrored his comfort with both cultures. Penny observed:

He had no problem East–West. That was a big thing. Most of the musicians have some problems. They go back to their hotels and they're in India again, then they go out and do the West. But with Panditji there wasn't any stepping over the bridge. I think he had it even more than his brother Uday.[45]

After the tour ended in Portland, Oregon, the party flew on December 17 to Los Angeles, which was to be Ravi's base for the next two months. Apart from the strain of the schedule, and his usual battles with allergies, he had been suffering from a problem with his right ear, which had been discharging pus and blood, and his already uneven hearing had been further impaired. In Hollywood he rented an apartment at 1716 North Fuller Avenue, not far from Grauman's Theatre, had his ear treated by a specialist, and took it easy for a couple of weeks. The other musicians checked into a nearby motel. "Alla Rakha is going squint by watching TV all the time," Ravi wrote to Kamala. "It's impossible to drag him away from it. He doesn't miss any cowboy, gangsters, biblical or costumes pictures & specially the cartoons that they show on TV." It was from the likes of *Bonanza* and *Ben Hur*, Ravi reckoned, that Alla Rakha learned his English. As for Nodu Mullick, he had "been sulking all along the tour. I give him hell at times. But it's too late to change him."[46] Mullick managed to pick up some work in Los Angeles repairing sitars and tanpuras.

After the New Year, having taken up Mantle Hood's invitation, Ravi began six weeks as visiting professor in the Department of Ethnomusicology at UCLA. He ran a practical seminar, consisting mostly of vocal music, on Tuesday evenings, and lectured in "History of North Indian Music" on Thursday evenings and "Form and Analysis of Indian Music" on Friday afternoons. This was a new experience for Ravi, and the preparation was stressful at first, but he was assisted by Penny, who worked "like a whirlwind."[47] Alla Rakha taught a class too. It seemed to Ravi "as if the gates of Indian music had been opened to American seekers."[48] *Time* reported that "local jazzmen are standing in line to enroll," and among nearly a hundred students was the jazz trumpeter Don Ellis.[49] He had been studying with Harihar Rao, who had opened up for Ellis "undreamed of new worlds of rhythm that he and his teacher, Ravi Shankar, had worked out."[50] Together Ellis and Harihar had recently formed the Hindustani Jazz Sextet, the first regular Indo–jazz fusion band, which also included the multi-percussionist Emil Richards.

Also in Ravi's classes was Lynn Gertenbach, a young American artist who had seen him perform in Madras the previous year. Ever since her return, she had been painting Indian subjects. He had sat for her during his short stay in Los Angeles in November, when she produced a number of studies. Two of her portraits, both based on photographs, were chosen for the covers of his next two World Pacific albums, *Portrait of Genius* and *Sound of the Sitar*. When she held an exhibition of sixty Indian-themed canvases in a Hancock Park residence, Ravi attended the opening. So too did the brilliant young conductor of both the Los Angeles Philharmonic and the Montreal Symphony Orchestra, Zubin Mehta, the son of Mehli Mehta.[51] He had grown up in a Westernized Bombay home and his first encounter with Indian music came only in his mid-twenties, when he discovered Ravi's records. "I couldn't stop listening," he says. "We musicians, as soon as we hear any music, we analyze, and with Ravi and his music there are rhythms that you can't even write down in our system."[52] Ravi recalled that they first met in Montreal—perhaps at his concert there in October—but it was now in Los Angeles that they got to know each other better, forging a firm friendship.

The two new albums were recorded in Los Angeles each side of New Year. *Portrait of Genius* is one of the best examples of Ravi raising the profile of percussionists. Of the six short tracks on side 1, three are built around tabla solos, while Ravi's sitar mostly takes a back seat. *Tabla-Dhwani*, absorbing in its deceptive simplicity, and recorded in a crisp stereo that still holds up, features a group of three tablas, Alla Rakha improvising freely while Phil Harland and Penny Estabrook play supportive phrases in *rela* style, mimicking a train on railway tracks. Elsewhere Harihar Rao plays tabla-tarang and dholak, and khartal and manjira also appear. On both albums Ravi draws on Indian folk music, including the tender and frolicsome *Pahari Dhun* on *Sound of the Sitar*, and *Song from the Hills* on *Portrait of Genius*. In the latter, based on a tune from the Kangra hills of Punjab, he deploys flute, played by the jazz artist Paul Horn, and santoor. On each album he also reserves a whole side to stretch out on a single *raga* himself.

Ravi was starting to be noticed by West Coast pop and rock musicians too. While guitarist Robby Krieger was still at high school, a year earlier, he had become obsessed with Ravi's album *In London*. Every night before he went to bed he put on the evening *raga Hamsadhwani* to relax, and it began to influence his guitar-playing. In November he heard Ravi play live at Royce Hall.[53] The same week, an observer at the *Portrait of Genius* session was David Crosby, then an emerging folk musician. He had been invited along by his producer Jim Dickson, who had free use of World Pacific Studios in the evenings and was working on demos by Crosby and his new band, the Jet Set. Dickson saw their potential and was trying to persuade them to record an as yet unreleased composition by Bob Dylan in an electric arrangement, inspired by the Beatles. Crosby was skeptical at first about covering Dylan, but instantly riveted by Ravi: "Jim Dickson turned me on to Shankar and blew my head out completely. I thought he was…one of the finest musicians on the planet."[54] Shortly afterward the fledgling Jet Set were signed to Columbia and took flight under their new name, the Byrds. Their recording of the Dylan song "Mr. Tambourine Man" became a number 1 hit and folk rock was born.

World Pacific was starting to thrive. Dick Bock had earned a reputation as a poor strategist that was not wholly deserved. Things had improved since his ill-fated alliance with George Avakian. In the opinion of Bock's son Ron, "He was a brilliant producer, he had perfect pitch and a great ear for talent, and he made a lot of excellent choices for the label."[55] Bock had wisely bought out his business partners, and when the opportunity arose in May 1965 he sold the company to Liberty Records, enabling him to move home from West Hollywood to Sherman Oaks. World Pacific remained a distinct label within Liberty, and he was retained as its producer and general manager on a five-year contract.

Bock's appearance—suit and tie, balding and bespectacled—was misleading. He was well connected among San Francisco intellectuals and ahead of the countercultural curve. Back in 1959 he had released a record by the philosopher Gerald Heard, a proponent of hallucinogenic drugs. Bock was captivated by Indian spirituality too. He met his second wife Leona at a talk on transcendental meditation on Catalina Island in 1961, and the next year he issued an album of lectures by Maharishi Mahesh Yogi. His commitment to Indian classical music was unimpeachable: Ravi was his star, but by 1965 he had also released records by Chatur Lal, Sharan Rani, Balachander and Ali Akbar Khan.

LSD, yet to be made illegal, was growing in popularity from its underground origins. In the summer of 1964 Ken Kesey and his Merry Pranksters had crossed America in their psychedelically painted bus, their mission to take the nation on a trip and turn it on. Bock had himself taken LSD, and encouraged Ravi to try it. "Ravi, it really expands the mind. You can do so much more with your imagination," he told him.[56] Ravi resisted, and in fact never took hallucinogens, but on this visit he was persuaded by Bock to provide the score to *The Psychedelic Experience*, a short film about a man taking a mescaline trip. There are voiceover extracts from the recent book of the same title by the psychologists Timothy Leary, Ralph Metzner and Richard Alpert, which was an instruction manual for taking psychedelic drugs safely and achieving enlightenment. The film also has an introduction by Leary, in which he advocates taking "a trip into the countless galaxies of your own nervous system" using chemicals or music.

Ravi subsequently regretted his involvement in the project and claimed that he had not been aware the film would promote the use of drugs. Much of the film consists of abstract footage such as kaleidoscopic montages or vividly colored inks in water, created by art teacher Jean Millay, with Ravi's soundtrack over it, and it is possible he saw it before the narration was added, which would have transformed its meaning. However, Ravi met both Leary and Millay beforehand, so he should have known what he was getting into. Perhaps he did not appreciate the full implications. At the time mescaline, like LSD, was still legal, and Ravi was aware of the experiments with these mind-expanding drugs conducted by intellectuals such as Gerald Heard and Aldous Huxley. The film won an award for "Film as Art" at the 1965 San Francisco Film Festival, but after that a furore broke around its advocacy of drugs, and it was little seen thereafter, except on university campuses, where it gained cult status.

Whether its practitioners liked it or not, Indian music was being adopted by the nascent counterculture, especially in California. The movement was challenging accepted values. It had many strands, including the embrace of psychedelic drugs, but it was rooted in a reaction against the stultifying effects of modern, secular, consumerist mass culture. Ian MacDonald called it a "generational yearning for a spiritual life beyond the banality of the material one...like a last gasp of the Western soul."[57] To many of the new hippies India represented an ancient, more enlightened culture. Allen Ginsberg, after a year soul-trekking around India, had returned singing the Hare Krishna mantra. Young Americans and Europeans started following his example and embarking on the overland route to South Asia. All over the West spiritual *gurus* such as the Maharishi were gaining followers. And Indian music was rising up through this efflorescence. Ravi found himself at the center of a psychedelically hued sunburst.

So by the spring of 1965, thanks to Ravi's relentless touring, musicians from the jazz, classical, folk and pop scenes in the West had all come under his influence. His connection with each one might be brief or lasting, but it was as if he were lighting touchpapers around the world and moving on; some time later would occur the musical eruptions.

His stint at UCLA finished on February 12, 1965 and, sad to leave Hollywood, he was soon on the road again, stopping to play in Honolulu en route to his first visit to Australasia. In New Zealand he played Christchurch, Dunedin, Wellington and Auckland; in Australia there were three sold-out nights at the Cell Block Theatre in Sydney, before the University of Melbourne, and then, on the way home, Singapore. From Christchurch he cabled Isadora Bennett that he was "feeling home sick for States already. Bring me back soon, Isy Dearest. Thanking for a glorious tour."[58] This time it would not be long before he returned.

Ravi arrived back in India on March 17. Even as he pitched himself straight into another furious schedule at home—Madras, Calcutta, Delhi and Bombay within his first fortnight back—four musicians were about to have their first encounter with Indian music on a film set on the other side of the world. The roads traveled by Ravi Shankar and the Beatles were converging.

IV
SUPERSTAR
1965–1970

Tuning his Nodu Mullick "Stradivarius" sitar at Rory McEwen's
Cathcart Road cottage, London, May 1967

14

THE SITAR EXPLOSION

We were entering the same door but from different sides.
PHILIP GLASS[1]

On the face of it, Philip Glass and George Harrison did not have a lot in common in 1965. One was an unknown graduate in composition from a New York classical music conservatory; the other had no formal musical training and was one of the four most famous pop stars on the planet. Yet both of them stumbled across Ravi's music by chance that year, and the impact on them both was intense and immediate.

It would be years before the impact on the young American would be felt by a wider public, as he developed a challenging new type of art music drawing on Indian rhythms. But for the Beatles guitarist the effects were swiftly apparent and so instantly appealing that within months, even before he had met Ravi, Indian music was being championed by numerous rock'n'roll musicians. As raga rock spiced up the charts in early 1966 and the hippies lit incense sticks, Ravi became the toast of the Western popular mainstream at the moment of its greatest fertility. There has never been a pop culture crossover like it. But for Ravi this triumph came tinged with a bitter taste, the sense that the meaning of Indian culture was being twisted.

In 1965, for the third year running, Ravi spent the summer in India, before leaving the country for a long tour in the autumn. He seemed to be becoming exasperated by his homeland. He marked Kinnara's third birthday with a concert at Bhulabhai Memorial Institute, but the school, lacking a major patron, was still operating from rented quarters and had not fulfilled his dreams. Kinnara was to stage no further theatrical productions and its activities were gradually wound down. Ravi was also losing patience with the constant sniping. He would doubtless have agreed with the opinion of one Indian columnist that "the more Ravi Shankar's fame grows, the less do people, especially in this country, consider it necessary to understand his music, its implications."[2]

These frustrations boiled over in October, when Ravi's Bombay apartment was raided by the police while he was away on a European tour. They appear to have been looking for evidence of financial impropriety. He did not know it at the time, but it was his wife who had contacted them. He wrote to Kamala from Zurich:

> I was shocked and sick to hear the news of events that happened
> in my flat. I can do so much more for my country outside than
> at home. I feel suffocated and so dead & uninspired when I go
> back & now to top it all I'm being labeled as bloody criminal or
> something![3]

He had left Bombay in mid-September for the Commonwealth Arts Festival in Britain. This huge 17-day international celebration was centered on four cities, London, Glasgow, Cardiff and Liverpool, and featured 1,400 performers from 22 countries. Other Indian artists included Bismillah Khan and the dancers Ram Gopal and Yamini Krishnamurti. Ravi made five appearances, with Kishan Maharaj as his tabla player. There was no East–West duet yet; Yehudi Menuhin had eventually commissioned a piece from Peter Feuchtwanger, a London-based German composer, but it was scheduled for 1966. Instead Yehudi compèred a variety concert entitled "Music of the Continents," which played once in each city, including at Liverpool Cathedral and the Royal Festival Hall. This featured Yehudi and his Bath Festival Ensemble playing Mozart's Clarinet Quintet and Dowland's *Lachrimae*; Ravi and Kishan Maharaj; musicians from the University of Legon, Ghana; and a Carnatic group led by the great mridangist Palghat Mani Iyer, on his first trip outside India. The Scottish *Daily Mail* called it the "oddest mixture of musicians and the most unusual variety of music one is ever likely to encounter in one evening," but praised Ravi's "prodigious feats on the sitar."[4] Ravi also played a solo show at the Festival Hall, during which he conjured up, according to *The Times*, "spiritual worlds unknown to occidental music."[5] Both Festival Hall shows were broadcast by BBC Radio.

On October 3 Ravi flew to New York for a short tour of five concerts, with Alla Rakha replacing Kishan Maharaj. The Asia Society having suspended its program, these dates were arranged by Isadora Bennett in tandem with the dance impresario Charles Reinhart. Ravi played in Massachusetts, Pennsylvania and Washington, but the biggest show was again at New York Town Hall. This concert had Robert Shelton wishing, in his *New York Times* review, for "an invasion of Indian musicians—if there be any like him." He added, "It is a mystery how a musical idiom so totally different from ours can be so compellingly communicative to Western listeners...Mr. Shankar is a fusion of the technical wizard with the musical poet and the philosophical mystic, all of which combine to make his performance remarkable."[6]

Before leaving India, Ravi had written to his New York girlfriend Hallie Scott, thanking her for a John Coltrane record she had sent him and telling her, "I want to meet him. Please read the letter I've written to him—and send it him immediately."[7] However, their schedules did not coincide. Ravi's tour was restricted to the northeast, and for the whole period Coltrane was out on the West Coast. By the 16th Ravi had reached Paris, where he began an eight-week European tour.[8] So he cannot have attended, as has been claimed, Coltrane's concert at the Village Gate in New York on November 10.[9]

After two performances at Salle Gaveau in Paris, Ravi moved on to Zurich, Geneva, Oslo, Stockholm and Lund. On November 7, back in London, he played the Festival Hall yet again. The next day *The Times* ran another a rave review that concluded, "What entertainment! What artistry!" and acclaimed Alla Rakha as "surely the greatest drummer in the world."[10] Basil Douglas sent the cutting to Humphrey Burton at the BBC, imploring him to film Ravi for television: "What more do you want? For the third time in two years the Festival Hall was full to capacity for one of his recitals. During his present tour he has televised recitals for the Americans and even for the Swedes; must the BBC be so timid?"[11] This did the trick. Burton, who was sympathetic, had recently been appointed as BBC Television's first head of music and arts, and he set the wheels in motion for a TV special, to be filmed on December 12 at Lime Grove. Lord Harewood was booked to introduce it.

Ravi pressed on with his tour, to Stuttgart, Berlin, Prague and Munich, but he was still feeling aggrieved and humiliated about the police raid in Bombay. "The whole incident has killed something within me," he wrote to Kamala on the plane between Munich and Rome.

> I want to return as soon as I can and straighten out things. I was disgusted to hear the attitude at home—but what else can one expect? What hurts most…is that even if they had anything against me, they should have given me the benefit of the doubt and waited till I returned. And then this ridiculous thing of reading all my letters written to me.[12]

It was only when he got back to India that he found out who had prompted the raid. Nothing untoward was found and the case was closed, but it was a mark of how badly the marriage had deteriorated.

After Rome and Vienna, in the last week of November he reached Paris, where he was to record the music to *Chappaqua*. This was the autobiographical debut movie by Conrad Rooks, about a man, played by Rooks himself, undergoing treatment for chronic alcoholism and drug dependency. The film has a cult following but, more importantly, with this commission Ravi unexpectedly lit another musical touchpaper—a slow-burning one, but with a huge fireworks display at its end.

Rooks had been through an epic battle with addiction. Alcohol had been his main problem, closely followed by cocaine, heroin and opium (in Thailand he smoked up to seventy-two pipes a day), and he "checked out on LSD when Dr. Timothy Leary was still in pre-flight school."[13] Eventually, in 1962, he underwent an unusual sleep cure at a clinic in Zurich, which was horrific but left him clean. He then used $750,000 of his $3 million inheritance to make a film based on his experiences. The result of this expensive piece of therapy is a disorient-ing, impressionistic recreation of his month-long treatment, shifting abruptly between brutal realism and black humor, freak-out para-noia and ecstatic visions. Ravi said it was "a slightly disturbing subject to provide music for" and it is intriguing that he agreed to it: this was a film about sobriety, but it served, as *The Psychedelic Experience* had the year before, to reinforce the links being made between Indian music and drug culture.[14] Consciously or not, he seems to have been drawn toward the subject of addiction.

The cast includes an array of counterculture icons, including William Burroughs, Allen Ginsberg, Peter Orlovsky, Moondog and Swami Satchidananda, and there is even a scene with Ravi, as the "Sun God," playing the sitar in a garden. Burroughs, who plays the sinister figure of Opium Jones, had taught Rooks his "cut-up" technique, a form of literary montage intended to break a writer or artist out of habitual thought patterns, and this approach influenced the editing of *Chappaqua*. The cinematography, by Robert Frank, is sublime.

Rooks had already commissioned music from Ornette Coleman. Although he loved what Coleman had produced, he decided that so much free jazz would be overwhelming for the viewer, and he turned to Ravi instead. The film was still unfinished when Ravi arrived in Paris, along with Keshav Sathe from London, who played pakhawaj, and Alla Rakha. A small ensemble of French musicians was mustered, including string- and wind players, piano, harp, guitar and percus-sion. Ravi, according to Rooks, "would create music to the absolute segment of the picture. We would project it on a big screen and he would sit there with the musicians. He cannot read music, so we had to hire a young guy to write it down."[15]

The "young guy" in question, appointed as musical assistant and conductor, was none other than Philip Glass. He was in Paris on a

Fulbright scholarship to study composition with Nadia Boulanger and had also immersed himself in the city's art-theater scene. Although he already practiced yoga, he had no knowledge of Indian music—a perfectly normal situation at the time for a graduate from a Western conservatory, which in his case was Juilliard.[16] By way of homework he bought one of Ravi's records, but he "couldn't make heads or tails of it," so, hoping to prepare himself for the sessions, he met Ravi in his room at Hôtel Bellman. Ravi was "bursting with energy" and delighted to discuss music over endless cups of tea, but, despite Glass returning every morning, it became clear that Ravi intended to compose by improvising. The only thing Glass learned in advance was how to play tanpura.[17]

Recording took place at a studio on the Champs-Élysées. Ravi sang or played each passage to Glass, one instrument at a time: first, say, the three-minute flute part, then the three-minute cello part, and so on. Glass was "impressed by Ravi's ability to hear all the individual parts of a piece composed on the spot entirely in his head and then dictate them note by note and line by line" without the intervening stage of a full score.[18] He thought he had coped well with the notation, but when they played the first piece Alla Rakha declared that the accents were wrong, explaining, "All the notes are equal." Glass tried rewriting phrases into different groupings, or moving the bar lines, but Alla Rakha interrupted each effort and said again, "All the notes are equal." Glass was flummoxed. The restless musicians began to make their own suggestions, and the session was in danger of descending into chaos. At last, about two hours in, he erased all the bar lines. "There before my eyes I saw a stream of notes, grouped into twos and threes. I saw at once what he was trying to tell me." He turned to Alla Rakha and said, "All the notes are equal!" The response was a warm smile.[19]

Glass now realized that the music was structured in a regular 16-beat rhythmic cycle—*teental*. This was the equivalent of lesson one in Indian classical music, but for him to discover it himself under pressure gave it the power of revelation. The session proceeded smoothly thereafter, and in free moments over the next few days Glass grilled Ravi about Indian music, its *ragas*, and especially its system of *talas*. He found Ravi to be open, curious and a natural teacher. "We clicked from the moment we met," said Ravi.[20]

This was a eureka moment for Glass as a composer. In Western music it is usually the interplay between melody and harmony that defines the structure, with rhythm generally subordinate. Glass saw that, in contrast, in Indian music rhythm plays a defining role through its interplay with melody. He began to think in terms of a new music that foregrounded rhythm as the controlling function, with harmony almost entirely absent, as in Indian music, and melody downgraded too.

Curiously, his breakthrough was based partly on a misapprehension about the structure of Indian music, since he believed initially that it was based on an additive process, in which beats can be added to or subtracted from a bar.[21] In fact this is not how Indian rhythm works; changes in the length of cycles are infrequent within any given piece, and clearly flagged. But as Brian Eno was to say, sometimes a musician should honor his error as a hidden intention. Glass went on to develop a radically new style using an additive approach. As he expressed it, "The epiphany for me was no matter what the *tala* was, the subdivisions would be groups of twos and threes."[22] Those twos and threes became his distinctive building blocks and it was the way he strung them together rapidly in different combinations that created his stripped-down, futuristically repetitive, neo-binary music.

Glass was also inspired by Ravi's dual role as composer and performer. During the previous century composition and performance had become viewed in the West as separate roles, and at Juilliard Glass had been encouraged to concentrate on writing and turn his back on playing. He now saw this as an unnatural division and resolved to resume playing the piano and to form his own ensemble. First, though, he began to implement his ideas in Paris with an austerely reductive composition on two saxophones for Samuel Beckett's *Play*. His new style would come to be labeled minimalism, but he preferred to call himself a theater composer, because that was where he first explored the possibilities of his new approach. He also made plans to visit India in autumn 1966.

Rooks was so exhilarated by what Ravi had created during the week in Paris that he decided to shoot more scenes, which meant that Ravi was obliged to return in May 1966 to revise and complete the commission. He described the indecisive Rooks as "one of the most difficult" directors he had worked with.[23] The film went on to win the Special Jury Prize at Venice Film Festival in September. Ravi's music, highly episodic in nature, reinforces the film's unsettling effect, and incidentally features, with *Om*, probably Ravi's first commercial recording as a singer. But the soundtrack LP, issued in 1968 on Columbia, is one of his less satisfying releases, the music losing its impact when separated from the torrent of images that it was written to accompany.

George Harrison's embrace of Indian music and spirituality originated in two incidents during 1965. In the spring the Beatles were at Twickenham Film Studios shooting their movie *Help!*, a comedy based, ironically, around a ghoulish Indian cult. On April 5 the group filmed a scene set in an Indian restaurant, featuring an unconvincing band of Indian musicians in the background, one of whom plucks inexpertly at a sitar. It was the first sitar that Harrison had seen and he messed around with it on set, simply intrigued by the sound it made. Later, during the summer he, his girlfriend Pattie Boyd and John and Cynthia Lennon had their first experiences of LSD, which was slipped into their coffee without their knowledge by a dinner-party host. For Harrison the acid trip left him with a permanently changed sense of spiritual awareness. "LSD was like just opening the door— and before, you didn't even know that there was a door there," he later said.[24] There was also a phrase that popped into his mind, as if it had been whispered to him: "The yogis of the Himalayas." It stayed with him afterward and made him curious to find out about Indian holy men.

"Somewhere down the line I began to hear Ravi Shankar's name," said Harrison. "The third time I heard it, I thought, 'This is an odd coincidence.' And then I talked with David Crosby of the Byrds and he mentioned the name."[25] This was in August, when the Beatles had a day off in Los Angeles, and Harrison, John Lennon and Ringo Starr spent it dropping acid with Crosby and Roger McGuinn of the Byrds. At one point talk turned to Indian music, and Crosby told Harrison about Ravi. "I'm not sure if it was me who did it, but there are people that tell me I turned him on to Indian music," wrote Crosby. "I know I was turning everybody I met on to Ravi Shankar because I thought that Ravi Shankar and John Coltrane were the two greatest melodic creators on the planet, and I think I was probably right."[26]

Back in England, Harrison bought a few LPs by Ravi and immersed himself in the music:

> I thought it was incredible. When I was a child we had a crystal radio with long and short wave bands and so it's possible I might have already heard some Indian classical music. There was something about it that was very familiar, but at the same time, intellectually, I didn't know what was happening at all.[27]

In fact while his mother was pregnant with him she had listened regularly to Indian music every Sunday morning on the BBC program *For the Indian Forces*.[28] Later he might even have heard Ravi playing on the BBC Third Programme, which Ravi had been doing since Harrison was thirteen.

Harrison went shopping at Indiacraft, on London's Oxford Street, where among the imported records, carvings and incense sticks he found a sitar, albeit "a real crummy-quality one."[29] He bought it for an inflated £70, began experimenting, and on October 12 brought it to the first day of studio sessions for the Beatles' next album, when they were recording "Norwegian Wood." Encouraged by Lennon, he doubled the melody line on sitar. His playing was amateurish by

Indian standards and, judging by his sound production, he might have been using a guitar pick rather than a sitarist's wire *mizrab*.[30] But the sitar had such a distinctive timbre that it caused a sensation when the album, *Rubber Soul*, was released in December, turbo-charging the embryonic fascination with India in pop culture. "It was such a mind-blower that we had this strange instrument on a record," said Starr.[31]

During the session Harrison broke a sitar string and needed a replacement. Producer George Martin knew the Asian Music Circle, and Starr volunteered to call them. Ayana Angadi answered the phone at home in Finchley, north London, and his daughter Chandrika, who was twelve at the time, overheard him saying, "Ringo? Ringo who?" in an exasperated voice. Frantically she signaled who he was, and in no time Ayana, Patricia and Chandrika Angadi were driving down to Abbey Road to deliver a sitar string. The Beatles invited them to watch the session and afterward Ayana, with his customary boldness, said to Harrison, "You must come to our house and join some Indian friends in making music together. And we'll give you a real Indian curry as well."[32] Harrison and Pattie visited about a week later and stayed until 1:30 a.m. That evening Angadi recommended a local sitar teacher, who was a student of Ravi's Delhi-based disciple Motiram, and Harrison began taking instruction.[33]

Patricia Angadi takes up the story in this account from her unpublished memoir:

> It happened that Ravi Shankar was coming over a few weeks later, to give a concert at the Festival Hall, so we said we would take them to the concert and introduce them afterward. We sat in the stalls and George was very nervous of being recognized and mobbed (I hadn't thought of that) but only a few young girls did a double-take when they saw him. Even so, there were such long queues waiting to meet Ravi that we decided to have them all to dinner at a later date and introduce them then.[34]

This chronology tallies with Harrison's own account, so it must have been Ravi's concert at the Royal Festival Hall on November 7 that they attended.[35]

After the *Chappaqua* sessions in Paris, Ravi was back in London between December 6 and 13, when he filmed the TV special for the BBC, and there were efforts by a publicist and a record company—probably Fontana, who were issuing Ravi's new albums in the UK—to arrange a meeting with Harrison, who was put off by the idea of a staged encounter. "I knew I was going to meet Ravi," Harrison said, "but I knew I must meet him the right way. A meeting for the sake of publicity would have been the wrong way."[36] Harrison was now a firm believer in karma, and it is as if the two were circling each other, at first unwittingly—as when the Beatles played the Palladium on the same day as Ravi had played the Festival Hall a mile away—and then more consciously over time, as their predestined meeting loomed closer. Meanwhile, Harrison and Pattie became regular guests at the Angadis' home in Finchley. A friendship was forged despite the age gap—George was twenty-two, Ayana sixty-two—and after the Harrisons married in January Patricia painted a double portrait of them.

As well as the sitar line in "Norwegian Wood," there are other traces of Indian music in Beatles songs of 1965 in the form of drones, or implied drones: in "Norwegian Wood" itself, in Harrison's "If I Needed Someone" and in "Ticket to Ride." The drone in "Ticket to Ride" is particularly intriguing since it was recorded back in February, before any of the Beatles had knowingly encountered Indian music. However, drones had been breaking through into the wider music culture—for example, in the early minimalism of Terry Riley and La Monte Young. Since late 1963 John Cale, later of the Velvet Underground, had been using electric guitar strings on his viola to play thunderous sustained notes in Young's Theatre of Eternal Music ensemble. In pop, there was a trend toward using the fewest possible chords in songs such as Dylan's "Subterranean Homesick Blues." Paul McCartney said that when the Beatles started listening to Indian music, "We liked the drone idea because we'd done a bit of that kind of thing in songs before." He added, about Indian music, "It's very hard to understand. But once you get into it, it's the greatest."[37]

Another British pop song that had employed a pseudo-Indian drone in 1965 was "See My Friends" by the Kinks. Ray Davies had recorded it in April by playing a chord on a twelve-string guitar and then using controlled feedback to sustain it. In the same month the Yardbirds, immediately after Jeff Beck joined them, had recorded "Heart Full of Soul," with hired Indian musicians playing the sitar and the tabla. But they were unhappy with the results, so Beck re-recorded it on his electric guitar, imitating a sitar by playing the melody on the middle G string, bending the notes and routing the signal through a fuzzbox.[38] That was the version released. Beck explained:

> There was something locked in my head that Ravi Shankar put there. He was playing scales on one thin wire—the rest are drone strings—and he was just doing the speediest scales. I was so impressed with the speed and intonation and the micro-tuning. I thought, "This could be used. This is a sound that people won't have heard applied to a pop record."[39]

Watching the Yardbirds' recording was Jimmy Page, at the time a prolific session musician. He claimed to be one of the first people in Britain to own a sitar, and a lifelong passion for Indian music commenced. Early on, possibly in 1963, he met Ravi backstage at a concert and told him that he had his own sitar but did not know how to tune it. "He was very nice to me and wrote down the tunings on a piece of paper," said Page.[40]

In January 1966 Ravi attended the Kumbh Mela at Allahabad. It is the world's largest religious festival and takes place every twelve years where three rivers meet: the Ganges, the Yamuna and the mythical, invisible Saraswati. The location is known as Triveni Sangam. Millions of devotees converge from all over India for ritual bathing at the most auspicious times. The Public Works Department constructs an entire tent city in the beds of the two earthly rivers after the annual monsoon floods have receded. In 1954 there had been about 5 million pilgrims and a terrible stampede had killed hundreds. Numbers attending in 1966 were probably even higher, and Ravi observed "hundreds of thousands of monks and religious men and women from all over the country." He greeted the heads of many religious orders, and performed on the sitar in the tents of two of them. One was Maharishi Mahesh Yogi, whom he had previously heard of only abroad. The other was Ma Anandamayi, the saintly woman he had first seen in his childhood, whom he now considered to be "like a mother" to him.[41]

Winter is a busy time for a musician in India as the cooler, drier weather heralds the principal music season. After the Kumbh Mela Ravi was touring regularly until the beginning of April. He was then in Calcutta for ten days to record the soundtrack to *Swapno Niye* for the Aurora Film Corporation. The fierce summer heat had arrived, and Ravi was none too impressed that Aurora's proprietor, Ajit Bose, had—"because of his *zamindari* aristocratic prestige"—arranged the session at his own studios, which had no air-conditioning. "Though the place has lovely atmosphere, *pukur*, and green lush, etc., it's hellish inside to record for 10–13 hours at a stretch," Ravi wrote.[42]

From there he flew to Manila for another musicology conference, this one jointly organized by UNESCO and the National Music Council of the Philippines. The subject was "Musics of Asia" and he deemed it the finest attempt to date in this field. Delegates included some of the usual suspects—Mantle Hood, Narayana Menon, Robert Garfias—as well as the composer Iannis Xenakis. Ravi told Yehudi Menuhin, who was absent, that the symposium was "really interesting" but wrote to Kamala that he also became "very bored & sad"— probably down to his being separated from her for an unplanned extra night.[43] His recital, which was intended to close the conference and was scheduled for just thirty minutes, was so warmly received that he was asked to stay on one more day to give a full concert. No doubt it was hard to say no to the honorary chair, who was Imelda Marcos. Her husband Ferdinand Marcos, in his honeymoon period after first being elected president of the Philippines, also attended some sessions.

In 1966 George Harrison's passion for Indian music was continuing to grow. He took his sitar with him on his honeymoon in Barbados and practiced while his wife sunbathed.[44] On their return to England he enthused to Maureen Cleave in the *Evening Standard* about Ravi's Festival Hall concert: "I couldn't believe it. It was just like everything you have ever thought of as great all coming out at once." He explained his struggles to play sitar cross-legged—"I wish I could sit on the floor like Ravi"—and revealed that he had considered going to India for six years to study properly. Dreamily, he told her, "Just before I went to sleep one night, I thought what it would be like to be inside Ravi's sitar."[45] Among the four Beatles, it was Harrison who led the fascination for Indian music, and he encouraged the others in the same direction. John Lennon also enthused about it to Cleave: "It's amazing, this—so cool. Don't the Indians appear cool to you?... This music is thousands of years old. It makes me laugh, the British going over there and telling them what to do."[46]

On April 6 the Beatles returned to Abbey Road Studios to create "Tomorrow Never Knows," the most startling leap forward of their whole career. Lennon's song, an aural recreation of an LSD trip, takes its lyrical inspiration from Timothy Leary's book *The Psychedelic Experience* (using lines different from those included in Ravi's soundtrack of the previous year). It opens with a tanpura drone, has no modulation and stays on a C chord throughout, with McCartney's bass guitar reinforcing the drone. "This was because of our interest in Indian music," said McCartney. "We would be sitting around and at the end of an Indian album we'd go, 'Did anyone realize they didn't change chords?... Wow, man, that is pretty far out.' So we began to sponge up a few of these nice ideas."[47] With this song, the drone was relaunched into the mainstream of Western popular music culture, and it is easy today, habituated as we are by its ubiquity in electronic music, to underestimate its impact then. As Ian MacDonald wrote, it was "like an unknown spiritual frequency tuning in."[48] Another psychedelic ingredient was the series of saturated tape-loops that were mixed into the song live—inspired, like Conrad Rooks, by the cut-up technique. One of these loops contained a sitar phrase played backward. Lennon's voice was even treated in order to sound like a Tibetan lama declaiming from a Himalayan mountaintop.

Harrison's song "Love You To," recorded the following week, makes its Indian influence even more explicit. It is like an Indian classical recital reshaped as a three-minute pop song. The opening passage on unaccompanied sitar, played by Harrison himself, represents a brief *alap*, and with the entry of the tabla segues into a medium-tempo *gat* in *teental*, before stepping up to a fast *gat* for the last 20 seconds. The scale has flattened third and seventh notes and is thus in Dorian mode—or, as a north Indian classical musician would put it, Kafi *thaat*. Indeed, his melody is based on a typical phrase of *Raga Kafi*. The tabla player Anil Bhagwat, who had been recommended by Ayana Angadi, was asked by Harrison to play the same rhythmic cycle as Ravi had used on a specific album track, almost certainly *Dhun-Kafi* from Ravi's album *In London*, which features an *alap* followed by medium and fast *gats* in *teental*.[49] The resemblance is closest from about 2 minutes 30 seconds to 3 minutes 5 seconds in *Dhun-Kafi*, and both pieces open with an arpeggio on the sitar's sympathetic strings. The most likely scenario is that, after hearing *In London*, George asked his sitar teacher to show him *Raga Kafi*, and then he worked out his own composition based on it. The result is still pop music, with overdubbed guitars, vocals and tambourine, and it is a composed piece, not improvised. Moreover, the rhythmic cycle is not authentic. It is *teental* quarter-sliced into 4 beats to the bar, and it does not run continuously throughout, as it would in Indian classical music, instead stopping three times for breakdowns, while the penultimate chorus comes in a beat early (on the twelfth beat rather than the thirteenth). But the song reveals that Harrison had absorbed a great deal from listening and from his initial lessons.

These new Beatles songs did not see light of day until *Revolver* was released to British radio in July, by which time the smoldering timber of "Norwegian Wood" had set off what Ravi came to call the "sitar explosion" in the world of rock and pop. In 1965 there was just a handful of pop stars tentatively exploring Indian music. In 1966 it became the flavor of the year.

When the Byrds had toured America in a motor home in November 1965, they took with them one of the newly available compact cassette players. They had just two tapes, which were on constant rotation, rigged via a Fender Showman amplifier to reverberate throughout the bus. One was John Coltrane, the other Ravi Shankar. Steeped in these sounds for a month, they recorded two new songs in December that took pop into the territory of modal improvisation. "Eight Miles High" is based around a recurring four-note guitar phrase lifted from Coltrane's Village Vanguard recording of "India"—itself an interpretation of Indian music. McGuinn plays long jazz-tinted solos on a Rickenbacker electric twelve-string against a bass-guitar drone, and the lyric has a deliberately druggy double meaning. If that was the Byrds playing Coltrane, then the second track was their Ravi Shankar number. "Why" has two extended guitar solos with a loosely Indian feel, again improvised modally by McGuinn on electric guitar over a bass drone.

When the two tracks were released as a single in March 1966, Columbia Records announced the invention of a new musical form called raga rock, "derived from the sitar music of Ravi Shankar." At the press launch McGuinn brandished a sitar, even though it had not been used on either track, and the event was delayed while the band struggled to tune it backstage. A wryly skeptical report in the *Village Voice* made it back to Ravi in Bombay, the cutting annotated in an unknown hand, "The Raga Rock? Do you believe it?"[50] He needed to, because in June World Pacific rush-released a cash-in album of pop covers entitled *Raga Rock* by a session band billed as the Folkswingers featuring Harihar Rao. Harihar guested on sitar amid a wail of fuzzbox guitars. If Ravi heard it, it is unlikely that he was impressed. The Byrds, however, were influential, David Crosby in particular. Renowned as a creative catalyst, he came to epitomize the brash, hedonistic side of the Californian counterculture. As Jackson Browne put it, "He had this legendary VW bus with a Porsche engine in it, and that summed him up—a hippie with power!"[51] He used that power to tell his friends about Ravi's music.

Another Californian group channeling its Indian fixation through Western instruments was the Doors. Keyboardist Ray Manzarek was, through another band, signed to World Pacific's pop subsidiary Aura Records, and at Dick Bock's suggestion he attended Maharishi Mahesh Yogi's transcendental meditation classes at a house in Pacific Palisades. There, in the summer of 1965, he met both Robby Krieger, who was about to join UCLA to take a course in Indian music, and drummer John Densmore. As Manzarek later wrote, "The Doors needed the other Doors. And we found each other in India."[52] The foursome was completed by his friend Jim Morrison. Their first demo (without Krieger) was recorded at World Pacific, and from the outset their sound was shaped by an Indian sensibility. They spent the first half of 1966 developing their repertoire in Los Angeles clubs, including the now iconic song "The End," which was conceived as a rock version of a *raga*. It has a modal structure, mostly staying on one chord, starts out slow and serene, and gradually develops over eleven minutes (an unprecedented length for a rock song) to its tumultuous climax. Krieger alternates his guitar melody line with playing open-tuned strings as though they are *chikari* drone strings on a sitar, and there is a moment when it shifts to double time that was likewise inspired by the *jhala* phase of a *raga*. "I got the idea for that from watching Ravi," says Krieger. "It's not based on a specific *raga*, just the structure and feel."[53] They also worked on "Light My Fire," which features a guitar solo modally improvised by Krieger using fingerings copied from sitar technique.[54] This became their first massive hit.

Pop music's Indian flowering was, if anything, thriving even more across the Atlantic. "How about a tune on the old sitar?" asked a *Melody Maker* headline on May 7. The new offering from the Yardbirds, "Over, Under, Sideways, Down," had a guitar distorted to sound like a sitar—not that the effect was exactly convincing. So did the Birmingham band the Move, who were reported to be playing "Brum-raga" sitting cross-legged on the stage.[55] Others incorporated a real sitar into their arrangements, although they tended to follow the example of "Norwegian Wood" in using it merely as a decorative element, usually replacing the role of a lead guitar. "Paint It Black" by the Rolling Stones was driven in this way by Brian Jones's sitar riff, offsetting a drawling vocal line by Mick Jagger, whose accent, according to *Melody Maker*, was becoming "progressively more curried."[56] Jones had taken up the sitar after trying out George Harrison's at his home. Meanwhile, Donovan had put sitars on his latest album, and a cover version of Simon and Garfunkel's "A Most Peculiar Man" was released by Adam, Mike and Tim with sitar lines played by Big Jim Sullivan, one of Britain's busiest session guitarists. Sullivan took sitar lessons in London from Nazir Jairazbhoy and subsequently recorded two albums of Indian-spiced pop covers. By 1968, the concept of *vinaya* having apparently passed him by, he had rebranded himself as Lord Sitar.

On the other side of the world in early 1966, Ravi was largely cut off from this trend. When he eventually caught up, it bemused him. Using Indian music to make pop songs, he said, was "like learning the Chinese alphabet in order to write English poems."[57]

15

WONDERLAND

You can't deny Indian music. It will win out in the end.

GEORGE HARRISON[1]

Ravi arrived in Paris on May 21 to find himself in the brightest of spot-lights. During the nine-and-a-half-week European trip that followed he finished his film-score work with Philip Glass, had his seminal first encounter with George Harrison and worked for the first time with Yehudi Menuhin as they pioneered crossover classical duets. It was Ravi's influence on those three musicians, above all, that had such a far-reaching impact on music around the globe in the late twentieth century. This was the summer when his long-term efforts at taking Indian arts abroad, and at breaking down cultural barriers, came to a fruition far richer and stranger than anyone could have foreseen.

It began inauspiciously enough. Ravi spent the first three days con-fined to the Hôtel Napoléon, sick with flu. He was still feeling weak when he went into the studio on the 25th, where he was reunited with Glass in order to complete the soundtrack for *Chappaqua*, now contain-ing the new scenes that Conrad Rooks had shot. "I had virtually to do the whole thing over again due to the many subsequent changes to the film," said Ravi.[2] His work was still unfinished on the 28th, when he had to leave for Norway, where he played the Bergen International Festival.

From Bergen he flew into London on the evening of the 30th. There, Indian music was unquestionably in vogue. "Paint It Black" was at the top of the British charts and the Soho boutique Adam West One was selling what it brazenly named a "sitar jacket."[3] Fontana had taken the unusual step of issuing two tracks from a classical LP on a seven-inch single, *Song from the Hills* backed with *Dhun*, both from Ravi's *Portrait of Genius*.

First came a day of press, and Ravi's ambivalence was obvious. "I don't really want to be associated with this 'pop.' People at home will criticize me," he said—and he was right. "I am delighted that young people here are interested in Indian music. But, you know, if George Harrison wants to play the sitar, why does he not learn it properly?"[4]

On June 1 Ravi played the Royal Festival Hall. The show had sold out two days in advance, and 300 extra seats were added on the stage itself. The crowd was noticeably younger than before, dominated by pop or jazz fans, and in Ravi's estimation only about 10 percent were from an Indian background. *India Weekly* reported on the prevalence of men with long hair and women in mini-skirts, while the *New York Times* observed "scores of young men and women in matching checked trousers who had heard of Mr. Shankar and the sitar through the Beatles."[5] Harrison himself was present; this was the second time he had attended a concert given by Ravi. He had left Abbey Road early to get there, allowing the other Beatles to finish off "Yellow Submarine" without him. This was the session when they threw a late-night party to generate the song's sound effects, using whistles, hooters and an old tin bath, so Harrison must have felt he was stepping from the ridiculous to the sublime. Still only twenty-three, he was half Ravi's age, but there was an old soul within him. He was already unhappy about the sitar becoming "another bandwagon gimmick," and in a wonderfully grumpy lament complained that the audience was "full of mods and rockers who, more likely than not, just went there to be seen at the Ravi Shankar show." He, in contrast, was deadly serious about learning Indian music.[6]

Ravi told Kamala the night was "a smashing success" and, according to the *Guardian*'s reviewer, the jazz critic Charles Fox, it was one of his finest London recitals yet: "One was left marveling at the way Shankar can move between gaiety—even wittiness—and serenity, letting a note sway as naturally as a leaf in the wind."[7] Ravi gave a prominent role, as ever, to Alla Rakha, who enthralled the audience with a tabla solo in the 17-beat cycle *shikhar tal*, a captivating polyrhythmic lesson in how to avoid the obvious.

Also in the audience was Jonathan Miller, formerly of the satirical revue *Beyond the Fringe* and now a prolific theater and television director. He had just persuaded the BBC to let him direct a TV film of *Alice in Wonderland* and was intrigued by the idea of using Indian music in it, having realized that a Victorian girl such as the original Alice Liddell would have heard dreamlike stories of colonial India. Miller knew nothing about Indian music but had been deeply affected by Ravi's soundtrack for *Pather Panchali* and had formed a mental association between the droning noise of insects on a hot summer's day in the country (the setting for his *Alice*) and the resonant buzz of the sitar.[8] Miller was sitting at the back of a box, reading a book, when he heard the first strains of Ravi's sitar. Immediately he announced to his companion, "That's it. That's the music we need."[9] Satirist approached sitarist, and within three weeks Ravi's commission was confirmed.

The next day Ravi flew back to Paris for a concert at the Théâtre des Champs-Élysées. Nostalgically he recalled appearing on the same stage in 1932 in Uday's ballet *Kalia Daman*. Backstage he was dazzled by an Indophile French writer, Mireille Ballero, beginning a long love affair with her. He then spent three days back in the recording studios, where he at last completed the *Chappaqua* score before returning to London on the 7th.

Rehearsals now began for his first duet with Yehudi Menuhin. Peter Feuchtwanger's piece for sitar and violin was to be premiered on June 25 at the Bath Festival, where Yehudi was artistic director. In May Ravi had proposed that they record it for EMI, but he was apprehensive about playing someone else's composition. "We must spend enough time for the piece we are to play together," he had written.[10] Yehudi assented to the recording—"provided, of course, that I do not make too great a fool of myself"—and reassured Ravi that the score was simply "a useful *point de départ*. Although superfluous for you, it is something for me to hang on to which I hope may in the course of our rehearsals also become superfluous for me; I can hardly hope, however, that in the course of a few hours I can acquire an art which takes years and years to master."[11]

Ravi's concerns were justified, as preparations for the performance were to become tense. On the morning of June 8 Ravi met with Feuchtwanger at the composer's Knightsbridge mews house. Feuchtwanger had written a piece based on *Raga Tilang* that he described as "not…a traditional rendering of an Indian *raga*, but a composition in my own style, with improvised variations and cadenzas."[12] Also present was a friend and pupil of Feuchtwanger, John Barham, a talented young pianist and trumpeter. The first hurdle was that Ravi could not sight-read Western scores, so they spent much of this meeting transcribing his part into Indian notation.

The next day Feuchtwanger visited Yehudi's beautiful Queen Anne house in Highgate for lunch and a rehearsal, following it up with an anxious letter to Yehudi. By this stage both musicians had rehearsed their improvised passages in front of him but neither had tackled the fixed element of the work, which he called his "*gat*":

> The way it was at rehearsal on Thursday could be compared to a composer having composed a double fugue in G minor which the performer substitutes by improvising a completely different fugue in the same key. Not one note of the written text was adhered to. Before and after playing the composed "*gat*" there will be sufficient scope for improvisation which is, of course, essential to Indian music, whereas the essence of Western music is the pre-conceived idea. Since this composition is a fusion of Eastern and Western music one factor should not dominate the other, but ideally a perfect balance should be maintained.

He added that he would be embarrassed if they ended up not playing his piece as written, given his role had already been publicized.[13] Clearly he did not see his work as simply a *point de départ*.

Ravi had a problem with playing these Western elements. "It was an interesting piece in which he had used the skeletal scale of the Indian *Raga Tilang*," he later wrote. "But somehow, from the point of view of the sitar and Indian music in general, it seemed quite strange to me—

especially if I had to perform it."[14] He was concerned about hurting the composer, but Yehudi encouraged him to develop his own piece in *Tilang*. Ravi had been impressed with John Barham, who had privately written a couple of *raga*-based arrangements for piano, and he invited him to a meeting at his hotel, the Leinster Towers in Queensway. There he asked him to transcribe his new *Tilang* composition into Western notation, and booked him for *Alice in Wonderland* as well. Barham recalls his surprise that Ravi was wearing a jacket and tie—his typical daily outfit in the West at the time—rather than the Indian clothes he wore on stage and in publicity photographs. He felt Ravi had "no affectation or attitude. He was just very simple, in the best sense of the word. Straightforward, calm, and as time went by I saw how incredibly professional and disciplined he was."[15]

At the time of the Festival Hall performance Ravi had not yet heard any sitar-embellished pop songs, but during the following week he was played "Norwegian Wood."[16] He thought it was "a strange sound that had been produced on the sitar," but interest in him was surging as a result of the song.[17] On the afternoon of the 8th, straight after meeting Feuchtwanger, he had his introduction to the pop world when he and Alla Rakha appeared on the BBC's youth-oriented TV show *A Whole Scene Going*, broadcast live at 6:30 p.m. After playing a three-minute *gat*, Ravi took questions about the sitar and its adoption by pop musicians from a panel including Jeff Beck and Keith Relf of the Yardbirds. He was frank about his ambivalence at being in vogue: "I am afraid that this sudden interest that there seems to be now might go away as suddenly. But on the other hand it will make me very happy if I see that some people take true interest and learn properly." He agreed that its use might just be a gimmick, asking, "Maybe it will be the Japanese koto tomorrow?" Also among the questioners was Darien Angadi, seventeen-year-old son of Ayana, who challenged him about his reported criticism of George Harrison's use of the sitar. "I just said one should learn properly. I am not criticizing it," responded Ravi.[18]

Next Ravi undertook a short tour of British folk-music societies, which had been booked by Basil Douglas. There were eight shows over eleven days, beginning on June 9 at the Islington Folk Club in London, in a room above the Fox pub on Upper Street, and followed the next night by Digbeth Civic Hall in Birmingham. On the 11th Ravi took an early train back to the capital for a morning rehearsal with Yehudi in Highgate, and then played the London Singers Folk Club on Tottenham Court Road, an evening run by Peggy Seeger. There followed Brentwood in Essex, Wolverhampton Public Library and the Suffolk Punch pub in Ipswich. After returning to London on the 15th, he had two free days, before taking the train up to Edinburgh and Glasgow for the last shows on the 18th and 19th.

The folk clubs were frequently located in rather cramped venues, and Ravi's experience was mixed. He was bemused by the audience's flamboyant clothing—hippie fashions were starting to proliferate—but what upset him was the beer-drinking and smoking of tobacco (and often marijuana), as well as the young people wrapped round each other. Writing in August, he said, "I liked the atmosphere of intimacy but put a stop to the smoking and drinking [during] the recital. I explained that our music was of a spiritual character and the whole atmosphere would be vitiated unless listened to in a more solemn and reverential attitude."[19] For the two Scottish recitals he laid down his conditions in advance: no necking, no smoking, no beer, no drugs and no Coca-Cola.

He even gave one of these lectures to Philip Glass, who was over from Paris on a short trip and attended one of Ravi's two London club concerts. Glass reassured him that he was drug-free. Afterward he visited Ravi in his hotel room and asked a question that had begun to fascinate him as a budding composer: "Raviji, where does music come from?"

Ravi turned toward the photograph of Baba on his bedside table and replied, "Thanks to the grace of my *guru*, the power of his music has come through him to me."[20]

Once again, Glass was struck with the force of a revelation. He realized that the Indian oral tradition, of direct teaching from *guru* to

(*clockwise from top left*) Ravi's father, Shyam Shankar, a Sanskrit scholar in New York, 1933. They did not meet until Ravi was eight.

Ravi, then Robindra (Robu), with his mother, Hemangini, at Sarnath in February 1930. Her early death left him with unresolved grief.

In plus fours, and clasping his beret, Robu is surrounded by his mother and his brothers Rajendra, Debendra and Uday, in Paris, 1932.

Uday Shankar with his French dance partner, Simkie. They were a global sensation in the 1930s.

Nine-year-old Robu, about to take an elephant ride with Alice Boner (center), in 1930, probably at Nasrathpur. Uday is on the left, the stylish returning hero.

The fledgling troupe's musicians in Paris, early 1931: Vishnudas Shirali on tabla, Annada Charan Bhattacharya (Bechu) on taus, Robu on a full-sized sitar, Timir Baran on sarod, and Rajendra on bansuri flute.

Uday's uncannily prescient double-exposure photograph of Robu as musician and dancer.
Madhavan Nair, Uzra Mumtaz, Uday, Simkie, Zohra Mumtaz and Robu, in 1936, perhaps at Dartington.

(*clockwise from top left*) Uday and Simkie (right) with Rabindranath Tagore, polymath titan of Indian culture, in about 1933. When Tagore blessed Robu, electricity seemed to course through him.

Simkie with the groundbreaking star of Bharatanatyam dance, Balasaraswati, in Calcutta, 1934.

Ravi, as he was now known, with his first wife, Annapurna, at Maihar, early 1942. She is pregnant with their son Shubho.

Even as he was drawn toward music, Ravi was earning acclaim as a dancer.

Ravi in 1945, at about twenty-five, while working at the Indian People's Theatre Association in Bombay, where he composed his first stage and film scores and wrote the melody for "Sare Jahan Se Accha."

Ravi, aged about thirty, with Narayana Menon, his mentor at All India Radio and a key early supporter.

Ravi on sitar, with his brother-in-law Ali Akbar Khan (right), back in Maihar to learn again at the feet of the latter's sarod-playing father, "Baba" Allauddin Khan, circa 1962.

The center of attention at the All-Union Agricultural Exhibition in Moscow, during India's cultural delegation, 1954. Jnan Prakash Ghosh is on the left in the long coat.

Watching a playback with Satyajit Ray (left) while recording the soundtrack for *Aparajito* in Calcutta, 1956.

A spellbound Yehudi Menuhin gets to grips with Ravi's sitar on their first meeting, Delhi, February 1952. Diana Menuhin watches on.

Ravi with his son Shubho and Baba's wife Madan Manjari.

Ravi and Marilyn Silverstone make a connection at the Resors' New York apartment, 1956, with Chatur Lal (left), James and Ann Laughlin (center) and Nodu Mullick.

Back to camera, Ravi thrills the New York jazz world gathered in Marshall Stearns's apartment in December 1956, including Willie "the Lion" Smith (on chair at left), Dizzy Gillespie (front row, in dark glasses), Roy Eldridge (speaking to Gillespie) and Quincy Jones (second row, at right).

George Avakian toasts Ravi upon his departure from New York on the *SS United States*, May 1957.

Peter Pears, contralto Norma Procter, Marion, Countess of Harewood, Benjamin Britten and the Earl of Harewood, with Ravi, his friend and tanpura player Prodyot Sen and the tabla maestro Alla Rakha, at Temple Newsam, Leeds, 1958. Britten, Pears and Harewood were early supporters of Ravi in the UK.

Ravi conducts the choir for *Melody and Rhythm*, Bombay, 1962. Second left in the back row is Penny Estabrook; just beyond her is Kamala Chakravarty.

(*clockwise from top left*) Ravi rehearses the "Nightingale of India," Lata Mangeshkar, for the soundtrack to *Anuradha*, 1960.

With folk singer and TV presenter Rory McEwen, outside the latter's London home, 1963.

Ravi with Jonathan Miller at BBC Television Centre, October 1966. *Alice in Wonderland* was a career high for both of them.

John Coltrane plays soprano saxophone at the 1966 Newport Jazz Festival. He studied briefly with Ravi and was strongly influenced by his music.

George Harrison with his new heroes: Alla Rakha, Ali Akbar Khan, Ravi and Bismillah Khan, backstage at the Hollywood Bowl, August 1967.

With Yehudi Menuhin, Alla Rakha and Prodyot Sen at Menuhin's Highgate home, in rehearsal for the Gandhi centenary concert at the Royal Albert Hall, October 1969.

Ravi and George Harrison jam on guitars aboard the motor yacht *Marala*, offshore from Cannes, May 1972.

The Dark Horse tour, 1974. Back row: T. V. Gopalkrishnan, Hariprasad Chaurasia, Alla Rakha, Ravi, Lakshmi Shankar, Vijji Shankar, Shivkumar Sharma, L. Subramaniam. Middle row: Gopal Krishan, Satyadev Pawar, Sultan Khan, Kartick Kumar. Front row: Kamalesh Maitra, Rijram Desad, Harihar Rao.

The perpetual traveler: Ravi, clutching his sitar in a soft bag, with Alla Rakha (left) and one of the great loves of his life, Kamala Chakravarty. A seat was often booked for the instrument in the name of Mr. Sitar.

Recording the music for *Gandhi* with George Fenton and Richard Attenborough, at CTS Studios, Wembley, January 1982.

Ghanashyam takes shape at 95 Lodhi Road, Delhi, 1989. From left: Shubhendra Rao, Ashit Desai, Ravi, Suresh Lalwani, Ronu Majumdar, Partho Sarothy, Durga Lal, Shanta Dhananjayan and V. P. Dhananjayan.

(*clockwise from top*) With Sukanya, his second wife, in 1997.

A lighthearted press call before the premiere of Ravi's second sitar concerto, with his friend, the conductor Zubin Mehta, New York, April 1981.

At home in Encinitas with Joshua Bell, 2007. Ravi was rehearsing him for the Verbier Festival.

With Philip Glass, exchanging musical themes for their album *Passages*, Santa Monica, 1989.

"These are like my two eyes." Ravi and Norah Jones, his daughter with Sue Jones, in Calcutta in January 1981; and with Anoushka Shankar, in Varanasi in January 1989, just before his wedding to her mother, Sukanya.

Anoushka, Norah, Ravi and Sukanya, at Lodhi Road, Delhi, during Norah's visit in early 2000.

Ravi gives his "semi-final" performance in London at Barbican Hall, 2008, with Anoushka assisting on sitar. Note his sitting position and shorter-necked sitar, adopted following the deterioration in his shoulder. Nick Able is on tanpura.

The bearded sage during his final concert in India, at the Premaanjali Festival in Bangalore on 7 February 2012.

shishya, had echoes within Western musical heritage and the lineage of composers that he himself was about to join. As he later put it,

> All of us had one teacher that we worked with. The transmission of the technique and the style of the music and the tradition of the music is done in the same way…My teacher was Nadia Boulanger. Her teacher was Fauré. It's a person-to-person transmission. You study with a teacher. That teacher studied with a teacher. We're probably only two or three teachers away from Beethoven.[21]

On the morning of Thursday, June 23 Ravi and Alla Rakha arrived at Yehudi and Diana Menuhin's suite at the Lansdown Grove Hotel in Bath. They cleared the chairs away, unrolled a rug that Ravi's entourage had brought, sat down and resumed rehearsals. With Ravi's favorite *agarbathi* burning, Yehudi likened the setting to a corner of Old Delhi. For the next two days, for ten and a half hours a day, they revised Feuchtwanger's piece and practiced assiduously, breaking only to refuel with Indian takeaways carted up the hill by Diana Menuhin and for post-prandial siestas, when they lay down "rolled up on the floor in varying positions like parcels at a poste restante."[22]

On the Saturday morning, the ensemble took their instruments, incense and rug to the city's Georgian Guildhall and squeezed in two hours' final practice in the committee room, before presenting their new offering at a 3 p.m. recital. In the first half Yehudi and his son-in-law Fou Ts'ong played violin and piano variations by Mozart. After the break, Ravi and Alla Rakha played two *ragas*, before Yehudi joined them on stage for the finale. He had changed out of his conventional concert wear and emerged, barefoot, in blue linen trousers and an embroidered Indian tunic lent to him by Ravi. Filled with dread, he sat down cross-legged onstage alongside his colleagues.

No score or recording exists of what they played, but we know they retained the first minute or two of Feuchtwanger's composition, billed as the *alap*, and thereafter segued into the new piece that Ravi had written, which continued through *gat* and *jhala* sections. It lasted about ten minutes in total.[23] *The Times* heard improvisatory violin passages, but Ravi later described these as "a few cadenzas for Yehudi written in such a way that, although it was not a free-improvisation piece, it sounded as if it was."[24] Yehudi was happy with how he acquitted himself, and the result was so infectiously joyful that they had to repeat it as an encore.

At the time Ravi publicly explained that there were "a lot of technical difficulties" with Feuchtwanger's composition.[25] In private he dropped the diplomacy. Writing to Kamala the day after the concert, he described the piece as "silly & stupid" and said that "Y.M. and myself both were disgusted!"[26] The uncharacteristically harsh tone— Feuchtwanger's was a serious effort, after all—suggests that this experience had jabbed at a particularly sensitive spot, where the Western composer's faith in his score bumped up against the Indian musician's emphasis on improvisation within a strict but unwritten framework. For Ravi it was not sufficient to argue that the "*gat*" represented the Western element of the piece and thus need not obey Indian rules. If it was billed as *Tilang*, he would not agree to breach the *raga*'s integrity as he had learned it.

The force of Ravi's reaction suggests that there was more to it than that. For one thing he was exhausted. In the same letter to Kamala he told her, "I want to sleep & sleep for weeks & months to make up for the sleepless years of my life." He was also "a worried man" with "self-doubts," in the judgment of the *Times of India*, which identified a fundamental conflict within him between his "unrivaled mastery over the classical idiom of Indian music" and his "bug to communicate his art to the West."[27] For years he had endured criticism back home of his overseas endeavors and he was sensitive to the charge (however unfair or ill-informed) that he was polluting the crystal waters of Indian classical music. He was not going to let those critics arraign him for someone else's crime. That summer he had battled the naive appropriation of the sitar by infatuated pop stars and the smoky, drug-laden atmospheres of folk clubs—and now this assault from the Western classical world. Constant firefighting was demanded of him. It was to be a long-running theme: his fervent drive to be faithful to Indian music in the face of accusations that he was doing the opposite was to cause him more anguish than anything else in his professional life. The Bath experience reinforced his instinct that if he was to collaborate with non-Indian musicians it should be on his own terms.

Three days later he played a three-and-a-half-hour private recital at Rory McEwen's Chelsea home that his audience, including Barbra Streisand and Jonathan Miller, seemed to sense on a profound level.[28] "It was a strange experience—which I felt after long time," he wrote to Kamala the following night.

> I didn't care where or for whom I was playing. I felt so humble and powerful; it was sensing the height of a musical, spiritual and sexual experience all at the same time. It was as if the sitar became the torso of a beautiful woman I love—and I was making love to it—tenderly—ardently & wildly! Oh what an ecstasy! I am still tingling with the afterthought. It is so rarely that these things happen! Everyone became mad & felt the reaction. I wish you were there.[29]

Ravi's letters to Kamala were more full of passion than ever. Despite his dalliances on the road, which he continued to share with her, he missed her deeply and they were now talking of her accompanying him on his 1967 tour. "Oh God, won't I be excited like a child to see Paris, Rome, London and so many other places," she wrote to him on July 1.[30]

It was in the cavernous Studio One at Abbey Road that Yehudi Menuhin, Alla Rakha and Ravi reconvened on July 4 for a historic session. Ravi had done a complete rewrite, removing all traces of Feuchtwanger's composition. *Swara-Kakali*, as it was now titled, became the centerpiece of the album *West Meets East*. It was still a duet, and still in

Raga Tilang, which is well suited to its intercultural task as a pentatonic *raga* (albeit using both natural and flat seventh notes) and thus relatively accessible to the Western ear. The main section is a *gat* in *teental*, with an urgent and catchy melody that develops over several phases, Ravi and Yehudi trading riffs in call-and-response style until they climax on a *tihai*—a thrice-repeated phrase, so characteristic of Indian music. There is the impression of improvisation, but Yehudi's parts here were composed. With his lack of training in Indian music, he does not produce much of the *gamak* ornamentation that an Indian violinist would employ, but the rapid and rhythmic nature of the *gat* means this textural difference is barely noticeable, and he does a fine job.

Indian listeners sometimes remark that Yehudi plays a strange variety of Indian classical music on this album. Earlier in this piece, he employs Western violin textures largely alien to his Indian counterparts: harmonics, to play very high notes; a tremolo, as the piece hangs in suspension; and *pizzicato* in the tumbling phrase leading toward the *gat*. He gives glimpses of vibrato too. There is also an unusual structural element, the minute-long segment sandwiched between the brief opening *alap* and the *gat* being described on John Barham's sleeve notes as a cadenza, Western terminology for a passage that allows for improvisation. Here Yehudi does extemporize, but his ascent to the heavens on harmonics surges far above the range normally covered by an Indian violinist, who would typically remain within the three-octave span of the human voice. At least he sticks to the notes allowed by the *raga*. Meanwhile, everything Ravi plays is faithful to it and beautifully rendered. He had obviously thought carefully about how he could showcase Yehudi's unique virtuosity in a work that remains Indian in character while allowing the violinist to make solo forays into exploratory terrain. Was this fusion music? There was no such genre label then, but the retrospective answer should be yes, because of Yehudi's idiosyncratic elements. Yet Ravi was clear that he did not seek a midpoint equilibrium. Here West meets East, but not at the border; the land underfoot is Indian.

"I've always loved violin and sitar together," Ravi reflected in 2011.

They are very different and very similar at the same time. I remember when I wrote and played with Yehudi Menuhin there was a sense that the two instruments would continuously come together at a sort of point and then diverge, weaving a remarkable pattern. The sound created by the sitar and violin is so compatible yet so different, it's the perfect improvisational match.[31]

Yehudi also recorded a second Indian piece, *Prabhati*, which Ravi had composed in an Indian restaurant in Bayswater, singing the Indian notation to Barham, who transcribed it into Western notation for Yehudi.[32] It is a short violin solo with tabla accompaniment in *Gunkali*, another pentatonic *raga*, this time with flattened second and sixth notes and no third or seventh, echoing folk or Romany laments. It was written in Ravi's sitar tuning of C sharp, and Yehudi seems to have retuned his violin down a semitone. It opens with a composed *alap*, soulfully played by Yehudi with more ornamentation (but noticeable vibrato), before moving on to another improvised "cadenza" and composed *jor* and *gat* sections. He remains mostly within an Indian's normal range, but in the cadenza he again rises up to a very high line on harmonics, and in the *jor* plays *pizzicato*. For the *gat*, he enlisted Barham on piano to rehearse him in its fast 14-beat rhythmic cycle (*chanchar tal*), roughly equivalent to a 7/8 time signature. He rises to the challenge admirably.

There was only one slip. On *Swara-Kakali*, stretched by the unfamiliar form, Yehudi made a scratchy sound in one place, and EMI demanded perfection. So Barham, who was supervising the editing, cloned a phrase from one part of the recording and spliced it in to replace the faulty notes. However, the violin and the tabla were on the same track, and Barham forgot that Alla Rakha was playing different permutations of drum syllables in each rhythmic cycle. By taking part of one cycle and dropping it into another, he spoiled the tabla's continuity. That was the version released. Fortunately, the glitch is hard to spot. "Nobody else noticed it probably, apart from Ravi and Alla Rakha, who was very upset, but polite. I was so embarrassed," says Barham.[33]

To complete the album Ravi performed *Puriya Kalyan*, while Yehudi and his pianist sister Hephzibah played Enescu's Sonata No. 3. The Enescu was a childhood favorite of Yehudi, chosen for what he called its Romanian "gypsy style" and the impression it gives of improvisation, even though, as with Ravi's compositions here, it is entirely composed. *West Meets East* proved to be a trailblazing triumph, probably the first great collaboration between virtuosos from different traditions—the precursor of Shakti, AfroCubism and many more. Released the following year, it occupied the summit of the *Billboard* classical charts for six months.

On July 8 Ravi departed on a brief European tour, which took in Aachen in Germany, the Jyväskylä Festival—his first time in Finland since the early 1930s—and Copenhagen. It was only when he returned to London on the 16th that the pace finally slowed down. In the previous eight weeks he had hurtled between TV shows, major concert halls, folk clubs and classical-music festivals, and recorded a film score and a historic album, but the most significant event of the tour happened near the end: finally meeting George Harrison.

A dinner party was specially arranged at 44 Fitzalan Road, the Angadi family home in Finchley. Harrison arrived in a Ferrari, and there was an extra guest that evening—Paul McCartney, who arrived separately and unannounced. News that two Beatles were visiting drew a crowd of neighbors onto the street. Ravi found McCartney to be "very charming and polite." McCartney was interested in Indian music, but it was with Harrison that the real connection was forged.[34] For Harrison, India and its music had the force of a life's quest. "George was very, very serious, very intense," recalls Shankara Angadi.[35]

George quizzed Ravi earnestly about both the music and the spirituality of India. Admitting that he was embarrassed about his playing on "Norwegian Wood," he asked Ravi to teach him the sitar. Ravi was struck by how humble the young star was, and the pair hit it off. "I knew nothing about the rock world before I met George," he later admitted.

> Like anybody brought up in a strictly classical thing I had a tremendous fear of it—the sound, the people associated with it, every aspect. I had seen a few characters connected with it and I was not very attracted to them—but, after George, I had to change my opinion. He had more of a respect.[36]

The Beatles were used to meeting politicians, royalty, film stars and their musical heroes, but George had always found those experiences hollow. Ravi was different. "He was so intriguing," recalled George in 1976, "because he's such a little person and yet had so much strength and so much power that I became so attracted to the music then through the person. And the deeper I got into it, the more there was."[37]

Ravi impressed on him the long road ahead if he were to understand Indian music and play the sitar well. He told him it was more like the training that a Western classical violinist or cellist goes through rather than a rock'n'roll guitarist. George was particularly moved by Ravi's declaration that learning never ceases. "I have given so many years of my life to sitar, and by God's grace I have become very well known," Ravi told him, "but still I know in my heart of hearts that I have a long way to go."[38] George said he was willing to devote the necessary time to learning, and on that understanding Ravi arranged to visit him at his home in Esher, Surrey, to begin teaching. In fact he went twice within about a week.[39]

In the first lesson George noticed how this virtuoso master had the patience to begin from scratch, to show him the correct way to sit and hold the sitar, and how to wear the *mizrab* pick (which George soon dubbed the "mizrable" because it pinches the forefinger so painfully). It was rare for Ravi to teach a beginner, an indication of how strongly he was drawn to his new student. George was completely self-taught on guitar, so beginning from the basics and playing *sargam* scale exercises on the sitar brought a new rigor to his music. He also had an instant lesson in the discipline required. When the telephone rang, he stood up to answer it, but as he went to step over his sitar Ravi slapped him on the leg and said, "The first thing you must realize is that you must have more respect for the instrument."[40]

Later that day, they were joined by John Lennon, Ringo Starr and their wives, as both families lived nearby, and Ravi and Alla Rakha played a three-and-a-half-hour recital for this select group. He began, of course, by asking them not to smoke or drink during the recital. George marveled at Ravi's sitar-playing. "If you see it up close it's just amazing, because it's like an orchestra in itself, with all the sympathetic strings," he said. "You just hit one note and this whole orchestra comes out of there."[41] The others were captivated too. At first Starr was bewildered to see Alla Rakha shaking his head at Ravi's playing, making the common mistake of thinking this signified disapproval. Then when the tabla entered he felt, like many a Western drummer, intimidated by the speed and complexity of the playing. "Ringo just sat there and watched Alla Rakha and then he ran a mile! He just didn't want to go near them!" remembered George, laughing sympathetically.[42] Ravi asked John Barham, whom he had invited along, to teach Starr how to count *teental* on his fingers.

The exact dates for the meeting in Finchley and the two lessons in Esher have always been difficult to pin down. June is usually given as the month for all of them, but both George and Ravi were exceptionally busy then and there were at most just three evenings when both were free in London: the 7th, 15th and 20th. However, Ravi did not mention meeting George in any of the eight letters he wrote to Kamala between May 30 and July 8, nor in any public statements. A more likely chronology has now come to light. In the program for two concerts Ravi gave at the New Empire, Calcutta, in mid-August, when events were still fresh, he contributed a report of his recent European tour, in which he wrote about George, "It was ten days prior to my leaving London that we met at a dinner party."[43] This dates their first meeting to Saturday, July 16—the day Ravi returned from Copenhagen—or perhaps Sunday the 17th. He also told the *New York Times* in May 1967 that the first lesson at George's home took place "with only three days left in England," which dates that to the following Saturday, July 23.[44] That still left time for a second visit to Esher before he flew home on the 26th. This timing is more plausible in that both parties had much more spare time in mid-July than they did in June. Interestingly, it would mean that the Beatles' first visit to India on July 6–8, when they stopped over in Delhi and George bought his first good-quality sitar from Bishandas Sharma, took place before he had met Ravi.

Arriving back in India, Ravi could reflect with satisfaction on his frenetic European summer. His nephew Kumar and niece Vijji were beside themselves with excitement at the news that their uncle was now teaching a Beatle. And there was more: Ravi had invited George to India for an extended period of study in the autumn.

Before that, there was little time to rest, and Ravi was feeling the strain again. A visit to Maihar in the first week of September plummeted him into melancholy. "Felt sad mostly mainly to see Baba, and then staying in the house the room all the details of past haunted me," he wrote to Kamala. "The thoughts of how by ill luck, mistakes & wrong moves I've messed up my, along with others lives." But daybreak brought the familiar view of Trikuta Hill and its promise of spiritual sustenance: "The *darshan* of my old and beautiful love "Ma Sharada" [*sic*] on the hills made feel much better since yesterday morning."[45]

On September 14 around the same time that Philip Glass was departing from Marseilles on the overland route to India via Turkey, Iran, Afghanistan and Pakistan, George Harrison and his wife Pattie flew into Bombay airport. Ravi was there to meet them. Just two weeks earlier George had returned from the Beatles' final tour, an ill-fated trip around America attended by hysteria, bans and death threats. The foursome's priorities were changing rapidly, George's fastest of all, and they had agreed to take three months off. By way of disguise he had cut his hair and—at Ravi's suggestion—grown a mustache, and the couple booked into Bombay's grandest hotel, the Taj Mahal, as Mr. and Mrs. Sam Wells. In his suite George's sitar practice was overseen by Ravi, or more often by Ravi's student Shambhu Das. He also had a yoga teacher to help him adjust to the demanding sitting position. At first he and Pattie managed to go out unmolested, so they visited temples and shops, wandered along Juhu beach and attended a five-hour recital by Ravi in Santa Cruz on the 17th.

This liberation from being a Beatle lasted about three days before a young lift attendant recognized him. When word leaked out, thousands of teenage Indian Beatles fans assembled on the pavement calling out, "Ravi Shankar! We want George!" Some even phoned his room or banged on his door. A frustrated George called a press conference on the 19th to appeal for privacy, explaining that he was in India to study the sitar with Ravi and to find out more about Indian religion. "You have the greatest culture, a great philosophy and a great artistic tradition. It's a pity really that people are overlooking it," he said.[46] Ravi, who was present, told the journalists, "I find him a wonderful student. He is very sincere in learning the sitar."[47]

As it was now impossible to study in Bombay, Ravi arranged a tour of several of India's finest sights instead. The press reported that George and Pattie had flown to Delhi on the 22nd and might leave India soon afterward. This sounds like a decoy story, and it is more likely that they traveled to Aurangabad, just two hundred miles away, for they were soon exploring, along with Ravi, Kamala and Shambhu Das, the ancient caves at Ajanta and Ellora.

They journeyed on to Varanasi, which had an overwhelming impact on George. It was the time of the annual Ramlila festival. A temporary camp is built on the east side of the river in Ramnagar to house huge crowds of pilgrims, and every night for a month plays are staged to tell Rama's story, using giant wooden effigies mounted on trolleys.

Ravi's friend Aruna Nand Dubey, known as A. N. Dubey, owned a shop that sold *bhang ki thandai*, a lassi drink made from yogurt, almonds, saffron, cashew nuts and cardamon, and laced with *bhang* (hashish). It is legal in the city, if sold under license, because of its association with Shiva and its sacramental function. On October 29, the last day of the festival, George drank a glass of Dubey's *thandai* and the group began exploring the city, including the riverside cremation *ghats*. At length they crossed the river to see the festival site. Spaced out from the *bhang*, George was spellbound by the scene: the thousands of dreadlocked *sadhu* renunciates, the pink dust rising in the air as the maharaja processed through the crowds on an elephant, the full moon ascending at dusk and the play celebrating Rama's final victory over the demon Ravana. He had the thrilling sense that he had gone back thousands of years.

After Delhi, where Ravi introduced them to the Bharat-Rams, the Harrisons continued without him to Jaipur, Udaipur and the Taj Mahal at Agra. They then flew from Delhi to Srinagar in Kashmir, where they were joined again by Ravi and Kamala, and the trip climaxed with fifteen days on an exquisitely carved houseboat on Dal Lake. Here, moored alongside the Mughal gardens of Naseem Bagh, with the chinar trees in their full autumn color, and nestled beneath the Himalaya that had mysteriously beckoned George, Ravi insisted they both follow the strict regime that he had learned from his own *guru*. In the early morning chill George woke to the sound of Ravi playing the sitar in the next room, and sat up in bed drinking tea brought by Ghulam Butt, proprietor of Clermont Houseboats. He took a bath before meditating or beginning sitar practice, so that he was ritually cleansed before worship—music being a form of worship. Breakfast followed only after the extended dawn session, and there was further practice throughout the day. They took day trips to the hill station of Gulmarg and to the ninth-century Hindu temple complex at Avantipur, where George's camera captured them on the steps of the ruined Avantiswami temple and posing with a goat and ten Kashmiri village children.

"His devotion to Raviji was something worth seeing," recalled Kamala.[48] Pattie was just as impressed by Ravi: "He had such a magnetic presence. A real alpha male and very attractive."[49] Traveling around India, the Harrisons watched, mesmerized, as he performed in public and in private homes—he once finished at four in the morning—and gave lessons to his disciples. Ravi played George LPs by other Indian soloists, and also a tape of *Nava Rasa Ranga*, which blew his mind all over again. It was the first time George had heard Indian music played by an ensemble rather than soloists or duos, and this piece of music was to haunt him.

For all that he loved the music, George realized that the spiritual side of India attracted him even more, and Ravi was his first guide in this area too. George was already reading Yogananda's *Autobiography of a Yogi*, which Ravi had given to him in London; thirty years later he was still calling it "the most incredible book of all time."[50] In Bombay Ravi's brother Rajendra gave him Swami Vivekananda's *Raja Yoga*, which asserted that religion was not a question of faith alone, as he had understood from his Catholic upbringing. Rather, God could be experienced directly, through yoga and meditation. He would always be fond of quoting this book's epigram:

> Each soul is potentially divine. The goal is to manifest this
> Divinity within by controlling nature, external and internal. Do
> this either by work, or worship, or psychic control, or philosophy—
> by one, or more, or all of these—and be free. This is the whole
> of religion. Doctrines, or dogmas, or rituals, or books, or temples,
> or forms, are but secondary details.[51]

On October 22 the Harrisons flew back to London, and Ravi returned to Bombay. He had spent about five weeks with them, and had even taken them to be blessed by Tat Baba, a sign of how dearly he valued this new friendship.[52] It was rare to find anyone, let alone a Westerner, so devoted to Indian music and philosophy. For all George's fame, it was this zeal that induced Ravi to give so much time to him:

My heart melted with love for him. His quest was beautiful, although at the same time it was more like a child's; he wasn't fully matured back then. Nevertheless his interest in and curiosity for our traditions, mostly in the fields of religion, philosophy and music, was quite genuine.[53]

"As soon as he started playing I realized that it was going to be a very important part of the film," said Jonathan Miller in 2005. "When I re-play the film nearly forty years later, that music brings back the whole occasion to me and I can't imagine the film without it."[54] Today Miller's television drama of *Alice in Wonderland*, featuring one of Ravi's finest soundtracks, is recognized as an arthouse classic. It presents the bizarre-ness of the adult world to a Victorian child, distorted by the surreal log-ic of dreaming. Screened on BBC1 on December 28, 1966, it drew 12.5 million viewers and was described by the *Daily Sketch* as "the most stun-ning and imaginative film to come from TV."[55] It was also embraced by the new LSD generation for its supposedly psychedelic child's-eye view, paralleling the Beatles' return to the inner child in their hallucinatory masterpieces "Strawberry Fields Forever" and "Penny Lane," recorded around the same time. Miller was in fact exploring the dreamscape of the 1860s, rather than the 1960s, but people saw what they wanted to see.

When Ravi flew in alone on October 25 to record the music, carry-ing his sitar in its waterproof bag, two people had arrived separate-ly at London Airport to meet him: from a black taxi stepped Miller himself, in a sheepskin coat, while from a dark blue Ferrari 275 GTB emerged George Harrison, who had been home from India just three days and was dressed in a kurta and raw silk waistcoat. Ravi, complet-ing a costume reversal with the latter, was sporting a dark suit, tie, raincoat and sunglasses.

The film's underlying theme, which would have struck a chord with Ravi, was the blessed but ephemeral nature of childhood and "the strange melancholy catastrophe of reaching adult life."[56] Miller also wanted to reference the British Empire in India, and in an inspired piece of casting he chose for his Alice a thirteen-year-old amateur with French–Indian ancestry, Anne-Marie Mallik, who was wonderfully grave and haughty. Previous treatments of Lewis Carroll's story had tended to interpret characters such as the White Rabbit and the Mock Turtle as animals, but Miller insisted they were human beings, distorted versions of real adults that the Victorian Alice knew. The BBC budget was generous and, Mallik apart, he assembled an all-star cast including John Gielgud, Peter Sellers and Peter Cook. None of them was paid more than £500, but terms restricted the BBC to just two screenings. Ravi received £315, plus £105 for the repeat.[57]

Ravi spent Saturday October 29 at BBC Television Centre, watching the edited film several times. He returned on Sunday morning with the oboist Léon Goossens, John Barham on piano, Keshav Sathe on tabla and Prodyot Sen on tanpura. Perched on a table in the dubbing theater, Ravi himself played the sitar and the swarmandal. An unknown dilruba player must have been present as well. Working closely with Miller, Ravi composed music on the spot, Barham notating it for Goossens page by page as Ravi wrote it.

Miller had hoped that Indian music would intensify the film's dreamlike mood, and he was not disappointed. Ravi's most striking contribution is to the early scene when Alice and her sister lie down in a meadow. Goossens plays a soporific pentatonic theme, perfectly creating the sweltering, torpid atmosphere on one of those endless Arcadian afternoons of childhood. As the theme is repeated, insects buzz more loudly and Alice sinks into a febrile sleep. Then comes the moment of greatest drama: she sits upright as an impatient top-hatted man (the White Rabbit) appears in the background to summon her, and Sathe's tabla rings out in a brisk, rousing solo. The dream has begun. It is a masterfully cinematic passage.

The film shows how accomplished Ravi had become over the previous decade at creating incidental music that accentuates atmosphere—from the circling piano motif that accompanies Alice running past billowing curtains to the harp-like timbre he produces on the sitar during the Mad Hatter's tea party. His soundtrack was described by Miller as "wonderfully reticent and not overdramatic."[58] The longest piece accompanies the closing titles, a bright three-minute composition led by the sitar that weaves in all the other instruments. Miller later chose this among his *Desert Island Discs*. "The film is beautiful," Ravi wrote to Kamala after the session. "The director Jonathan Miller is GREAT! A rarely gifted man—as an actor, playwriter & director. So witty and humorous—& a mimic."[59]

Life and *Vogue* magazines ran features on *Alice*, and it was also previewed on television in BBC2's *New Release*, which included footage of the music recording. With Ravi so topical, the same channel also scheduled for December 30 his TV special made a year earlier, which had yet to be screened. In the run-up to the broadcast of *Alice* the press leaped to the incorrect conclusion that Miller had turned an innocent national treasure into a Freudian sexual psychodrama, encouraged by Peter Cook quipping that it should be titled "Analysis in Wonderland." After transmission the controversy dissipated amid the positive reviews. Miller, despite all his later achievements in television, theater and opera, considers *Alice* "one of the best things, if not the best thing, I ever made."[60]

For his London stay, Ravi had rented Rory McEwen's studio apartment on Hollywood Road in Chelsea, which he thought was "a dream."[61] In the mid-1960s McEwen and his wife Romana were known for throwing parties at their home around the corner on Tregunter Road, with guests including John Lennon, Princess Margaret and a young David Dimbleby, and Ravi played at least twice at these. He continued teaching George Harrison, who also attended part of the *Alice* recording.[62]

On November 1, suffering from flu, Ravi flew to Paris for a UNESCO general meeting, where he performed and took part in another panel discussion on the music of East and West. He then flew into Calcutta on the 5th. There he stayed with Lala Sridhar, but on the

8th he checked himself into the Woodland Nursing Home for three days as he was concerned about repeated stomach upsets over a long period. He was given a sigmoidoscopy, an examination of the lower intestine carried out rectally. "Boy! It was painful. A hollow rod nearly 13 inches long was completely pushed in," he reported to Kamala. He also had a barium enema ("I hate it!"), before an X-ray of his colon.[63] Nothing of concern was found, but his symptoms recurred the following week. "After all the tests I went through would you believe that they have found absolutely nothing!" he grumbled. The best diagnosis was that his lower intestine was hypersensitive and the slightest mental, physical or muscular strain could trigger an attack of diarrhea. He resolved to be more cautious with his diet and was advised not to overexert himself, which went against his nature. He suspected that part of the problem was his "insatiable appetite"—for music, for new experiences, for sex, for love.[64]

Over the next five weeks he made trips to Calcutta and Chengail in West Bengal, Rourkela in Orissa, Pune, Bombay, Delhi, Patna, Varanasi and Calcutta again, before returning to Bombay. Most of these were for concerts, but in mid-November he spent three days at HMV's Dum Dum studios in Calcutta re-recording *Abhogi Kanada* and *Tilak Shyam*, two *ragas* that he had attempted and rejected back in April. This time the results were sublime, and he passed them for an HMV India LP.

His abdominal problems did not stem the flow of passionate letters to Kamala, whom he was missing greatly. She responded with deep feeling, looking ahead to their plans for 1967: "I could ask for nothing more than to be with you for a whole year. Because being with you means having EVERYTHING at once."[65]

"It was like wildfire," according to Ravi.[66] The reports of a Beatle in Bombay had echoed around the world, and most loudly of all in America. "Interest in Indian music is snowballing," Richard Bock told *Billboard* in December, as World Pacific issued five albums by Asian artists, all packaged handsomely in gatefold sleeves. These included his first release by M. S. Subbulakshmi, who had spent almost three months touring Europe and America in the autumn, and a reissue of Ravi's 1957 EMI album *Three Ragas*. The strongest markets, he explained, were Los Angeles, San Francisco, Chicago, Boston and New York.[67]

It was in New York that Bock recorded the next album by Ravi, who flew in on December 18, direct from Bombay. Ravi had been booked to play three successive nights at Philharmonic Hall, within the four-year-old Lincoln Center complex. Still using his five-act format, he played different *ragas* each night from the 21st to the 23rd. "Unbelievable success. All three sold-out houses," he cabled home. Extra seats had been added due to demand, and he played to over three thousand each night, described by *Newsweek* as "a houseful of U.S. devotees—hippies, haut monde and hoi polloi paying homage to their longtime teacher."[68] His World Pacific album *In New York*, taped live at these concerts and issued the following April, features three classic, contemplative performances: the devotional *Bairagi*, his own creation from 1949; the Carnatic *raga Nat Bhairavi*; and a particularly solemn and exquisite rendering of *Marwa*, a *raga* of the sunset hour that conveys "feelings of renunciation, loneliness and desolation."[69]

Ravi's U.S. management was in transition. These concerts were promoted jointly by Jay K. Hoffman, a New York classical agent, and the Asia Society, who threw a reception in Ravi's honor after the first concert. The flyers announced that Ravi was represented by Isadora Bennett and Charles Reinhart, as in 1965, but the baton was being passed to Hoffman, who had sensed the potential in Asian music after his first venture in that direction, his Japan Week at Philharmonic Hall in 1964.[70] He had reached out to Ravi via World Pacific. "The bottom line was that I heard his music and I loved it. The way he composed, the way he played," said Hoffman in 2012.[71]

Richard Goldstein, who reported for the *Village Voice* from the function at Asia House, noted that Ravi looked like "a man who has patiently endured all the praise-without-comprehension an alien culture can bestow. He has been Martian-in-residence for years." Even with all the acclaim, Ravi still had to reach for his firefighter's suit. An advertisement in the concert program had encouraged readers to sample "the primitive folk sounds" of India. "I do not play folk or primitive songs," he declared pointedly. "This is classical music."[72]

As soon as Ravi had arrived in New York he had called John Coltrane. They had remained in contact over the years but their schedules had not coincided during Ravi's American tours in 1964 and 1965, so it was probably five years since they had met. In that time Coltrane had created *A Love Supreme*, the pinnacle of his achievement with the classic John Coltrane Quartet, which had been recorded in December 1964. Two things reveal that Ravi's music was part of its inspiration. First, the album is conceived as a spiritual offering and resolves to a sense of ultimate peace, echoing what he had told Ravi were the elements he found most attractive in Indian music. Second, almost exactly nine months after the recording his partner Alice McLeod gave birth to their second son—whom they named Ravi.

Coltrane had then pushed on with a demanding musical and spiritual quest. During 1965 he began taking LSD, and he moved into free-jazz territory on the albums *Ascension* and *Om*, the latter featuring chants from the *Bhagavad-Gita*. His music was becoming ever more avant-garde, with unmetered rhythms and impenetrable, discordant solos. Once again he met with hostility from American audiences, some of whom began to walk out of his concerts.

"He sounded very sad," said Ravi, "and I told him I was disturbed after hearing his latest record he had sent me. He told me that he was feeling extremely frustrated, that he was still trying for something different but he did not know what he was looking for."[73] The record was most likely *Meditations*, which had appeared three months before and saw Coltrane playing in free-jazz style, mixing some exquisite passages with much overblowing of his tenor saxophone, the shrieking sound that Ravi found so uncomfortable.

"I was so impressed," Ravi told him, "and found it amazing and touching as well, but in places I felt you were crying out through your instrument and it was like a shriek of a tormented soul…But seeing and knowing you I thought that the interest in and love of our tradition and music has helped you to overcome this."

Ravi never forgot the expression on Coltrane's face as he replied, "Ravi, that is exactly what I want to know and learn from you. How you find so much peace in your music and give it to your listeners."[74]

Ravi suggested Coltrane came to India to learn, but this wasn't possible, so they agreed to meet in Los Angeles the following summer, when Ravi was planning to open a Californian branch of Kinnara and would be able to teach Coltrane for six weeks. "We embraced and parted with such love," said Ravi.[75] It was a firm arrangement, but Coltrane never came because he contracted liver cancer. He declined rapidly and died in July 1967, aged just forty, before they could see each other again.

Ravi remained perplexed about the turmoil he had heard in Coltrane's music. In truth, though, he had not listened that widely to his body of work. It would be another thirty-four years before he gained more insight. In 2001 the writer Ashley Kahn, who was working on a book about *A Love Supreme*, discovered that Ravi had never heard it, so he mailed him a copy. "I played it again and again," said Ravi, "and I was so moved by the beautiful resolution of this great work and his sleeve notes in the form of a prayer. Here was the peace he had been looking for. At last it seemed to make sense."[76]

For Christmas 1966 George Harrison bought Ravi a two-volume edition of the *I Ching*, and signed and dedicated both volumes to him. He tried to meet Ravi at London Airport on December 27 as he changed planes en route from New York to India, but he had the wrong flight information.[77] This conjures up an image impossible to envisage twelve months earlier, that of a Beatle disciple hovering in the transit lounge at Heathrow with a bulky gift-wrapped package, realizing with disappointment that he has missed his jet-setting *guru*. For Ravi, it had been that kind of year, and 1967 would be no less improbable.

16

IT HAPPENED IN MONTEREY

The kings of rock and roll abdicated. To Ravi Shankar and the Maharishi.
GITA MEHTA[1]

By 1967 Ravi's fame in India as a classical musician was unrivaled. Abroad, jazz, folk and classical audiences had embraced him. In May the *New York Times* declared he was "in as high a virtuoso class as anything this century has heard from Horowitz, Heifetz, Casals or Menuhin."[2] And now the hippie generation loved him for being a Beatle's *guru* and providing the soundtrack for their acid trips, even while he lamented them using drugs. At the height of the Summer of Love came the most spectacular concert of his career: Monterey Pop. The thousands thronging the arena at this first great rock festival were astounded by his virtuosity, and a wider legend was sealed in the staggering closing sequence of D. A. Pennebaker's movie. "I became a superstar!" Ravi later recalled, and he was right.[3]

He was back in India for just seven weeks in early 1967, during which time he played to fifteen thousand at the Harballabh Festival in Jalandhar, gave recitals in the major cities and received the Padma Bhushan, India's third-highest civilian honor, on Republic Day.[4] Then, as if embarking on a new life, he finally left his marriage and, in mid-February, headed west.[5] He had a schedule mapped out for a full year abroad, starting with an eleven-week European tour, followed by summer in Los Angeles, where he would rent a house and open a branch of Kinnara, and autumn in New York, where he had accepted the position of visiting professor at City College for the fall semester. As he had promised, he took Kamala with him for the duration.

Ravi's split with Annapurna occurred shortly before his departure. Neither of them ever recounted exactly what was said that day, but

Ravi later stated that from 1967 onward he was asking Annapurna for a divorce, which she was to refuse for thirteen years. There was surely a residue of love amid all the hurt, and a letter from Annapurna two years later shows she was still hoping he might change his mind and return to her.[6] Given that Ravi's relationship with Kamala had been established for close on a decade, not to mention all his other affairs, the surprise is not that he left Annapurna at this point, but that he had delayed so long. This is some indication of how difficult he had found it to break his deep attachment to her and—perhaps even more so— to her father. Ravi does not seem to have told Baba that the marriage was over.

At a Calcutta press conference on the eve of departure, Ravi was challenged as to why he was not staying in his homeland to encourage the growth of Indian music there. He explained that his long-standing aim had been to expand the horizons of Indian music around the globe, and "he felt it improper on his part to leave his task half done." He also revealed that the Bhulabhai Memorial Institute building was to be demolished and replaced, and this announcement signaled the effective closure of Kinnara in Bombay.[7] After a 26-story residential apartment block, Akash Ganga, was completed on the site in 1970, M. F. Husain held Soli Batliwala responsible for terminating a great cultural center by agreeing to the sale of the land.[8] Although Ravi purchased two sixth-floor apartments in the tower, he never moved in.

The European tour was built round a 28-date British leg that included the Royal Festival Hall again, but also took Ravi to the kind of major provincial venues that had previously been deemed too risky. The brief folk-club experiment of 1966 had been dropped. A special concert, and a poignant one, took place beneath Graham Sutherland's enormous tapestry, *Christ in Glory*, in the nave of the new Coventry Cathedral—a symbol of reconciliation after the destruction of the medieval building during the Second World War.

When Ravi played Luxembourg's Théâtre Municipal in mid-April, up in the circle was the nineteen-year-old Marc Bolan, with his bandmates from John's Children and their manager Simon Napier-Bell. This notoriously unruly pop group had arrived hotfoot from Munich, where they had been sacked from their support slot on the Who's tour after inciting a riot in the auditorium. Napier-Bell, who also managed the Yardbirds, spotted a poster for Ravi's concert that evening and bought tickets. Bolan watched from the edge of his seat. According to Napier-Bell,

> It was an incredible contrast to what we'd just experienced on the John's Children tour. This man played to a hushed, reverential audience in the simplest way imaginable—seated on a carpet and surrounded by joss sticks which filled the air with a pungent smell. That really tripped Marc's mind. I think that was the moment he realized what he should be doing.[9]

Back in the UK that summer, Bolan drew on this memory of Ravi to reinvent his act as an acoustic duo with oriental tinges, playing guitar cross-legged on the stage, with just a bongo player and incense tapers for company. So began Tyrannosaurus Rex, favorite of influential DJ John Peel and psychedelic folk precursor of Bolan's glam-rock phenomenon T. Rex.

The unhappiest stop on Ravi's tour was Russia, where he went on an official Indian cultural-exchange visit. To his frustration, no public concerts had been arranged, only private performances for VIPs. At the All-Union Composers' Club he played to 250 mostly elderly musicians, and it was no better at Moscow's Gnessin Music Institute, nor at a similar musicians' club in Leningrad. The nadir came at a reception, when the composer Sergey Balasanian, who had written a ballet about Shakuntala, acclaimed Ravi with vodka toasts and told him, "We know your music very well. We appreciate the folk music of India very much. Shankar-Jaikishen and Sachin Dev Burman are very popular here, and Raj Kapoor's 'Awara Hoon' is the most popular song."[10] Ravi realized they knew only India's folk and film music. The Indian ambassador begged him not to make a scene, but Ravi insisted on courteously explaining that India, like Russia, had very rich folk music, but he was not a folk musician, and he hoped other Indian classical musicians would be invited to play for the Russian public. The whole trip was "a disaster and a let-down," for which he blamed the civil servants in both countries.[11]

Gerry Farrell has argued that British interest in the "sitar explosion' had peaked by September 1966.[12] If so, it had a long tail. Groups such as Traffic, the Moody Blues and the Incredible String Band continued to take up the sitar. Jimi Hendrix, rock's new supernova, had three of Ravi's albums in his collection and was depicted as an incarnation of Vishnu on the sleeve for *Axis: Bold as Love*.[13] It was not until June 1967 that raga rock's most famous song of all appeared. The Beatles' *Sgt Pepper's Lonely Hearts Club Band* was the soundtrack to the surge of youthful optimism, social upheaval and mind expansion that was the Summer of Love, and George Harrison's "Within You Without You" was, in the words of Howard Goodall, "the most unexpected, and as it turns out most visionary, of all the many surprises on the album."[14] Musically, as a unique mash-up of Indian classical and semi-classical styles, it is the most radical outlier in the entire Beatles catalog, with its use of an Indian scale (*Khamaj thaat*, with its flattened seventh note), the 16-beat *teental* and 10-beat *jhaptal* rhythmic cycles, and a complex instrumental palette, with sitar and dilruba to the fore. The dilruba shadows George's vocal line like a sarangi accompanying a *khyal* singer.[15] George, having absorbed Ravi's recommended reading, had written lyrics imbued with spiritual profundity. As he laments those who cannot see beyond the illusions of the material world, it seems that the combination of Indian music and philosophy has liberated him to express his most serious thoughts. Some find the sentiments too pious, and, as Ian MacDonald put it, the song has often been "described by those with no grasp of the ethos of 1967 as a blot on a classic LP."[16] But its premise, the need to take sides in an inner revolution, is central to the outlook that shaped the album and the era.

During March and April, when "Within You Without You" was recorded, Ravi was in and out of London. He rented again from Rory McEwen, this time a cottage at 10 Cathcart Road, and he continued George's sitar instruction. Ravi was not involved in the creation of the song, but it was based on what George described as a suite-like composition of Ravi's for All India Radio. The original has never been identified, but it is likely his inspiration was not so much a melody as an arrangement—that is, the use of several Indian instruments in an ensemble. If so, he was probably referring to *Nava Rasa Ranga*, which Ravi had given him on a spool tape and which he mistakenly believed was an All India Radio piece.

Elsewhere on *Sgt Pepper*, tanpura drones are present on "Getting Better" and "Lucy in the Sky with Diamonds," while for the cut-out heroes on the sleeve George chose to depict only four people—all of them Indian yogis. In May he reflected:

> I've got the Indian thing more in perspective now. I don't fancy myself as the next Ravi Shankar. I met so many sitar students and players over there—well, it sort of made me realize when I got home I probably wouldn't ever be a star sitar player. But I still prefer Indian music to any other form of music... Ravi has taught me a lot. He's been great. Every time I see him, it makes me want to go home and play more and get better.[17]

In fact George barely picked up a guitar in 1967 except when in a recording studio, preferring the sitar.

While Ravi was in London he worked on two commissions. One was the BBC Radio production of *A Touch of Brightness*, Partap Sharma's groundbreaking play, which had been banned in India because of its gritty depiction of slum life. It had its world premiere in March at the Royal Court Theatre, and was quickly recorded for broadcast. The other project was *Viola*, an experimental short horror film by Dunstan Pereira, told through still photographs. It was based on a story by British writer–producer Richard Davis about a paranoid man who believes his dead wife has returned to torment him in the form of a cat. Again John Barham assisted Ravi. Also featured were the Baschet brothers from Paris, a pair of French musicians who invented the instruments they played in their ensemble Les Structures sonores. Their most famous creation was the Cristal Baschet, which is fashioned from glass rods of different lengths and played with moistened fingers. With fiberglass and sheet metal cones for acoustic amplification, it looks more like a sculpture than a musical instrument and creates what Ravi called "weird sounds, but beautiful, celestial, spacey."[18] It is used to great effect on one piece, entitled *Fantasy* on the soundtrack album (released in 1973 as *Transmigration Macabre*). Elsewhere Ravi displays astonishing speed and dexterity but, as with *Chappaqua*, the more experimental, disturbing elements of this soundtrack do not work so well without the images.

After stopping over in New York for two nights, Ravi arrived in Los Angeles on May 17, where he was renting a detached, three-bedroomed 1920s house for the summer at 177 South Vista Street in the Fairfax district. Waiting for him on arrival was an advance copy of *Sgt Pepper*. George had sent it via Amiya Dasgupta, who had come over to run the new Kinnara, just as he had the Bombay original. En route Dasgupta had spent six weeks staying with George in England, before reaching the West Coast a month ahead of Ravi to set things up. The school had been Richard Bock's idea, and World Pacific was involved at the start, Bock writing the first press release himself. A single-story venue had been found at 8718 West 3rd Street, directly opposite World Pacific Studios, and it was there on May 19, following "an authentic Indian buffet," that Ravi held the press launch.

In these "very modest quarters" teaching began the following week.[19] Students sat on the floor Indian-style. Classes were initially limited to two hours each weekday evening, in two strands: introductory lectures by Ravi twice a week on Indian music history and appreciation, at $5 per lecture, which attracted between fifty and seventy-five students; and group tuition, at $10 per lesson. The three main performance disciplines were sitar, which Ravi taught in classes of up to twenty-five, tabla with Alla Rakha, which attracted about a dozen, and vocal. Smaller classes were offered for sarod and flute, and individual lessons could be arranged. At first there were just four instructors: Ravi, Alla Rakha, Amiya Dasgupta and Kamala.[20] It was announced that Ravi would teach at Kinnara on weekdays throughout the summer and play recitals at the weekends, but in practice his time was not so neatly divided. Even in that first week, he played on the Friday at the San Francisco Civic, where his concert was recorded by World Pacific. His new agent, Jay K. Hoffman, had booked thirty concerts for him across North America. As in Bombay, Ravi was not going to be a full-time head of school. Dasgupta covered his classes when he was away.[21]

As so often in his life, Ravi's timing was uncanny, for he had arrived in California, epicenter of the hippie scene, just in time for the Summer of Love. *Sgt Pepper* was released the following week, and on June 25, in the first global TV broadcast, the Beatles told the world that love was all you needed. There was a heady sense of a new age embodied by a mixture of rock music, mind-expanding drugs, communal living, free love, civil rights campaigns, Vietnam war protests and a revolt against authority. Ravi sympathized with some of these sentiments. "Often, I too am overcome by the hatred, the jealousy and envy, the wars, all the ugliness that is part of our world," he wrote. "I seek out all that has a quality of inner beauty, and I am immediately repulsed by anything ugly that sends out bad vibrations."[22] He certainly needed no teaching about free love.

But he soon realized that his new students' fascination with Indian music was confused with all these other issues, especially the experimentation with drugs. "Before I accepted them," he said, "I had to make them understand again and again the whole background of our music, so that they don't have the misconception that they have had all this time, that our music is part of the psychedelic experience."[23] He saw the same attitude applied to India's wider culture too: "I felt offended and shocked to see India being regarded so superficially and its great culture being exploited. Yoga, tantra, mantra, kundalini, ganja, hashish, Kama Sutra—they all became part of a cocktail that everyone seemed to be lapping up!"[24]

Initially Ravi committed only to running the summer courses, finishing in late August, but there was clearly a demand for the school to continue all year round. "At first it seemed like a good idea and I was swept along," he said. Plans were made to find Kinnara a bigger venue for the fall semester, and he even had a dream of founding an ashram-style institution outside the city—another reincarnation of Almora. But Ravi's passion for the school gradually dissipated as he assessed the hundreds of students who had enrolled:

> I found only one or two of them genuinely interested in the music and working hard at it. Most of them were doing it simply because it was the fad or the vogue. Within a few weeks of its opening I had realized that the school was not going to work, but I couldn't stop it at that point.[25]

An early visitor to Ravi's new home was Marlon Brando, who came round to invite Ravi to participate in a UNICEF gala in Paris. Those who visited Kinnara to bestow their blessings included Zubin Mehta, Yehudi Menuhin and Peter Sellers. In early June Ravi gave a dinner and private recital for Satyajit Ray and Sellers. Ray, lodging at Chateau Marmont, had been summoned to Los Angeles after hearing that Columbia would back *The Alien*, his ill-fated script about an extraterrestrial with magical powers whose spacecraft splashes down in a Bengali village. He was keen to offer the role of a Marwari industrialist to Sellers, who was in town to shoot his new comedy *The Party*, in which Sellers played a Clouseau-like Indian man who unintentionally spreads havoc. During the title credits he was required to pluck at a sitar, so Ravi had offered to play for him and show him how to hold the instrument. According to Ray, throughout the "splendid recital" that followed dinner "Sellers sat cross-legged on the carpet,

intently watchful, and simulated learned response by judicious inter-
jections of wah-wahs."[26] Sellers's sitar technique in *The Party* is amateurish, and appropriately so, but Ray found his hammy, brownface
impersonation "quite the most tasteless, heavy-handed caricature of
an Indian ever put on the screen," and went off the idea of casting
him.[27] For a while Ravi considered Sellers to be "a very good friend,"
and they were known to do a double act at parties where each imitat-
ed the other's accent. Sellers also introduced him to Henry Mancini,
who composed the music for *The Party*, including its Indian-spiced
pop title song.[28]

By the spring of 1967 Indian music was playing a ritual role for many
of the new psychedelic explorers. When the writer Joan Didion sat in
to observe a group of friends taking an LSD trip, she noted that four
hours passed with no sound except for the sitar music on the stereo.[29]
Jon Savage says Indian music had become "the central aural metaphor
for LSD and the wider hallucinogenic experience."[30] Many of the very
musicians so attracted by Indian music were using the drug, including
members of the Beatles, as Paul McCartney revealed to *Life* magazine
in June, and the Doors, who took their name from Aldous Huxley's
book *The Doors of Perception*, his own ode to mescaline. Mike Heron
of the Incredible String Band recalls first hearing Ravi's music on a
turntable at his hashish dealer's flat in Edinburgh.[31]

One city in particular became a magnet for the youth of America,
many of them very young, who were running away from their families
to drop out in the mecca of LSD: San Francisco. When a curious Ravi
paid a visit to Haight-Ashbury, hub of the city's scene, he was horrified. "It chilled me inside," he said.[32]

Ravi insisted time and again, in interviews and on concert plat-
forms, that psychedelic drugs should not be taken before listening to
Indian music, although in the main he avoided being judgmental
about what people chose to ingest at other times. He explained:

For years people thought I took drugs myself. They saw how involved I became while playing, and they jumped to the wrong conclusion…I don't want to be a preacher. Let these youngsters take anything they like. But I don't want them to have their "visions" while listening stoned to our music…You don't have to fortify yourself for it in an artificial way, any more than you have to "stone" yourself for Beethoven's "Choral" Symphony or Bach's B minor Mass.[33]

He seemed to be fighting against the odds. As David Crosby once countered, "Well, he didn't understand how good it was to listen to that music when you smoked pot."[34]

Ravi identified four "great *gurus*" who were encouraging the use of LSD or other psychoactive drugs. Three were in America—Timothy Leary, Allen Ginsberg and Alan Watts, who was a proponent of Zen as well as of psychedelic exploration—and one was in London, the Scottish psychiatrist R. D. Laing. Ravi once visited Laing's residential center, Kingsley Hall in London's East End (the same building, oddly enough, where Gandhi had stayed for three months in 1931). Laing advocated the use of LSD instead of anti-psychotic medicines, arguing that schizophrenia was rooted in childhood trauma and as such was a rational response to an insane world.[35] "I'll never forget that scene," remembered Ravi. "I spent two hours and I had to run away from there. They were all high on drugs. And such weird characters."[36] It is fascinating that Ravi should make a point of visiting Kingsley Hall. It fits a pattern, along with his work on *Chappaqua* and *The Psychedelic Experience*: he was drawn to the issue of drugs and their effects. The vehemence and consistency with which he sought to dissociate Indian music from drug use only underline how the subject seemed to find his pressure point.

Speaking to the *Oracle*, Southern California's pillar of the new, alternative press, he explained the spiritual bliss he felt when he played, and how this could make others high too:

It's very hard to explain, but it is that feeling of extreme sadness that is the first awareness of what I go through. It is that sad longing to be with something that I have not been able to attain. And that's what I try to do to my musical notes. I try to get nearer and nearer, and when I feel I am nearer, I feel a certain peace. When I really do feel like I have found what I seek, it does go out of me, and it can be felt by people who are hearing me. Provided that they are in the right mood or receptive enough, that they are in their clear, sober mind.[37]

The Monterey International Pop Festival was the first and greatest of the counterculture's mass gatherings, and Ravi was key to it. He was no mere exotic sideshow to this parade of the new rock royalty; in fact the festival was initially built around him. The venture was the brainchild of two booking agents, Alan Pariser and Ben Shapiro, who wanted to stage an outdoor pop-music event at the same fairgrounds as the annual Monterey Jazz Festival, a hundred miles south of San Francisco. At the time Shapiro was arranging Ravi's West Coast concerts and, according to Richard Bock, he had the idea,

> because Ravi was at that point very hot and very much a peer figure for the rock musicians, that if Ravi Shankar would agree to do an afternoon concert, on the strength of that he could get all the other artists that he wanted, which was somewhat true. And Ravi agreed, after a lot of persuasion. He didn't want to do it. I talked him into it because I thought that it would be very good for him to expand his audience...and that it wouldn't compromise his music because he would have the afternoon to himself. He wouldn't be playing before or after rock acts.[38]

And so during the winter or early spring Ravi had signed for a fee variously reported as $3,000 or $5,000. He actually had to push for his afternoon slot, because the first press release went out announcing he would close the festival on the last night.[39] He also made it a condition that he could have his own set filmed and recorded.

Soon the Byrds, the Grateful Dead and Jefferson Airplane were lined up too, all of them Ravi fans, but before any of them were signed the festival was taken over by Lou Adler and John Phillips, producer and leader of the Mamas and the Papas. They bought out Shapiro and other investors in what Derek Taylor, the festival's publicist and former press officer to the Beatles, described as "a classic Hollywood palace coup."[40] They ramped it up into an ambitious artist-led, three-day festival over the weekend of June 16–18, bringing together the hitherto discrete San Francisco and Los Angeles scenes in an epochal celebration of "Music, Love and Flowers." A foundation was set up and all of the acts were asked to perform for expenses only—except Ravi, whose contract was honored.

Ravi asked Bock to arrange the filming, and suggested they also shoot some of his other summer concerts—such as Expo '67 in Montreal and Philharmonic Hall in New York—and make a film out of them. Bock called up Martin Ransohoff, the founder of Filmways, a major producer of film and television whose credits included *The Cincinnati Kid*:

> He was receptive, and I called Ravi's agent and he was agreeable, and Ravi was agreeable—he was going to get one-third of the profits and a nice fee up front. There was not enough time to get the contracts drawn up but there was a verbal agreement over the telephone with Jay Hoffman, his manager, and with Ravi, and he was all excited about the prospects of this. With that, and my word, Ransohoff sent a film crew up to Monterey and I had to battle with Lou Adler to allow them to film the Monterey concert.[41]

Adler had separately sold film rights to D. A. Pennebaker, whose classic Bob Dylan documentary *Dont Look Back* had just been released, and ABC Television had stumped up a $200,000 advance for his film, which became *Monterey Pop*.

Sunday in Monterey was cool and gray after overnight rain. There was another light shower shortly before Ravi took the stage at 1:30 p.m., but it halted just in time. The arena held about seven thousand and was mostly full, while tens of thousands more milled around the adjacent fairgrounds, a temporary town of the gentle people with flowers in their hair, famously easy to police. There was a last-minute attempt to stop Ransohoff's crew from filming, but Bock insisted that Ravi would not play unless that agreement was honored, and so it was. Ravi settled down, surrounded by joss sticks and thousands of Hawaiian orchids, and took his time to tune his sitar, earning him, in a foretaste of the Concert for Bangladesh, a ripple of applause. At times such as this, the ritual served a double function: it was not only a matter of precise pitch control of his instrument, essential as that was; it also had the effect of calming and settling the listeners before he began. It was about tuning in, as well as tuning up. Ravi asked for no smoking and no photographs, and prayed for no rain. "I love all of you," he proclaimed, "and how grateful I am for your love of me. What am I doing at a pop festival when my music is classical? I knew I'd be meeting you all at one place, you to whom music means so much. This is not pop—but I am glad it is popular."[42]

Abandoning his five-act formula, he began with the late-afternoon *raga Bhimpalasi*, taking his time through a contemplative *alap*, continuing to probe his deepest tones during the *jor*, and accelerating into the concluding *jhala*. Half an hour had passed without any tabla, the audience was fully attuned and all the seats were taken now. He moved on to *Raga Todi*, at last bringing in Alla Rakha for a *gat* in *rupaktal*, before introducing a tabla solo in a fast 12-beat *ektal*, which Alla Rakha concluded by voicing a *tukra* (rhythm composition) and then playing the same rapid-fire syllables on the drums. Ravi picked up his sitar again for *Raga Shuddh Sarang* in *teental*, before they reached their climax, a light classical *dhun* in *Pancham Se Gara*. After Ravi's briefest of *aochar alaps*, they played a medium-tempo *gat* in 6-beat *dadra tal* and then shifted gears into a turbocharged *teental*, Ravi improvising on what is surely his most famous instrumental melody. He was on fire by now and he entranced the whole crowd. Footage shows Jimi Hendrix, Jerry Garcia, Mike Bloomfield, Juliette Greco and Micky Dolenz looking transfixed. Others present included Brian Jones and Jackson Browne. As the duo neared the end of a three-hour set, their *sawal–jawab* exchanges drew gasps and ovations, and as they finished the arena rose as one. "He mesmerized," said Michelle Phillips. "The result was endless, grateful applause, tears of joy, flowing flower petals, and, if you were looking for it, a religious experience."[43]

"It was an extraordinary epiphany and had a lot of heavy spiritual overtones," said Pennebaker. In *Monterey Pop* he intercuts shots of Ravi and Alla Rakha during this nineteen-minute climactic sequence with audience footage, filmed with synchronized sound, so what we see are authentic reaction shots. There is no better document of Monterey's spirit of discovery and rebirth. The scene has an emotional crescendo and an ecstatic peak; it is the high point of the whole movie. Pennebaker put it at the end, explaining, "You couldn't follow this with anything, no matter how interesting it was."[44]

Ravi, privately if not publicly his own harshest critic, said that for once he was "almost satisfied" with how he had played.[45] The festival was his first close-up experience of the flower children en masse, and he approved of their calls for love and peace, their interest in spirituality, and of course their enthusiasm for Indian music. As he toured the bazaar stalls that surrounded the arena he was showered with love and reverence. Of the other acts—he had arrived on the Friday to watch them—he loved Simon and Garfunkel, Otis Redding and the Mamas and the Papas, and admired Janis Joplin, who "sang from her guts, like some of the olden-days jazz singers."[46] But two acts on Sunday evening left a bad taste: the Who and Jimi Hendrix, in both cases because of the way they abused and destroyed their instruments as part of their acts. To Ravi that was sacrilege.

Ransohoff's rival film crew shot Ravi's performance and three or four days of other footage around the fairgrounds and the Monterey Peninsula. According to Bock,

> The footage came out very well, so well in fact that when Jay Hoffman saw it and Ravi saw it they both said that *they* wanted to do [produce] the film and that I should get them out of the agreement. And of course I had given Ransohoff my word, and he had spent about $15,000 in filming at that particular point.[47]

Ransohoff, who had arranged for Ravi's film to be released through MGM, was furious, but he handed over the footage once they had paid his costs.

It was around this time that Nancy Bacal told Ravi, "We should be making a film of your life."[48] Bacal was a Canadian broadcast journalist who had met Ravi through George Harrison and filmed a long TV interview with him for CBC when she lived in London. During her colorful life there she had helped start the British Black Power movement with her former partner Michael X. She and Ravi arranged to meet up at Expo '67, the World's Fair in her home city of Montreal, where Ravi played in early July, and they met again in New York, and along the way began a relationship. On a shoot in Kenya, she worked with a young filmmaker named Howard Worth and told him of her idea for a documentary on Ravi. She insisted he should direct it, and she would write it. Worth knew nothing of the subject and felt Indian music sounded "like sitting on a cat's tail," but back in New York she took him to a private recital, with her oldest friend Leonard Cohen also present, and five minutes into the *alap* Worth realized he was crying. Bacal wrote a treatment while she was staying in the Manhattan apartment of Judy Collins. The big change from the Filmways concept was that, rather than just filming scenes in America, the production would go on to India in the spring. Ravi was eager to take viewers back to the source of his music. At first Ravi thought Worth was too young for the role of director, but he was persuaded, and they gained the approval of Jay K. Hoffman and Ravi's accountant Gary Haber too, edging out interest from Pennebaker, among others. Hoffman said they did not want "just another *cinéma-vérité* documentary of a musician on tour."[49] The film, eventually to be titled *Raga*, was up and running. There was only one problem: who was paying for it?

Beneath flock wallpaper sit five musicians, all smiling at the camera. Each is distinguished in his own field. In the middle of the shot, the customary location for a Beatle being photographed in 1967, is George Harrison. Mustachioed, wearing an Indian shirt, he looks contented, tranquil. To the left, nearest to the camera, is the plump, chuckling Sancho Panza figure of Alla Rakha.[50] Alongside him is Ali Akbar Khan, head tilted, his smile somewhat quizzical. To the right, beyond Harrison, are Ravi and the master of the shehnai, Bismillah Khan.

They were captured backstage at the Hollywood Bowl on August 4, seven weeks after Ravi's triumph at Monterey. It was interval time for the four Indians, who were performing in a five-hour concert promoted by Ben Shapiro and billed as the "Festival from India." There was also a south Indian trio on the bill: vocalist K. V. Narayanaswamy, violinist V. V. Subramaniam and Palghat Raghu on the mridangam drum. Ravi was the headline act, of course, and was thrilled to be playing the huge venue. He had been there a few weeks earlier to watch Margot Fonteyn and Rudolf Nureyev dancing *Romeo and Juliet.*[51] It had been his initiative to book the others as he was keen to spread awareness of India's wider musical riches. He had personally paid a $10,000 fee to Bismillah Khan to come over from India with his five accompanists for a month's tour, which was organized by Hoffman.[52]

The picture was taken by Eric Hayes, a young Canadian studying photography in Santa Barbara. He had been sitting in the audience, taking shots for his own pleasure. Having heard that George Harrison was in Los Angeles, he guessed that he would attend the concert and that he might be able to photograph him there. Shortly before the interval Hayes was approached by an official, but rather than being told to stop taking photographs, he was informed that "Mr. Harrison" would like him to come to the dressing rooms and take some snaps of him with Ravi Shankar and the other musicians. Evidently there was no camera backstage. So Hayes's image is not what it seems. Usually a photograph from 1967 featuring a Beatle surrounded by other people exists because they wanted their picture taken with him. But here it was George Harrison who wanted to be pictured with his new heroes.[53]

George had come over from London especially to attend Ravi's show. They gave a joint press conference at Kinnara, and there was time for more sitar lessons. George was staying in a rented house above the Sunset Strip, and it was there that he wrote "Blue Jay Way" for the Beatles, its title taken from the address. On record the song's instrumentation is all Western, a cello taking the lead, but Indian music structures it, with its organ drone in C and modal melody. It is inspired by *Raga Marwa*, and George had probably been listening to Ravi's exposition of it on his recent record, *In New York*. George already knew and loved a piano piece based on *Marwa* that John Barham had played for him.[54]

George's friendship with Ravi was deepening. At this point his enthusiasm for Indian music was still bound up with his wider psychedelic exploration, but there was a step change a few days later in San Francisco, where, like Ravi before him, George was shocked by the Haight-Ashbury scene. He had anticipated a creative community happily running artisan stalls, but instead found large numbers of young, disturbed dropouts who were numbing their consciousness rather than expanding it, and who treated him as some kind of messiah. He was on acid himself and the experience frightened him, changing how he felt about the drug. "I needed it the first time I had it," he said. "It was a good thing but it showed me that LSD isn't really the answer to everything. It can help you go from A to B, but when you get to B you can see C and you see that to get really high you have to do it straight."[55] Alan Watts had a phrase for this insight: "When you get the message, hang up the phone."[56] So it was meditation now for George, and with perfect timing along came Maharishi Mahesh Yogi. George and the rest of the Beatles met him in London in late August. With their characteristic groupthink, they promptly announced to the world that they were all giving up drugs in favor of the Maharishi's transcendental-meditation system. For the public, this new association sealed the deal: India was the fountainhead now.

In the wake of Monterey, sales of Ravi's records soared. On its release in July *West Meets East* became the fastest-selling LP in Angel Records' history, shifting 15,000 copies in America in its first six weeks. After gliding to the top of the *Billboard* classical album charts, it stayed there for 25 consecutive weeks. *In New York* pushed into the top 200 of the main U.S. album chart, peaking at 148—an apparently unremarkable statistic, but it was unusual to find classical albums amid the rock and pop discs. His back catalog of LPs, U.S. lifetime sales of which had passed 100,000 in May, enjoyed a surge, and World Pacific even brought out his 1961 recording of the *Pather Panchali* theme as a single.

Since Ravi did not have an exclusive deal, other record companies joined the bandwagon. In New York Columbia scoured its vaults and unearthed George Avakian's unused recordings from 1957 and issued them in October under the title *The Genius of Ravi Shankar*. In London EMI launched a fine new series entitled *Music from India*, eventually comprising eleven titles, with two LPs by Ravi among the first four released. The second was a reissue of Ravi's 1965 HMV India album of duets with Ali Akbar Khan, and the fourth was a solo disc that Ravi had recorded in London earlier in the year, pairing *Khamaj* with *Lalit*. Back in Los Angeles, Bill Miller, director of Capitol's international A&R, found his own source of Ravi Shankar masters at HMV India.[57] In August Capitol released *Two Raga Moods*, and in October four more imports followed, including *Abhogi Kanada/ Tilak Shyam* from the previous year, and *A Sitar Recital*.

In the autumn World Pacific's edit of Ravi's Monterey set was the focus of a $45,000 promotion, at the time the biggest campaign in Liberty's history. This featured six-foot-tall dealer display portraits of Ravi and a "win a sitar" competition that gave away $16,000 worth of instruments.[58] The Monterey album reached number 43 in the main album chart, the highest placing of his career. Also issued in this campaign was the triple set *Anthology of Indian Music*, one of Ravi's favorite releases of his whole career, which sold 20,000 in its first week. Two of its six sides are given over to his impressive spoken introduction to Indian music, while there are performances by ten musicians across both north and south Indian systems, including Ali Akbar Khan, Balachander and Ravi himself, and tabla performances by Alla Rakha, Shankar Ghosh and Kanai Dutta. A 24-page color booklet was included, for World Pacific's releases were prepared with care.

In total a dozen Ravi Shankar albums appeared in the USA during 1967. The market became completely flooded and he was competing against himself to a ridiculous degree. He had no control over many of the releases. The front cover of *The Genius of Ravi Shankar* featured a strange faux-Indian pattern (actually more Greek in style), while its liner notes were a babble of groovy lingo: "Here are some more of Ravi Shankar's enthralling psychedelicacies... One *tunes in* at the first exhilarating run of the cool waterfall of a *raga—turns on*—but one never wants to *drop out*."[59] An even more psychedelic sleeve followed on Capitol's 1968 import *Six Ragas*, a blur of DayGlo illustration in which the title puffs out of the end of Ravi's sitar in a bell-bottom typeface.

"Bombay has joined the ranks of New York, San Francisco, Nashville and London as a leading, influential music city," declared *Variety*.[60] Indian instrument-makers enjoyed an unprecedented export boom. Sitars started appearing in trade shows, and an Indian workshop with a capacity of 50 sitars per month had to decline an order for 10,000.[61] There was also a craze for the so-called "electric sitar," a modified electric guitar made in New Jersey by Danelectro under the brand name

Coral Sitar. It had six normal guitar strings on a standard neck and thirteen sympathetic strings placed alongside them (not underneath, as on a real sitar) on a pinewood body. It was used on several pop records, including Stevie Wonder's "Signed, Sealed, Delivered I'm Yours." A "Baby Sitar" model was also produced, without sympathetic strings but using a "buzz bridge." Ravi was bemused by the fad, for these objects had nothing to do with sitars. Real electrified sitars had been used in Bombay film music for about twenty-five years, and Ravi even owned one himself, but he was dissatisfied with their tone.

Ravi could scarcely walk down the street without being mobbed, and there were occasions when he needed police or security guards in hotel corridors.[62] "Outrageously implausible as it is, he has become a pop hero in America—the delight of teenagers, the adored of hippies," declared *Life* magazine in a five-page feature in August. Ravi remained dubious about this rage for *ragas*. "One lifetime is not enough to learn how to play the sitar," he told the magazine, while adding that he appreciated the hippies' love for Indian music, even if many of them misunderstood it. And then—perhaps coining a phrase—he said, "It's not their fault they are looking for instant karma."[63]

Through the summer Ravi was regularly away from Los Angeles playing concerts. There were festivals in Aspen and Washington DC during August, and a three-day "Weekend with Ravi Shankar" at Esalen, the retreat center built on the hot springs at Big Sur. As a haven of Eastern philosophy and the emerging Human Potential movement, Esalen dovetailed neatly with the counterculture, and its influence was considerable. At first Ravi liked it a lot, because he sensed the innocence of the search, but disillusionment came when he saw how prevalent drug use was there at the time. It didn't help when some residents told him they had had sex with alien visitors who arrived in UFOs.[64]

Prime-time television wanted him too. In September he appeared live on the season opener of *Hollywood Palace*, ABC's TV variety show, playing a three-and-a-half-minute version of *Mishra Piloo*. Host Bing Crosby admitted he felt "a little more than awed" by his guest's musical mastery. "When Ravi played at the Hollywood Bowl," he said, mispronouncing his name "Rav-eye," "well, you couldn't get a seat out there, it was pack-jammed with admirers. And when he played the Monterey festival the kids all over the country they found themselves a new hero."

"The job of educating audiences is almost over, I don't have to worry about understanding and acceptance. Now I can play as I please," Ravi had declared at the beginning of the year.[65] With this bold statement Ravi was rather glossing over his consummate knack of judging an audience, but it was true that the format of his overseas concerts had changed by 1967. When Lincoln Center booked him for another three consecutive nights in September, again all sold out, he played notably longer *ragas*. In the last concert on the 15th he referred to criticisms that in America he wasn't playing the same way he did in India, and then proceeded to play *Jhinjhoti* for 65 minutes. He was given a six-minute standing ovation.[66]

He had moved to New York the previous weekend to take up his visiting professorship at City College. It was the university's white-haired, rosy-cheeked musicologist Elise Barnett who was responsible for the appointment.[67] She had known both Ravi and Uday in the 1940s when, as a refugee from Austria following the Nazi *Anschluss*, she had lived for several years in India and given piano recitals at All India Radio in Calcutta. Since Ravi had been appointed for only one semester, he did not attempt to teach the sitar. Instead he lectured in "Music in Indian Culture, Theory and Practice" to a graduate class of 24 students and "Introduction to Oriental Music" to an undergraduate class of 40. There was such curiosity about him that 250 extra students attended without gaining credit, so the classes were moved into the college's Aronow Auditorium, a former chapel at 135th Street. Ravi found that the students' standard of musicality was "very high."[68]

One of the students, Misha Schreiber (later Misha Dasgupta Masud), recalls how Ravi began each lecture:

He sat there as still as anyone can imagine and helped all of us, coming from these wild New York lives and being young college students, to become quiet inside of ourselves. He created this beautiful atmosphere, with his famous incense too. It was a way for us to understand the mindset we needed to be in. His desire to teach was so passionate. You could see it and feel it in his tone of voice, his body language and his facial expressions. *I want you to know there's something very great here.*[69]

Ravi would discuss music history, play recordings, lead the students in vocal and rhythmic exercises, demonstrate occasionally on the sitar or ask Alla Rakha to demonstrate on the tabla. The depth of preparation was evident in the number of mimeographed handouts he distributed. The *New York Times* described him as "quiet and businesslike, less of a performer than many a science or history professor."[70]

Philip Glass, who had returned to New York in May, recalls how the sound of people playing the sitar drifted out of apartment windows all around the East Village at this time.[71] He attended some of Ravi's lectures uptown, and also joined a private tabla class that Alla Rakha ran for a few weeks in a downtown music store, House of Musical Traditions at 414 East 9th Street. In the same class were Misha Schreiber, Hallie Scott and Collin Walcott, a Kinnara sitar student who became Ravi's first American disciple. Glass bought his own tabla and found these lessons "riveting and immediately rewarding."[72] They directly informed his new approach to composition, and he began what became a seven-year project to integrate Nadia Boulanger's instruction in Bach and Mozart with the language of the Indian *tala* system and thus create a single musical expression. "The result was I had the ability to write music that was so radical that I could be taken for an idiot. And I was often!" he said.[73] In 1968 the Philip Glass Ensemble began playing concerts, mostly in SoHo lofts, and built up a cult following.

Meanwhile, across in Los Angeles, Kinnara reopened for the fall semester in its new home at 5882 West Pico Boulevard, just off

South Fairfax. With Ravi away, no lectures were scheduled, but instrumental lessons continued and Bharatanatyam classes were added. Among the new students were Robby Krieger and John Densmore from the Doors. This was a sure sign of their serious interest in Indian music, given that "Light My Fire" had reached number 1 in July, but they squeezed in a couple of four-week tuition blocks between tours. Krieger was taught the sitar by Harihar Rao but recalls the excitement when Ravi once turned up to give a lecture, probably after the New Year.[74] Contrary to Ravi's later account, Jim Morrison never attended Kinnara, but two other rock musicians who learned the sitar there were Russ Titelman, who later became a major record producer and songwriter, and Lowell George.

In New York Ravi was also supposed to be writing a book.[75] *My Music, My Life* was to be an autobiographical introduction to Indian music and had been commissioned by Simon & Schuster on the initiative of the twenty-three-year-old assistant to the managing editor, Carlie Hope Simon, who was fresh out of grad school. She was no relation to the late Richard Simon, who had co-founded the publishing house (nor, therefore, of the singer Carly Simon, who was Richard's daughter), but she soon learned that the name could work to her advantage. "This is Carlie Simon from Simon & Schuster," she would begin her phone calls, and in the summer it seemed to work with Jay Hoffman when she called him to pitch her proposal. Without even talking to Ravi, Hoffman said, "This is great, we'll do it." The contract was signed but months then passed with no sign of a manuscript, and when she met Ravi in New York in the autumn she realized there was no way he was going to sit down at a typewriter and grind it out himself. So, in a process that became familiar to me twenty-seven years later, she cleared her decks and sat down with Ravi and a tape recorder.

At the time he was living in some style in a four-story town house at 6 Sniffen Court, a gated, Civil War-era mews off East 36th Street, which he rented from the jazz pianist Mary Lou Williams. Sniffen

Court has plenty of showbiz history. Cole Porter had lived at number 2, and shortly before Ravi moved in Joel Brodsky had shot a group of street performers in the mews courtyard for the cover of the Doors' second album, *Strange Days*. Ravi's house had a mezzanine level where he worked with Carlie Simon at a coffee table, Carlie recording their interviews and then editing and rewriting the transcripts into copy. Ravi was usually in town for only half the week, so she also went on the road with him to continue the work.

The book was divided into four sections, only one of which— amounting to 38 pages—was about Ravi's own life. There were fine sections on "My Heritage" (Indian music theory, practice and instruments) and "My Masters" (great musicians in history, including Allauddin Khan), which were the logical end point of Ravi's many presentations to musicologists, students and the general public, but they needed to be heavily shaped by Simon. There was also a sitar manual, which had benefited from earlier work by Amiya Dasgupta and Collin Walcott and needed minimal editing. For Ravi, the manual was probably more important than telling his life story, Simon now thinks, and its publication helped to establish his style of notation for Indian music and sitar playing as an industry standard.

Simon sensed a pervasive melancholy in Kamala, who was always around, but her mood did not seem to affect Ravi: "He would just kind of bounce along in his usual way." She found him fascinating to work with, and was struck by how he embodied both materialism and spirituality to a high degree. On the material side, he showed his worldliness in his appreciation for beautiful, well-crafted objects, and he was generous with gifts. He was also practical and professional. "One would think when he's playing a concert he goes off in a trance, absorbed in the music," she says, "but he always knew exactly what time it was," so he always finished on schedule.

His spiritual side was even more striking, and it had a remarkable effect on her:

Every single time he mentioned Tat Baba's name, things happened. I'll give you one example. We were working in our suite in the Brown Palace Hotel in Denver. It was a new part of the hotel with glass walls looking out on snowy mountains. As he started to talk about Tat Baba, the entire room filled up with undulating gold waves. I know that sounds strange. Each wave was composed of tiny particles of gold—not as fine as dust but definitely granular and reflective, as though light were shining directly on them. The waves would undulate back and forth horizontally across the room, floor to ceiling.

The first time this happened, we were working in the town house in Manhattan, sitting in the small mezzanine room that looked down onto the double-height living room. The waves weren't so intense or so large and didn't fill up the whole space, but they were like a horizontally flowing backdrop behind Raviji. In great surprise, I asked him what was happening. He asked me to describe what I was seeing. Then he just smiled and said something like, "Very good," and left it at that.

The music that Ravi wrote in New York included "Mahji Re," a Bengali boatman's song for Carolyn Hester. He coached her in the pronunciation and oversaw her recording session for Columbia. A visitor to Sniffen Court, from late November onward, was Yehudi Menuhin. For four days and nights they sat together in the living room as Ravi taught him a new violin–sitar duet piece he had written based on *Raga Piloo*. They then performed it in a concert in the General Assembly Hall at the United Nations building to mark UN Human Rights Day on December 10. The running order was much the same as in their previous concert at Bath. Yehudi and his sister Hephzibah played first (Franck's Sonata in A major for violin and piano), then Ravi performed two solo *ragas* accompanied by Alla Rakha, before Yehudi joined them, dressed in a kurta, for their duet finale in *Piloo*. "It was a thunderous success!" said Ravi, and it certainly made an impact.[76] The audience of two thousand were mostly diplomats and UN staff, including Secretary General U Thant, and the concert was broadcast live in the USA on public-service television and radio.

Ravi was happier with the new duet: "It is definitely not only a better piece, but more appropriate and Yehudi feels much more at home now and I think the whole thing went off much better."[77] The pair went into Angel Records' New York studios to record it for *West Meets East: Album 2*, where it appeared alongside Ravi's solo renditions of *Raga Ananda Bhairava* and a *Dhun*, and Bartók's Six Duos for Two Violins performed by Yehudi and Nell Gotkovzky.[78] Yehudi's performance on *Piloo*, despite some vibrato and a brief use of harmonics, comes closer to an Indian violinist's style, and the piece has space for both musicians to display their virtuosity. Of the four duets Ravi recorded with Yehudi, this is the one they would perform live most often, and the one Ravi chose for his retrospective box set *In Celebration*.

As Ravi had promised Marlon Brando, he flew to Paris for the UNICEF gala at the Palais de Chaillot on the 15th. Ravi had a fifteen-minute slot on a variety bill that featured everyone from the Beach Boys to Johnny Hallyday, Lena Horne to Elizabeth Taylor and Richard Burton. A Christmas Eve TV broadcast of the show went out to 250 million people in 21 countries. Back in New York, Ravi's year then closed with three more nights at Lincoln Center, making ten concerts there in twelve months. There seemed to be no slackening in the public's enthusiasm. "I felt the same magic which I felt in Monterey," he told *Rolling Stone*.[79]

It had been a second successive *annus mirabilis* for Ravi, and it was capped by *Billboard*'s announcement that he was its "Artist of the Year," an award based not on record sales (although World Pacific's turnover had doubled during 1967) but on wider impact.[80] The magazine's editors acclaimed him for nationalizing music across the genres. The citation read:

Shankar's World Pacific albums do not rise to the top of the charts. But their influence on contemporary music far transcends their commercial appeal ... Shankar has demonstrated that popular music belongs to no one society or culture, and that it is not the exclusive province of a trans-Atlantic society. And that is no mean achievement.[81]

17

WOODSTOCK DEGENERATION

I wonder how much they can understand,
and where all this will lead to.
RAVI SHANKAR[1]

At this time of his most prodigious success, Ravi used his position to showcase the wider riches of Indian music and dance. One of his two main projects for 1968 was the Festival from India, a hugely ambitious tour of North America by an ensemble of India's finest musicians, which he organized and underwrote. The other project was his film *Raga*. Although it was conceived as a documentary about him, he sought to cast its net wider: "It is not about me. I am only the medium for introducing the spirit behind our musical tradition," he told the Indian press.[2] "Ravi wanted to make a film on all the music of India," remembers Nancy Bacal, "and I said no, this film is about you."[3] The same tension applied to the book he was working on, an "autobiography" of which only one quarter was about his own life.

According to Bacal, the plan was to fund the film using the profit from the Festival from India shows, which, all too optimistically, was expected to be huge. Effectively this meant Ravi was now financing his own film, but he does not seem to have realized the extent of his commitment. There is no evidence of any other investor at this stage. And the shoot was well under way. In New York Bacal and Howard Worth had filmed Ravi lecturing at City College, in concert at Lincoln Center and in rehearsal with Yehudi at Sniffen Court, and they also obtained footage from the UN recital. The Indian shoot would start in March.

In Los Angeles, Kinnara returned to a full syllabus in its new term, which started in late January, and Ravi gave a few lectures. Misha

Schreiber, who had enrolled at his suggestion (and met her first husband Amiya Dasgupta there), says, "Raviji would come periodically and suddenly the school would be bursting at the seams with students."[4] This was the same pattern as in Bombay. Teaching classes could never be Ravi's top priority, as he told one of his City College students in December 1967:

> It's a bit difficult when, like myself, one is a performer-artist, because as long as one has the energy to travel and perform, there's nothing like it, you know. To play for a live audience—that's number one. And then I'm also interested in composition and things like that, so at present the only problem I have is that I'm overworked.[5]

Before he went to India there were three more composition projects. First was a Broadway adaptation of R. K. Narayan's Malgudi novel *The Guide*, with Zia Mohyeddin in the lead role. This had been a bestselling book and a hit film in India, but the play failed to generate the same excitement. Ravi was commissioned to supervise the music, although it is unclear whether he recorded the soundtrack himself. He was already abroad by the time the play opened at the Hudson Theater on March 6, and still away when it closed after only five performances.

Then there was the deftly named *Rich à la Rakha*. Richard Bock had the idea for a percussion showdown between what he billed as the greatest jazz drummer and the master of Indian tabla—Buddy Rich and Alla Rakha—and the resulting World Pacific album is an early fusion classic. Rich plays drumkit on two tracks and dholak on a third. Ravi was closely involved, composing and conducting two of the pieces, including the arresting *Rangeela*, which climaxes in a *sawal–jawab* dialogue between tabla and drumkit. Kinnara supplied the additional line-up—Taranath Rao, plus Ravi's disciples Shamim Ahmed, Collin Walcott, Amiya Dasgupta and Nodu Mullick—while Paul Horn appears on flute.

The third project was the film *Charly*, a science-fiction variation on the Pygmalion myth. Cliff Robertson, who starred opposite Claire Bloom, won the best actor Oscar for his portrayal of an innocent, doomed creation of hubristic science, in what director Ralph Nelson called "a love triangle between two people."[6] Apart from a few *raga* phrases that illustrate love scenes with sitar, shehnai and flute, Ravi's restrained, decorative soundtrack is not particularly Indian. "If the screenplay has nothing to do with India, one must use the sitar only as a 'sound'; why should one shove in a 'dhrupad' for no reason?" he explained.[7] Richard Bock produced the session at MGM Studios. Ravi arrived without a score, which was normal for him, but Nelson began to panic when only one of the thirty music cues had been recorded after three hours. "I suppose we violated every tenet of traditional scoring," wrote Nelson. "But the results were unique, and Ravi Shankar finished on time, a trifle disappointed in me that I had ever doubted that he would."[8] *Variety* judged it "one of the year's more interesting film scores." The main theme is appealingly wistful, but Ravi's genius, like that of the film's protagonist, is apparent here only fleetingly.[9]

Straight after the MGM sessions, Ravi left for a whistle-stop Asia-Pacific tour en route to India, taking in Hawaii, Tokyo, Hong Kong, Kuala Lumpur, Singapore and Bangkok. While he was in Japan he heard that *West Meets East* had won him his first Grammy Award, for best chamber-music performance. He arrived in Calcutta in mid-March, after a year away "conquering the musical world," as *Cine Advance* reported, and a large photo of him in the newspaper was headlined "Veni Vidi Vici."[10] Among the crowd welcoming him at Dum Dum airport was his film crew, who had arrived earlier to scout locations and prepare for a shoot of about seven weeks. The core team was Howard Worth, Nancy Bacal, cinematographer Jimmy Allen, soundman Chris Newman, assistant cameraman Malcolm Vinson and Indian coordinator Sovendu Roy, with Shambhu Das assisting. They were poised to capture the moment of Ravi's triumphant touchdown, as this elegant figure emerged from the aircraft in his trademark Bengali-style dhoti. "Finally the plane arrives and he walks out of it—in a green American sports jacket," remembers Bacal. "It was like an omen, because everything went wrong."[11]

Not quite everything. Ravi was keen to document the diverse wonders of India that had helped form him, and he had agreed to a tremendously ambitious schedule covering the length and breadth of the country. The result was wonderful footage of him roaming along the *ghats* in Benares, seeking the blessing of Tat Baba at the hill station of Lonavala, or conducting a new piece for an ensemble of eighteen stellar musicians in Bombay, including Shivkumar Sharma, Hariprasad Chaurasia, Alla Rakha and his young son Zakir Hussain. In Chengail, West Bengal, Ravi initiated a new disciple. At an ashram outside Madras, priests chanted Vedic hymns. In the Keralan village of Cheruthururthy, a Kathakali troupe performed outdoors through the night, illuminated by oil lamps. This scene runs for five minutes in the finished film—too long by any standard filmmaking rulebook, but riveting nonetheless.

The most touching episode is Ravi returning to see Baba at his home in Maihar on March 24. Cleverly, the crew did not allow the two to meet first off-camera, instead sending Sovendu Roy ahead, so when Ravi enters the courtyard and greets his *guru* it is the actual moment of reunion, and the raw emotion is obvious. "It's like returning to my own family. I wonder how he will receive me," says Ravi on the voiceover. (This was the first time they had met since he had left Annapurna.) The unplanned bonus was when Baba's wife Madina Begum emerged, sobbing, and Ravi embraced her and began crying too. Jimmy Allen kept shooting. It is a beautiful moment. The film cuts to Baba, perched on his bed, teaching a vocal composition to Ravi, who squats on the floor below him, and then to a concert in Maihar where Ravi plays, sublimely, in front of Baba.

Many location shoots did not make the cut. Among the Eastman-color 16 mm reels in the Shankar archives today are outtakes of Uday Shankar's dance school in Calcutta, the Golden Temple at Amritsar, the Kullu Valley and the temple sculpture at Khajuraho. There is also an all-night concert at Allahabad on March 27–28, which was intended to be the climax of the film. At treatment stage, Bacal had proposed to Ravi that there should be a piece of music running like a thread throughout, starting with him composing it and finishing with him performing it in a set-piece concert. Nalin Mazumdar, a disciple of Ali Akbar and director of Allahabad's Jhankar music school, arranged an outdoor concert beside the Ganges at Rasulabad Ghat, near Triveni Sangam, where the Kumbh Mela takes place. A packed audience watched as Mazumdar opened the show at 9:30 p.m. with a recital on the Hawaiian guitar. There followed Kathak dance by Manjushri Bannerji, sarod by Aashish Khan and vocal music by Lakshmi Shankar, all building up to Ravi's appearance at 3:30 a.m.

He began by playing *Raga Lalit* for an hour and a half. During the ensuing short coffee break, Mazumdar noticed Ravi's drink was untouched and he was pacing up and down. "Is there a problem with the coffee?" he asked. Not at all: rather, Ravi had suddenly had an idea for a new *raga*. It was the offspring of his *Raga Kameshwari*, which had come to him two weeks earlier in Chengail.[12] The new one, which he named *Gangeshwari* after the river, was created by shifting the tonic note using the *swara bheda* system, a kind of modulation. Feeling inspired, he played it through until dawn, before moving on to *Bhairavi* and concluding at 7:30 a.m. This first rendition of *Gangeshwari* was eventually released in 2010 on Ravi's album *Nine Decades Volume I*, and it is utterly electric. But around him things were falling apart. Cameras were breaking down, Ravi was glowering at Bacal because the crew had miscalculated where the sun came up, and she was despairing because he was not playing the piece they had planned all along. As it transpired, none of the footage shot at Allahabad was usable anyway, because of the lighting and camera problems.

Summer had arrived and most shoots began at dawn to avoid the fiercest heat. "We were getting three hours' sleep and working hard," says Bacal. "We were dragging ourselves around. Then Ravi would show up fresh as a daisy. Amazing stamina, and always a lot of fun."[13] The logistics of filming were demanding. Every time a camera was set up a crowd appeared, so they started deploying dummy cameras. They even hired a railway carriage on the Kashi Express from Bombay to Maihar in order to film the scenes of a pensive Ravi sitting alone. The train did not normally halt at Maihar, but it made a special stop for Ravi.[14] The carriage was uncoupled and shunted into a siding for 36 hours, before being coupled up to the train to Allahabad, their next location. Another challenge was the local fauna. While shooting at night on the Ganges there were so many flying bugs that the cameraman jumped overboard, and there was a near-mutiny by the crew when filming the Kathakali due to the heat and their fear of eighteen-foot king cobras in the jungle. Bacal, who ended up contracting tuberculosis, hepatitis and malaria, says, "I've filmed in Africa, I've filmed everywhere, and it was the most difficult. That was 1968, and there's probably still an ox cart bringing a generator to Triveni Sangam now as we speak."[15]

Before Ravi arrived in India, the news had broken that the Beatles were in Rishikesh learning meditation at Maharishi Mahesh Yogi's ashram, bringing to a boiling point the world media's fascination with India. The two band members who stayed longest were John Lennon and George Harrison. Lennon, suddenly disillusioned by the Maharishi, wrote his attack on him that became "Sexy Sadie," and returned to England. But George, who always defended him, flew down to south India with Pattie to see Ravi, having agreed to take part in his film. They met in Cochin, where Ravi was playing a concert the evening after the all-night Kathakali shoot. Penny Estabrook greeted the Harrisons at the airport, and it was not hard for her to spot them: in a city where almost everyone wore white, Pattie arrived wearing green see-through harem pants and George was in a green top and tiger-stripe trousers.[16] Ravi arranged a special *puja* ceremony in Trivandrum for his guests, and they went together to the Temple of Devi at Kanya-kumari, the southernmost point of India. And it was here, where three oceans meet, that Ravi composed *Raga Parameshwari*, another relative of *Kameshwari*. Unfortunately George was taken ill with dysentery and he flew home on April 21 without having filmed his scene, but he promised to rendezvous with the cameras in America.

The final shoots took place in California in June and July. These included sitar, vocal and tabla classes at Kinnara, and a light-hearted passage in Griffith Park, where a prancing Ravi has a mock swordfight to the accompaniment of Alla Rakha's vocal percussion. "We prodded them to play up because he was always doing silly things and you had to get that in somewhere," says Bacal.[17] On June 9 Ravi was filmed receiving an honorary doctorate from the University of California, Santa Cruz, in its open-air Quarry Amphitheatre. Alfred Hitchcock, who regularly made a cameo appearance in his own movies, now made one in Ravi's, as the director was also being awarded a degree. "I just met him briefly," Ravi said. "He looked so serious, but I know that he had a naughty mind—of that, I'm very sure."[18]

The next day the crew shifted fifty miles south to Big Sur to meet up with George and Pattie Harrison, who had flown out specially, along with Ringo and Maureen Starr. On the cliff top at Esalen was filmed the sequence that has become the one most commonly shown of Ravi and George, in which Ravi teaches a new sitar phrase that George, unprepared and under the gaze of the camera, struggles to play. "Thank God they edited it down a bit, otherwise we'd still be there now," George later joked.[19] In a second Esalen sequence, Ravi teaches a vocal composition, "Vande Guru Deva," to a large group including not only George, Kamala and Lakshmi Shankar, but also Fritz Perls, founder of Gestalt therapy, and Alan Watts, who were both scholars in residence. While in Big Sur, further scenes were shot at the Nepenthe restaurant, where Ravi's rictus grimace screams "get me out of here" as a band jams for him, and on the beach, where he was filmed from a helicopter.

The initial title had been *Ravi Shankar: East Meets West*, but while Ravi was in India it had changed to *Messenger Out of the East*. Fortunately that was only another working title, but its messianic undertone seems appropriate for a period when the craze for India was getting out of proportion. Ravi felt that he kept his head pretty well at the center of a typhoon of events spiraling around him. "At forty-seven I was mature enough to cope with it. I would have gone completely bonkers if I had been younger!" he later wrote.[20] But he could not control what he had unleashed, and some of it upset him deeply.

Also being shot in India in early 1968 was *The Guru*, Merchant Ivory's tale of an English pop star, played by Michael York, who visits India to study sitar with an Indian master. The story drew inspiration from George Harrison's 1966 visit to India to study with Ravi. The *guru*, played by Utpal Dutt, was even dressed like Ravi in a long black Nehru jacket or white dhoti paired with sunglasses. He seems torn between upholding his tradition and exploiting the opportunities that a famous student will bring. Not surprisingly, Ravi was irritated by this characterization. James Ivory, director of *The Guru*, says, "Because of its subject, it was basically deplored by a lot of people in India, musicians and so on, for the fact that we'd shown the *guru–chela* [teacher–student] relationship in such a way. And I heard that Ravi was dismayed at this movie."[21] It probably didn't help that its music was by Vilayat Khan.

Another episode offended Ravi more. While he was in India, World Pacific's sales manager Macey Lippman ran a massive, month-long U.S. promotion, in which Ravi's albums were displayed in all 950 Thom McAn shoe stores nationwide, while the chain launched a "Raga Buckle" shoe and paid for saturation radio advertising. With a value of $1.5 million, the campaign was one of the largest tie-ins to date involving any record company.[22] "When Ravi saw that he hit the ceiling," said Richard Bock.

He was ready to sue, because to associate his music with feet was something that was almost like a sacrilege. And of course Macey didn't know this. He had no idea of anything about Indian culture. All he was doing was merchandising something. I didn't even know it was done—that was not my department—and Ravi was furious. He held me accountable and it strained our relationship for a while, but by the time he got wind of it the whole promotion was out there and finished.[23]

A $750,000 lawsuit was in fact filed on Ravi's behalf against both Thom McAn and World Pacific for using his name without authorization. But Ravi withdrew the suit during 1969 and stayed with the label.[24]

It is fair to say that sometimes Ravi had only himself to blame. Anyone who watched the films *Chappaqua* or *The Psychedelic Experience* could be forgiven for making the very link between Indian music and drugs that so aggrieved him. And anyone who read the serialization of *My Music, My Life* in *Playboy* magazine in October 1968 might have wondered why he had a problem with overt sexual behavior at his concerts. "I was so busy at the time that I couldn't think properly," he later wrote. "It was as if I was completely in the hands of my managers, with all the dates fixed by them. Everything was a blur."[25]

The passion for all things Indian was like an inflationary boom, and a bust was round the corner. UCLA warned the Asia Society, "Prices now being asked for Shankar and all the various Khans are ridiculous, and will eventuate in a reversal of the current tide of interest running in the direction of Asia."[26] In July both Ali Akbar Khan and Indrani flopped at the Schaefer Music Festival in New York's Central Park, heralding a downturn.[27]

Meanwhile, the unstable mixture of elements that made up the counterculture, from spiritual seekers through hedonistic rock fans to Maoist revolutionaries, was disintegrating. The mood of the Summer of Love, so open and optimistic, and so welcoming to Indian culture, was fading away. Instead 1968 brought a growing sense of chaos and violence in Western politics: from the Tet Offensive in Vietnam, the assassination of Martin Luther King in April and the widespread urban riots that followed across America, the May *évènements* in France and the student rebellions in West Germany, the gunning down of Robert F. Kennedy in June, through to the Soviet crushing of the Prague Spring and the violence at the Democratic National Convention in Chicago in August. Anarchy was loosed upon the world.

For a while longer Ravi could dine out on the boom, and he invited others to join him. He was keen to challenge his audience. "The time has come for Westerners to try to understand and appreciate Indian music on its own terms and not through the music they know," he announced in May.[28] Sixteen other Indian musicians were booked for his summer project, billed as "Ravi Shankar and His Festival from India." Jay K. Hoffman, who had spent a week with Ravi in India listening to some of them, set up a three-month American tour at twelve different venues, forty-three shows in all. Many of them joined the Kinnara faculty for a few weeks, staying together in a sorority house near UCLA. Under Ravi's direction, they also recorded an eponymous double album that captures wonderfully the range and quality of the ensemble, and reflects Ravi's role as enabler rather than star: he performs on only two of its fourteen tracks.

The tour was, as *Time* put it, "the first time that so many Indian musicians had been seen west of Bombay on one Oriental rug."[29] Ravi had handpicked artists of the highest class, drawn from all corners of India. There was Sabri Khan on sarangi, Shamim Ahmed on sitar, Aashish Khan on sarod, Sharad Kumar on shehnai, flute and rabab, and Miskin Khan on shehnai and tota (an Afghan flute). Vocal music was represented by Jitendra Abisheki and Lakshmi Shankar, Shivkumar Sharma played santoor and tabla, and there were other awe-inspiring drummers in Alla Rakha, Shankar Ghosh and Taranath Rao on tabla, Palghat Raghu on mridangam and Fakir Mohammad on dholak. Nodu Mullick and Kamala slotted in on tanpura, as usual, and Ali Akbar Khan was a special guest on sarod at four venues. They mostly performed in solos and duets, except on *V 7½*, a piece that Ravi created for the whole ensemble in *Raga Vachaspati* with a 7½-beat *tala*.

Shivkumar Sharma, who like several of the others was making his first overseas tour, says Ravi sought to give "a glimpse of what happens in India, how in one evening so many musicians perform. He wanted the American audience to experience that."[30] Santoor was unknown in America and Sharma felt fortunate to be chosen, but his star was in the ascendant. He had recently released *Call of the Valley* with Hariprasad Chaurasia and Brijbushan Kabra. This concept album, themed around a day in the life of a Kashmiri shepherd and styled as "a symphony in Indian classical music," was an international hit and became HMV India's best-selling album.

The tour opened on June 24 with seven nights at the open-air Greek Theatre in Los Angeles, where the guest of honor was Tat Baba, who flew in for a week and also blessed Kinnara. Indrani made two special appearances with her troupe. After three nights at the Stanford Festival and two in Chicago, most of the rest of the dates were in the northeast. One highlight was the Tanglewood Festival, summer home of the Boston Symphony Orchestra, where Ravi was moved by a meeting with Pablo Casals, whom he recalled from his childhood. In September he played six consecutive nights in New York—four at Lincoln Center followed by two at Carnegie Hall.

Einstein, Churchill, Picasso, Bardot, Kennedy, Indira Gandhi—and now Ravi Shankar. To be photographed by Karsh of Ottawa was a sign that you had made it. In the middle of the run of shows at Lincoln Center, Ravi visited Karsh's New York apartment for a session.[31] In one frame, taken in Karsh's trademark pin-sharp black-and-white, Ravi is in profile, wearing a light-colored "*guru* shirt," the style he'd made so popular in America. His Stradivarius sitar rests in his lap, the cipher "Nodu" clearly legible on its neck, and he is tuning one of its *chikari* strings. Head held high, he is at his most regal. Philip Glass has talked of Ravi's winning combination of "strength and gentleness," and for all his refined delicacy the strength should not be underestimated.[32] Karsh liked to look for what he called the "inward power" of his subjects, and he has found it, but the sense is also of the outward power of this diminutive man. Ravi is a supreme artist, still at his physical peak. And yet there is something about his far-off look that hints at unease.

"Just as suddenly, the fad passed," confirmed *Time* magazine a week later, reviewing his Manhattan concerts. "The teeny-boppers returned to their Bee Gees, and the hippies began playing Erik Satie at their acid parties." Ravi was dismayed at the abruptness of the shift, but he had seen it coming and all was not lost. *Time* delivered a rave review, and called Ravi "the foremost practitioner of one of the world's oldest and most sophisticated musical arts."[33]

For Richard Bock, the day it all changed was May 14, when John Lennon and Paul McCartney dissociated themselves from the Maharishi on national TV. On the *Tonight* show, speaking to guest hosts Joe Garagiola and Tallulah Bankhead, Lennon said, "We made a mistake there." While confirming they still believed in meditation, they portrayed the Maharishi as just another human being with the same faults and weaknesses as everyone else. According to Bock,

> The record sales took an immediate nosedive in Indian classical
> music. Within six months from when you could sell a hundred
> thousand copies of Ravi, you could sell ten thousand. There were
> millions of Nehru jackets out there in the marketplace, and they
> were all finally sold for a dollar apiece. The Beatles were that
> powerful an opinion-maker.[34]

Nancy Bacal's memory is that the Festival from India tour "crashed." This overstates it. Ticket sales might not have reached expectations, but those expectations were probably unrealistic. Reviews were consistently strong. Ravi's duet with Ali Akbar Khan on the opening night was "the most exciting musical experience I have ever witnessed," wrote the *Hollywood Reporter*'s critic. "We were playing to packed halls," said Shivkumar Sharma. "Westerners were keenly receptive to our music."[35] *Variety* reported that across the six consecutive nights in New York

10,320 seats were sold out of a 16,800 capacity, and judged that "the take was impressive...though the six-night hand was overplayed."[36]

After the U.S. leg finished in San Antonio, Texas, on September 21, the ensemble promptly crossed the Atlantic for a European tour. Over the next two months they played London, Amsterdam, Rotterdam, The Hague, Stockholm, Budapest, Milan and Paris, and numerous other venues. The tour culminated with ten concerts in Britain and Ireland in late November, including Ravi playing solo at the Royal Festival Hall, which was vividly described by Geoffrey Moorhouse: "It had tempo. It had fantastic dexterity. And it had infinity; it was a minor surprise when any of the pieces stopped." Moorhouse, who was about to embark on his fine history of Calcutta, concluded that "India has got us by the...er...long hairs."[37]

Two pieces of bad news reached Ravi during the British tour. Richard Bock, who had been in Scotland on a separate trip, was taken ill en route to London, and by chance was discovered by some musicians from Ravi's tour party who were on the same train. They took him to hospital, where a heart attack was diagnosed. Ravi visited him on his ward as he recuperated.[38] It seems this gave Ravi an intimation of mortality because he wrote to Dr. Martin Schickman at UCLA and asked to be admitted in December to a Los Angeles clinic "for about fifteen days or so, for a thorough medical check-up and a complete rest." He did not specify any problem except to say that he'd had a very tiring tour of Europe, but Schickman was a professor of cardiology.[39]

Even more worrying for Ravi was that Uday, who was on his last U.S. tour, suffered a heart attack and stroke on November 24 in San Diego. After being discharged from Mercy Hospital, he stayed on in Los Angeles for about six weeks, convalescing in Ravi's new home at 314 North Vista Street, a five-bedroom modern bungalow into which he had recently moved (after a summer spell on Castilian Drive in the Hollywood Hills). Amala and their children, twenty-five-year-old Ananda and thirteen-year-old Mamata, remained there to care for Uday, helped by Kamala, who did not join Ravi on his European tour.

When Ravi arrived back on December 8, Uday's sixty-eighth birthday, he was shocked at his brother's condition: "To see him like that was such a pity. I felt like crying, because I couldn't forget him from earlier years when he was absolutely like fire—this handsome superstar, so strong and virile."[40]

It did not seem to Mamata that the vogue for all things Indian had passed. She marveled at how popular Ravi was: "I remember going with him to the farmer's market one day. Young people recognized him and it was a crazy scene. People started getting him to sign autographs on whatever they could find—paper plates and cups. The store ran out of paper plates."[41] Ananda, who had been learning sitar in Benares, stayed on with Ravi in Los Angeles and made the most of the opportunities. After jamming with Jimi Hendrix in a Beverly Hills hotel suite, he developed his own pop fusion sound combining the sitar with a rock band and a Moog synthesizer. He released an album for Reprise Records, including a version of "Light My Fire." It was not to Ravi's taste, but Ananda gained a cult following.

During 1968 Ravi was a regular on American network TV, appearing on shows presented by Dick Cavett, Mike Douglas, Merv Griffin and the Smothers Brothers. *My Music, My Life* was published in November, and all the while new albums continued to appear. Seven were issued in 1968: Angel's sequel to *West Meets East*, the *Chappaqua* soundtrack, two Capitol imports (*Ravi* and *Six Ragas*) and three World Pacific releases—*In San Francisco*, which was the live set from May 1967, the *Charly* soundtrack and *Festival from India*. World Pacific also released *Rich à la Rakha*, and there was a fascinating reissue from RCA Victrola, which took the five 78 rpm discs of the Uday Shankar troupe from 1937 and released them in LP format for the first time, under the title *Ragas and Dances*. These featured the sixteen-year-old Ravi on the sitar and esraj. Also recorded at World Pacific Studios during the summer, in a single day, was *Song of God*, an album of music by Aashish Khan that accompanies twenty-one verses from the *Bhagavad Gita*. Shivkumar Sharma played the santoor. Ravi himself recited the texts, which were translated from Sanskrit into English by a musician friend of Aashish Khan, Rooshikumar Pandya, who occasionally played tanpura on stage for Ravi. Of all these new albums, the most successful were *In San Francisco*, which reached number 140 in the main *Billboard* album charts in August, and *West Meets East: Album 2*, which reached number 2 in the classical album charts the same month.

The production company for *Raga* at the time of the principal photography was Perdan Films Inc., of which Jay K. Hoffman was head. In June 1968 he had told *Variety* that the movie's budget was "in the mid-six-figure area" and admitted there was no distribution deal as yet, but said "a very big distributor" was interested. He was confident that public interest in Indian music and Ravi was no passing fad, so he did not intend to rush the completion of the film.[42]

Later Hoffman said, "Ravi had told me he could raise money for it. But like most feature films, it cost more than we had anticipated. He was not happy about it."[43] If the plan really was to raise the film's finance through touring, Ravi would have done far better taking just three musicians on the road (Alla Rakha, Kamala and himself), as he usually did, rather than seventeen. Looking back in 1977, Ravi admitted that the tour was one of several ventures on which he'd "lost money miserably," although he didn't regret it.[44]

Editing *Raga* was a huge task: the ratio of raw footage to final film was around 50 to 1. In late 1968 or early 1969 funds ran out and the team had to shut down in the middle of editing. This was probably because Ravi pulled the plug when he at last realized how much the project was costing him. In 1967–8 he relied on Hoffman and his accountant Gary Haber to manage his American affairs. "They kept my account, and I was so stupid as usual, as I am still, as far as money and everything is concerned," he said in 2006. He was earning large sums of money, but the film was eating up a huge chunk of this income. There is no question of any fraud, but Ravi's inattention to matters financial was a lifelong trend. "I realized only afterward what a big amount [it was]—something like $300,000 or $350,000...Jay K. Hoffman and Gary Haber, both of them—it was an honest attempt and I am grateful to them for having done it. But you see, I was not aware that the finance was my own."[45]

Ravi later wrote that *Raga* "was not and could not have been a box-office success."[46] But Richard Bock's original plan with Filmways had been to rush out a film in November or December 1967, when Ravi's popularity was at its height. "Had that come out at that time," said Bock,

> I think it could have been a sizable success because you could have beaten the Monterey Pop Festival film if we had gotten really down and done it. But it didn't work out that way, and in the meantime Ravi spent the next four years and almost all of the profits that he got from the record royalties. He put over $300,000 of his own money into *Raga*, and it still wasn't finished. And what burned me up was that he wouldn't have had to invest anything. The other film wouldn't have cost him a penny and he would have gotten a third of the profits, and I think something like $35,000 or $50,000 for performing in it, if he had let it be. But they had a better idea. They were going to control it. So they lost everything with it, and it blew the relationship with Jay Hoffman and Ravi. It just was a disaster.[47]

"I am going through a lot of problems with the film that Hoffman produced and it will take me a little while to get out of the entanglements mostly created by him," Ravi wrote to Yehudi Menuhin on May 22, 1969, adding, "I have even decided to have a new manager."[48] So, barely two years after Ravi had appointed Hoffman, their relationship had unraveled. Ravi set up a new company, Tatra Corporation, to represent him exclusively in the USA and Canada, and lawyer Phillip Chronis became its president and his personal manager. The hiatus on *Raga* lasted for about nine months before work resumed. When it was eventually released in 1971, Perdan Films was not credited, although Hoffman was named as his concert agent for a little longer.

By the time work resumed on *Raga* many things had changed, including Nancy Bacal's relationship with Ravi, which had ended amicably, as had America's hitherto stratospheric demand for Indian music. Pennebaker's movie *Monterey Pop* had its theatrical release in December 1968, giving Ravi a boost but stealing some of *Raga's* thunder.

There were now two major creative problems with the film. The script that Bacal had written, peaking in triumph in India, was no longer authentic, and its structure had been ruined by the fiasco in Allahabad. Ravi's performance of *Raga Desh* at the Lincoln Center concert was substituted as the new conclusion, and a rapid-cut section was created portraying the frenzy and confusion of the period, with a musical suite by Collin Walcott that segued from raga rock to avant-garde sensory overload. Bacal also interviewed Ravi about what had gone wrong. "It was very hard for him," she says. "This is painful, for a man of his stature to say, 'I took on more than I could handle.' Honest and raw. Not everyone would do that."[49] She then edited this interview into a voiceover script, and in February 1970 Ravi recorded these narrative lines at Ryder Sound in New York during a ten-day visit. "We sat in the studio for days and he was in a little booth," says Worth. "He finally separated himself from the world and he says, 'OK, let's go now.' I think it was so heroic of him."[50]

The results are deeply impressive, as Ravi reflects on the consequences, both exhilarating and perturbing, of his period of extreme fame. In his final passage, spoken over the helicopter footage of him walking on the beach at Big Sur, he says,

> I wonder if I tried to do too much, if I took on a false role in America. Somehow I simply could not let it go. I keep asking myself if all this terrible distortion could have been avoided. You cannot just brush the surface of a culture and pretend that you

have found an answer. We must turn inward to the deepest of our own roots to find the very best of who we are.

He then concludes with a line that could be his personal credo, encapsulating his life's quest, musical and spiritual: "It is a constant search, trying to reach something that I can see and feel, that I can almost touch but never hold on to."[51]

Howard Worth feels this honest self-examination takes *Raga* to another level. It was Peter Sellers who brought this home to him after watching a screening. "We know the story about Ravi and his brilliance," said Sellers, "but the most important thing is the subplot, which is: all of us have dreams; very few of us go after them. And going after them and not getting them doesn't matter, as long as you go after your dreams."[52]

However, three years after being commissioned the film still had no distributor. Worth was getting desperate. When George Harrison came to New York in late October 1970 he attended a private screening at 1600 Broadway, but afterward he and his entourage walked out without comment, and Worth went home more despondent than ever. At ten the next morning George rang. "I have to apologize," he said. "I was so moved I couldn't talk. Would you come down to the office?" Worth rushed over, trying to play it cool. He explained that all he was requesting was for George to call United Artists and encourage them to distribute *Raga*. "Well, we're not going to do it," said George. "Here's what we're going to do. The Beatles are going to finance the rest of the film, put out the album and distribute it worldwide."[53] The movie would be distributed by their own company, Apple Films, and the soundtrack released on Apple Records. It was a hugely generous action—Richard Bock estimated the cost at $50,000—and it led to an even more significant venture.

In 1969, thanks to Hoffman's forward planning, Ravi had a packed schedule all over North America for the first two-thirds of the year.

By February, when his concert at the Santa Monica Civic was only about half full, it seemed the waning of interest was having an impact on ticket sales.[54] But he honored all his bookings, and demand remained strong, and in fact on August 15 he played to his biggest ever audience—at Woodstock.

The festival was the brainchild of Michael Lang, a head-shop owner from Miami who used Ravi's music to accompany his acid trips and had previously presented him at a concert on Key Biscayne. He wanted Ravi at Woodstock because of his significance at Monterey, and he booked him for a $4,500 fee—far below the top-priced Jimi Hendrix, who received $30,000.[55] Ravi had just returned from Montreal, where he had played three shows at "Man and the World," the renamed Expo '67 site. Kamala was ill, and at short notice her role as tanpura player was filled by Maya Kulkarni, a twenty-two-year-old master's student at NYU. She was also a fine Bharatanatyam dancer and knew Ravi from Bombay, where she had performed in *Chandalika*.

On August 14 Ravi, Alla Rakha, Kulkarni and tour manager Frank Wicks were driving toward upstate New York when they became stuck in a traffic jam. A crowd of 200,000 was expected at Max Yasgur's farm, but as the numbers mushroomed the highways ground to a halt. Eventually a helicopter was sent to pick up Ravi's party and take them to the musicians' quarters at the Holiday Inn in Liberty, New York—dubbed Tranquility Base after the site of the Moon landing three weeks earlier. The next day they reassembled at a nearby farmhouse for onward transit. As they waited, Kulkarni was bemused to see a man crazily chasing the chickens. "Then we got into the helicopter, and he was sitting right in front of me, and this guy started pulling hairs out of his chest!" she says. "I didn't know where to look. Raviji started teasing me, and Alla Rakha was laughing. Later I was told it was Jimi Hendrix."[56]

They flew over the enormous festival crowds, upward of 400,000, and touched down backstage. Richard Bock, who was in the helicopter, wrote that Woodstock was "one of the most wonderful experiences of a lifetime."[57] Ravi disagreed. He felt that if Monterey had heralded the beginning of a new movement, Woodstock marked its end. At least he was scheduled on folk night, with no rock bands in earshot, but rather than having a whole afternoon to himself, as at Monterey, he came on at 10 p.m. in a forty-minute slot sandwiched between Tim Hardin and Melanie. There was thunder and lightning, and driving rain, and the water pooling on the canopy over the stage threatened to bring it down. His set consisted of *Raga Puriya Dhanashri* in *chartal ki sawari*, a tabla solo by Alla Rakha in *jhaptal*, and *Manj Khamaj* in *keherwa tal*. He did his best, but the atmosphere was wrong. He was worried about his sitar getting wet, and he found it impossible to connect to the vast crowd:

> It was drizzling and very cold, but they were so happy in the mud; they were all stoned, of course, but they were enjoying it. It reminded me of the water buffaloes you see in India, submerged in the mud. Woodstock was like a big picnic party, and the music was incidental.[58]

Kulkarni, who played several more tour dates, saw what a superb foil Alla Rakha was for Ravi: "Their relationship was so incredible. Between them there was a lot of playfulness and teasing and a quick appreciation of what the other was doing. He would play something and Raviji could finish it, and vice versa. It was like finishing each other's sentences."[59] As with Ravi, the evident joy Alla Rakha took in music was infectious, and reflected a similarly childlike nature. One reviewer in September wrote that he played tabla "with all the pride and joy of a two-year-old playing a tom-tom but with the precision of a space age engineer."[60] When Ravi and Alla Rakha stayed later in the year at Harewood House, and played in its Gallery, Lord Harewood's second wife Patricia was amused by how Alla Rakha, when served a crème brûlée at dinner, played its hard sugar topping as if it were a tabla.[61]

On tour Ravi rose as early as 4 a.m. to set himself up for the day with his morning *puja* (worship) and his sitar practice. "That was the Raviji who was very disciplined, anchored in the history and traditions of music," says Kulkarni, who sometimes watched. "His day started with that whole ritual—and then he was OK. He was now a modern man out there."[62] After a concert, he was transformed. Usually there would be a reception, and he thrived on the camaraderie. Kulkarni says,

> I was sitting next to him, and he would say to me in half English, half Hindi, "That girl has beautiful eyes," or comment on somebody's hair. There was always this about beauty, about aesthetics. It's like going into the garden and seeing beautiful flowers and trees—that spontaneous appreciation of beauty. There is no calculation there.[63]

According to Saeed Jaffrey, "Ravi was quite a reincarnation of the Hindu lover god Krishna in those days, with his curly long black locks, his large bedroom eyes and his sensuous mouth," and he had "many *gopis*…in the Brindaban of America."[64] Ravi's girlfriends Nancy Bacal and Hallie Scott both described him as a Krishna figure too. "There is a whole tradition of horny gods and goddesses," says Bacal. "It's not about the morality that we bring to these things now. There really was a spiritual aspect to it. There was always something sacred and beautiful about everything he did."[65]

Ravi's Woodstock set was released on LP, although a better snapshot of this period, infused with spirit and play, is the private concert he recorded at home two weeks later, issued in 2011 as *Reminiscence of North Vista*. Following the years of plenty, Indian music was now suffering a slowdown in the record industry. In April 1969 World Pacific had put out *A Morning Raga, An Evening Raga*, a fine studio recording of Ravi's own *raga Nat Bhairav* paired with *Mishra Piloo*, but it was his only release of the year. After the Woodstock album came out in 1970, Richard Bock's five-year contract expired and Liberty, which was moving away from jazz as well as from Indian music, did not renew it. The World Pacific catalog was subsumed into the parent company. Bock was left unemployed and bereft, while Ravi had lost his most important producer, who in the last dozen years had released eighteen albums either by him or to which he contributed significant-ly. Ravi still had a worldwide relationship with EMI, but he could never hope to find another label as passionately supportive.

Ravi became disillusioned with the rock scene as it descended from the peak Indophilia of 1967. After Woodstock he'd had enough of un-ruly audiences and longed to return to concert halls. The last show of his 1969 summer tour, at the iconic rock venue of the Fillmore East, had an end-of-term feel to it. For once he neglected to give an intro-ductory talk, "because there is no point to it at this stage." His set was unusually long and he even sang a couple of songs, including a trib-ute to Gandhi in *Mohankauns* to mark his centenary.[66] Two grander commemorations of the Mahatma followed—first at Washington National Cathedral, and then at the Royal Albert Hall in October, in the middle of Ravi's eight-week European tour.

It was also end of term at Kinnara, and for good this time. In *My Music, My Life* Ravi wrote that he dreamed of having a whole series of rural ashram-like schools, but even before the book was published he was debating whether to close down his one branch. "Help me to decide what to do!" he had beseeched Kamala in a letter from Stock-holm in October 1968.[67] The contrast with his brother-in-law was instructive. Ali Akbar Khan had founded a branch of his music college in Berkeley the same year as Kinnara opened. They had agreed that Ali Akbar should concentrate on northern California while Ravi took the south. But Ali Akbar was, as George Ruckert once said, "more of a backwoods kind of guy," and running a school suited him in a way it never did the far more restless Ravi. The Ali Akbar College of Music became a hub for Indian music, with the early faculty including Nik-hil Banerjee and Shankar Ghosh. It is going strong today in San Rafa-el, whereas Kinnara was shut down in the summer of 1969. But Ravi still wanted to be involved with music education. He taught a few special classes at Ali Akbar College—Ruckert found them "a very in-vigorating experience"—and soon another door opened.[68] In 1970 he joined the brand-new California Institute of the Arts to head north Indian music teaching. Cal Arts, the vision of Walt Disney, opened on a temporary site in Burbank, before moving to its purpose-built university campus at Valencia in the high desert north of Los Angeles. Ravi brought in Amiya Dasgupta and Taranath Rao, and once the department was established he left it to them to take charge, returning to play occasional recitals. He was learning where his strengths lay.

On November 29, 1969 Ravi arrived in Calcutta from Beirut, where he had stopped over after his European tour. It was his first time in India for eighteen months and he felt he had something to prove. On his last visit he had been criticized for being abroad too much, so he planned to stay for nearly five months. But absenteeism was just one of the charges against him. The self-appointed purists who had been attacking him for years for supposedly Westernizing his music had a field day after the raga-rock explosion. Allegations circulated that he had been jamming with the Beatles or had sold out. "At home I was torn to pieces," he said. "They thought I'd gone mad, and didn't have any confidence in me. They thought I was getting involved with hippies and drug addicts, and so there was a lot of propaganda against me."[69]

Among fellow musicians, the most frequent thorn in his side was still Vilayat Khan. An unimpressed Ravi perceived this as obsessive jealousy: "It was like Salieri with Mozart." Vilayat took his sniping to another level now, as Ravi recalled: "In every program he would say, 'This is not Beatle sitar, this is the real sitar,' directly taking my name." Ravi also heard reports of Ali Akbar Khan bad-mouthing him to his acolytes. "These two people were always hurt by me without my trying to do anything," he said. "I never tried to hurt."[70]

Shivkumar Sharma says,

Some people were very critical of Raviji. But I had seen what he was doing: he had not diluted our music, but he presented it according to the requirements of the listeners where he was playing our music for the first time…I watched—he was playing pure classical music. And his contribution was immense.[71]

"Criticism doesn't bother me," Ravi asserted at the time.[72] But he was deceiving himself. He became obsessed with setting the record straight. "He was a softie. Yes, it did hurt him," says Penny Estabrook. "You couldn't say to him, 'Forget it, it doesn't matter.' He would grab onto it, and be upset and hurt. The main thing is, it was jealousy. People couldn't accept him as he was."[73]

"A bit of paranoia set into me for those few years," Ravi later admitted. "With all the fuss, I started believing some of the propaganda being leveled against me."[74] After playing the Dadar Matunga Music Circle in Bombay, he was stung by a harsh review by Mohan Nadkarni. So Ravi arranged an additional date in the city, invited Nadkarni and gave an extra-long recital. The critic gave a glowing notice second time around.[75] For the rest of this tour, and for some years to come in India, Ravi returned to playing two or three *ragas* stretched out over four or five hours.[76] "I am going through a hectic tour, with marathon performances at most places," he wrote to Yehudi Menuhin in January, "and though it is trying at times, it is also a great joy."[77]

Ravi had also raised hackles by comparing making music to lovemaking. "When you know a *raga* really well," he once told the London *Times*, "you can start anywhere—it doesn't matter. You're quite free. It is like the art of making love with real finesse. You just do as the mood takes you."[78] This was no mere provocation. For Ravi it expressed something deeply felt and spiritual at root, and had nothing to do with the West: "It created a great furore when I said that. I was misunderstood, but it's really true—it is the height of ecstasy on me. It becomes one, the spiritual feeling and sensual feeling."[79]

By the late 1960s Westerners were increasingly coming to India to immerse themselves in its culture rather than to impose their own. Cultures still clashed, though. Gita Mehta described the numerous hippie pilgrims as a "caravanserai of libertine celebrants who were wiping away the proprieties of caste, race and sex by sheer stoned incomprehension."[80] The friction they caused was dramatized in the hit film of 1971, *Hare Rama Hare Krishna*. In this morality tale, matinee idol Dev Anand warns India's youth not to be waylaid by foreigners corrupting their religion with drugs, drink, free love and rock music. Ironically its big song was R. D. Burman's "Dum Maro Dum," an invitation to "Take another toke" set to a superb rock backing.

Conscious that some Indians associated him with these scruffy tourists, Ravi lamented how India was now "overrun by unwashed, rebellious young…Americans and Europeans from good families and backgrounds" who were latching onto what he saw as the wrong kind of role models. At the Kumbh Mela, he noted, instead of directing themselves to the "good and saintly persons" present, they had tended to follow the ash-smeared *aghori* and the naked, dreadlocked *naga sadhus*—mendicant holy men who often indulged in drugs or alcohol, and of whom many Hindus were wary.[81] In *My Music, My Life* he can sometimes sound like a social conservative. At one point he says, defensively, "It warms me to hear high government officials or other eminent people tell me that I am a good influence on the young people of their country."[82]

Later he admitted that he had gone too far in trying to distance himself from his new fans overseas:

> In endeavoring to please one camp, I hurt the other. With some justification, the young faithful in the West objected to what must have seemed like my ingratitude in turning my back on those who had made my name and fortune. It was a unique situation to be in, and at times it was not easy.[83]

His Indian tour was interrupted by two overseas trips. In January 1970 he was away for ten days performing in Beirut and at the Cannes MIDEM festival, which had a classical focus that year. The Russian cellist Mstislav Rostropovich was there. Ravi was "dog-tired," he wrote to Kamala from Cannes, putting it down to the longer recitals he had been playing, plus cumulative lack of sleep. "Do rest as much as you can before Hurricane R hits Bombay again!" he told her.[84] Then in February he was in New York to record the *Raga* voice-over and also to play the Fillmore East again. This concert was notable as the U.S. debut of the eighteen-year-old prodigy Zakir Hussain, who accompanied Ravi instead of his father, who was ill. Afterward Ravi told him of an opening as tabla instructor at the University of Washington under Robert Garfias, and Zakir began his teaching career in America.[85]

"I got a strange letter from A[nnapurna]," Ravi wrote to Kamala. "Such devotion all of a sudden!"[86] In this letter, sent in October 1969, Annapurna had acknowledged that he was living with another woman, yet divorce was still far from her mind. "Always remember one thing, you are my husband, you are my everything. Without you I have no one in this world," she wrote.[87]

The marriage was definitely over for Ravi, and yet it seems he still had not told Baba and Madina Begum about the separation, for he deliberately made plans to visit Maihar before he reached Bombay, so that they would not ask him whether he had seen Annapurna there.[88]

In the same letter Annapurna also encouraged Ravi to get more involved with Shubho's musical progress. She wrote,

> Remember, you can do whatever you want about me, but it is very important that you take Shubho with you and sit and teach him sitar...If he can play, then your music will survive. In our country the condition of music is very bad. If you don't create, then it will all be over. Please think about this.[89]

Shubho was still living with his mother in Pavlova, and Ravi's separation from her only accentuated the gulf between father and son. When Shubho wrote to him in November, he complained that he had sent three letters without getting a reply.[90]

For several years Annapurna had been giving Shubho serious instruction on the sitar. He was talented but didn't have Ravi's drive. So, as if she were her father drilling Ali Akbar, Annapurna became the sternest of teachers, and Shubho improved greatly over time. Ravi felt Shubho's left hand was better than his right. Like his mother, he had a superb touch on the *meend* (when bending the notes), but he needed more work on rhythmic aspects and playing with an accompanist. He struggled under her intense regime and, Ravi reflected, "Maybe it became like a bitter medicine."[91]

Matters came to a head in early January. It seems Shubho could no longer cope with his mother's temper, and in desperation he claimed he had taken "eight to ten" strong sleeping pills. According to Ravi (and Shubho later confirmed the account to his wife), a doctor pumped Shubho's stomach.[92] According to Annapurna, the doctor examined him and said nothing was wrong.[93] Either way, this does not sound like a determined attempt to kill himself, as Shubho told somebody that he had taken pills—but it was unarguably a cry of pain. Ravi received "an SOS call" at his hotel from his son. Alarmed, he rushed over to Pavlova, where he found Shubho lying down, looking sick. "He clung to me desperately, like a little boy, and begged me to take him away with me to America," Ravi wrote. "Coming from a man of twenty-eight, this both melted my heart and angered me."[94] Shubho (actually twenty-seven at the time) was about the same age as Ravi had been when he had considered suicide. "Seeing his desperation, I had to take him away, though I knew that this might later be portrayed as me forcing him away from his mother and harming his musical career."[95] As Ravi left the apartment, Annapurna shouted at him, "You have ruined my life and now you are ruining your son's life."[96] She later claimed it was all a plot by Ravi, stage-managed to malign her and prize Shubho away from her.[97]

"They always blamed each other. Shubho was a ping-pong between the two of them," says Kumar Shankar, who was close to his cousin. "My heart went out to him. I think he got bounced around quite a bit, and he got affected and it made him quite timid. Plus whose shoes are you stepping into? That's always a big deal for most kids of famous parents."[98] It was Kumar who, at Ravi's request, collected Shubho and his belongings from Pavlova and brought him back to recuperate at Rajendra and Lakshmi's apartment in Santa Cruz. Ravi was staying there too, but shortly afterward left for Cannes, where he had time to think about Shubho. "Have never missed him like this. I felt quite sad!" he wrote to Kamala.[99] He was back in Bombay by January 25, and at length Shubho moved to Bangalore to stay for a few weeks with Ravi's disciple Rama Rao.

This act of filial insurrection hurt Annapurna deeply and accelerated her withdrawal from contact with other people. However, the episode has been framed in some accounts as if it were a child custody battle, or even a nefarious attempt by Ravi to scupper his son's musical destiny. Annapurna later said Shubho had needed another eighteen months of her training before he would be ready to go abroad, but she herself, in her recent letter, had raised the idea that Ravi take him away to teach him. In truth, Shubho was a man of twenty-seven who needed to move on, or to run away, and who wanted to live in California like his father, his uncle Ali Akbar Khan and his cousins Aashish and Pranesh Khan. As in 1956, the trauma of this rupture persisted in Annapurna, and prevented her from accepting that her son was finding his own path.

Ravi had no direct contact with Annapurna for the next decade. She would not countenance divorce, and he was unwilling or unable to push for it, so he supported her financially through a lawyer and gave her the ocean-facing apartment in Akash Ganga (he gave the adjoining flat to Shubho). He also encouraged Jamshed Bhabha and Narayana Menon, founder and first director respectively of the National Centre for Performing Arts in Bombay, to offer her some teaching there. She already had a few disciples of her own, including the vocalist Vinay Bharat-Ram and Hariprasad Chaurasia, who at her insistence switched to playing flute left-handed so that she could teach him from scratch. But she had not, as has sometimes been claimed, taught Ravi. Gradually she became a recluse, never performing again, never recording. Music, she resolved, was her private offering to God rather than something to be sold to the public. This approach suited her. So did her role as a *guru*. She was a rigorous teacher, loving but uncompromising; sometimes her father's fury would rise in her, and once she even broke a tanpura over Chaurasia's head.[100] But over time she created a fine legacy, with several disciples of the top rank. They revered her.

In April, shortly after his fiftieth birthday, Ravi left India on another arduous itinerary: Malaysia, Singapore, seven U.S. concerts in eight days, then back to Japan and Australia. After a third crossing of the Pacific Ocean, he played Canada and eventually reached Los Angeles on June 15. Shubho, who traveled from India via Japan with Kamala, arrived two days later to begin his new life.[101] At first the three stayed in another rented property on a short let, but soon Ravi set up Shubho with his own apartment, a Ford Mustang and a monthly stipend. Within weeks Ravi moved too, this time buying a three-bedroomed Spanish villa at 327 North Highland Avenue, just south of Hollywood. He was abroad during September: first in Iran, where he played the Shiraz Arts Festival, a showcase for the international avant-garde held in the ruins of Persepolis; then Berlin, to record the score to Manfred Durniok's film *Unterwegs nach Kathmandu*, and London.

Back in Los Angeles, he gave Shubho the freedom to choose his own future, but plainly wanted him to continue with the sitar. So Shubho hedged his bets. He enrolled at Otis Art Institute to study graphic arts, and in November appeared on stage for the first time, accompanying Ravi, Alla Rakha and Zakir Hussain in a fathers-and-sons concert in New York. But as Shubho sometimes said in later years, when you debut at Carnegie Hall, where do you go after that?[102]

V
PERPETUAL ORBIT
1970–1987

In London, 1974

18

DREAM, NIGHTMARE AND DAWN

I am missing you, oh Krishna, where are you?
Though I can't see you, I hear your flute all the while.
RAVI SHANKAR, "I AM MISSING YOU"[1]

Ravi began the new decade with the intention of pulling back from the rock and pop world and repositioning himself in classical concert halls, and focusing more on India. He already had a major commission that complemented this shift: a concerto for sitar and orchestra, opening up a new landscape of Western orchestral composition that he was to return to intermittently for the rest of his life. As it transpired, his key collaborator over the next five years would be none other than George Harrison, who became the driving force behind two films, five albums and a stadium tour of North America, all of which featured Ravi prominently.

In Ravi's mental picture of the musical world, he visualized two great mountain peaks: Indian classical music and Western classical music. Could a bridge be constructed from one summit to the other? Over the previous few years his opinion on what he had called "this East–West-*bhai-bhai* stuff" had fluctuated. In his 1964 paper at Delhi he had suggested that improvisatory passages could be introduced into Indian orchestral works. But melding Indian and Western systems was a step further. "If one hopes to retain the individual character of each music there can never be a fusion," he wrote in 1967. "The melodic character of Indian music and the harmonic character of Western music are like oil and water. They will not mix…Nor should there be any fear that one will harm the other. If anything, the study of both sharpens our musical awareness."[2] But after his triumphant duets with Yehudi Menuhin, he started to see the possibilities: if Yehudi could play cadenzas on violin in Indian music, why couldn't Ravi play *raga* improvisations on the sitar within a Western format? In many ways, composing for a Western orchestra was a logical move after two decades of writing for Indian ensembles.

It was André Previn who made it happen. Previn was a young meteor who spanned the worlds of jazz, classical and Hollywood film scores, and had won four Oscars and five Grammys by the age of thirty-five. He admired Ravi's music, without claiming expertise in the field, and as far back as 1963 had presciently suggested that Indian music might be more happily coupled with Western concert music than with jazz.[3] After the London Symphony Orchestra appointed him as its principal conductor in 1968 he brought his adventurous spirit to bear on the orchestra's programming and invited Ravi to write a concerto for sitar and orchestra. This had been commissioned by May 1969, when Ravi referred to it in a letter to Yehudi.[4]

This was to be the first ever sitar concerto, although there were some notable precursors. In 1958 the Anglo-Indian composer John Mayer had written a *Dance Suite* for sitar, flute, tabla, tanpura and orchestra that was premiered by the Royal Liverpool Philharmonic, but it had little impact. In spring 1969 Ravi met Alan Hovhaness in New York to discuss *Shambala*, a work for violin, sitar and orchestra that the American wanted to write for Yehudi and Ravi. Although he liked and respected Hovhaness, Ravi told Yehudi he wanted nothing to do with the project. "Let us not please perform anything that doesn't sound right and again go through the misery that we did at Bath," he wrote. Ravi had an alternative suggestion for Yehudi: "I am sure that with your help I could write an ideally beautiful piece for you and me along with a chamber or symphony orchestra."[5] This was an intriguing proposal but surely unrealistic, because Yehudi had never composed. Either Yehudi did not pass on Ravi's rejection to Hovhaness or he persuaded him to reconsider, because when the score was delivered in November Yehudi said he would discuss it with Ravi. It was not until March 1970 that Hovhaness heard, via Leopold Stokowski, that

Ravi would not play the work, and he started looking for another soloist. Ultimately *Shambala* remained unperformed during Hovhaness's lifetime. Its belated premiere came in 2008, with Ravi's disciple Gaurav Mazumdar playing the sitar part. Ravi also turned down other offers to perform concertos by Western composers. "I might still do it (play such concerto) in future," he wrote in late 1970, "but before that I wanted to play a sitar concerto which should be basically Indian in nature."[6] He preferred to be the composer himself, which made Previn's commission much more attractive.

He wrote the work in two and a half months during 1970. As with any concerto, it alternates the focus between the orchestra and the soloist—who in the premiere was Ravi himself—with the difference that the solo passages were mostly improvised, ending with Ravi giving a cue for the return of the orchestra. Essentially he used the orchestra to play Indian music, as he had with the All India Radio ensemble. The work is uncommonly long for a concerto, at 40 minutes, and has four movements, one more than usual, each of which is based on a different *raga*. The opening movement, which is structured like an *alap–jor* progression, is in *Khamaj*, the second in *Sindhi Bhairavi*, the brief third in the night *raga Adana*, and the fourth closes the circle with *Manj Khamaj*, which is related to *Khamaj*. There is minimal counterpoint and harmony, to avoid obscuring the flavor of each *raga*. Instead the focus is on Ravi's gift for melody and rhythmic intricacy. Melody lines are played solo or in unison, the baton passed from one instrument to another, with liberal use of *sawal–jawab* exchanges and *tihais* by both sitar and orchestra. With no tanpura involved, the drone is provided by two harps or the strings, and the tabla's role is allocated to bongos and other percussion.

There are gestures toward the structures of Western music: the key does change between movements, from D to B to E and back to D, for which reason Ravi used a sitar tuned to D (his master sitar was tuned to C sharp). Otherwise he avoided modulation, although in the second movement the strings briefly and luxuriantly shift from

B to A, in a technique known as *Avirbhava-Tirobhava* (appearance and disappearance), which occurs in the semi-classical *thumri* style. Ravi also seems to have drawn on some favorite Western influences. His rapid unison string passages recall Aaron Copland's *Hoedown*, while the opening of the last movement evokes the natural world of Beethoven's "Pastoral" Symphony, Ravi's flutes chirping like hoopoe birds and his sustained horns resounding like distant elephant calls.

Ravi's formal study of Western music had been limited to a brief spell in Paris in his youth, so he needed a music assistant. Initially he worked with John Barham, in London in September 1970. Ravi composed in Indian notation or on the sitar or piano, and Barham transcribed into a Western score. After a while Barham felt that his role had stretched from notating to writing orchestration, and he withdrew on amicable terms.[7] Ravi turned to his American student Fred Teague to help him complete the score.

The first draft of the score still needed much work. Previn, who never formed much of a bond with Ravi, responded by listing 21 queries for Teague, in a letter that betrays his anxiety seven weeks before the premiere.[8] Some of these problems were the product of inexperience, and easily fixed, but others arose from differences between Indian and Western music. Ravi included a demonstration cassette along with his answers, and he knew that the rehearsal phase would be crucial in ensuring that the musicians grasped the rhythmic patterns and rendered the note embellishments in an authentically Indian style.

The premiere took place at the Royal Festival Hall on January 28, 1971. While the reviews were mostly positive, they did divide into two camps. Felix Aprahamian, the long-serving *Sunday Times* critic, applauded "a continuously fascinating as well as a novel musical experience," while in the *Daily Telegraph* Colin Mason gave qualified approval, noting how much the orchestral players had evidently enjoyed it.[9] Others were unconvinced. Watching the premiere, Edward Greenfield observed "one of my sourer-faced colleagues looking as though he was suffering from an overdose of sugar, and I imagine the custodians of Indian culture might have been having qualms of conscience too, but the rest of us were able to sit back and enjoy sweet music."[10]

The concerto had its U.S. premiere in Denver in October, and further outings later in the year, and it then gained a new profile with the release of the album, which had been recorded at Abbey Road at the end of May. Capitol Records claimed that "it sold like a pop record," which was perhaps a different kind of embellishment, but it did reach number 6 in the *Billboard* classical chart.[11]

For years the only way the concerto could be heard in India was on record. Ravi attended an album launch at the Taj Mahal Hotel in Bombay in January 1972, which generated much enthusiasm, although *Onlooker* magazine sniffily declared that "this type of music is gall and wormwood," satisfying neither East nor West.[12] Some musicians were disconcerted by the limited scope for improvisation, but in later years several leading Indian soloists followed suit and wrote their own concertos.[13]

Western detractors have tended to attack the concerto as a misuse of the orchestra. Perhaps the starkest critic was Previn himself, who later grumpily attacked the recording as "absolute, total, utter shit...I knew it was nonsense."[14] Naresh Sohal, an Indian composer trained in the Western system who admired Ravi's solo sitar performances, was also dismissive, although in more respectful terms. "Concerto is a form of Western classical music," he said. "To partake in it, if you are going to ignore the most fundamental of Western music's tenets, harmony—if you are not going to indulge in it, and you *cannot* indulge in it—how are you writing a concerto?" He argued that it should simply be called an ensemble piece.[15]

"Coming from an Indian ensemble background, it's very difficult to use all the resources of a Western orchestra in a way that does them justice," says the conductor David Murphy, who worked with Ravi on several later orchestral works.

On the other hand, if you use a symphony orchestra to play an early symphony by Mozart, you're using the resources in a very light, delicate way, which is exactly what Raviji did. People were expecting different things. The way music was going in the mid-twentieth century, with twelve-tone music, which is so alien to Indian music, the academic musicians were persuaded that was the way you *had* to go. So Raviji coming up with something that was beautiful, simple, diatonic, delicate, elegant, with the expression *between* the notes rather than in huge orchestral textures—they didn't get it.[16]

The Western musician whose endorsement mattered most to Ravi was Yehudi Menuhin, who had been skeptical about him orchestrating Indian music, but was won over. "Dearest Ravi," Yehudi wrote to him in 1997:

> The works you composed for solo sitar and Western orchestra are absolutely superb. To use the Western orchestra to produce the rhythms, the sounds, the colors of Indian classical music is a great achievement and brings us all much closer to the true Indian tradition which you represent, especially when it is carried by your playing and your virtuosity.[17]

The day after the London premiere, Ravi sat down with Roy Plomley to discuss his *Desert Island Discs* for the BBC. His selection feels rather calculated: he picked three pop or blues songs and three Western classical pieces, and only one Indian classical work. His final choice, "if he could choose only one," and telling for its lyrical theme, was "Jamuna Ke Teer" by Abdul Karim Khan, a spellbinding favorite of Ravi's childhood. It is the song of a *gopi* searching for Krishna on the banks of the River Jamuna (or Yamuna), another story of earthly and heavenly yearning intertwined. As a restless extrovert with few practical skills, Ravi admitted he was singularly ill-equipped for life as a desert-island castaway. Yet, intriguingly, he said it might be appealing to "leave behind this pressure on the mind and time, of being haunted all the time by commitment."[18]

Ravi almost never took holidays, and rarely allowed himself time off. But a week earlier, in another interview, he had floated the idea of retiring from international touring. Escape was on his mind. His new plan was to return to Benares, motivated in part by love for the spiritual aura of his home town and in part by that recurring desire to recreate Almora in the form of his own ashram for music. This time, though, it would not be a school. "Soon I intend to retire there and just take a small handful of students who are prepared to take the time to study," he said.[19]

For Ravi, the Bangladesh liberation struggle of 1970–71 revived the most painful memories of his life. With its streams of traumatized and starving refugees, and a communal conflict accompanying the birth pangs of a new nation, it was like an awful echo of Partition and brought back the time of his deepest despair twenty-three years earlier.

The seeds of the conflict were sown in the retreat from empire. The British first partitioned the Indian state of Bengal as a punitive measure in 1905, but reversed course due to resistance. At independence Bengal was again divided, but this time East Bengal was yoked together in a new country—on the basis of its Muslim majority—with the culturally and geographically remote West Pakistan. Ever since, the less populous western half had shut the east out of power, and tensions had risen over attempts to impose Urdu as the national language at the expense of Bengali. After a cyclone struck East Pakistan in November 1970, killing at least a quarter of a million, its Bengali population blamed the central government for a lackluster humanitarian response. In December, in Pakistan's first free general election, the Awami League, which favored autonomy for East Pakistan, gained a clear majority in the National Assembly, but the military regime in the west annulled the results.

Ravi's Bengali identity was always important to him. Throughout his life many of his closest friends were Bengalis and, wherever he was in the world, he always wanted to know what was happening culturally in Calcutta. The singer Sanjukta Ghosh, who was teaching at Ali Akbar College in the Bay Area at this time, recalls being startled by just how many Bengali magazines and books there were in the bathroom at Ravi's Highland Avenue home.[20] According to Janet Bock Bicker, who visited Ravi there over Christmas 1970 with her husband Richard Bock, he was already expressing concern about the suffering in East Pakistan.[21]

Those anxieties escalated after a vicious and probably genocidal crackdown by the Pakistan army. The territory declared independence on March 26, 1971 under the name Bangladesh, and a national liberation struggle ensued, in which India gave covert support to the Mukti Bahini freedom-fighters. The death toll that year is disputed, but it was certainly in six figures, possibly seven. Ten million fled. The Indian government opened its borders and set up refugee camps, and the streets of Calcutta absorbed the new arrivals. Among them were some of Ravi's distant relatives, as both his father and his father-in-law came from the affected area. A second humanitarian catastrophe unfolded among these hungry and desolate refugees. The Indian government appealed for international assistance, to little avail. But Ravi was determined to help.

In June 1971 Ravi was finalizing the soundtrack for *Raga* in a Hollywood studio with George Harrison. This was their first musical collaboration. Much had happened in the three years since they had filmed at Esalen. Shortly after that, George gave up serious practice on the sitar, accepting that he couldn't dedicate the time it required. Returning with renewed enthusiasm to the guitar, he blossomed as a songwriter during the Beatles' final majestic flourish, for which he gave credit to his training in Indian music: "It really did help me as far as writing strange melodies, and also rhythmically it was the best assistance I could ever have had."[22] He thrived in the initial post-

Beatles era too, and in early 1971 he simultaneously topped the singles charts with "My Sweet Lord" and the album charts with *All Things Must Pass*—on both sides of the Atlantic. All the while, his love for Indian music was undimmed. After seeing Ravi give a "transcendental" recital at Rory McEwen's house, he had written to Kamala, "He is becoming more celestial each time I see him."[23]

On June 12, in the midst of the soundtrack sessions, Ravi gave a morning recital for friends at home. "Being a Bengali myself," he said, as he introduced a Bengali *dhun*, "we are very much disturbed at present with all that is happening, the whole Bangladesh thing." George was present, and later that day they discussed Ravi's plan to stage a benefit show for the refugees.[24] On his own Ravi thought he could raise only about $20,000—a drop in the Bay of Bengal compared to what was needed. "After half an hour he talked me into being on the show," said George, who was so moved by his friend's distress that he took over responsibility for it.[25] With a Beatle in charge, they could raise a lot more money—and awareness. "The war had been going on for a bit, and I had hardly even heard of it, so he fed me a lot of newspaper articles about it," said George. "The priority was to attract world attention to what was going on."[26]

Throwing his energy into the cause, George booked New York's Madison Square Garden on August 1 for afternoon and evening performances, jointly titled the Concert for Bangladesh. He then set about persuading his friends among the new rock aristocracy to take part without a fee. He arranged for the concerts to be recorded and filmed, and rush-released a charity single, "Bangla Desh," in which he sang of how Ravi had informed him of the catastrophe, and appealed for support for the afflicted land.

Ravi wrote and recorded his own musical response in the form of two folk-style songs in Bengali, each potent in sentiment and fascinating in musical style. In "Joi Bangla" he takes up the rallying cry of the liberation movement. It opens with brief phrases on the ektara and bansuri flute, characteristic Bengali instruments and subtle echoes of the music of *Pather Panchali*. But it is most notable for its vocals by Sanjukta Ghosh and Ravi's son Shubho, his sweetly rich *filmi* tones accentuated by the backing strings. Double-tracked, the pair trade lines, merge into unison and even diverge into that rarest of phenomena in a Ravi Shankar recording, harmony. This is not classical music, but it is an urgent, busy and joyful celebration of the motherland.

In contrast "Oh Bhaugowan" is a lament written from the viewpoint of a Bengali boatman.[27] Ravi takes the lead vocal himself and in a unifying gesture appeals to God using both the Hindu name "Bhaugowan" and the Muslim "Khoda": "Oh God, where have you gone, leaving us alone?...Who counts how many die / Who hears our cry?" The spare arrangement, with G. S. Sachdev on flute and Harihar Rao twanging the ektara again, and an uncredited santoor player, is underpinned by a drone C chord on an organ that is so reminiscent of the opening of "Blue Jay Way" that it is surely played by George, who was producing the sessions. The affecting melody builds at a stately pace until it peaks with Shubho and Sanjukta Ghosh singing in counterpoint against Ravi's melody. Ravi also recorded a short instrumental piece that drew on Bengali folk tunes, this one a light classical sitar–sarod duet in *Mishra Jhinjhoti* with Ali Akbar Khan, himself a Bengali Muslim with his own relatives in Bangladesh. The three tracks were released in August as an extended-play (EP) single on Apple Records.

George worked tirelessly to arrange the concert, but as it approached he was unsure which musicians would show up. A Ticketron advertisement billed the concert as "George Harrison, Ravi Shankar and..." but all seats sold out within hours anyway, such was George's drawing power. In the event he secured a stellar line-up, including Bob Dylan, Eric Clapton, Ringo Starr and Billy Preston, their presence a tribute to the worthiness of the cause as well as George's tenacity and boldness. He needed extra courage on the day itself because it was the first time he had ever fronted a band, let alone organized and compèred a show.

The concert began with a duet between Ravi and Ali Akbar, accompanied by Alla Rakha on tabla, with Kamala on tanpura. Ravi prefaced it by speaking briefly of the agony of the Bangladeshi refugees. After the musicians spent a couple of minutes tuning up, a wave of applause surged around Madison Square Garden. Ravi dissolved the awkwardness of the moment with playful humor, perhaps because he'd had practice; it was not the first time Western audiences had applauded him merely for tuning up. Leaning into his microphone, he said, "If you appreciate the tuning so much, I hope you will enjoy the playing more."

The crowd reminded Ravi of the audience at Monterey Pop—younger than he usually drew, but attentive.[28] The Indian maestros played two pieces. The first, at least in the matinee concert, was the afternoon *raga Shuddh Sarang*, but no recording of it has been released. Then they turned to a semi-classical piece that drew on Bengali folk melodies, simply titled *Bangla Dhun*. First Ravi and Ali Akbar presented a brief *alap*. Then, joined by Alla Rakha, they explored a medium-tempo *gat* in 6-beat *dadra tal*, followed by a fast *gat* in *teental* in which all three performed with passion and precision. It was over in fifteen minutes, but this became arguably the most famous piece of Indian classical music ever performed in the West.

To Ravi, their performance was "a conscious statement for peace through our music."[29] It was a deliberate public display of Hindu–Muslim harmony, and, if one watches the footage today, what it represents is still powerful and supremely relevant. From a musical point of view, too, there remains something intensely moving about this duet between two masters, forged more than thirty years earlier in the music room at Maihar, reaching its apotheosis in one of the greatest concerts of the century—and documented in a feature film and a number 1 hit album. Indian music had truly arrived at the heart of Western popular culture.

Having finished his second set of the day, Ravi took his seat in the front row for the rest of the evening concert. Footage of the refugees had been screened in the arena during the interval, and he sensed a special atmosphere in the house. He was thrilled by the concert, appreciating the "soulful" selection of numbers and the lack of hard rock. He was now used to mixing with rock musicians, although there were still moments when attitudes and behavior clashed. Ravi had asked the audience not to smoke during his recital, but almost all the rock musicians were puffing away during their sets. At the after-party at Ungano's nightclub Keith Moon smashed up a drumkit, and Ravi remonstrated with Eric Clapton about his heroin habit—an act of tough love, as he admired Clapton's guitar playing and they were later to become friends.[30]

Ravi was touched deeply by what George had created for Bangladesh. This was the first big rock charity concert, and coverage was overwhelmingly positive; the event was interpreted as a revival of the peace-and-love spirit of the 1960s, after two post-Woodstock years in which the Beatles had split up and rock had been tainted by increasing avarice, hard drugs and the deaths of Brian Jones, Jimi Hendrix, Janis Joplin and Jim Morrison. According to *Life* magazine, it was "an occasion of almost devotional intensity."[31] The box-office receipts of over $243,000 were given straight to UNICEF's Bangladesh fund, and millions more were eventually raised from the film and album. Above all, it gave an instant global profile to the name "Bangladesh" and the nascent country. "It was a miracle, really," Ravi reflected later.[32]

It took a war to resolve the political crisis. As the repression continued, India began making preparations to intervene, and by the autumn conflict seemed inevitable. On December 3 Pakistan carried out pre-emptive air raids on India's northwestern front, triggering a large-scale air, land and sea conflict. India triumphed in under a fortnight. Bangladesh gained its independence, and India soon withdrew its own forces. Ravi and George were hailed as heroes by Bangladeshis, and on Ravi's three later visits to the country he was left in no doubt as to their lasting appreciation.

Popular music had been inspired to find its conscience. In September London staged its own Concert for Bangladesh at the Oval cricket ground, headlined by the Who, and countless major multi-artist benefit shows followed in subsequent years for other good causes—all with their roots in Ravi and George's bold act of imagination. When Live Aid was being planned in 1985, Bob Geldof called up George for advice. George's main tip was to set it up properly as a charitable venture in advance, as he had had to fight long-running battles with the tax authorities, which delayed some payments to UNICEF for years, and involved a huge personal tax bill for him. Funds continue to be raised today through sales of the album and the 2005 DVD.

In November 1971 *Raga* finally had its premiere, at a press view at Carnegie Hall cinema in New York attended by George and Pattie Harrison, and John Lennon and Yoko Ono. Ravi himself felt ambivalent about the film, but the *New York Times* did not. "See *Raga*," ran its review, praising it unreservedly as a "quietly penetrating, beautifully made color documentary...Everything about it is admirable."[33] Apple Records put out the soundtrack LP in North America and Japan, while Ravi and George appeared together on the Dick Cavett and David Frost talk shows to promote both *Raga* and the Bangladesh cause. Sadly, *Raga*'s theatrical release was very limited, probably because, as Richard Bock put it, "The bloom was off the rose."[34] Yet even though the mania for all things Indian had passed, the Bangladesh projects brought Indian music to a huge new audience, and in terms of public impact represented the high-water mark of Ravi and George's alliance.

"There is so much I have to tell you reg. the visit to India," Ravi wrote to Harihar Rao at the end of February 1972, after a two-month stay in his homeland. "I was so happy—and felt very optimist[ic] for the first time in years for the future of our country & people!"[35] The main reason for this positivity was probably pride at India's intervention to resolve the suffering among his fellow Bengalis, and the ongoing relief efforts. There was also the elation of the new homemaker. In 1970 Ravi had purchased a three- to four-acre mango grove beside the road at Shivpur, halfway between the *ghats* of Benares and the airport, and he now began building a house there.[36] Kamala, tired of constant traveling, assumed the role of overseeing its construction and design, and she opted to remain in India while Ravi was abroad for the next nine months touring Japan, Mexico, North America and Europe—the longest time they had spent apart. A new phase in their relationship had begun. Ravi admitted to Harihar that he was dreading being in his Los Angeles home because he would miss Kamala so much.[37]

Ravi's life in California was well established. He owned a home, he had friends and family nearby, including his son, and he had brought over his favorite cook from India, Vasudevan Nair. He had also started a music circle, which grew out of the recitals that he gave or hosted at Highland Avenue. This was one of those smaller ventures of which Ravi was particularly proud. He was always passionate about Indian classical music being played on an intimate scale for connoisseurs and enthusiasts. In 1973 he and Harihar Rao stumbled on Herrick Chapel at Occidental College. With its clean, modernist aesthetic and vibrant stained glass, the chapel, which had a capacity of five hundred, struck Ravi as an ideal home for what became a formal, nonprofit-making organization, incorporated as the Music Circle. For many years he gave an annual fundraising concert, and it thrived. "Every one of the great artists that you'll ever hear about played in the Music Circle in the early days," says Paula Rao, who was a key mover alongside her husband Harihar.[38] Later Richard Bock helped, more as evangelist than businessman, by issuing live recordings on cassette under the name of the Ravi Shankar Music Circle.[39] At the time of writing the Music Circle continues to host first-rank Indian musicians at Herrick Chapel.

Despite putting down these roots, Ravi found his restlessness resurfacing. "When I first visited California I thought it was an earthly paradise—I loved the climate, the variety of people. But now I feel different about it," he said in the autumn of 1972.[40] He missed being surrounded by Indian culture, language and food. Much had changed in his American set-up. Demand for his records and film scores had receded from the zenith of 1967. World Pacific was gone. His concert bookings remained strong but they had now been taken over by George Schutz and Gary Haber in New York, and he was relying less on his Los Angeles lawyer, Phillip Chronis. Shubho had fallen in love with a woman from South Carolina, Linda Justice. On their first date he showed up two hours late and had his car stolen while they were at the cinema, but she still fell for him, and they moved in together in Hollywood.[41] Most important of all, there was no Kamala to make it feel like home. Over the next couple of years Ravi repeatedly told journalists of his intention to move to Benares, and said that it would take him two to three years to effect the change because of contractual commitments. "This is a period of life when one has to travel. It will be over soon," he said in February 1973.[42] A new dream loomed ahead of him, still just out of reach for the moment.

"A *guru* never dies," wrote Ravi. "He lives on enshrined in the heart of his disciples."[43] On September 6, 1972 Allauddin Khan died. For Ravi, who was in Los Angeles, the news was not unexpected, but the loss of his *guru* and father figure still distressed him profoundly. In a letter published in the *New York Times*, he acclaimed Baba's contribution to reviving north Indian instrumental music and his indirect role—through his pupils—in the music of India reaching Western ears.[44] Baba's official age at his death was a hundred and nine. His real age was probably ninety-one but, more to the point, as Ravi and Ali Akbar wrote, "What does it really matter if he was over a hundred or not? What he accomplished in his lifetime many others could not have done in three hundred years."[45]

Shortly afterward Ravi held a musical function in Baba's memory at Highland Avenue, and in October he and Ali Akbar Khan played a tribute concert at Lincoln Center. They chose two *ragas* composed by

Baba, *Hem Bihag* and *Manj Khamaj*. The performance was released by Apple Records as the double album *In Concert 1972*, mixed beautifully by George Harrison with Zakir Hussain and engineer Phil Mac-Donald. A powerful photograph of Baba by Mireille Ballero adorned the inside of the gatefold sleeve, opposite a eulogy by Ravi and Ali Akbar. When the duo played at the Royal Albert Hall three weeks later—surprisingly, the first time they had appeared together in London—the concert was again dedicated to Baba.

To reinforce the sense of an era closing, Tat Baba died the following year. Latterly Ravi had become disenchanted by some of his behavior and he ultimately stopped believing in him. But Tat Baba's gift had been incalculable: he had inspired Ravi's recovery from his lowest ebb, and for twenty-five years had been instrumental in filling him with a spiritually rooted confidence.

By this time Ravi had met Sathya Sai Baba. In early 1972 Richard and Janet Bock, who were already devotees of the spiritual *guru*, took Ravi to meet him at his ashram in Puttaparthi, near Bangalore. Sai Baba, famous for materializing objects out of thin air, conjured up a diamond ring on this occasion and presented it to Ravi. On a later visit he produced a ruby ring for him. Such feats were controversial, but Ravi, who was instinctively attracted to him, seems to have believed in them.[46] "With any Baba, any *sadhu*, any *ma*, any spiritual person, he was carried away very much," said Kamala, "and I always calmed him down: be careful because tomorrow this whole thing might change." What he valued more than the magic tricks, though, was the spiritual guidance. Sai Baba told him that his music gave people an experience of bliss, or God, even if they were unaware of it happening. This chimed with Ravi: "I feel God mostly in the musical notes. That is my approach and that is my way of worshipping God, my way of trying to feel him."[47] He later became disillusioned by Sai Baba too, but for some years he regularly returned to Puttaparthi to play for him on his birthday, November 23. Afterward Sai Baba would press some *vibhuti* (holy ash) on Ravi's forehead. On one occasion, Ravi prompted

Kamala, who spoke Telugu, to ask if he would put some *vibhuti* on his sitar too. Sai Baba declined, saying, "There are hundreds of sitars, but there is no other Ravi Shankar."[48]

After the Bangladesh concert, George Harrison was on a new mission to help Ravi. He, Ringo Starr and their wives accompanied Ravi and his French *amour* Mireille Ballero to the Cannes Film Festival in May 1972 to promote *Raga*. Ravi was warming to the film, and a distribution deal was struck with New Line Cinema, which specialized in U.S. campus theaters.[49]

In London George loaned Ravi a large townhouse at 27 Charles Street, which had exquisite Georgian fittings and kitchen graffiti by John Lennon. More significantly, there was a new album, which George produced and released as the first offering from his new label, Dark Horse. In April 1973, still glowing from their success at the Grammys, where the Bangladesh box set had just won Album of the Year, they assembled at A&M Studios in Hollywood, a state-of-the-art facility occupying Charlie Chaplin's old film studios, to record *Shankar Family & Friends*. The album is Ravi's deepest foray into what we now call fusion. It was still based largely on Indian *ragas* and *talas*, and Ravi was in charge, but thirty-eight musicians were involved. There was an Indian ensemble to rival that of the 1968 tour, a peerless line-up of Western rock and jazz players, and even a Moog synthesizer. Key musicians Ravi brought in included Emil Richards and the flutist and saxophonist Tom Scott, both of whom had played on *Charly*.

Ravi was nothing if not ambitious. Side 2 comprises a three-part suite he conceived as music for an unstaged ballet. "He was *obsessed* with doing ballets," according to Kamala.[50] He created it spontaneously over two days in Studio A, and it saw the first appearance of what he described as his favorite narrative theme, a variation on paradise lost/paradise regained. The first part, Dream, represents the utopia of times gone by, the joy of young lovers, and "the golden past which we recall with nostalgia, times of childlike innocence."[51] The music here peaks with a romantic *pas de deux* between two sitars, representing the lovers' sensuous dance, before the second part, Nightmare, ushers in the exploitation, conflict and despair of the present. The highlight here is *Dispute and Violence*, which opens with a vocal percussion battle between Ravi and Harihar Rao, before switching to a jazz-funk tussle between marimbas, saxophone and bass. The final part, Dawn, brings hope for a better future. This is heralded with a multi-faith call for peace in *Awakening*, which features, in succession, Gregorian chant, a Jewish cantor, Buddhist incantation, the Muslim call to prayer and a Vedic chant.

The tripartite theme of Dream, Nightmare and Dawn had profound resonance for Ravi, and he would return to it. It was undoubtedly prompted by the recent traumas of Bangladesh, with its echoes of Partition, erasing the utopian vision of a Golden Bengal. But it was also rooted in his own life experiences, from his childhood ordeals to his suicidal low point in his twenties. He had earned the knowledge that life is marred by appalling suffering, but that one can be rescued from the brink and redeemed, and ultimately there is the potential for bliss.

Side 1 showcases a set of songs on devotional themes, with four compositions (and three new lyrics) by Ravi. The running theme here, surely Ravi's second favorite, is a lover's paean to Krishna. Above an all-star cast of Indian musicians, including Shivkumar Sharma, Hariprasad Chaurasia and the brilliant young violinist L. Subramaniam, Lakshmi Shankar's voice floats ethereally, pining for her absent beloved. The one song breaking the theme is *Jaya Jagadish Haré*, in which Jitendra Abisheki sings an eleventh-century text in praise of Vishnu's ten incarnations. Ravi's arrangements, here using almost exclusively Indian instruments, are consistently superb.

Unusually, Ravi wrote an English lyric for one track, *I Am Missing You*. George was so taken with the song that he recorded a second, better-known version with his own rock arrangement, in which

Lakshmi's voice was backed by Ringo Starr, Billy Preston, Klaus Voormann and Jim Keltner. They were in town recording Starr's album, and had all been in George's Bangladesh band. George himself (credited as Hari Georgeson) played the guitar and autoharp. He must have particularly loved this version's opening, with its attention-grabbing piano chord, because a very similar arrangement begins Starr's number 1 hit "Photograph," which George wrote and produced shortly afterward. For all its instant appeal, the rock version of I Am Missing You sits slightly uneasily on the album. Ravi always felt ambivalent about it, as George enjoyed relating. When he told Ravi, "It's fantastic. It sounds to me like a hit record. You should write more of these," the reply came back, "George, I've been trying *not* to write them for years."[52]

Among those who played on the album was Shubho, but he was losing interest in the sitar. Ravi was upset when he found out that he planned to marry Linda. He felt Shubho was not ready for marriage, as he was a student—now taking a BA in art at Occidental College—and Ravi was still supporting him financially. Ravi was also initially disappointed that Shubho was not marrying an Indian woman. In June Shubho returned to India for the first time since his departure. On arrival he discovered that his father had set up meetings with various eligible Indian women, but he was adamant that he was marrying Linda. He also went to seek his mother's blessing, but she was upset, perhaps because it was now clear he wanted to settle permanently in America, and their last meeting was a disaster, when she refused to let him in.[53] He was still, as Kumar Shankar put it, "between a rock and a hard place with his parents."[54] He and Linda went ahead with their wedding in August, a small civil ceremony at Harihar Rao's home in Pasadena, followed later by Indian rituals. Neither of his parents attended.

At least Shubho's rapport with Kamala had improved. In Bombay, she helped him buy all the wedding clothes and ornaments. After initially staying in Kumar's apartment, he moved downstairs to her sitting room, explaining that Kumar's room was too dirty—not realizing, said Kamala, that he was the one who had made the mess. But he was so charming that she couldn't get angry.[55] "Myself and Shubho, we are great friends now," she wrote to Ravi.

> I have tried my best to do everything possible for him, keep him comfortable, nurse him in his sickness, pack, shop, run around, and do all. Be a mother for him. It is almost like having a *kutti* [baby] edition of you "all the while" (I hear your flute!). I shall miss him like mad for some time. God help Linda![56]

Kamala had also sung on the album, and she traveled with Ravi to Mexico in May, but after that they spent seven more months apart as he went on to Peru, Chile, Argentina, Brazil, New Zealand, Australia, Tunisia and Switzerland. Kamala's letters in this period are chatty and yearning; one was signed "insatiably in love with you."[57] Another concluded, in a rather poignant little musical joke, "Your *Mishra Gara* (I hope you *are* coming back to the main theme!)"[58] But even as Ravi's Krishna fixation seemed to intensify, separation made her reassess one aspect of their relationship. The previous year, on the back of an envelope from him, she had written out the names of sixteen of his past or present girlfriends, with her name at the top, as though she was keeping a tally of the significant ones.[59] His habit of relating his amorous encounters on the road was wearing thin, and after he ignored a request to stop writing to her about them, she snapped. "It's entirely your emotional problem," she wrote in October 1973. "Because don't you see, it's not physical after thirty-five years of liaisons, affairs and 'beautiful bonds' and sex? It's a disease which you alone will have to cure *yourself*, and act mature." Her love remained undiminished, but she added, "This is my *last request*. After this, it's simply hopeless."[60]

Her antennae must have been well calibrated, because it was during this period that Ravi met both the women who were to become the great loves of the latter part of his life. When he played Southern Methodist University in Dallas in March he met Sue Jones, a twenty-five-year-old concert producer who was working for Schutz and Haber on the Texan part of his tour. When Ravi met her again in November the relationship intensified. After Kamala realized that this one was more serious than the other "beautiful bonds," she was upset, but she remained devoted to Ravi.

The other woman was Sukanya Rajan. Ravi first met her in October 1972. She was a friend of his niece Vijji Shankar and had grown up in Madras immersed in Carnatic music and Bharatanatyam. Her grandmother was a first cousin of the dancer Rukmini Arundale, the greatest of Bharatanatyam's revivalists. Having recently moved to London, Sukanya was invited by Vijji to meet Ravi at his London house, and remembers vividly how awed she was by the "godlike figure" walking down the stairs.[61] At first, because of her connection through Vijji, she called him Uncle ("Kaku"). She was then asked to play tanpura for him at the Royal Albert Hall in late November 1973. With his typical attention to detail, he told her that it was important for a tanpura player to pluck the strings with fingertips rather than fingernails, and insisted on cutting her nails himself. "He only needed to cut two, but he cut all ten of my fingers," she says. "I used to tease him, 'You just wanted to hold my hand.'"[62] These encounters had a similar effect on Ravi. "I will never forget when I saw you first in Charles Street," he wrote to her years later. "You were like a ripe Alfonso mango—with such shining fragrance!"[63]

He was impressed by her ability to follow the 17-beat *tala* he played in the concert, and she became part of his circle of London friends. Shortly before, she had married Narendra Kotiyan, a forty-one-year-old Indian who had settled in London. It was a pragmatic match, affectionate but not close. Sukanya had her own income—she worked in a bank—and maintained an independent life, pursuing her interests in music and dance. She was by her own admission very innocent, and might have been content with this passionless life.[64] But over the next few years, whenever Ravi came to London she attended his concerts and accompanied him to films and restaurants, and she loved cooking for him or ironing his clothes. "Nothing ever happened, but I suppose subconsciously I must have loved him all along, because even then the day he would arrive in London would be the most important date in that year for me," she said.[65]

In Benares Kamala was overseeing the decoration and design of the new house and trying to get the electricity connected in time for Ravi's arrival. They were reunited in Sri Lanka, where he was performing, and in January 1974 they joined a big gathering in Calcutta to celebrate the wedding of Uday's son Ananda to Tanusree. It was the first time in almost twenty-seven years that all four Shankar brothers had been together.[66] Other guests included George Harrison, his manager Denis O'Brien and fellow musician Gary Wright, who then took the train up to Benares with Kumar Shankar for Ravi's house-warming ceremony. The home, named Hemangana after Ravi's mother, was inaugurated by eight south Indian Brahmins who blessed it with Vedic chants. Rajendra, Lakshmi, Debendra and Krishna also stayed, as did Deepak Choudhury, an upcoming sitar disciple of Ravi.[67]

At Hemangana there was time to make plans. Still haunted by the beauty of *Nava Rasa Ranga*, George proposed to Ravi that they reenact a version of it by bringing Indian musicians to Europe, sponsored by his new charitable foundation. They would go on to North America for a joint tour of arenas with George, taking Indian music out to the American heartlands. Ravi set about putting together a stellar ensemble: several of the previous year's line-up returned, including Lakshmi Shankar, Shivkumar Sharma, Hariprasad Chaurasia, L. Subramaniam and Alla Rakha, and they were augmented by the wonderful sarangi maestro Sultan Khan, Gopal Krishan on the vichitra veena and ten others. Shubho opted out. He had already given up playing publicly. He felt unable to emerge from the shadows cast by his family—especially his father, but also his mother, his uncle, his late grandfather and his cousins. He wanted to escape those expectations.

Ravi and Kamala spent that summer in London, staying in another house that George loaned them, at 39 Eaton Mews North in Belgravia. Ravi told Yehudi Menuhin that the city would be his headquarters for the next few years, supplanting California. The musicians came over early to record an album at Friar Park, George's home in Henley-on-Thames. Every morning George sent his Mercedes-Benz stretch limousine down to the Imperial Hotel in Henley to pick up the musicians. Simultaneously Ravi was traveling up by car from London, a journey of around an hour, during which he prepared that day's compositions. The album *Ravi Shankar's Music Festival from India* was recorded live in the drawing room, with George producing. At breaks there was sumptuous Indian food prepared by Ravi's chef Vasudevan Nair, and the music reflects a relaxed atmosphere of joy and creativity. The album opens with *Vandana*, a beguiling chant in praise of Ganesh, Saraswati and other auspicious entities. Ravi wrote in a range of styles: there are *dhamar*, *tarana* and *bhajan* songs, a rainy-season folk melody played on the shehnai by Anant Lal, and two longer works for the ensemble, one in *Raga Jait* and another, *Dehati*, inspired by Indian folk melodies and rhythms. The most unusual piece, *Naderdani*, is in a contemporary style with vocal harmonies reminiscent of the Swingle Singers and a rapid-fire instrumental finale.

In the middle of these sessions Ravi was invited to provide the score to the television film *Forbidden Image*. In this, the documentary-maker Jeremy Marre contrasts the tradition of erotic art in India and Nepal with its chaste counterparts in European art of the same era. He had filmed at Khajuraho, Konarak, Elephanta, Ajanta, Benares and Kathmandu. The subject held an obvious fascination for Ravi, if done tastefully, and his one condition was that the film must show no (live) nudity. With George's permission, he took eight members of the ensemble and they recorded the soundtrack in one afternoon at Denham Studios in Buckinghamshire, with Ravi composing live to the screened footage. "At one point when he seemed to have run out of inspiration, he disappeared into the toilet and returned with an idea," says Marre.[68] He was thrilled with Ravi's music, and it makes a fascinating codicil to the album. The program was broadcast in the UK in an edited form on ITV's *Aquarius* series in February 1976, with Peter Hall narrating.

In September Ravi led the Indian musicians on a short European tour, starting at the Royal Albert Hall, and traveling to Paris, Brussels, Frankfurt, Munich and Copenhagen. In these performances they came closest to fulfilling George's dream. Ravi conducted them in seventeen short items, including all the pieces they had just recorded at Friar Park. In the first half, as in *Nava Rasa Ranga*, the program worked its way through classical styles, with an emphasis on vocal music, while the second half had a more contemporary flavor, with percussion and folk influence to the fore. There were three items for the whole ensemble, leaving plenty of scope for solo improvisation. George had the Albert Hall show filmed, and, although the picture quality leaves something to be desired, it is an invaluable record of a historic event.

Kamala then returned to India, and a slightly reduced, fifteen-strong group flew to Los Angeles and began rehearsing at A&M Studios' soundstage with George and his rock band for the Dark Horse tour. In this they had just seven numbers, but that did not stop Ravi introducing two new compositions, *Anourag* ("Love"), which featured a four-minute sitar spot for himself, and *Zoom Zoom Zoom*, which was arranged for both Indian and Western groups, as were *I Am Missing You* and *Dispute and Violence*. Apart from *Anourag*, the other all-Indian pieces were *Vandana*, *Naderdani* and *Chatpaté*, a shortened and revised version of *Dehati* renamed after the spicy street snack. Shivkumar Sharma, who was a skeptic about Indian orchestral music, told Ravi that he was uncomfortable about playing it, but there was insufficient time for solo numbers.[69]

If the Indians found the American tour musically less fulfilling than the European performances, they were all overwhelmed by the lavish travel arrangements. George had chartered a Boeing 707, which had an "Om" symbol on its nose cone and was decked out inside like a maharaja's lounge. They usually flew at night, straight after a concert, Indian and Western musicians winding down together. Emil Richards recalls learning complex *tihais* from Alla Rakha mid-flight.[70] Champagne flowed and Indian vegetarian food was served on board by Vasudevan. Once they landed they were whisked off in limousines to five-star hotels.

Meanwhile, *anourag* was in the air. In Los Angeles George, whose marriage to Pattie had ended, met and fell in love with his future wife, Olivia Arias, who was working for his label and joined him on the tour. L. Subramaniam and Vijji Shankar, vocalist daughter of Lakshmi and Rajendra, also revealed they were in love. As for Ravi, he was accompanied by Sue Jones, who was acting as his secretary and helping to manage the Indian musicians, and their relationship had become close. Flouting instructions, Ravi wrote about her to Kamala. So too did Lakshmi, who described her as "a very nice intelligent girl…She does much more than the usual g.f. [girlfriend] for Robu."[71]

If the tour was exhilarating, it was also punishing. There were 47 shows in 49 days, often two houses a night. George, who disliked being a front man, was burdened by a perfect storm of divorce, overwork, Beatles legal disputes and the towering public expectations for the first American tour by an ex-Beatle. Something had to give, and it was his voice, which went hoarse before the tour even began. "It was a very rigorous tour and George was not in the best shape. In fact that's an understatement," says Olivia Harrison. "George felt tremendous responsibility. His relatively new manager really didn't know the man. If he had, he would never have booked that type of tour. I don't think people tour like that now."[72]

The opening night on November 2 in Vancouver was, according to Lakshmi, "a fiasco, soundwise & everything."[73] George's voice was one problem. Another was that his revue-style setlist was challenging to the masses of Beatles fans present. He played mostly solo material, with only four Beatles songs, and he opted to share the spotlight with the jazz-funk of Tom Scott and the exuberant soul of Billy Preston. The Indians too were integrated into the main show, at the insistence of their champion. "George wanted so badly for people to hear what he had heard," says Olivia, "and honestly he was going to make sure you listened to it whether you liked it or not."[74]

After Vancouver it was clear the running order was an issue. There were too many shifts of genre. The Indians came on twice and they met with hostility from some rock'n'roll fans. It was Ravi who proposed the restructuring. Thereafter the show opened with a tape of *Vandana*, and the six other Indian pieces (down from seven) were delivered consecutively through the second quarter of the show, finishing at the interval. "Now the show's slick," wrote Lakshmi.[75] Promoter Bill Graham still felt the audience "didn't get to go back in the time machine enough" and tried in vain to persuade George to play more old songs.[76] But George was adamant: he was no longer Beatle George. Certainly most of the audiences enjoyed themselves hugely, and Bob Dylan, Peter Sellers, David Bowie, John Lennon and Paul McCartney all attended concerts. Some of the press was very favorable—*Billboard* deemed the Oakland show "a well-executed, high-inducing musical experience" and said the Indian segment was "a genuine curiosity"—but many other critics were harsh, dubbing it the "Dark Hoarse" tour.[77]

"There were a lot of less than positive reviews," says Olivia Harrison. "George felt that people were coming to see an ex-Beatle and maybe not so much an Indian classical recital, even though it was bluesy and rocking and powerful. I think that really got to Ravi, having all those musicians out there, and him being responsible for them and their wellbeing—although they were all having a great time."[78] Ravi acknowledged the strain in a letter to Kamala. "This tour has done a great deal to me," he wrote. "For the first time I'm shocked to find (after many years!) all those depths of feelings I have. Such as anger, ego, jealousy—pettiness, being hurt."[79]

In Chicago on November 30, having played 26 shows in 29 days, Ravi had a more serious physical reaction. After the second house that night he was rushed to hospital with an irregular pulse and kept in intensive care for five days.[80] George, with a light touch, explained that "Ravi's heart, with these Indian time signatures, happens to beat in seven and a half beats or something."[81] Perhaps because he wanted to get back on stage, Ravi also played the episode down, deeming it a reaction to the ear-splitting volume of the stage speakers. It seems that he had actually suffered a minor heart attack; in later years he counted this as his first such episode. In his absence the tour had continued, with Lakshmi conducting the ensemble, while Sue Jones stayed back with him in Chicago. He rejoined the tour in Boston on the 10th.[82]

There was a memorable outing in Washington. Jack Ford, son of the new U.S. president Gerald Ford, had come backstage at Salt Lake City and invited them to visit the White House when the tour reached the capital. George, who insisted on calling it the Black and White House, commended its good vibrations four months after Nixon's departure. The entourage was shown around, and Billy Preston got to play "God Bless America" on the presidential Steinway, before at noon a lunch of cold ham, roast beef and cheese platters, potato salad, vegetable salad, fresh fruit and cookies was served in the family quarters. A handwritten White House memo notes against Ravi's name: "Not completely a vegetarian." The inner circle (George, his father Harry, Olivia, Ravi, Preston, Tom Scott and Denis O'Brien) then had a fifteen-minute audience with the president in the Oval Office, where the two leaders surreally exchanged gifts. George's offering to the president was a button bearing the "Om" symbol, which the *Washington Post* reported was Sanskrit for "the complete whole." Ford responded in kind with a button featuring the slogan "WIN," which was Republican for "Whip Inflation Now."[83]

The tour had been breathtaking in so many ways, with boldness as its keynote. "It was very ambitious, twenty years before its time," says Olivia Harrison.[84] It capped four remarkable years in the public alliance between Ravi and George. And it had nearly destroyed them both. Never again, they concluded—but their friendship was to endure.

19

PARALLEL LIVES

I was born with this loneliness and
it lives in my heart always.
RAVI SHANKAR[1]

"I've never experienced anything so Indian," said Satyajit Ray when he visited Hemangana in late 1977, while filming *Joi Baba Felunath* in Benares.[2] Ravi's new house had stone floors and high ceilings and was tastefully adorned with sculptures, prints and vibrant murals of Indian deities. The main part was two stories high, but its tiered terraces rose up to a third and fourth floor on the roadside facade. The huge mango *bageecha* had been adapted into a restful walled garden, with colorful flowerbeds and cool stone benches, space for music students or picnic parties to sit in the shade of the trees, and an open-air stage. There were colonnades and arches, and the roof terraces were edged with carved stone *jali* screens.

Hemangana was conceived as a *gurukul*, a home with space for disciples in residence. Ravi had moved on from teaching beginners, and here the only students were highly talented, mostly Ravi's own disciples. As ever, he charged no fees for them, and provided board and lodging in the house's student quarters. "I want to work on fewer people, maybe only three, four, five and give more time like in the old system," he said. "If I can, by God's grace, leave behind a couple of fine musicians that would do more than having a hundred half-baked."[3]

Once a year Ravi would gather a larger group of up to two dozen disciples and instruct them en masse. As a teacher he was very serious, often stern, and by all accounts inspirational. He would give masterclasses of perhaps three hours in the morning, and another two in the afternoon after his siesta. At dinner the mood would lighten and afterward there would be parlor games. Ravi particularly loved charades, although Kamala said people could never work out what he was trying to convey.[4] Sometimes there would be another teaching session before bed.

He set up a new foundation based at the house, the Research Institute for Music and Performing Arts, or RIMPA for short, its purpose to provide opportunities for younger performers. As his secretary he appointed his Banarasi friend A. N. Dubey, whose family ran the Mishrambu soft drinks business. Dubey had coordinated all the building work at Hemangana, and he now managed the house and organized the workshops. From 1979 onward, he ran the annual festival that Ravi instituted in the city. "I completely gave him carte blanche," said Ravi.[5] Dubey also became the main coordinator of Ravi's diary and concerts in India, taking over from Rajendra, who had had this responsibility since 1968.

In the wake of his heart scare in Chicago, Ravi hoped that this new environment would remove some of the pressure. "When I have time to myself in Benares, I like to be as lazy as possible," he said, rather wishfully.

> I get up as early as I can, but I relax more. Even if I try, I cannot sleep more than to seven or seven-thirty. The first thing I do is to take my bath and do my meditation before taking breakfast. And then I have my students come to me, and I teach, and I practice for a couple of hours, and read as much as is possible—classical literature or light novels. And I like to see good films.[6]

The reality was often different in the early years at Hemangana, as is explained by Kartik Seshadri, a child prodigy on the sitar who became Ravi's disciple in 1974, beginning a lifelong connection. "I was led to expect a very traditional set-up in Varanasi, but the reality was quite different," says Seshadri. He was seventeen and had never before encountered a celebrity-focused world. "I was shocked by the discrepancy between the ideology and the reality. He himself lived a very worldly life but wanted his disciples to live in an austere way (one almost of the mythological times)." Ravi was by all accounts—including Seshadri's—a loving *guru*, but it was as though he felt his disciples needed to go through the same experience as he had in Maihar, an ascetic lifestyle of "music and nothing but music." And yet, as Seshadri continues,

> There was a constant flux of a press corps, PR, TV and camera crews, visits by ministers and other social elites. This was also a time when he was juggling multiple affairs in his personal life. I had read his book *My Music, My Life* and had idealized the *guru–shishya* relationship. The reality was jarring and confusing for me as a kid.[7]

Ravi was certainly famous in Benares. When he stayed at Clark's Hotel in town, during the construction of Hemangana, it displayed a large banner over its entrance with the greeting, "Welcome, Pandit Ravi Shankar."[8] Local instrument-makers all swore that they had built Ravi's latest sitar, although none of them had.[9]

In a 1977 interview Ravi said he would soon be spending seven or eight months of the year in India and touring in the West for only three or four months.[10] Yet in practice he rarely stayed in Benares for more than a month each year. According to Kamala, "If he comes to a place and stays even for a week he gets fidgety and says, '*Chalo*, let us go to Bangalore.' And at Bangalore after a few days he'd say, 'Come, we're off to Calcutta.'"[11] One thing that frustrated him at Hemangana was getting a telephone line. Calling there from America was "harder than talking to someone on the Moon!" he told her.[12] Even though he had dreamed of a bucolic music ashram, when it came to it he disliked the feeling of being cut off. "He would want to buy *Time* magazine the moment it came to the market, but it was possible only two days later," said Kamala. "He would keep a person posted in the airport, and the moment that *Time* arrived he would bring it to him."[13]

Another complication, which he did not publicly voice, was that at this point he was legally non-resident in India, which restricted him to spending 59 days in the country per financial year, or 89 days from 1977, when the limit was increased. Hemangana was expensive to run, and most of his income came from abroad. "I want to curtail hyperactivity in my life," he said on his sixtieth birthday, "but I cannot stop it all of a sudden. It is a vicious circle and I do not know when I will be able to free myself."[14]

After the Dark Horse tour, Ravi began 1975 with two months in India. He had canceled his concerts because of his heart scare, but only part of his time was spent at Hemangana. There was a memorable first visit to the Kamakoti Shankaracharya of Kanchi, head of an ancient Hindu monastic order in Tamil Nadu. Ravi played the sitar for him, and felt as though time was standing still. "His eyes exuded such love. Seeing him was like taking a cold bath in an extremely hot weather," he said.[15] But otherwise the return home seemed to stoke up his melancholy. "I've a strange feeling after visiting India this time—a very sad, lonely and 'ghabraot' [agitated] feeling," he wrote to Kamala in March from Tokyo, where he was making his fifth tour of Japan. He mentioned several causes of his ennui, including discussions he'd had with her, Tat Baba's death and concerns about his own heart, liver and digestive system. It came to a head with "the madhouse Calcutta... It was all too much—I'm having delayed reactions! But mostly missing you! Remember that I love you whatever happens."[16]

At least he had not lost his gallows humor. In Los Angeles, he had a car accident when he drove into a parked van while momentarily distracted. His nose hit the steering wheel and started bleeding profusely. It was broken in three places and needed surgery to set it. "This has taught me to keep my nose out of trouble," he wrote to Kamala on a postcard of a rhinoceros. "This picture is to suggest the state of affairs of my nose."[17]

What was happening in this period was not so much the shift back to India that Ravi's interviews repeatedly heralded. Rather, as illustrated by his 1975 schedule, he was gradually establishing

parallel lives. In America there was Sue Jones, now a regular partner, and spring 1975 was spent with her. She met him in Los Angeles
before his American tour. New York, where she was now living and
working for Gary Haber, was assuming greater importance in Ravi's
American life, and with her assistance he began a music circle there
too, although it proved to be a tougher market than southern California. Meanwhile, he had become unhappy with George Schutz as
his agent. Schutz was mining the new crossover market between classical and pop music with his other acts, such as Claude Bolling and
Jean-Pierre Rampal, who had just had a massive hit with their *Suite
for Flute and Jazz Piano Trio*, and Collin Walcott's group Oregon,
with its Indian-infused chamber jazz.[18] What Ravi wanted instead
was a leading classical impresario. So he embarked on a career reset
in America, disappearing from the regular concert circuit for the
next two seasons, during which he performed only the concerto and
occasional special recitals. The most spectacular of these was his all-
night concert in August 1976 at New York's Cathedral of St. John the
Divine, organized by the new music circle. Determined to reclaim
his reputation as a classical virtuoso, he then relaunched his career
with Herbert Barrett Management.

In his other existence there was Kamala. She joined him in London in June 1975, when he put his American life on the back-burner
and decamped to Eaton Mews for the summer. His life with her was
focused mostly on India, where Rajendra or Dubey coordinated his
concert bookings with music circles, festivals and promoters around
the country. Important new figures there were Robin Paul in Calcutta,
who arranged one of Ravi's favorite ever concerts, at Marble Palace
in February 1976, and Mohan Hemmadi in Hyderabad. Kamala also
traveled abroad sometimes if the trip was not too grueling. Kamala
and Sue had become the two main focal points of his life, and bal-
ancing them to everyone's satisfaction (even if he had had lots of
practice at it) was going to be an increasing source of tension—and
hypertension.

In career terms there was a third axis in London, from where Basil Douglas ran Ravi's bookings all over Europe. And there were other women. He had a deep, loving relationship with Mireille Ballero in France for over ten years. Despite his other lovers, she never felt jealous and found him to be very loyal. He was full of love and always searching for more, she says.[19]

In 1977 the Calcutta journalist Sankarlal Bhattacharjee persuaded him to open up about his love life in a way that was unusual for an Indian public figure. When asked if he suffered from loneliness, Ravi replied,

> You have touched my nerve center. I was born with this loneliness and it lives in my heart always. I have received so much love, but my loneliness has not disappeared...Somehow I got it by inheritance, and I'm carrying it all the time in my life. But I can't tolerate it any more. That's why I build close relationships with people—to avoid loneliness.

He added—and one can imagine the accompanying glint in his eye— "Of course it has its advantages too," before continuing, more reflectively, "That's why I move on from women, but it's my addiction to be attracted to people. What's the reason for it? Because I didn't have any other addictions. No alcohol, no cigarettes, no gambling, no *bhang*."[20]

He liked to talk about the exquisite, melancholic yearning for something or someone out of reach. This was the feeling he craved most in music, as well as love. The Portuguese have a word for it, *saudade*, which the seventeenth-century writer Francisco Manuel de Melo defined as "a pleasure you suffer, an ailment you enjoy." But deep attachment to lovers, Ravi had concluded, ultimately exacerbated his unbearable loneliness. It was not that he had decided to become a renunciate monk. The answer, he told himself, was to avoid becoming too dependent on one lover. For companionship he relied heavily on his male friends, as well as some women with whom he had no physical relationship. Of the men, he named Biman Ghosh in Calcutta and

Prodyot Sen in London as his great confidants, and mentioned his sadness at the death the previous year of his cousin Jogu Chatterjee.

The feeling of yearning permeates *Twilight Mood*, which Ravi recorded at Capitol's Hollywood studios in April 1976, in a duet with Yehudi Menuhin. It is based on *Puriya Dhanashri*, a *raga* associated with dusk, and is one of four new pieces that make up the third volume of *West Meets East*, Ravi's major release of this period. He had now played several live duets with Yehudi, including recitals at Yehudi's Gstaad Festival in 1973 and 1975, and his admiration for his friend had continued to grow. "He is like a *rishi* (sage) in his heart. In fact he is much more Indian than most of us are," said Ravi.[21] At Gstaad in 1973, the pair had played two new pieces that Ravi had written, one of them in *Puriya Dhanashri* and the other in Ravi's own *raga Nat Bhairav*. As the original manuscripts at the Royal Academy of Music show, these were the first outings for, respectively, *Twilight Mood* and *Tenderness*, the duo's two collaborations that make up side 1.[22] Although Yehudi still uses harmonics and *pizzicato* on these recordings, his playing is more Indian in feel, and on *Tenderness* he copes impressively with some intricate cross-rhythms within the 7-beat *rupaktal* cycle. Indeed, the whole album is a more consistently satisfying meeting of musical cultures than its two better-known predecessors, in which the duets were bolstered by solo pieces in the separate traditions.

Side 2 was recorded in Paris in August with Jean-Pierre Rampal, the French flutist who was now such a crossover star. *Enchanted Dawn*, a duet between the heavenly pairing of flute and harp, based on *Raga Mian Ki Todi*, is a rare example of Ravi writing for Western instruments alone. The harp is played by Martine Géliot and effectively takes the role of tabla and tanpura combined, while Rampal's flute takes the lead. The last track on the album is the best known. *Morning Love*, a duet for flute and sitar, is a superb foray into light-classical territory that *Billboard* judged "one of the most striking musical unions ever conceived."[23]

*

In 1976 the Indian government founded its first national television network, Doordarshan. Television had been introduced in India in 1959 as part of All India Radio's services, but at first it was restricted to the Delhi area and broadcast for only one hour per day, mostly showing public information films. Gradually coverage, broadcast time and programming range improved until there were eight regional stations reaching 45 million people, and the government decided to unify them into a national network, under the aegis of the Ministry of Information and Broadcasting. Until then, both radio and television networks had used the same signature tune, but Ravi now recorded a new one for the founding of Doordarshan. This haunting instrumental theme, an arrangement of the first two lines of Ravi's own melody to "Sare Jahan Se Accha," was played on the shehnai by Ali Ahmed Hussain Khan. At 60 seconds long, it is a miniature masterpiece, the restrained setting giving a sense of space that allows the shehnai to work its evocative magic.

The usual story is that Prime Minister Indira Gandhi asked Ravi to compose it. This may be the case—he seems to have visited Delhi specially to meet her in February 1976—but that his theme was not guaranteed to be accepted is clear from a letter to Ravi from his brother Rajendra, written just the day before Doordarshan began services on April 1. "Congratulations!" he wrote. "Against expectations, the 'sare-jahan-se-achhhha' [*sic*] has been selected for TV and will be played from tomorrow."[24] For years thereafter Ravi's theme accompanied the famous swirling Doordarshan logo as transmission began and finished each day. It retains a special resonance for the first generation of national television viewers in the late 1970s and 1980s, when there were no other channels.

Doordarshan was launched in the middle of the Emergency, the controversial two-year period when Indira Gandhi suspended the constitution in favor of direct rule, and the new state broadcaster, despite its notional autonomy, was at first seen as the mouthpiece of an undemocratic government. Ravi always distanced himself from party politics. "That is one thing to keep away from. I think it is so dirty. And what is today changes tomorrow. So how could I be involved with any party or person?" he said in 1977. "The way I traveled—today America, tomorrow a Communist country or a dictatorship—I see all sides of it and that has cleansed me of any interest in politics."[25] Nevertheless, he was certainly a favorite of Indira, as he had been of her father. After she returned to office in 1980, following three post-Emergency years in opposition, he was bestowed with India's second-highest civilian honor, the Padma Vibhushan, in the next Republic Day awards. He approved of her support for cultural liberalism, and even seemed to have some influence over her. In 1981 he appeared at the Gunidas Sangeet Sammelan, a classical music festival in Bombay founded by the vocalist C. R. Vyas. Vasant Sathé, Indira's minister for information and broadcasting, was guest of honor, and when he came backstage he had a request for Ravi: "Panditji, please come and bless us in our Doordarshan studios." Ravi replied, "I will definitely come, but please try to get color in your studios." Indian television was still broadcast in black and white. "Panditji," said Sathé, "please lift the phone and tell Madam. Once you tell Madam things will happen!"[26] Whether he did call her is not known, but Doordarshan began color transmission in 1982.

One aspect of Ravi's career that was in its twilight was film music. Abroad he was now less sought after by filmmakers, and was focusing more on live performances and selected studio recordings. In India he had not worked on a feature film since 1966, although he had turned down offers for lack of time. Now that he was theoretically based in Benares, Ravi announced that he hoped to do more film work, and a choice project arose in late 1976. *Meera* is a biopic of Meera Bai (or Mirabai), the medieval Rajput queen who became a great poet-saint of the *bhakti* tradition, defying conservative conventions and embracing the lower castes as she pursued her ecstatic religious devotions. Today there exist hundreds of songs in praise of Krishna that she is said to have composed. The 1945 film about her that had made a star of M. S. Subbulakshmi had also enshrined Mirabai as a national icon. Ravi threw himself into this new version, no doubt relishing the subject matter. It was made in Hindi for what was now known as Bollywood, and the director was Gulzar, himself a noted poet and lyricist.

As is common in Bollywood, the recording was done in two stages. The songs were taped before the film was shot, so that its song sequences could be synchronized to the soundtrack. Later, after filming was completed (there were long delays), Ravi added the background music. The song sessions began at Mehboob Studios in Bombay at the end of November, and lasted two weeks. Ravi wrote new arrangements for nine of Mirabai's *bhajans*. His first-choice vocalist, Lata Mangeshkar, was unavailable, so he engaged Vani Jairam, who was making a name in both Hindi and south Indian cinema. Vijay Raghav Rao assisted and the soloists included Shivkumar Sharma. Among the observers was George Harrison, who had been to Puttaparthi with Ravi a week earlier, and was staying on in Bombay for Vijji Shankar's wedding to L. Subramaniam. Another guest was Ashwini Bhide Deshpande, today a leading vocalist, but then just a schoolgirl, watching her mother Manik Bhide and aunt Sarala Bhide record backing vocals.[27]

On screen Mirabai was played by Hema Malini with the cool composure of the righteous, while Vinod Khanna portrayed the husband she rejects in favor of Krishna. The film took a while to find its audience, but the music was much loved. Its lead song, *Mere to Giridhar Gopal*, won Jairam her first Filmfare award for best female playback singer. As it transpired, *Meera* was the last film score Ravi recorded in India, and he went out in some style.

The work on *Meera* undermined Ravi's plan to spend more time resting at Hemangana on this trip.[28] He managed barely ten days there in total, split into two visits. At least he had squeezed in an eight-day break in Bali in October (in the midst of touring Indonesia and Singapore), a sign that he was trying to take care of his health. He had also lost some weight, cutting down on sugar and switching to artificial sweeteners, which he asked Harihar Rao to bring in bulk from California.[29] On arrival in Calcutta he took a day off to revisit places about which he felt sentimental. He told Sankarlal Bhattacharjee, whom he invited along with him, that he wanted to see them because he might not have much longer to live.[30]

Uday's situation was encouraging this morbid mood. After his heart attack and stroke in 1968, Uday had produced only one more stage production, *Shankarscope* in 1970. He fell out with his family and moved into a tenth-floor flat in Ballygunge Place, Calcutta, where he lived alone, cared for by his faithful servant Menon. He was unhappy, artistically frustrated, short of money and in declining health. "He was a shadow of the person I knew when I was young," said Ravi, who used to see him whenever he was in the city.[31] As gifts he brought large bottles of 4711, Uday's favorite German eau de cologne, and he helped out with medical expenses. But on his March 1975 visit he had been "completely shaken & unnerved" by Uday's condition.[32] Together with Kalpana Sen and his nephew Bhudeb Shankar, he then set up the Shankar Foundation for Creative Arts, the initial priority of which was to make Uday's remaining years comfortable. He persuaded Yehudi to become a patron, and on December 18, 1976 he played a benefit for a crowd of 14,000 at Calcutta's Netaji Stadium. Indira Gandhi sent a supportive message.

But Uday continued to deteriorate. In September 1977 he was taken into the intensive cardiac unit at Calcutta Hospital, and he died on the 26th. Ravi was in London with Kamala. "The news came at about five o'clock in the morning that he had passed away," said Kamala. "I took the message, so I had to wake him up. Because they wanted him on BBC and Calcutta TV. So I said, 'Raviji, bad news.' He said, 'Dada?'"

Zohra Segal, who was also in London, arrived shortly afterward. "I wanted to come and see you and Robu just now," she said. "I am crying so much. I want to be with people who know who he was."[33]

About three days before, realizing the end was approaching, Uday had asked to see Amala, Ananda, Mamata and Ravi. According to Mamata, every day her father would say, "Where's Robu? Call him. I have so many things to tell him." Later Mamata tearfully told Ravi she felt hurt that he had not come. "You have to understand that I couldn't come," he replied. "It was not that I didn't want to come, it was that I just couldn't."[34]

Ravi's rationale was that he had a concert to play and he had a responsibility to his audience to be there if he could. It was a lesson he had learned originally from Uday himself. Later, when Anoushka Shankar was growing up, Ravi talked about this episode as an example of what it meant to be a performing artist—that on the night his brother died, he still played his concert.[35] This was the measure of his professionalism, but it could at times be taken to unhealthy extremes.

Sankarlal Bhattacharjee is a midnight's child, born on the day of India's independence. Ravi liked the man, he admired his music columns for the esteemed Bengali literary journal *Desh*, and he particularly enjoyed his article in the *Hindusthan Standard* about their day exploring Calcutta. As 1977 dawned he agreed to expand the project into *Raag-Anuraag*, a volume of reminiscences in Bengali. Bhattacharjee would interview Ravi on tape and the Ananda Bazar publishing house would release the transcripts as a book. "I'm leaving the day after tomorrow for Madras and then Delhi," Ravi told him. "Can you accompany me?"[36] He could, but a few days' work in transit around India proved insufficient, so Ravi asked him to come to London in July. He stayed till November.

"He was a typical Bengali," said Kamala. "Everything was all right, never get up on time, never be ready on time. So I used to tell him, 'Sankar, I will wake you up at seven.' I knew he would be ready at nine. If there was anything that Raviji hated it was not being on time."[37] Bhattacharjee himself recounted how he frequently arrived an hour late, to find his subject looking at his watch. "I'm fed up with you," Ravi would say, but he couldn't help adding, in Bengali, "*Tomar shaath khun maaf.*" ("You could commit seven murders and still be forgiven.")[38]

They worked well together. Ravi loved telling stories and his memory was phenomenal. Here in London, as they walked on Kensington High Street or relaxed in his apartment in Chelsea Cloisters on Sloane Avenue, he spoke more freely. Also with them in London for some of this time was the Calcutta photographer Aloke Mitra, who much later published a collection of photographs that concentrates on this year.[39] Work on *Raag-Anuraag* continued during further sessions in India: on a *bajra* boat on the Ganges at Benares, beside the pool at Bombay's Centaur Hotel, or by candlelight during power cuts in Calcutta.

There was much laughter along the way. At the Windamere Hotel in Darjeeling, where they completed their work, Ravi would break for a massage every afternoon. One day, when Ravi was face down, having his back rubbed, the masseur spotted his sitar in the corner of the room.

"Oh, do you play the sitar, sir?" he asked.

"A little."

"You should play more! There is a man called Ravi Shankar. Have you heard of him?"

"Mmmm."

"He goes round the world and earns pots and pots of money, just by playing the sitar," the masseur blundered on. "Keep on doing it!"

"OK, I will practice."

Eventually Kamala told the masseur to look at his client's face. He jerked upright, begging forgiveness, as Ravi fell about laughing.[40]

The candor of the finished book, on matters of love and music, was unprecedented for an Indian musician. Ravi not only acknowledged his relationship with Kamala, which was an open secret in Calcutta; he also revealed his parallel life with Sue Jones. Described by *India Today* as "a musical-erotic autobiography," *Raag-Anuraag* stirred up disquiet among the more conservative readers of *Desh*, where it was serialized over a remarkable thirty-one weeks in 1978.[41] "The magazine sold like hot cakes in Calcutta," said Kamala.[42] In 1980 it appeared in book form, with some minor amendments. In his foreword, Ravi acknowledged the controversy, but said, "I don't have regrets. I am not after all a god. Those who used to think that I was godlike now know that I am a man of flesh and blood; if they still love me, I shall feel satisfied."[43] He said he did not want to be a hypocrite. He did not want people to place him on a moral pedestal.

Ravi no longer had the Eaton Mews house in London. With typical generosity, George Harrison had offered to give it to him outright. Separately, however, George's manager Denis O'Brien had been implying that Ravi was taking advantage of George financially, and Ravi took offense. "Denis was very resentful of anyone that George helped. I know he was trying to look after George in some sense," says Olivia Harrison. "But Ravi was a main target of his resentment really."[44] Ravi gently declined the gift and returned the house in 1975, which probably put paid to his idea that London might serve as his global headquarters. He still spent extended periods of time in the city over the next couple of years, but in rented flats at Chelsea Cloisters or Dolphin Square. After that he saw a little less of London and of George over the next few years as their paths diverged, but the friendship was still precious to both of them, and when George and Olivia's son Dhani was born in 1978 Ravi stopped at Friar Park during his autumn tour. The new arrival was named after the sixth and seventh notes of the Indian scale, *dha* and *ni*, and Ravi improvised a song based around the two notes, which they recorded privately with Alla Rakha on tabla and George on guitar.

The three months at Chelsea Cloisters in the summer of 1977 had helped Ravi to unwind, but the benefits were lost as he grieved for Uday. An arduous schedule the following winter increased the pressure on him. In October he flew to New York to be with Sue. In

November he began a seven-week tour of India and Sri Lanka. January 1978 brought three weeks in Europe, where he was joined by Sue, before he resumed his Indian concert itinerary for six weeks, squeezing in Mamata's wedding in Calcutta. March found him back in London for another three weeks, before he returned to India yet again, arriving in Delhi late on April 1. "I'm in a shattered condition healthwise & mentally," he wrote to Kamala in January. "I need lots and lots of rest & peace. But when & where that's the question!"[45] And again in March, he was "exhausted, mentally, physically, emotionally I've been going through a torture," although he tried to reassure her he was all right.[46]

He had overdone things this time. On April 2 he played for 4½ hours at Lal Kothi, the grand family home of the Bharat-Rams on Sardar Patel Marg, in front of an audience of ambassadors and ministers. The next day he was taken ill with chest pain and high blood pressure. He spent ten days at the Sir Ganga Ram Hospital nursing home and was diagnosed with coronary ischaemia (a constricted supply of blood to the heart), caused by heart disease. An electrocardiogram in Calcutta confirmed the condition. He also reported some numbness in one of his fingers around this time.[47] "It was the stress, all the traveling & jet lag exhaustion plus the prog was like the last straw!" he wrote to Harihar.[48] Ravi's concert itinerary for April was canceled and on doctor's orders he spent four weeks at Hemangana, relaxing, reading and listening to music. There he saw the best heart specialist in Benares, who warned him that he was at risk of a heart attack, advised him to build in longer rest periods after his concerts and his trips, and said that he might be a candidate for a coronary bypass graft. It was the first time that Ravi had heard of this procedure, which had been developed in the late 1960s and was available in India only in Bombay and Vellore, but was becoming quite common in America.

He had recovered sufficiently by mid-May to fly to Japan, where he recorded an album with Alla Rakha and two Japanese instrumentalists. One was Hozan Yamamoto, a master of the shakuhachi, the end-blown bass flute, which Ravi felt had an even richer sound than the Indian bamboo flute. The other was Susumu Miyashita on the koto, the 13-string zither that is Japan's national instrument, which had gained some popularity in the West during the 1960s, when Richard Bock had released five albums by Kimio Eto. On his many visits to Japan Ravi had noticed how Japanese music uses modal structures, as well as the similarities between its scales and certain pentatonic *ragas*, which encouraged him to explore a crossover project. He named the album *East Greets East*, a nod to his series with Yehudi.

The previous decade had seen the tentative emergence of what is today commonly labeled fusion music—the interplay between artists of different world traditions in order to create new combined forms. Ravi was not exactly the instigator of this trend, given how he liked to collaborate on his own musical turf, but he was an obvious precursor for it. The most common early pairing was Indian classical musicians with Western jazz players, as seen in the improvisations between Ali Akbar Khan, John Handy and Zakir Hussain on *Karuna Supreme*, and between L. Shankar, Zakir Hussain, Vikku Vinayakram and John McLaughlin on the Shakti albums. McLaughlin, a scintillating jazz guitarist who had made several albums with Miles Davis, became an informal student of Ravi, who took him under his wing, as he often did with bright talents. From about 1975 onward Ravi regularly invited McLaughlin over when he was in New York, and one day decided to teach him south Indian music theory. "I cannot overestimate the impact he had on me as an individual and as a musician," says McLaughlin.[49]

East Greets East mostly follows the *West Meets East* formula of Ravi composing the material in Indian *ragas*, regardless of the instrumental combinations. There is a koto solo, *Padhasapa*, which Ravi based on *Raga Durga*; a piece for shakuhachi and tabla in *Shivaranjani*; a sitar solo in *Kaushik Dhwani*; and a tabla solo. But one track stands out. In *Rokudan* the koto, shakuhachi and sitar take turns playing improvised solos based on a seventeenth-century Japanese melody, making this an unusual example of Ravi playing sitar on foreign musical territory, thus a kind of fusion. Ravi was particularly satisfied with this album, which was released by Deutsche Grammophon (Polydor in India), following the end of his long-running deal with EMI. Over the next three years the German-based multinational issued three more LPs of new classical recordings by him featuring *ragas Hameer* and *Gara* (1979) and *Jogeshwari* (1980), and then a double tribute album in 1981 that featured *Hemant*, under the title *Homage to Baba Allauddin*, and his first recording of *Mohankauns*, titled *Homage to Mahatma Gandhi*.

Ravi again leaned toward fusion with *Jazzmine*, his own Indo-jazz venture. It was performed live at Bombay's open-air Rang Bhavan on the closing night of Jazz Yatra, a week-long international festival in February 1980. He assembled and conducted five jazz musicians, a nineteen-piece Indian orchestra and a remarkable quartet of vocalists, including future playback star Hariharan, Ashit Desai, who would be a key collaborator over the next decade, Sarala Bhide and her niece, nineteen-year-old Ashwini Bhide. The jazz section comprised the American saxophonists John Handy and George Adams, bassist Mike Richmond, Bombay's own pioneering jazz keyboardist Louis Banks and a young Ranjit Barot on drumkit. The five-part suite began with invocational chants in *Hamsadhwani* and progressed through light-classical and folk-based ensemble pieces, the jazz quotient rising as it went on. In the extended finale the jazz soloists improvised freely around a theme written by Ravi in *Jog*, a pentatonic *raga* with a blues feel. The beat swung and by the end this music had left Indian soil and was halfway to Dixieland. *Jazzmine* was recorded (rather amateurishly) and released on Polydor only in India. There was soon a sequel: the middle piece in the suite was a rhythm ensemble with north and south Indian percussionists, always a favorite lineup of Ravi's, and the following year he revisited the format with a full *Tala Vadya Kacheri* concert at the same venue.

It would be an exaggeration to say that Ravi had found a stable equilibrium between his parallel lives. Both Kamala and Sue had accepted the arrangement, but it could be emotionally very hard for each of them. As for Ravi, he tended to nurture feelings of guilt and to avoid conflict, and by now the strain was telling on him physically, too.

In 1978 two events conspired to upset the uneasy balance. With each visit to London Ravi had become closer to Sukanya Rajan. In October 1975 she had played the tanpura for him on the BBC TV program *New Life*, filmed at the Pebble Mill studios in Birmingham. Being with her that day was "a delicious torture" for him, he later told her.[50] Eventually he could no longer resist his feelings: in March 1978, during a concert at Greenwich Town Hall, he played *Yaman Kalyan*, her favorite *raga*, and stared at her in the audience. So began their affair. "That was it for me! If I had had my way I would have left my husband right then, because for me it was absolutely clear that I was in love for the first time," said Sukanya. "I had an insatiable and burning passion for her and could never have enough of her," said Ravi. "We were so much in love with each other."[51] But for now she was another parallel life.

Then in June, after the *East Greets East* sessions in Tokyo, Ravi spent a couple of weeks with Sue Jones in Los Angeles, and she became pregnant. When he returned to India in August for the long-postponed background music session for *Meera*, he was unable to find the right moment to tell Kamala in person, probably because of his perennial fear of confrontation. So he broke the news in a letter from London in late September at the start of his European tour. When Kamala received it in Madras she was deeply hurt, and she debated whether to end the relationship. It was not until Ravi reached India at the end of December that they talked it through and found a modus vivendi for a while longer. On March 30, 1979 Sue gave birth in New York to a girl, named Geetali Norah Jones Shankar—who shared a birthday with Shubho. Ravi heard by telegram in India. "I was so happy when she arrived," he later wrote.[52] Soon he visited them, and there is a photograph dated April 22 of Norah, or Geetu as he called her, in her cradle, while Ravi plays the sitar.[53]

In London the relationship with Sukanya intensified too. "I wanted his child," she said. "I knew I would never find a love like that again in my life."[54] In October 1980, during the Durga Puja (Dussehra) holidays, she became pregnant. It was a deliberate choice to have his baby. Ravi made it clear that he could not be involved as a parent, but he was happy with her decision, and his second daughter, Anoushka, was born on June 9, 1981. There was never any doubt about paternity, but Narendra acted in public as though she was his child, while never discussing the subject with Sukanya. "Men act conveniently deaf when they don't want to hear something," she once observed.[55] Ravi first visited Anoushka three months later, and gave her the middle name Hemangini, after his mother. On that visit he performed at Southwark Cathedral on Sukanya's birthday. Once again, he played *Yaman Kalyan* for her.

By this time Kamala had finally ended their twenty-four-year relationship. The immediate cause was Ravi welcoming Sue and Norah to India in January 1981, which crossed a boundary that Kamala had set. The parallel lives had converged, and for Kamala it was more than she could bear. In truth, this was just the last straw. In recent years she had several times considered leaving him. "I know how difficult & complicated life is…for anyone who loves me," he had written to her in July 1976. "But then you have been so brave all these years & weathered it so far & given me so much & spoiled me so utterly that I pray to God that you don't back out now—& that I can give you at least a little happiness in return."[56] Sankarlal Bhattacharjee paints a rather telling tableau of the pair in London in 1977, when they watched Ingmar Bergman's gripping miniseries *Scenes from a Marriage*, a bracing examination of modern matrimony that was supposed to have caused a surge in Swedish divorce rates. After each episode Kamala would leave the room in tears, while Ravi would sit in silence, the subject matter uncomfortably close to home.[57] The same year, Kamala sold her Bombay apartment. Although Hemangana remained her principal home, while Ravi was away she started spending some time in Madras with Lakshmi and

Rajendra, who had relocated there—a return to her Tamil roots possibly giving her more psychological distance.

For both parties the split was accompanied by anger. Each wrote letters to Dubey or Prodyot Sen complaining about the other being unresponsive, and they did not speak for nearly two years. For a while Ravi was in a dark place. For all that the relationship had always been on his terms, he was very dependent on Kamala, perhaps more than he realized but not quite as much as she thought. In March 1981 he wrote to Dubey, "I have not requipped [*sic*] yet from the mental agony & the physical effects yet. But time heals everything. This was indeed a tremendous crisis."[58]

It was a sad irony that Ravi—who had stated that he would have married Kamala long ago if he had been free to—now learned from Annapurna that she was at last consenting to a divorce. Robin Paul set up their first meeting for a decade. Annapurna invited Ravi to Bombay for lunch, which passed amicably. After some time she wrote to ask for a quiet divorce, and they met again a few days later to agree it. Paul took a photograph of the two together at Akash Ganga on November 14, 1980, at what was probably the second of these meetings, the last time they ever met. On that occasion Ravi asked if she had found a new partner. "No! Men are all the same," she replied.[59] But after the divorce went through, in 1982, her sitar student Rooshikumar Pandya, whom Ravi knew from *Song of God* in 1968, proposed to her. He had become a specialist in therapeutic hypnosis and counseling, and went on to be a motivational trainer and management *guru* in India. They married in December 1982. Despite everything that had passed, there was a part of Ravi that was unsettled by the news, as Sukanya could see at the time. "I think he truly loved her," she says.[60] Nevertheless, he was happy for them. "He was one of the first persons to congratulate me," said Pandya.[61] "I thought now she would be at peace," said Ravi. "For some time she was."[62]

Ravi was fifty-eight when Norah was born, and sixty-one when Anoushka arrived. The obvious question is, why did he deliberately have two children at this stage in his life, and by different mothers on different continents? There is no single reason. The decision might have been sparked by the arrival of his first grandchild in 1975, Shubho and Linda's son Somnath, known as Som. Ravi, who gave him his name, was overjoyed and told Kamala that when he took Som in his hands, "I felt very awkward as I am out of practice for so long (since Shubho) holding a baby!"[63] He also named his granddaughter, Som's sister Kaveri, who was born in September 1979; she was given the middle name of Sue. His acute sense of his own mortality was a possible spur too, the creation of new life serving as an instinctive response to a fear of death. He had barely recuperated from his 1978 heart scare when Sue became pregnant. Moreover, having a baby was the ultimate satisfaction for a man, he told Sukanya, adding that all three of his brothers had daughters, and he had long hoped for one too.[64] Kamala would not have contemplated having his child unless he had married her. That possibility had gone; Kamala turned fifty in 1978. So one factor was that two women had come along, both of whom he loved deeply, and who both wanted his child. Ultimately, however unusual the decisions Ravi took, there is much cause to be grateful for the results, in the form of his two extraordinarily creative daughters. Ravi would undoubtedly have applied to both Sue and Sukanya the term that Allauddin Khan had used to describe Ravi's own mother, on that most emotional day of his childhood: *ratnagarbha*, one who creates a jewel.

By 1981 a new geometry had formed in which Ravi was again living parallel lives. He spent more time with Norah as a young child than with Anoushka, but he acknowledged neither of them publicly, and most of the time he was elsewhere, still restless as a nomad. Although he loved being with them, it was as if he could not help but play out his own father's absentee approach to parenting. This new arrangement was one that, unsurprisingly, never found an equilibrium.

20

HEART STRAIN

There is yet so much to do.

RAVI SHANKAR[1]

In the early 1980s India's fascination with Ravi showed no signs of declining. He was arguably the world's most famous Indian, Indira Gandhi probably his only rival for the accolade. He was the conqueror of the West, the revered elder statesman of Indian music, and a personality who kept gossip columnists busy. On his sixtieth birthday *India Today* described him as a "part-*sadhu*, part-playboy."[2] He was also spending more time in his homeland. Indeed, the 1980s were dominated professionally by a series of high-profile commissions from India. The decade began, however, with two major international projects: the biggest film of his career, and perhaps his greatest work for a Western orchestra.

Ravi had become keen to make a new foray into concerto territory, and it was Zubin Mehta who gave him the opportunity to do so. As early as 1968 Ravi had talked with his compatriot about collaborating on an orchestral work.[3] Mehta had his reservations. "His first sitar concerto just confirmed my view that these two worlds of East and West can't mix," he said. "But Ravi and I have always been friends…He said he'd learned a lot from his first encounter, and wanted to try another."[4] When Mehta became music director of the New York Philharmonic in 1978 he prompted the orchestra to commission Ravi.

In preliminary work during the summer of 1979 Ravi was aided briefly by Fred Teague, and Mehta even transcribed a few of Ravi's themes himself. In search of an assistant in New York, Ravi sought the help of Elise Barnett. She had retired from City College, but her former colleagues there recommended a twenty-six-year-old recent graduate, José-Luis Greco. Before turning to music Greco had, like Ravi, been a child dancer in a family troupe—the José Greco Spanish Ballet, run by his father. In June 1980 Ravi rented an apartment in Gramercy Park, near to Sue Jones's, and installed a piano. "For the next three months I worked with him just about every day. It was really wonderful," says Greco, who has since made a successful career as composer:

> I would sit at the piano and he would sit next to me on a piano bench, with his legs crossed, and his sitar. He would either play or sing or tap things and I would try to imitate them on the piano. The most difficult thing was to try to get some of the rhythmic inflections.[5]

That summer Ravi spent time listening to the orchestra in rehearsal. Mehta introduced him to its leading players, so that he could get to know their strengths, and he wrote for them what Mehta calls "quasi-improvisations," fully composed solos with the impression of spontaneity.[6] As in his first concerto, Ravi also gave himself several passages where, between agreed cues, he improvised on the sitar.

Mehta, who carried a small tin of chilies with him to liven up bland food, urged Ravi to add more spice than he had on his first concerto. "Make it difficult," he told him. "Like hot chili."[7] Ravi complied happily, and the finished work features rhythmic cycles of 6, 6½, 7½, 8, 10, 13½, 14 and 16 beats, sometimes overlapping, and a total of thirty different *ragas*, the melody line nevertheless remaining "unabashedly loyal" to Indian classical music, as Shubha Mudgal has observed.[8] His use of harmony and counterpoint was again minimal, but any suggestions that this work might be considered insubstantial were nullified by this extraordinary melodic and rhythmic complexity. Greco deserves credit too; the orchestration is superb.

Once again Ravi wrote a four-movement concerto, this time running to upward of 52 minutes. The first movement is based on *Raga Lalit*, which makes for a moody and dramatic opening, but gave problems to the orchestral players, particularly the violinists, who had to master the unfamiliar scale, with its flattened second and sixth notes, both fourths (natural and sharp), and no fifth. After exploring five *ragas* in the second movement, the concerto reaches divine heights of lyricism in the third, with serene passages played by the sitar, flute, harp and strings in *Raga Yaman Kalyan*, which Ravi included for Sukanya. A virtuoso solo on the trumpet (Phil Smith in the premiere) then heralds a rousing theme led by the timpani in a 7½-beat cycle. During the section that follows in *jhaptal*—5/4 in Western notation— there is also a remarkable jazz-infused solo on the clarinet in *Raga Marwa*, played originally by Stanley Drucker, before it closes with *Raga Desh* in a cycle of 13½ beats. The final movement commences with the monsoon *raga Mian Ki Malhar* and timpani swells that suggest an approaching storm. It progresses through twenty-one different *ragas*, played in *raga mala* style, sometimes in flashes as short as eight bars, and many consequent changes of key, as it builds to its tempestuous resolution.

The premiere of the concerto, under the title *Raga Mala*, was given on April 23, 1981 at Avery Fisher Hall, the renamed Philharmonic Hall. It was a triumph. The *New York Times* hailed it as "racy, complex, inexhaustibly interesting" and compared its "climax of virtuosity" to another New York-born orchestral crossover by a composer–performer: Gershwin's *Rhapsody in Blue*.[9] It played to four sellout houses that week, and this experience, along with seeing his daughter, lifted Ravi out of the depression that had dogged him since the split with Kamala in January. "This has brought back some happiness & joy in me," he wrote to Dubey. "Of course some of it was after coming to NY and spending time with darling Geetu. May God protect her, *nazar na lage* ['let there be no evil eye']! She is so special; so intelligent, observant, sensitive, humorous, emotional and passionate!"[10]

The following year he recorded the concerto for EMI at Abbey Road, with Mehta conducting the London Philharmonic. Over the next decade Ravi performed it at a number of venues, including in

London and Paris. Sometimes there were problems because of the work's sheer complexity. Ravi was used to being absolutely in control on stage, and an incorrect accent from anywhere in the orchestra could distract him into making an error in his own part. "I am scared of the second concerto," he later admitted.[11] He toured it to India in April 1989, along with Mehta and the European Community Youth Orchestra, but it seems Indians wanted more *raga* development than the concerto allowed. There was a cool reaction at Calcutta's 12,000-seater Netaji indoor stadium (surely an inappropriate venue). "He got off the stage and they wouldn't even call him back," says Mehta. "It was not appreciated. I was so sorry for him."[12] After that he ceased playing the work, concentrating instead on the less challenging first concerto. It was his daughter Anoushka who revived the second. Since she took it up in 2012, it has become her favorite among her father's orchestral works to play, and she has brought it to a wider audience. Major orchestras have embraced it, and it certainly offers them more to grapple with than the first concerto. Ravi's performance fears aside, he was proud of the composition, and rightly so: it is a *tour de force* that is maturing well with age. Stephen Slawek, professor of ethnomusicology and sitar disciple of Ravi, believes it is his masterpiece.[13]

Gandhi was the highest-profile, most commercially successful film that Ravi ever worked on. It won eight Academy Awards and revived global awareness of the father of the Indian nation. Ravi was the obvious choice as its composer and it gained him the only Oscar nomination of his career, as well as an Ivor Novello Award. Yet the experience left him feeling underemployed. "I could have done so much more for that film really, I'm sorry to say," he later reflected.[14]

As a boy in the 1930s, Richard Attenborough heard a British cinema audience jeering as they watched newsreel footage of Mahatma Gandhi visiting London. He always remembered how his father told him, "Dick, they are such fools, they have no concept of the quality of this man. He is a great man."[15] Attenborough had first begun trying to make his film about Gandhi in 1962. The subject was so sensitive in India that he needed top-level approval. Nehru was encouraging, but after he died the project stalled. Attenborough was both producer and director; his persistence was phenomenal. Eventually Indira Gandhi green-lit the film in 1980, and it is thought that she insisted on Ravi providing the music. There might be some truth in that, but Attenborough had wanted Ravi ever since the early 1960s, when he watched the *Apu Trilogy*.[16] In January 1973 they had met at the Hyde Park Hotel in London and come to an agreement in principle.

Attenborough approached Ravi again once the film was in post-production. He agreed a fee of £25,000 and arranged to meet him in Bombay in October 1981. However, Ravi felt there was "a slightly discordant feeling from the outset" because Attenborough wanted him to work alongside a Western composer.[17] The film required some British music to evoke imperial pomp, and Attenborough felt that Indian music would be wrong for the South African scenes, but he also worried that too much Indian music would alienate an international audience, so he wanted an orchestral presence throughout. Initially Carl Davis was engaged, but after he dropped out Attenborough called up George Fenton, a thirty-one-year-old British composer in rising demand from theater and television. *Gandhi* was his first big film.

On October 14 the three of them viewed the first "fine cut" of the film in a projection theater at BR Studios in Juhu. Afterward, at the Taj Mahal Hotel, they discussed how they would work together. Fenton, who understood his role was subordinate to Ravi's, would mostly orchestrate Ravi's themes but also write a few passages himself. Ravi was keen that his *Raga Mohankauns*, which he had composed after Gandhi's death in 1948, should be used prominently.

Fenton then returned to Bombay for ten days in November. In his room at the Taj he, Ravi and Vijay Raghav Rao, who was engaged as Ravi's assistant, worked every day from late afternoon until about 10 p.m., with piano, sitar and flute to hand. Fenton taped each session and transcribed it the next morning. "This was the highlight for me," he says.

Having been a long-time fan, to sit on the floor in front of him and witness his technique and mastery of the sitar so close up was amazing. I would constantly ask him questions about the effect the orchestra would have on the Indian music. If I moved the bass line it would change the *raag*. Could I do that? What instruments meant culturally, and so on.[18]

Fenton had not studied Indian music formally, but he had done some homework. "What a sensitive musician George is," Ravi wrote to Attenborough afterward. "I have become very attached to him!"[19]

The recording sessions took place in January 1982 at CTS Studios in Wembley. Ravi oversaw his nine chosen Indian soloists, while Fenton conducted the Wren Orchestra. Attenborough was present and even joined in when Ravi needed a humming chorus.[20] There are three places in the film where Indian classical music is given free rein: the sitar- and sarangi-led *Discovery of India*, which accompanies Gandhi's train journeys; in the improvisations by the tabla, sitar and shehnai that cover the intermission and in the *bhajans* of *For All Mankind*, beautifully sung by Lakshmi Shankar and Ashit Desai over the closing credits, which won the Ivor Novello Award. Elsewhere the Indian instrumentalists and vocalists are used in the background, or in short snippets, or are incorporated into the orchestral sound, which dominates most of the arrangements.

In April, after watching a preview screening on his birthday, Ravi wrote to Attenborough to say that he was "deeply moved by the film" but disappointed by the music. "I do feel sad that you have not made the best use of my abilities," he explained. He pointed out that the film had fragmented his *Mohankauns* theme "beyond recognition" and distorted the spirit of the shehnai piece that plays in the aftermath of the Jalianwala Bagh massacre. This could have been the most agonizing moment of the film, comparable to the tar-shehnai's sustained lament in *Pather Panchali*, but it is mixed at a medium volume and is edited to under 30 seconds, reducing its effect. "I wanted it to be of piercing intensity to be gradually faded out after the scene ended," Ravi wrote. He further complained that the music was generally low in the sound mix, which remains true in places. Attenborough made at least one change in response to the letter: Ravi's sitar level in *Discovery of India* seems to have been boosted.[21]

Mixing aside, Ravi's frustrations arose from the constraints imposed on him by the process itself. There was an industry assumption that what was needed for an epic movie was an epic Hollywood score. Attenborough didn't want this, but he was having to resist pressure to be conservative in his use of Indian music. Today, after A. R. Rahman's Oscar win with *Slumdog Millionaire*, it is easy to underestimate how powerful this attitude once was. On the first day at CTS Studios the control room was full of studio executives, and commercial expectations were high. Fenton also feels that Attenborough was used to a traditional approach to film scoring, whereby "The film is finished, we are all set, the studio is booked, the orchestra comes in, someone waves, they play, everyone says, 'Great!' and we all go home."[22] There was little scope for the music to grow in the studio, which was Ravi's preferred approach. He had worked to rigid music cues before on films such as *Charly*, but his greatest soundtracks, from the *Apu Trilogy* to *Alice in Wonderland*, had evolved through improvisation in the studio.

It is also significant that Ravi was not involved in the initial "spotting" session, when decisions are made about which scenes will have music and what effect each passage should have. These music cues had already been prepared by Attenborough before the meeting in Bombay. They were revised after those discussions, but the overall approach was already established, and it is noticeable how little music there actually is in the film. Attenborough preferred to foreground the actors' performances. He loved stillness. As a result, Ravi felt that he never had sufficient chance to express what Gandhi meant to him personally. He had visited some of Gandhi's associates in Ahmedabad and Rajkot to collect his favorite *bhajans*, but in the end only the two best known were used, *Vaishnava Janato* and the *Ram Dhun*. "I really wanted to bring more spirit of Gandhi and the simplicity in his life," he said in 1985. However, he added, "The net result seems to be very good and people love it."[23]

When I visited Ravi in 2009, he mentioned that Attenborough had recently given "a nice interview," expressing some regrets.[24] "I know Pandit Ravi Shankar was very upset with me as I did not use his compositions in *Gandhi*," Attenborough had said. "I thought that the...orchestra would prove more effective than his music. It was one of my biggest miscalculations."[25] It does not follow that Ravi was right all along, for films have their own needs and dynamics. When I put Attenborough's comment to George Fenton, he said:

I think and thought then that he could have given both Ravi and me more scope. He was very restrained in his appetite for music in the film generally. And the success of the film would suggest he was right. Beyond that, it was a remark made in hindsight and the Western world's rapport with Indian music has changed radically in the last thirty years. I'm not sure he was ever in a position to do what he described.[26]

Fenton and Ravi both attended the 1983 Academy Awards, at which they were jointly nominated, although they lost out to John Williams's classic soundtrack to *E.T.* Attenborough's film proved to be a big break for Fenton, who has gone on to compose for over a hundred films and several BBC natural history series, including *The Blue Planet*. For Ravi, it was almost his last hurrah in cinema: he was to compose for only one more feature film.

The film exceeded all expectations in bringing Gandhi's story to new generations and overwriting the old imperial narratives. Its release marked a moment when Western culture was refocusing on the history of the subcontinent, thirty-five years on from independence. If Attenborough was in the vanguard of this process, so too was Philip Glass, who, having broken through with his postmodern opera *Einstein on the Beach*, followed it up in 1980 with a similarly abstract portrait of Gandhi in *Satyagraha*. Attenborough's success then unleashed a wave of Raj dramas in Britain, including *The Jewel in the Crown* (with music by Fenton), *The Far Pavilions* and David Lean's *A Passage to India*. Whereas the 1960s' fascination with India had been about discovering aspects mostly ignored by the colonialists, and *Gandhi* had honored their nemesis, these adaptations seemed to be giving the Raj a makeover. "In Britain today the refurbishment of the Empire's tarnished image is underway," wrote Salman Rushdie, whose 1981 novel *Midnight's Children* addressed post-colonial history from a very different angle.[27] Imperial revivalists were emboldened by a striking feature of Anglo-Indian relations after 1947: the swiftness with which most Indians forgave or moved on. For the British, as the journalist Ian Jack recently noted, "the foundations of the relationship, which lay in conquest and trade, were obscured by a cloud of fond feeling that was part E. M. Forster, part Ravi Shankar and (for a few) part *bhang*."[28]

Ravi's status as musician of choice for the Indian establishment was confirmed over the next few years. In March 1982 he helped launch the Festival of India in Britain, the first in a series of such cultural initiatives by the Indian government across the world. Nineteen exhibitions and numerous other events were held around the UK. The inaugural concert at the Royal Festival Hall opened with Carnatic music by M. S. Subbulakshmi, before Ravi gave the European premiere of his second sitar concerto, with Zubin Mehta conducting the London Philharmonic. Backstage it was like a soft-power summit as Ravi was congratulated by Prime Ministers Indira Gandhi and Margaret Thatcher, as well as the Prince of Wales. Also present were Richard Attenborough, Yehudi Menuhin and Jacqueline du Pré, who sat next to Sukanya and held her hand throughout.

By this time Ravi had also been appointed as musical and artistic director of Asiad '82, the Olympic-style Asian Games staged in

Delhi in November and December 1982, with thirty-three nations competing. It was a huge event in India and televised live in color by Doordarshan. Indira Gandhi took a close personal interest. With about ten thousand people involved in creating the opening and closing ceremonies, including nearly seven thousand dancers, she felt martial rigor was needed and appointed three senior army officers to organize the performers. The theme was India's unity in diversity, and at the heart of the opening ceremony was a ninety-minute cultural pageant of folk dances from all over the country, each state allocated its own slot. This was the responsibility of Major-General Narindar Singh, who spent much of 1981 touring the country and urging chief ministers to provide their best artists. In Bombay in February 1982 he presented his ideas to Ravi, who was impressed. "Shankar was the first one to support me," said Singh. "After his approval, things became much easier."[29] Ravi made some specific recommendations, such as bringing in Trichur elephants and Kathakali dancers.

As well as advising on this pageant, Ravi was tasked with writing the principal musical elements. These proved to be a runaway success. The hymn of welcome, "Swagatam, Shubha Swagatam," has become probably Ravi's best-known song in India after "Sare Jahan Se Accha." It took shape during an intensive two-week spell in May and June, when he had flown in specially from New York for composing sessions, site visits and meetings, including an audience with the prime minister. "It still gives me gooseflesh to recall how the theme song was composed," says Tanusree Shankar, whom Ravi had brought in to work on choreography.[30] They were all staying at the Ashok Hotel in Delhi, and one evening Ravi called her to his room. She found him there composing the tune, sitting with Pandit Narendra Sharma, who was writing the Hindi lyric, and Ashit Desai, who was notating the song. What he needed urgently was a female voice.

"Ashit, you sing the first line, 'Ata Swagatam,'" said Ravi, "and then Tanusree will respond with the second line, 'Shubha Swagatam.'"

"I can't sing to save my life!" complained Tanusree.[31]

But Ravi insisted, and he liked what he heard. He then flew down to Bombay to record the hymn at HMV Studios, with massed voices led by Ashit and Hema Desai. Ravi's remit also covered three more versions—an arrangement for naval band, another for Indian instruments, and an English recitation of it by the Bollywood star Amitabh Bachchan—and music for other numbers: a mass dance number with Orissan umbrellas; the dance of the birds and animals; and, as the showpiece of the closing ceremony, a three-part suite in tribute to the Games' mascot, Appu the elephant. At the end of the fortnight, just before returning to New York, he sent rough cuts of everything to the prime minister for approval, explaining, "In all these compositions I have maintained the deep spiritual quality of India that the whole world respects and looks up to—as well as strength and a positive attitude."[32] He knew his patron well.

As with London's 2012 Olympics, the opening ceremony rendered mute all but the most die-hard critics of the Games. *India Today* acclaimed "a dazzling feat of skilled management and brilliant creative artistry."[33] As the flame was lit Ashit Desai conducted a 200-strong choir singing "Swagatam," although they were not miked up because all of Ravi's music in the ceremonies was pre-recorded. The hymn became the ubiquitous refrain of the Games, and when EMI rushed out the album *Sound of Asiad '82* it shifted 10,000 copies within 18 hours.[34]

Among the musicians and choreographers, Ravi was the only one who did not charge for his services, viewing his contribution as a gift to the nation. Two years later he was among just twenty-two people who received the Asiad Vishisht Jyoti, a one-off honor from the Indian president. More immediately, his reward came in the form of a government house in New Delhi allocated to him by Indira Gandhi from the quota for "prominent persons." This was a spacious bungalow in attractive grounds on the Lodhi Estate. It was widely reported that he now planned to settle in Delhi and spend eight months a year in India.[35] He was also nominated to the board of the Sangeet Natak

Akademi, although he declined its chairmanship because he dreaded the administrative burden.[36]

Ravi's euphoria after the opening ceremony had been cut short by a call from Kamala—the first time he had heard from her for two years. She told him Rajendra was seriously ill. Ravi rushed to Madras to find his brother lying in a coma in a nursing home. Three days later, he died. With Kumar in America, it was Ravi who carried out the funeral rites that are usually the duty of the eldest son. "I felt numb and empty after this for quite a long time," he said.[37]

Outwardly, he still exuded a positive attitude. "After seeing the Asiad and the inherent strength of the Indians," he told *Screen*, "my earlier acute depression and frustration have given place to a new kind of dynamic optimism about the future growth of the nation."[38] The Asiad had coincided with the world premiere of *Gandhi*, also in Delhi, so Ravi's profile was flying high. He had just started a brief Indian tour with Ali Akbar Khan too. Relations between them had improved to the extent that in May 1982 they had performed live together for the first time in a decade, in a four-hour Carnegie Hall concert produced by Sue Jones. Excerpts from their sublime *jugalbandi* in *Mishra Piloo* were released on an Angel Records LP. They then agreed to team up for their first Indian duets for almost two decades, playing major venues in Delhi, Calcutta and Bombay, where Ravi told a press conference that their rapport had "ripened."[39] Alla Rakha and Zakir Hussain both accompanied them. A homecoming recital followed in Maihar in February 1983.

When India unexpectedly won the 1983 cricket World Cup in London—sparking the nation's love affair with the one-day format of the game—it was Ravi who hosted a reception for the homecoming team at the Bharat-Rams' home in Delhi.[40] And when the Chinese government wanted to invite an Indian musician, it was Ravi they approached. In August he arrived for his first visit to the country, where he gave well-attended concerts and lecture-demonstrations in four cities: Beijing, Chengdu, Shanghai and Guangzhou. He also watched the Peking Opera, visited the Great Wall and the Leshan Giant Buddha, and gorged on the food. But his strongest impression was of how China's traditional music, which was what most interested him, had stopped developing long ago and been superseded by Western music and its conservatories. "All the arts in China appeared to be a matter of heritage only," he said.[41] The contrast with India only reinforced his love for his own musical tradition—ancient but still evolving.

His next big creative venture was Uday Utsav, a four-day festival of dance and music in memory of his eldest brother. Fearing that Uday was being forgotten, Ravi was the principal force behind the event. It opened on December 8—Uday's birthday—at the Siri Fort Auditorium in Delhi, which had been built for the Asiad, and, almost inevitably, Indira Gandhi inaugurated proceedings. Numerous dance stars took part. There was a Kathakali troupe, Odissi dance by Kelucharan Mahapatra, and Bharatanatyam by Vyjayantimala. Amala Shankar restaged several works by Uday, including *Samanya Kshati*, and there were shows by the dance troupes of Sachin Shankar, Uma Sharma, Mamata Shankar, Narendra Sharma and Ananda and Tanusree Shankar.

It was a vast collective effort, but Ravi's imprint was all over it. Each day began with an overture he had composed, and there were three substantial new works from him. These included the closing extravaganza, *Rasa Ranga*, which featured dancers, visuals and eighty musicians on stage, including All India Radio's choir group and Vadya Vrinda, and emerging *khyal* vocalists Rajan and Sajan Mishra. There was also a sitar ensemble in *Raga Tilak Shyam* (*Sitar Vrind*), in which he was assisted by his disciples Deepak Choudhury, Kartick Kumar, Sunil Kumar Das and Shubhendra Rao. The other piece was a vocal and instrumental suite, *Manoharini*, with Lakshmi Shankar and Ashit Desai as the lead voices, which was performed to the accompaniment of a multimedia slideshow devised by the American photographer Alan Kozlowski. Ravi had sent him around India to shoot numerous locations especially for the show, including Ajanta, Ellora and the Taj Mahal.

Manoharini was a tribute to Uday but saw the reappearance of Ravi's favorite narrative theme: Dream, Nightmare and Dawn. Perhaps his trip to India's nuclear rival China had prompted it, for in this piece spiritual invocations and a Radha–Krishna love song give way to impressions of violence, pollution and ultimately nuclear holocaust, before resolution arrives with inner peace. It was paired with *Sitar Vrind* on his next Indian album, *New Offerings from Ravi Shankar*. The cover illustration, in which a group of sitarists in echelon face off against a mushroom cloud, was a slightly bizarre representation of a message that he now took very seriously, that music could point the way out of conflict: "The solution lies in the quest to find inner peace, and in loving."[42]

Events in 1984 would have tested that belief. On October 31 Ravi was in a hospital in Pittsburgh (the reason is not known) when the news reached him of the assassination of Indira Gandhi. In June she had ordered the military to storm the Golden Temple in Amritsar, Sikhism's holiest shrine, to root out the separatist militants sheltering there. In revenge for this she was gunned down in cold blood by two of her Sikh bodyguards. There followed a horrific pogrom against Sikhs in Delhi, with thousands killed. In December Ravi sent a letter to her son, Rajiv Gandhi, who had succeeded her as prime minister and was about to win a landslide election victory. "I pray to God to save you from any harm and give you the strength and wisdom so that you can steer the people in the right direction," he wrote.[43]

Rajiv was like his mother in that, although he was no connoisseur of the arts, he valued them and respected Ravi greatly. When, in February 1985, Ravi played the first ever classical concert inside Calcutta's Victoria Memorial, it was staged in remembrance of Indira, and he subsequently presented a copy of the live recording, entitled *Shanti Dhwani* ("The Sound of Peace"), to the new prime minister. In June Ravi and Ali Akbar played in front of Rajiv and U.S. Vice President

George Bush at the Kennedy Center to inaugurate the Festival of India's American incarnation. Then, in October, a year to the day after her death, Ravi gave the Paris premiere of his second sitar concerto. From the rostrum Zubin Mehta dedicated the evening to Indira's memory, and the Salle Pleyel audience responded with seemingly endless applause. "They just wouldn't stop!" Mehta said, his voice still cracking with emotion at the recollection thirty years later. "That was a profoundly felt performance on his part. He gave everything."[44]

Another marker of his standing in India followed. At any one time the Rajya Sabha, the Indian parliament's upper chamber, includes twelve appointees, distinguished figures from the arts or sciences. In 1986 Rajiv Gandhi nominated Ravi for this role. He began his six-year term as an MP alongside R. K. Narayan and M. F. Husain.

For all this recognition in his homeland Ravi was never a conventional member of the establishment. The government had provided his home, of which he had taken possession in early 1984, and now parliamentary sessions tied him to Delhi more than before, but he remained, both at heart and in practice, a traveling musician. Much as he loved India, he retained a cosmopolitan perspective.

"I think he's probably always been an outsider who wanted to belong, and someone who belonged who wanted to be free," Anoushka says today. This applied to his musical identity too:

> It was a key theme for him that he wanted to be in the purest sense
> a presenter and promoter of the classical tradition and heritage,
> but he also rebelled against the restraint that implied, and fought
> to be creatively free and experimental. Interestingly, though,
> he was also very stringent about the way in which he would do
> that, which was his classical side coming out. He had his own
> internal borderline around what it meant to be artistically free.
> For him, even when writing for orchestras or for other musicians,
> experimenting with new instruments and sounds, it was always

in the *raga* form. Even when he was being experimental there was something deeply classical about him.[45]

This duality was partly the product of a lifetime straddling cultures. He knew he meant different things to different people: here an insider, there an outsider; here a purist, there a pioneer. A musical piece that was considered in the West to represent ancient tradition might be deemed as innovative or controversial in India. He was certainly intrigued by cross-cultural juxtapositions, which constituted much of his daily life. Not all artists shared this sentiment. Satyajit Ray, for example, had little interest in portraying those who were "fifty–fifty," preferring to concentrate on those rooted in Bengali culture.[46] Ravi demanded the right to have it both ways: as a performer he rigorously applied the Indian classical tradition, but in his creative experiments embraced hybrid forms—as long as he could dictate the boundaries.

By the 1980s a new generation of south Asian migrants in the West was starting to express what it was like to grow up between two cultures. In 1984 Ravi was involved in a groundbreaking British dance production that mined this territory. *The Adventures of Mowgli*, which toured nationwide for three seasons, was a landmark in the development of a contemporary British Asian dance style, refashioning Indian solo classical forms with group choreography, elements of contemporary dance, a theatrical production and a non-mythological subject, Kipling's *Jungle Book*. The choreographers were from India— the Dhananjayans, who are Bharatanatyam experts from Madras, and Kathak master Pratap Pawar, disciple of Birju Maharaj—but the other dancers were all based in the UK. Ravi agreed to provide the music, but later had to pull out as he was too busy. Instead he recommended Vijay Raghav Rao, while retaining a credit as artistic adviser. The cast included Shobana Jeyasingh and Pushkala Gopal. It also saw the debut of the ten-year-old Akram Khan, who remembers the young Anoushka hanging around rehearsals copying his movements. "Encourage him," Ravi told Akram's father. "One day he will be great."[47]

Ravi's creatively open mindset was in evidence on his album *Tana Mana*. His interest was piqued when Alan Kozlowski introduced him to Frank Serafine, a cutting-edge sound designer who had recently worked on *Tron* and *Star Trek: The Motion Picture*. In Serafine's Santa Monica studio Ravi discovered samplers, emulators and synthesizers. "For a long time I have wanted to do experimentation with sounds," he told the *Los Angeles Times* in May 1983, mid-project. "I have done everything else," he said, before adding, "Almost."[48]

Ravi played the synthesizers himself, as well as the sitar, and sang on several pieces, most movingly on the title track, a homage to his mother. As guest artists he brought in Aashish Khan, Lakshmi Shankar, Harihar Rao, Swapan Chaudhuri on tabla, and on sitar and vocals Shubho, who, to Ravi's satisfaction, had started playing again after many years. Fortunately, unlike many first-time experiments with synthesizers during that era, Ravi handled them with deft judgment. Only on *Memory of Uday* do the sampled vocals now sound slightly dated. Otherwise the electronics support the organic elements beautifully, without overwhelming them, and "without compromising on the solid foundation of our classical music," as he later explained.[49] A later track, *Friar Park*, recorded at George Harrison's home, partners Ravi's sitar with Ray Cooper's marimba, to hypnotic effect.

The resulting collection of pieces was an indefinable hybrid of Indian, jazz and electronic sounds, and was programmed like a pop album, with no track longer than six minutes. No record company knew how to pigeonhole it, and it sat on the shelf for three years. "Thank God the New Age was born in the meantime," said Ravi.[50] It was eventually heard by Peter Baumann, former keyboard player in Tangerine Dream, who signed Ravi to his eclectic new label, Private Music, in 1986.[51] At least one more track was added at that stage, the playful *West Eats Meat*, produced by Baumann himself, before the album was released in June 1987. Although it didn't trouble the charts, it stands up as a coherent, melodic and constantly intriguing experiment.

If *Tana Mana* was the most innovative of his creative projects overseas in these years, two others are of interest. One saw him return to writing for Japanese musicians, when a ninety-minute piece was commissioned for a festival in June 1985 at the Japanese American Cultural and Community Center, located in Los Angeles's Little Tokyo. Japanese musicians playing the koto, the shakuhachi and the big o-daiko drum were integrated into a group of ten Indian musicians, mostly his disciples, four of whom he brought over from India for the first time: Tarun Bhattacharya on santoor, Ramesh Mishra on sarangi, Daya Shankar on shehnai and Vishwa Mohan Bhatt on his customized slide guitar or "mohan veena." To date the only music released from this work is the finale, which is reminiscent of the ensemble style of *Music Festival from India*.[52]

The other project was *Genesis* (1986), his final feature film soundtrack, on which he at last worked with Mrinal Sen, a major figure of Bengal's Parallel Cinema. For this parable of the rise and fall of a utopian community in a ruined village, Ravi was given a free hand, and his background music, recorded in Paris, employs a broad palette of instruments and styles, from Rajasthani folk tunes to the haunting emulator-driven theme music.

In parallel with this experimentation, and as a balance to it, was a trio of solo classical albums that he issued through the Stuttgart-based label Chhanda Dhara, which compiled a wonderful catalog of Indian music over two decades. Ravi's first for them was his last album with Alla Rakha, a classical recording of *Charukauns* laid down at the BBC in London.

In Delhi, Ravi invited a new wave of younger disciples to live and learn with him in the *gurukul* style, at 95 Lodhi Road, his new house. The first two were the sarod player Partho Sarothy from Calcutta, who was about twenty-four, and nineteen-year-old sitarist Shubhendra Rao, who was the son of Rama Rao (and had been named after Ravi's son). They assumed integral roles in Ravi's Delhi life. Partho was responsible for running the household, and according to Sukanya his care for Ravi epitomized the concept of *seva*, or selfless service. Ravi nicknamed him the Home Minister. Shubhendra took care of outside matters, from running errands to acting as Ravi's personal assistant for the Rajya Sabha. He was the External Affairs Minister. Subsequent disciples residing there included the sarod player Aditya Verma and the sitarist Gaurav Mazumdar, who later took over as Rajya Sabha secretary.

Living with the *guru* enabled intensive commitment to music. Teaching could take place at almost any hour. Ravi usually went to bed around midnight but read into the small hours, and managed on about four hours' sleep, plus his daily forty-five-minute nap after lunch. Shubhendra Rao recalls one occasion when Ravi reappeared half an hour after retiring to bed. "Shubhendra? Partho?" he called out. "I'm not able to sleep for some reason. Come, let's practice." That night they finished at 4 a.m.[53]

Ravi still had Hemangana but in the main used it as a retreat for masterclasses and the festival. He had evolved his ideas on how best he should teach, and to make the most out of his limited time he now regularly assembled his disciples in groups and taught them together. These workshops sometimes took place in Delhi, Ahmedabad, Bangalore, Hyderabad or Madras, but the biggest gatherings were in Benares. Here disciples assembled once a year from all over India or overseas, for ten intensive days. As well as the wave of new students, there were established regulars, including Deepak Choudhury, Kartick Kumar, Shamim Ahmed, Rama Rao, Gopal Krishan, Uma Shankar Mishra, Kartik Seshadri, Ramesh Mishra, Daya Shankar, Manju Mehta, Vishwa Mohan Bhatt and Tarun Bhattacharya. By the 1980s, Seshadri recalls, the media interest had waned at Hemangana and it was an ideal atmosphere for learning music. "It was divine, that place," says Gaurav Mazumdar. "The smell of *agarbathi* everywhere, small gods and goddesses, the music room. That whole house was like a true ashram."[54]

Every year RIMPA also ran the four-day festival of music and dance in the city, with world-class line-ups curated by Ravi himself. Sanjay Guha, a sitar disciple of Deepak Choudhury (and later of Ravi), remembers one year when Ravi played the first day of the festival, Ali Akbar Khan day two, Zakir Hussain day three, and the final night was Vilayat Khan with Kishan Maharaj. After Vilayat's set ended at 6:30 a.m., a profoundly moved Ravi embraced him on stage, both of them in tears.[55]

Gradually Ravi realized that Benares had lost some of its enchantment. The locals showed less appreciation for music. "By nature Banarasis are very macho people: even if they have no muscles, they walk as if they do," he said. This aggressive streak seemed to have become more pronounced.

> We had wonderful audiences for the music festivals, but there were also many people who just wanted to get in free. They wouldn't buy a ticket, and if they weren't given one they would just tear up the side of the marquee and sneak in. The city officials claimed a large number of free passes. Sometimes, if we didn't offer someone a ticket, we were threatened: "Or else…!" This hurt me. I remembered how in earlier days Benares had cherished its musicians and scholars.[56]

When the photographer Raghubir Singh visited the festival in November 1986, he noticed that the hall was never full, and Western visitors outnumbered locals in the audience. Ravi told him he was disillusioned with the indifference of Banarasis to what he had tried to create. As they walked around Hemangana together, he said, "I feel I have wasted my money."[57] There was a similar sense of defeat on his face when he showed a French film crew around his home. "I sank all my money, as much as I could, but then I couldn't do it any more. It needs so much more money to bring it up to my dream. I am an optimist, but still it's unfinished," he said. "Especially this place," he added, gesturing to the site of a planned indoor stage, studio and archive complex. Only a depression in the grass marked where excavation had begun and then been called off.[58]

For the first time in many years, money was an issue. Ravi was becoming concerned about what he called "the shambles of my business ways and finances." There were problems on both sides of the ledger. Throughout his years of frantic touring, money had rolled in, so he had never worried about it, but health problems were starting to limit what he could take on. He was accustomed to living a good life and generous in the extreme. "I have always loved to entertain and to give presents, and never like to eat alone; I would rather take ten persons with me," he said.[59] Hemangana was expensive to maintain, and for some time Ravi had been urging Dubey to economize.[60] The problems went deeper. A global strategy was needed to structure his finances. Ravi's affairs were particularly disorganized in India, where he had always been closely involved in his own concert arrangements. After he moved to Delhi Ravi asked Harihar Rao, who was good with money, to become his manager in India, but Harihar did not want to leave Los Angeles.[61]

In 1983 Ravi engaged Kuldeep Drabu, a young accountant in Delhi recommended by Arun Bharat-Ram, to review his situation. By this time Ravi was an Indian resident again, but he was being taxed in India, the USA and the UK, and withholding taxes were applied when he toured elsewhere. Drabu, who visited New York and London to gather information, found he was sometimes paying taxes more than once on the same income. The only property he owned was Hemangana, which he rarely visited. Rent at Lodhi Road was nominal, but even after moving in he lived much of his life in hotels, friends' houses or leased apartments. "I would say that he was completely reckless and negligent as far as his financial matters were concerned," says Drabu.[62] Drabu improved matters by setting up a company, Vistar Presentations, to engage Ravi as an artist for his Indian commitments, but Ravi was still financially vulnerable. Drabu also pointed out some discrepancies in the figures. It took many years for Ravi to accept the unwelcome conclusion. "In every possible manner so many people had fleeced me," he eventually admitted.[63]

At least his reassertion of his classical identity overseas had paid off. Audiences might not have been as huge as in the 1960s but they were still very healthy, and they were generally more serious about Indian music. He changed his U.S. booking agent again, to Sheldon Soffer, but still played the best concert halls. In New York he gave an annual concert at Carnegie Hall. In London he played at the Festival Hall or Albert Hall every year till 1984. Basil Douglas and Maureen Garnham were still his mainstays there, and Ravi's relationship with them was excellent. But Douglas, who turned seventy that year, was losing touch a little and looking to sell the business. "He was very old school, a real gentleman, rather grand and superior," says Angela Sulivan, who started working for him in 1983 and handled Ravi's next two London concerts. "It was partly that era, but it was almost like the artists were working for the manager, not the other way round." When the larger Albert Hall was booked in September 1984 Angela pressed for advertising on the London Underground and PR. "What's PR?" asked Douglas.[64]

Angela soon found herself going the extra mile for Ravi. Douglas had a fine carpet that was used to cover the dais whenever Ravi played in London, and when there was no longer space to store it at the office he asked Angela to keep it at her home. She was sharing a house in Kentish Town, where it served as her living-room rug. So in the run-up to the Albert Hall concert she handwashed it at home. "It took me a week after work," she says, "and then the weather became cold and I was terrified it wasn't going to dry in time. So I spent night after night with a hairdryer, blow-drying this beautiful carpet!"[65]

Meanwhile, there was a changing of the guard on the road. Nodu Mullick, so long Ravi's sober sidekick and master luthier, had retired from touring and was ailing physically. Ravi also reluctantly concluded that he needed to travel with a tabla player younger than Alla Rakha. He was criticized for this decision, but the logic was undeniable:

We were both in our mid-sixties and touring was getting harder:
the days had passed when I could tour with my sitar wrapped
in plastic in one hand and my travel bag in the other. Now I was
feeling pain in my shoulder, and at the same time I had decided to
use the sitar case on tour, which was much heavier. We could not
afford to tour with a large entourage.[66]

Typically he still traveled abroad as part of a trio: tabla player, tanpura
player and himself, with no tour manager. Often it was just a duo and
he relied on a local tanpura player. Occasionally there was an extra
instrumentalist, usually a disciple.

Ravi put off the difficult conversation with Alla Rakha, but confided to a close Bengali friend in London, Nishith Ganguly, that he
was going to ask the tabla maestro to retire. "Nishith is a wonderful,
humorous fellow but he has a fault—he talks too much," Ravi later
said. Directly before the last concert of the 1985 tour, Ganguly went
to Alla Rakha's dressing room.

"Khansahib," he said, jovially. "I heard that you are going to retire!"

"What?"

"Ravi said you are going to retire."[67]

It was not how Ravi had intended the news to be broken. "He was
such a sweet person, and he felt rejected, which made me feel very bad,"
Ravi later reflected.[68] The bitterness subsided in time. In Alla Rakha's
place Ravi took on Kumar Bose, a dynamic thirty-two-year-old disciple of Kishan Maharaj from Calcutta. For the next few years he was
Ravi's main touring accompanist overseas, and with this younger accompanist Ravi was able to continue to keep up a strenuous pace.

"I have the sweetest memory of Norah," says Misha Dasgupta Masud.
"When she was tiny, Raviji would practice sitar, and Norah had her
little banjo and would sit across from him copying his sitting position
and listening intently."[69] Sue recognized Norah's musical aptitude
early on, and she had her first piano lessons with Elise Barnett. Ravi

also had a little sitar made for her, although she never took to Indian music. He had many happy memories of her first years, but aside from the long summer when he worked on the concerto, his visits were mostly brief. There was something that made him hold back from building a parental relationship with his children. He adored them when they were in a good mood, but could not cope with tears and tantrums. And always he felt the need to move on. "Psychologically it has something to do with my never having my own father," he said. "I don't know what a father is. It's a case for any psychiatrist to find out why I have been like this. I couldn't give enough time to them."[70]

Sue worked now as a freelance concert producer—she managed Ravi's Carnegie Hall concerts during the 1980s—but she tired of New York and moved to Grapevine, Texas, when Norah was about three, keen to be nearer her own parents in Oklahoma. Ravi visited them there once, perhaps twice, and they met in other cities too. "We took a trip to New Mexico once, where he was on tour," says Norah. "We would often meet him in hotels when he was on tour in the States. I remember coming to New York once a year and seeing him at the Lexington Hotel: my mom cutting his toenails and him pretending it hurt like a baby, making me laugh."[71] Sue and Norah visited him in India again in March 1984, spending time in Delhi before traveling around with him and ending up in Kashmir for a stay on a houseboat. Norah recalls this trip sketchily. "I remember riding an elephant, and locking my mom in some room and being a brat!" she says. "I ate a lot of bananas because I wouldn't eat anything else."[72]

Ravi was committed to the life of an itinerant musician. Despite the earlier talk of retirement from touring, he just kept going. It was his career: he had to maintain his audience and his income, and he lived for the sensation of creating music live. There was also the deep-rooted restlessness that made him largely an absentee father and partner. "I think for a long time it was a way of avoiding things," says Norah.[73] "I cherish the time that Sue and I had together," Ravi later wrote. "But at the same time I was busy traveling the world and sharing my love with others, so I was not always there. My life was an emotional mess, and I hurt people."[74]

The reason Ravi saw less of Anoushka in her early years than he did of Norah was that Sukanya was married. Prodyot Sen, who had his ear, kept warning Ravi of the damage that scandal could bring to his reputation. Sukanya, who would bring Anoushka to Ravi's London hotel whenever he visited, respected his wishes and told only her closest friends that he was Anoushka's father. Ravi kept it a secret from most people—including Sue, who did not find out for about three years, and unsurprisingly found it very difficult to accept. When Anoushka was two Sukanya took her to Madras, where Kamala revealed she was aware of the child's existence. But she added, "I would have known anyway, just by looking at her." A few others noticed the striking resemblance, including Anoushka herself; Sukanya recalls her watching Ravi on television when she was about two and saying, "Baba looks just like me."[75]

Sukanya, sticking to her promise that she would bring up Anoushka alone, did not ask Ravi for any financial support. Kamala also cautioned Sukanya not to depend on him emotionally: "He's not going to marry you. Find someone else." She told her she had kept a tally of Ravi's past girlfriends, who numbered 186 in all. Sukanya knew Ravi had had many lovers but this was still a shock, so she asked Ravi whether it was true.

"Who told you?" he asked.

"Kamala."

"Those are just the ones she knows about."[76]

Sukanya wanted to know why he was like that, but she did not judge him: "With women he put his cards on the table—and he was free by then. Why not?"[77] Her love for him was such that she could accept this Krishna figure with all his "beautiful bonds." Indeed, her nickname for him was Shyam (or Shyamu), another name for Krishna. "He was traveling a lot and there were always women, but they knew what to expect," she has said. "He is also a deeply caring person. All the women he has been with agree when I say this. He made them feel very special."[78]

Anoushka's first clear memory of her father is from 1985, when her mother threw a party for her fourth birthday and he arrived, bringing four party dresses for her. She had been waiting for him all afternoon by the upstairs window. She was very close to her mother and sensed her excitement. "It was a big deal when he showed up, so it obviously wasn't happening very often," she says. She also recalls dancing around the living room to *Tana Mana*. Sukanya told her, as soon as she was old enough to understand, that Ravi was her father and that she had a sister in America.

> The thing I can't analyze is what the word Father meant to me, because I called him Baba right from the beginning. But at the same time, in Indian culture we never call an elder by name. There were dozens of aunties and uncles, there were a couple of grandmothers who weren't really my grandmothers. So he was Father, and he was someone I loved. I shifted to Bapi a few years later at his request, after my parents married. Bapi is a bit more intimate, like Daddy. I don't remember being confused, even through some very dramatic changes like having my surname changed. I was young and I was a smiler and nodder. I remember being "fine" about everything, and then having to unpick a lot of stuff much later.[79]

Eventually Sukanya decided to end her marriage to Narendra. They had been living separate lives for years, staying in separate rooms, and he was often away (once for thirteen months), but there was the public facade of a normal marriage. "It was like a show we were putting on, and in the end it just became too much for me," she says.[80] Prodyot Sen, revealing a manipulative streak, warned her not to leave her husband, but in 1986 she obtained a divorce on the grounds of five years' separation. Narendra became bitter, but Sukanya encouraged Anoushka to maintain a relationship with him, which continued for some years.

By this time Ravi had reached the end of his three-decade-long butterfly lifestyle. Sukanya is confident that he had no affairs after 1985. He could no longer bear the strain of maintaining all his relationships and could see the pain he had caused to some of his lovers. But this brought no solace. He was beset by guilt, snared in what he called "a mixed-up phase."[81] Sukanya's divorce unsettled him, and he blew hot and cold toward her. When she and Anoushka visited India in September 1986 they stayed at 95 Lodhi Road for a month because Anoushka caught chickenpox, but he was away and did not see them.

There should have been plenty to look forward to that autumn: Shubho was spending several months in India and making his Indian debut at the RIMPA festival; there was Ravi's first parliamentary session; and another prestigious commission in Delhi, for the December opening of the city's Baha'i temple, a lotus-shaped architectural marvel. No instruments were allowed there, so he wrote ten Hindi songs to be sung *a cappella* by three choirs, Indian, Iranian and English. In the event, they were performed in his absence, with Ashit Desai overseeing things, because Ravi was at that moment lying in Lenox Hill Hospital in New York, in mortal peril.

The physical crisis had developed as the emotional stress on him increased in tandem with worsening angina. In an effort to tackle both aspects of this strain on his heart, in September he took himself off for several weeks to an Ayurvedic center in Coimbatore, Tamil Nadu, where he adopted a vegetarian diet and had his hair shaved off. He returned feeling even worse, his physical decline now accompanied by mental anguish. "I started believing that someone had performed some witchcraft on me," he said. "I was angry with everyone—with myself more than anyone else—but all my emotional problems had reached such a climax that I couldn't cope with the stress."[82]

Playing the closing session of his RIMPA festival in Benares on November 15, he felt a pain in his arm.[83] He was admitted to the National Heart Institute in Delhi, and learned that he had suffered a "mild" heart attack. His worried doctors advised him to have bypass surgery if possible. The best place to have it was in America. At first Ravi resisted, but he was becoming weaker, and the need for surgery more urgent. Shubhendra Rao was liaising with Narasimha Rao's ministry on his behalf, trying to secure government help. Over in California, a fretful Ali Akbar Khan was calling to find out how he was, trying to reach Rajiv Gandhi.[84] The prime minister visited Ravi in hospital, and eventually the government generously provided three airfares. On December 8, the day Ravi had been due to give his maiden speech in the Rajya Sabha, he left the country with Shubho and an accompanying doctor. His flight was front-page news in India.[85]

As he waited for surgery in New York, he was buoyed up by a phone call from Satyajit Ray, who had been through the same operation two years earlier.[86] Both Sukanya and Kamala wanted to fly in, but he asked them not to. Sue did come, but there was an unhappy meeting at his hotel. She did not visit him in hospital, and the relationship seemed to be over.[87]

On December 30 he had a successful quadruple heart bypass. He stayed on in the city to recuperate, but, lonely in wintry New York, he felt the absence of a partner. To keep him company Kartik Seshadri arrived from Washington DC, and the perennially upbeat Nishith Ganguly flew out from London. Ganguly stayed with him for over four months, accompanying him when he transferred to San Diego in February to stay with his friends Sheila and Prem Trikannad, whom he had known since his Los Angeles days, and who were very close to Shubho. Gradually Ravi's strength returned.

VI
EVENING SUN
1987–2012

At the Ravi Shankar Centre, Delhi, 2006

21

SHANTI MANTRAS

Basically I really am a one-woman man.
RAVI SHANKAR[1]

"He never imagined he would be such a long-lived person," says Sankarlal Bhattacharjee. "He was always worrying about the next year, the year after that."[2] Ravi could so easily have died in late 1986, at the age of sixty-six. A year earlier, Nikhil Banerjee, his *gurubhai* and the only contemporary sitarist who could rival Ravi and Vilayat Khan, had suffered a fatal heart attack in Calcutta, aged just fifty-four. A year later Richard Bock also died of a heart attack on an airplane between Los Angeles and San Francisco, at the age of sixty-one.[3] If the sliding doors of life had closed on Ravi in Delhi's National Heart Institute, or on the operating table in New York, how would we assess his life and work?

Most of the musical achievements for which he is best known were behind him. He had revitalized Indian classical music in its homeland. He had taken it to five continents, promoting an image of India in its most cultivated and noble incarnation. He had composed great scores for feature films and pioneered Indian orchestral and ensemble music. He had a number of close disciples trained in his style. But he would also have died personally unfulfilled, as Uday had, laid low by emotional turmoil. The restlessness that had driven him to supreme heights of artistry and sensual experience had also left him lonely and unhappy. He had no partner; he had an awkward relationship with his son, and he was largely a stranger to his two daughters, neither of whom he publicly acknowledged.

As it transpired, he would live for another twenty-six years, and there was so much more to come in this long final act. He reached the pinnacle of his achievements with Indian ensemble works, wrote his finest vocal music, and returned to Western classical forms for his most sustained engagement with them. He trained his greatest disciple and established Indian music's place with a new generation. Commercially his greatest success as a performer also lay ahead of him. There would be tragedy and pain, but also a long and largely successful process of emotional resolution—including a second marriage.

On Ravi's sixty-seventh birthday he played Cornell in his first concert since his surgery. Another dozen North American concerts followed, at a pace surprisingly intense for a recovering heart patient. But in other respects he knew he could not go on as before. In late July 1987 he returned to India for the Rajya Sabha's monsoon session. Sitting in parliament, between distractedly voting on motions, he wrote a letter to Sue Jones, acknowledging his mistakes and asking her to marry him. But it was too late for her; it really was over.[4] "When she said no, I felt so lonely and so dejected," he said. "I was tired of being this bumbling bee. I'd had enough of that life and complications everywhere."[5]

Who then to settle down with? Ravi feared that he was too Westernized for most Indian women, but too Indian for a Western woman. However, Sukanya, who had lived half her life in Madras and half in London, was comfortable in both his worlds. At first, ever wary of confrontation, he worried that he would not be able to cope with her direct and fearless nature.[6] But he started warming to her again, and called her from Delhi with increasing frequency. On her birthday he rang her seven times.

In November he did something very uncharacteristic. After playing in Moscow, he sent his sitars back to Delhi with his fellow musicians, and flew to London alone, just to be with Sukanya. They spent what he described as "four crazy days at Bailey's Hotel in bliss."[7] He told her, "This time if I make up my mind about anybody it will be serious and final." But he was promising nothing yet. She in turn was noncommittal. When he asked her if she thought she would find any-body, she demurred. "I loved him with all my heart but I didn't want to show it. I think that helped in our relationship," she says.[8]

Ravi returned to London in the spring, after wintering in India. Prodyot Sen, perhaps sensing that his position as Ravi's closest London confidant was under threat, was livid with him for reviving his affair with Sukanya. There followed a furious argument in Ravi's hotel suite as Ravi confronted his friend over his controlling behavior. Sen walked out and followed up with two vitriolic letters, despite Ravi's attempt at reconciliation. He blamed Sukanya for the breakup of their thirty-year friendship, but this time Ravi had made his choice. If Sen would not accept Sukanya, then they could not be friends. They never saw each other again.

With his customary sense of timing Ravi had showed up in the Soviet Union just in time for *glasnost*. Mikhail Gorbachev came to power in Moscow in 1985, just months after Rajiv Gandhi's accession in Delhi. The two leaders shared a modernizing instinct, and used culture as one means of pursuing a closer friendship between their nations. When Ravi arrived that year on a short tour organized through the ICCR, accompanied by Alla Rakha, his experience was the polar opposite of his previous visit eighteen years earlier. Rather than performing for the conservatory elites, he played sold-out public recitals in Moscow (in Tchaikovsky Hall), Leningrad and Kiev. The paranoid atmosphere had receded somewhat, and he was startled to discover there were now hippies in the USSR. They embraced him with flowers and chanted "Om," as if in a long-delayed echo of the Summer of Love. Fans even chased after his train as it left Leningradsky station. When he returned in 1987, for the tour that preceded his London tryst with Sukanya, he took Kumar Bose and had a similarly delirious reception, this time playing the Bolshoi Theatre in Moscow and two concerts in Latvia, where he even found an Indian music club in Riga.

In July 1988 Ravi staged a massed orchestral–choral concert in the Palace of Culture in the Kremlin. This was the first of three projects in three years that saw him reach the apotheosis of his work with Indian ensembles. Perhaps love had given him new creative inspiration. Perhaps the brush with death, too; certainly he felt physically rejuvenated, like many successful bypass patients. The occasion was the closing event of the Festival of India in the USSR, the latest in India's series of cultural campaigns, after the UK, France and the USA. Rajiv Gandhi saw the soft-power potential of these festivals. The Soviets, determined to outdo the Americans, extended their own festival to eighteen months and reciprocated by sending an unprecedented array of their own artists to India.

For the prestigious role of headlining the opening ceremony in Moscow, the first-choice artist proved uncooperative. "I discovered why Vilayat Khan was not so popular as Ravi Shankar, and why he was not so well known," says Lalit Mansingh, then Director General of the ICCR.[9] The notoriously difficult Vilayat was the only artist who insisted on being paid a commercial fee rather than the modest honorarium that was on offer, and the festival committee, headed by Indian President Venkataraman, refused on principle. Instead they recruited Bismillah Khan, who shared the bill with M. S. Subbulakshmi and the Kalakshetra Bharatanatyam group. When Mansingh approached Ravi about the closing ceremony, he asked for no fee at all, only for his flights and accommodation.

The finale was repeated over three nights in front of Venkataraman and Soviet president Andrei Gromyko, and each performance was divided into two parts, both highly ambitious: a dance show choreographed by Kumudini Lakhia, and a musical gala composed and arranged by Ravi. Ravi brought twenty musicians from India, many of them his own disciples, and enlisted three Russian ensembles: the Government Chorus of the Soviet Ministry of Culture, the Chamber Orchestra of the Moscow Philharmonic and the Boyan Folk Ensemble of traditional instrumentalists. Ashit Desai assisted with arranging the Indian parts and conducting, while the Bombay violinist and arranger Suresh Lalwani handled the Western orchestration. In all there were about a hundred musicians on stage. Ravi had composed the music back in Delhi with them all in mind. "Both Kumudini and Ravi Shankar are very meticulous artists," says Lalit Mansingh. "When you see the finished product it looks effortless, but a lot of fine tuning goes into it."[10]

The theme of the concert was peace and "commonalities," and Ravi called his work *Swar Milan*, "the meeting of musical notes," symbolic of the harmonious encounter between peoples. It launched with *Prarambh*, a rapid exposition of several *ragas* that showcased both Indian and Soviet musicians. There was a single piece written for Russian chamber orchestra, *Three Ragas in D Minor*, featuring a gorgeous swooping melody on strings, while two pieces were performed by the Indians alone: another exercise in the *tarana* style of singing, which employs meaningless syllables at a medium to fast tempo; and *Sandhya Raga*, one of Ravi's favorites among all his ensemble pieces, a lively exploration of *Raga Yaman Kalyan* (inspired again by Sukanya). The finale brought together Indian and Russian instruments in a colorful twenty-five-minute suite, *Bahu-Rang*, with Ravi's sitar solo at its heart. The concert was televised back in India and it also became Ravi's second release on Private Music, titled *Inside the Kremlin*. It is a superb album and there are plenty—including Ashit Desai—who consider it to be Ravi's finest achievement.

Standing out above everything was *Shanti Mantra*, the first of Ravi's three greatest vocal works, all of them *dhrupad*-based—and all composed after his sixty-eighth birthday. This deceptively simple song is based on *Raga Devagiri Bilawal*, approximating the Western major scale. It employs the *num-tum* classical style of singing, which has a measured pulse; it is the vocal equivalent of the *jor* section in instrumental *dhrupad*. Vocals are by Ashit and Hema Desai, Ravindra Sathe and the south Indian Ratna Mala, while the Russian choir hums and chants in washes of harmony. Running through it is the droned chant of the *Shanti Mantra* itself, a Sanskrit prayer for peace (*shanti*) in the universe. It was reprised as an encore, this time with dancers from the Bolshoi and the symbolic lighting of lamps. "The feeling of peace and love flowed in the hearts and minds of everyone," recalled Ravi.[11] There were many tears in the hall, including some on Ravi's own cheeks. Listening to this heavenly piece of music, I am reminded of Picasso's description of Chagall: "He must have an angel in his head."[12]

From Moscow Ravi flew to the UK. In the Sussex town of Crawley Sukanya was co-organizing Britain's first national festival of Indian arts, the Nayee Kiran. Most of the performers were British Asians. A year earlier, at a time when Ravi's affection toward her had cooled, she had booked him at his full professional fee through Basil Douglas. He gave a recital and a workshop and stayed all week in the role of chief guest, attending many shows, including the Pakistani *qawwali* singer Nusrat Fateh Ali Khan, who was becoming an international star, and even a *bhangra* concert. Although they had separate rooms Ravi wanted Sukanya to be with him all the time, and was frustrated because, as festival director, she was too busy to spend time with him. She also gave a couple of dance workshops herself. "He was moving toward me and I was pretending to hold back," she says. "It was a game, trying to find out."[13]

At St. James's Court Hotel he said, "If I proposed to you, what would you say?"

"I'd say no," she replied, "and don't joke."

"Really? Why are you doing all this for me?"

"Because I love you and you're a great artist."

One day in October he stopped their taxi on impulse and entered an Indian jeweler's on Kilburn High Road, where he bought her a single diamond ring. When she showed it to her friend Anna Farlow, she said, "He's going to marry you." Sukanya responded, "No, Anna, he's just given me a gift."[14]

Sukanya did not know what to make of it. "Nothing seemed real," she says. She feared that Ravi might still suddenly change his mind, but then he asked her to accompany him to Budapest, where he played a huge indoor arena, the Sportcsarnok. At his hotel, with Kumar Bose also in the room, he introduced her to his Hungarian disciple András Kozma, with the words, "Meet Sukanya, my fiancée."[15]

He asked the others to keep the news to themselves, wanting to avoid it leaking out before he had told other people, primarily Sue. He does seem to have made up his mind. "I was feeling so guilty about Anoushka and Sukanya—and by that time I really loved Sukanya very much," he explained.[16] But Sukanya still didn't feel certain. She planned to visit India that winter, but Ravi went ahead of her, and it was only when he rang her from Delhi in January and suggested that they get married on the 23rd that she understood it really was happening. She was so startled that she put the phone down. He kept phoning back.

"I was in bed upstairs. She came off the phone and came upstairs and said, 'Your wish came true,'" says Anoushka. She was seven at the time and could see how much her mother loved Ravi, so his picture was on her wall and she had been praying at night that they would get together. "I knew she loved him and wanted to marry him and that would be the fairy-tale ending," she says. "I just didn't know what it was going to mean."[17]

The wedding took place outside Hyderabad, at Chilkur Temple. It was relatively small, fifty guests in all, close friends and disciples. They had a mixture of Bengali and south Indian rituals, beginning at 4 a.m. In a photograph taken that morning, Ravi sits cross-legged at the temple, meditative and solemn in expression, eyes downcast, as Daya Shankar plays his shehnai to create an auspicious mood. Ravi took his commitment seriously and he knew he was doing the right thing at last. "I felt very loved," said Sukanya.[18]

For Anoushka it was a day of great excitement. "I had matching clothes to my mum for every event, outfits cut from the same silk," she says, laughing. "She wore yellow, I wore yellow. She wore red, I wore red. She was great that way, she really kept me involved. It was all very thrilling."[19] But it was also, initially at least, unsettling to be the secret daughter that no one knew about. She remembers particularly the meeting in Benares with her uncle Debendra and aunt Krishna, who were completely in the dark:

> This was me meeting my uncle for the first time, who didn't know I existed. Basically we walked in, they saw us and cried out, "Geetu!" That's how alike Norah and I looked. Then my dad had to go, "No, this isn't Norah, this is my other daughter, Anoushka, and this is my fiancée, Sukanya"—it was crazy. They could have done that separately and then brought me in later! I felt very self-conscious, like I was some kind of replacement daughter. But they didn't think like that. I think they were just so happy, and this happiness was like a big love bubble.[20]

Fortunately Debendra immediately fell in love with Sukanya and Anoushka, and asserted his role as older brother, telling Ravi, "If you let this girl down, that's the end of you!"[21]

With Ravi's permission, Sankarlal Bhattacharjee covered the wedding for *Ananda Bazar Patrika*. No other press were invited, but they got wind of it anyway. It became a big story throughout India, with interest stirred by the thirty-four-year age gap between the couple, as well as the first public acknowledgment of Anoushka. After one erroneous press report, Ravi put out a statement confirming unambiguously that she was his daughter.[22] Later that year the Bombay women's magazine *Savvy* ran a ten-page cover article in which Sukanya explained her whole story with her characteristic candor.

The wedding startled many who thought Ravi would never marry again, especially Kamala. "I was really surprised," she reflected. "But then I thought a time in his life has come—maybe he needs someone more strong. Afterward I thought maybe she is the right kind of person, because I treated him like a god, and she treated him like a human being, which was good for him."[23]

In America there was a poignant corollary to this outbreak of joy. Before the wedding Ravi had traveled there to break the news in person to Sue and Norah. "In New York he told me I had a sister and that he was getting married," says Norah. She remembers that he was wearing a neck brace—he was suffering from spondylitis—but the news was too much to take in for a nine-year-old.[24] "After that I didn't see him again or talk to him again until I was eighteen," says Norah. "I don't think it was because I cut him out, and I don't think it was because my mom cut him out. But they both had very different perspectives on this."[25] Over the next few years Ravi sent birthday cards and money regularly but had to do so through an intermediary, and after they moved house he was denied their new address. He was adamant that Sue had prevented him from communicating with his daughter. "He tried his best to find her because he loved her," says Sukanya.[26] Norah feels that he was "probably afraid to try a little harder," that he wanted to contact her but he felt he must respect Sue's wishes, which also involved not talking publicly about her. "I'm sure he wanted to," says Norah. "I definitely know that much, but it is what it was. It's complicated."[27]

From my perspective that was kind of awkward. I got a letter once from Sukanya inviting me to visit, and it just felt weird, and I think it got pushed off. It's not like I wasn't welcome, but it's not like he beat down the door to make sure I knew I was. It's nuanced. Everybody has a different perspective of it, but that's mine.[28]

"When we married," says Sukanya, "I told him nothing should change. I marry you for what you are. I'm not expecting you to change for me."[29] At first it was almost as though they were not married. Anoushka was at school in London, so she and her mother were mostly living at Sukanya's home, 38 Osborne Road in Willesden. Meanwhile, Ravi was fulfilling his existing commitments, which that year comprised the sitar concerto tour of India with Zubin Mehta in April, and concert tours of America and Europe, including a major recital at the Barbican in London to celebrate fifty years as a solo artist. But gradually he was able to spend more time at Osborne Road, where Sukanya prepared everything the way he liked it. Once, when he stayed there shortly before they married, he had turned to her with misty eyes and said, "Thank you. I'd forgotten what a home was."[30] They even had a family break in Cornwall, the first time Ravi and Sukanya had taken a holiday together.[31] He still struggled to relate to their child on some levels, and was conscious that he was too old and fragile to play with her in the way a younger father might. But in London he put on his beret to go and pick her up from school, and he sang her to sleep. He found he enjoyed the role.

One thing that brought Ravi closer to Anoushka was music. She noticed that people kept asking her parents, "Has she started playing yet?" and she sensed the pressure of expectation. Initially he was reluctant to teach her, having never previously taught a child from scratch, and he worried about pushing her in case she was not interested. She is unsure of the exact chronology, but it was sometime during 1989, and at her mother's suggestion, that she first plucked a sitar string. She enjoyed music, without feeling an overwhelming passion for it at first.

> There was lots of me sitting and keeping time while he taught other students, and hours of sitting listening or playing tanpura. I very much enjoyed listening to the music and it was very comforting and familiar to me; however, in no way did I have an inbuilt, instant hunger for playing it myself.[32]

It did give her a separate, one-to-one connection with her father. He soon noticed what a fast learner she was and became inspired by her potential. When she was nine her interest stepped up a level, and gradually she began studying more seriously.

Something else that was new to Anoushka was her father's celebrity. Aged seven, she was taken by her parents to Rashtrapati Bhavan. There she played in the gardens as freely as if she was at a friend's house and met President Venkataraman, who took to her immediately, and actually gave her his hotline phone number, telling her to ring him any time. She did once, and he answered, saying, "I've been waiting for your call." The next year she was at a private recital in London that her father gave during Venkataraman's state visit to Britain. As well as the Indian president, the audience included the Queen, Prince Philip, Prince Charles, Princess Diana, Prime Minister Margaret Thatcher and Deputy Prime Minister Geoffrey Howe. She was introduced to them afterward and then sent off home before the banquet. All the Queen said was, "Shouldn't she be in bed?"[33] If that wasn't surreal enough, a couple of years later her father took her to see *Wayne's World* and they howled with laughter as Mike Myers asked Tia Carrere, "Will you still love me when I'm in my hanging-out-with-Ravi-Shankar phase?"

For the first three years the family split their life between London and Delhi. Anoushka began and ended each academic year at her local state primary school in Willesden, but in between she attended the British School in Delhi, where they spent the winter music season. By 1991–2, the third year, they spent most of it in Delhi and just a few weeks in London.

Ravi and Sukanya had to make the inevitable adjustments to each other's idiosyncrasies. She found, for example, that he spent an inordinate amount of time in the bathroom, perhaps improvising a rhythmic composition sparked off by the sound of brushing his teeth, or, in obsessive-compulsive fashion, reorganizing his bottles of toiletries in order of height. She realized more than ever how music dominated his existence, night and day. Sometimes he could not sleep because he was haunted by a rhythmic or melodic motif. She might wake in the middle of the night to find him silently mouthing or tapping away as he improvised the phrase in bed.

Ravi, in turn, appreciated her directness and clear thinking, but, not used to being told what to do, he took a while to become accustomed to it on a daily basis. This was partly her personality, and partly cultural differences: south Indians do not indulge so much in the exaggerated decorum of north Indians. "She can be brutally frank at times and can be misunderstood, but people who have come to know her love her for this quality, as well as adoring her for her spells of gutsy laughter," he explained.[34]

Sukanya had sound business sense, which was invaluable as she began managing his affairs. "That was very advantageous for him," says Kuldeep Drabu. "There was someone who could actually tell him about and control things that were happening."[35] For the first time in his career Ravi had somebody with a single, global perspective. Sukanya was shocked to discover how meager Ravi's savings and assets were, and she pointed out some irregularities. She also crucially appreciated that if he was to remain productive as he grew older, his time needed to be rationed. "He was being exploited left, right and center, and she came and shielded him from that," says Tanusree Shankar.[36] Many great artists have thrived on the back of such protection. Like Hélène von Breuning, the patron who protected Beethoven from social parasites, Sukanya understood the need to "keep the insects off the flowers."[37]

This gatekeeper role made Sukanya unpopular with those who had been draining Ravi's energies or, worse, swindling him. If he cut ties with them, she usually got the blame, which upset him: "She has become the villain while I remain the good person in their eyes. This is not fair. I have seen what has happened with my own eyes."[38] As he wrote to her later, "You have earned a bad name from many who [go] on to say Sukanya has changed Panditji—he cannot go to bathroom even without her permission." He added, "If the world knew how much time…I spend in the bathroom!"[39]

Nor was she, as some claimed, trying to control his life for her own benefit, a classic accusation against a second wife. Her devotion to him was transparent. If he really wanted to see someone, she was happy to enable access. She also encouraged the healing of personal strains and wounds: for example, the sarod maestro Amjad Ali Khan credits her with reviving his friendship with Ravi after periods of public frostiness.[40] Her main priorities when it came to allocating his time were close family and the making of music, which she knew was what Ravi really lived for.

In Delhi Ravi served out his six-year term as a parliamentarian, and to mark its conclusion he composed a new *raga*, *Rajya Kalyan*. He found the political process dispiriting. It was a time of economic crisis for India, as the country neared bankruptcy, and there was Rajiv Gandhi's assassination. At least politics gave Ravi some perspective. He wrote to Sukanya in 1991,

> Sitting in this turmoil within this august house, where everyone is trying to out-shout each other, I am separating myself from this cacophony and entering deeply within my mind where you are present so vividly & brightly... You and Anoush have filled my life so completely—which was sometime empty & sometime quarter or half filled! I love you both so much.[41]

Ghanashyam: A Broken Branch, his first creative work after his marriage, was a delight for Ravi. In the summer of 1988 Sukanya introduced him, via Britain's Arts Council, to City of Birmingham Touring Opera. This new company, which took opera out to community audiences, was looking for a project that embraced ethnic diversity, while Ravi wanted to return to the stage with what he called a "musical theater," a dance-drama with Indian music. The two ideas converged and the work was quickly commissioned.

It took shape during ten days in Delhi in February 1989. Ravi came up with a tale about a pair of neighboring dancer couples, one north Indian and one south Indian, with Kathak, Bharatanatyam and Kathakali styles all incorporated. The central theme was the danger of drug abuse. The protagonist Ghanashyam, a Kathak dancer played by Durga Lal, spirals into decline through taking *ganja* and *bhang* supplied to him by a fake *sadhu*. He suffers a fatal heart attack, before his spirit returns to possess his neighbor's wife. Ravi created most of the music during sessions at Lodhi Road, gathering his disciples and team around him and, when the sacred hour arrived in late afternoon, improvising his compositions. He also took an active role in suggesting dance moves to Durga Lal and the Dhananjayans, who were the three choreographers and lead dancers. The piece was honed into theatrical form during six weeks of rehearsals at Aston University in Birmingham in the autumn, the music and dance refined in response to each other through an improvisational process.

Evidently the subject of addiction continued to intrigue Ravi. The story, he explained, was his response to the damage that he had seen drugs and alcohol cause to people he knew. But it had supernatural elements to it too (inspired by a late-nineteenth-century ancestor of his, who had been possessed), and underlying it was his favorite narrative structure. After the death of Ghanashyam's wife, which enables his troubled spirit to escape, there is an uplifting finale with the message that life goes on, as the survivors cast off their sadness and resume dancing. Graham Vick, the artistic director, sensed that this scene, in which both cultures come together to dance to Ravi's music, expressed something very personal to him, and describes it as

> a fantastically moving finale of synthesis, really beautiful. It was nothing to do with the story of a wasted life. It was a very different message and a very potent one. I think it represented everything that he was trying to do with his work with Western music and Indian classical music, with north and south India, trying to keep it all open and not close anything down. They found a way of dancing to the same tune. It's a very simple metaphor but profoundly beautiful.[42]

The music, for which Ravi drew on the traditions of folk theater and classical dance, was played live by a stellar ensemble, including Ashit and Hema Desai, and Ravi's disciples Vishwa Mohan Bhatt, Ronu Majumdar, Ramesh Mishra, Daya Shankar, Partho Sarothy, Shubhendra Rao and Shubho. The production opened in October and toured to sixteen UK venues. It sold well, was very positively reviewed and won the prestigious Prudential Award for the Arts. It was truly groundbreaking work. "It was ten years before anybody else was doing this kind of stuff again," says Vick, who is today one of the world's foremost opera directors.[43]

There was a chilling postscript when weeks later Durga Lal, after a marathon solo show in Lucknow, and aged just forty-two, dropped dead of a heart attack, just like his character. Ravi was devastated and could not avoid a strange sense of responsibility. Vick had been awestruck by Durga Lal: "We had a flame dazzling bright at the moment of this piece. He was up there with the two or three greatest artists I have ever worked with. An unprepossessing man, bald, vain, not attractive particularly, but when he breathed a light came on."[44]

A year later Ravi toured *Ghanashyam* to Madras, Bombay, Calcutta and Delhi in a revised production with a new cast. Durga Lal's role was taken by Maulik Shah, a disciple of Kumudini Lakhia, while Kumudini's academy and that of the Dhananjayans provided many of the dancers. The budget was lower and the logistics challenging, but ticket sales were again strong. "There was an overwhelming response, not all of it complimentary," said V. P. Dhananjayan, who received threatening letters in Madras from people protesting on religious grounds about the negative depiction of the *sadhu*.[45] Despite the aggravation, Ravi relished the overall experience of *Ghanashyam*, which took him back to his days in Uday's troupe. Certainly the soundtrack album, which the company recorded at HMV Studios in Calcutta, is profuse with catchy tunes and shows him at his most imaginative.

Indeed, he was on a roll, for even before *Ghanashyam* was staged he had begun his next project, and it was perhaps the most interesting collaboration of his composing career. Private Music, looking for a follow-up to *Inside the Kremlin*, proposed that Ravi work with Philip Glass on an album of new material. This was their first musical encounter since *Chappaqua*. The prolific Glass had built a worldwide reputation in the interim, his best-known works being his operas, his film scores (especially *Koyaanisqatsi*) and his album *Glassworks*. India continued to inspire him. He was a regular visitor to the Madras Music Academy, where Narayana Menon would help by whispering the *talas* in his ear, and he often said that his two most important teachers had been Ravi and Nadia Boulanger, the distinction between them being "One taught through love and the other through fear."[46]

At first Ravi did not see how they could collaborate. He had a strange mental block in that he thought of Glass only as a composer. "He never figured out I played the piano," laughs Glass today.

> He said, "It's too bad you don't have an instrument." I was out doing thirty to forty concerts a year! I never corrected him. Sometimes when we were at the piano together and he was playing something, he'd say, "Someone give Philip a pencil. You think better when you have a pencil in your hand."[47]

Perhaps this misunderstanding was helpful, as it meant they collaborated as composers rather than as performers. It was Peter Baumann's suggestion that they exchange musical themes. When they met at Alan Kozlowski's house in Santa Monica in June 1989, Glass presented Ravi with two short motifs, eight or sixteen bars long, to take away and flesh out in his own arrangements. Ravi, who had not prepared anything in advance, reciprocated by sitting down at the piano and improvising two *raga*-based themes. Each of them agreed to write and record an extra piece of his own, making six tracks on the album, which they titled *Passages*. Glass recorded his three pieces in New York, employing a chamber orchestra and small chorus. Ravi recorded his in Madras, using a core of his disciples—Partho Sarothy, Ronu Majumdar, and Shubho playing the sitar part—augmented by local musicians, with Suresh Lalwani as arranger and Glass in attendance. Although the two halves of the album thus differ in instrumentation, the tracks are integrated and they reinforce each other like warp and weft. "The reason why I think *Passages* works so well," Glass has said, "is that when I listen to those four pieces we did together, I don't know whose music I'm hearing."[48]

Despite their co-writer status, Glass found they naturally fell back into a master–student relationship. He wryly recalls the session in New York when Ravi listened to the playback of Glass's first arrangement: "He said, 'It's fine...but you've murdered the *raga*.' You have to understand something: he had his own ideas about music. He allowed that I had my own—but not when it was *his* music."[49] Glass's view is that Ravi was a great teacher but not a great collaborator, in that he felt compelled to work within *raga* form and policed his strict boundaries around it.

Yet one secret of Indian music is that constraints can be creatively productive, and Glass agrees that *Passages* is a very successful work. It features some of Ravi's finest work with ensembles, such as in *Ragas in Minor Scale*, where his elaboration of the Glass theme segues from 6- to 8-beat cycles to thrillingly seductive effect. The true masterpiece is *Prashanti* ("Peacefulness"), the track that Ravi both wrote and arranged. Yet again he employs his favorite three-part structure, and this time, after the frolicsome instrumental opening and the descent into apocalypse, the hopeful dawn comes in the form of a sublime prayer for peace and love. Ravi wrote its words, in Hindi, and he sings them himself with agonizing tenderness before the south Indian playback singer S. P. Balasubramanyam reprises them in his richer tones. This song, which constitutes the latter part of *Prashanti*, has been separately released under the title "Hey Nath" and, like *Shanti Mantra*, is written in *num-tum* style. It is the second of Ravi's three great vocal works, and perhaps his finest moment of all on record. The sense of space and peace is otherworldly.

Ravi was disappointed by the album's sales and dreamed in vain of it being made into a ballet, but from an early cult following its reputation has blossomed to the point where it is now one of his best-known albums. Its belated live premiere came at the BBC Proms in 2017, courtesy of the Britten Sinfonia, with Gaurav Mazumdar singing

"Hey Nath." Anoushka, who worked with David Murphy to rearrange it for this live performance and played the sitar lead, had watched the original sessions when she was eight, and sees it as a seminal work for the originality with which two traditions meet. "It doesn't have a genre sometimes, even though the melodies are often totally, sweetly Indian," she says. "I think it's some of the most beautiful, syncretic music that he wrote."[50]

When Shubho had returned to playing the sitar it had been after years of rejecting the role of musician. During that time he still loved listening to music. He and Linda had a huge and varied LP collection; he particularly adored Indian film songs, while she loved country music and was an early enthusiast for the Moog synthesizer. He played the sitar at home occasionally but had given up performing. After Occidental College he had started a master's degree at Cal State Long Beach, but he left without completing it. Thereafter he rarely had a job. The one he held down longest was a staff position at the Yellow Pages art department, where he drew advertisements, but that was for less than a year. His father had paid his college fees and for a long time gave him an allowance. The main breadwinner was Linda, who after studying hard at night school had begun a career in programming. "Shubho didn't understand money. I don't think he ever had to think about it growing up," says Linda.[51] What Shubho did have was charm, a gift for languages and a growing passion for cooking Indian food; he was frequently shrouded by a cloud of chili smoke in the kitchen. He happily saw his father when he was in town, but he didn't want to make music with him.

Around 1984 there was a sudden change. "Something happened to him where he decided, wait a minute, music *is* the most important thing," says his son Som Shankar. He started playing recitals at friends' homes and composing music for the Shakti Dance Company run by Viji Prakash, who also found him some music tuition work around southern California. One venue for his sitar lessons was in Encinitas, just north of San Diego, at the home of Purna and Gopa Patnaik, who had become friends through the Trikannads. Shubho found he loved teaching. "That's when he was happy," says Som.[52] He didn't teach his children, but then Som had gravitated early toward electronic music. Kaveri played some flute but preferred baton twirling, and Shubho was delighted when at the age of eleven she took up Bharatanatyam with Viji Prakash.

Shubho also resumed studying with Ravi whenever he was in town. He had a superb touch in the slow *alap* movement, when the left hand dominates, which his mother, with her surbahar style, had inculcated in him. Ravi now worked on his weaker side, his right-hand strokes, and his *layakari*—the myriad of rhythmic patterns and variations that Ravi deemed essential for a performing artist. Shubho improved considerably, and rejoined his father on tours and recordings. This, according to Ravi, was the period when he came closest to his son, when they spent more time together and indulged the childlike sense of fun that they shared. Shubho also had a fabulous voice, and a knack for writing spontaneous tunes reminiscent of his father, which he put to use for Viji Prakash. "Shubho had the type of talent which blossomed late," said Ravi, who was impressed with his creative side.[53] In retrospect he felt that his son could have made an excellent playback singer or music director in Bombay cinema. Meanwhile, Shubho began to heal his relationship with his mother, visiting her on two trips back to India. "I was very glad. He hadn't seen or spoken to his mother for many years," says Linda.[54]

But Ravi and Shubho never completely overcame their dysfunctional father–son relationship. Whenever his father lectured him about his chain-smoking, the normally placid Shubho seethed. He even resented his allowance as a mark of his failure to break free. Sukanya noticed that he didn't hug his father. "There was no warmth in the relationship between Raviji and Shubho," she says. "All that I knew was lessons. It was very strange to me."[55] In the end music pushed them apart. The stern *guru* in Ravi could not help but show his disappointment when Shubho lagged behind. Shubho, for his part, felt the fastest passages were showy. He preferred his mother's style.[56] That was all very well when one was playing for God alone, Ravi reasoned, but an earthbound audience expected some virtuosity, especially at a Ravi Shankar concert.

There was a big argument at a friend's house, when the two of them disappeared into a room and were heard shouting at each other, before Shubho emerged and told his family, "We're leaving."[57] He never repeated what had been said, and Linda feels the issue remained unresolved. Things came to a head during Ravi's American tour in autumn 1991. Shubho asked his father to play familiar compositions in the fastest passages so that he could keep up, but Ravi would not compromise on improvisation, telling him, "I have an audience." After the concert in Philadelphia, Shubho vowed never to play with him again. He relented, but after playing the Orange County Performing Arts Center, it was over.[58] Shubho returned home and cut himself off completely from Ravi.

The year 1992 was immensely difficult for Ravi. It was bad enough that he lost two old friends and key collaborators. On April 23 he spent the day in Studio Synthesis in Delhi recording two solo classical *ragas* for a new album. That night he returned home to the news that Satyajit Ray had died from heart failure. It was not unexpected because three weeks earlier, when Ray had accepted his Honorary Oscar from his Calcutta hospital bed, he was already gravely ill. But Ravi was so emotionally affected that he returned to the studio later that week to deliver an impassioned tribute in the form of a semi-classical *dhun*, weaving together his theme from *Pather Panchali* with *Raga Ahir Bhairav*. He called it *Farewell, My Friend*.

In October Basil Douglas died. Over thirty-one years, through all the changes in Ravi's management in different parts of the world, and all his triumphs and trials, Douglas had been a constant. Latterly he had reduced his roster, but he had continued to represent Ravi until his retirement earlier in the year, at which point he was still thinking of his client's future. Douglas set up a meeting at St. George's Terrace with Angela Sulivan, who had left his agency in 1985 to co-found Tennant Artists, and Ravi invited her to represent him. She accepted. "I felt very honored and I adored Raviji, so I was thrilled," she says.[59]

Ravi's own health was causing concern. His angina had returned and was becoming unstable. The family spent part of the summer staying with the Patnaiks in Encinitas. Ravi loved the quiet suburban area, nestled between the Pacific Ocean and the hills. Conscious that Indian summers were now too fierce for him, London winters too long, and Los Angeles too hectic and smoggy, he and Sukanya decided to move to Encinitas. They asked if there was a suitable house for sale. "The only criterion is it should be walking distance from your house," he told Purna Patnaik.[60] A modern Spanish villa was quickly located. Ravi bought it, and Sukanya, with typical energy, decided on the renovations it needed, which Purna supervised over the next few months.

Encinitas offered clean air, a year-round climate and an SRF ashram beside the sea. The other attraction was the world-class healthcare in nearby San Diego, and for Sukanya this was a vital consideration. A cardiologist there had been recommended to Ravi: Dr. Maurice Buchbinder, a nationally known pioneer of angioplasty, which was a new procedure to relieve angina, in which narrowed coronary arteries are unblocked through inserting and inflating a tiny balloon. Ravi's angina worsened during the summer, and on August 19, under Buchbinder's care, he underwent a double angioplasty.

Before the procedure Ravi became anxious about his son, who had fallen ill with a persistent chest infection but was still incommunicado. He had been sick off and on for a long time, and Linda couldn't persuade him to return to the doctor because previous visits had not seemed to help. Shubho did not have medical insurance, but Linda does not think this was a factor in his eschewing medical care because he never worried about money. The day before Ravi entered hospital, he and Sukanya arrived unannounced at Shubho's Garden Grove home, where they found him in bed, looking very ill. Anoushka waited outside in the car as her anxious parents called a doctor. Soon Shubho was admitted to hospital with advanced bronchopneumonia. Ravi was so concerned about his condition that he immediately called Rooshikumar Pandya in Bombay, spoke to him at length about Shubho and asked for Annapurna to come urgently. It was probably an unrealistic request. She was now such a recluse that she would barely leave her flat, let alone travel to California. Later it became a source of contention between them that neither of them was with Shubho during his illness.

Even if Shubho had wanted him there, Ravi was in no state to sit with him anyway. His angioplasty passed off successfully, but during convalescence at the Patnaiks' house he became dangerously ill with diverticulitis (an infection of the large intestine) and was rushed by ambulance into intensive care. He recovered after five days on antibiotics, but after he was discharged he was very weak, and George Harrison took him to Massachusetts to rest further at a Maharishi Ayurveda centre, while Sukanya flew ahead to London with Anoushka, whose school term was starting. On the morning of September 8 Ravi woke with blurred vision, a drugged sensation and a loss of power in his legs. He did not realize it immediately but he had suffered a stroke. He remained unsteady on his feet, but traveled to London as planned, arriving on the 14th. When Sukanya met him at the airport, George was pushing him in a wheelchair.

The following day, at the Los Alamitos Medical Center, Shubho died. It was Purna Patnaik who had to break the news to Ravi. Sukanya took his call at Osborne Road during the night, then disconnected all the phones. In the morning she waited until Ravi had had his breakfast and morning medication before she said to him, "I need to talk to you." Immediately he said, "Shubho?" Sukanya confirmed his worst fears. Anoushka, who was eleven, remembers going up to see him in his room later and finding him shaking and crying, barely able to speak.[61] He was taken to Clementine Churchill Hospital in Harrow out of concern for his fragile state, and he was unable to travel to

California for the memorial, where Gopa Patnaik read out his eulogy. To Sheila and Prem Trikannad he wrote,

> The sad news struck me hard, followed by dismay, disbelief and then anger toward destiny for this cruel & untimely decision…
> I found in him a beautiful & sensitive soul and a childlike quality which touched me. We all found lately that he had a hidden creative talent which was emerging gradually. Even he was excited by it like others—but just when this was happening came this cruel blow![62]

On Valentine's Day 1993 a house-warming ceremony took place at the new home in Encinitas. A Brahmin priest chanted prayers to bless the house. For Ravi, urban creature that he had become, it was the first time since Borivli nearly forty-five years earlier that he had lived in suburbia. But this was no retirement move; it was more like making a new start. At last he made a concerted effort to break out of his cycle of constant movement. He embraced the role of father and family man, and his focus turned increasingly to teaching the highly promising Anoushka.

Even so, he was still pledged to work on the three parallel fronts— performing, teaching and composing—that had shaped his life for fifty years. He still spent much of the year away from Encinitas, basing himself in London for a month or two every summer during his European concert season, and in India for three to four months each winter.

There was much change for him in his homeland. He decided at last to give up Hemangana. In 1988 he had sold part of its land to the Dubey family business for a bottling plant. He continued to visit sporadically for student workshops into the 1990s, but eventually he sold it. He had lost heart, and now that he had a new home in California it made no sense to retain this remote and expensive asset. He never recouped his huge investment in the site.

He still had ambitious plans in Delhi. He retained 95 Lodhi Road, although it was soon to embroil him in controversy. When he had become an MP back in 1986 he had been entitled to a government house. However, since he already occupied one, he simply remained where he was. After finishing his term, his name was included in error on a list of former parliamentarians who had not relinquished their grace-and-favor homes. Unfair as the charge against Ravi was, he was unable to counter it because no paperwork existed to corroborate Indira Gandhi's transfer of the house to him. He was billed for overstaying, and the Indian press repeatedly mined a story of celebrity discomfort.

His new dream was to build his own *gurukul* residence in the capital, a purpose-built space much larger than he had at Lodhi Road. In 1988, thanks to the intervention of President Venkataraman, the government sold him a prime plot of land in the diplomatic district, Chanakyapuri, at a nominal price, for what was to be a nonprofit-making institution run by RIMPA. (The foundation, which was now re-registered in Delhi, was subtly personalized, the "R" in RIMPA hereafter standing for "Ravi Shankar" rather than "Research.") But after a change of government the terms of the sale were altered, and the project became mired in bureaucracy. In January 1993, unable to get a response from the authorities, Ravi went public with his frustration, threatening to take the project abroad. "The *gurukul* should have been ready by now," he declared. "I want to do something for my country, for my own people. I am not exactly forty or fifty. There is not much time."[63]

It is not surprising he should have felt like that. The stroke that he had suffered left him less steady on his feet, although his ability to play music was not affected. In April 1993 a recurrence of his angina led him to see a cardiologist urgently in Tucson, and in August he underwent his second angioplasty, again under the care of Maurice Buchbinder. Despite this, by November he was complaining again of angina. The angioplasties were serving as maintenance rather than cure, and over the years to come he would have the procedure time and again, on each occasion gaining some medium-term relief.

He had to cancel many recitals in 1993, but in between he managed to stage two events in aid of a new charity close to his heart, the Rajiv

Gandhi Foundation, and used them to draw attention to the war in Bosnia. One was at Washington National Cathedral and the other at the Royal Albert Hall. He called each of them the Concert for Peace— a *Shanti Mantra* in another form.

22

THE INNER LIGHT

It's just our bodies that are old. Inside we're about six years old.
GEORGE HARRISON[1]

In December 1994 the Shankar and Harrison families were holidaying together in Rajasthan. They stopped in Udaipur, the most romantic of Rajput cities with its lakeside marble palaces. One day, when they were exploring the city's streets on foot, Ravi was recognized and a crowd of college students gathered. They jostled each other to get near him, good-natured but over-enthusiastic. Concerned for Ravi's safety—and relishing not being the target of such hysteria himself for once—George took on the unlikely guise of bodyguard, holding back the mob, shielding Ravi and shepherding him into the car. When the door was closed, both families dissolved in laughter. If only the crowd had recognized the minder.

There was always a father–son element in Ravi's relationship with George Harrison, but who was playing which role varied constantly. "He's always been like a *guru* and a father figure," said George, "but at the same time I think mainly of him just as a friend, because we joke around most of the time. Sometimes *I'm* like *his* dad. He can be so childlike."[2] After the death of Shubho, George increasingly assumed filial duties. He flew in to visit Ravi during his increasingly frequent stays in hospital or during his periods of recuperation. He pleaded with him to stop touring, to protect his health. When Ravi responded that he had to tour, George said, "I'll pay you not to do it!"[3] Of course, although Ravi had plenty of bills to pay, it was not only about the money. He still craved the audience, the high of spontaneous creation. With his new family life he was taming some of his restlessness, but it was still there in his need to make and perform music.

George's devotion to Indian spirituality and music was unwavering, and with the deepening of their long-standing friendship there came a renewal of their creative partnership, so that what turned out to be the final years of George's all too short life formed a coda to the heady days of 1966–74. As Ravi approached seventy-five, the two families hatched plans for three projects to mark the milestone: another concert at St. John the Divine in New York (which sadly never happened), an autobiography and a box-set retrospective co-produced by George, which also opened the way to Ravi's last major creative studio project, a labor of love for both of them, *Chants of India*.

However, Ravi's ailments proliferated in 1994. In May he had surgery to repair a hole in his right eardrum. The procedure was successful, but it had the side effect of making more obvious the problem with his left eardrum, which had been perforated since childhood and was irreparable. He had barely 10 percent hearing in the left ear, and what he heard in that ear was at a different pitch from that in the right ear, so he now needed mentally to block out the sound in his left ear when performing. Then, in August, while taking his regular walk in the garden at Encinitas, he slipped and fell heavily on his right arm and shoulder. An X-ray revealed no broken bones, so he continued his schedule: teaching students, practicing the sitar, giving a lecture-demonstration, even traveling to Canada to receive a doctorate from the University of Victoria. It was three weeks before an MRI scan revealed that he had badly torn the rotator cuff in the shoulder. He needed surgery and three to six months of rehabilitation and rest—with no sitar-playing. For Ravi this restriction was torture. He had just resumed playing when he suffered an electric shock, due to faulty wiring, while taking a shower at a friend's home in Calcutta. He survived, but he injured his head as he fell and had to rest for eight more days.

It was around the end of the no-sitar period that I arrived in Encinitas for my first meeting with Ravi. I was twenty-three, the same age as George had been when he met Ravi, but there the parallels ended. I was an editor at Genesis, his new publisher, and had been given

the job of assisting him with writing his autobiography. My qualifi-
cations stretched not much further than a month's preparation, a love
of 1960s music and, helpfully, a Bengali girlfriend named after a *raga*,
Shohini. On arrival, I shed my shoes at the threshold and was ushered
up to the music room, where he was giving a sitar lesson to Anoushka,
then thirteen, and another disciple. Gregarious from the first, he encouraged me to join them on the pristine carpet, so I sat down, cross-
legged in imitation. "Ah, you sit Indian style," he said approvingly.

Ravi was a lean, hawk-like seventy-four-year-old, still handsome,
with the broad Shankar nose. His hair was thinning now but worn
like a flourish, while the sideburns that he had sported since the late
1960s were like a proud vestige of an earlier era. He was immaculate-
ly presented in a smart *kurta*, *pajama* trousers and socks; no shoes,
of course. It was absorbing to study him in motion: his gestures and
facial expressions revealing delight, impatience or playfulness as the
lesson progressed, the dancer in him very much present. There was
an aura about him that I have never encountered in anyone else. He
could command a room without apparent effort.

At the conclusion of the lesson he rose to his feet, and I was struck
by his physical slightness. Standing five foot three (so he liked to
claim), he moved with a frailty that had not been apparent during the
lesson. He and I adjourned downstairs to begin our work. We sat on
one of several cream sofas in the spacious White Room, dominated
by wooden sculptures of the goddesses Lakshmi and Saraswati, and
I began interviewing him. He settled my nerves by taking the lead,
mischievously launching into a story about wetting his bed in Paris,
aged ten. He was happy to talk, and he was fun.

It was soon clear that the age gap between us was of little consequence. He was naturally curious, comfortable working with people
of all ages, used to teaching students younger than me. I often felt like
his pupil, but equally he deferred to me over the written word. I soon
observed his democratic spirit, how he could relate equally to a shop
assistant or a president. But it went further than that: he just seemed

to trust me. Later, when others told me how they got to know him, what resonated was the openness with which they felt welcomed into his life. As Shuchi Bhatt, a London friend of both Sukanya and Ravi, told me, "Once he made room for you in his heart, he really meant it."[4] Our target was to create the text of his autobiography, *Raga Mala*, and over the next couple of years the book took shape. Ravi shared some of his deepest confidences with me. Strangely, from that very first meeting, he raised some matters that he did not want included in the book, explaining, "This can come out after I die." Without asking for it, I was being assigned a future role.

One thing immediately apparent to me was how much hope Ravi was now investing in Anoushka. He said she had all the *lakshana*, the right signs. As she recalls:

> He was a very detailed teacher. He was unbelievably controlling and exacting, to give us the grounding and the shape and the technique, and in some ways I had more of that than anyone else, because he'd started with me from the very beginning. Only many years later did he start asking me to let go, encouraging me to express more freely, after at least ten years of showing me exactly how to inflect my improvisations, with exact pacing and phrasing. Everything was very shaped. Now when I play freely, I feel the vocabulary I have is so strong because of that.[5]

Anoushka's new life in Encinitas gave her more stability and she started to flourish at school. Her musical training took place in a strict environment, but there are plenty of prodigies in the East and West who have started younger and faced much more pressure. Periodically Ravi would check in with her, as she recalls:

> He would say, "Do you love this? It's OK if you stop. I want you to be happy." And then after a pause, "Of course I will be very sad if you don't continue, but it's your choice." Oh Bapi! Back to smiling and nodding. Of course I was going to say I wanted to continue.[6]

Her immersion in music was gradual—there was no sudden plunge—and the deeper she went, the more she loved it. Between the ages of ten and sixteen she was also playing the piano, and for a while she enjoyed the piano more than the sitar. "It felt more private, more safe," she says. "It felt like I could just go and play in a room and no one was watching. There weren't reviews happening. It felt like my own thing in a way, which I think is important at that age."[7]

She would often learn the sitar alongside other disciples, and became used to a stream of visitors. Ravi had few boundaries between his musical and family lives, and there were always people staying on for dinner. "It was always exciting and the creative input was amazing," says Anoushka, but the flipside was that she had to share her parents in what she called this "caravan ideal." "I don't think he knew how to do it differently. He put a huge amount of sweet and touching effort into being Dad, but the way he knew that was a very particular way."[8]

"Uncle George" gave her encouragement but was also sensitive to the pressure she was under. According to her,

> In that sea of people saying, "Is she playing yet? She must play!" he would always find a minute to pull me to the side, even if we were all in the same room together, and ask, "Are you really OK? Are you enjoying playing?" If I'd needed to say, "No, I don't like it," he made it clear that he would have been in my corner.[9]

Soon it was apparent to all the disciples just how gifted she was. The sitarist Paul Livingstone, who became Ravi's disciple in 1995 after his previous *guru* Amiya Dasgupta died, is a fine musician himself but admits affectionately that sharing a lesson with Anoushka "was humiliating in a way because I'd been playing much longer than her!"[10]

In February 1995 a concert was held at Siri Fort in Delhi to celebrate Ravi's seventy-fifth birth year. Many of his disciples played, and in the middle Anoushka performed a sitar solo, with Zakir Hussain on tabla. She was very nervous. "I remember Zakir Uncle being amazing that day," says Anoushka. "He was sweet and caring, and talked to me about his debut aged eleven, when he had played with his dad and Ali Akbar Khansahib. I felt like he was holding my hand throughout that day and the actual performance."[11] Her solo was framed as one element in a celebratory concert, but it was effectively a very public debut. There were TV cameras, and the next day many Indian newspapers carried a picture of her on the front page. Before this, Anoushka had sometimes played tanpura for her father in concert, but from now on she regularly assisted on sitar in a disciple's typical role: shadowing his melody lines, filling in and responding, gradually being given more responsibility, along the way learning matchless lessons in public performance.

When Angela Sulivan became Ravi's agent she took over a few concerts already booked by Basil Douglas, but soon she put a new strategy in place. "He was very clear what he wanted: the best concert halls, his tradition to be treated with respect, and he wanted financial security. It was also very important for Raviji to be seen with core Western classical [musicians]," she says.[12] He no longer wanted any of his concerts to be "own promotions"—meaning that Ravi took the financial risk—as they had occasionally been under Douglas. The risk had previously been tolerable because his concerts always sold well and he was reliable. "Raviji was unbelievably professional," she says. "The show must go on. He would never cancel for anything except health reasons, and then only in extreme cases."[13] But by the early 1990s Ravi could no longer get cancelation insurance because of his poor health. Her first move was to persuade the London Symphony Orchestra to promote a concert at the Barbican Hall in July 1995 as part of their subscription series, paying Ravi a fixed fee. It was an unusual arrangement for an orchestra, but Ravi and the LSO had a long shared history. It was a sell-out success and became an annual event for the next six years, and then continued sporadically for the rest of his life. Elsewhere in the UK Angela sought to work directly with venues, obtaining guaranteed advances against a split of the box office. Demand remained high. "He was becoming a sort of legendary figure," she says.[14]

The net effect was a big boost to Ravi's earnings. Ravi used to tell Angela, "You earn your money in America but you build your career in Europe."[15] But by now he was earning just as much in Europe. Angela took on responsibility for Ravi's representation in the whole world excluding India and North America—and during the 1990s she managed concerts as far afield as Singapore, Bangkok, Japan, Taiwan and Israel. She became close to the whole family and occasionally accompanied them on international trips, but mostly remained in London. "When he came over I would always spend quite a lot of time with them, in a way that I wouldn't with any other artist. There was always a drama whenever there was a Ravi Shankar concert! Problems with visas, or someone losing their passport." She adored working with him. There was just one special request he made every year that she struggled to fulfill: "Please get me back to the Théâtre des Champs-Élysées in Paris."[16]

The box set *Ravi: In Celebration* appeared on Angel Records during Ravi's seventy-fifth birthday year. The selection had been compiled by George Harrison and Alan Kozlowski, who presented it for Ravi's approval. Kozlowski had also become very close to Ravi, who entrusted him with looking after his U.S. film and music archive. He was a disciple and friend who credited Ravi with transforming his life. When he had filmed Uday Utsav in 1983 he was broke. A decade later he had a thriving post-production house in Santa Monica with three hundred staff and three Oscars on the mantelpiece, and he put it down to the blessings of his *guru*. The album's five hours of music, which were mastered at Kozlowski's P. O. P. Sound, drew on forty years of recordings from multiple labels, divided into four thematic discs: classical sitar, orchestral and ensembles, East–West collaboration, and vocal and experimental. It remains an unrivaled curation of Ravi across all his different guises. Two of the previously unreleased tracks are particularly fascinating, in different ways: *V 7½*, the ensemble tour de force from the 1968 *Festival from India* sessions, and *Adarini*, the recording debut of Anoushka. Her inclusion on her father's retrospective, playing one of his compositions in *Khamaj*, signified that she was now being presented by him. As she recorded it in an Encinitas studio, he was watching from the mixing room. "He was exacting about every note and shadow and beat," she recalls.[17]

While *In Celebration* was in progress, Angel's president Steve Murphy put another idea to Ravi. The label had recently enjoyed an enormous and unexpected hit with *Chant*, an album of Gregorian plainchant by the Benedictine monks of Santo Domingo de Silos in Spain. Murphy suspected there was a market among the chill-out generation for a similar album of Indian chants and invocations. As a Brahmin, Ravi was familiar with such chants, and he had featured them as elements in larger works, from *Melody and Rhythm* to *Manoharini*, but he had long wanted to explore them more. With George also an advocate for Vedic chanting, they decided to work together on it. George took the initiative, not only serving as studio producer, but also, after the first recordings in Madras in January and March 1996 produced some unsatisfactory results, hosting the remaining sessions at Friar Park in July. As in 1974, the musicians set up in his drawing room, with cables running upstairs to the studio.

George's meticulous approach as a producer was likened by George Martin to that of a fine Persian carpet-maker, and he was ideally suited to *Chants of India*, which was, according to Ravi, the most time-consuming album he ever worked on.[18] He wanted to create all-new musical settings with a universal appeal, while remaining faithful to the spirit of each chant. The texts were mostly Sanskrit invocations for peace, love and the harmony of the universe: some traditional, some from the Vedas or Upanishads. He was careful to select appropriate words—some mantras should never be vocalized—and assiduous in ensuring that they were rendered with the necessary precision, typically sung using just the three magic notes: the tonic, flattened seventh and flattened second notes (*sa*, *komal ni* and *komal re*). The arrangements, stately and spare, allow space for the chants to take their meditative effect, with prominent use of drones and judicious layering of Indian instruments, bamboo flute and south Indian veena to the fore, plus a harp, string quartet and three different choruses. Additional aural space was created by three instrumental interludes.

Two tracks stand out, both for their musical distinctiveness and because they feature new lyrics by Ravi. "Mangalam," written in Sanskrit with scholarly assistance from Dr. M. N. Nandakumara, director of London's Bharatiya Vidya Bhavan, is an insistent chant built around an extended percussion duel that gives it a driving rhythm. The other is a song written in Hindi, "Prabhujee," that Ravi sang in duet with Sukanya. This is the third of his great vocal works of later years, once again based around slow-tempo, *dhrupad*-style *num-tum*. Unlike the spiritual chants, it is a devotional song, an appeal to "Prabhujee" (God, or perhaps a lover) to "fill this empty pot with the nectar of love." Although it is an expression of longing and yearning, the feeling it creates is that of the tenderest love and overwhelming peace, an indication that Ravi had this time managed to grasp that elusive heaven that usually seemed just out of his reach. He knew that it was special. Ten years later, on Sukanya's fifty-second birthday, he wrote to her, "Please remember the songs I created in some blessed moment! 1) Hey Nath & 2) Prabhujee. Specially the 2nd one—which you & I sang—that created such a magic."[19] He would return to it.

Ravi used the album as an opportunity to involve Anoushka as his creative assistant. She transcribed as he spontaneously composed, and she rehearsed and conducted the ensembles and choirs. He was impressed with how swiftly and intelligently she learned. Once the mixing phase started, she and her mother returned to California, but Ravi stayed on with George for a fortnight, working with me on the autobiography manuscript in between giving feedback on mixes. When George was away one weekend, Ravi suggested a cinema outing. I let him choose the film, of course. Shohini and I picked him up and, after a hunt for 4711 cologne in Boots the Chemists, we settled down at the local multiplex—to watch *Mission Impossible*.

Ravi was thoroughly satisfied with *Chants of India*. After listening to the playback of the first four tracks to be mixed, he wrote to Anoushka:

When I heard it with closed eyes it gave me goose bumps—real good & very effective. George became very high & emotional—embraced me again & again with tears in his eyes, thanking me many times for [this] music. It brought tears to my eyes also & touched me deeply—and I felt rewarded for all these months of agony I have gone through.[20]

It was the last collaborative project between the duo, and George gave a number of joint interviews with him to promote its release in 1997. On the American television network VH1 they even performed "Prabhujee" live, with Ravi on sitar, George on acoustic guitar and Sukanya sharing vocal duties with the pair. It was George's last public performance of any kind. Hopes of matching the exceptional sales of *Chant* were unrealistic but, aided by the promotional push, the album sold well enough, going platinum in India.

One person who was underwhelmed by *Chants of India* was Yehudi Menuhin. After listening to only "parts" of it, he wrote to Ravi, "I found the sounds on this CD somehow a little alien to your tradition and did not feel it carried me away as when I hear you alone with your incredible Tabla players improvising and transported."[21] It was a shame that he had not seen *Melody and Rhythm* or *Nava Rasa Ranga*, in which Ravi had illustrated how Indian classical music in all its complexity evolved from Vedic chants. But their austere purity is not for everyone, and Yehudi's candor was the mark of an honest, close bond. "In the forty-three years of our friendship, Ravi and I have never had an argument," he said in 1995. "He is just my dearest friend," responded Ravi.[22]

It was not as though Yehudi was uninterested in the evolution of musical forms. For his final collaboration with Ravi, they co-curated *From the Sitar to the Guitar*, a two-night festival in Brussels in November 1995 on the development of Romany gypsy music and dance from Indian origins. This was the connection that had so fascinated Ravi in Leeds in 1958 and Bardejov in 1960. While it is now accepted that Romany peoples are descended from Indian nomads, the validity of their musical connection is disputed, but there are striking similarities: for example, in the use of wooden hand percussion, the castanets of flamenco echoing the khartal beloved in India.

Ravi selected the Indian performers. "There are gypsies or semi-gypsies all over India," he wrote to Yehudi, "but their music and dance is very poor in quality, except Rajasthan, Punjab and Haryana. Rajasthan stands out [as] unique because of their rich and very high standard."[23] During the holiday that the Shankar and Harrison families took in Rajasthan, Ravi organized a tented private concert near Jodhpur by two groups of hereditary folk musicians from the desert, the Langas and Manghaniyars. Both groups are Muslims whose culture also embraces Hindu traditions, and their music expresses an ecstatic devotion that is kindred to *qawwali* singing. Thirteen-year-old Anoushka was mesmerized (this was one seed of her later solo album *Traveller*), but she did not realize at the time that they were auditioning for Ravi. "See, you could never just have a holiday with him!" she laughs today. "There I was thinking we were having a lovely family holiday, and it was a work trip."[24]

As well as compèring the show alongside Yehudi, Ravi opened it himself with a classical sitar recital accompanied by Kumar Bose, each night performing a new *raga* he had created, *Banjara* on the 24th and *Piloo Banjara* on the 25th. After the Rajasthani troupe, there were performers from Slovakia, Russia and Algeria, and the flamenco dancer Blanca del Rey with her shawl dance, before Ravi arranged and conducted the music for her grand finale using the Indian, Russian and flamenco musicians.

Yehudi had recently retired from playing the violin in public, but he was still a prolific conductor (112 concerts in 1996, the year he turned eighty) and a restless firefly committed to realizing music's healing power. "He has been looking old and quite frail, but he is still driven like the devil," said Ravi. "As far as work is concerned, my nature is the same as his, but I've had a couple of heart attacks and have had to slow down…I look at Yehudi's schedule and it's scary."[25] But Yehudi would not change. "I couldn't imagine life without the whirlwind," he told his daughter Zamira.[26] He came once more to India, in January 1998, appearing as chief guest at a concert Ravi organized at Siri Fort to mark India's golden jubilee year. That evening Anoushka performed two duets with Jean-Pierre Rampal: on *Morning Love* she played the sitar, while on *Enchanted Dawn*, rearranged for flute and piano, she played the piano part. Philip Glass happened to be in town and joined the dinner party at the Taj Mansingh afterward, completing a remarkable quartet.[27]

That summer there was a happy echo of the past when Ravi played the New York Jazz Festival. He was booked on a double bill at Town Hall, the other attraction being saxophonist Ravi Coltrane, the son of John Coltrane, in what was dubbed the "Two Ravis" concert. Ravi Coltrane had just released his first album. Although he had been named after his father's mentor, and had heard many stories about him, he had never met Ravi—until a month before the concert, when they bumped into each other at the Juliet Hollister Awards, where Ravi was being honored alongside the Dalai Lama, Swami Satchidananda and others.

India's attainment of its half-century in August 1997 came at a time of growing national self-confidence. Like Ravi himself, the country had embarked on a new course at the beginning of the decade. It had shrugged off the era of the "Licence Raj" by liberalizing its economy, and the lasting boost given to growth rates was already apparent, although—as in other countries—rising inequality and pollution has dogged the country since, and the impact of rapid change on its culture has been problematic. India's new assertiveness was symbolized by the shedding in this period of British place names, so that Madras became Chennai, and Bombay became Mumbai. It was in Mumbai that Ravi marked the anniversary, playing a midnight concert with Anoushka and Zakir Hussain at the NCPA. He unveiled a new *raga*, *Suvarna*, and a new *tala*, *Jayanti*, the latter a mind-boggling 50-beat cycle divided, in a palindromic structure, 3–4–5–6–7–7–6–5–4–3. The next morning's newspapers lauded Ravi in their Independence Day special issues, the Calcutta *Telegraph* naming him one of ten people in independent India who had made "a positive difference," and the *Times of India* hailing him as "the Sun who rose in the West."[28] In the UK the BBC marked the independence of both India and Pakistan by televising his concert at Birmingham Symphony Hall, and he played in a gala at the Albert Hall. He also had a déjà-vu experience under a big top at the Womad festival. Initially he was perturbed to be confronted by the kind of unruly festival crowd that he thought he had escaped years before. "Sit down!" he called out, which succeeded in stilling the hubbub, and then he added, by way of explanation, "I am your grandfather! I love you all."[29] A memorable recital followed, with George and Dhani Harrison in the audience.

Meanwhile, in another echo of the 1960s, Indian music was once more breaking through in British pop music. The difference this time was that it was being driven by second-generation south Asians. Moreover, thanks to the new ubiquity of electronic dance music, nobody in the West was startled by the drone any more—a long-term shift that could be traced back, reversing past house music, disco, Krautrock, minimalism and modal jazz, to the Indian music that Ravi had introduced in the 1950s and 1960s. The so-called Asian Underground brought together Indian instruments, rhythms and melodies with the sounds of drum'n'bass or jazz-funk. This music bore a tenuous relation to what Ravi was doing, but at the age of seventy-seven he remained a touchstone for its protagonists. East Londoner Talvin Singh, whose compilation album *Anokha* and eponymous club night were definitive expressions of the movement, was a classically trained tabla player who revered Ravi. In 1999, shortly after DJing at Anoushka's eighteenth birthday party, he won the Mercury Music

Prize for his album *OK*, taking the movement overground. When the Midlands indie band Cornershop recorded a cover of "Norwegian Wood" with Punjabi lyrics, there was the feeling of a circle being completed. Ananda Shankar, whose raga-rock songs now had cult status, was also enjoying a revival. Although there was an element of gimmick in the way that Indian music was co-opted by some pop stars, music culture had become much more heterogeneous, and recent years have seen a proliferation of Indian-influenced musical exploration under the broad banner of fusion, much of it of very high quality. The Renaissance man to emerge from this movement was Nitin Sawhney. He was trained in both Western and Indian classical systems, as well as in flamenco guitar and jazz, and was another big Shankar aficionado. "In the 1990s I was making a strong point of integrating Indian classical music into everything I did," he has said.[30] His breakthrough fourth album *Beyond Skin* in turn earned Ravi's appreciation.

The most significant development of 1997 was Norah's return to Ravi's life. After no direct contact for six years, she had called him in 1995, but it was solely to request his authorization to drop "Geetali" and "Shankar" from her legal name, as she simplified it to Norah Jones for her first driving license. It must have saddened him, and the conversation was brief. A year later, when he performed in Houston on Anoushka's birthday and played "Happy Birthday" for her on the sitar, Norah was in the audience incognito and did not come backstage. But when she turned eighteen she received a letter from him through a lawyer and took up the invitation to call. This time, it was Anoushka who answered the phone at home. She introduced herself, and they laughed awkwardly, before the phone was handed over to her father. He spoke for a while, but was rather overwhelmed and was about to hang up when Sukanya grabbed the handset and invited Norah to come and stay. She agreed and soon after arrived in Encinitas.

That first week together was a success, for which Ravi always gave the credit to Sukanya and Anoushka. They both went out of their way to welcome Norah, and Sukanya made a point of treating both sisters equally. Norah recalls how she instantly bonded with Anoushka:

We used to say this thing to each other, "You're the best sister I never had." We got really close at first, and then we had typical sistery fights for a while, but it always felt really good. I'm really thankful that we became so close. I feel that we had that sister chemistry, even though we didn't have that growing up together.[31]

Ravi then invited Norah to join them for about three weeks on his summer tour of the UK, Turkey and Budapest, and it was now that Norah tried to get answers from him about the past. One day the two of them locked themselves in a room for hours. Anoushka remembers:

I remember hearing the noise from outside and thinking, "Oh, you can shout at him?" I didn't know you could do that. Because to me, the way my mother raised me and the way the atmosphere was growing up around his disciples, he was the God, the legend, the love, the father, the *guru*. You didn't shout at that. I felt oddly jealous and surprised that she came and was able to have a real experience, sharing her anger and moving through her difficulties with him. That seemed really healthy to me. I ended up talking about that stuff with her a lot over the years.[32]

"When I first got reunited with him I was eighteen, and I was kind of angry," says Norah. "I was like, 'Where have you been?' But it didn't really work with him, approaching him like that. Maybe I got some frustration out."[33] "He didn't like conflict," confirms Anoushka:

The idea of someone confronting him in a room was anathema to him, but he had to hear it out. At that point he possibly didn't know how to deal with that. But I could see he was also thrilled. It always felt like there was a hole in him that she wasn't there all those years, and so when she came back it did complete something for him. He loved her.[34]

"We had a lot of fun and a lot of laughs, and also a lot of difficult moments," says Norah.

> But it was still one of the most fun experiences for me because I got to see him play music so much. I got to go to every show. It was beautiful and it was inspiring. I was just starting to write songs and figure out my own self musically. I loved it, and it kind of seeped in, and it was great to actually experience that side of him.[35]

The time spent with Ravi, Sukanya and Anoushka was Norah's first serious exposure to Indian culture, which had been absent from her life in Texas. "Growing up I really struggled a lot with my identity," she says.

> I like to pretend that I didn't, but I think I did, because nobody ever knew what I was, and they always wanted to know, "What are you?" Which is a silly question, but everybody thought I was Mexican, and I watched Apu in *The Simpsons* and I didn't know what to think! It was just me and my mom, and we didn't really talk about my dad to anybody.[36]

She had instinctively gravitated to music, but for her it was country, jazz and blues, her heroes Billie Holiday, Willie Nelson or Aretha Franklin. She attended a performing arts high school in Dallas, and on that first visit to Encinitas the whole family was smitten when she played the piano and sang for them. Her voice, according to her father, was "like liquid gold."[37] Linda Shankar, who brought Kaveri down to see her, remembers Norah singing all the time.[38] When Ravi introduced me to Norah in London that summer, he said she was a talented jazz singer and pianist. That autumn she began majoring in jazz piano at the University of North Texas.

Norah continued to visit the Shankars regularly. Sometimes she felt jealous watching their concerts—there was the unavoidable thought that "I could have been taught by him"—but she concluded that she liked the music she played. "I felt a lot of conflicted feelings but in the end I don't have any regrets, because I am who I am and I grew up the way I grew up, and it was different. I am happy that we all were able to become close." In January 2000 she flew to Delhi to stay with them for four weeks. This was her first adult trip to India. There was the predictable culture shock, but she enjoyed a warm welcome, and was particularly struck by her father's status there: "It was like he was a king."[39]

Anoushka was going from strength to strength. At sixteen she was signed to Angel Records by Gilbert Hetherwick, who had arrived to run the label after Steve Murphy's departure. In May 1998 she recorded her first solo album, very much under her father's wing: not only did she play his *ragas* and compositions, which he had taught her, but he produced it too. She recorded it over one weekend at Alan Kozlowski's P. O. P. Studios in Santa Monica, and then it was back to school on Monday. She was getting used to having a dual identity: one moment a sitar-playing disciple touching her father's feet, the next a Californian teenager. "They felt like the on–off switches on electrical lights. A lot of people of mixed culture learn how to do that," she says. "It wasn't that one was fake, or more me or less really me, but more that those aspects were compartmentalized."[40] She started touring in her own right, and increasingly at Ravi's recitals she would play solo for the first half, and he would appear only after the interval. Her second album followed in 2000, and that summer she played a memorable free concert in New York's Central Park on the same bill as drum'n'bass star Roni Size.

Hetherwick persuaded Ravi that Angel should issue a new live album by him, and arranged for the Carnegie Hall concert on October 6, 2000 to be recorded. For his set, which features *ragas Kaushi Kanhara* and *Mishra Gara*, Ravi was accompanied by Anoushka on sitar, and by Bickram Ghosh and Tanmoy Bose, who had become his regular tabla accompanists on foreign tours. The album, named *Full Circle* after his eightieth birthday tour, won Ravi his third Grammy, for Best World Music album, in February 2002. Angel also recorded

Anoushka's solo set earlier in the evening, and released that a year later. Hetherwick, who considers Ravi "the greatest musician I have ever known in my life," gave his artists good support. When signing Ravi for the live album, he told EMI's lawyers, "This contract has to be overly fair and right. This is Ravi Shankar. If you do anything wrong you will go to hell, you do realize that?"[41] He also set in motion a remastering and reissue program for Ravi's back catalog across various EMI labels (including World Pacific), most of these albums appearing in digital format (initially on CD) for the first time—an invaluable contribution to his recorded legacy.

When Angel had signed Anoushka, Hetherwick had recommended Earl Blackburn, then at IMG Artists, to be her first manager. Blackburn, who had been attending Ravi's concerts since the age of seven, flew out to Encinitas and explained to Sukanya and Anoushka what his management would entail. On the spot, they confirmed their agreement. As the meeting finished, Ravi joined them. "I'm so happy that you are going to be managing my daughter," he said. "I am just wondering, would you be able to manage me as well?" Blackburn almost fell off his chair. Like Angela Sulivan in London a few years earlier, he felt sure Ravi's agent could be doing more for him at this stage in his career. "I didn't think that there was a clear plan for where he should be playing and I felt that, frankly speaking, he was being underpaid," he says.[42] Sukanya agreed; she had already been pushing for his fees to be raised. When Blackburn took Ravi on, they tripled his fee, and the market accepted it. With Blackburn handling North America and Angela Sulivan the rest of the world bar India, Ravi's fees hit their highest ever levels. The strategy was fewer concerts, at prestige venues. Audiences responded to the sense that this was a unique artist at the end of his life. "Last chance to see" is a strong motivation.

Concert schedules and arrangements were carefully managed to alleviate the strain on Ravi, and for almost the first time he was traveling with a tour manager. This concentration on his health was important. In the summer of 1999 he was admitted to London's

Royal Brompton Hospital as an emergency. This was an occasion that Angela Sulivan remembers as particularly frightening because for once Sukanya was away, in India. George Harrison spent a lot of time at his bedside. Ravi recovered, after being given more angioplasties. Even though this was becoming a familiar pattern for the family, it still meant a great deal of anxiety. "What was it, seventeen angio-plasties by the end? I remember at one time thinking the honorary doctorates and angioplasties were neck and neck," says Anoushka.

> There were so many experiences over the years. For example, once when we were in the shuttle from our Encinitas home on the way to the airport, he felt pains in his heart, and my mum and dad sent me and the tabla players to do the shows without them, whilst he went to the hospital to have another life-threatening surgery. In fact my very first solo concerts aged eighteen were accidental ones, in Spain and Italy, for huge outdoor audiences who had been expecting my dad and got me instead. Invariably, of course, after any of these incidents he'd soon be on the road again.[43]

Medicine aside, nobody was in much doubt that what kept him going was music.

Looking back, Anoushka realizes that she was having to deal from a young age with her father's fragile mortality.

> It did create a kind of extended state of intensity. He never knew how much time he had, so there was always a depth and weight to our connection. One of the hardest conversations I remember was in Encinitas, when an ambulance had just been called and my mum went to the bedroom quickly to get a hospital bag together. My dad held my hand and said, "You know I'm fighting to stay alive for you. I have so much more to give you." I felt such a mix of emotions in that moment, including love, gratitude, pressure and a sense of his pain and physical struggle. I replied to him that I

didn't want him to fight if it was too painful. I felt guilty for years afterward, as if I'd told him to go, but I think I meant I didn't want him to struggle. Looking back, I think the lighter moments of laughing and hanging out being silly felt really precious to me— they felt like the real father–daughter connection.[44]

The risks posed by grueling tours had been underscored in March 1999 by the death of Ravi's great friend Yehudi Menuhin, who had kept up a relentless pace until a heart attack felled him in Berlin—on tour to the end. In his violin case, along with family mementos, he was found to be carrying a silk scarf given to him by Ravi.[45] A couple of years later, Hetherwick told Ravi over dinner about the Italian conductor Giuseppe Sinopoli, who had recently died on the podium while conducting *Aida*. At this Ravi lit up and declared, "That's how I want to go!" Sukanya tossed her napkin at him, telling him to stop.[46]

Two other bereavements during this period were especially hard to take. His nephew Ananda died far too young at fifty-six, following complications after appendix surgery, while Alla Rakha's passing at eighty was made all the more painful by the circumstances: he suffered a heart attack after learning of the death of his daughter Razia during cataract surgery, and died while his ambulance was stuck in Mumbai's traffic. Ravi was in Trivandrum with Sukanya, Norah and Anoushka when he heard the news, and he flew in to be present at the burial. They had made their peace, and Ravi penned a long, affectionate tribute in *India Today*, reflecting that "Bhaiya was a happy man and that inner bliss communicated itself in his playing."[47]

Ravi's greater financial security now enabled him to proceed with RIMPA's new institution in Delhi. To fund it, he donated the prize money from three awards—the Ramon Magsaysay from the Philippines, Japan's Praemium Imperiale and Sweden's Polar Music Prize— and there were grants from the Ford Foundation and other bodies. He also set up a nonprofit in the USA, the Ravi Shankar Foundation (its motto, "Peace through Music"), which enabled him to play benefit concerts in America and transfer funds to India to build the center. Even after official authorization was given in Delhi, progress was slow and bureaucracy tortuous. Ravi did consider building in California instead. But as the millennium drew to a close an impressive stone structure arose on José P. Rizal Marg, comprising indoor and outdoor auditoria on an intimate scale, with Jaipur-style *jali* stone screens, a recording studio, an archive, five student rooms and separate family quarters. The final cost was six times the original estimate. On April 7, 2001, Ravi's eighty-first birthday, he played during the first public function of the Ravi Shankar Centre.

A further trio of awards set the seal on his international reputation. France presented him with the Légion d'honneur, the UK gave him an honorary knighthood, and, most cherished of all, in 1999 India awarded him its highest civilian honor, the Bharat Ratna. He was only the second musician to receive it, after M. S. Subbulakshmi the year before. Even though Ravi stated publicly that Vilayat Khan should have been given the same award, Vilayat attacked him for accepting it, arguing with breathtaking discourtesy that he was a better musician than Ravi, from a "superior" *gharana*, and moreover that Ravi knew it.[48] "If there is any award for sitar in India, I must get it first," said Vilayat.[49] Ravi held his tongue. Vilayat's bluntness was part of his appeal to some people, and it was true that he never received the official recognition that his extraordinary talent deserved, but he was also his own worst enemy, and he still saw Ravi at the heart of a conspiracy to deny him his due. Otherwise most responses to Ravi's Bharat Ratna were positive. Playwright and director Girish Karnad said that Ravi had been the single most influential figure in India's cultural life during the previous fifty years.[50]

Ravi was renowned among friends for his impish sense of humor, bad puns and corny jokes. Mark Kidel, who directed the award-winning 2002 documentary *Ravi Shankar Between Two Worlds*, said that he had "a marvelously light touch and a strong spiritual core."[51]

Cellist Barry Phillips, who became Ravi's disciple in 1996, provides a couple of examples. Once, when they were touring, Ravi bit into an airport sandwich that Phillips had brought him. Finding the French bread too stale, he started singing in a surprisingly good Bob Dylan impression: "It's hard, it's hard..." Ravi also liked to ask what voice Phillips sang in: "The answer was, of course, Barry-tone."[52]

The love of wordplay was something he shared with George Harrison, who nicknamed Ravi the Pundit. "They made each other laugh as if they shared a secret. And I'm sure they did," said Olivia Harrison.[53] The closeness of their friendship intensified further in George's final years. His cancer first appeared in his throat in 1997, shortly after *Chants of India* was released. He had surgery and radiotherapy and was given the all-clear, but on December 30, 1999 he was brutally attacked in his own home in the middle of the night by a mentally disturbed intruder, who stabbed him repeatedly. He came within about an inch of dying that night. Even amid such horror, he maintained his Pythonesque sense of humor; as he was wheeled off to hospital, drenched in blood, he asked a new staff member, "So what do you think of the job so far?" His wounds healed, and he was well enough to attend Ravi's Barbican concert the following summer. But the attack drained him emotionally and physically, and his son Dhani quite reasonably blames it for the return of his cancer.

While George was recuperating from the attack he stayed with various friends, including Ravi in Encinitas. "George revered him. He felt he was a really important person in the world, and loved his music," says Olivia.[54] Ravi wrote the Harrisons a touching letter in which he recommended a book he had recently read, Mitch Albom's *Tuesdays with Morrie*, which was full of philosophical perspectives on life. "Truly speaking, I am an illiterate person & have read more stupid books than the meaningful ones! But this book touched me & that's why I wanted to share it with you," wrote Ravi, concluding, "I love you dearly & pray for your good health & *best* of everything."[55] They remained in contact, and even as George was being treated for the cancer that had reappeared in his lungs and his brain, he faxed birthday greetings to Ravi. Ravi flew to Switzerland to perform a last private recital for him, and as the end drew near he, Sukanya and Anoushka visited him one final time in Los Angeles, where Ravi sat at his bedside holding hands and saying farewell. George died the following day, November 29, 2001.

"I feel I have been cheated by George," wrote Ravi a week after his death. "Why did he have to go so soon at such a young age when I really wanted to go first?"[56] The irony was that George had been anxious when he attended Ravi's concerts in later years because he was terrified Ravi would collapse on stage. He had kept trying to persuade him to retire. Ravi said that if he didn't achieve everything he wanted to in this life, he hoped for another life to finish it. George didn't want to come back. He told Ravi he had done enough, and there was a better world. For years George had said that his ambition was to have no ambition. It was a spiritual lesson that Ravi struggled with.

The Concert for George, a memorial celebration organized by Olivia along with George's great friends Eric Clapton and Brian Roylance, was held at the Royal Albert Hall a year to the day after his death. The evening opened with the closing track from *Chants of India*, for, as Olivia said, "At the end of his life George said to me that all he could listen to was *Sarve Shaam*. After all the sounds and sights and tastes you experience over a lifetime, it came down to the purity of *Sarve Shaam*."[57] Ravi gave an introductory speech, telling the audience that he was sure George was present that night. Ravi did not perform himself, Anoushka playing the sitar parts, but he gave the greatest gift in the form of *Arpan*, a superlative twenty-three-minute suite that he composed and arranged for a mixed Indian and Western ensemble, conducted by Anoushka. It featured a solo sung by Sukanya, and another on acoustic guitar by Clapton. The lyric sang of George, or rather of "Jayaraj Harisana," Ravi's playful Indian name for his Krishna-loving rock'n'roll saint of a friend. The concert was the perfect homage to George's life, presenting Ravi's Indian ensemble music that had so inspired him on the same bill as classic rock songs by other close friends, with a couple of *Monty Python* sketches to ward off the sadness. "He would have thought dying was worth it just to see Eric on stage playing a solo in *Arpan* and all those musicians who finally were so deeply moved by that music," says Olivia. "If you go back to George and *Nava Rasa Ranga* and finish that bookend with *Arpan*, it was such a life cycle."[58]

23

A STUDENT OF MUSIC

*Obviously I am approaching my last great journey. I have no fear and will
greet the Ferryman with glorious music! But, hopefully, not yet.*
RAVI SHANKAR[1]

"India Calling!" read the poster for the Hollywood Bowl, and at the age
of eighty-nine Ravi was still doing the calling on his country's behalf.
It was late summer 2009, and when I arrived in Encinitas for my final
interview with Ravi he was in an upbeat mood, preparing a new Indian
ensemble composition for the gala concert. He was going through a
surge of productivity that belied any assumptions about his age.

We sat down in the White Room, as we had on our first meeting,
and spent several hours catching up. He ranged freely across musical
projects, family developments and his lengthening medical history,
but there was one thing he said that struck me forcefully. "I feel very
strongly that I am now a much better musician than ever before, so
much more creative," he said. "Maybe I don't have the same speed or
stamina of youth, but believe me, I have trouble sleeping these days
because so much music is going through my head."[2]

If old age had some musical benefits, it also brought the sense of
being the last one standing at the party after too many friends had
left without him. It was George Harrison he missed the most. "I don't
know why he had to leave so early," he said.[3] He talked also of his
brother Debendra, who had died in 2003, aged ninety-five. "Still the
longest-lived among us brothers," said Ravi. "It's one record I would like
to break."[4] He lamented the recent death of his close disciple Deepak
Choudhury, and that of Ali Akbar Khan barely two months before.

When Ravi had been ill in 2006, Ali Akbar had driven five hundred miles from the Bay Area to check on him. Ravi had reciprocated

two years later when his *gurubhai* was ailing. He was upset by his condition. "I can't see him like this," Ravi told Swapan Chaudhuri. For all the decades of tension with Ali Akbar there was a deep fraternal bond. "They had a very funny relationship," says Chaudhuri, who was close to both. "They could criticize each other, but you cannot poke your nose in there. If you say anything to Khansahib about Raviji, he is going to kill you! Same thing with Raviji. Their love was intense."[5]

At one point, Ravi and I were joined by Suki, the family dog. Ravi's eyes lit up. Suki was such an intelligent, sensitive creature that she would watch his concerts silently from the front row before leaping up on stage at the end to take the applause with him. "Hello, Suki! Now she is the life force. Her love for Sukanya is something which I am so jealous of," he said. At this point Suki nuzzled up to me. "She won't come to me," he smiled. "They can be very obstinate, these poodles. She is a Maltese and poodle combination, a Maltipoo...I remember one of my English girlfriends used to call me Ravipoo." He had a twinkle in his eye now. "No one called you Olliepoo?"[6]

Ravi's last decade had begun with the most startling development. Norah had moved to New York in 1999 to pursue a career as a musician. After a year of playing in bars and cafes, she was spotted by an accounts executive at Blue Note, who made sure that Bruce Lundvall, head of the label, heard her demo tape. Lundvall, who had first met Norah at the "Two Ravis" concert, was bowled over and signed her up. To Ravi's delight, this meant that both his daughters were now in the EMI family with him. Norah's first album, *Come Away with Me*, was released in February 2002. From the start, it turned heads with its seductive late-night country/blues sound, and Norah's voice, all honey and smoke, captured hearts by the millions. It entered the Contemporary Jazz chart at number 1, where it remained all year. By January 2003 it reached the summit of *Billboard*'s Top 200 national album chart. In February it earned a remarkable eight Grammy Awards. The photograph of her clutching the five she herself had won, wearing a delightfully bemused expression, was the image of the night. Ravi's pride was doubled by Anoushka's nomination for *Live at Carnegie Hall*, which made her the youngest ever nominee in the World Music category. Norah's album was everywhere, and it kept on selling. To date it has shifted over 27 million copies. She was the world's best-selling female artist of the decade.

She was unprepared for success on this scale. The endless promotion was demanding enough, but she also had to cope with press curiosity about her relationship with her father. When she told *Rolling Stone* that he had nothing to do with her or her music, journalists identified a sore spot and repeatedly probed it.[7] Although she thanked all her family at the Grammys, they leaped on the fact that she did not mention him by name. There were false stories of a rivalry with Anoushka, and veteran Bollywood star Dev Anand even announced that he intended to make an unauthorized biopic about Norah.

Ravi, who watched the ceremony on television from Delhi, put out an immediate statement. "There is no rift between us," he declared.

> There have been stories to that effect, but the truth is just that…
> I couldn't find her when her mother moved away, and Sue didn't
> want me to be in touch with her. But we are the best of friends
> now. She is an adoring big sister to Anoushka. She is my daughter
> and I love her.[8]

"I was wary of talking about my dad because he's very famous," Norah said two months later in a phone interview from Encinitas, where she was visiting him.

> I didn't want my lineage to be the first thing people knew about
> me because it would set up expectations and comparisons before I
> played any music. I've never said anything negative about my dad,
> but people twist things… We are very close now. For the past five
> years we've reconciled and it's been really good.[9]

"It caused a lot of bumps in my relationship with my father, my sister, my stepmom and my mom, which is why it was so frustrating, because I couldn't say anything that would please everybody," Norah says now.

> People asked me this question all the time, and I didn't really know what to say any more, so I finally shut down, and I said, "I can't talk about this." I thought that it wasn't key to my story or my music. Maybe it was, but in my mind at the time the fact that he was my dad was separate. It was a cool little anecdote, but it wasn't the story to me.

She adds, with self-deprecating laughter, "I thought *I* was the story!"[10] Her refusal to answer questions about her private life initially fed the press suspicion that she was covering up a feud, and rumors continued to circulate that he had abandoned her, but she felt silence was the sanest option and the feeding frenzy did pass. "It turned me from a very open, say-whatever type of person, publicly, to a super-guarded person, because it caused so much anguish," she says. "Honestly, things could be worse, for all of us. But it was just not worth it."[11]

Gradually things were smoothed over with her father. "We sorted it out," says Norah.

> I think it made me a little bit distant from him for a while, but after he got really sick once and I came, and he pulled through, after that I feel like we all came together a lot more. Everybody got some distance and saw that there was some aspect of bullshit to it all that we just can't let in our little bubble, including my mom. My mom over the years made lunches for them, and welcomed them, and tried really hard to mend it all. I think they did it for my sake, but I'm sure it was healing for them too.[12]

Sue and Sukanya got to know each other better when Norah played the Hard Rock in Las Vegas, and when Ravi celebrated his ninetieth birthday with a party in Carlsbad, near Encinitas, Sue came to stay with them, and Sukanya gave her the seat next to Ravi at the dinner.

There was a lightness to Ravi and Norah's relationship that allowed them to shake off the burden of the past. "I remember sitting down and trying to ask him about John Coltrane, because I loved his music," she says.

> He told me a little bit, but I always felt like those moments where we tried to talk about his history were a little forced for me and him. My favorite moments with him were just sitting around and being silly. Because he was a really silly person, actually, and those were when we had the most fun. It had nothing to do with his musicianship or his past or his legendary status, it was just us goofing off, dancing, doing little eyebrow dances or watching movies. He always wanted me and Anoushka to dance around and be silly, to the point where we sometimes felt we were being told to perform for him like monkeys! But we also loved it.[13]

For a long time it seemed that Ravi was not going to write again for Western classical musicians. There were no suitable commissions and his time was filled with other commitments. But while composing he often visualized orchestral possibilities—he might tell Sukanya, "If only I had ten violins there!"[14] He continued to perform his first concerto up until 1997, when he and Anoushka shared the soloist's duties in a Barbican recital, with Zubin Mehta conducting. At one point that evening Ravi's improvisation went off into uncharted territory, and briefly Mehta did not know where he was in the score. Anoushka started playing the violin part on her sitar to show him. Afterward Mehta hugged her and said, "Thank you for saving my life!"[15] It was a watershed moment. Ravi had to acknowledge that the time was approaching to pass the concerto torch to Anoushka. He played it only once more, in Lille. Anoushka took on the role—initially with the first concerto—in Berne in 2005, and performed it that summer at the BBC Proms.

One project that interested Ravi was to arrange his first sitar concerto for solo guitar and orchestra. He approached John Barham about it in 1993. Reasoning that a classical guitarist cannot replicate a sitar's overtone sonorities nor its sympathetic-string resonance, nor slide nor bend notes to comparable effect, Barham instead exploited the guitar's unique coloristic qualities, using chords, harmonics, arpeggios and multiple stops. While Ravi appreciated Barham's work, he was unimpressed by the test recording done by an unnamed guitarist, which Barham admits was unsatisfactory. "All the ornamentations, intonations and accents are wrong," said Ravi.[16]

Ravi was attracted instead by working directly with a soloist, and he revived the idea after meeting the German classical guitarist Hucky Eichelmann in 1995 in Bangkok, where he was a long-term resident. In late 1998 Eichelmann spent about two weeks in Encinitas working closely with Ravi on a completely new guitar part, followed by a further fortnight in Delhi. Ravi instructed Eichelmann to avoid microtones; he did not want the guitar to imitate a sitar. Days were spent on the *alap* alone. What Ravi really needed was to work face to face with a guitarist on the detail of every note. Eichelmann loved the collaboration. What stunned him, apart from Ravi's constant creativity—"he was like a fountain, music constantly pouring out"—was that he had every note of the score in his head.[17] Ravi was satisfied with the guitar part they devised, and there was interest from Australia in arranging a performance, but the project lost impetus while Ravi was having a series of angioplasties. The guitar version of the concerto has yet to be recorded or performed, but the score does exist.

The germ of another project emerged in 1995, when Sukanya's mother Parvati Rajan was staying with them in Delhi. One day Ravi mentioned how much younger he had felt since marrying. "I named you right, then," Parvati told her daughter. Ravi asked what she meant. So Parvati told him the story of Sukanya from the *Mahabharata*, a princess who married a much older man, the sage Chyavana, who was subsequently transformed into a young man as part of a test for her.

Ravi delighted in the parallels. "I would love to make a dance-drama—or maybe an *opera* about it!" he said. However, for now it was merely an idea. "He was always building castles in the air," says his wife.[18]

Ravi's fallow period came to an end with a notable composition in *Raga Palas Kafi* for cello and sitar, which he wrote for the Russian virtuoso Mstislav Rostropovich to play with Anoushka at the 1999 Evian Festival. It is one of Anoushka's favorites among her father's duet works:

> It's as if he found this incredible balance: it's perfectly in a *raga* and yet it doesn't sound like you've taken solo Indian structure and transposed it to a Western instrument. Also I hadn't heard anything of his with cello and sitar before, and that was hugely influential on me.[19]

She subsequently recorded it with Barry Phillips on cello for the album *ShankaRagamala*, a three-volume collection of Ravi's works performed by his disciples that was prepared for his eightieth birthday.

Ravi's third collaboration with Philip Glass took place in 2004. Around this time Glass was writing a lot of film soundtracks. When he had to visit Los Angeles for sessions, he liked to take the early plane from New York and drive down to Encinitas for lunch. This was partly because he revered Ravi, and partly because he loved Sukanya's cooking. She would prepare special south Indian vegetarian dishes for him. After lunch they would adjourn to the music room with whichever disciples were visiting at the time. "We'd sit down and he'd actually start giving a class," says Glass. "He couldn't help himself! Those were priceless visits for me."[20] Glass had a commission to write *Orion*, a suite for the Athens Cultural Olympiad, and the movement *India* was born on one of these visits. Following the *Passages* precedent, Ravi played him a theme on the piano in the Carnatic *raga Nat Bhairavi*, with shades of the morning *raga Jaunpuri*, and Glass went away and arranged it. This time there was no reciprocal exchange, and Ravi was not involved in the performance. The sitar part was played by Gaurav Mazumdar in the premiere, which was recorded live, while on a subsequent tour it was played by Kartik Seshadri. As before, when Glass played the piece back to Ravi he could see that he was about to be chastised for his treatment of the *raga*. "I was at his place in Encinitas," says Glass. "I played it for him and he said, 'Well…' with a loud sigh. He let me go. I think I was just too old at that point."[21]

In the next Shankar–Glass collaboration, it was Anoushka who co-wrote a sitar–piano duet with Glass. They performed it (along with a reworked version of her piece *Voice of the Moon*) as a surprise for Ravi at an event in New York in 2007—he was being honored by the Asian Cultural Council in front of an audience that included Mikhail Baryshnikov. "It's not always a good idea to have surprises for Ravi. He didn't like it that much," says Glass. "But we did not want to play it for him before, because we knew that he would make us rewrite it! So she timed it so that there was no time to play it for him. He took it very well. He smiled. I'm sure he had comments."[22] Later Ravi wrote a solo piano piece for Glass, but delivered it slightly too late for Glass's concert, and it has yet to be performed.

A commission for the 2004 Dartington Festival triggered Ravi's return to the orchestral world. It was apt that, seventy years on from his first appearance at Dartington, his residency was funded by William Elmhirst, son of Leonard and Dorothy. Ravi composed a suite entitled *Sanmelan*, meaning "a meeting," for a mixed ensemble of twenty Western instrumentalists, drawn from Dartington's summer school, and eleven Indian classical musicians, some provided by the Bharatiya Vidya Bhavan, which hosted the London sessions where the piece took shape. One passage featured five different rhythmic cycles, in 3, 5, 7½, 10 and 15 beats, overlapping and coinciding every 30 beats. There was a *tarana* section, and also a gripping demonstration of *konnakol* (Carnatic vocal percussion), while another part featured an uplifting devotional song in Bengali, "O Parun Bondhu" ("My Dear Friend"), which Ravi wrote in a folk-style melody.

Ravi's assistant on *Sanmelan*, after initial notation by Barry Phillips, was David Murphy, a British conductor who had become attracted to Indian music in his youth through violin masterclasses with Yehudi Menuhin. He had worked with Indian musicians before but had to raise his game to another level now. "Raviji had the most incredible ability to compose a sublime melody at the drop of a hat. It just came pouring out, in the same way that Mozart and to some extent Beethoven could do," he says.[23] Initially Murphy used Western notation (later he became fluent in Indian notation too), and learned to keep track of all Ravi's ideas, even those that had apparently been discarded, because he sometimes changed his mind. "Raviji worked at lightning speed," he says. "I had practically no sleep for a month. He didn't seem to need any sleep either. It was just one long creative burst."[24] It was a superb training and opened Murphy's eyes to new creative possibilities. At the premiere on August 12, Ravi, who neither performed nor conducted, allowed him to take the rostrum. There were twice as many queueing outside Dartington's Great Hall as it could accommodate, so the musicians simply performed it twice. The joyous torrent of music was received with rapture, and it seemed to renew something within Ravi.

Murphy now became Ravi's key associate in a new surge of composing, taking on a role previously filled by Anoushka, Ashit Desai, Vijay Raghav Rao, José-Luis Greco and John Barham. According to Anoushka,

> You just had to turn on the tap and he'd be flowing out with these new ideas, and because he was so creative he wouldn't remember the thing he'd composed a minute ago, so you really had to be present catching things. Sometimes as a teenager, when he'd ask me to play him something I hadn't practiced enough, I'd just ask him to write me something new and he could be distracted for an hour! He couldn't help himself composing.[25]

In 2006 Murphy obtained an Arts Council grant enabling him to spend time with Ravi in Delhi and Encinitas. Ravi had proposed re-editing his second concerto, but did not proceed with it (and never disclosed what he had intended to change).[26] Instead they notated a piano piece that Ravi wrote in *Yaman Kalyan*, designed to introduce a pianist to aspects of Indian *raga* and *tala* forms. They also created a score for "Prabhujee," because Ravi felt it was important. These pieces were both incorporated into his final work, the opera *Sukanya*, so this marks the start of their collaboration on it, but at this stage he kept the project secret from his family as he wanted it to be a surprise for his wife, and he had not yet decided on it taking operatic form. It was sometimes referred to as "the ballet."

The next significant work was a sitar–violin duet that he composed for Anoushka to play with Joshua Bell at the Verbier Festival in August 2007. This was very much Indian music, but he worked with Barry Phillips and David Murphy to produce a Western score for Bell when he visited Encinitas for a couple of days of Ravi's coaching, along with Anoushka. They also rehearsed Ravi's duet in *Raga Piloo*, which he had made famous with Yehudi. Ravi was inspired by the way Bell picked up his ornamentations so instinctively. He told Anoushka that the new piece was written about her, and she feels it embodies a father's idealization of his daughter. "It's a really sweet piece, and also a beast of a piece to play, really challenging for both of us, and it *is* beautiful." However, she feels it does not have the three-dimensional depth of some of his best writing for sitar. "It's in a really sweet *raga* called *Vachaspati*, and he called it *Variant Moods*—so it's meant to have variant moods!" she says.

> But on the whole I find it quite light and sweet. If I step back and analyze it alongside his other compositions, I can see that when he wrote for me as opposed to for himself the music could have more sweetness but usually less fire. We did the show at Verbier and people loved it, but it felt clear that the *Mishra Piloo* piece got a much stronger reaction.[27]

*

Throughout his last decade Ravi's performances became more selective and sporadic, but he remained a big draw and he never contemplated retirement. His summer tour in 2003 was a memorable one, with four concerts in the UK, including Salisbury Cathedral, as well as Lisbon, Athens and the emotional peak of the Théâtre des Champs-Élysées in Paris, a return to where it had all started. It was the first time he had played there since 1966, and Angela Sulivan had worked hard to make it happen through the promoter Saïd Assadi. In 2004, the year of Dartington, he scaled back his concert appearances because Anoushka was having a year away from touring, but he made up for it a year later with an ambitious eighty-fifth birthday tour that took him from Morocco to Lebanon to St. Petersburg.

There were dramas that summer: for the first time he needed oxygen after performing at the idyllic Beiteddine Festival, up in the verdant hills above Beirut. Then, after the Air France flight back to Paris, there was the discovery that both his sitar and Anoushka's had been broken in transit, and the tour was rescued only by replacements being flown out from India. Before the open-air Paléo Festival in Switzerland, he found out he was scheduled directly after Lenny Kravitz and refused to play unless the running order could be reversed, which fortunately it could. Touring so often came with such stresses, but he was still addicted to it. August brought the high point of the BBC Proms—amazingly, his first appearance at the great festival—with much consequent press attention. He played a solo set after Anoushka had delivered his first concerto, and earned that rarity at the Proms, a standing ovation.

In the autumn he took a fourteen-strong ensemble around the USA in what he called Festival of India III. It had neither the scale nor the profile of its 1968 and 1974 precursors, but instead he gave an opportunity to some gifted younger musicians, such as the shehnai player Sanjeev Shankar (son of Daya Shankar), vocalist Aditya Prakash (son of Viji Prakash) and the mridangam drummer Pirashanna

Thevarajah, along with a core of superb senior artists, such as Tanmoy Bose and Partho Sarothy. He composed and arranged all the pieces, and Anoushka conducted their half of the show.

For Nick Able, a twenty-three-year-old new sitar disciple from Newcastle-upon-Tyne who was traveling as a tanpura player, this tour gave him unforgettable insights into his *guru*. He noticed with awe how uncomplainingly the eighty-three-year-old Ravi dealt with a twelve-hour delay at San José airport followed by a flight cancelation, even as the younger musicians were wilting. Able himself struggled with exhaustion, lack of privacy and the general grind of touring, and several weeks into the tour he went to unburden himself to Sukanya and broke down in tears. It was 2 a.m. in Toronto. He was surprised to find that Sukanya was still working, preparing for the next day, as she so often did into the small hours. She listened, and in reply told him about what Ravi had gone through in his early touring years, wedged into trains and busses, sharing rooms, paying his dues, and how he had discovered coping mechanisms.

To illustrate this she took him into the bedroom, where Ravi was sleeping. Able saw that he was wearing an eye mask and earplugs and had wrapped a towel around his head—habits picked up on the road long ago, absorbed into his sleep routine. "What was even more crazy," says Able, "was that his picking hand was above the covers, and the finger that he wore the *mizrab* on was moving as if he was playing or practicing. I felt bad about complaining now—he was on another level! It wasn't twitching. His whole hand was moving. He was playing in his sleep."[28]

Ravi was not entirely superhuman. He had long suffered badly from nerves before concerts. Kumar Bose recalls this being the case back in the 1980s, and saw it as a function of his perfectionism.[29] As is not uncommon for older artists, Ravi's concert anxiety seemed to increase with age. Anoushka recalls how there was always a different atmosphere on the day of a recital:

Right to the end, he would get so tense. I think it was part of his process, how he would get into the zone of needing to play for people, but it came with so much stress. He would always be worried that he wouldn't be able to do a good show and cared so deeply about giving each audience his best.[30]

Those audiences would watch nervously as a frail old man was helped on stage, only for the spotlight to bring on a transformation in him. The older he became, the more astonishing the effect. "Instantly, once he starts playing, his face has this weird glow to it where I just don't see the wrinkles any more," said Anoushka in 2003. "He's kind of on fire."[31]

Ravi's welfare was Sukanya's top priority, and her care was unquestionably responsible for him living as long as he did. His own medics called her Dr. Sukanya. She saw it as devoted and selfless service to her husband and *guru*. He was still coping with chronic heart problems and high blood pressure, as well as the stomach upsets that had always dogged him, and many other issues: more ear surgery in 2004, for example, and a nasty bout of food poisoning in India in early 2006. A big scare came that September, when he spent twenty-five days in intensive care with double pneumonia. This time there was a long convalescence, during which he needed oxygen and a wheelchair at home. His morale was raised by the new addition to the household, Suki the Maltipoo.

One consequence of this illness was that his left shoulder, which had long suffered from inflammation, had deteriorated to the point where he could no longer move his left hand all the way up the neck of the sitar. This threatened to end his career, but an instrument-maker came to his aid. Ravi already owned a shorter-necked sitar designed by Bishandas Sharma with a flatter, smaller main *tumba* made of wood (rather than gourd) and no secondary soundbox, but it was not of concert quality. Bishandas had died, but his son Sanjay Sharma now adapted this smaller design and improved the sound. The tone of this new instrument was inferior to that of Ravi's best sitars, but its *meend* (string-bending) quality was superb and overall he was satisfied. With this, and a new sitting position with him perched on the edge of a platform rather than sitting cross-legged on a flat surface, he was able to reach all the notes with his left hand. Seven months of concerts were canceled, but in April 2007, armed with his new concert sitar, Ravi returned to the road. Having been impressed by a luxury tour bus that Norah had used for her concerts, he adopted a similar vehicle for his subsequent U.S. trips, as he could sleep on the bus and avoid the aggravations of air travel—and take Suki with him.

That autumn, while he was away on another tour, there was a different kind of scare. A brush fire threatened the Encinitas home for a few days while the Santa Ana winds blew from the east. The winds changed direction in time, but not before the Shankars' assistant Jennifer Braxmeyer had gained hero status by crossing the police cordon around the house to rescue Ravi's sitars.

The tours were regularly named to hint that each might be the last. After the Full Circle and eighty-fifth birthday tours, there was a Farewell to Europe in 2008, an Australian Farewell in 2010, and several Tenth Decade concerts after that. Much of the Farewell to Europe tour actually had to be canceled due to Ravi's poor health. At the Barbican, where he played a particularly emotional set, he told the audience with his customary wit that although the concert had been announced as his final one in London, he hoped it would be his "semi-final," a wish that was to be fulfilled. In Toronto the following year there was a dramatic scene an hour before the show, when a doctor declared Ravi unfit to perform, but he went ahead anyway, saying, "All these people are here for me. I have to play." He told his accompanist Pirashanna Thevarajah, "It doesn't matter what happens to me on stage, you guys just carry on playing."[32]

Ravi spent three to four months every winter in India, except for 2006–7 and 2010–11, when he was too unwell to travel. The Ravi

Shankar Centre was open all year round but would come alive when he was present, with students in residence, a stream of visitors and constant demands on his time. The showpiece annual event was a four-day festival of music and dance, first staged in 2003 and named in memory of George Harrison. Here, yet again, Ravi was giving a platform to a mixture of established and rising artists. It took place in the outdoor amphitheater in the middle of the center, with the audience seated *baithak*-style on floor cushions, and entry was free. Ravi's hopes for the future of Indian classical music alternated between optimism and pessimism, but he always believed strongly in this kind of intimate event in front of a connoisseur crowd.

The center also ran lessons for serious students, which were usually conducted by Delhi-based disciples, including Parimal Sadaphal and Barunkumar Pal (and are continued at the time of writing by Gaurav Mazumdar). Ravi taught his own disciples and led occasional events. There might be a lecture-demonstration to a room of schoolchildren or a workshop with visiting musicians. In 2005 he brought over Jazzmin, a group of San Diego jazz-rock musicians to whom he had been teaching Indian music, and presented them in concert with Anoushka in Nehru Park. Ravi Coltrane played at the center the same year. In 2009 he ran a masterclass for Herbie Hancock, Anoushka, Chaka Khan, jazz singer Dee Dee Bridgewater, keyboardist George Duke and students from the Thelonious Monk Institute of Jazz. Hancock gave a demonstration, and Ravi discussed the system of *tala*, as well as teaching the Americans Gandhi's favorite *bhajan*, the *Ram Dhun*, which they sang the following week at a concert to mark the anniversary of Martin Luther King's 1959 visit to India.

Ravi's commitment to music teaching was instinctive and reflected his untiring curiosity. As a patron of the Bharatiya Vidya Bhavan in London, he regularly dropped in on classes to watch and offer encouragement. For a couple of summers he rented an apartment in West Hampstead, where he would take daily walks. One day when he went into a pharmacy he was recognized by a young British Asian staff member, who offered a *pranam* greeting to him. When Ravi found out that the boy was a tabla student, he gave him an impromptu ten-minute lesson, there in the aisles, to assess his standard. This finished with a homework assignment: Ravi left him with a *tihai* phrase to practice, and vowed to return to test him two days later—and he kept his promise.[33]

Another student who benefited from Ravi's openness was the emerging British conductor and composer Duncan Ward. After meeting in London, Ravi invited him to come and study in Encinitas in July 2010. For nearly a month Ward, who was only twenty-one, had twice-daily one-on-one lessons with Ravi, exploring just one *raga*, *Yaman Kalyan*, from scratch. Gradually Ravi led him through an extemporization on piano, which grew into a half-hour piece that he performed on his last day for a select audience: Ravi, Sukanya, Anoushka and Suki. Ravi thrived on this interaction with one so eager and gifted, and his health improved noticeably over the month. "He was an incredible teacher and an incredible giver, and clearly he was getting some reward from that process," says Ward. "I have never been struck so much by someone so old seeming so young and so curious."[34]

Once during these final years, at a lecture-demonstration that he gave at Delhi University, Ravi had a question for the audience: "It looks like there are a lot of university students here. How many of you are students of music?" A scattering of hands was raised. Ravi responded by raising his own hand and saying, "I am also a student of music."[35]

24

LATE STYLE

*In some ways I have never enjoyed playing more. There is no boundary
between the music and myself. The thin layer that separated me from
it has dissolved. Now, I am the music. This is a time of great joy.*

RAVI SHANKAR[1]

"Maybe a psychologist or psychiatrist can answer this: is it possible
when you want to forget something very unpleasant you really forget
other things along with it of that period?" Ravi asked his Canadian
filmmaker friend Art Makosinski in 2005. "Because it has happened
to me. It's amazing, because I have a very good memory, but there are
certain spots which have been very unpleasant and when I think of a
lot of things in that period that I did, they have been almost erased."[2]

One of the many benefits Sukanya brought to Ravi was a sense of
security that allowed him to confront, at long last, his deep-buried
wounds. Ravi kept it vague when he was talking to Makosinski, but he
was most likely alluding here to events in his childhood, as in his later
years he was privately taking stock of them. It was in the mid-1990s,
Sukanya recalls, that he revealed to her his most tightly guarded
secret: the repeated episodes of rape he had suffered in childhood.
"If only people knew," he told her. "I have to say it to somebody before
I die." He was not normally one to shed tears, but she recalls he had
"misty eyes" as he unburdened himself. She cried and found the news
difficult to take, but he said it was "such a good feeling" to be able to
unburden himself to her about it, and he felt at peace afterward.[3]

Ravi's youth was shaped not just by the thrill of treading the world's
stages but also by a number of traumatic experiences. There was the
rejection by his father, who withheld both his physical presence and
his love; the parting from his mother in Paris at the age of twelve, and

again on the Bombay docks at fifteen; the unbearable confrontation with death in the demise of his favorite brother, and then the loss of both parents in swift succession, suddenly and at a distance. Above all, there was the sexual abuse. These ordeals provide the context for some of the phenomena that defined his adult life: his surprising sense of loneliness, his suicidal feelings, his obsessive relationship with music, his spiritual quest, his workaholism, and what for so long seemed like an unquenchable thirst for love. Some of these characteristics could easily be missed among the overwhelming bounty of his music-making and the warmth of his charisma, but they were there all along.

Anoushka learned about the abuse her father had suffered only after his death, but her mature insight, in her late thirties, was that all these elements added together—cause and effect—fit the pattern of addiction triggered by childhood trauma. She brings her own perspective to this. "I've been in a twelve-step program and in recovery from addiction for some years," she says,

and through my experience with that, I believe addiction is something fundamental within the person as opposed to being about the substance or the activity itself. It's about something lacking in the self. So it can easily be alcohol or a drug or sex or love or work or shopping or gambling—any of those things are the person's way of looking for something to fill that lack. Looking back at my father, and with my understanding that addiction is a family illness, I feel a new compassion for what he may have struggled with in silence. I see it in his relationships and in his need to work endlessly. I think there may have been a kind of bottomless pit in him, needing that love and validation. I don't think he could do without it for a day. What's interesting is that, even though I'd say he was addicted to his work, I'd draw a separation between the "work" and the music itself, because the music was very spiritual for him, and was therefore healing to anything like addiction. I imagine the paradox must have created a very real struggle, for the very thing that brought him to his closest sense of connection also triggered an addictive high.[4]

Although there is no evidence that Ravi ever had a problem with alcohol, as a young man with the dance troupe he did drink and, as he later told Sukanya, he sensed his relationship with alcohol was becoming unhealthy, or at least had that potential. He worshipped Uday but he didn't want to end up like him. It was a lasting source of pain that such a great artist had done so much to destroy himself. But Ravi had an inner strength that drove him to escape Uday's influence in favor of that of Allauddin Khan, who saw music as his religion. A decade later, when Ravi was rescued from the deepest crisis of his life, he realized just how spiritually powerful music could be. It was through music that he rebuilt himself, and thereafter he became a global proselytizer for its healing benefits, as well as for the joy it can bring. He came to idealize a vision of the world in which suffering is overcome by music, love and spiritual ecstasy. This is the Dawn that succeeds the Nightmare—in the ultimately optimistic theme that recurs again and again in his later works. Peace through music.

When he talked of his loneliness, despite having so many friends and lovers, when he wrote all the songs about Krishna and his frustrated yearnings, he was revealing his ongoing need for a healing spiritual connection. "The interesting thing," says Anoushka,

> is that in many ways he found a solution himself through his music and through his spiritual practice, without any kind of therapy or recovery program, and when he was in it, it would soothe him. But then I feel he would put his music down, put his instrument down, and he would be restless again, always seeking that connection.[5]

In the words of the addiction specialist Dr. Gabor Maté, there is an "ever-agitated, ever-yawning emptiness" at the heart of addiction, and workaholism is an often overlooked manifestation of it.[6] "The work, the need to perform in that propulsive way, going and going and not being able to stop—that is the other side that needs to be fed by the high of performing, of moving," says Anoushka. "The inability to sit still for more than a week in one city, which Kamala Auntie talks about, comes from the inability to sit with oneself."[7] Ravi kept touring, kept moving on, even when it meant he didn't see his children or it was damaging to his relationships.

The perfectionism that manifested itself in his music was allied to a sense of perpetual dissatisfaction, a combination that has inspired much great art but has also destroyed many musicians. "It's a beautiful thing," says Anoushka, "but also potentially tragic. But in his case, blessedly, because drugs and alcohol weren't a part of his story, it didn't go the way it does for so many people."[8]

Apart from the abuse, Sukanya remembers him speaking of two other deep sources of his pain. One was an unresolved grief for his mother, for what she had gone through and how she had died too soon. "I wish I could have done more for her," he would say.[9] Anoushka says he would speak about his mother with intensity, as if something were still missing. His relationships with his younger daughter and his mother seemed emotionally bound together; he had given Anoushka the middle name of Hemangini, and the nickname Hemoushka, and he used to tell her that she looked like his mother when she put her hair up. "There was something unusually childlike and tender in the way he talked about her," she says.[10]

The other origin of his pain was his feeling that he had been denied a childhood, that he had missed out on the innocent joy of youth. It was all curtailed—first through the abuse, and then through being immersed too early in a very adult world, and effectively abandoned by his parents.[11] Sukanya says now:

> When I found out what he had been through, and how he came
> to terms with it on his own—there was no counseling available
> in those days—my admiration for him went up a thousand times.

That's the reason I've decided to talk about this now. He could have become a bitter and twisted person, but he found a way to help himself. Through his music and spirituality he was able to make something positive out of all those trials, and he became such a compassionate person.[12]

Somehow, because of a deep *joie de vivre* that had survived everything, and perhaps because the frivolity was good at soothing a deeper pain, the mature Ravi had a childlike, playful side. In old age the quality he prized most in others was that of remaining young at heart. In interviewing people about Ravi, I found this theme arising repeatedly. Simran Mangharam, who worked as his tour manager in 1998, still treasures his parting message before she returned home: "Don't ever change. You have this beautiful childlike quality to you—keep that always."[13] The south Indian flutist Ravichandra Kulur, who became a regular accompanist from 2005, says that the biggest thing he learned from Ravi was to "be curious about music like a child."[14] Ravi himself, in a handwritten memo from near the end of his life, offered the advice: "Don't grow up, but if you do, don't lose those wonderful qualities you have!!!"[15] This was a veteran musician preaching the value of an inquisitive mind in his profession. But it was also the wisdom of an old man remembering how his own childhood was truncated and reflecting on how many problems in our world would disappear if we retained a child's-eye view.

Being able to share these traumas with Sukanya was a mark of how much she had helped him to come to terms with himself. On their eighteenth wedding anniversary he wrote her the most beautiful letter: "How amazing that growing with age all these years my love for you has grown so much more," he wrote.

Sweetheart—think how blessed we are in so many aspects—specially when I LOVE YOU so much and your fathomless love & *seva* [devoted service] for me!!!! I don't want any complication in my next life. I JUST WANT YOU AND NO ONE ELSE—

Don't let me wait too long—promise to come soon! I pray for your health & happiness always. I LOVE YOU / ADORE YOU / my passion for you has become even more. I kiss you all over & bless you! Kiss you madly, Shyamu.[16]

There was also the joy of having Norah and Anoushka in his life, and the satisfaction of seeing them both blossom musically. "These are like my two eyes, really," he said.[17] He even extended the Encinitas house so that Norah had her own bedroom when she stayed. There was Anoushka's marriage in 2010, to Joe Wright, and the following year she had her first son. Ravi doted on Zubin—named after the conductor Zubin Mehta—and loved to play his sitar for him.

"I think he derived a great deal of contentment from feeling like he had a family life in a way that he hadn't managed to have before," says Anoushka.

But creatively, he was always hungry. He couldn't be happy for long without an instrument, without music, without a new show or a new project to plan toward. I feel a lot of artists are workaholics, and it's so much more impressive-looking than bog-standard workaholism, but it's kind of the same thing! He just couldn't not do it.[18]

"Even when we were sitting at breakfast he couldn't just have a con-versation," says Norah. "He had to start tapping on the table and say, 'OK, you do five over three, and you do six over three.' It was really fun, but it was proof that his brain never shut off in that way." She adds, "I think music is what kept him alive so long."[19]

Along with airing the skeletons in his closet, Ravi was also sorting out the music in his attic. In the late 1990s Philip Glass had been shocked to discover that Ravi had no idea how many records he had on the market, and they were generating hardly any income. He did have a music publishing company, Anourag, which had been in existence for about a decade, succeeding an earlier incarnation, Saira Music, but it covered only part of his backlist. "He had been completely exploited for years," says Glass, who, in contrast, had held on to his copyrights and set up his own publishing company, Dunvagen Music.[20] Glass decided to do Ravi a big favor. He employed a researcher, Cat Celebrezze, who located 234 releases with Ravi's name on them, many of them low-quality sub-licenses, lacking proper credits, or repackaged as music for meditation or well-being. Some even had the image of him reversed on the cover so he appeared to be playing left-handed. Most were generating no publishing income. Glass then set up a new publishing company, St. Rose Music. Its first two artists were Ravi and Tom Waits. Today it has eight, including Nico Muhly and Anoushka. Celebrezze worked closely with Ravi identifying recordings, and St. Rose began assigning the copyrights to him and collecting the money on behalf of Anourag. Ravi started to receive an income. "You always want to do something for the *guru*," says Glass.[21]

With his business affairs on a better footing, and the center up and running in Delhi, Ravi and Sukanya could focus on some legacy projects. By now Ravi had a large and important archive. Alan Kozlowski had organized and restored his holdings before returning them to Ravi in 1998. Sukanya had reclaimed several other collections and solicited donations of material from friends and disciples. As well as film reels, documents, photographs, instruments and other objects, she had amassed a huge collection of unreleased music, ranging from vintage reel-to-reel tapes to digital files. She regularly recorded Ravi's new live performances. Art Makosinski cataloged the audio-visual materials, while Celebrezze, after she left Dunvagen, began logging the other items.

The music business having been transformed by the internet, Ravi decided to set up his own company, East Meets West Music. He liked the idea of music going direct from the artist to the audience. The plan was to release archival highlights, and perhaps some emerging musicians, and to control the quality so that the label would become the signature brand on the market. With Celebrezze as chief executive, it launched in 2010 with the first DVD release of *Raga* and the first CD in the series *Nine Decades*. Over the next two years this program of previously unreleased gems included Ravi's epic performance of *Gangeshwari* in Allahabad in 1968, the 1969 home concert at North Vista and a selection of orchestral works from his Vadya Vrinda days. There was attention to detail: Ravi wrote his own sleeve notes, while Barry Phillips did most of the restoring and remastering, under Ravi's supervision. Separately Ravi also helped to get Uday's film *Kalpana* restored by bringing it to the attention of Martin Scorsese, whose World Cinema Foundation took on the task.

When Ravi received an honorary doctorate from the New England Conservatory in 1993, there was an extraordinary moment when he passed a statue of Beethoven and spontaneously touched his feet. Turning to Sukanya, he said, "He would understand what I go through."[22] What did he mean? Conceit would be out of character. He might have been referring to their common struggle with hearing problems, but more likely it was the sense of being constantly pregnant with musical ideas, tortured by their possibilities.

Suburban Encinitas was somewhat off the beaten track, and at times Ravi felt isolated, especially in periods when his health kept him at home. He wished more of his disciples could spend time with him, to feed his creative juices, but he recognized that they had to build their own careers, just as he had done on leaving Maihar. His great hope was to work on another dance production; he often talked about *Ghanashyam*, which was perhaps the project he had most enjoyed in his life. Dance still mesmerized him. "Whenever I play music I see movements. I dance quite a lot today even," he told Makosinski, adding, chuckling, "but mostly in the bathroom."[23]

One creative outlet was his work with David Murphy, who was by now an eager disciple. At last there was a commission for a new sitar concerto, Ravi's third, from the Orpheus Chamber Orchestra, a New York-based ensemble that performed without a conductor. Ravi wrote a programmatic work, his music expressing a simple story about the love between a lonely, rich princess and a poor servant boy who was her only childhood friend.[24] He had Anoushka in mind, with her sitar part representing the princess. He conceived it as a potential ballet, and its three movements are preceded by an orchestral overture. At about thirty minutes, it was shorter than his previous concertos, and musically it drew much more on folk melodies, while still being firmly rooted in *raga* forms. One innovation Ravi employed was to instruct the timpanist to play sometimes with sticks, sometimes with the flat of the hand and sometimes with a finger stroke, effectively translating some tabla techniques for the orchestral percussion section.

It came together in 2008, during Murphy's visits to Delhi in February and Encinitas in April and August. The process of orchestration had been revolutionized since the second concerto by computer software (Murphy used Sibelius), which meant that Ravi could hear a playback and make adjustments as he went along. "He loved the idea of feeding the music into the computer and letting the computer digest it," says Murphy.[25] The concerto was premiered in January 2009, in a short tour that opened at Pick-Staiger Concert Hall near Chicago and concluded at Carnegie Hall. It was broadcast live on the radio, but has yet to be recorded.

Ravi then moved on to writing his first and only symphony, commissioned by the London Philharmonic Orchestra following an approach from Murphy. One inspiration was Prokofiev's Classical Symphony. Murphy says Ravi wanted to "look at the Western classical symphony through the prism of Indian music, in the same way that Prokofiev had used his viewpoint as a twentieth-century composer looking back at eighteenth-century forms."[26] Ravi adopted the traditional four-movement structure, following sonata form in the bold opening *Allegro*—mostly based on *Raga Kafi Zila*, which uses the notes of the natural minor scale. A slow second movement follows with a gorgeous melody in *Raga Ahir Bhairav* and two scored sitar passages in dialogue with the orchestra.

The highlight is the third movement, which follows a playful scherzo form. It has a rhythmically intricate opening, as a side-drum plays a 5-beat cycle, the bongos 7½ beats and the cellos and basses 10 beats. The three cycles swell and surge along in overlapping waves as oboes and piccolos surf above on a beguiling melody that Ravi spontaneously composed to fit the syncopated pulse. After a trio passage between sitar, xylophone and marimba, the overlaying of rhythmic cycles returns and the movement builds to a thrilling close. The *raga* here is *Doga Kalyan*, Ravi's own creation, which uses both third notes in the scale (hence "Doga," literally two *ga* notes). The final movement is based on *Raga Banjara*, which Ravi had written for the 1995 *From the Sitar to the Guitar* shows, and it similarly explores rhythm in the context of Indian folk music. Like *Kafi Zila* and *Doga Kalyan*, *Banjara* had featured in *Sanmelan*, and the way in which that work prefigured the symphony is particularly evident toward the end, when much of the orchestra breaks out into *konnakol* vocal percussion— believed to be a first for a Western orchestra.

The symphony was originally conceived as a work for orchestra alone, with an optional Indian ensemble, and Ravi decided relatively late to rework the ensemble lines into a sitar part, adding an extra dimension. The premiere, given at the Royal Festival Hall on July 1, 2010, featured this sitar version, with Anoushka as soloist. Characteristically, Ravi was still adjusting her part up until the night before the premiere.[27] The concert was recorded live and released as an album by the LPO. An alternative version was scored for orchestra alone, and has also been performed.

Reviews were again split between those who deemed it a triumph and those who could not see beyond the absence of harmony. However, six decades after Imogen Holst had yearned for someone who could explore "Indian counterpoint to suit Indian tunes," Ravi was doing just that: while he maintained his lifelong fealty to *raga* rules, the symphony has more counterpoint than any of his earlier works, particularly toward the end of the third movement.[28]

"In the early days I would do what I thought was textbook interesting orchestration," says Murphy. "I'd come back the next morning pleased with what I'd done, and he'd say, 'David, no, you've put too much makeup on the *raga*. She had a beautiful face and you've plastered it with all this stuff. We can't see the pristine beauty any more.'"[29] Through trial and error, Murphy absorbed from Ravi what could be done while respecting *raga* purity, and helped him push the boundaries:

> I was beginning to learn how you could orchestrate things in sometimes a far more complex way than concerto number 1 and still manage to keep that beauty. That is really breaking new ground. It's to do with the important notes and the less important notes of the *raga*, and how you can combine them simultaneously in counterpoint and building up chords, but you have to be so subtle with that. If only he'd only lived another ten or twenty years, that would have been an amazing journey to go on. At some point hopefully that will be undertaken.[30]

Ravi seemed to be thinking along the same lines; at ninety-one he told one of his staff, Jessica Young, with startling specificity, that he still had eleven years' worth of ideas left.[31] His late surge of creativity, which had already yielded a sitar concerto and a symphony, now led on to an opera—all three projects completed after his eighty-eighth birthday. He had decided that *Sukanya* would be a Western opera with Indian dance, and, although it was obviously a tribute to his wife, it would tell the story of the character in the *Mahabharata*. In October 2010 he was taken into hospital again with fluid on the lungs, a consequence of his ailing heart, but with treatment and physiotherapy he bounced back, and work on the opera began in earnest in January 2011, when Murphy spent two weeks in Encinitas. The following summer they worked on it daily in London, where Ravi rented a flat in Limehouse for a couple of months.

By this time the impression of him as a venerable sage, a real-life Chyavana, was accentuated by a full white beard. "I hope you recognize me. I have gained some weight here," he joked to his Barbican audience that summer, gesturing to his face. This time it really was his final London concert, and in a pair of rare treats he not only began with a chanted invocation, "Hari Om," he also sang Tagore's "Sedin Dujone" in tribute to his 150th birth anniversary. Anoushka was in the front row with four-month-old Zubin.

His heart remained a constant concern. When he had no musical project to work on his spirits dropped and he tended to fall sick. After the autumn 2011 tour Sukanya had a brainwave and asked Tanmoy Bose to stay back in Encinitas, where he and Ravi spent four days recording classical *ragas* together. They set up in the White Room: Ravi on sitar, Bose on tabla and Kenji Ota, who had become a devoted and much loved disciple over the previous decade, on tanpura. Barry Phillips was responsible for the recording. The result is a close-miked snapshot of Ravi's incredible late-period inventiveness, drawing on a lifetime's knowledge. There is an appealing intimacy: you can hear comments between the musicians, and during *Sindhi Bhairavi* Ravi breaks out in song and vocal percussion. Other high points include *Raga Satyajit*, a development of his *Ahir Bhairav* melody from *Farewell, My Friend*, and a *Raga Mishra Kafi* of stunning delicacy, while on *Bhairavi*, innovator to the last, he plays his sitar with a cloth laid over the strings, giving it a percussive timbre. The seven *ragas* filled two albums, named *The Living Room Sessions*. These were Ravi's first solo albums for two decades to be recorded in studio conditions, and the first releases of new material by East Meets West. *Part 1* received the Grammy for Best World Music album, while *Part 2* was nominated a year later. Not bad for a ninety-one-year-old "fooling around at home," as he put it.[32]

Ravi was well enough to travel to India that winter, and gave a memorable concert with Anoushka in Bangalore in February 2012, which was his last ever appearance in India and has been released on

DVD. Simran Mangharam, with whom the family stayed, was amazed to discover that Ravi was still practicing every day.[33] His ongoing commitment to encouraging others was enshrined in his center's annual festival, which he hosted for a last time. Younger musicians were encouraged, as ever: from London came the sarodist Soumik Datta and percussionist Bernhard Schimpelsberger, whom he had invited after they played privately for him the previous summer.[34]

Back in San Diego in March Ravi fell ill and had surgery to open a heart valve, which meant the cancelation of a concert at Long Beach. When David Murphy visited in April Ravi continued working on the opera from his hospital bed. He was told the cardiac problem would keep recurring and worsening unless he had a transcatheter aortic valve replacement (TAVR), a risky procedure at his age, although as a keyhole procedure it was less dangerous than open-heart surgery. Understanding that he might not have long to live, he told his wife about the opera that would carry her name, having intended to keep it a surprise until it was completed. By now he and Murphy had moved on to organizing already notated material, and they continued when Murphy returned in August. If necessary, Ravi reassured Sukanya, Anoushka would be able to finish it.

In London, where she was now living, Anoushka had been writing and recording a new album in collaboration with Nitin Sawhney, but, sensing that her father's time was running out, she flew out to Encinitas four times during 2012. Other visitors included Gaurav Mazumdar, who stayed for the first week of October. By now Ravi was on oxygen all the time, with an extra-long tube connecting him to his cylinder so that he could wander about the house. "I heard him play a beautiful morning *Bhairavi*," says Mazumdar.

> He watched a lot of television series, movies, spoke a lot. My favorite was always sitting next to him for lunch. As a gesture he would always take something and put it on my plate, like *prasad* for me, like a blessing. I felt so sad that here is a mind which is

200 percent alive and young, and because of this body which is ninety-two years old we have to say goodbye to this brilliant brain which can create so much music.[35]

When Satish Vyas visited for dinner the following week Ravi was cracking jokes, and he asked after Vyas's *guru*, Shivkumar Sharma.[36]

Ravi still had plans for the future; there were tour dates lined up for 2013. First, though, aware that he had the surgery ahead of him, he was determined to rearrange the canceled concert at Long Beach. This time he knew it really might be his last one, and November 4 at the Terrace Theater was a night of overwhelming emotion. For Ravi even to make it on stage was a minor miracle, because he had to be brought on in a wheelchair, with a nasal cannula for his oxygen supply during the concert. "Maybe for other artists who didn't live for playing to that degree it would have been one more holiday at that age, one more pretty sunset, one more family dinner," says Anoushka. "I'm not saying that with any negative feeling. It's so staggeringly beautiful how much music he still had to share."[37]

Accompanying him were Tanmoy Bose, Ravichandra Kulur, B. C. Manjunath on mridangam, Kenji Ota and Barry Phillips on tanpura, and—happily—Anoushka herself, who, following years of playing every tour, had missed all his shows during 2011 after having Zubin, and was grateful that it was possible for her to join Ravi for his final two concerts. His performance was "transcendent," she says. "The music was exquisite. It was one of the most perfect shows I remember us doing."[38]

At the end Ravi set his sitar down and was overwhelmed by emotion and exhaustion. As Anoushka checked on him, he seemed to be half laughing, half crying. He stood to take a bow, blessed each of his fellow musicians and waved to the audience, who were giving him a continuing ovation. At length Sukanya appeared on stage with his wheelchair and maneuvered him out, still waving and blowing kisses to the auditorium, his oxygen cable trailing behind him. Backstage he was in a loving mood. Kulur remembers how Ravi held on to him and stroked his head affectionately as he thanked him.[39]

"He would pull on his reserves to do these incredible shows, finding energy that he didn't even have to walk up and down the stairs at home," says Anoushka. "Afterward we would see how flattened he was by it. But at that show it was particularly worrying because of the visible oxygen tank and because he was so unwell."[40] There were two doctors backstage, Ravi's pulmonologist Scott Eisman and cardiologist Martin Charlat, and they were concerned at how low his blood oxygen level was afterward. In fact there was no way he should have been capable of playing the concert.

"I feel so happy that the program last Sunday went off well," Ravi wrote four days later. "Having been critically ill for such a long time I had given up the idea of performing again. But this was possible because of my wife Sukanya only. With her constant care overlooking my health, giving me courage, confidence, strength & her priceless love!"[41]

All the family agreed the heart surgery was necessary as Ravi was having such difficulty breathing. "I remember him being keen to do it," says Anoushka. "He was getting unwell so frequently at that point that it just felt really clear—and there was a potential for him to feel even better than before for a while, if the surgery succeeded."[42] On November 17 she had to give a concert in Leipzig, playing Ravi's second concerto for the first time—another torch being handed over—but she then returned to be with her parents. Nitin Sawhney came out to Encinitas in December so that Anoushka could continue working on her album in a studio there. Norah had been on a world tour since May, which moved on to South America at the end of November.

The surgery was arranged for December 6 at Scripps Memorial Hospital in nearby La Jolla. Ravi rang a number of people beforehand. These were not goodbye calls as such, but when Philip Glass promised he would fly over to welcome Ravi out of the hospital, he had a feeling that he would not see him again: "It wasn't a long conversation, nor did it need to be. Things were said that had been said before but needed to be said one last time."[43] Ravi called Lata Mangeshkar, and even Amitabh Bachchan, who was surprised to be in his thoughts— he had known Uday better—and described the call as "one of my most privileged moments."[44] In fact Ravi had been watching Bachchan in *Kaun Banega Crorepati* (the Indian version of *Who Wants to Be a Millionaire?*) at home and simply wanted to offer his appreciation and blessings. That week Ravi also heard that he was going to be awarded a Grammy for lifetime achievement. Meanwhile, Anoushka, understanding that this surgery was different, prepared a list of people to inform if it didn't go well, and I received a heartbreaking request from her to prepare an obituary that the family could have ready for the media—just in case.

Ravi's attitude remained positive. He told Sukanya that he did not want to be resuscitated if things went wrong, but he also said that he would take her on a holiday once he had recovered. The night before the surgery itself she gave him a pedicure, and then he put both hands on her head and held her with deep feeling. He took "the longest shower ever," she recalls, and ate his porridge before bed.[45] From midnight he was nil by mouth.

The surgery next day went very well in that the heart valve was successfully replaced. But at the age of ninety-two Ravi's recovery was always going to be a huge challenge. His doctors kept him sedated on a ventilator. He came round the following day and opened his eyes. He managed to interact with visitors and to smile at videos of Zubin, although he could not speak as he was intubated. He remained critically ill throughout the aftercare period. By the 10th he was still on a ventilator, sedated, in pain, and with a feeding tube in place. He was deteriorating, and on Tuesday December 11 his condition took a fatal downturn.

"When it was finally the last afternoon and the last moments, my mum and I were there and it just felt *right*," says Anoushka. "In a very sacred way I was watching someone pass away." She had been coming in and out of hospital with Zubin over the past five days and she felt grateful that she was there at the end. They managed to get hold of Norah, who was in her hotel room in Brazil, and held the handset close to Ravi in the hope that he could understand what she was saying. "She spoke to him very openly and sweetly on the phone," says Anoushka.[46]

"I was glad I could be there in some way with them," says Norah. "He had been in the hospital so many times and bounced back so many times, like a cat with nine lives, that it was a shock, actually."[47]

Anoushka continues:

As the struggle started to leave him it became very peaceful, and as it became peaceful it became very subtle, and my mum and I instinctively started saying certain prayers together. We were reciting them through the process of him passing away. I remember it being this finer and finer and finer point of watching him, right down to this paper-thin moment of being there and not being there. It was so profoundly clear and so subtle at the same time. It was painful and beautiful.[48]

Shortly afterward Nitin Sawhney came in, and he had an overpowering sensation: "It felt like you were walking into a vacuum where something amazing had been but was no longer there. It was such a strong feeling of absence." He continues:

When I was about seven years old I remember my dad was playing a Ravi Shankar album. I kept going over this one bit of his sitar-playing and I said to him, "How have they done this trick?" I was already a classical pianist by then. My dad said, "What trick are you talking about?" I said, "It sounds like he is playing really, really fast, but you have got this at normal speed." I couldn't get my head round it. My dad said, "No, that's Ravi Shankar, he plays at that speed." I said, "But that's impossible, no one can move their fingers like that." When I was by his bedside, he had passed away by this point, and I was holding his arm. That was one of the strangest moments in my life, thinking, "I am holding the very arm that did those incredible things that blew me away when I was seven, and now it has no life."[49]

Ravi used to tell Sukanya that he thought of her as his fourth wife, after Annapurna, Kamala and Sue. Kamala once told her that she had been with Ravi at his peak, which was true in a way. But Sukanya was happy with how it worked out. "I'm glad I came in the end to him," she says.

I feel so blessed to have taken care of him, to have his complete love, to be able to serve him. I saw what a beautiful soul he was. I met that gorgeous, handsome fellow, but when I think of him it's that man with the beard. I see such kindness in his eyes, that saintliness. Even when he passed I just put my head on his feet and I said, "May I be there again for you. Bless me to be there again."[50]

In contrast with this cocooned, intense experience of private loss, the world was soon reverberating with the news of his death. It reached India on the morning of December 12. There were public tributes and private letters of condolence from India's prime minister and president. The Lok Sabha stood to remember him in silence. Obituaries, memories and instant verdicts flooded the world's media. Lata Mangeshkar described him as the Tansen of his generation.[51] Despite a lifetime of getting used to the attention her father attracted, Anoushka still felt the aftermath went "eye-of-storm-level crazy."[52]

After Norah arrived from Brazil, having canceled her concerts there, a Hindu funeral ceremony was held at home in Encinitas for immediate family and close friends, about forty people in all. It was led by Dr. Nandakumara, who had flown in from London. The cremation took place locally. Norah and Anoushka performed the final rituals for their father. "We held hands through the whole thing and did all the last rites together, and every time I sobbed she just held my hand even more firmly," says Anoushka. "That was the exact moment I decided to have another child."[53]

On December 20 there was an open-air memorial held at the SRF ashram in Encinitas, with a large crowd turning out to hear speeches by family members and close friends, including Olivia Harrison and Zubin Mehta. There was an even bigger memorial in Delhi's Nehru Park in March, with thousands attending and an intense media focus. In between the commemorations, Norah and Anoushka accepted two Grammy Awards on their father's behalf, for *Living Room Sessions Part 1* and for lifetime achievement.

Norah also gave her first ever concerts in India. Ravi had always wanted her to play there, and had been excited to hear the shows were booked. So it was a bitter-sweet experience for her, but still satisfying, and she stayed on for a holiday in Rishikesh. Today she feels more comfortable talking about her father, and her memories are warm. "He would always take my hand and be very affectionate, which I needed from him. He would call me Baby," she says.

> He was a very sweet, fun person, and I don't know if people really know that about him because he's this king, this legendary serious musician. And I get it, he's a serious person. But to me, he was not that serious. Even at the memorial I kept on thinking, "I hope they show something of him being goofy!"[54]

The day after the Nehru Park event a small group flew to Benares: Sukanya, Anoushka, Joe, Norah and her partner, Angela Sulivan and her husband Lawrence Mallinson, Arun Bharat-Ram, Alan Kozlowski, Richa Aniruddha and Simran Mangharam. There they met up with Sting and Trudie Styler, who were friends of Anoushka and happened to be in India. Ravi had once promised Sting that he would take him to Benares, so they wanted to be there. Along with two Brahmin priests, the party boarded a *bajra* boat on the Ganges. Prayers were chanted, and then Norah and Anoushka together released their father's ashes into the Ganges. It was almost the perfect completion of his journey, the real Full Circle, returning him to the holy city that had nurtured a sweet, playful boy touched by genius, to the waters he had bathed in during his lonely childhood. If the moment was slightly marred by the paparazzi, whose long lenses captured the image of his ashes being poured overboard, even this had a certain logic. Ever since leaving the city at the age of ten Ravi had lived in the public eye, and Benares, of all places, is the least squeamish about death and its leveling processes. And, as Ravi always said, his was an imperfect mission; he was always being driven to seek something just out of reach. But what music he created in that quest.

EPILOGUE
THE SUN WON'T SET

*Seeing a great man die is like watching a sunset. For me, he was
the greatest of the great and the best of the best.*
PHILIP GLASS[1]

It is May 9, 2017, a cool, bright afternoon in London. Four and a
half years have passed since Ravi Shankar died. At the Henry Wood
Hall, a former Greek Revival church in Southwark that serves today
as a rehearsal venue, the first orchestral rehearsal gets under way for
the opera *Sukanya*. Present are the two people most responsible for
bringing Ravi's parting gift to the stage: David Murphy runs proceedings from the podium, while Sukanya Shankar sits up in the balcony,
alone. It is the first time that she has heard this music in full. Until
now, the score has existed only on the printed page.

Early in Part Two there is a long scene in which the old sage
Chyavana, sung by Alok Kumar, gives a music lesson to his young
bride, the Princess Sukanya (Susanna Hurrell). The music here is
based on the piano score of *Yaman Kalyan* that Ravi prepared in
2006 as a teaching exercise, and carries a discursive prose text by
the librettist Amit Chaudhuri, extracted from his own novel *Afternoon Raag*.[2] The scene builds over about thirteen minutes to a sublime climax. *Yaman Kalyan* was the love song of Ravi and Sukanya
Shankar, so listening to it is intensely moving for her, but there is
a moment when it becomes too much—when she recognizes one
of the lines. Years before, when Ravi must have been writing that
melody, he asked her to try singing it for him, without revealing
what it was for.

*

Sukanya had its world premiere three days later at the Curve, Leicester, and three further UK performances followed, concluding at the Royal Festival Hall. Its theme is the rejuvenating power of mortal love in the face of jealous and meddling demigods, and, in keeping with Ravi's fondness for romantic songs about Krishna, it is both love letter to his wife and devotional hymn to love divine. Given its choice of *ragas* and reworked compositions from earlier in his career, it is also a reflective piece about his own life and art, and, with that music lesson at its center, it honors the making and teaching of music itself.

Ravi's last session with David Murphy had been in August 2012, by which time he had completed all the primary composition work and left instructions in case of his death, which Murphy later followed in completing the orchestration. Ravi made it clear that the singers should employ their Western operatic voices and not try to imitate Indian vocal style, apart from some occasional ornaments. He wanted the audience to hear Indian music from another perspective. So *Sukanya* is written for six operatic voices, chorus and Western orchestra, as well as five Indian instrumentalists: sitar, shehnai, tabla, mridangam and ghatam. The co-producers were the Royal Opera House, the London Philharmonic Orchestra and the Curve, and the development phase was eased by sponsors and a crowdfunding campaign.

Following Ravi's wishes, the production incorporated projected backdrops—turning the setting from temple to forest to music room—and liberal use of Indian dance. The five dancers, who deployed Bharatanatyam, Kathak and contemporary styles under the choreography of Aakash Odedra, were a central focus, weaving their way through and in front of the orchestra, who were seated on stage, under Murphy's baton. The overall effect achieved by director Suba Das from the Curve—a British Bengali whose father had migrated to the UK decades before, carrying two of Ravi's records in his suitcase— was a rush of thrilling movement and saturated color, rather belying the production's description as merely semi-staged.

Unusually for an opera, the music had preceded the libretto. Amit
Chaudhuri had been chosen in early 2012, but Ravi died before they
met and at that point the text was unwritten. Chaudhuri, who is also
an Indian classical vocalist (and a Bengali), knew little about opera
but, after seeing Philip Glass's *Satyagraha* at the London Coliseum, in
Murphy's company, he felt encouraged to take a literary approach. He
chose to rework texts by other writers on the subject of desire in old
age, including passages by Kalidas and Walter Benjamin, and extracts
from Sophocles' *Antigone* and from *The Two Noble Kinsmen*, which is
attributed in part to Shakespeare. He was given a free rein: he structured his libretto according to Ravi's scene-by-scene framework, and it
was Murphy's role to fit the words to the music line by line afterward.[3]

The libretto is not, Chaudhuri stresses, an allegory of the relationship between Ravi and his wife. However, Ravi inserted several self-
reflective elements within the music. It refers to *Sanmelan* and the
symphony in featuring passages in his own *ragas Doga Kalyan* and
Banjara and sections in *tarana* and *konnakol* styles. A chanted invocation was repurposed from an ensemble piece he had written for his
"India Calling!" concert at the Hollywood Bowl in 2009. There was
personal significance in other *ragas* chosen: his own *Bairagi*, haunting-
ly played by the shehnai to open both Part One and Part Two; *Piloo*,
on which he had duetted with Yehudi Menuhin at the United Nations;
and, in the final scene, *Pancham Se Gara*, with which he had closed his
Monterey set. There are even a couple of moments when his orchestration consciously pays tribute to the style of Philip Glass, which he had
done much to influence—in effect, returning the compliment.

The only textual elements that Ravi composed himself are two
songs that he reused: "Prabhujee" from *Chants of India* and "O Parun
Bondhu" from *Sanmelan*. "Prabhujee," sung in a majestic arrangement as part of the wedding scene between Chyavana and Princess
Sukanya, is an emotional high point. Originally this was a devotional
song, on which Ravi himself shared the vocals with the real Sukanya.
Here it becomes the marriage song of the princess and her new hus-

band. "O Parun Bondhu" was written as another devotional song, to Krishna, but here it can also be read as a message from beyond the grave. When the princess asks where her husband is, the reply comes back, "I am in your heart…When you think of me, you will hear the sound of my flute." In the text, there is the familiar playful ambiguity about whether the beloved who replies is Krishna or an absent lover— perhaps one who has departed this world. Once again, mortal love rhymes with spiritual love.

The subtlest musical message, hiding in plain sight, is the three-note theme on clarinet and oboe, D, F sharp and C sharp, that accompanies the first appearance of Chyavana and recurs on various instruments at significant moments, such as the close of Part One or the end of the music lesson. The notes are the tonic, third and seventh of the scale, or *sa*, *ga* and *ni* in Indian *sargam* terminology. This is a musical cryptogram, akin to the four-note B–A–C–H motif that Bach sometimes employed, or indeed the three-note *ga–ni–dha* that Ravi himself used to honor Gandhi in his *raga Mohankauns*. Here he has chosen the three syllables approximating to the name of his muse, *sa–ga–ni* signifying Sukanya. The seventh note, *ni*, is always left hanging, like a question that needs an answer, or a perfection just out of reach, until the final note of the opera, when it resolves up to top *sa*, the tonic note D. As his friend George Harrison once sang, the answer's at the end. It is an exhilarating, love-affirming conclusion.

Inevitably one wonders how different the opera would have been had Ravi lived to complete it and supervise its production. He would surely have rewritten elements, because he always made changes right up to the deadline if he was allowed to. I suspect he would have expanded on the relatively restrained use of the Indian instruments. But *Sukanya* is authentic to his late-period style, and as a total artwork, involving Indian and Western music, story, dance and projections, it was a project he would have loved. "Can you imagine how excited he would have been to be there?" asks Sukanya Shankar.[4]

*

In his latter years Ravi sometimes feared for the survival of Indian classical music. He knew that times had changed in India, that no *guru* could now expect his disciples to study music in the same way as he had in Maihar, up to sixteen hours a day and renouncing all distractions. Indian state institutions still supported classical music, but not to the same degree as they did in the 1950s, and, as Ravi lamented, many Indian sponsors were turning away from music in favor of Bollywood, cricket and fashion. When they did support music events, they were more likely to choose fusion music rather than classical.

Ravi's generation of Indian musicians who emerged in the early years after independence burned so brightly that their successors often remained in the shadows. This was, at least, the international perspective. In 2008 the critic Simon Broughton wrote about the peril this threatened. "Ask a man in the street in the UK to name an Indian musician and you will get one answer—Ravi Shankar," he said. Ravi was almost eighty-eight then. "Ask someone a little more up on their classical instrumentalists and they might also proffer Ali Akbar Khan, Vilayat Khan, Bismillah Khan, perhaps Amjad Ali Khan, Hariprasad Chaurasia and Shivkumar Sharma." The first four of these are now dead, and of the last three the youngest, Amjad Ali Khan, is seventy-three at the time of writing. Even Zakir Hussain, omitted from that list but probably the most famous living Indian classical musician, is now sixty-eight. "Is this the end of one of mankind's most sublime achievements?" asked Broughton.[5] He was exaggerating for effect, but the generation gap he had identified was troubling.

Sensitive to the last, Ravi could sink into negativity at times, but usually he expressed optimism for the future. As he said in one of his last interviews, "More than ever before there is an abundance of talent today."[6] He retained such love for Indian classical music that he felt it would continue to flourish as long as students dedicated themselves to exploring its depths and audiences were given opportunities to hear it. Interestingly, he argued that young musicians today tend to learn more quickly because technology exposes them to so much variety in music at an earlier age. Their challenge is to maintain their focus despite the distractions, and it remains essential to be guided by a good *guru*. Despite his fears, he did not sit back and complain. Right to the end he engaged with young musicians. He would find out who were the budding talents and try to hear them himself. He asked them to play for him privately or provided a platform for them. He invited a chosen few on stage with him or accepted them as disciples. He took heart from this generational renewal.

His hope was that Indian classical music could sustain a position in India similar to that of Western classical music in the West, attracting healthy audiences and sponsors regardless of how fashions in popular music shifted. Abroad, he had long ago accepted that it would never recapture its brief position in the popular mainstream, but he was happy that in many countries it has settled into an influential niche, gaining students of all nationalities and attracting audiences who are more knowledgeable than ever.

Ravi's own influence shows no signs of disappearing. During 2012, when Ravi was composing his opera even as his health was in terminal decline, Anoushka wrote the song "The Sun Won't Set" about him and invited her sister Norah to sing it. It is the ballad of a daughter who wishes she had known her father in the bright morning of his life. It is also about his refusal to fade away and her reluctance to let him go.

In the years that followed his death, rather than receding into darkness, the Indian Sun continued to spread his warming rays and exert his gravitational pull. The coverage given to the premiere of *Sukanya*, which included national television news reports, showed that Ravi was posthumously still a draw, as did the first live performance of *Passages* at the BBC Proms, which was televised in full. Anoushka took on her father's mantle as the world's best-known sitar player and continued to champion his orchestral works. The most popular is now his second sitar concerto; within the span of four months in 2016–17, for example, the Philharmonic Orchestras of New York, Los Angeles, Berlin and Luxembourg all performed it, with Anoushka as soloist.

In 2015–16 the Grammy Museum in Los Angeles mounted a year-long retrospective exhibition on Ravi. New archival releases have emerged from East Meets West Music, including a 1971 recital recorded at home (*In Hollywood*), his 1976 concert at the Cathedral of St. John the Divine, New York, and an expanded edition of his *Ghanashyam* soundtrack.

The younger generations of classical musicians are so diverse in approach now that it is difficult to generalize about them, but it does seem that the best of them are comfortable about combining the rigorous training of their ancestors with the liberal approach to musical forms that has become the norm in the interconnected world— the world that Ravi helped to create. It is fascinating to see how some of these musicians have embraced forms such as minimalism, modal jazz or electronic dance music that had earlier been molded by influences from Indian music, and from Ravi in particular. Many circles have been completed. If no one in the new generation approaches Ravi's level of name recognition, Anoushka comes closest to doing so. Like him, she is prodigiously creative and voyages in her own directions. The high profile of both his daughters helps to stimulate interest in Ravi among new audiences.

The vocalist Kaushiki Chakraborty, a contemporary of Anoushka who is one of the rising stars of Indian classical music, recently described Ravi as "the god who has showed us the direction forward to take our music globally," and admitted that she had watched all his online interviews. "Every single comment never fails to inspire," she said, "to make me feel that tomorrow morning I will get up one hour earlier and sit for my practice and try to get better. He has shown us how to dream."[7]

Bickram Ghosh concurs. Having formally become Ravi's disciple during their touring years, he is now one of India's most respected percussionists and film composers. "As time flows," he says, "the world will realize what he did, what unlimited possibilities he opened up and what an incredible task he eventually accomplished in a single lifetime."[8] He released his own musical homage to Ravi in the form of his 2016 album *Maya*. Others who have recorded tributes to Ravi include John McLaughlin and Talvin Singh.

Ravi's enduring impact extends beyond his musical legacy to his example as a kind of global citizen who traveled relentlessly, breaking down barriers between peoples, introducing them to the best of India. This makes him as relevant today as sixty years ago. "He represents hope, because he is a person who embraced everyone," says Nitin Sawhney.

> Boundaries to people like him feel superfluous and actually inhibit growth, and we have so many people at the moment in the world who are trying to do that. From that point of view, what he represents is so incredibly important right now and will continue to be. In that respect he must be preserved as more than just a memory, but as an inspiration.[9]

Stephen Walsh has argued that, contrary to the common view of radicals as figures who exist at the margins, most musical revolutionaries tend to be popular.[10] Ravi fits the bill, following in the tradition of Beethoven, Wagner and Debussy, and paralleling his contemporaries (and adherents) the Beatles. Emerging at a time of flux for India and its arts, he bridged the old and the new. More than anyone else, he was responsible for establishing standards and practices for Indian classical music, and for creating a mass market for it—first in India, and then worldwide. That his success met with so much criticism at times can be seen as one measure of his radical impact. Those who claimed he had sold out were far wide of the mark. He was the most scintillating, persuasive exponent of the form, and the most revolutionary.

"Right now, the kind of world we are living in is so fast paced that people forget very soon, and they move forward," says Shivkumar Sharma. "But whenever you will talk about taking Indian classical music to the whole world, Raviji's name will be there."[11]

*

In the *New Yorker*'s obituary, Taylor Ho Bynum wrote, "Ravi Shankar reminds us of the real standard of musical genius: total individual commitment, dedication, and mastery joined with a collaborative generosity and a beginner's open mind."[12] After knowing Ravi for eighteen years and immersing myself in his life for the past six, the image of him that stands out above all for me is of that open mind, ever curious, playful like a child. He embraced the creed that learning never ends, and he expressed it in an unquenchable thirst for musical exploration. Despite his formidable musical erudition, for him, as for Tansen five centuries ago, music was a vast ocean of promise in which his knowledge remained a mere drop.

Ravi was once asked in an interview whether he believed in reincarnation. "Absolutely," he replied. What would he like to return as in his next life? There was only one possible answer: "I would like to come back as a better musician."[13]

REFERENCES

Ravi Shankar is identified within the references as RS. Unless otherwise credited, all interviews and telephone conversations referred to were carried out by the author, and all letters and emails were written to the author.

Ravi Shankar wrote two autobiographies in English, *My Music, My Life* (first published in 1968) and *Raga Mala* (1997), and one in Bengali, *Raag-Anuraag* (1980). *Raga Mala* was later revised for a French edition, *Raga Mala: Ma vie en musique* (2010). This revised version subsequently appeared in an Italian edition but has yet to be published in English, hence the references below to *Raga Mala: Ma vie en musique*.

For full details of all books cited below, see the Bibliography.

Abbreviations

BOOKS BY RAVI SHANKAR

MMML	*My Music, My Life*
RA	*Raag-Anuraag*
RM	*Raga Mala*
RMMVM	*Raga Mala: Ma vie en musique*

ARCHIVES

AP	Avakian Papers; George Avakian and Anahid Ajemian Papers, JPB 14–28, Music Division, New York Public Library
BBC WAC	BBC Written Archives Centre, Reading
BPL	Britten–Pears Library, Aldeburgh
DBD	Dokumentationsbibliothek Davos; Alice Boner papers
FMA	Foyle Menuhin Archive, Royal Academy of Music, London
HA	Holst Archive, Britten–Pears Library, Aldeburgh
IBC	Isadora Bennett Collection, (S) *MGZMD 22, Dance Division (Special Collections), New York Public Library for Performing Arts
PRC	Paula Rao Collection, Los Angeles
RAC	Rockefeller Archive Center, Sleepy Hollow, New York

RAP   Richard Attenborough Papers, University of Sussex. From the collection of Lord and Lady Attenborough. Accepted in lieu by HM Government in 2018 and allocated to the University of Sussex.

SA   Shankar Archives: collections of the Shankar family, California and Delhi

SZ   Stadtarchiv Zurich; vii.389: Alice Boner Nachlass 1929–48

Introduction: An Unending Quest

1   RS in Anoushka Shankar, *Bapi: The Love of My Life*, p. 15.

2   L.E., "Ravi Shankar" (typescript report on 30 June press conference), July 7, 1966 [SA].

3   *Billboard*, December 30, 1967, p. 10.

4   Sadanand Menon, "Pancham-taar may have snapped, but the dhwani remains," *The Hindu*, December 13, 2012.

5   RS, Foreword to Claude Sauvageot and Mireille Ballero, *Inde*, p. 10.

6   Sumit Mitra and Chitra Subramaniam, "Return of the maestro," *India Today*, April 16–30, 1980, p. 90.

7   Ronald Bergan, "Richard Attenborough obituary," *Guardian*, August 25, 2014.

8   E. M. Forster, *A Passage to India*, p. 77.

9   Alfred Frankenstein, "Two unusual concerts: Paris boy singers, India players here," *San Francisco Chronicle*, April 12, 1957, p. 14.

10 RS, "You cannot treat a Raga" (signed memo, late 1970s) [SA].

11 *MMML*, p. 30.

12 Subroto Roychowdhury, quoted in Chandrima S. Bhattacharya, "A home in music," *Telegraph* (Calcutta), January 6, 2013.

13 Peter Lavezzoli, *The Dawn of Indian Music in the West: Bhairavi*, p. 433.

14 "The sun who rose in the west," *Times of India*, August 15, 1997.

15 Vishwa Mohan Bhatt, quoted in Sandip Roy, "Ravi Shankar, 90," *India Abroad*, April 16, 2010, p. M4.

16 "The maestro speaks out," *Northern Indian Patrika*, April 7, 1980.

17 Yehudi Menuhin, quoted in flyer for RS's concerts at Friends House, London, October 12 and 17, 1956 [SA].

18 Zubin Mehta, interview, Florence, September 4, 2016.

19 Philip Glass, "Foreword" in *MMML*, p. 12.

20 David Sheppard, *On Some Faraway Beach: The Life and Times of Brian Eno*, p. 5n.

21 Tanmoy Bose, in "Ravi Shankar 1920–2012," *Songlines*, March 2013, p. 17.

22 Amit Chaudhuri, "My hero: Ravi Shankar," *Guardian*, December 12, 2012.

23 Shubhendra Rao, conversation, Delhi, February 18, 2017.

24 Peggy Holroyde, *The Music of India*, p. 12.
25 RS, speaking in *Ravi Shankar Reflects* (series on BBC Bengali Service radio), cited in *Telegraph* (Calcutta), April 4, 1983.
26 Padmini S. Kirtane and Donatus de Silva, "An hour with Ravi Shankar," *Himmat*, January 25, 1974.
27 RS, voiceover narration in *Raga* (1971, directed by Howard Worth).

1 Benares

1 RS, voiceover narration in *Raga* (1971, directed by Howard Worth).
2 Jerry Camarillo Dunn, *My Favorite Place on Earth: Celebrated People Share Their Travel Discoveries*, p. 213.
3 Ibid., p. 211.
4 *MMML*, p. 71.
5 Shyam Shankar, "To my children to be carefully preserved," undated, *c.* 1928–35 (copy) [SA].
6 Sankarlal Bhattacharjee in Aloke Mitra, *Ravi: The Colours of the Sun*, p. 3.
7 Shyam Shankar, "To my children."
8 *RM*, p. 19.
9 *RMMVM*, p. 24.
10 *MMML*, p. 70.
11 RS, interview, Delhi, January 6, 2006.
12 *RA,* p. 162.
13 RS interview, January 6, 2006.
14 *RA*, p. 162.
15 *RM*, p. 25.
16 Ibid., p. 26.
17 Ibid.
18 Joan L. Erdman, "Rajputana influences on Uday Shankar's oriental ballets," paper presented at International Seminar on Rajasthan, Mohanlal Sukhadia University, Udaipur, December 17–21, 1991.
19 V. H. Jones, "A Short Sketch of the Career of Pandit Shyam Shankar (Hara Chowdhuri), M.A. (London) Bar at Law," *c.* 1928 [SA].
20 "The Italian ballet," *The Times*, March 20, 1924, p. 12.
21 At Queen's Hall, London, June 11, 1928. Advertisement in *The Times*, June 2, 1928.
22 *RM*, p. 27.
23 Shyam Shankar, "To my children."
24 Ibid.
25 RS, "My Hols," *Sunday Times*, September 14, 1997.

26 *MMML*, p. 70.

27 RS interview, January 6, 2006.

28 *MMML*, p. 76.

29 *RM*, pp. 17–18.

30 RS interview, January 6, 2006.

31 Mohan Khokar, *His Dance, His Life: A Portrait of Uday Shankar*, p. 25.

32 Basanta Koomar Roy, "Shan-Kar," *Encore* (New York), April 1933, p. 25.

33 Alice Boner to Anna Boner, December 17, 1928 [DBD 5.19].

34 In the Alice Boner collection at Museum Rietberg, Zurich.

35 Alice Boner, *Indien, Mein Indien: Tagbuch einer Reise*, p. 16.

36 Joan L. Erdman, "Rajputana influences on Uday Shankar's oriental ballets."

37 Alice Boner to Anna Boner, August 25, 1930 [DBD 6.10].

2 Dancing Comes First

1 Benjamin Britten's diary entry for May 6, 1933, in John Evans (ed.), *Journeying Boy: The Diaries of the Young Benjamin Britten 1928–1938*, p. 139.

2 RS, voiceover narration in *Ravi Shankar: One Man and His Music* (1986, directed by Nicolas Klotz).

3 Alice Boner to Anna Boner, October 31, 1930 [DBD 5.29]. Author's translation.

4 *MMML*, p. 72.

5 RS, "A Brother Speaks," in Mohan Khokar, *His Dance, His Life: A Portrait of Uday Shankar*, p. 10.

6 RS, "Some recollections," *India Weekly*, October 23, 1975.

7 Alice Boner to "Mlles Boner," March 4, 1931 [DBD 6.4].

8 "Sinuous Sidelight," British Pathé newsreel, March 23, 1931.

9 Emile Vuillermoz, "Les événements musicaux," *Candide*, March 12, 1932, quoted in Ruth Abrahams, "Uday Shankar: The early years, 1900–1938," *Dance Chronicle*, vol. 30 no. 3 (2007), p. 405.

10 Jan Murray, "You cannot brush the surface of a culture," *Time Out*, October 20–26, 1972.

11 Charles Reid, "Ravi Shankar and George Beatles," *New York Times*, May 7, 1967, p. 54.

12 There is a copy in the British Library.

13 RS, "A Brother Speaks," in Khokar, *His Dance, His Life*, p. 10.

14 Mamata Shankar, interview, Kolkata, February 13, 2016.

15 Khokar, *His Dance, His Life*, p. 165.

16 Rajendra Shankar to Alice Boner, November 14, 1931 [SZ 1.1.26].

17 Ibid., November 17, 1931 [SZ 1.1.29].

18 Ibid.

19 "Amala Shankar's love story," *Telegraph* (Calcutta), July 3, 2013.

20 Rajendra Shankar to Alice Boner, February 14, 1932 [SZ 1.1.56].

21 Ibid., March 13, 1932 [SZ 1.1.63].

22 Photograph in Alice Boner's collection at Museum Rietberg, ref. ABF 0-35.

23 RS, "The life of Pandit Ravi Shankar," *Outlook Traveller*, December 22, 2015.

24 Alice Boner to Anna Boner, June 26, 1931 [DBD 6.14].

25 Ibid., October 31, 1931 [DBD 6.17].

26 *MMML*, p. 77.

27 George Harrison, "Foreword," in *RM*, p. 7.

28 "Dancer from Hindustan," *Time*, January 9, 1933, p. 62.

29 RS, "Dada—My Brother," in Dibyendu Ghosh (ed.), *The Great Shankars: Uday, Ravi*, p. 11.

30 "Hindu music and dance," *The Times*, April 5, 1933, p. 12.

31 *RM*, p. 45.

32 Evans (ed.), *Journeying Boy*, p. 139.

33 Khokar, *His Dance, His Life*, pp. 89–90.

34 Shyam Shankar to Alice Boner, May 23, 1933 [SZ 1.1.137].

35 Rajendra Shankar to Alice Boner, undated (June 23, 1933?) [SZ 1.1.145].

36 Ibid., from Rangoon, undated (June 23, 1933?) [SZ 1.1.144].

37 RS, "Some recollections," *India Weekly*, October 23, 1975.

38 RS, "My Hols," *Sunday Times*, September 14, 1997.

39 *Times of India*, c. May 1933, quoted in Khokar, *His Dance, His Life*, p. 75.

40 Shyam Shankar to Debendra Shankar and RS, July 14, 1934 [SA], reproduced in *RM*, p. 55.

41 RS, speech in Chennai, April 2, 2001 [SA, video, ref. 1448].

42 RS, "My Hols."

43 Shyam Shankar to RS, December 23, 1933 [SA], reproduced in *RM*, p. 55.

44 Sol Hurok to Rajendra Shankar, September 17, 1935 [SZ 1.1.201].

3 The Call of Music

1 Padmini S. Kirtane and Donatus de Silva, "An hour with Ravi Shankar," *Himmat*, January 25, 1974.

2 G. K. Seshagiri, quoted in John Martin, "The dance: Art of India," *New York Times*, April 2, 1934, p. 8.

3 Uday Shankar, quoted in Martin, "The dance: Art of India."

4 Rajendra Shankar to Alice Boner, August 27, 1934 [SZ 1.1.172].

5 Alice Boner to the Boner family, January 24, 1935 [DBD 9.15].

6   RS with Sankarlal Bhattacharjee, *Smriti*, translated and quoted in Chandrima S. Bhattacharya, "A home in music," *Telegraph* (Calcutta), January 6, 2013.

7   *RA*, p. 162; Sukanya Shankar, conversation, London, October 8, 2019.

8   Alice Boner to George Boner, April 20, 1935 [DBD 9.21].

9   RS, interviewed by Mita Nag, Delhi, March 23, 2005, and Mita Nag, interview, Kolkata, February 2, 2017.

10   *MMML*, p. 80.

11   *RM*, p. 63.

12   Douglas M. Knight Jr, *Balasaraswati: Her Art and Life*, p. 95.

13   Rajendra Shankar to Alice Boner, June 17, 1935 [SZ 1.1.141].

14   "Pandit Shyam Shankar," *The Times*, October 19, 1935.

15   Alice Boner to Anna Boner, November 21, 1935 [DBD 9.11].

16   "The Bombay man's diary," *Evening News of India*, December 16, 1935 [SZ 2.1.17].

17   Mohan Khokar, *His Dance, His Life: A Portrait of Uday Shankar*, p. 95.

18   RS, interview, Delhi, January 8, 2004.

19   *RM*, p. 68.

20   RS, "The sound of God," *Oracle* (July 1967), p. 5.

21   *RMMVM*, p. 76.

22   RS, "The sound of God," p. 28.

23   Allan Kozinn, "Ravi Shankar," *New York Times*, December 12, 2012.

24   Vishnudas Shirali to Alice Boner, December 2, 1936 [SZ 1.1.261].

25   Zohra Segal to Alice Boner, November 29, 1936 [SZ 1.1.256].

26   RS to Alice Boner, December 1, 1936 [SZ 1.1.260].

27   Uday Shankar to Alice Boner, January 7, 1937 [SZ 1.1.162].

28   Joan L. Erdman with Zohra Segal, *Stages: The Art and Adventures of Zohra Segal*, p. 80.

29   RS to Alice Boner, January 7, 1937 [SZ 1.1.285].

30   Uday Shankar to Alice Boner, undated letter, shortly before December 1, 1937 [SZ 1.1.449].

31   Jan Murray, "You cannot brush the surface of a culture," *Time Out*, October 20–26, 1972, p. 22.

32   Erdman with Segal, *Stages*, p. 83.

33   Britten's diary entry for July 19, 1937, in John Evans (ed.), *Journeying Boy: The Diaries of the Young Benjamin Britten 1928–1938*, p. 443.

34   RS, "Dada—My Brother," in Dibyendu Ghosh (ed.), *The Great Shankars: Uday, Ravi*, p. 10.

4 The Path of Most Resistance

1 RS, voiceover narration in *Raga* (1971, directed by Howard Worth).

2 Joan L. Erdman with Zohra Segal, *Stages: The Art and Adventures of Zohra Segal*, p. 90.

3 Karun Kumar Chakravarty and Nabarun Chatterji, interviews, Nasrathpur, February 5, 2017.

4 Zohra Mumtaz to her uncle Memphis, June 27, 1938, in Erdman with Segal, *Stages*, p. 82.

5 Mark Kidel, "Remembering Ravi Shankar," December 13, 2012 (www.theartsdesk .com/classical-music/remembering-ravi-shankar-1920-2012).

6 *MMML*, p. 82.

7 *RM*, p. 84.

8 RS, "A great musician," 1962 [SA].

9 RS, "Some recollections," *India Weekly*, October 23, 1975.

10 *MMML*, p. 83.

11 Ibid.

12 RS, interview, Delhi, January 8, 2004.

13 *MMML*, p. 62.

14 RS, interviewed by Gavin Esler on *Hardtalk* (BBC World (TV), broadcast July 29, 2005).

15 Padmini S. Kirtane and Donatus de Silva, "An hour with Ravi Shankar," *Himmat*, January 25, 1974.

16 Lajwanti Gupta, interview, Mumbai, February 10, 2017.

17 Ira Landgarten, "Ravi Shankar: Genius of the sitar," *Frets*, November 1979, p. 32.

18 Sandy Schurter, "Star course audience enjoys Indian music," *News-Gazette* (Champaign-Urbana), November 3, 1961.

19 Landgarten, "Ravi Shankar: Genius of the sitar," p. 32.

20 Ibid.

21 Girish Mehra, *Nearer Heaven than Earth: The Life and Times of Boshi Sen and Gertrude Emerson Sen*, p. 533.

22 Utpal K. Banerjee, "Mind of a legendary maestro" (manuscript of interview with RS), *c.* 2004 [SA].

23 Kumudini Lakhia, telephone interview, October 10, 2018.

24 Anita Pai, "Interview with Smt. Lakshmi Shankar," *Kathaka*, October 9, 2010 (www.kathaka.wordpress.com/2010/10/09/interview-with-lakshmi-shankar).

25 Kamala Chakravarty, interview, Chennai, March 21, 2014.

26 V. Ramnarayan, "Ravindra Sangeet," *Sruti*, May 2009, p. 17.

27 Gertrude Emerson Sen, "A beacon on the Himalayas," *Asia*, December 1941, p. 694.

28 Alice Boner to Georg Boner, March 14, 1941 [SZ 1.1.861].

29 Swapan Kumar Bondyopadhyay, *An Unheard Melody: Annapurna Devi, An Authorised Biography*, p. 31.

30 RS to Alice Boner, June 26, 1942 [SZ 1.1.934].

31 Debendra Shankar to Alice Boner, January 7, 1943 [SZ 1.1.956].

32 RS to Alice Boner, June 26, 1942 [SZ 1.1.934].

33 Ibid.

34 Ibid.

35 *RM*, p. 102.

36 Ibid.

37 Aneesh Pradhan, *Hindustani Music in Colonial Bombay*, p. 103.

38 RS, "What set Allah Rakha Khan apart was his musicality," *India Today*, February 21, 2000.

39 Vinay Bharat-Ram, *From the Brink of Bankruptcy: The DCM Story*, p. 42.

40 Vinay and Arun Bharat-Ram, interview, Delhi, March 28, 2014.

41 Debendra Shankar to Alice Boner, January 7, 1943 [SZ 1.1.956].

42 *RM*, p. 105; price given in *Link*, September 14, 1958 [SA].

43 Charles Fox, "Review: Ravi Shankar recital at the Royal Festival Hall," *Manchester Guardian*, June 20, 1966.

44 Landgarten, "Ravi Shankar: Genius of the sitar," p. 32.

45 K. A. Abbas, *I Am Not an Island: An Experiment in Autobiography*, p. 264.

46 Ibid., p. 265.

47 Jawaharlal Nehru, *The Discovery of India*, p. 499.

48 Debendra Shankar to Alice Boner, January 7, 1943 [SZ 1.1.956].

49 Mohan Khokar, *His Dance, His Life: A Portrait of Uday Shankar*, p. 112.

5 Mumbai Made Me

1 RS, "Scope of classical music in films," *Sunday Standard*, November 23, 1947.

2 Narendra Kusnur, "Mumbai made me," *Mid-Day*, December 18, 2001.

3 See, for example, Sunil Khilnani, *The Idea of India*, p. 136.

4 *RM*, p. 105.

5 RS, speaking alongside Lata Mangeshkar at the Nehru Centre, London, June 2000, video [SA, ref. 1444].

6 "Ravi Shankar misses Mumbai's 'Baithaks,'" *Times of India*, August 13, 1997.

7 Dev Anand, *Romancing with Life: An Autobiography*, p. 52.

8   *RM*, p. 105.

9   RS, "The central cultural troupe," in *India Immortal* programme, 1946 [Misha Dasgupta Masud collection].

10 Rekha Jain, "Shantida—my mentor," in Gul Bardhan (ed.), *Rhythm Incarnate: Tribute to Shanti Bardhan*, p. 61.

11 RS, "Experiments in film music," *Filmfare*, March 14, 1958.

12 Ibid.

13 V. A. K. Ranga Rao, "The other sides," *Indian Express* (Madras), April 25, 1970.

14 Ibid.

15 Dilip Bobb and Sumit Mitra, "Ravi Shankar: An amorous odyssey," *India Today*, February 15, 1979.

16 *MMML*, p. 86.

17 Partha Bose, interview, Kolkata, January 23, 2017.

18 *RM*, p. 99.

19 Ajoy Chakrabarty, speaking from the stage at Bharatiya Vidya Bhavan, London, November 19, 2017.

20 RS, "Scope of classical music in films."

21 Gaurav Mazumdar, interview, London, September 19, 2014.

22 Sukanya Shankar, *Ravi Shankar: 75 Years, A Celebration*, p. 62.

23 Krishna Ramkumar, interview, Delhi, March 23, 2014.

24 *Asian Relations: Being Report of the Proceedings and Documentation of the First Asian Relations Conference, New Delhi, March–April 1947* (New Delhi: Asian Relations Organization, 1948), p. 23.

25 "The talk of the town: Sitarist," *New Yorker*, October 14, 1961, p. 45.

26 Sakuntala Narasimhan, *Kamaladevi Chattopadhyay: The Romantic Rebel*, p. 103.

27 *RM*, p. 111. Damu Jhaveri recalled there being eighteen shows in Bombay (Jhaveri, "Discovery of India," in Bardhan (ed.), *Rhythm Incarnate*, p. 86).

28 *RM*, p. 112.

29 "Ravi Shankar misses Mumbai's 'Baithaks.'"

30 *RM*, p. 112.

31 RS, "The sound of God," *Oracle* (July 1967), p. 28.

32 *MMML*, p. 88.

33 Ibid., p. 89.

34 *RM*, p. 311.

35 *MMML*, p. 90.

36 Kamala Chakravarty, interview, Chennai, March 21, 2014.

37 RS to Harihar Rao, February 3, 1949 [PRC].

6 All India Star

1   Sumit Mitra and Chitra Subramaniam, "Return of the maestro," *India Today*, April 16–30, 1980, p. 93.
2   U. L. Baruah, *This Is All India Radio: A Handbook of Radio Broadcasting in India*, pp. 1–8.
3   Figures from David Lelyveld, "Upon the subdominant: Administering music on All India Radio," *Social Text*, 39 (summer 1994), pp. 115–16; Ramachandra Guha, *India After Gandhi: The History of the World's Largest Democracy*, p. 739.
4   Baruah, *This Is All India Radio*, p. 9.
5   RS, "Scope of classical music in films," *Sunday Standard*, November 23, 1947.
6   *RM*, p. 118.
7   Shubhendra Rao, interview, Delhi, March 25, 2014.
8   Balwant Rai Verma, interview, Delhi, March 25, 2014.
9   *MMML*, p. 93.
10 Ibid.
11 Utpal K. Banerjee, "Mind of a legendary maestro" (manuscript of interview with RS), *c.* 2004 [SA].
12 *RM*, p. 171.
13 Quoted in Aneesh Pradhan, *Hindustani Music in Colonial Bombay*, p. 198.
14 Nalini Ghuman, *Resonances of the Raj: India in the English Musical Imagination, 1897–1947*, pp. 283, 301.
15 Lelyveld, "Upon the subdominant," p. 120; Ghuman, *Resonances*, p. 299.
16 RS to Harihar Rao, undated (February 1949) [PRC].
17 Ghuman, *Resonances*, p. 283.
18 Imogen Holst to Leonard Elmhirst, January 2, 1951 [HA, ref. HOL 5/1/3/9].
19 Philip Reed (ed.), *The Travel Diaries of Peter Pears, 1936–1978*, pp. 31–2.
20 Lalit Mansingh, interview, Farnham, June 13, 2014.
21 Baruah, *This Is All India Radio*, p. 131.
22 Mansingh interview.
23 RS, "The life of Pandit Ravi Shankar," *Outlook Traveller*, December 22, 2015.
24 Aashish Khan, interview, Los Angeles, April 13, 2016.
25 Birju Maharaj, interview, Delhi, March 28, 2014.
26 RS, "The life of Pandit Ravi Shankar."
27 Vinay and Arun Bharat-Ram, interview, Delhi, March 28 2014.
28 Ibid.
29 Ibid.
30 Sunil Khilnani, *Incarnations: India in 50 Lives*, p. 528.

31 RS to Rao, May 1, 1950 [PRC].
32 Kavita Chhibber, "Pandit Ravi Shankar and Sukanya Shankar," March 18, 2005 (www.kavitachhibber.com/2005/03/18/pandit-ravi-shankar-and-sukanya -shankar).
33 Ibid.
34 Kavita Chhibber, "Ustad Imrat Khan," March 19, 2004 (www.kavitachhibber .com/2004/03/19/ustad-imrat-khan).
35 Kavita Chhibber, "Pandit Ravi Shankar and Sukanya Shankar."
36 RS to Rao, August 3, 1952 [PRC].
37 Quoted in Namita Devidayal, *The Sixth String of Vilayat Khan*, p. 4.
38 Sukanya Shankar, *Ravi Shankar: 75 Years, A Celebration*, p. 62.
39 Sakuntala Narasimhan, "Songs from strings," *Deccan Herald* (Bangalore), April 11, 1993.
40 Gaurav Mazumdar, speaking from the stage at Ravi Shankar Centre, Delhi, February 15, 2019.
41 Pirashanna Thevarajah, interview, London, June 14, 2016.
42 RS to Rao, March 18, 1954 [PRC].
43 Ibid., March 22, 1954.
44 Ibid., June 12, 1950.
45 Shuchi Bhatt, interview, London, April 27, 2014.
46 RS to Rao, August 25, 1953 [PRC].
47 *RM*, p. 130.
48 Yehudi Menuhin, quoted in *RM*, p. 138.
49 Ibid., p. 317.
50 RS to Rao, April 23, 1954 [PRC].
51 Khilnani, *Incarnations*, p. 493.
52 RS to Rao, October 5, 1954 [PRC].
53 RS, "My Hols," *Sunday Times*, September 14, 1997.
54 RS to Rao, October 5, 1954 [PRC]. 8 Barter Street has since been demolished.
55 Narayana Menon, letters to Peter Crossley-Holland and Philip Bate, both October 8, 1954 [BBC WAC: RCONT1, Ravi Shankar file 1, 1954-62; and TVART2, Ravi Shankar misc. pre-1963].
56 John Linton to RS, October 26, 1954 [BBC WAC: RCONT1, Ravi Shankar file 1, 1954–62].

7 The World of Apu

1   Dolly Rizvi, "Pandit Ravi Shankar: Behind the screen," *Filmfare*, May 4, 1962.

2   RS, "This dangerous epidemic of cheap film music," *Ananda Bazar Patrika* cinema supplement, October 1957.

3   *RM*, p. 121.

4   Satyajit Ray to Norman Clare, May 22, 1948, quoted in Andrew Robinson, *Satyajit Ray: The Inner Eye*, p. 64.

5   Folke Isaksson, "Conversation with Satyajit Ray," *Sight and Sound* (summer 1970), p. 116.

6   See Andrew Robinson and Nemai Ghosh, *Satyajit Ray: A Vision of Cinema*, pp. 292–9, and Sandip Ray (ed.), *Satyajit Ray's Ravi Shankar: An Unfilmed Visual Script*, pp. 43–74.

7   Sankarlal Bhattacharjee, "Unheard melodies," in Sandip Ray (ed.), *Satyajit Ray's Ravi Shankar*, pp. 1–40.

8   "*Pather Panchali* music by Ravi Shankar was written and recorded in one shift," *Screen*, October 19, 1956.

9   Robinson, *Satyajit Ray*, p. 92.

10   Satyajit Ray, "Background music in films," in *Speaking of Films*, p. 110.

11   Bert Cardullo, *World Directors in Dialogue: Conversations on Cinema*, p. 156.

12   Satyajit Ray to RS, August 12, 1955 [SA]; Sukanya Shankar, telephone conversation, July 28, 2019.

13   Satyajit Ray, *My Years with Apu: A Memoir*, pp. 75–6; *RM*, p. 121.

14   See Bhattacharjee, "Unheard melodies," p. 6; and RS, interview with Mark Kidel, Delhi, March 2000 [SA].

15   "*Pather Panchali* music by Ravi Shankar was written and recorded in one shift."

16   Ibid.

17   Satyajit Ray, sleeve notes for Ravi Shankar, *Music from Satyajit Ray's Apu Trilogy* (EMI, 1978).

18   Shubha Mudgal, "Remembering Pandit Ravi Shankar through some of his work for films" (2012) (www.shubhamudgal.com/remembering-pandit-ravi-shankar-through-some-of-his-work-for-films).

19   RS, "Working with Satyajit Ray," in Sandip Ray (ed.), *Satyajit Ray's Ravi Shankar*, p. 95.

20   Martin Scorsese's contribution to Nemai Ghosh, *Satyajit Ray at 70*, pp. 116–17.

21   Satyajit Ray, sleeve notes for *Music from Satyajit Ray's Apu Trilogy* (HMV India, 1978).

22 Ian Firth, "An interview with Ravi Shankar," *Film Digest* (WEA Film Study Group, Sydney, Australia), issue 3, September 1965 [SA].

23 "Ravishanker to tour Europe," *c.* September 24, 1956, unidentified cutting [SA].

24 Tapan Sinha, "Ravishankar: Total musical personality," from Dibyendu Ghosh (ed.), *The Great Shankars: Uday, Ravi*, p. 92.

25 "*Pather Panchali* music by Ravi Shankar was written and recorded in one shift."

26 RS, "Experiments in film music," *Filmfare*, March 14, 1958.

27 RS, interviewed by Art Makosinski, Encinitas, August 23, 2005.

28 Satyajit Ray, "Some aspects of my craft" (1966), in his *Our Films, Their Films*, p. 71.

29 RS, "My first break," *The Hindu*, October 7, 2010.

30 RS, "This dangerous epidemic of cheap film music."

31 *RMMVM*, p. 123.

32 Partha Bose, interview, Kolkata, January 23, 2017; Monoj Shankar, interview, Kolkata, January 27, 2017.

33 Bose interview.

34 Renuka Vyavahare, Akshata Shetty and Swasti Chatterjee, "Panditji treated me like his daughter," *Times of India*, December 13, 2012.

35 See Shubha Mudgal, "Songs of the little road," December 2012 (thebigindianpicture.com/2012/12/songs-of-the-little-road).

36 RS to Kamala Chakravarty, September 26, 1960 [SA].

37 "Ravi Shankar's music," *Cine Advance*, February 24, 1961.

38 "Pandit Ravi Shankar for a film role," *Cine Advance*, October 30, 1959.

39 "Big plan," *Screen*, November 6, 1959.

40 "Three masters join hands," *Cine Advance*, September 16, 1960; "L. Vijayalakshmi to star in Ravi Shankar's film," *Screen*, April 14, 1961; "Ravi Shankar to make film on himself" and "To production," undated cuttings [SA].

41 V. A. K. Ranga Rao, "The other sides," *Indian Express* (Madras), April 25, 1970.

42 Firth, "An interview with Ravi Shankar."

8 Going Solo

1 RS to Harihar Rao, October 1, 1955 [PRC].

2 Yehudi Menuhin to Narayana Menon, first of two undated telegrams, forwarded to RS on March 5, 1955 [SA].

3 Menuhin to Menon, second of two undated telegrams, forwarded to RS on March 5, 1955 [SA].

4 RS to station director, AIR, March 18, 1955 [SA].

5   Tathagata Ray Chowdhury, 'Every note Annapurna Devi plays is like an offering: Rooshikumar Pandya,' *Times of India*, September 7, 2014.

6   RS, interviewed by Art Makosinski, Encinitas, August 23, 2005.

7   *RM*, p. 270; Radha Rajadhyaksha, "An unequal music?," *Times of India*, July 25, 1999, p. 4.

8   RS, Makosinski interview.

9   Suanshu Khurana, "Notes from behind a locked door," *Indian Express*, May 16, 2010.

10   Tathagata Ray Chowdhury, "Pandit Ravi Shankar was unhappy as I was drawing more applause: Annapurna Devi," *Times of India*, September 1, 2014.

11   Ibid.

12   Aalif Surti, 'Annapurna Devi: The greatest living exponent of the surbahar and the sitar,' *Man's World* (India), April 7, 2016 (first published 2000).

13   We discussed it in London in July 1995.

14   RS, Makosinski interview.

15   *RM*, p. 138.

16   Ibid.

17   Peter Lavezzoli, *The Dawn of Indian Music in the West: Bhairavi*, p. 58.

18   Ibid., p. 61; Menuhin, "The music of India—an ancient art form," *New York Times*, April 17, 1955, p. X9.

19   John Coast to P. A. Narielwala, October 7, 1955 [SA]; *Times of India*, August 21, 1955, p. 10.

20   *Times of India*, August 21, 1955, p. 10.

21   RS to Menuhin, August 26, 1955 [FMA].

22   *RM*, p. 141; John Coast to P. A. Narielwala, September 5, 1955 [SA].

23   Paul Willetts, *Rendezvous at the Russian Tea Rooms*, pp. 141–2, 153, 441–2; Laura Noszlopy, "Railroad of death: An introduction," in John Coast, *Railroad of Death*, pp. xiv–xxxv; Laura Noszlopy, telephone interview, July 27, 2016.

24   Laura Rosenberg, telephone interview, August 12, 2016.

25   David Attenborough, *Life on Air*, pp. 221–2.

26   Coast to Narielwala, October 7, 1955 [SA].

27   RS to Coast, November 30, 1955 [SA].

28   *MMML*, p. 96.

29   Information from Laura Noszlopy and Laura Rosenberg, 2016.

30   See Mervyn Cooke, *Britten and the Far East: Asian Influences in the Music of Benjamin Britten*.

31   *RM*, p. 118.

32   Benjamin Britten to Menuhin, December 22, 1963, in Philip Reed and Mervyn Cooke (eds.), *Letters from a Life*, vol. 5: *1958–65*, pp. 541–2.

33   Philip Reed (ed.), *The Travel Diaries of Peter Pears, 1936–1978*, p. 30.

34   Britten to Imogen Holst, January 4, 1956, in Philip Reed, Mervyn Cooke and Donald Mitchell (eds.), *Letters from a Life*, vol. 4: *1952–57*, p. 382.

35   Britten to Mary Potter, December 23, 1955, ibid., pp. 373–4.

36   Nigel Williamson, "My world: Quincy Jones," *Songlines*, 121 (September 2016), p. 70.

37   RS, telephone interview, March 24, 2000, and interview, London, June 19, 2003.

38   "Festival in the Pandal: Making music in Madras," *The Times*, January 13, 1956.

39   Sakuntala Narasimhan, "Songs from strings," *Deccan Herald* (Bangalore), April 11, 1993.

40   *RM*, p. 141.

41   RS, Makosinski interview.

42   Ashwini Kumar, interview, Delhi, March 24, 2014.

43   RS, Makosinski interview.

44   Telegram from Amiya Dasgupta to Rao, January 17, 1956 [PRC].

45   Swapan Kumar Bondyopadhyay, *An Unheard Melody: Annapurna Devi, An Authorised Biography*, p. 92.

46   RS, Makosinski interview.

47   Ibid.

48   RS to Rao, January 28, 1956 [PRC].

49   RS, Makosinski interview.

50   *RM*, p. 276.

51   Ibid., p. 221.

52   RS to Rao, March 8, 1956 [PRC]; author's conversation with RS, London, July 1995.

53   RS, annotated draft of resignation letter, undated, *c.* June 1956 [PRC].

54   *Times of India*, July 15, 1956, p. 3.

55   "Ravi Shankar's tour," *Times of India*, July 20, 1956, p. 6.

56   Coast to Miss Divall of EMI Ltd, August 9, 1956, reproduced in *RM*, p. 142.

57   Menuhin, quoted in a flyer for RS's concerts at Friends House, London, October 12 and 17, 1956.

58   Satyajit Ray to RS, June 28, 1956 [SA]

59   "Ravi Shankar to leave Bombay for tour on Oct. 5," *Indian Express*, September 26, 1956; *New York Times*, April 30, 1957, p. 25.

60   RS to Menuhin, undated, *c.* July–August 1956 [SA].

9 Like Driving Through a Mist

1   Jay S. Harrison, "Shankar and Lal perform on sitar, tabla at Y.M.H.A.," *New York Herald Tribune*, December 7, 1956.

2   RS to Harihar Rao, October 9, 1956 [PRC].

3   Stella Alexander in *Times of India*, November 25, 1956, p. 5.

4   "The Earl of Harewood" (obituary), *Daily Telegraph*, July 11, 2011.

5   Lord Harewood, *The Tongs and the Bones: The Memoirs of Lord Harewood*, pp. 145, 252.

6   John Coast, unpublished memoir (courtesy of Laura Rosenberg).

7   *RM*, p. 144.

8   Shankara Angadi, interview, London, May 22, 2015.

9   *MMML*, p. 97.

10 Contract, November 14, 1956 [BBC WAC: TVART2, Ravi Shankar, misc. pre-1963] and miscellaneous contracts in BBC WAC: RCONTI, Ravi Shankar, file 1, 1954–62.

11 RS to Rao, October 23, 1956, and undated letter not earlier than November 5, 1956 [both PRC].

12 Stella Alexander, *Times of India*, November 25, 1956, p. 5.

13 RS, interview, Delhi, January 8, 2006.

14 RS, "Experiences in musical life," 1957 [SA].

15 In the USA Angel marketed it as volume 2 in a "Music of India" series. In 1967 it was retitled *Three Ragas*.

16 Bhaskar Menon, email, April 10, 2016.

17 RS, original liner notes to *Music of India: Three Classical Ragas*.

18 RS to Rao, October 9 and 23, 1956 [both PRC].

19 Alex Ross, *The Rest Is Noise*, p. 409.

20 Saloni Mathur, "Charles and Ray Eames in India," *Art Journal Open*, May 29, 2011 (artjournal.collegeart.org/?p=1735).

21 See Nicolas Nabokov, *Bagázh: Memoirs of a Russian Cosmopolitan*, pp. 242–6; Richard Taruskin, "In from the cold," *Times Literary Supplement*, August 5, 2016, p. 3.

22 Yehudi Menuhin to Nabokov, May 14, 1966, quoted in Frances Stonor Saunders, *Who Paid the Piper? The CIA and the Cultural Cold War*, p. 408.

23 RS to Rao, October 23, 1956 [PRC].

24 Ian S. MacNiven, *"Literchoor Is My Beat": A Life of James Laughlin, Publisher of New Directions*, p. 325; MacNiven, email and telephone communications, December 8, 2016.

25 *Perspective of India*, pp. 51–5, issued with *Atlantic Monthly*, vol. 192, no. 4 (October 1953).

26 James Laughlin, interviewed by Charles T. Morrissey for Ford Foundation Oral History Project, May 22, 1973, p. 58, in folder 192, box 36, Subseries 4, Series IV, FA618, Ford Foundation Archives [RAC].

27 MacNiven, *"Literchoor Is My Beat,"* p. 325.

28 Laughlin to Tennessee Williams, November 10, 1956, in Peggy L. Fox and Thomas Keith (eds.), *The Luck of Friendship: The Letters of Tennessee Williams and James Laughlin*, pp. 211–12.

29 Gunther Stuhlmann (ed.), *Diary of Anaïs Nin*, vol. VI: *1955–1966*, p. 57.

30 *New York Times*, December 6, 1956, p. 59.

31 "Indian sitar recital given by Rani Shankar," *New York Times*, December 7, 1956, p. 32.

32 *RM*, p. 145; *New York Times*, December 9, 1956, p. 66.

33 "Sitar jam session," *Life*, February 4, 1957, p. 113.

34 RS to Rao, January 16, 1957 [PRC].

35 R. K. Narayan, *My Dateless Diary: American Journey*, pp. 184–5.

36 Travis Elborough, *The Long-Player Goodbye*, p. 86.

37 George Avakian, letter, June 27, 1995 [author's collection].

38 *RM*, pp. 147–8.

39 Gil McKean, "A conversation with Conrad Rooks," sleeve notes to RS's *Chappaqua* soundtrack LP (CBS, 1968).

40 Avakian, letter, June 27, 1995.

41 Ron Bock, telephone interview, November 18, 2017.

42 Richard Bock, "Ravi Shankar," in *Ravi Shankar*, concert tour program, 1967 [SA].

43 Peter Lavezzoli, *The Dawn of Indian Music in the West: Bhairavi*, p. 433.

44 McKean, "A conversation with Conrad Rooks."

45 Penny Estabrook, interview, Delhi, March 26, 2014.

46 *RM*, p. 149.

47 Rosette Renshaw to Ken Wright, March 10, 1957 [BBC WAC: TVART2, Ravi Shankar].

48 RS to Rao, January 16, 1957 [PRC].

49 Avakian, letter, June 27, 1995; undated memos in AP.

50 RS to Avakian, August 6, 1957 [AP].

51 Avakian, letter, June 27, 1995.

52 *MMML*, p. 97.

53 RS's liner notes for *In Celebration* (1996). It is the first track.

54 Bock, interviewed by Ira Landgarten, Los Angeles, May 1979.

55 Avakian, letter, January 8, 1997 [author's collection].

56 RS to Avakian, August 3, 1957 [AP].

57 Stuhlmann (ed.), *Diary of Anaïs Nin*, vol. VI, p. 57.

58 McKean, "A conversation with Conrad Rooks."

59 *Billboard*, May 6, 1957, p. 41.

60 Mantle Hood, "The challenge of bi-musicality," in *Ethnomusicology*, vol. 4 no. 2 (May 1960), pp. 55–9.

61 Robert Garfias, interview, Irvine, California, April 21, 2016.

62 *RM*, p. 148.

63 RS, "An introduction to Indian music," track 1 on *The Sounds of India*.

64 "Sitar jam session," *Life*, February 4, 1957, p. 113.

65 George Avakian to Richard Bock, April 19, 1958 [AP].

66 Quincy Jones, email interview, October 12, 2016.

67 *RM*, p. 53.

68 Garfias, email, April 22, 2016.

69 *RM*, p. 149.

70 Terence Dobson, *The Film Work of Norman McLaren*, p. 148.

71 Norman McLaren, "Music" (1974), in Donald McWilliams, *Norman McLaren: The Creative Process*, p. 33.

72 McLaren, "A Chairy Tale" (1957), a 1957 text (rewritten 1984) in McWilliams, *Norman McLaren*, pp. 63–4; recording schedule from memo by Grant McLean, "To whom it may concern," March 7, 1957 [NFB Canada archives].

73 James Ivory, interview, London, March 18, 2016.

74 Bock, Landgarten interview.

75 Marilyn Silverstone to RS, June 30, 1957 [SA].

76 Silverstone to RS, May 3, 1957 [SA].

77 Silverstone to RS, June 30 and June 24–5, 1957 [SA].

78 RS, interview, Delhi, January 8, 2004.

79 "Sitar recitals," *The Times*, June 10, 1957.

80 RS, "Experiences in musical life," 1957 [SA].

81 Ibid.

82 RS to Avakian, August 6, 1957 [AP].

83 "Sitar player," *Time*, March 25, 1957, pp. 56–8.

84 *MMML*, p. 98.

10 A Hero's Welcome

1 RS to George Avakian, October 8, 1957 [AP].

2 Marilyn Silverstone to RS, August 7, 1957 [SA].

3 "Indian theme holds glamour in West," *Times of India*, June 20, 1957, p. 6.

4 "Raga associated with monsoon," *Times of India*, August 24, 1957, p. 5.

5 "The social whirl," *Times of India*, August 25, 1957, p. 3.

6 "A classical concert," September 13, 1957; and "Sitar exponent," September 6, 1957, unidentified cuttings [SA].

7 *American Reporter*, September 11, 1957.

8 Ibid.

9 RS, "Experiences in musical life," 1957 [SA].

10 *American Reporter*, September 11, 1957.

11 RS to Avakian, October 8, 1957 [AP].

12 Silverstone to RS, September 26, 1957 [SA].

13 RS to Avakian, October 11, 1957 [AP].

14 Aashish Khan, interview, Los Angeles, April 13, 2016.

15 "Ravi Shankar to give music recitals," *Cine Advance*, week ending June 6, 1963.

16 Nemai Ghosh, emails, February 16–24, 2016.

17 RS to Avakian, October 11, 1957 [AP].

18 *RM*, p. 139.

19 Ed Murrow, from *The Lady from Philadelphia*, in the *See It Now* series (CBS, broadcast December 30, 1957).

20 RS, "Experiments in film music," *Filmfare*, March 14, 1958.

21 RS to Avakian, October 8, 1957 [AP].

22 Ibid.

23 RS to Avakian, April 1958, from Akasaka Prince Hotel, Tokyo [AP].

24 RS to Harihar Rao, January 6, 1958 [PRC].

25 Ibid.

26 Jawaharlal Nehru to RS, March 6, 1958, in *Selected Works of Jawaharlal Nehru*, series 2, vol. 41 (January 1–March 31, 1958), p. 252.

27 *RM*, pp. 153–4.

28 RS to Avakian, April 1958, from Tokyo [AP].

29 RS to Rao, January 6, 1958 [PRC].

30 "Japs applaud Bharatanatyam," April 5, 1958, cutting [SA]; RS to Avakian, April 1958, from Tokyo [AP].

31 *MMML*, pp. 98–9; *RM*, pp. 154–5.

32 RS to Avakian, October 8, 1957 [AP].

33 Sue C. Clark, "Ravi Shankar: The *Rolling Stone* interview," *Rolling Stone*, March 9, 1968.

34 RS to Avakian, April 1958, from Tokyo [AP].

35 Avakian to Richard Bock, April 24, 1958 [AP].

36 RS telegram to Avakian, July 16, 1958 [AP].

37 Bock to RS, August 15, 1958 [SA].

38 Agreement between The Gramophone Company Limited and Pandit Ravi Shankar, December 26, 1958 [SA].

39 Silverstone to RS, September 26, 1957 and April 13, 1958 [SA].

40 Annapurna Shankar to RS, June 4, September 18 and 24, 1958 [SA].

41 Ibid., June 4, 1958.

42 Ibid., August 9, 1958.

43 Allauddin Khan to RS, August 22, 1958 [SA].

44 Annapurna Shankar to RS, September 24, 1958 [SA].

45 "Sitar–sarod duet: Delightful team-work," *Times of India*, September 29, 1958, p. 3.

46 "Heart-warming Raksha Bandhan ceremony," 1958 cutting [SA].

11 A Compromise to Suit Other Purposes

1 RS's diary, October 4, 1958 [SA].

2 Ibid.

3 Ibid., October 1, 1958.

4 Ibid., October 2, 1958.

5 Tapan Sinha, "Ravishankar: Total musical personality," in Dibyendu Ghosh (ed.), *The Great Shankars: Uday, Ravi*, p. 92.

6 RS's diary, October 4, 1958.

7 John Coast, unpublished memoir (courtesy of Laura Rosenberg).

8 RS's diary, October 4, 1958.

9 Ibid., October 6, 1958.

10 Ibid., October 11–14, 1958.

11 Ibid., October 12, 1958.

12 Lord Harewood, *The Tongs and the Bones*, p. 252.

13 RS to Harihar Rao, October 17, 1958 [PRC].

14 RS to Rao, January 16, 1957 [PRC].

15 Hariprasad Chaurasia, interview, Rotterdam, March 29, 2017.

16 Annapurna Shankar to RS, February 8, 1959 [SA].

17 Shubho Shankar to RS, February 24, 1959 [SA].

18 Annapurna Shankar to RS, October 29 1958 [SA].

19 *RM*, 157.

20 RS interviewed by Art Makosinski, Encinitas, August 23, 2005.

21 RS to Kamala Chakravarty, September 26, 1960 and July 4, 1961 [SA].

22 Chakravarty to RS, November 14, 1966 [SA]. See also Chakravarty to RS, October 20, 1959 [SA].

23 RS to Chakravarty, November 10, 1960 [SA].

24 RS to Chakravarty, January 18, 1961 [SA].

25 RS to Chakravarty, August 20, 1961 [SA].

26 RS, interview, Delhi, January 8, 2004.

27 RS to Chakravarty, August 23, 1960 [SA].

28 Jimmy Fox of Magnum Photos, email, October 13, 2005.

29 *Times of India*, October 7, 1960, April 23, 1960, March 10, 1959, August 9, 1958 and October 30, 1960.

30 RS interview, January 8, 2004.

31 Nemai Ghosh, emails, February 16–24, 2016.

32 RS interview, January 8, 2004.

33 "Ravi Shankar opts for Indo–Japanese decoration," June 1960, cutting [SA].

34 Lajwanti Gupta, interview, Mumbai, February 10, 2017.

35 Shivkumar Sharma, interview, Kolkata, January 24, 2017.

36 "Ravi Shankar for Prague to attend Spring Fete," *Screen*, May 20, 1960 [SA]; "Ravi Shankar is back from Czechoslovakia," *Screen*, June 24, 1960 [SA]; "Ravi Shankar hailed at Prague Festival," undated cutting [SA]; *Kultura* (Prague), June 2, 1960 [SA].

37 Birju Maharaj, interview, Delhi, March 28, 2014; Kumudini Lakhia, telephone interview, October 10, 2018.

38 *Ceylon Daily News*, August 3, 1960, p. 1.

39 RS to Chakravarty, August 7, 1960 [SA].

40 Penny Estabrook, interview, Delhi, March 26, 2014.

41 RS to Chakravarty, November 10, 1960 [SA].

42 RS to Chakravarty, January 18, 1961 [SA]; *RM*, pp. 160–61.

43 RS, interview, London, July 29, 2005.

44 Allen Hughes, "Dance: Hindu company at City Center," *New York Times*, September 27, 1962, p. 32.

45 "Tollygunge: An hour with the master," *Cine Advance*, May 5, 1961; RS, interview, December 1994.

46 *Screen*, April 14, 1961.

47 RS to Chakravarty, January 18, and February 17, 1961 [SA].

48 RS to Chakravarty, August 16, 1961 [SA].

49 *Link*, September 14, 1958, cutting [SA].

50 *RM*, p. 21.

51 RS to Chakravarty, September 26, 1960 [SA].

52 Martin Clayton, "Allauddin Khan," in *New Grove Dictionary of Music and Musicians*, 2nd edn, vol. 13, p. 563.

53 RS to Chakravarty, November 23, 1960 [SA].

54 Ibid., July 9, 1961.

55 Ibid.

56 Ibid., August 16, 1961.

57 Ibid., August 20, 1961.

12 Coast to Coast

1 RS, "My dream," September 1, 1961 (Kinnara 1962 scrapbook [SA]).

2 *RM*, p. 159.

3 RS, liner notes to *In Celebration* CD box set (1996), p. 37.

4 RS to Basil Douglas, August 10, 1961 [BBC WAC: RCONT12, Ravi Shankar file 2, 1963–7].

5 RS to Kamala Chakravarty, October 20, 1961 [SA].

6 "India's man-of-music comes to the United States," Asia Society press release, June 1961 (1961–2 scrapbook [SA]).

7 John Martin, "Dance: Threesome," *New York Times*, October 1, 1961, p. X17.

8 Beate Sirota Gordon, *The Only Woman in the Room: A Memoir of Japan, Human Rights, and the Arts*, pp. 154–5.

9 Martin, "Dance: Threesome."

10 RS to Isadora Bennett, October 3, 1962 [IBC].

11 Sukanya Rahman, *Dancing in the Family: An Unconventional Memoir of Three Women*, pp. 124, 129.

12 Isadora Bennett to "Carol," May 14, 1963 [IBC].

13 Figures from "Performing Arts Program: Report on the first experimental year" in folder 5346, box 509, Subseries 5, Series 6, FAI10, Asia Society Archives [RAC].

14 Cindy Hughes, "Ravi back again with raga-time," *New York World-Telegram and Sun*, October 2, 1961.

15 Carolyn Hester, Radio France, April 6, 2010.

16 Bennett to Rekha Menon, June 8, 1965 [IBC].

17 "The tiger raga," *Village Voice*, October 5, 1961.

18 Robert J. Landry, "Ravi Shankar Trio from India presents a 'bash,'" *Variety*, October 11, 1961, p. 2.

19 RS to Chakravarty, November 7, 1961 [SA].

20 *Harvard Crimson*, December 12, 1961, cutting, 1961–2 scrapbook [SA].

21 Louis Hayes, telephone interview, October 13, 2016.

22 Press release, January 24, 1962 [SA].

23 "Brief reviews of new disks," *New York Times*, April 1, 1962, p. 124.

24 Walter Arlen, "Ravi Shankar gives dazzling performance," *Los Angeles Times*, November 21, 1961, p. 10.

25 RS to Chakravarty, November 24, 1961 [SA].

26 B. K. Nehru, *Nice Guys Finish Second*, pp. 384–5.

27 Gil McKean, "A conversation with Conrad Rooks," sleeve notes to RS's *Chappaqua* soundtrack LP (CBS, 1968).

28 Lewis Porter, *John Coltrane: His Life and Music*, p. 209; Peter Lavezzoli, *The Dawn of Indian Music in the West: Bhairavi*, p. 277.

29 John Tynan in *Down Beat*, November 23, 1961, p. 40, quoted in Cuthbert Ormond Simpkins, *Coltrane: A Biography*, p. 138.

30 Porter, *Coltrane*, p. 209.

31 RS, "Reminiscences about John Coltrane," 2001 (www.ravishankar.org/reflections/reminiscences-about-john-coltrane-2001).

32 J. C. Thomas, *Chasin' the Trane: The Music and Mystique of John Coltrane*, p. 142.

33 *RM*, p. 178.

34 Simpkins, *Coltrane*, p. 114. The venue of the Jazz Gallery is given by both Simpkins and Peter Watrous, "John Coltrane: A life supreme," in Carl Woideck, *The John Coltrane Companion*, p. 63. Neither of them gets the date right, but there was no other occasion when Ravi could have heard Coltrane live—as I conclude from comparing my own chronology of Ravi's life with Coltrane's timeline in Chris Devito, Yasuhiro Fujioka, Wolf Schmaler and David Wild, *The John Coltrane Reference*.

35 Thomas, *Chasin' the Trane*, pp. 142, 141.

36 Don Demicheal, "John Coltrane and Eric Dolphy answer the jazz critics," *Down Beat*, April 12, 1962, pp. 20–23.

37 Jean Clouzet and Michel Delorme, "Entretien avec John Coltrane," *Les Cahiers du Jazz*, vol. 8 (1963), pp. 1–14; quoted in Porter, *Coltrane*, p. 211.

38 Terry Riley, interviewed in Lavezzoli, *Dawn*, p. 258.

39 Ross, *The Rest Is Noise*, pp. 532–3.

40 Steve Reich in Edward Strickland, *American Composers: Dialogues on Contemporary Music*, p. 46.

41 Philip Glass, *Words Without Music*, p. 260; Ross, *The Rest Is Noise*, p. 542; "Steve Reich," *The South Bank Show* (LWT, directed by Matthew Tucker; broadcast December 10, 2006, ITV1).

42 Riley, in Lavezzoli, *Dawn*, p. 256.

43 La Monte Young, in *The World According to John Coltrane* (1990, directed by Robert Palmer and Toby Byron).

44 On drones, see Ian MacDonald, *Revolution in the Head: The Beatles' Records and the Sixties*, p. 191.

45 Riley, in K. Robert Schwarz, *Minimalists*, p. 39.

46 Basil Douglas to RS, January 24 and February 16, 1962; RS to Douglas, February 7 and 25, 1962 [all SA]. The quote is from February 25.

47 Richard Bock to RS, February 7, 1962; Mantle Hood to RS, July 12, 1962 [both SA].

48 "Ravi Shankar impresses U.S. audiences," January or February 1962, unidentified cutting [SA].

49 "Ravi Shankar's tour of the U.S.," *Sunday Standard*, February 4, 1962.

50 RS, interviewed by Reginald Massey, *Mayur*, November 1973, p. 25.

51 See 1961–2 scrapbook [SA].

52 Uma Vasudev, "Ravi Shankar: A modern and yet a traditionalist," *Times of India*, November 19, 1961.

53 RS, "My dream," September 1, 1961, in Kinnara 1962 scrapbook [SA].

54 Bennett to RS, February 15, 1962, and his undated reply [both SA].

55 RS to Chakravarty, April 9, 1962 [SA].

56 Annapurna Shankar to RS, May 1, 1962 [SA].

57 Douglas to RS, January 24, 1962; RS to Douglas, February 7, 1962 [both SA].

58 RS to Chakravarty, undated letter, probably summer 1962 [SA].

59 Ibid., June 13, 1962.

60 *Screen*, July 20 and August 3, 1962.

61 Penny Estabrook, interview, Delhi, March 26, 2014.

62 *Screen*, August 3, 1962.

63 "Pandit Ravi Shanker [*sic*] on good listening," cutting in 1962–4 scrapbook [SA].

64 "Two sitar maestri," *Screen*, June 28, 1963.

65 *Screen*, September 7, 1962.

66 *RM*, p. 170.

67 Shanta Gokhale (ed.), *The Scenes We Made: An Oral History of Experimental Theatre in Mumbai*, pp. 33, 37, 40.

68 Meera Menezes, *Vasudeo Santu Gaitonde: Sonata of Solitude*, from an extract in *The Hindu*, May 7, 2016.

69 RS to Bennett, October 3, 1962 [IBC].

70 *Ustad Allauddin Khan* (1963, directed by Ritwik Ghatak for Sangeet Natak Akademi).

71 RS, "A great musician," cutting, 1962 [SA].

72 "Experiment in music to help war effort," c. November 19, 1962, unidentified cutting in 1957–64 scrapbook [SA].

73 *RM*, p. 171; *Melody and Rhythm* programme, 1962 [SA].

74 "Experiment in music to help war effort"; "Search for new forms of music," *Times of India*, November 19, 1962.

75 "Mr. Menuhin on Indian music today," *The Times*, May 24, 1962.

76 *Melody and Rhythm* program, 1962 [SA].

77 R. M. Kumtakar, "Pandit Ravi Shankar's creative adventure in music," *Screen*, November 16, 1962.

78 *RM*, p. 171.

79 Vyjayantimala Bali with Jyoti Sabharwal, *Bonding: A Memoir*, p. 194.

80 "Lasting impressions of beauty in Chandalika," *Times of India*, December 24, 1962.

81 RS to Chakravarty, undated (probably summer 1962) and January 5, 1963 [SA].

82 Lajwanti Gupta, interview, Mumbai, February 10, 2017.

83 RS to Bennett, February 5, 1963 [IBC].

84 Estabrook, interview, Delhi, March 26, 2014.

85 RS to Chakravarty, June 18 and 30, 1963 [SA].

86 Estabrook, email, April 13, 2014.

13 Propagandist-in-Chief

1 Rory McEwen, "On detecting the sound of the sitar," *Listener*, June 24, 1971, pp. 827–8.

2 Douglas M. Knight Jr, *Balasaraswati: Her Art and Life*, p. 198.

3 Philip Rawson, *An Exhibition of Music and Dance in Indian Art*, exhibition catalogue.

4 "Hindustani fare," *The Times*, August 31, 1963; *Daily Telegraph* cited in "UK critics' high praise for Ravi Shankar and Alla Rakha," c. September 1963, unidentified cutting in 1952–68 binder [SA].

5 "When Indian masters improvise," *The Times*, September 3, 1963.

6 RS to Kamala Chakravarty, September 2, 1963 [SA].

7 McEwen, "On detecting the sound of the sitar."

8 William Mann, "Indian music," *Musical Times*, October 1963.

9 Ibid.

10 Narayana Menon, "The Edinburgh Festival in retrospect," *Times of India*, November 17, 1963.

11 Lord Harewood, *The Tongs and the Bones*, p. 189.

12 Carolyn Hester on Radio France, April 6, 2010.

13 Narayana Menon, "Western interest in Indian music," *Bharat Jyoti*, August 22, 1971, p. iv.

14 "Ekstase und Meditation," *Die Welt*, October 1, 1963.

15 Colin Mason, "Indian music," *Guardian*, October 14, 1963.

16 RS to Chakravarty, October 24, 1963 [SA].

17 "J'ai entendu improviser Chopin": Jacques Longchampt, "Splendeur de la musique indienne," *Le Monde*, February 13, 1964.

18 "Artist in search of an audience," *Hindustan Times*, December 13, 1963.

19 André Previn, quoted in *Down Beat*, November 7, 1963, p. 17.

20 "Questions for Christmas," *The Times*, December 24, 1963.

21 Yehudi Menuhin to RS, September 27, 1963 [SA].

22 Menuhin to Benjamin Britten, December 16, 1963 [BPL, ref. BBA/MENUHIN_Y].

23 Britten to Menuhin, December 22, 1963, in Philip Read and Mervyn Cooke, *Letters from a Life*, vol. 5: *1958–65*, p. 542.

24 Sorab K. Modi, "Ravi Shankar on Ellington," *Times of India*, September 22, 1963.

25 RS to Menuhin, February 22, 1964 [FMA]. The score is in FMA.

26 Robert Garfias, interview, Irvine, California, April 21, 2016.

27 RS to Chakravarty, February 13, 1964 [SA].

28 Nicolas Nabokov to Joseph Alsop, February 18, 1964, in Vincent Giroud, *Nicolas Nabokov: A Life in Freedom and Music*, p. 352.

29 RS, "Hindustani classical music and the demands of today," in Roger Ashton (ed.), *Music East and West*, pp. 158–65.

30 "Indian music and orchestration," *Cultural News from Asia*, no. 25 (Congress for Cultural Freedom, May 1964), p. 20.

31 See RS to Chakravarty, December 13, 1963 [SA]; RS to Miss Kitchlu, December 20, 1963 [IBC].

32 *RM*, p. 176.

33 RS to Isadora Bennett, May 25, 1964 [IBC].

34 "Musical show," *Screen*, July 10, 1964.

35 *RM*, p. 174.

36 Ibid.

37 RS to Chakravarty, October 15, 1964 [SA].

38 Elaine Moss, *The JDR 3rd Fund and Asia*, pp. 34, 113.

39 RS to Chakravarty, October 15, 1964.

40 Alan Rich, "Enchanting, exciting: India classical music," *New York Herald Tribune*, October 12, 1964.

41 Robert Shelton, "Propagandist-in-chief," *New York Times*, November 8, 1964, pp. X26–7.

42 K. Neel Kant, "Ravi Shankar enthrals Australian audience," *Screen*, c. March 1965, cutting [SA].

43 *Time*, November 6, 1964, p. 84.

44 Penny Estabrook, interview, Delhi, March 26, 2014.

45 Ibid.

46 RS to Chakravarty, December 23, 1964 [SA].

47 RS to Chakravarty, January 9, 1965 [SA].

48 Kant, "Ravi Shankar enthrals Australian audience."

49 *Time*, November 6, 1964, p. 84.

50 Liner notes for Don Ellis Orchestra, *Live at Monterey!* (1967).

51 Lynn Gertenbach, interview, Calabasas, California, April 21, 2016.

52 Zubin Mehta, interview, Florence, September 4, 2016.

53 Robby Krieger, telephone interview, April 19, 2016.

54 David Crosby and Carl Gottlieb, *Long Time Gone: The Autobiography of David Crosby*, p. 98.

55 Ron Bock, telephone interview, November 18, 2017.

56 *RM*, p. 182.

57 Ian MacDonald, *Revolution in the Head: The Beatles' Records and the Sixties*, pp. 31, 37.

58 RS to Bennett, February 26, 1965 [IBC].

14 The Sitar Explosion

1 Philip Glass in Joshua M. Greene, *Here Comes the Sun: The Spiritual and Musical Journey of George Harrison*, p. 241.

2 Shani, "Let music prevail," unidentified cutting, 1965 scrapbook [SA].

3 RS to Kamala Chakravarty, October 23, 1965 [SA].

4 David Harper, "A most unusual musical evening," *Daily Mail* (Scotland), *c.* September 30, 1965.

5 "Indian players' subtle art," *The Times*, September 25, 1965.

6 Robert Shelton, "Ravi Shankar plays music of India here," *New York Times*, October 11, 1965, p. 48.

7 RS to Hallie Scott, September 6, 1965 [Hallie Goodman collection].

8 RS, telegram to Isadora Bennett, October 18, 1965 [IBC].

9 J. C. Thomas (*Chasin' the Trane: The Music and Mystique of John Coltrane*, p. 142) seems to be the origin of this story.

10 "Breathtaking performance by Indian virtuosi," *The Times*, November 8, 1965, p. 14.

11 Basil Douglas to Humphrey Burton, November 8, 1965, BBC WAC: T13/288/1, "Ravi Shankar," broadcast December 30, 1966.

12 RS to Chakravarty, November 14, 1965 [SA].

13 Press kit for the DVD release of *Siddhartha* (dir. Conrad Rooks, 1972).

14 *RM*, p. 179.

15 Gil McKean, "A conversation with Conrad Rooks," sleeve notes to RS's *Chappaqua* soundtrack LP (CBS, 1968).

16 Philip Glass, *Words Without Music*, p. 106.

17 Ibid., pp. 130–31.

18 Philip Glass, *Opera on the Beach*, pp. 17–18.

19 Glass, *Words Without Music*, p. 132.

20 *RM*, p. 179.

21 Tricycle, "First lesson, best lesson" (1992), in Richard Kostelanetz (ed.), *Writings on Glass*, p. 318.

22 Philip Glass, interview, New York, December 12, 2016.

23 Sue Clark, "Ravi Shankar: The *Rolling Stone* interview," *Rolling Stone*, March 9, 1968.

24 George Harrison to Anthony DeCurtis of *Rolling Stone*, June 1987, reproduced in Olivia Harrison, *George Harrison: Living in the Material World*, p. 190.

25 Timothy White, "A portrait of the artist," *Billboard* (December 5, 1992), p. 23.

26 David Crosby and Carl Gottlieb, *Long Time Gone: The Autobiography of David Crosby*, p. 101.

27 The Beatles, *The Beatles Anthology*, p. 196.

28 Mark Lewisohn, *All These Years, Volume One: Tune In (Extended Special Edition)*, p. 84.

29 The Beatles, *The Beatles Anthology*, p. 196.

30 Gerry Farrell, *Indian Music and the West*, p. 172.

31 The Beatles, *The Beatles Anthology*, p. 197.

32 Patricia Angadi, unpublished memoir (courtesy of Shankara Angadi and Chandrika Casali).

33 *RM*, p. 189.

34 Patricia Angadi, unpublished memoir.

35 George Harrison, interview, Friar Park, February 13, 1995.

36 Charles Reid, "Ravi Shankar and George Beatles," *New York Times Magazine*, May 7, 1967.

37 Paul McCartney interviewed by WKLO-Louisville radio DJ Ken Douglas, Chicago, August 12, 1966.

38 Brad Tolinski, *Light and Shade: Conversations with Jimmy Page*, pp. 34–5.

39 Kory Grow, "Jeff Beck talks Eric Clapton rivalry and what Motown taught him," *Rolling Stone*, May 16, 2018.

40 Chris Salewicz, *Jimmy Page: The Definitive Biography*, p. 20.

41 *MMML*, p. 92.

42 RS to Chakravarty, April 5, 1966 [SA].

43 RS to Yehudi Menuhin, May 16, 1966 [FMA]; RS to Chakravarty, April 19, 1966 [SA].

44 Steve Turner, *Beatles 66*, p. 83.

45 Maureen Cleave, "George Harrison: Avocado with everything," *Evening Standard*, March 18, 1966.

46 Maureen Cleave, "How does a Beatle live? John Lennon lives like this," *Evening Standard*, March 4, 1966.

47 Barry Miles, *Paul McCartney: Many Years From Now*, pp. 290–91.

48 Ian MacDonald, *Revolution in the Head: The Beatles' Records and the Sixties*, p. 191.

49 Anil Bhagwat in Turner, *Beatles 66*, p. 149.

50 Sally Kempton, "Raga rock: It's not moonlight on the Ganges," *Village Voice*, March 31, 1966, annotated copy [SA].

51 Barney Hoskyns, *Hotel California: Singer-Songwriters and Cocaine Cowboys in the LA Canyons, 1967–1976*, p. 18.

52 Ray Manzarek, *Light My Fire: My Life with the Doors*, p. 136.

53 Robby Krieger, telephone interview, April 19, 2016.

54 Peter Lavezzoli, *The Dawn of Indian Music in the West: Bhairavi*, p. 158.

55 *Melody Maker*, June 28, 1966, quoted in Farrell, *Indian Music and the West*, p. 173.

56 *Melody Maker*, May 14, 1966, quoted in Farrell, ibid.

57 Joseph Lelyveld, "Ravi Shanker [*sic*] of India lends inscrutable West a new sound," *New York Times*, June 20, 1966.

15 Wonderland

1 *Disc and Music Echo*, May 27, 1967.

2 RS, "Tour of Pandit Ravi Shankar to Europe, May–June–July 1966," uncorrected draft of programme notes, New Empire Calcutta, August 14–15, 1966 [SA].

3 *Disc and Music Echo*, June 11, 1966.

4 William Alden, *Evening Standard*, June 1, 1966; quoted in RS, "Tour of Pandit Ravi Shankar to Europe" [SA].

5 "Ravi Shankar," *India Weekly*, June 9, 1966; Joseph Lelyveld, "Ravi Shanker [*sic*] of India lends inscrutable West a new sound," *New York Times*, June 20, 1966.

6 *Disc and Music Echo*, June 11, 1966.

7 RS to Kamala Chakravarty, June 12, 1966 [SA]; Charles Fox, 'Review: Ravi Shankar recital at the Royal Festival Hall,' *Manchester Guardian*, June 2, 1966.

8 Jonathan Miller, interview, London, June 23, 2016; director's commentary on *Alice in Wonderland* DVD (BBC, 2003).

9 Kate Bassett, *In Two Minds: A Biography of Jonathan Miller*, p. 155.

10 RS to Yehudi Menuhin, May 16, 1966 [FMA].

11 Menuhin to RS, May 23, 1966 [FMA].

12 Peter Feuchtwanger to Menuhin, June 10, 1966 [FMA].

13 Ibid.

14 *RM*, p. 183.

15 John Barham, interview, London, October 4, 2016.

16 *New Musical Express*, June 3, 1966; *Melody Maker*, June 11, 1966.

17 *RM*, p. 189.

18 RS interviewed on *A Whole Scene Going*, BBC1, broadcast June 8, 1966.

19 RS, "Of my recent Europe tour," program notes, New Empire Calcutta, August 14–15, 1966 [SA].

20 Philip Glass, *Words Without Music*, p. 134.

21 *Glass: A Portrait of Philip in 12 Parts* (2007, directed by Scott Hicks).

22 Diana Menuhin, *Fiddler's Moll: Life with Yehudi*, p. 216.

23 RS, "Of my recent Europe tour"; Sue Clark, "Ravi Shankar: The *Rolling Stone* Interview," *Rolling Stone*, March 9, 1968; *MMML*, p. 95.

24 "Menuhin with Ravi Shankar in concert of Indian music," *The Times*, June 27, 1966; *RM*, p. 183.

25 RS, "Of my recent Europe tour."

26 RS to Chakravarty, June 26, 1966 [SA].

27 K. C. Khanna, "Beatniks hail master of the sitar," *Times of India*, July 10, 1966, p. 8.

28 James Fox, "Rory McEwen: His life and music," in Martyn Rix (ed.), *Rory McEwen: The Colours of Reality*, p. 27.

29 RS to Chakravarty, June 29, 1966 [SA].

30 Chakravarty to RS, July 1, 1966 [SA].

31 RS, "My world," *Songlines*, October 2011, pp. 10–11.

32 The original is in FMA.

33 Barham interview.

34 *MMML*, p. 100.

35 Shankara Angadi, interview, London, May 22, 2015.

36 James Johnson, "A sitar is born," *New Musical Express*, September 21, 1974.

37 George Harrison, interviewed by Don Ellis, KCET-TV, March 1976 (archive.org/details/calauem_000057).

38 *RM*, p. 189.

39 Ibid., p. 190.

40 George Harrison, *I Me Mine*, p. 55.

41 Harrison, Ellis interview.

42 Ibid.

43 RS, "Of my recent Europe tour."

44 Charles Reid, "Ravi Shankar and George Beatles," *New York Times Magazine*, May 7, 1967; see also *MMML*, p. 101.

45 RS to Chakravarty, September 9, 1966 [SA].

46 Pollux, "In person," *Times of India*, September 25, 1966, p. 3.

47 "Beatle fans storm hotel as George meets press," *Times of India*, September 20, 1966, p. 3.

48 Kamala Chakravarty, interview, Chennai, March 21, 2014.

49 Ajoy Bose, *Across the Universe: The Beatles in India*, p. 80.

50 Harrison, TV interview on *This Morning* (CBS, June 12, 1997).

51 Swami Vivekananda, *Raja Yoga*, p. vii.

52 Bose, *Across the Universe*, pp. 81–2.

53 *RM*, p. 193.

54 "Guru: How Ravi Shankar brought Indian music to the West," BBC Radio 3, broadcast August 3, 2005.

55 *Daily Sketch*, quoted in *Radio Times*, March 30, 1967, p. 13.

56 Director's commentary on *Alice in Wonderland* DVD (BBC, 2003).

57 Fee from BBC contract, July 6, 1966 [BBC WAC: TVART 4, Ravi Shankar misc. 1963–70].

58 Miller interview.

59 RS to Chakravarty, November 5, 1966 [SA].

60 Miller interview.

61 RS to Chakravarty, November 5, 1966.

62 Barham interview.

63 RS to Chakravarty, November 9, 1966 [SA].

64 RS to Chakravarty, November 22, December 13 and 15, 1966 [all SA].

65 Chakravarty to RS, November 14, 1966 [SA].

66 *RM*, p. 196.

67 "India's rhythm captures World Pacific," *Billboard*, December 17, 1966, p. 4.

68 RS to Chakravarty, December 24, 1966 [SA]; *Newsweek*, January 2, 1967.

69 RS, liner notes to this recording on *In Celebration* (1996).

70 Raymond Ericson, "Go East, young man," *New York Times*, September 1, 1968.

71 Charles Passy, "How Ravi Shankar found his fame: A promoter's memories," *Wall Street Journal*, December 14, 2012.

72 Richard Goldstein, "Ravi and the teenie satori," *Village Voice*, January 5, 1967, reproduced in Goldstein, *Goldstein's Greatest Hits*, p. 83.

73 RS, quoted in J. C. Thomas, *Chasin' the Trane: The Music and Mystique of John Coltrane*, p. 154.

74 RS, "Reminiscences about John Coltrane," 2001 (www.ravishankar.org / reflections/reminiscences-about-john-coltrane-2001).

75 Ibid.

76 *RMMVM*, p. 166; RS, interview, Delhi, January 8, 2004; Ashley Kahn, *A Love Supreme: The Creation of John Coltrane's Classic Album*, p. xxiii.

77 Harrison to Chakravarty, January 8, 1967 [SA].

16 It Happened in Monterey

1 Gita Mehta, *Karma Cola: Marketing the Mystic East*, p. 6.

2 Charles Reid, "Ravi Shankar and George Beatles," *New York Times Magazine*, May 7, 1967, p. 29.

3 *RM*, p. 196.

4 For Harballabh, see *Newsweek*, January 2, 1967.

5 K. C. Vajifdar, "Ravi Shankar: The sweet smell of success," *Times of India*, December 17, 1967.

6 Annapurna Shankar to RS, October 5, 1969 [SA].

7 "Ravi Shankar aims to spread appeal of Indian music abroad," *Screen*, February 24, 1967.

8 M. F. Husain with Khalid Mohamed, *Where Art Thou*, pp. 206–8.

9 Mark Paytress, *Bolan: The Rise and Fall of a 20th Century Superstar*, p. 89.

10 RS, transcript of an unpublished 1990 interview apparently prepared as an introduction for a planned new edition of *MMML* [SA].

11 *RM*, p. 196.

12 Gerry Farrell, *Indian Music and the West*, pp. 177–8.

13 *India's Master Musician, Portrait of Genius* and *Sound of the Sitar*—given to him by Brian Jones along with *The Sounds of Subbulakshmi*. Displayed in Hendrix Flat museum, 23 Brook Street, London.

14 *Sgt Pepper's Musical Revolution with Howard Goodall*, directed by Francis Hanly, BBC2, broadcast June 3, 2017.

15 George Harrison applies a similar effect on guitar in 'Lucy in the Sky with Diamonds'; see Peter Lavezzoli, *The Dawn of Indian Music in the West: Bhairavi*, pp. 178–80.

16 Ian MacDonald, *Revolution in the Head: The Beatles' Records and the Sixties*, p. 244.

17 *Disc and Music Echo*, May 27, 1967.

18 *RM*, p. 203.

19 *MMML*, p. 98.

20 Bock's press release, *c.* April 1967 [SA]; K. C. Vajifdar, "Ravi Shankar: The sweet smell of success," *Times of India*, December 17, 1967.

21 Hank Fox, "Indian music school to open on W. Coast," *Billboard*, April 29, 1967, p. 14.

22 *MMML*, p. 103.

23 RS, "The Seriousness of It," on the original soundtrack to *Raga: A Film Journey into the Soul of India*.

24 *RM*, p. 203.

25 Ibid., pp. 197, 203.

26 Satyajit Ray, "Ordeals of The Alien," *Statesman* (Calcutta), October 4 and 5, 1980.

27 Ray to Marie Seton, July 25, 1968, in Andrew Robinson, *Satyajit Ray: The Inner Eye*, p. 291.

28 *RM*, p. 204; Howard Worth discussing *Raga* at a screening, Ojai, 2010 (www.youtube.com/watch?v=-VVi6sC54kA).

29 Joan Didion, *Slouching Towards Bethlehem*, p. 106.

30 Jon Savage, *1966: The Year the Decade Exploded*, p. 125.

31 Mike Heron and Andrew Greig, *You Know What You Could Be: Tuning into the 1960s*, p. 24.

32 Sue Clark, "Ravi Shankar: The *Rolling Stone* interview," *Rolling Stone*, March 9, 1968.

33 Reid, "Ravi Shankar and George Beatles."

34 Lavezzoli, *Dawn*, p. 166.

35 Sean O'Hagan, "Kingsley Hall: RD Laing's experiment in anti-psychiatry," *Guardian*, September 2, 2012.

36 RS, transcript of interview with Mark Kidel, Delhi, March 2000 [SA].

37 RS, "The sound of God," *Oracle*, July 1967, p. 7.

38 Richard Bock, interviewed by Ira Landgarten, Los Angeles, May 1979.

39 For "first press release," Derek Taylor, *It Was Twenty Years Ago Today*, p. 79.

40 Ibid., p. 78.

41 Bock, Landgarten interview.

42 Michael Lydon, "Monterey Pop: The first rock festival" (1967), reprinted in Lydon, *Flashbacks: Eyewitness Accounts of the Rock Revolution 1964–1974*, p. 32.

43 Michelle Phillips, "Afterword," in Harvey and Kenneth Kubernik, *A Perfect Haze: The Illustrated History of the Monterey International Pop Festival*, p. 242.

44 D. A. Pennebaker's audio commentary for the *Monterey Pop* DVD (2002, Criterion Collection).

45 RS, "The sound of God," p. 5.

46 *RM*, p. 199.

47 Bock, Landgarten interview.

48 Nancy Bacal, interview, Los Angeles, April 20, 2016.

49 *Variety*, June 5, 1968, p. 5.

50 Reid, "Ravi Shankar and George Beatles," p. 29.

51 RS, interview, Delhi, January 6, 2006.

52 *Billboard*, August 5, 1967, p. 54; RS in conversation with Satish and Shashi Vyas, June 2007 (www.ravishankar.org/reflections).

53 Eric Hayes, "How I met George Harrison and Ravi Shankar," email, April 13, 2005.

54 Simon Leng, *The Music of George Harrison: While My Guitar Gently Weeps*, p. 17.

55 *Melody Maker*, autumn 1967, quoted in Derek Taylor, *It Was Twenty Years Ago Today*, pp. 134–5.

56 Alan Watts, *The Joyous Cosmology: Adventures in the Chemistry of Consciousness*, p. 26.

57 *Billboard*, September 16, 1967, p. C-30.

58 Ibid., October 18, 1967, pp. 3, 8.

59 Liner notes to RS, *The Genius of Ravi Shankar* LP (Columbia, 1967).

60 *Variety*, October 11, 1967, p. 93.

61 "Ravi Shankar and the raga rage," *Span* (Delhi), vol. 8, no. 2 (November 1967).

62 C. Y. Gopinath, "Ravi Shankar has started something," *Dateline Delhi*, December 28, 1969, p. 8.

63 Jon Borgzinner, "How a shy Pandit became a pop hero," *Life*, August 18, 1967, p. 36.

64 *RM*, p. 210.

65 *Newsweek*, January 2, 1967.

66 *Billboard*, September 30, 1967, p. 22.

67 Elenore Lester, "Shankar, unnerved by the hippies' adulation," *New York Times*, October 22, 1967.

68 Don Heckman, "Conversation with Ravi Shankar," interview, late December 1967, reprinted in "Ravi Shankar and his Festival from India" tour program, 1968.

69 Misha Dasgupta Masud, interview, New York, December 13, 2016.

70 Lester, "Shankar, unnerved by the hippies' adulation."

71 Philip Glass, tribute to RS for Encinitas memorial, December 19, 2012.

72 Glass, *Words Without Music*, p. 215.

73 *Glass: A Portrait of Philip in 12 Parts* (2007, directed by Scott Hicks).

74 Robby Krieger, telephone interview, April 19, 2016.

75 This section draws on my telephone interview with Coriolana Wolters Simon, September 21, 2016, and our emails between July and September 2016.

76 Liner notes to *In Celebration* (4-CD set, 1996).

77 Clark, "Ravi Shankar: The *Rolling Stone* interview."

78 The UK edition, subtitled *Volume 2*, does not feature the *Dhun*, and Menuhin plays a different Bartók piece.

79 Clark, "Ravi Shankar: The *Rolling Stone* interview."

80 *Billboard*, February 3, 1968, p. 24.

81 Ibid., December 30, 1967, p. 10.

17 Woodstock Degeneration

1   RS, voiceover narration in *Raga* (1971, directed by Howard Worth).
2   Razia Ismail, "Maestro denies 'pop' label," *Indian Express*, March 29, 1968, p. 3.
3   Nancy Bacal, interview, Los Angeles, April 20, 2016.
4   Misha Dasgupta Masud, interview, New York, December 13, 2016.
5   Don Heckman, "Conversation with Ravi Shankar" (interview, late December 1967), reprinted in "Ravi Shankar and his Festival from India" tour program, 1968.
6   "*Charly* goes to Berlin," *Daily Cinema*, May 1, 1968.
7   Ismail, "Maestro denies 'pop' label."
8   Ralph Nelson, liner notes to *Charly* soundtrack LP.
9   *Variety*, July 3, 1968, p. 6.
10 *Cine Advance*, March 28, 1968.
11 Bacal interview.
12 Sukanya Shankar, liner notes to *In Hollywood, 1971* CD.
13 Bacal interview.
14 Zakir Hussain in conversation with Nasreen Munni Kabir, *Zakir Hussain: A Life in Music* (Noida: HarperCollins, 2018), pp. 65–6.
15 Bacal interview.
16 Penny Estabrook, interview, Delhi, March 26, 2014.
17 Bacal interview.
18 *RMMVM*, p. 194
19 George Harrison, interviewed in *Sangeet Ratna* (2013, directed by Alan Kozlowski).
20 *RM*, p. 204.
21 James Ivory, interview, London, March 18, 2016.
22 *Billboard*, March 9, 1968, pp. 1 and 8.
23 Richard Bock, interviewed by Ira Landgarten, Los Angeles, May 1979.
24 *Variety*, January 22, 1969, p. 49.
25 *RM*, p. 204.
26 Undated survey of colleges in folder 5346, box 509, subseries 5, series 6, FAIIO, Asia Society Archives [RAC].
27 *Variety*, July 31, 1968, p. 2.
28 Alfred G. Aronowitz, "Ravi Shankar: 'I walk a tightrope,'" *Saturday Evening Post*, August 10, 1968, pp. 55–7.
29 "Utter joy uninhibited," *Time*, September 20, 1968, p. 86.
30 Shivkumar Sharma, interview, Kolkata, January 24, 2017.

31 Yousuf Karsh, *Faces of Our Time*, p. 174.

32 Philip Glass, tribute to RS for Encinitas memorial, December 19, 2012.

33 "Utter joy uninhibited," *Time*, September 20, 1968, p. 86.

34 Bock, Landgarten interview.

35 Shivkumar Sharma with Ina Puri, *Journey with a Hundred Strings: My Life in Music*, p. 100.

36 *Variety*, September 18, 1968, p. 56.

37 Geoffrey Moorhouse, "Ravi Shankar at the RFH," *Guardian*, November 19, 1968.

38 Janet Bock Bicker, telephone interview, August 3, 2018.

39 RS to Dr. Schickman, November 20, 1968, sent from Edinburgh via Kamala Chakravarty in Los Angeles.

40 *RM*, p. 232.

41 *India Abroad*, April 16, 2010, p. M7.

42 *Variety*, June 5, 1968, pp. 5, 19.

43 Charles Passy, "How Ravi Shankar found his fame: A promoter's memories," *Wall Street Journal*, December 14, 2012.

44 RS quoted in Francesco Scavullo, *Scavullo on Men*, p. 169.

45 RS, interview, Delhi, January 6, 2006.

46 *RM*, p. 210.

47 Bock, Landgarten interview.

48 RS to Yehudi Menuhin, May 22, 1969 [FMA].

49 Bacal interview.

50 Howard Worth discussing *Raga* at a screening, Ojai, 2010 (www.youtube.com / watch?v=-VVi6sC54kA).

51 RS, voiceover narration in *Raga*.

52 Worth discussing *Raga*.

53 Ibid.

54 Karen Monson, "Ravi Shankar plays in Santa Monica," *Los Angeles Times*, February 17, 1969, p. 21.

55 Michael Lang with Holly George-Warren, *The Road to Woodstock*, pp. 22, 25, 83.

56 Maya Kulkarni Chadda, interview, New York, December 12, 2016.

57 Richard Bock, liner notes to *Ravi Shankar at the Woodstock Festival* LP (World Pacific, 1970).

58 *RM*, p. 211.

59 Maya Kulkarni Chadda, interview, New York, December 12, 2016.

60 *Billboard*, September 20, 1969, p. 25.

61 Patricia, Dowager Countess of Harewood, email interview, January 10, 2017.

62 Chadda interview.

63 Ibid.

64 Saeed Jaffrey, *Saeed: An Actor's Journey*, p. 139.

65 Hallie Goodman, interview, New York, December 11, 2016; Bacal interview.

66 *Billboard*, September 20, 1969, p. 25.

67 RS to Kamala Chakravarty, October 8, 1968 [SA].

68 George Ruckert in Peter Lavezzoli, *The Dawn of Indian Music in the West: Bhairavi*, p. 396.

69 Ray Connolly, "Ravi Shankar now that the Indian summer is over," *Evening Standard*, January 23, 1971.

70 RS, interview, Encinitas, August 31, 2009.

71 Shivkumar Sharma, interview, Kolkata, January 24, 2017.

72 C. Y. Gopinath, "Ravi Shankar has started something," *Dateline Delhi*, December 28, 1969, p. 8.

73 Penny Estabrook, interview, Delhi, March 26, 2014.

74 *RM*, p. 213.

75 Satish Vyas, interview, Bombay, February 23, 2015.

76 *RM*, pp. 212–13.

77 RS to Menuhin, January 25, 1970 [FMA].

78 "Ravi Shankar explains his art," *The Times*, October 8, 1965.

79 Aronowitz, "Ravi Shankar: 'I walk a tightrope.'"

80 Gita Mehta, *Karma Cola: Marketing the Mystic East*, p. 5.

81 *MMML*, p. 103.

82 Ibid., p. 105.

83 *RM*, pp. 213–14.

84 RS to Chakravarty, January 15, 1970 [SA].

85 Hussain and Kabir, *Zakir Hussain: A Life in Music*, p. 67.

86 RS to Chakravarty, November 6, 1969 [SA]. The Bengali is "Hotat Khub Bhakti!"

87 Annapurna Shankar to RS, October 5, 1969 [SA].

88 RS to Chakravarty, November 6, 1969 [SA]. In the end he did not visit Maihar; the last time he met Baba was in 1968, when he was filming *Raga* (see *RM*, p. 221).

89 Annapurna Shankar to RS, October 5, 1969 [SA].

90 Shubho Shankar to RS, November 17, 1969 [SA].

91 RS, interview, Delhi, January 6, 2006.

92 *RM*, p. 260; Linda Shankar, interview, Los Angeles, April 16, 2016.

93 Aalif Surti, "Annapurna Devi and her music of silence," *Mumbai Mirror*, October 14, 2018.

94 *RM*, pp. 259–60.

95 Ibid., p. 260.

96 Surti, "Annapurna Devi and her music of silence."

97 Ibid.

98 Kumar Shankar, interview, Simi Valley, April 15, 2016.

99 RS to Chakravarty, January 15, 1970 [SA].

100 Tathagata Roy Chowdhury, 'Every note Annapurna Devi plays is like an offering: Rooshikumar Pandya,' *Times of India*, September 7, 2014.

101 RS to Chakravarty, May 15, 1970 [SA].

102 Linda Shankar, interview, Los Angeles, April 16, 2016.

18 Dream, Nightmare and Dawn

1 RS, "I Am Missing You," released on *Shankar Family & Friends* (1974).

2 "Ravi Shankar and the raga rage," *Span* (Delhi), vol. 8, no. 2 (November 1967).

3 André Previn, in *Down Beat*, November 7, 1963, p. 17.

4 RS to Yehudi Menuhin, May 22, 1969 [FMA].

5 Ibid.

6 RS, draft of "Program Note" (liner notes) on RS, *Concerto for Sitar & Orchestra* LP [SA].

7 John Barham, interview, London, October 4, 2016.

8 Previn to RS, December 6, 1970 [SA].

9 Felix Aprahamian in the *Sunday Times*, January 31, 1971; Colin Mason, "Lively orchestration in sitar concerto," *Daily Telegraph*, January 29, 1971.

10 Edward Greenfield, "Ravi Shankar and the LSO at the Royal Festival Hall," *Guardian*, January 29, 1971.

11 *Billboard*, November 4, 1972, p. 51.

12 "On the turntable," *Onlooker*, March 1972.

13 Stephen Slawek, "The urge to merge," in Victoria Lindsay Levine and Philip V. Bohlman (eds.), *This Thing Called Music*, p. 451.

14 Philip Clark, "André Previn," *Guardian*, March 1, 2019.

15 Naresh Sohal, interview, London, June 19, 2016.

16 David Murphy, interview, Harpenden, July 20, 2016.

17 Menuhin to RS, September 11, 1997 [FMA].

18 RS on *Desert Island Discs*, BBC Radio 4, broadcast February 27, 1971 [BBC WAC: Scripts, Ravi Shankar].

19 Ray Connolly, "Ravi Shankar now that the Indian summer is over," *Evening Standard*, January 23, 1971.

20 Sanjukta Ghosh, interview, Calcutta, January 30, 2017.

21 Janet Bock Bicker, telephone interview, August 3, 2018.

22 George Harrison, *I Me Mine*, p. 58.

23 Harrison to Kamala Chakravarty, November 17, 1969 [SA].

24 RS, "Hollywood Dhun," and liner notes by Sukanya Shankar, both on his album *In Hollywood, 1971.*

25 Harrison on *The Dick Cavett Show*, November 23, 1971.

26 Harrison in *RM*, p. 220.

27 The different spelling "Oh Bhagawan" was used when it was reissued in 1996 on *In Celebration.*

28 Harvey Kubernik, 'With a little help from his friends: George Harrison and the Concert for Bangla-Desh,' *Rock's Backpages*, July 2011.

29 Peter Lavezzoli, *The Dawn of Indian Music in the West: Bhairavi*, p. 432.

30 Graeme Thomson, *George Harrison: Behind that Locked Door*, pp. 229–30.

31 Albert Goldman, "An epiphany that went flat," *Life*, February 18, 1972.

32 RS interviewed on *Concert for Bangladesh* DVD extras disc.

33 Howard Thomson, "Screen: Ravi Shankar," *New York Times*, November 24, 1971.

34 Richard Bock, interviewed by Ira Landgarten, Los Angeles, May 1979.

35 RS to Harihar Rao, February 29, 1972 [PRC].

36 A. N. Dubey to RS, February 22, 1981 [SA].

37 RS to Harihar Rao, February 29, 1972 [PRC].

38 Paula Rao, interview, Los Angeles, April 17, 2016.

39 *Billboard*, February 24, 1979, p. 67.

40 Jan Murray, "You cannot brush the surface of a culture," *Time Out*, October 20–26, 1972.

41 Linda Shankar, interview, Los Angeles, April 16, 2016.

42 Patricia Anstett, "Ravi winds down the road," *Chicago Sun-Times*, February 26, 1973.

43 RS, "In sacred memory of my Guru Baba Allauddin Khan," *Indian Express*, November 6, 1972.

44 RS, "The legacy left by Allauddin Khan," *New York Times*, September 24, 1972.

45 RS and Ali Akbar Khan, sleeve notes to *In Concert 1972* album.

46 Janet Bock Bicker interview.

47 Kamala Chakravarty, interview, Chennai, March 21, 2014; Padmini S. Kirtane and Donatus de Silva, "An hour with Ravi Shankar," *Himmat*, January 25, 1974.

48 Chakravarty interview.

49 RS to Chakravarty, May 18, 1972 [SA].

50 Chakravarty interview.

51 RS, liner notes on *Shankar Family & Friends.*

52 *Sangeet Ratna* (directed by Alan Kozlowski, 2013).

53 Linda Shankar interview.

54 Kumar Shankar, interview, Simi Valley, April 15, 2016.

55 Chakravarty to RS, August 13, 1975 [SA].

56 Chakravarty to RS, August 3, 1975 [SA].

57 Chakravarty to RS, October 7, 1973 [SA].

58 Chakravarty to RS, September 10, 1973 [SA].

59 RS to Chakravarty, May 22, 1972 [SA].

60 Chakravarty to RS, October 17, 1973 [SA].

61 Sukanya Shankar in *RM*, p. 265.

62 Sukanya Shankar, interview, London, June 13, 2015.

63 RS to Sukanya Shankar, January 23, 2007 [SA].

64 Sukanya Shankar, telephone conversation, February 6, 2019.

65 Sukanya Shankar in *RM*, p. 267.

66 RS to Harihar Rao, February 2, 1974 [PRC].

67 Kumar Shankar, interview, Simi Valley, April 15, 2016.

68 Jeremy Marre, telephone conversation, December 6, 2018.

69 Shivkumar Sharma with Ina Puri, *Journey with a Hundred Strings: My Life in Music*, p. 104.

70 Emil Richards and Tom Di Nardo, *Wonderful World of Percussion*, p. 54.

71 Lakshmi Shankar to Chakravarty, November 7, 1974 [SA].

72 Olivia Harrison, interview, Henley, August 31, 2016.

73 Lakshmi Shankar to Chakravarty, November 7, 1974 [SA].

74 Olivia Harrison interview.

75 Lakshmi Shankar to Chakravarty, November 7, 1974 [SA].

76 Ben Fong-Torres, "George Harrison: Lumbering in the material world," *Rolling Stone*, December 19, 1974.

77 *Billboard*, November 30, 1974, p. 22.

78 Olivia Harrison interview.

79 RS to Chakravarty, November 18, 1974 [SA].

80 "Notes on People," *New York Times*, December 10, 1974, p. 53.

81 Keith Badman, *The Dream Is Over*, p. 150.

82 *Rolling Stone*, January 16, 1975, p. 20.

83 Box 40, folder "Ford, John—Events—George Harrison Visit 12/13/74" of Sheila Weidenfeld Files at Gerald R. Ford Presidential Library; Don Shirley, "Harry's son and Jack's dad," *Washington Post*, December 14, 1974, p. C1.

84 Olivia Harrison interview.

19 Parallel Lives

1 *RA*, p. 159.

2 *Sruti*, May 2009, p. 21; Sandip Ray, "Preface" in his *Satyajit Ray's Ravi Shankar: An Unfilmed Visual Script*, p. viii.

3 Padmini S. Kirtane and Donatus de Silva, "An hour with Ravi Shankar," *Himmat*, January 25, 1974.

4 Kamala Chakravarty, interview, near Chennai, March 21, 2014.

5 RS, interview, Delhi, January 8, 2004.

6 RS in Francesco Scavullo, *Scavullo on Men*, pp. 168–9.

7 Kartik Seshadri, email, October 18, 2018.

8 George Avakian, letter, June 27, 1995.

9 Paul Roberts, "Holy water of life and death," *Canberra Times*, December 30, 1990, p. 20.

10 RS in Scavullo, *Scavullo on Men*, p. 169.

11 *Sruti*, May 2009, p. 21.

12 RS to Chakravarty, December 11, 1975 [SA].

13 Chakravarty interview.

14 "The maestro speaks out," *Northern Indian Patrika*, April 7, 1980.

15 *RM*, p. 116.

16 RS to Chakravarty, March 22, 1975 [SA].

17 RS to Chakravarty, April 10, 1975 [SA].

18 *Billboard*, March 13, 1976, p. 32.

19 Mireille Ballero, telephone interview, September 26, 2019.

20 *RA*, p. 159.

21 Kirtane and de Silva, "An hour with Ravi Shankar."

22 RS to Chakravarty, September 1, 1973 [SA]; the original scores are in folder 128172-1001 (Ravi Shankar *Ragas*) in FMA.

23 *Billboard*, March 26, 1977, p. 82.

24 Rajendra Shankar to RS, March 31, 1976 [SA].

25 RS in Scavullo, *Scavullo on Men*, p. 169.

26 Satish Vyas, interview, Mumbai, February 23, 2015.

27 Ashwini Bhide Deshpande, interview, Mumbai, January 17, 2018.

28 RS to Rajendra Shankar, October 8, 1976 [SA].

29 RS to Harihar Rao, September 13 and 30, 1976 [PRC].

30 Sankarlal Bhattacharjee, interview, Kolkata, January 31, 2017.

31 RS interviewed by Art Makosinski, Encinitas, August 23, 2005.

32 RS to Chakravarty, March 22, 1975 [SA].

33 Chakravarty interview.

34 Mamata Shankar, interview, Kolkata, February 13, 2016.

35 Anoushka Shankar, conversation, London, August 1, 2017.

36 Bhattacharjee interview, January 31, 2017.

37 Chakravarty interview.

38 *RA*, pp. 9–10.

39 Aloke Mitra, *Ravi: The Colours of the Sun*.

40 Bhattacharjee interview, January 31, 2017.

41 Dilip Bobb and Sumit Mitra, "Ravi Shankar: An amorous odyssey," *India Today*, February 15, 1979.

42 Chakravarty interview.

43 *RA*, pp. 7–8.

44 Olivia Harrison, interview, Henley, August 31, 2016.

45 RS to Chakravarty, January 4, 1978 [SA].

46 RS to Chakravarty, March 12, 1978 [SA].

47 *RM*, p. 271.

48 RS to Rao, May 1, 1978 [PRC]

49 Ian Patterson, "John McLaughlin: Risk, magic and mystery," *All About Jazz*, January 7, 2013.

50 RS to Sukanya Shankar, January 23, 2007 [SA].

51 *RM*, p. 268.

52 *RMMVM*, p. 264.

53 Photograph in Robin Paul's collection, Calcutta.

54 Anoushka Shankar, *Bapi: The Love of My Life*, p. 117.

55 Sukanya Shankar, "I believe," *Savvy* (Bombay), December 1989.

56 RS to Chakravarty, July 1, 1976 [SA].

57 Sankarlal Bhattacharjee in Mitra, *Ravi: The Colours of the Sun*, pp. 14–16.

58 RS to A. N. Dubey, March 5, 1981 [SA].

59 *RM*, p. 269.

60 Sukanya Shankar, interview, London, June 13, 2015.

61 Tathagata Roy Chowdhury, 'Every note Annapurna Devi plays is like an offering: Rooshikumar Pandya,' *Times of India*, September 7, 2014.

62 RS, Makosinski interview, August 23, 2005.

63 RS to Chakravarty, December 11, 1975 [SA].

64 Sukanya Shankar, telephone conversation, January 10, 2019.

20 Heart Strain

1   RS, quoted in Sorab Modi, "Ravi Shankar: Master of the sitar," *Ovation*, 1981.
2   Sumit Mitra and Chitra Subramaniam, "Return of the maestro," *India Today*, April 16–30, 1980, p. 90.
3   Ashoke Chatterjee, "Ravi Shankar," *Illustrated Weekly of India*, February 16, 1969, p. 23.
4   John Rockwell, "Ravi Shankar brings his sitar to the Philharmonic," *New York Times*, April 19, 1981, p. 24.
5   José-Luis Greco, telephone interview, November 12, 2016.
6   Zubin Mehta, interview, Florence, September 4, 2016.
7   *RM*, p. 237.
8   Shubha Mudgal, "World music, but not fusion," *The Hindu*, December 14, 2012.
9   Irving Kolodin, "Shankar's rhapsody in beige," *New York Times,* April 25, 1981.
10 RS to A. N. Dubey, April 26, 1981 [SA].
11 *RM*, p. 238.
12 Zubin Mehta interview.
13 Stephen Slawek, telephone interview, July 24, 2018.
14 RS, interviewed by Marian Foster on *Ravi Shankar: Maestro and Guru*, BBC2, broadcast June 10, 1985.
15 Simon Hattenstone, 'Richard Attenborough on laughter, levity and the loss of his daughter,' *Guardian*, September 6, 2008.
16 *Gandhi* press release, November 4, 1981 [RAP, ref. SxMs180/4/29/8/8/5].
17 *RM*, p. 239.
18 George Fenton, email, July 8, 2015.
19 RS to Richard Attenborough, November 18, 1981 [RAP, ref. SxMs180/4/29/8/8/5].
20 Ashit Desai, interview, Mumbai, February 10, 2017.
21 RS to Attenborough, April 13, 1982 [RAP, ref. SxMs180/4/29/8/8/7].
22 George Fenton, interview, London, July 15, 2015.
23 RS, Foster interview.
24 RS, interview, Encinitas, August 31, 2009.
25 "Sir Richard Attenborough opens up," *Times of India*, August 17, 2009.
26 Fenton email.
27 Salman Rushdie, "Outside the whale," *Granta*, 11 (March 1, 1984).
28 Ian Jack, "Perhaps India, rather than China, should be the target of Britain's charm offensive," *Guardian*, October 24, 2015, p. 31.

29   Sunil Sethi, "IX Asiad opening day ceremony in New Delhi leaves die-hard critics speechless," *India Today*, December 15, 1982.

30   "Add special spices for George Harrison," *The Hindu*, December 13, 2012.

31   Tanusree Shankar, interview, Kolkata, January 27, 2017.

32   RS to Indira Gandhi, undated but *c.* June 12, 1982 [SA].

33   Sunil Sethi, "IX Asiad opening day ceremony."

34   N.K.G., "Ravi Shankar: Optimistic about the future," *Screen*, December 31, 1982.

35   For example, "Ravi Shankar to live in India," *Times of India*, November 28, 1982.

36   Raman Swamy, "Ravi Shankar may settle down in Delhi," *Sunday Observer*, January 6, 1983.

37   *RM*, p. 242.

38   N.K.G., "Ravi Shankar: Optimistic about the future."

39   "Rapport with Ali Akbar better: Ravi Shankar," *Times of India*, February 6, 1983.

40   Alan Kozlowski, interview, Santa Barbara, April 19, 2016.

41   *RM*, p. 243.

42   RS, sleeve notes to *New Offerings from Ravi Shankar* (1984).

43   RS to Rajiv Gandhi, December 19, 1984 [SA].

44   Mehta interview.

45   Anoushka Shankar, interview, London, March 4, 2016.

46   Andrew Robinson, *Satyajit Ray: The Inner Eye*, pp. 2–3.

47   Amit Roy, "Dance of discovery," *Telegraph* (Calcutta), October 23, 2011.

48   Daniel Cariaga, "Ravi Shankar still experimenting at 63," *Los Angeles Times*, May 27, 1983, p. 11.

49   RS, conversation with Satish and Shashi Vyas, June 2007 (www.ravishankar.org /reflections/excerpts-from-a-conversation-between-raviji-and-satish-and-shashi -vyasjune-2007).

50   *RM*, p. 249.

51   *Billboard*, October 25, 1986, p. N22.

52   Released on RS, *In Celebration* box set (1996).

53   Shubhendra Rao, interview, Delhi, March 25, 2014.

54   Gaurav Mazumdar, interview, London, September 19, 2014.

55   Sanjay Guha, interview, London, June 17, 2016.

56   *RMMVM*, p. 218.

57   Raghubir Singh, *Banaras: Sacred City of India*, pp. 19–20.

58   *Ravi Shankar: One Man and His Music* DVD (1986, directed by Nicolas Klotz).

59   *RM*, p. 280.

60   For example, RS to Dubey, March 9, 1981 [SA].

61   Paula Rao, interview, Los Angeles, April 17, 2016.

62   Kuldeep Drabu, interview, Delhi, January 15, 2018.

63   *RM*, p. 280.
64   Angela Sulivan, interview, London, May 24, 2016.
65   Ibid.
66   *RMMVM*, pp. 235–6.
67   RS, interview, Encinitas, August 31, 2009.
68   *RMMVM*, pp. 235–6.
69   Misha Dasgupta Masud, interview, New York, December 13, 2016.
70   RS, interview, Delhi, January 6, 2006.
71   Norah Jones, telephone interview, January 16, 2019.
72   Ibid.
73   Ibid.
74   *RMMVM*, p. 265.
75   Sukanya Shankar, interview, London, June 13, 2015.
76   Sukanya Shankar, telephone conversation, January 10, 2019.
77   Ibid.
78   Kavita Chhibber, "Pandit Ravi Shankar and Sukanya Shankar," March 18, 2005 (www.kavitachhibber.com/2005/03/18/pandit-ravi-shankar-and-sukanya-shankar).
79   Anoushka Shankar, interview, London, September 7, 2016.
80   Sukanya Shankar, interview, London, June 13, 2015.
81   *RM*, p. 268.
82   Ibid., p. 272.
83   Singh, *Banaras*, p. 19.
84   Swapan Chaudhuri, interview, Kolkata, January 31, 2017.
85   "Ravi Shankar rushed to New York: Suspected heart condition," *Mid-day*, December 26, 1986.
86   Sankarlal Bhattacharjee, "Unheard melodies," in Sandip Ray (ed.), *Satyajit Ray's Ravi Shankar*, p. 26.
87   RS, interview, Delhi, January 7, 2006.

21 Shanti Mantras

1   *RM*, p. 284.
2   Sankarlal Bhattacharjee, interview, Kolkata, January 31, 2017.
3   *Billboard*, February 20, 1988, p. 6.
4   RS, interview, Encinitas, August 31, 2009.
5   RS interviewed by Art Makosinski, Encinitas, August 23, 2005.
6   Sukanya Shankar, interview, London, June 13, 2015.
7   *RM*, p. 273.

8 Sukanya Shankar interview, June 13, 2015.

9 Lalit Mansingh, interview, Farnham, June 13, 2014.

10 Ibid.

11 RS, liner notes to *In Celebration*, p. 51.

12 Quoted in Sidney Alexander, *Marc Chagall: A Biography*, p. 33.

13 Sukanya Shankar interview, June 13, 2015.

14 Ibid.

15 Ibid.

16 RS, Makosinski interview.

17 Anoushka Shankar, interview, London, September 7, 2016.

18 Sukanya Shankar, "I believe," *Savvy* (Bombay), December 1989.

19 Anoushka Shankar interview, September 7, 2016.

20 Ibid.

21 *RM*, p. 276.

22 Sukanya Shankar, "I believe."

23 Kamala Chakravarty, interview, Chennai, March 21, 2014.

24 Norah Jones telephone interview, January 16, 2019.

25 Ibid.

26 Sukanya Shankar, telephone conversation, April 10, 2019.

27 Norah Jones, telephone interview.

28 Ibid.

29 Sukanya Shankar, telephone conversation, April 10, 2019.

30 Sukanya Shankar interview, June 13, 2015.

31 Sue Fox, "My hols: Anoushka Shankar," *Sunday Times*, April 29, 2012.

32 Anoushka Shankar interview, September 7, 2016.

33 Ibid.

34 *RM*, p. 279.

35 Kuldeep Drabu, interview, Delhi, January 15, 2018.

36 Tanusree Shankar, interview, Kolkata, January 27, 2017.

37 Edmund Morris, *Beethoven: The Universal Composer*, p. 33.

38 *RMMVM*, p. 321.

39 RS to Sukanya Shankar, September 5, 2006 [SA].

40 Amjad Ali Khan, *Master on Masters*, p. 77.

41 RS to Sukanya Shankar, September 12, 1991 [SA].

42 Graham Vick, interview, London, November 24, 2016.

43 Ibid.

44 Ibid.

45 Tulsi Badrinath, *Master of Arts: A Life in Dance*, p. 214.

46 Philip Glass, *Words Without Music*, p. 149.

47 Glass, interview, New York, December 12, 2016.

48 *RM*, p. 251.

49 Glass interview.

50 Anoushka Shankar, interview, London, January 14, 2019.

51 Linda Shankar, interview, Los Angeles, April 16, 2016.

52 Som Shankar, interview, Los Angeles, April 14, 2016.

53 *RMMVM*, p. 259.

54 Linda Shankar interview.

55 Sukanya Shankar, interview, Encinitas, April 21, 2016.

56 Linda Shankar interview.

57 Ibid.

58 Sukanya Shankar interview, April 21, 2016.

59 Angela Sulivan, interview, London, May 24, 2016.

60 Purna Patnaik, interview, Encinitas, April 25, 2016.

61 Anoushka Shankar, *Bapi: The Love of My Life*, pp. 118–19.

62 RS to Sheila and Prem Trikannad, September 17, 1992 [SA].

63 Kalpana Jain, "Ravi Shankar may leave India to set up 'gurukul' abroad," *Times of India*, January 23, 1993.

22 The Inner Light

1 TV interview for *Chants of India*, May 1997 (www.youtube.com/watch?v=V3l9awv1yhA).

2 George Harrison, "Foreword," in *RM*, p. 7.

3 Olivia Harrison, interview, Henley, August 31, 2016.

4 Shuchi Bhatt, interview, London, May 5, 2014.

5 Anoushka Shankar, interview, London, September 7, 2016.

6 Ibid.

7 Ibid.

8 Anoushka Shankar, interview, London, March 4, 2016.

9 Anoushka Shankar interview, September 7, 2016.

10 Paul Livingstone, interview, Los Angeles, April 14, 2016.

11 Anoushka Shankar interview, September 7, 2016.

12 Angela Sulivan, interview, London, May 24, 2016.

13 Ibid.

14 Ibid.

15 Ibid.

16 Ibid.

17 Anoushka Shankar interview, September 7, 2016.

18 George Martin, *Playback: An Illustrated Memoir*, p. 182.

19 RS to Sukanya Shankar, September 5, 2006 [SA].

20 RS to Anoushka Shankar, August 1, 1996 [SA].

21 Yehudi Menuhin to RS, September 11, 1997 [FMA].

22 Sue Fox, "How we met: Yehudi Menuhin and Ravi Shankar," *Independent*, October 1, 1995.

23 RS to Yehudi Menuhin, January 11, 1995 [FMA].

24 Anoushka Shankar interview, September 7, 2016.

25 Fox, "How We Met."

26 *Sunday Telegraph*, October 31, 1999, quoted in Humphrey Burton, *Menuhin: A Life*, p. 486.

27 Sukanya Shankar, interview, London, October 3, 2016.

28 Aveek Sarkar to RS, August 20, 1997; "The sun who rose in the west," *Times of India*, August 15, 1997.

29 Sukanya Shankar, telephone conversation, April 10, 2019.

30 Ammar Kalia, "The birth of Asian underground," *Guardian*, January 11, 2019.

31 Norah Jones, telephone interview, January 16, 2016.

32 Anoushka Shankar interview, September 7, 2016.

33 Norah Jones telephone interview.

34 Anoushka Shankar interview, September 7, 2016.

35 Norah Jones telephone interview.

36 Ibid.

37 *RMMVM*, p. 319.

38 Linda Shankar, interview, Los Angeles, April 16, 2016.

39 Norah Jones telephone interview.

40 Anoushka Shankar interview, September 7, 2016.

41 Gilbert Hetherwick, telephone interview, November 25, 2016.

42 Earl Blackburn, interview, New York, December 15, 2016.

43 Anoushka Shankar interview, March 4, 2016.

44 Ibid.

45 Now in FMA.

46 Gilbert Hetherwick, email, November 25, 2016.

47 RS, "What set Allah Rakha Khan apart was his musicality," *India Today*, February 21, 2000.

48 Ustad Vilayat Khan with Sankarlal Bhattacharjee (trans. Gargi Dutta), *Komal Gandhar*, p. 39.

49 "Vilayat Khan declines award," *The Hindu*, February 8, 2000.

50 "No music to the ear," *Tribune*, March 13, 1999.

51 "Mark Kidel," *India Abroad*, April 16, 2010, p. M7.

52   Phillips, quoted in Sandip Roy, "Ravi Shankar, 90," *India Abroad*, April 16, 2010, p. M4.

53   Olivia Harrison speaking at memorial to RS, Encinitas, December 20, 2012.

54   Olivia Harrison interview.

55   RS to George and Olivia Harrison, August 16, 2000 [SA].

56   RS, "George Harrison," *New York Times*, December 9, 2001.

57   Nigel Williamson, "My world: Olivia Harrison," *Songlines*, 138 (June 2018), p. 90.

58   Olivia Harrison interview.

23 A Student of Music

1   RS, "My Hols," *Sunday Times*, September 14, 1997.

2   RS, interview, Encinitas, August 31, 2009.

3   *RMMVM*, p. 323.

4   Ibid.

5   Swapan Chaudhuri, interview, Kolkata, January 31, 2017.

6   RS interview.

7   Erik Hedegaard, "The hot side of a cool chanteuse," *Rolling Stone*, July 4, 2002, p. 52.

8   RS in John Cassy, "I was blown away," *Guardian*, February 26, 2003.

9   Sumit Bhattacharya, "Keeping up with Jones," *Times of India*, April 30, 2003.

10   Norah Jones, telephone interview, January 16, 2016.

11   Ibid.

12   Ibid.

13   Ibid.

14   Sukanya Shankar, interview, London, September 30, 2016.

15   Sukanya Shankar, telephone conversation, April 11, 2019.

16   RS to John Barham, October 19, 1993 [SA].

17   Hucky Eichelmann, telephone interview, April 14, 2019.

18   Sukanya Shankar interview.

19   Anoushka Shankar, interview, London, January 14, 2019.

20   Jane Graham, "Philip Glass," *The Big Issue*, February 6, 2018.

21   Philip Glass, interview, New York, December 12, 2016.

22   Ibid.

23   David Murphy, *Sukanya* press launch, Royal Opera House, London, September 20, 2016.

24   David Murphy, interview, Harpenden, July 10, 2016.

25   Anoushka Shankar, email, April 17, 2019.

26 David Murphy interview.

27 Anoushka Shankar interview, January 14, 2019.

28 Nick Able, telephone interview, March 5, 2019.

29 Kumar Bose, interview, London, September 19, 2016.

30 Anoushka Shankar, interview, London, March 4, 2016.

31 Vikram Dodd, "Sitar turn," *Guardian*, May 15, 2003.

32 Pirashanna Thevarajah, interview, London, June 14, 2016.

33 Able telephone interview.

34 Duncan Ward, interview, London, November 16, 2016.

35 Parimal Sadaphal, interview, Delhi, March 25, 2014.

24 Late Style

1 Douglas Heselgrave, "Remembering Ravi Shankar (1920–2012)," *Paste*, December 12, 2012.

2 RS interviewed by Art Makosinski, Encinitas, August 23, 2005.

3 Sukanya Shankar, telephone interview, April 2, 2019, and conversation, London, August 26, 2019.

4 Anoushka Shankar, interview, London, January 14, 2019.

5 Ibid.

6 Gabor Maté, *In the Realm of Hungry Ghosts: Close Encounters with Addiction*, p. 230.

7 Anoushka Shankar interview, January 14, 2019.

8 Ibid.

9 Sukanya Shankar, interview, London, September 14, 2017.

10 Anoushka Shankar interview, January 14, 2019.

11 Sukanya Shankar interview, September 14, 2017.

12 Sukanya Shankar, telephone conversation, August 29, 2019.

13 Simran Mangharam, interview, Delhi, January 12, 2018.

14 Ravichandra Kulur, telephone interview, June 22, 2016.

15 RS, handwritten note, *c.* 2011 [SA].

16 RS to Sukanya Shankar, January 23, 2007 [SA].

17 Irene Lacher, "Riffing on the classics," *Los Angeles Times*, March 18, 2012.

18 Anoushka Shankar, interview, London, March 4, 2016.

19 Norah Jones, telephone interview, January 16, 2016.

20 Philip Glass, interview, New York, December 12, 2016.

21 Ibid.

22 Sukanya Shankar, telephone conversation, February 6, 2019.

23 RS, Makosinski interview.

24 RS, "A note from Ravi Shankar," programme for Williams Center of the Arts, Easton, Pennsylvania, January 29, 2009.

25 David Murphy, *Sukanya* press launch, Royal Opera House, London, September 20, 2016.

26 David Murphy, interview, Harpenden, July 10, 2016.

27 Sukanya Shankar, interview, London, September 30, 2016.

28 Imogen Holst to Leonard Elmhirst, January 2, 1951 [HA, ref. HOL 5/1/3/9].

29 David Murphy, *Sukanya* press launch.

30 David Murphy interview.

31 Jessica Young, email to Sukanya Shankar, April 7, 2016 [SA].

32 RS, sleeve notes to *The Living Room Sessions Part 1*.

33 Simran Mangharam, interview, Delhi, January 12, 2018.

34 Bernhard Schimpelsberger, interview, London, June 30, 2014.

35 Gaurav Mazumdar, interview, London, September 19, 2014.

36 Satish Vyas, interview, Mumbai, February 23, 2015.

37 Anoushka Shankar interview, March 4, 2016.

38 Anoushka Shankar interview, January 14, 2019.

39 Ravichandra Kulur telephone interview.

40 Anoushka Shankar interview, January 14, 2019.

41 RS, handwritten note, Encinitas, November 8, 2012 [SA].

42 Anoushka Shankar interview, January 14, 2019.

43 Philip Glass, tribute to RS for Encinitas memorial, December 19, 2012.

44 Amitabh Bachchan's official blog, December 5, 2012.

45 Sukanya Shankar, telephone interview, April 2, 2019.

46 Anoushka Shankar interview, January 14, 2019.

47 Norah Jones telephone interview.

48 Anoushka Shankar interview, January 14, 2019.

49 Nitin Sawhney, interview, London, November 14, 2016.

50 Sukanya Shankar, interview, Delhi, March 28, 2014.

51 Renuka Vyavahare, Akshata Shetty and Swasti Chatterjee, 'Panditji treated me like his daughter,' *Times of India*, December 13, 2012.

52 Anoushka Shankar interview, January 14, 2019.

53 Ibid.

54 Norah Jones telephone interview.

Epilogue: The Sun Won't Set

1 Philip Glass, tribute to RS for Encinitas memorial, December 19, 2012.

2 Amit Chaudhuri, *Afternoon Raag*, pp. 42–5.

3   Chaudhuri, interview, Kolkata, January 28, 2017.

4   Sukanya Shankar, interview, London, September 30, 2016.

5   Simon Broughton, "A near death experience," in *Songlines*, March 2008, p. 41.

6   Tithi Sarkar, "Pandit Ravi Shankar: Sitar maestro who took Indian music to global audiences," *India Today*, December 13, 2012.

7   Kaushiki Chakraborty speaking from the stage at Swami Haridas–Tansen festival, Delhi, January 11, 2018.

8   Bickram Ghosh, Facebook post, June 29, 2017.

9   Nitin Sawhney, interview, London, November 14, 2016.

10 Stephen Walsh, *Debussy: A Painter in Sound*, p. 321.

11 Shivkumar Sharma, interview, Kolkata, January 24, 2017.

12 Taylor Ho Bynum, "Ravi Shankar, open mind," *New Yorker*, December 12, 2012.

13 RS in Francesco Scavullo, *Scavullo on Men*, p. 169.

BIBLIOGRAPHY

Abbas, K. A., *I Am Not an Island: An Experiment in Autobiography* (Delhi: Vikas, 1977)

Alexander, Sidney, *Marc Chagall: A Biography* (London: Cassell, 1979)

Anand, Dev, *Romancing with Life: An Autobiography* (Delhi: Penguin, 2007)

Ashton, Roger (ed.), *Music East and West* (Delhi: ICCR, 1966)

Attenborough, David, *Life on Air* (London: BBC Books, 2009)

Badman, Keith, *The Dream Is Over: Off the Record 2* (London: Omnibus, 2002)

Badrinath, Tulsi, *Master of Arts: A Life in Dance* (Gurgaon: Hachette, 2013)

Bali, Vyjayantimala, with Jyoti Sabharwal, *Bonding: A Memoir* (New Delhi: Stellar Publishers, 2007)

Banerji, Bibhutibhushan, trans. T. W. Clark and Tarapada Mukherji, *Pather Panchali: Song of the Road* (London, Folio, 1971)

—, *Aparajito: The Unvanquished*, trans. Gopa Majumdar (New Delhi: HarperCollins, 1999)

Bardhan, Gul (ed.), *Rhythm Incarnate: Tribute to Shanti Bardhan* (Delhi: Abhinav, 1992)

Baruah, U. L., *This Is All India Radio: A Handbook of Radio Broadcasting in India* (Delhi: Publications Division, 1983)

Bassett, Kate, *In Two Minds: A Biography of Jonathan Miller* (London: Oberon, 2012)

Beatles, The, *The Beatles Anthology* (London: Cassell, 2000)

Bharat-Ram, Vinay, *From the Brink of Bankruptcy: The DCM Story* (Delhi: Viking, 2011)

Bondyopadhyay, Swapan Kumar, *An Unheard Melody: Annapurna Devi, An Authorised Biography* (New Delhi: Roli, 2005)

Boner, Alice, *Indien, Mein Indien: Tagbuch einer Reise* (Zurich: Werner Classen, 1984)

Bose, Ajoy, *Across the Universe: The Beatles in India* (Gurgaon: Viking, 2018)

Boyd, Pattie, with Penny Junor, *Wonderful Today: George Harrison, Eric Clapton and Me* (London: Headline Review, 2008)

Brenscheidt gen. Jost, Diana, *Shiva Onstage: Uday Shankar's Company of Hindu Dancers and Musicians in Europe and the United States, 1931–38* (Berlin and Zurich: LIT, 2011)

Burton, Humphrey, *Menuhin: A Life* (London: Faber and Faber, 2001)

Cardullo, Bert, *World Directors in Dialogue: Conversations on Cinema* (Lanham, Maryland: Scarecrow Press, 2011)

Chaudhuri, Amit, *Calcutta: Two Years in the City* (London: Union Books, 2013)

—, *Afternoon Raag* (London: Oneworld, 2015)

Coast, John, *Railroad of Death* (Newcastle upon Tyne: Myrmidon, 2014)

Cooke, Mervyn, *Britten and the Far East: Asian Influences in the Music of Benjamin Britten* (Woodbridge: Boydell Press, 1998)

Crosby, David, and Carl Gottlieb, *Long Time Gone: The Autobiography of David Crosby* (London: Heinemann, 1989)

Devidayal, Namita, *The Sixth String of Vilayat Khan* (Chennai: Context, 2018)

Devito, Chris, Yasuhiro Fujioka, Wolf Schmaler and David Wild, *The John Coltrane Reference* (New York: Routledge, 2008)

Didion, Joan, *Slouching Towards Bethlehem* (New York: Farrar, Straus & Giroux, 2008)

Dobson, Terence, *The Film Work of Norman McLaren* (Eastleigh: John Libbey, 2006)

Dunn, Jerry Camarillo, *My Favorite Place on Earth: Celebrated People Share Their Travel Discoveries* (Washington DC: National Geographic Books, 2009)

Dutta, Krishna, and Andrew Robinson, *Rabindranath Tagore: The Myriad-Minded Man* (London: Bloomsbury, 1995)

Elborough, Travis, *The Long-Player Goodbye* (London: Sceptre, 2008)

Erdman, Joan L., with Zohra Segal, *Stages: The Art and Adventures of Zohra Segal* (Kali for Women, Delhi, 1997)

Evans, John (ed.), *Journeying Boy: The Diaries of the Young Benjamin Britten 1928–1938* (London: Faber and Faber, 2009)

Farrell, Gerry, *Indian Music and the West* (Oxford: OUP, 1997)

Forster, E. M., *A Passage to India* (Harmondsworth: Penguin, 1970)

Fox, Peggy L., and Thomas Keith (eds.), *The Luck of Friendship: The Letters of Tennessee Williams and James Laughlin* (New York: Norton, 2018)

Ghosh, Dibyendu (ed.), *The Great Shankars: Uday, Ravi* (Calcutta: Agee Prakashani, 1983)

Ghosh, Nemai, *Satyajit Ray at 70* (Brussels: Eiffel Editions, 1991)

Ghuman, Nalini, *Resonances of the Raj: India in the English Musical Imagination, 1897–1947* (Oxford: OUP, 2014)

Giroud, Vincent, *Nicolas Nabokov: A Life in Freedom and Music* (Oxford and New York: OUP, 2015)

Glass, Philip, *Opera on the Beach* (London: Faber & Faber, 1988)

—, *Words Without Music* (London: Faber and Faber, 2015)

Gokhale, Shanta (ed.), *The Scenes We Made: An Oral History of Experimental Theatre in Mumbai* (New Delhi: Speaking Tiger, 2016)

Goldstein, Richard, *Goldstein's Greatest Hits* (Englewood Cliffs: Prentice Hall, 1970)

Gordon, Beate Sirota, *The Only Woman in the Room: A Memoir of Japan, Human Rights, and the Arts* (Chicago: University of Chicago Press, 2014)

Greene, Joshua M., *Here Comes the Sun: The Spiritual and Musical Journey of George Harrison* (London: Bantam, 2006)

Guha, Ramachandra, *India After Gandhi: The History of the World's Largest Democracy* (London: Macmillan, 2007)

Harewood, Lord, *The Tongs and the Bones* (London: Weidenfeld & Nicolson, 1981)

Harrison, George, *I Me Mine* (London: Weidenfeld & Nicolson, 2002)

Harrison, Olivia, *George Harrison: Living in the Material World* (New York: Abrams, 2011)

Heron, Mike, and Andrew Greig, *You Know What You Could Be: Tuning into the 1960s* (London: Riverrun, 2017)

Holroyde, Peggy, *The Music of India* (New York: Praeger, 1972)

Hoskyns, Barney, *Hotel California: Singer-Songwriters and Cocaine Cowboys in the LA Canyons, 1967–1976* (London: Fourth Estate, 2005)

Husain, M. F., with Khalid Mohamed, *Where Art Thou* (Mumbai: M. F. Husain Foundation, 2002)

Hussain, Zakir, in conversation with Nasreen Munni Kabir, *Zakir Hussain: A Life in Music* (Noida: HarperCollins, 2018)

Jaffrey, Saeed, *Saeed: An Actor's Journey* (London: Constable, 1998)

Kahn, Ashley, *A Love Supreme: The Creation of John Coltrane's Classic Album* (London: Granta, 2003)

Karsh, Yousuf, *Faces of Our Time* (Toronto: University of Toronto Press, 1971)

Khan, Amjad Ali, *Master on Masters* (New Delhi: Penguin Random House, 2017)

Khan, Ustad Vilayat, with Sankarlal Bhattacharjee (trans. Gargi Dutta), *Komal Gandhar* (Kolkata: Sahityam, 2006)

Khilnani, Sunil, *The Idea of India* (London: Penguin, 1998)

—, *Incarnations: India in 50 Lives* (London: Allen Lane, 2016)

Khokar, Mohan, *His Dance, His Life: A Portrait of Uday Shankar* (New Delhi: Himalayan Books, 1983)

Kildea, Paul, *Benjamin Britten: A Life in the Twentieth Century* (London: Penguin, 2014)

Knight Jr, Douglas M., *Balasaraswati: Her Art and Life* (Chennai: Tranquebar, 2011)

Koch, Lars-Christian, *Sitar and Surbahar Manufacturing: The Tradition of Kanailal & Brother, Kolkata* (Berlin: Ethnologisches Museum, 2011)

Kostelanetz, Richard (ed.), *Writings on Glass* (New York: Schirmer, 1997)

Kubernik, Harvey and Kenneth, *A Perfect Haze: The Illustrated History of the Monterey International Pop Festival* (Solana Beach: Santa Monica Press, 2011)

Kuratli, Andrea, and Johannes Beltz, *Alice Boner: A Visionary Artist and Scholar Across Two Continents* (New Delhi: Roli, 2014)

Lang, Michael, with Holly George-Warren, *The Road to Woodstock* (New York: HarperCollins, 2009)

Lavezzoli, Peter, *The Dawn of Indian Music in the West: Bhairavi* (London: Continuum, 2006)

Leng, Simon, *The Music of George Harrison: While My Guitar Gently Weeps* (London: Firefly, 2003)

Levine, Victoria Lindsay, and Philip V. Bohlman (eds.), *This Thing Called Music* (Lanham, Maryland: Rowman & Littlefield, 2015)

Lewisohn, Mark, *All These Years, Volume One: Tune In (Extended Special Edition)* (London: Little, Brown, 2013)

Lydon, Michael, *Flashbacks: Eyewitness Accounts of the Rock Revolution 1964–1974* (London: Routledge, 2003)

MacDonald, Ian, *Revolution in the Head: The Beatles' Records and the Sixties* (London: Pimlico, 2005)

MacNiven, Ian S., *"Literchoor Is My Beat": A Life of James Laughlin, Publisher of New Directions* (New York: Farrar, Straus and Giroux, 2014)

McWilliams, Donald, *Norman McLaren: The Creative Process* (Montreal, National Film Board of Canada, 1991)

Manzarek, Ray, *Light My Fire: My Life with the Doors* (London: Century, 1998)

Martin, George, *Playback: An Illustrated Memoir* (Guildford: Genesis, 2002)

Maté, Gabor, *In the Realm of Hungry Ghosts: Close Encounters with Addiction* (London: Vermilion, 2018)

Mehra, Girish, *Nearer Heaven than Earth: The Life and Times of Boshi Sen and Gertrude Emerson Sen* (Delhi: Rupa, 2007)

Mehta, Gita, *Karma Cola: Marketing the Mystic East* (New York: Vintage, 1994)

Mehta, Zubin, *The Score of My Life* (New Delhi: Roli, 2008)

Menezes, Meera, *Vasudeo Santu Gaitonde: Sonata of Solitude* (Mumbai: Bodhana, 2016)

Menuhin, Diana, *Fiddler's Moll: Life with Yehudi* (London: Weidenfeld & Nicolson, 1984)

Miles, Barry, *Paul McCartney: Many Years from Now* (London: Vintage, 1998)

Mitra, Aloke, *Ravi: The Colours of the Sun* (New Delhi: Alchemy, 2013)

Moorhouse, Geoffrey, *Calcutta* (London: Phoenix, 1988)

Morris, Edmund, *Beethoven: The Universal Composer* (New York: HarperCollins, 2005)

Moss, Elaine, *The JDR 3rd Fund and Asia* (New York: JDR 3rd Fund, 1977)

Nabokov, Nicolas, *Bagázh: Memoirs of a Russian Cosmopolitan* (London: Secker & Warburg, 1975)

Nadkarni, Mohan, *Music to Thy Ears: Great Masters of Hindustani Instrumental Music* (Mumbai: Somaiya, 2002)

Narasimhan, Sakuntala, *Kamaladevi Chattopadhyay: The Romantic Rebel* (New Delhi: Sterling, 1999)

Narayan, R. K., *My Dateless Diary: American Journey* (New Delhi: Penguin, 1964)

—, *The Guide* (London: Penguin, 1988)

Natt, Kulbir S. (ed.), *Darbar: Arts Culture Heritage* (Leicester: Darbar, 2008)

Nehru, B. K., *Nice Guys Finish Second* (Delhi: Viking, 1997)

Nehru, Jawaharlal, *The Discovery of India* (Delhi: Jawaharlal Nehru Memorial Fund, 1994)

Paytress, Mark, *Bolan: The Rise and Fall of a 20th Century Superstar* (London: Omnibus, 2006)

Perspective of India (New York: Intercultural, 1953)

Porter, Lewis, *John Coltrane: His Life and Music* (Ann Arbor, Michigan: Michigan University Press, 1998)

Pradhan, Aneesh, *Hindustani Music in Colonial Bombay* (Gurgaon: Three Essays, 2014)

Rahman, Sukanya, *Dancing in the Family: An Unconventional Memoir of Three Women* (New Delhi: HarperCollins, 2001)

Ranade, Ashok Da., *Hindustani Music* (New Delhi: National Book Trust, India, 2005)

Rawson, Philip, *An Exhibition of Music and Dance in Indian Art* (Edinburgh: Royal Scottish Museum, 1963)

Ray, Sandip (ed.), *Satyajit Ray's Ravi Shankar: An Unfilmed Visual Script* (Noida: Collins, 2014)

—, *The Pather Panchali Sketchbook* (Noida: HarperCollins, 2016)

Ray, Satyajit, *Our Films, Their Films* (Delhi: Orient Longman, 1976)

—, *My Years with Apu: A Memoir* (Delhi: Penguin, 1996)

—, *Speaking of Films* (Delhi: Penguin, 2005)

—, *Travails with the Alien* (Noida: HarperCollins India, 2018)

Reed, Philip (ed.), *The Travel Diaries of Peter Pears, 1936–1978* (Woodbridge: Boydell, 1995)

—, and Mervyn Cooke (eds.), *Letters from a Life: The Selected Letters of Benjamin Britten 1913–1976*, vol. 5: *1958–65* (Woodbridge: Boydell, 2010)

—, Mervyn Cooke and Donald Mitchell (eds.), *Letters from a Life: The Selected Letters of Benjamin Britten 1913–1976*, vol. 4: *1952–57* (Woodbridge: Boydell, 2008)

Richards, Emil, and Tom Di Nardo, *Wonderful World of Percussion* (Albany, GA: Bear Manor, 2013)

Rix, Martyn (ed.), *Rory McEwen: The Colours of Reality* (Kew: Royal Botanic Gardens, 2015)

Robinson, Andrew, *Satyajit Ray: The Inner Eye* (London: I. B. Tauris, 2004)

—, *The Apu Trilogy: Satyajit Ray and the Making of an Epic* (London: I. B. Tauris, 2011)

—, and Nemai Ghosh, *Satyajit Ray: A Vision of Cinema* (London: I. B. Tauris, 2005)

Ross, Alex, *The Rest Is Noise* (London: Harper Perennial, 2009)

Roy, Anjana, *Acharya Ustad Allauddin Khan: Musician for the Soul* (self-published, 2010)

Sadie, Stanley (ed.), *New Grove Dictionary of Music and Musicians*, 2nd edn, vol. 13 (London: Macmillan, 2001)

Salewicz, Chris, *Jimmy Page: The Definitive Biography* (London: HarperCollins, 2018)

Sauvageot, Claude, and Mireille Ballero, *Inde* (Paris: Albin Michel, 1974)

Savage, Jon, *1966: The Year the Decade Exploded* (London: Faber, 2015)

Scavullo, Francesco, *Scavullo on Men* (New York: Random House, 1977)

Schwarz, K. Robert, *Minimalists* (London: Phaidon, 1996)

Sen, Mrinal, *Always Being Born: A Memoir* (New Delhi: Stellar Publishers, 2006)

Shankar, Anoushka, *Bapi: The Love of My Life* (New Delhi: Roli, 2002)

Shankar, Ravi, *Learning Indian Music: A Systematic Approach*, ed. Elise B. Barnett (Fort Lauderdale: Onomatopoeia Inc., 1979)

—, *Raag-Anuraag* (Calcutta: Ananda Publishers, 1980)

—, *Raga Mala: The Autobiography of Ravi Shankar* (New York: Welcome Rain, 1999)

—, *My Music, My Life* (San Rafael: Mandala, 2007)

—, *Raga Mala: Ma vie en musique*, trans. Catherine Baldisserri (Paris: Editions Intervalles, 2010)

—, *Raga Mala: La mia vita, la mia musica*, trans. Riccardo Battaglia (Rome: Arcana, 2011)

—, with Sankarlal Bhattacharya, *Smriti* (Kolkata: Prativash, 2012)

—, with Penelope Estabrook, *Music Memory* (Bombay: Kinnara, 1964)

Shankar, Sukanya, *Ravi Shankar: 75 Years, A Celebration* (Delhi: RIMPA, 1995)

Sharma, Shivkumar, with Ina Puri, *Journey with a Hundred Strings: My Life in Music* (New Delhi: Viking, 2002)

Sheppard, David, *On Some Faraway Beach: The Life and Times of Brian Eno* (London: Orion, 2008)

Simpkins, Cuthbert Ormond, *Coltrane: A Biography* (New York: Herndon House, 1975)

Singh, Raghubir, *Banaras: Sacred City of India* (London: Thames & Hudson, 1987)

Stonor Saunders, Frances, *Who Paid the Piper? The CIA and the Cultural Cold War* (London: Granta, 1999)

Strickland, Edward, *American Composers: Dialogues on Contemporary Music* (Bloomington, Indiana: Indiana University Press, 1991)

Stuhlmann, Gunther (ed.), *Diary of Anaïs Nin*, vol. vi: *1955–1966* (New York: Harcourt Brace Jovanovich, 1976)

Taylor, Derek, *It Was Twenty Years Ago Today* (London: Bantam, 1987)

Thomas, J. C., *Chasin' the Trane: The Music and Mystique of John Coltrane* (London: Elm Tree Books, 1976)

Thomson, Graeme, *George Harrison: Behind that Locked Door* (London: Omnibus, 2016)

Tolinski, Brad, *Light and Shade: Conversations with Jimmy Page* (London: Virgin, 2012)

Turner, Steve, *Beatles 66* (New York: Ecco, 2016)

Vivekananda, Swami, *Raja Yoga* (London: Kegan Paul, 1922)

Walsh, Stephen, *Debussy: A Painter in Sound* (London: Faber & Faber, 2018)

Watts, Alan, *The Joyous Cosmology: Adventures in the Chemistry of Consciousness* (New York: Vintage, 1970)

Willetts, Paul, *Rendezvous at the Russian Tea Rooms* (London: Constable, 2015)

Woideck, Carl, *The John Coltrane Companion* (London: Omnibus, 1998)

LIST OF ILLUSTRATIONS

PHOTO SECTION ONE

Page 1 (clockwise from top left)
Ravi's father, Shyam Shankar.
Courtesy of the Shankar family.

Ravi, then Robindra (Robu), with his mother, Hemangini.
Museum Rietberg Zürich, Legat Alice Boner, ABF 413-14.

Robu with his mother and his brothers Rajendra, Debendra and Uday, in Paris, 1932.
Courtesy of the Shankar family.

Uday Shankar with his French dance partner, Simkie.
Courtesy of the Shankar family.

Page 2
Nine-year-old Robu with Alice Boner in 1930, probably at Nasrathpur.
Museum Rietberg Zürich, Legat Alice Boner, ABF 413-5.

The fledgling troupe's musicians in Paris, early 1931.
Courtesy of the Shankar family.

Page 3
Uday's double-exposure photograph of Robu as musician and dancer.
Courtesy of the Shankar family.

Madhavan Nair, Uzra Mumtaz, Uday, Simkie, Zohra Mumtaz and Robu in 1936.
Museum Rietberg Zürich, Legat Alice Boner, ABF 0-47.

Page 4 (clockwise from top left)
Uday and Simkie with Rabindranath Tagore, in about 1933.
Courtesy of the Shankar family.

Simkie with Balasaraswati, in Calcutta, 1934.
Museum Rietberg Zürich, Legat Alice Boner, ABF 271-1.

Ravi with his first wife, Annapurna, at Maihar, early 1942.
Courtesy of the Shankar family.

Ravi as a dancer.
Courtesy of the Shankar family.

Page 5
Ravi in 1945, while working at the Indian People's Theater Association in Bombay.
Courtesy of the Shankar family.

Ravi with Narayana Menon.
Courtesy of the Shankar family.

Ravi on sitar, with his brother-in-law Ali Akbar Khan (right) and "Baba" Allauddin
Khan, *c.* 1962.
Courtesy of the Shankar family.

Page 6
Ravi at the All-Union Agricultural Exhibition in Moscow, 1954.
Courtesy of the Shankar family.

With Satyajit Ray in Calcutta, 1956.
Courtesy of the Shankar family.

Page 7
Yehudi Menuhin with Ravi's sitar on their first meeting, Delhi, 1952.
Keystone/Hulton Archive via Getty Images.

Ravi with his son Shubho and Baba's wife Madan Manjari.
Courtesy of the Shankar family.

Ravi and Marilyn Silverstone with Chatur Lal, James and Ann Laughlin
and Nodu Mullick, New York, 1956.
Courtesy of the Shankar family.

Page 8
Ravi thrills the New York jazz world, December 1956.
Paul Schutzer, The LIFE Picture Collection via Getty Images.

George Avakian with Ravi on the SS *United States*, May 1957.
Courtesy of the Shankar family.

LIST OF ILLUSTRATIONS

Page 5
Recording the music for *Gandhi* with George Fenton and Richard Attenborough,
Wembley, January 1982.
Tom Hanley, courtesy George Fenton.
Ghanashyam takes shape, Delhi, 1989.
Courtesy of the Shankar family.

Page 6 (clockwise from top)
With Sukanya, his second wife, in 1997.
Courtesy of the Shankar family.
With conductor Zubin Mehta, New York, April 1981.
Jack Vartoogian, Getty Images.
With Joshua Bell, 2007.
Art Makosinski.
With Philip Glass, Santa Monica, 1989.
Alan Kozlowski.

Page 7
Ravi and Norah Jones, Calcutta, January 1981.
Sue Jones.
Ravi and Anoushka Shankar, January 1989.
Courtesy Anoushka Shankar.
Anoushka, Norah, Ravi and Sukanya, at Lodhi Road, Delhi, 2000.
Alan Kozlowski.

Page 8
Ravi gives "semi-final" performance at Barbican Hall, London, 2008.
Shaun Curry, AFP via Getty Images.
Final concert in India, Premaanjali Festival, Bangalore, February 2012.
Chethan Ram.

ACKNOWLEDGMENTS

Ravi Shankar is a dream as a biographical subject, and I have been spoiled for life. It was a privilege to spend so much time with him over eighteen years, talking, watching, listening, feeling the world open up. Raviji (as I always called him) was generous, engaged in life, full of energy and playful spirit. I miss him and I shall always be deeply grateful to him.

For the initial introduction twenty-five years ago, and for years of mentorship and friendship, I remain indebted to the late Brian Roylance, who typically followed his instincts rather than convention in taking a punt on me.

To be the first person to write Ravi Shankar's biography has been a mammoth undertaking and a weighty responsibility. For years I resisted the role, but Raviji must have known me better than I knew myself for he had planted the seed early. After he died, I realized I was ready. A few weeks later, I called Sukanya Shankar, nervous to find out whether she would approve. I'm sure she has a sixth sense. Before I had voiced the question, she said, "You know, you must write something more about him."

Sukanya granted me unfettered access to the family collections, which are of international significance. They are the most important archival source for this book, and it was a sustained thrill to be the first writer to explore them in depth. Sukanya hosted me on research visits to Delhi and California, and provided me with numerous interviews and introductions, but encouraged me to make my own judgments. She has an enlightened attitude to the past. At my request, she read and corrected the full manuscript and answered many queries. I am profoundly grateful for her cooperation over the past six years, as I am fortunate to have had her friendship and guidance over a quarter of a century.

This book could not have taken its final shape without the cooperation of Raviji's remarkable daughters. Anoushka Shankar has been extremely supportive, granting me multiple interviews and meetings, and encouraging me to explore her father's psychological development. She, too, read and commented on my draft. I greatly value her friendship. I was also touched by the thoughtful interview that Norah Jones gave me, and am grateful to her for reading extracts.

Annapurna Devi, who sadly died during the writing of this book, had declined to be interviewed due to ill health but wished the project well. Sue Jones also opted not to talk to me. She has never spoken publicly about Raviji. She played a very important role in his life and I have attempted to recount it as accurately and fairly as possible. I am conscious that she must have different takes on some matters.

I conducted more than 125 other interviews with family members, disciples, friends, musicians or other collaborators. The earliest (apart from Raviji himself) were in 1995, for *Raga Mala*, with George Harrison, Yehudi Menuhin, Romana McEwen and Alexander McEwen. Since 2014 the following kindly agreed to be interviewed. In India: Ahasan Ahmed, Sujata Banerjee, Arun Bharat-Ram, Vinay Bharat-Ram, Sankarlal Bhattacharjee, Ashwini Bhide Deshpande, Partha Bose, Tanmoy Bose, the late Kamala Chakravarty, Nabarun Chatterji, Amit Chaudhuri, Swapan Chaudhuri, Ashit Desai, V. P. and Shanta Dhananjayan, Kuldeep Drabu, Penny Estabrook, Bickram Ghosh, Nemai Ghosh, Sanjukta Ghosh, Lajwanti Gupta, Nityanand Haldipur, Ravichandra Kulur, the late Ashwini Kumar, Kartick Kumar, Kumudini Lakhia, Birju Maharaj, Simran Mangharam, Udhai Mazumdar, Kanhaiyalal Mishra, Mita Nag, Barun Kumar Pal, Robin Paul, Krishna Ramkumar, Shubhendra Rao, Maharajapuram Ramachandran, Parimal Sadaphal, Saswati Sen, Mamata Shankar, Monoj Shankar, Tanusree Shankar, Shivkumar Sharma, L. Subramaniam, Balwant Rai Verma and Satish Vyas.

In the USA: Nancy Bacal, Earl Blackburn, Ron Bock, Janet Bock Bicker, Cat Celebrezze, Maya Kulkarni Chadda, Madalaine and Michael Charnow, Misha Dasgupta Masud, Pedro Eustache, Robert Garfias, Lynn Gertenbach, Philip Glass, Hallie Goodman, Louis Hayes, Gilbert Hetherwick, Aashish Khan, Alan Kozlowski, Robby Krieger, Ira Landgarten, Quincy Jones, Paul Livingstone, Art Makosinski, Kenji Ota, Purna, Gopa and Shalini Patnaik, Barry Phillips, Paula Rao, Laura Rosenberg, Tom Scott, Kartik Seshadri, Kaveri Shankar, Kumar Shankar, Linda Shankar, Som Shankar, Stephen Slawek, Jan Steward and Coriolana Wolters Simon.

In the UK: Nick Able, Shankara Angadi, John Barham, Shuchi Bhatt, Tarun Bhattacharya, Kumar Bose, Ajoy Chakrabarty, George Fenton, Sanjay Guha, the late Patricia, Dowager Countess of Harewood, Olivia Harrison, James Ivory, Viram Jasani, Lalit Mansingh, Ronu Majumdar, Jeremy Marre, Gaurav Mazumdar, Manju Mehta, Jonathan Miller, David Murphy, Dr. M. N. Nandakumara, Laura Noszlopy, Nitin Sawhney, Bernhard Schimpelsberger, Sanjeev Shankar, Talvin Singh, Naresh Sohal, Angela Sulivan, Pirashanna Thevarajah, Graham Vick, Jay Visvadeva and Duncan Ward. Elsewhere I spoke to Hariprasad Chaurasia, Jose-Luis Greco, Zubin Mehta, Mireille Ballero and Hucky Eichelmann.

I am grateful to all the interviewees for sharing their thoughts and memories and for further helpful suggestions.

I would like to thank the archives and libraries where I researched or wrote the book: Ravi Shankar Centre in Delhi (special thanks to Anshuman Pandey and Joyita Dutta); Ravi Shankar Foundation in California (Cat Celebrezze, Art Makosinski); British Library; BBC Written Archives Centre (Louise North); Britten–Pears Foundation (Sarah Bardwell, Judith Ratcliffe); London Symphony Orchestra (Libby Rice); Royal Academy of Music (Ilse Woloszko and Andrew Neilson); School of Oriental

ACKNOWLEDGMENTS

and African Studies; Southbank Centre (Clare Wood, Annette Mackin); University of Sussex (Richard Wragg); Museum Rietberg (Johannes Beltz, Esther Tisa, Andrea Kuratli, Nanina Guyer); Stadtarchiv Zürich (Angelika Ruider); Library of Congress, Washington, DC; National Archives at College Park, Maryland; New York Public Library for Performing Arts (Dave McMullin, Phil Karg); Rockefeller Archive Center (Renee Pappous); Staatsbibliothek zu Berlin; NYU Abu Dhabi; and American University of Beirut. Other archives that provided information were American Dance Festival (Dean Jeffrey); Dokumentationsbibliothek Davos (Timothy Nelson); ITV Archives; National Film Board Canada (Pierre Boucher); and Prasar Bharati (T. S. Ramakrishna, with thanks to Shailaja Khanna).

Many people provided company and hospitality during my research trips. On an unforgettable visit to Maihar, Rajesh Ali Khan kindly arranged for me to stay in Allauddin Khan's home, ascend to the shrine of Ma Sharda, enjoy a private performance by the Maihar Band, and visit Maihar Palace—where I was grateful to HH Kaviteshwari Devi, the Rajmata Maihar, for the tour of the palace and stories of Baba and Brijnath Singh. Raviji's cousin Karun Kumar Chakravarty and nephew Nabarun Chatterji took me to Nasrathpur. Tim and Tom Shread helped me hunt for Raviji's birthplace in Varanasi. Jan Steward hosted me in Los Angeles, and Alan Kozlowski in Santa Barbara. Faryal Ganjehei showed me around the former A&M Studios. Bruno Kavanagh, Preeti Vasudevan and Ambaalika gave me a warm welcome in wintry New York. Nuri Akgul did his best to show me Marshall Stearns's apartment. During all-night sessions at the Dover Lane Music Conference, Mostafa Baha was an expert *raga*-spotter and Peter Lavezzoli provided many insights over coffee. Peter's book *The Dawn of Indian Music in the West: Bhairavi* was an invaluable resource.

I am very grateful to the following for granting me permission to reproduce extracts from unpublished material: Paula Rao for thirty years' worth of letters from Ravi Shankar to Harihar Rao; Art Makosinski for his interviews with Ravi Shankar, and for help with other audio-visual sources; Ira Landgarten for his 1979 interviews with Richard Bock and Ravi Shankar; Mark Kidel for his 2000 interview with Ravi Shankar (and the title of chapter 4); Kumar Shankar for letters from his parents and his aunt Kamala Chakravarty; and Bhaskar Menon for his memorial tribute to Raviji.

The following also kindly granted permissions (with extract details in brackets): Shankar Angadi and Chandrika Casali (memoir by Patricia Angadi); BBC (documents in BBC Written Archives Centre; BBC copyright content is reproduced courtesy of British Broadcasting Corporation. All rights reserved); Ron Bock (the words of his father, Richard Bock); Britten–Pears Foundation (letters and diaries of Benjamin Britten and Peter Pears); Dokumentationsbibliothek Davos (letters from Alice Boner); Michael Garady (letter from Peter Feuchtwanger); Olivia Harrison (words of George Harrison); Holst Foundation (letter from Imogen Holst); Immediate Media and

Christabel Holland on behalf of the Rory McEwen Estate (article by Rory McEwen); Reed Karen (letters by Isadora Bennett); Dilgo Khyentse Fellowship, with thanks to Brian S. Garrison (letters from Marilyn Silverstone); Jeremy Menuhin (letters from Yehudi Menuhin); Museum Rietberg (Alice Boner's diary); Musicians' Benevolent Fund (letter from Basil Douglas); Laura Rosenberg (unpublished memoir by John Coast); Royal Academy of Music (letters in the Foyle Menuhin Archive); Robert Schatzkin of Norton, with thanks to Peggy Fox and Ian S. MacNiven (letter from James Laughlin); Linda, Som and Kaveri Shankar (letters of Shubho Shankar); Stadtarchiv Zurich (letters to Alice Boner in VII.389 Alice Boner Nachlass 1929–48).

Extracts from the following lyrics by Ravi Shankar are © Anourag Music and are reproduced by kind permission: "Oh Bhaugowan," "I Am Missing You," "Prabhujee" and "O Parun Bondhu."

Others who helped in various ways include: Preetha Narayanan (for a violinist's insights into the Shankar–Menuhin scores), Shukti Karmakar (unsung hero), Mark Lewisohn (so generous with sources), Bruce Adolphe, Catherine Berge, Richard Blurton, Aaron Bremner, Sue Cheetham, Jonathan Clyde, Rachel Conroy, Alex Cserhat, Suba Das, John Kameel Farah, Anna Farlow, Bickram and Jaya Seal Ghosh, Shambhu and Punita Gupta, Mamoun Hassan, Raymond Head, Nicholas Hogg, Nasreen Munni Kabir, Digvijay Sinh and Swati Kathiwada, Sheema Kermani, Don Kirby, Ian S. MacNiven, Saskia Rao-de Haas, John Reader, Catherine Riboud, Dan Saccoccio, Bernhard Schimpelsberger, Mary Scott, Suddhaseel Sen, Supriya Shah, Jasdeep Singh Degun, Isambard Thomas and Lynn Tungate. Over several years Andrew Robinson encouraged me to write this book. At Southbank Centre I thank Vicky Cheetham, Gillian Moore, Madani Younis, Clare Wood, Maddy Mills, Georgia Ward, Rachel Harris and others. Heartfelt thanks to Jenny McKinley and Tim Clarke for granting me a sabbatical from Scala, and for being so reasonable when I didn't return. A special *pranam* to my Hindustani vocal music *guru* Chandrima Misra, and to all at Bharatiya Vidya Bhavan, London, especially Dr. Nandakumara, Sanjay Guha and Rajkumar Misra. Thanks to Willa Gebbie for her wonderful drawing of a sitar and map of India.

Shohini Chaudhuri provided essential love and support throughout a very long process, and superb critical comments on the entire manuscript. The rest of my family has patiently suffered my absences, and I am grateful to them all for loving support, in particular my mother, Gwyneth Craske. My father-in-law Amal Chaudhuri also provided invaluable expertise on Bengali culture. My extended family in Kolkata always offers the warmest of welcomes, and endless supplies of tea and *mishti*.

As well as Sukanya, Anoushka and Shohini, Richard Hamson also read the entire manuscript, while Nina Chang, Julith Jedamus, James Lever, Mark Lewisohn, Andrew Lycett, Claire Reihill, Andrew Robinson and Angela Sulivan read chapters. Sujata Banerjee, Amal Chaudhuri and Anupam Roy assisted with translation from Bengali,

ACKNOWLEDGMENTS

Andreas Corcoran from German, and Gaurav Uniyal from Hindi. Cath Proctor transcribed interviews. The final responsibility for the text is mine, of course.

Many thanks to my agent David Godwin, and to Philippa Sitters. I have been lucky to find two wonderful publishers for this book. It was commissioned by Faber & Faber, and I am grateful to all the team there, especially my wise and patient editor Belinda Matthews, managing editor Anne Owen, and tabla-playing CEO Stephen Page. Being copy-edited by Jill Burrows is a bit like having a music lesson with Raviji: she misses nothing. Thanks also to Jill for the typesetting and indexing. In the USA, Ben Schafer's enthusiasm is inspiring and I am delighted to be part of the music list at Hachette Books.

London, October 2019

To hear some of the music discussed in this book, please visit indiansun.co.uk, where you will find a curated playlist of music that can be streamed, and related news and information.

INDEX

Ravi Shankar is abbreviated as RS. Relationships, e.g., "brother," are to Ravi Shankar. Musical terms and instruments are indexed only when they are defined or described. References to photographs and captions are in italics. The plate sections are identified as ONE and TWO, with pages in each section numbered 1–8.

INDEX

Private Music, 449, 467, 477
Privy Council, London, 61
Prasad, Rajendra, 204
Presidency Court, Calcutta, 220, 223
Preston, Billy, 394, 403, 410–11
Previn, André, 386, 388–9
Procter, Norma, *two/1*; 216
Prohibition, 48
Prokofiev, Sergey, 536; Classical Symphony, 536
Prudential Award for the Arts, 477
Pudovkin, Vsevolod, 100
puja, 359, 373
Pune, 96, 106, 322
Punjab, 110, 276, 498; Kangra hills, 276; *tabla gharana*, 209
Purana Qila, Delhi, 107
Pushkin, Alexander, 135
Puttaparthi, 400, 421

Qasim, Abd al-Karim, 227
qawwali, 498
Queens Hotel, Leeds, 216
Queen's Own Cameron Highlanders, 262
Quit India movement, 82
Qureshi, Zakir, *see* Hussain, Zakir

Radha, 27, 221, 233, 446
Radhakrishnan, Sarvepalli, 109, 228, 252, 257, 259
Radio Ceylon, 121
Radio City Music Hall, New York, 48
Rafi, Mohammed, 150
raga, 4–5, 52
Raga (film), 342, 354, 368–71, 379, 392, 397, 401 soundtrack album and DVD, 371, 397, 535
"Raga Buckle" shoe, 361
raga mala (musical style), 78–9
Raga Rock (album, Folkswingers), 299
raga rock, 283, 298, 330, 370, 501
Ragas
  Abhogi Kanada, 322, 344; Adana, 387; Ahir Bhairav, 175, 482, 537, 539; Ananda Bhairava, 352; Bairagi (RS), 106, 323, 550; Banjara (RS), 498, 537, 550; Bhairav, 106; Bhairavi, 226, 358, 539–40; Bhimpalasi, 207, 339; Charu Keshi, 129, 188, 195, 201; Charukauns (RS), 450; Deepak, 11; Desh, 139, 142, 270, 370, 435; Devagiri Bilawal, 467; Dhani, 238; Doga Kalyan (RS), 537, 550; Durga, 427; Gangeshwari (RS), 358, 535; Gara, 428; Gunkali, 311; Hameer, 428; Hamsadhwani, 68, 233, 276, 428; Hem Bihag, 400; Hem Kalyan, 271; Hemant, 106, 428; Jait, 407; Janasanmodini (RS), 149; Jaunpuri, 518; Jhinjhoti, 347; Jogeshwari (RS), 428; Jogiya, 215; Kafi, 233, 297; Kafi Zila, 536–7; Kameshwari (RS), 358, 360; Kaushi Kanhara, 504; Khamaj, 344, 387, 495; Kirwani, 129, 239, 248; Lalit, 344, 358, 434; Madhuvanti, 239; Malkauns, 111, 248; Manamanjari, 127; Manj Khamaj, 126,

149, 373, 387, 400; Marwa, 106, 323, 343, 435; Megh Malhar, 10; Mian Ki Malhar, 127, 201, 435; Mian Ki Todi, 418; Mishra Gara (RS), 404, 504; Mishra Jhinjhoti, 394; Mishra Kafi, 539; Mishra Mand, 239; Mishra Piloo, 187–8, 195, 346, 374, 444, 521; Mohankauns (RS), 111, 375, 428, 437–8, 551; Nat, 106; Nat Bhairav (RS), 106, 267, 374, 418; Nat Bhairavi, 267, 323, 518; Nat Kirvani, 226; Palas Kafi (RS), 518; Pancham Se Gara (RS), 248, 339, 550; Parameshwari (RS), 360; Patdeep, 142; Piloo, 351–2, 521, 550; Piloo Banjara (RS), 498; Puriya Dhanashri, 373, 418; Puriya Kalyan, 212, 312; Rageshri, 239; Rajya Kalyan (RS), 475; Ramkali, 233; Satyajit, 539; Shivaranjani, 427; Shuddh Sarang, 339, 395; Simhendra Madhyamam, 68, 129, 175; Sindhi Bhairavi, 387, 539; Sindhu Bhairavi, 149; Suvarna (RS), 499; Tilak Shyam (RS), 149, 322, 344, 445; Tilang, 304–5, 308, 310; Todi, 139, 339; Vachaspati, 129, 363, 521; Yaman Kalyan, 248, 429–30, 435, 467, 521, 527, 548
Ragas and Dances (album, Uday Shankar troupe), 367
Raghu, Palghat, 263, 342, 363
Raghupati Raghav Rajaram (bhajan), see Ram Dhun
Ragini Todi (miniature), 139
Rahman, A. R., 439
Rahman, Indrani, 134, 234–5, 255, 362, 364
Raj, British, 16, 89–90, 108, 147
Raj Bhavan, Calcutta, 229
Rajagopalachari, C. (Chakravarti), 108
Rajan, Parvati, 517
Rajan, Sukanya, *see* Shankar, Sukanya
Rajasthan, 488, 498
Rajasthani music, 450, 498
Rajiv Gandhi Foundation, 486–7
Rajkot, 323
Rajput culture, 31, 139, 195, 420, 488
Rajya Sabha, 447, 451, 460, 464
Rakha, Alla, *two/1, 3, 4*; and All India Radio, 86, 121; death, 507; documentary film, 357, 360; and Philip Glass, 288, 348; and Zakir Hussain, 271, 357, 382, 444; performances with RS, 86, 214–15, 217, 270, 275, 288, 302, 305, 307, 314, 339, 351, 382, 395, 444; recordings: 215, 275, 309, 311–12, 345, 425–6, 450, *Rich à la Rakha*, 355; relationship with RS, 8, 229, 373, 454–5; RS on, 209, 274, 455, 507; tabla player, 2, 125, 261, 263, 273; and Tat Baba, 131; teacher, 333, 348; tours with RS, 208–9, 227, 272–4, 285, 287, 302, 305, 307, 342, 363, 368, 372–3, 406, 409, 465
Raksin, David, 187
Ram Dhun (bhajan), 63, 440, 526
Rama, 26, 28, 316–17
Ramachandran, Alangudi, 263
Ramamatya, 268
Ramayana, 28, 227, 270
Ramlila festival, 26–7, 316
Ramnagar, 316